Darfur and the Crisis of Governance in Sudan

D1560808

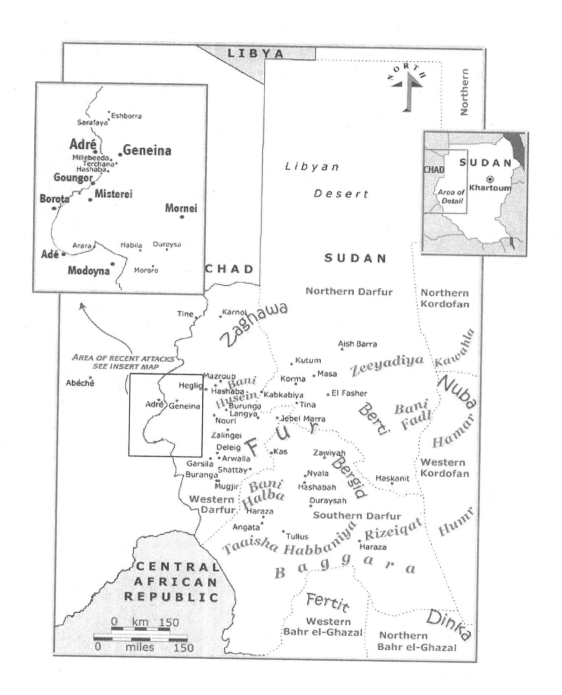

Map of Sudan: Darfur Region Ethnic Groups and Major Towns
Source: Human Rights Watch, http://www.hrw.org/campaigns/darfur/map.htm

Darfur

and the Crisis of
Governance in Sudan

A Critical Reader

Edited by
Salah M. Hassan
Carina E. Ray

Prince Claus
Fund Library

Cornell University Press
Ithaca and London

To the people of Darfur and to all Sudanese who are aspiring for a democratic and united Sudan.

Editors: Salah M. Hassan and Carina E. Ray
Book Design: Irma Boom Office
Cover Photography: Issam A. Abdel Hafiez,
Young Boy, Kalmah Camp, Color Photo, 2006.

The publisher and editors gratefully acknowledge
permission to reprint the following essays:

Abdullahi Osman El-Tom, "Darfur People: Too Black
for the Arab-Islamic Project of Sudan," *Irish Journal
of Anthropology*, 2006, 9(1): 12–18; 2006, 9(1): 5–11.

Alex de Waal, "Who Are the Darfurians? Arab and
African Identities, Violence, and External Engagement,"
African Affairs 2005 104 (415): 18–205.

Mahmood Mamdani, "The Politics of Naming:
Genocide, Civil War, Insurgency," *London Review
of Books*, 8 March, 2007.

Rogaia Mustafa Abusharaf, "Competing Masculinities:
Probing Political Disputes as Acts of Violence against
Women from Southern Sudan and Darfur," *Human Rights
Review*, January–March 2006, 7(2): 59–74.

First published 2009 by Cornell University Press
Printed in the Netherlands

ISBN 978 0 8014 7594 8

Librarians: Library of Congress Cataloging-in-Publication
Data are available.

Generous support for this publication provided by

Fonds

Prince Claus Fund *for*
Culture and Development
The Netherlands

Contents

PART 2

Appendices

Foreword

Andreas Eshete

As we enter Ethiopia's new millennium, it is important to attend to what merits celebration in the Ethiopian and wider African past. It is even more important to pause for collective reflection, care, and concern over our intractable troubles. It is noteworthy that, like African institutions, African public intellectuals have demonstrated deep engagement in the tragedy unfolding in Darfur.

Although nobody can be justly convicted of haste, the tragic events in Darfur have, over time, captured the moral imagination of individuals, governments, and international institutions everywhere. The immense suffering in Darfur is particularly poignant for Ethiopians. The Sudanese people have sheltered us in times of war and repression ever since the fascist occupation (1935–1941). Robert Frost famously remarked that "home is the place where, when you have to go there, they have to take you in." Since it is by now unthinkable that if we go to Sudan they will not take us in, it would be fair to say that Sudan has a claim, more than any other place, to be called home by Ethiopians. Against this background, it is deeply painful for us to witness, in Darfur, Sudanese citizens denied a home in their own country. It is plain that the iniquity in Darfur is not just a calamity for Sudan, its neighbors, and the rest of Africa; it is a moral and political affront to humanity.

While Western talk about Africa often tends to focus on the sensational, transitional, and, most of all, the generic, our own talk about ourselves is overly confined by national isolation. This courts the loss of cosmopolitanism in our thoughts and solidarity in our deeds.

In conjunction with the *Darfur and the Crisis of Governance in Sudan* conference, held at the Institute of Ethiopian Studies, Addis Ababa University (February 21–23, 2008), in collaboration with Cornell University's Africana Studies and Research Center and Fordham University's History Department, this volume is a true historic and intellectual milestone. Together, the conference and this volume throw light on Darfur's pressing, contested issues: the genealogy of the crisis; the identification of the wrongs; divided public perspectives; unusual war crimes or unusual guises of familiar crimes, such as crimes committed against women; and divergent paths in the quest for peace and justice. This volume, to say the least, will certainly sharpen our understanding of the conflict in Darfur and fortify our personal commitment to proactively addressing the insufferable plight of the people of Darfur.

The conference and this volume also renew the commitment of the Africana Studies and Research Center at Cornell University and Addis Ababa University to embark jointly on issues that are pertinent to the African continent.

I should add that throughout the course of this project we Ethiopians saw much to emulate in our Sudanese colleagues: forthrightness; a readiness to disagree, happily free of a trace of rancor; attention to what Darfur and the political fate of Sudan spells for Africa; hope in the face of grim burdens. These are wonderful traits, especially in light of Francis Deng's cited observation: "What we are silent about is what divides us." The exchanges at the conference and within this book exemplify the value of conversation among African citizens and intellectuals across national borders.

Finally, benedictions never come easy. Still, surely, you will join me in congratulating all our contributors and, of course, Carina E. Ray of Fordham University and Salah M. Hassan of Cornell University, for the remarkable feat of coordinating the conference across many countries and continents, and following up most swiftly in producing this diligently edited and thoughtfully designed book. Elizabeth Wolde Giorgis and her colleagues at our Institute of Ethiopian Studies worked very hard to make the necessary preparations for the conference in Addis Ababa. The erudition and passion on display – virtues seldom encountered together – have made the conference and this groundbreaking edited volume a success.

Acknowledgments

The editors wish to acknowledge the following individuals and institutions whose goodwill, hard work, and enthusiasm made this publication and its sister-conference, *Darfur and the Crisis of Governance in Sudan* in Addis Ababa (February 22–23, 2008) a reality. We are indebted to our gracious hosts in Addis Ababa, Andreas Eshete, President of Addis Ababa University, and Elizabeth Wolde Giorgis, Director of the Institute of Ethiopian Studies for collaborating on this project and for doing everything possible to organize the conference and make it a pleasant experience as well. We are particularly grateful to have been able to inaugurate this project on African soil. Symbolically, Ethiopia was the nation where the Addis Ababa Peace Agreement of 1972 was brokered, which paved the way for peace in South Sudan – albeit temporarily, before the war flared up again in 1983 as a result of the perverse actions of Numeiri's regime. It is our hope that the conference and this publication become one step among many toward peace in Darfur and an end to another unjust chapter of senseless killing and bloody conflict in Sudan. Embarking on this project in Addis Ababa was also ideal because it facilitated the participation of Sudanese scholars and activists who are based in Sudan and their counterparts in Europe and the United States who otherwise, as Africans, would have faced difficulties in obtaining visas to the United States or Europe. In addition, the conference strengthens the institutional ties of Cornell University and Fordham University with an important African-based counterpart and advances our efforts to establish linkages and exchange programs with African universities.

The success of the conference and seeing this book to fruition could not have been possible without the contribution of several institutions and a host of individuals. We would like to acknowledge and thank those who provided generous support: The Prince Claus Fund for Culture and Development, The Netherlands, supported us with a major grant that enabled us to fund the conference and this publication. Thanks to Els van der Plas, Director of Prince Claus Fund, whose vision and tireless support shaped this publication in the best way possible. The conference was co-sponsored by Cornell University's Africana Studies and Research Center; Society for the Humanities; Office of the Vice Provost for International Studies; and College of Arts and Sciences Dean's Office. Fordham University's Dean of Faculty, Dr. Robert Himmelberg, and Professor Doron Ben-Atar, Chair of the History Department, also provided generous support.

Our ultimate gratitude goes to the conference participants – the presenters, chairs, and discussants – all of whom contributed in one way or another to the success of this volume. Their contributions during the conference have enriched this volume and made it intellectually viable. We thank them all for enduring the hazards of travel and crossing borders and for taking time out of their busy schedules to write papers, prepare comments, and engage in vigorous dialogue. We would like to express our gratitude to our two keynote speakers, Dr. Mansour Khalid, the former Sudanese minister of foreign affairs, and Professor Mahmood Mamdani of Columbia University. Dr. Khalid's talk eloquently unpacked the crisis in Darfur as a problem within a problem rooted in the legacy of the colonial state. Prior to his own keynote address, Professor Mamdani gave an insightful and intellectually provocative series of lectures in Addis Ababa, which galvanized audience attendance and paved the way for one of the most dynamic exchanges at the conference.

We are particularly grateful to Professor Abdullahi Osman El-Tom for his valuable suggestions and advice with regard to contributors and for supplying us with rare documents, some of which are reproduced in the appendices of this book. A special note of thanks goes to Mustafa Adam, who beautifully translated Kamal El-Gizouli's essay from Arabic into English, and to Rogaia Abusharaf, who kindly assisted us in editing and shortening the translated version. Yasir Arman, Deputy Secretary-General, Sudan People Liberation Movement (SPLM) and Deputy Member of the SPLM's Darfur Task Force, provided valuable advice on the conference and the SPLM's effort to unify the Darfur resistance movements, but could not attend due to a scheduling conflict. We are indebted to the generosity of Issam A. Abdel Hafiez, the prominent Sudanese artist, for permitting us to use his photographs in the publication material for the conference, the cover of this book, and for contributing a remarkable visual essay.

In Addis Ababa, our appreciation goes to the discussants whose intellectual energy and insightful interventions made the discussions more stimulating and assisted our contributors in refining their essays. We offer our special thanks to Zenebework Tadesse, Director of the Forum for Social Science Studies and Coordinator for UNISA, Addis Ababa; Bahru Zewde, Professor, Historian, and President of the Forum for Social Science Studies; Timnit Abraha, Regional Coordinator, Inter-Africa Group; Ambassador Nureldin Satti, UNESCO Representative to Ethiopia, Djibouti, the African Union, and IGAD, Addis Ababa, Ethiopia; Jean-Bosco Butera, Chair of Peace and Security Studies, Addis Ababa University, and Former Director of the Africa Program of the United Nations–affiliated University for Peace (UPEACE); Meaza Ashenafi, Member, Economic Commission for Africa, Founder and Former President of Ethiopian Women Lawyer's Association, Addis Ababa; Tamerat Kedebe, Director of Inter-Africa Group, Addis Ababa; Mogobe Ramose, Regional Coordinator, UNISA, Addis Ababa. We also thank our friend the Ethiopian historian Takalign Wolde-Merriam for being so generous with his time and for introducing our guests to Addis Ababa.

In the United States many individuals worked tirelessly behind the scenes to make this project a success. Ms. Cindy Telage, administrative manager of the Africana Studies and Research Center, and Ms. Lesley Andrews and Ms. Linda Charles, of the Cornell Business Center, navigated all kinds of bureaucracies to ensure that financial and logistical matters were taken care of. We are most grateful to Jeff McCord, who with grace and efficiency helped prepare the manuscript by coding the essays and assisting us with the index. In the world of publishing, a well-edited final product depends on the keen eyes of a good copy editor. In this regard, we are grateful to Susan Barnett for working through an earlier draft of this book to correct many errors, and to Karen Tongish for her acumen and promptness in copyediting the book's final draft. Possessing a keen sense of aesthetics and an eye for perfection, Ramez Elias designed the posters, brochures, and website for the conference.

Working with Irma Boom, the prominent Dutch designer, and her assistant Sonja Haller was a tremendous pleasure and an honor.

Finally, we would like to thank Roger Haydon and John Ackerman from Cornell University Press for their enthusiasm and commitment to this project.

Young Woman Kalmah Camp
Nyala, 2006

Introduction
Critically Reading Darfur and the Crisis of Governance in Sudan

Salah M. Hassan and Carina E. Ray

Violence can never be understood solely in terms of its physicality – force, assault, or the infliction of pain – alone. Violence also includes assaults on the personhood, dignity, sense of worth, or value of the victim. The social and cultural dimensions of violence are what give violence its power and meaning. Focusing exclusively on the physical aspects of torture/terror/violence misses the point and transforms the project into a clinical, literary, or artistic exercise, which runs the risk of degenerating into a theater or pornography of violence in which the voyeuristic impulse subverts the larger project of witnessing, critiquing, and writing against violence, injustice, and suffering.

Nancy Scheper-Hughes and Philippe Bourgois, *Violence in War and Peace* (2004)[1]

The ongoing conflict in the western Sudanese region of Darfur has received unprecedented attention, especially in the West, from the international media and human rights organizations, and it has captured the attention of millions of ordinary citizens around the world. Those seeking to learn about the conflict, as well as those who have reported on it, often rely on information produced by the various governmental bodies and nongovernmental organizations (NGOs) that are involved in addressing the humanitarian crises spawned by the conflict. As a result, much of what has been written about the conflict tends to be either aid-oriented or journalistic in nature and often lacks a strong understanding of the historical, economic, political, sociological and environmental factors that have contributed to the conflict. While newer scholarship on the conflict has increasingly included more Sudanese voices, the perspectives of those who are directly affected by the war – most specifically the people of Darfur – and, more generally, Sudanese women – have not been adequately heard.

    This volume includes essays that explore the multiplicity of factors that have given rise to what has been called "the first genocide of the twenty-first century." Composed of essays that have been specially written for this volume as well as key previously published essays, the collection brings together many of the leading thinkers and civil society activists involved in understanding and proactively addressing the situation in Darfur and in Sudan. The essays engage in careful analysis of the historical, geopolitical, military, social, environmental, and economic roots of the conflict, and reflect on the contemporary realities that shape the experiences of those living in the region. It is our hope that this kind of cross-disciplinary dialogue will foster a comprehensive yet nuanced understanding of the root causes, manifestations, and implications of the ongoing conflict, and help generate more informed prospects for a just and comprehensive resolution to the conflict. Importantly, as several of the essays demonstrate, formidable pre-existing as well as newly formed multiregional and multiethnic movements and civil society organizations within Sudan have organized themselves around the issue of Darfur. This often-neglected development is but one indication that if solutions to the conflict are to be found they must be developed in dialogue with ongoing internal efforts to deal with the range of issues that have given rise not only to the war in Darfur but also to the larger interlocking political crises in Sudan.

Reportage on Darfur typically glosses over the strong sense of self-reliance and responsibility among the thousands of Sudanese aid workers who form the backbone of relief organizations, in favor of highlighting the work of a much smaller number of foreign counterparts. It is precisely this kind of skewed representation that perpetuates the false notion that Sudanese, and by extension Africans, are not actively involved in addressing and resolving their own problems. Indeed, the deep extent to which Sudanese, both in Sudan and abroad, have been and continue to be engaged in what is happening not only in Darfur but throughout the nation was brought into sharp focus during the international conference *Darfur and the Crisis of Governance in Sudan*, convened at the Institute of Ethiopian Studies at Addis Ababa University, Ethiopia, on February 22–23, 2008. Our goal in convening this conference was to create a space for contributors to this volume – leading scholars, civil society members, and activists – to discuss and debate the factors that have given rise to the Darfur crisis. Strikingly, even with such a diverse group of presenters from various walks of life and with different political orientations, a clear consensus was reached that despite the multiplicity of factors that have contributed to the conflict, its root causes lie at the doorstep of the failed Sudanese state. Equally so, the different panels at the conference underscored the fact that Sudan continues to have a strong civil society base that remains engaged in all issues related to Darfur and the larger crisis of governance in Sudan.

Characterized by different emphases and varying degrees of analysis, several existing works on Darfur have examined its history, ethnic politics, and the conflicts that have characterized much of its devastating recent history. These include the work of Abdel Ghaffar M. Ahmed and Leif Manger; Martin Daly; Alex de Waal; Alex de Waal and Julie Flint; Sulayman Hamid; Douglas Johnson; Mahmood Mamdani; and Mohamed Suliman.[2] Together, these authors have shed light on Darfur's complex internal history, as well as its complicated relationship with the larger Sudanese nation-state. In the process they have advanced our understanding of the various dynamics at work in the current conflict. This volume, however, departs in focus by bringing together essays on the discourse and activism around the Darfur crisis, along with contributions that delve into quite focused examinations of particular aspects of the war from a range of different perspectives.

A Word about Terminology

Several editorial issues surfaced in relation to the terminology, names, and concepts used throughout the different essays included in this book. Some of these issues are simple matters of inconsistency in spelling the names of ethnic groups, individuals, and places, in addition to other terms related to Darfur and Sudan. Since most of these words have their origin in Arabic and other Sudanese languages, the inconsistencies mostly emanate from the difference between the standardized spelling of such words on the one hand, and their correct transliteration in Roman letters on the other hand. In such cases, we have streamlined the spelling throughout this volume by employing the most standardized English language spellings, especially where names of cities, towns, and places are concerned. For instance, we have used *El Fasher*, the most common spelling of the name of the North Darfur capital, rather than *al-Fashir*, even though the latter is the most accurate transliteration of the same name.

With regard to names of individuals and major figures, where possible we have adopted the way in which such persons spell their own names. An example of this is the name of the veteran politician and Darfur activist Mohammed Ibrahim Diraig, whose last name is often spelled in more than three ways: Diraige, Diraig, and Direge. We resorted in this case to the spelling Diraig himself used when he signed the Declaration of the Darfur Salvation Front, a copy of which is included in the appendices to this volume. In the case of the former military dictator Ja'far Muhammad Numeiri, contributors have used widely different spellings of his last name; we streamlined these into the most common spelling Numeiri. We have also used Omar Hassan Al Bashir as the most accurate spelling for the current president of Sudan. We opted to use *Darfurian/s* rather than *Darfuri/s* to reference the people of Darfur and *riverian/s* rather than *riverean/s* to reference the northern and central people of Sudan. In the case of the infamous government-sponsored militia, we use *Janjawid* rather than other renderings of the same term, such as *Janjaweed* or *Janjawiid*.

More challenging has been encountering terms that we ourselves would not employ in our own work because of their conceptually and intellectually problematic histories, meanings, and usage. A good example of this is *tribe*, a term that has been subjected to much-needed criticism within anthropological and social science discourses.[3] For well over three decades, Africanists have debated the uses and abuses of the word *tribe*. One of the earliest critiques of the term came from the great South African anthropologist and Pan-Africanist Archie Mafeje, who in 1971 argued that "if tribalism is thought of as peculiarly African, then the ideology itself is particularly European in origin."[4] Later generations of scholars have gone on to show how in many instances so-called tribes were indeed colonial creations and thereby question the efficacy of using *tribe* as a unit of analysis when studying African societies.

While today few Africanists use *tribe* in their scholarship and teaching, it is still rampant in public discourse about Africa, particularly in the Western media's coverage of conflicts in Africa. Slapping the word *tribal* on African conflicts is not only analytically lazy but irresponsible and dangerous. Deeply embedded in a colonial lexicon of racism, the use of such inaccurate terminology naturalizes and further exoticizes violence in Africa in ways that preclude a true understanding of the root causes and manifestations of violence, and forecloses the possibility of generating more informed prospects for just and comprehensive resolutions to violent conflicts. This could not be more evident than in the case of Darfur as many of the essays included in this volume illustrate.

The use of *tribe* in the context of Darfur is especially troubling because it gives the wrongheaded impression that the conflict is rooted in primordial identities. The casual use of the term *tribe* obscures rather than clarifies our understanding of how ethnic identities and groups have evolved and interacted with one another over time, and in relation to such factors as state and class formation; economic, social, and political change; environmental factors; as well as more mundane facts of life such as migration and intermarriage. While there is no doubt that ethnic tensions, which have a long history in Darfur, have affected how the violence has unfolded, to characterize the violence as a "tribal" or "race" war neither speaks to the ethnic dimensions of the violence nor to other important factors, such as unequal access to political and economic power, that have coalesced to bring about this unprecedented wave of destruction at this particular moment. Nor does it acknowledge the leading role that violent conflicts play in concretizing previously fluid categories of ethnic identity and creating new forms of ethnic affiliation, which in turn can intensify existing conflicts or become fodder for future ones. Indeed, as Mohamed Suliman points out:

> Most violent conflicts are over material resources, whether these resources are actual or perceived. With the passage of time, however, ethnic, cultural and religious affiliations seem to undergo transformation from abstract ideological categories into concrete social forces. In a wider sense, they themselves become contestable material social resources and hence possible objects of group strife and violent conflict.
> Usually by-products of fresh conflicts, ethnic, cultural and spiritual dichotomies, can invert with the progress of a conflict to become intrinsic causes of that conflict and in the process increase its complexity and reduce the possibility of managing and ultimately resolving and transforming it.[5]

Having clarified our own position on *tribe*, we made an editorial decision not to interfere with the use of *tribe* or *tribal* by many of the contributors to this volume because of our understanding of the problem of translation. The equivalent of the word *tribe* in Arabic is *qabilah*, which neither harbors colonial stereotypes of savagery and primordialism nor connotes the external imposition of group identities associated with colonial policy. Rather, *qabilah* is self-referential in most cases and indicates a sense of ethnic identification. It is important to note, however, that in contemporary Arabic scholarship *tribe* is increasingly being replaced by the Arabic word *ithniya* (ethnicity) and *ithny* (ethnic), signaling a growing awareness that *qabilah* is often misinterpreted by Western audiences when translated as *tribe*. Given that our contributors are generally substituting *qabilah* with *tribe* rather than intentionally using it as part of the lexicon of colonial racism, we are hopeful that readers will not misinterpret its usage herein.

Just as the use of the term *tribe* obscures rather than clarifies the dynamics of the conflict in Darfur, so too does the use of *African* or *Black African* and *Arab* to describe not only the involved parties, but also to explain the root of the conflict. Let us be clear from the beginning that we take the position that this is not a "race war" and that the multiple parties involved are all indigenous Africans whose ethnic identities have increasingly become racialized as a result of the conflict, but are by no means the sole cause of it. Alex de Waal unpacks the extent of this misleading characterization as follows:

The story is not as simple as the conventional rendering in the news, which depicts a conflict between "Arabs" and "Africans." The Zaghawa – one of the groups victimized by the violence and described in the mainstream press as "indigenous African" – are certainly indigenous, black and African: they share distant origins with the Berbers of Morocco and other ancient Saharan peoples. But the name of the "Bedeyat," the Zaghawa's close kin, should alert us to their true origins: pluralize in the more traditional Arab manner and we have "Bedeyiin" or Bedouins. Similarly, the Zaghawa's adversaries in this war, the Darfurian Arabs, are "Arabs" in the ancient sense of "Bedouin," meaning desert nomad, a sense that has only in the last few decades been used to describe the Arabs of the river Nile and the Fertile Crescent. Darfurian Arabs, too, are indigenous, black, and African. In fact there are no discernible racial or religious differences between the two: all have lived there for centuries; all are Muslims (Darfur's non-Arabs are arguably more devout than the Arabs); and until very recently, conflict between these different groups was a matter of disputes over camel theft or grazing rights, not the systematic and ideological slaughter of one group by the other.[6]

In Mahmood Mamdani's essay "The Politics of Naming: Genocide, Civil War, and Insurgency," included in this volume, he underscores how the twinned processes of depoliticizing and racializing the war in Darfur have enabled various international actors to paint it as a genocide perpetrated by "Arabs." One needs little education in the politics of fear and anti-Arabism in the post-9/11 world to understand that demonizing Arabs has been a critical component of legitimizing America's "War on Terror."

Given what is at stake here we want to emphasize that while many of our contributors use *Arab* and *African* to refer to the different parties involved in the Darfur conflict, typically they do so in ways that either reference the multiple meanings that both labels have in Sudan, or reflect how those involved in the conflict have adopted and deployed these categories to further their own causes both nationally and internationally. We would have preferred to use *Arabized* to denote that ethnic groups routinely called *Arab* in the context of Darfur, who are in fact indigenous Africans and who through processes of cultural change, intermarriage, language acquisition, and mode of livelihood, have become culturally rather than racially "Arab" over time. Yet, it is our hope that as readers encounter the term *Arab* they will disentangle it from the contemporary meaning assigned to it by the West's vernacular of fear.[7] Similarly, in the case of "*Zurqa*," (or "*Zuruq*") a locally used name for the non-Arabized population of Darfur derived from the Sudanese Arabic word for "black," we always place it inside quotes to signal our awareness that this term emerges out of what de Waal calls "the casual racism of Arabs in Darfur."[8] The widespread use of "*Zurqa*" in some of the essays is indicative of the process through which many words with derogatory connotations become normalized through their repetition; we hope that as readers encounter the term in quotes they will be reminded that in the context of Darfur it is not simply a neutral descriptor.

Organization of Chapters
Presented in two parts, the first part of this book consists of five thematic sections with essays written by leading Sudanese academics, intellectuals, activists, civil

society representatives, and members of government and Darfur rebel factions, along with essays by scholars based in Europe and the United States.

The first section of the book, "Origins and Evolution of the Conflict," opens up with an essay by Mansour Khalid that addresses the continued failure of post-independence governments in Sudan to re-conceptualize the model of governance inherited from the colonial state, which in turn has led to the state's sanctioned policy of monopolizing power at the center. Khalid brings his long-standing experience not only as a scholar and leading member of the Sudan People's Liberation Movement (SPLM), but also as former Minister of Foreign Affairs, to his analysis of the multitude of factors that spawned the war in Darfur. As such, Khalid argues that what is now needed is a complete restructuring of the state in order to repair the domestic space, making it conducive to peace by coming to terms with the internal heterogeneity of the Sudanese people. In his well-researched and comprehensive essay, Atta El-Battahani elucidates the convergence of local, national, and environmental factors that have led to horrific crimes against humanity in Darfur. He argues that while these factors have led to actual homicide in Darfur, the increasing potential for genocide must be understood as a product of the role of the state in perpetuating injustice in the first place. Armed with figures and statistics, Benaiah Yongo-Bure compares and analyzes the conflict in Darfur in relationship to the North/South civil war by looking at the similarities in the structural inequalities between South Sudan and Darfur, on the one hand, and what is known in Sudanese political discourse as "Hamdi's Privileged Triangle" of Dongola – El Obeid – Sennar riverian elites, on the other hand. Yongo-Bure concludes that the wider practice of marginalization by the Sudanese state, which excludes the majority of Sudanese from political participation and neglects their socioeconomic and cultural needs, accounts not only for the war in Darfur, but for the multiplicity of protracted conflicts that have plagued Sudan since its independence in 1956. Abdullahi Osman El-Tom, a member of the Justice and Equality Movement (JEM) and respected anthropologist, takes a hard look in his essay at the implications of the racial politics of exclusion, practiced by both the Sudanese state and Darfur's Arab Gathering, for ethnic cleansing and restructuring of land ownership in Darfur. El-Tom argues that the paradox of Muslim fighting Muslim in Darfur is the result of a deliberate effort by the hegemonic forces of the center to create an Arab-Islamic belt in the region by displacing Darfurian groups who are perceived as non-Arab. This is followed by Ali B. Ali-Dinar's contribution, which makes a call for greater analytical clarity in discerning patterns of continuity and change within the history of conflict in Darfur. Ali-Dinar contends that while the current conflict in Darfur shares common denominators with past conflicts, its size, scale, and the nature of destruction set it apart from previous patterns of violence. He also eschews the characterization of the conflict as a war over natural resources intensified by drought and desertification in favor of looking at the deeper layers of dysfunction embedded in the structure of governance.

Together, the essays in this section enumerate the multiplicity of factors that have contributed to the rise of this horrifying chapter in the history of Sudan. Although each of the authors has focused on a specific aspect of the conflict, they all emphasize the need to point out its complex roots and evolution over time. Above all, each has come to the same conclusion that the state's monopolization of power and wealth at the center and the hegemony of the riverian Arabized elites, who have held power in Sudan since independence, are to blame for the perpetuation and escalation of the marginalization and oppression of the people of Darfur.

The second section, entitled "Representations of the War in Darfur" includes four essays that focus on the politics of representation and identity discourses that inform the various ways in which the war is constructed and understood. Alex de Waal's comprehensive essay is a study of the overlapping historical processes of identity formation in Darfur. De Waal argues that the recent polarization of "African" and "Arab" identities that has come to misleadingly represent the fault lines of the current conflict in Darfur marks a sharp break with earlier models of identity formation that were absorptive in nature and thus heterogeneous and constantly evolving in outcome, particularly as a result of Darfur's long history of stable state formation prior to British conquest in 1916 and the Sultanate's subsequent incorporation into Sudan in 1922–1923. Darfurians' political and economic marginalization by both the colonial and postcolonial Sudanese state has increasingly set the stage for identity politics to emerge as a potent weapon in their struggle for greater access to wealth and power. This has manifested itself in the emergence of what de Waal describes as a "historically bogus, but disturbingly powerful" dichotomy between "Arabs" and "Africans" in Darfur. De Waal concludes his essay with an examination of how contemporary local, regional, national, and international networks are exploiting this false dichotomy in pursuit of their own agendas.

The essays by Mahmood Mamdani and Salah M. Hassan highlight the selective ways in which the conflict has been presented, represented, and used by a range of actors in and outside of Sudan to promote their own agendas and interests. Mamdani's essay provides a nuanced analysis of the politics of conflict in and around Darfur by drawing attention to their global dimensions and long-term consequences for conflict resolution and sovereignty. Mamdani provides a powerful critique of the Save Darfur movement and its misleading representation of the war in Darfur. While unequivocal in his condemnation of the large number of civilian deaths, he contends that the huge discrepancy in numbers being reported in the Western media and quoted by organizations such as Save Darfur as proof of genocide, on the one hand, and the lower but still significant numbers reported by the UN Commission on Darfur, on the other hand, deserves to be scrutinized because it tells us something about the agenda behind some of those who have taken up the Darfur cause. He also problematizes the push by Western constituencies to internationalize the conflict through the deployment of a hybrid UN/AU force, which came at the heels of a deliberate effort to undermine the capabilities of the AU force. Mamdani further cautions those inside Darfur who are calling for an "outside" solution that external military intervention under the guise of protecting civilians may end up being a permanent occupation. Salah M. Hassan draws attention to the urgency of apprehending the politics of representation around Darfur "from within." Focusing on Sudan's historically strong civil society, Hassan elucidates how Sudanese civil society's analysis of the country's conflicts eschews oversimplified binary oppositions, such as "Arab North" versus "Christian/Animist South," or "Arab" versus "African" as in the case of Darfur. He argues in favor of looking at the origins of these conflicts

Darfur and the Crisis of Governance in Sudan

as manifestations of unequal development and historic injustices perpetrated against the margins by the ruling class of Arabized elites. In the process, Hassan reveals the vigorous engagement of Sudanese at all levels in the Darfur crisis, as well as other areas of conflict currently engulfing Sudan. His essay points to the need to foreground Sudanese voices if a genuine resolution to the country's manifold conflicts is to be pursued. Carina E. Ray's essay comprehensively surveys the reportage on Darfur in the (English-language) African press. Her exhaustive research turned up more than 1,500 articles published between early 2004 and December 2007, unequivocally demonstrating the great extent to which Africans, continent wide, have been reading and writing about Darfur over the last four years. Ray's essay analyzes how Darfur has been discussed in a wide cross-section of African newspapers, and concludes by probing what the African press can tell us about African understandings, opinions, and concerns in relation to Darfur.

The essays in this section emphasize the shifting and fluid nature of Darfurian identities and how their evolution over time has both shaped and been shaped by how the conflict is represented. Also emphasized are the politics of naming the conflict in and outside Sudan, and the far-reaching effects the media's coverage of the conflict has had on its development. Therefore, deconstructing the politics of representation and the role identity politics plays in shaping the conflict in Darfur is as crucial to its resolution as any other factor.

The third section, which focuses on issues related to gender, war, and violence, looks collectively at a particularly troubling aspect of the war in Darfur: its devastating effects on women. Based on ethnographic fieldwork among internally displaced women from the South and Darfur, Rogaia Mustafa Abusharaf's essay provides a comparative study of the ways in which violence against Southern Sudanese and Darfurian women has been used as a mechanism by which men seek to prove their masculinity and power over other men. While persistent violence has forestalled the promotion of women's rights, Abusharaf also contends that it has sharpened women's awareness of themselves as political subjects and in the best-case scenario may lead to new avenues of self-empowerment. Karin Willemse's essay analyzes how the Sudanese government's quest to mark the boundaries of an exclusive form of citizenship has relied on the twinned processes of otherizing groups it deems inferior – that is those who do not live up to the religious, class, and cultural standards of the Arabized elite – and then committing violence against such groups in an attempt to dislocate them from the nation. Willemse uses both gender and race as units of analysis in order to demonstrate how in the context of Darfur the politics of marginalization are manifested in raced and gendered discourses that adversely affect both men and women in particular ways. Willemse's essay is particularly compelling in its examination of the way in which the increasingly bleak economic picture in Darfur has produced a "crisis of masculinity" in which young men on both sides of the conflict are drawn to battle as a way of defending their manhood, and in the process often commit horrific crimes against women. Based on her experience as founder and director of the Salmmah Women's Resource Centre in Khartoum, Fahima A. Hashim provides an in-depth overview of how grassroots organizations in the Sudan are responding to gender-based violence in the context of the war in Darfur. Despite her own location within civil society, Hashim warned that the "NGO-ization" of society is creating a dangerous pattern of co-dependency, especially in light of the government's creation of its own well-funded parallel NGOs (known as GONGOs, i.e., governmental NGOs). She highlights the way in which GONGOSs have become the only space in which the government authorizes the activities of civil society, and thereby binds it to the state's agenda. This has made the task of providing services to victims of gender-based violence extremely difficult since the Sudanese state refuses to acknowledge the extent of such violence in Darfur.

As consistently emphasized by the human rights community, violence against women is one of the most pervasive human rights abuses across many societies, and more specifically in the context of war and in conflict zones. The essays in this section confirm that Darfur is not an exception. As in other sites of conflict, violence against women is rooted in the structural inequities between women and men, and is intended, as the papers have fully explained in the context of Darfur, to perpetuate masculine power and control. The essays also highlight the difficulties Sudanese NGOs and Sudanese women must cope with in the face of the government's denial of sexual violence in Darfur.

Section Four, "Darfur: Law, Human Rights, and Prosecution," begins with noted Sudanese lawyer, writer, and activist Kamal El-Gizouli's astute analysis of what he deems the "erroneous" confrontation between the NIF-controlled Sudanese government and the International Criminal Court (ICC) over the prosecution of war crimes in Darfur. El-Gizouli clearly articulates the array of ever-shifting "erroneous" excuses that the Sudanese government has used to evade facing the ICC, including the claim of national sovereignty. In an uncanny way, El-Gizouli seems to have anticipated the July 2008 referral by the chief prosecutor of the ICC, Luis Moreno-Ocampo, of the President of Sudan, Omar Hassan Al Bashir, to the ICC court on charges of genocide, crimes against humanity, and war crimes committed in Darfur. This, as El-Gizouli warns us, will have far-reaching implications on the future of a democratic and united Sudan. At the same time, he notes that demanding Khartoum's compliance is also complicated by the double standard of the international community toward the prosecution of war crimes in places such as Palestine and Iraq, and the refusal of the United States to sign the ICC Charter. The jointly authored essay by Adrienne L. Fricke and Amira Khair documents the significant difficulties involved in prosecuting sex crimes in the context of the ongoing conflict in Darfur, and in Sudan more generally, as well as the great risks women face in bringing such charges to official notice. Sudan's current legal code conflates rape with adultery (zina), thereby exposing women to punishment for adultery if they are not successful in proving that they have been raped. Evidentiary stipulations that require a minimum of four witnesses to substantiate a rape claim give some insight into just how perilous the legal system can be for survivors of rape. Munzoul A. M. Assal concludes this section with an effort to explain why both national (Sudanese) and international responses to the conflict in Darfur are flawed and/or complacent and have in effect escalated rather than de-escalated it. He notes that the government has not been willing to launch a credible effort to end the conflict because from the beginning it refused to acknowledge the roots of the conflict, choosing instead to paint it as a "tribal" conflict, and because it regards problems in peripheral regions as nuisances rather than legitimate national concerns. At the international level, he notes that while the condemnations have often been loud, an effective response has not been forthcoming primarily because of the inability of the international community to name what is actually happening in Darfur. Assal concludes his essay by recommending a way out of the current crisis that starts with the unity of purpose among the different armed rebel groups, and calls for the government to move beyond the stalemate and to engage the international community in a meaningful way that will allow it to find the tools and necessary structures to facilitate a meaningful settlement.

Together, the essays in this section navigate the legal terrain and the importance of prosecuting injustices in the context of Darfur as a crucial step toward peace. Moving from the confrontation between the ICC and the Al Bashir regime to the legal obstacles to prosecuting gender-based violence to the way in which national (Sudanese) and international responses have exacerbated the conflict, the essays underscore the importance of identifying the multiplicity of actors involved and assessing how their actions/inactions have deepened the crisis in order to undertake the hard work of bringing justice to Darfur.

The fifth and final section entitled "Sudanese Civil Society, the State, and the Struggle for Peace in Darfur," opens with a thought-provoking philosophical meditation on civil society, sovereignty, and violence by Grant Farred. While reflecting on the role that civil society might play in the political process of bringing about resolution to the war in Darfur and Sudan, Farred urges us to consider what happens to the "political" when civil society is championed so vigorously. In other words, he asks: Can the "civil" bring an end to violence without instituting the end of the "political"? It is not an easy question to answer, but certainly one worth thinking through if we are to comprehend the tenuous relationship between the "civil" and the "political." Musa Adam Abdul-Jalil's essay probes how the strategic niche that schoolteachers fill in Sudanese society, and particularly in North Darfur, has allowed them to play a particularly prominent role in shaping how the conflict in Darfur has unfolded. In many instances Abdul-Jalil points out that schoolteachers have acted in ways that have led to the escalation of the conflict by furthering ethnic polarization in the region. Al-Tayib Zain Al-Abdin's contribution draws upon a recent experience of organizing a workshop on the crisis with Sudanese NGOs and academic units – in his capacity as General Secretary of the Sudan Inter-Religious Council (SIRC) – to illustrate the considerable extent to which the government is intervening in the activities of civil society organizations, reinforcing a point made earlier by Fahima Hashim. Nonetheless, the success of the workshop, which brought together leading figures from Darfur, including intellectuals, members of parliament, leaders of the native administration who were specially invited from their respective regions to take part, and student activists, in addition to government officials, NGOs working in the region, and the media, serves as a testimony to the strength and perseverance of Sudan's civil society. Finally, Abaker Mohamed Abuelbashar, a leading member of the Sudan Liberation Movement/Army (SLM/A), draws on his firsthand experience as a representative of the SLM/A at the Abuja Peace Talks (2004–2006) in order to provide an account of why the lengthy talks were unable to successfully broker a resolution to the war. While confirming the SLM/A's position that a political rather than military solution is needed, Abuelbashar notes that the political solution offered at Abuja did not meet the minimum standards for addressing the root causes of the conflict. Ending on a more hopeful note, Abuelbashar reports that efforts by the SPLM in 2007–2008 have helped to reunify what was increasingly becoming a very fragmented rebel movement. Read together, the essays in this last section highlight the complex and often tense relationship between the state, civil society, and pro-Darfur movements. What is clear is that the state, and more specifically the NIF, remains the main obstacle to resolving the crisis in Darfur. Its denial of its own actions coupled with its repression of civil society organizations trying to proactively address what is happening in Darfur and the lack of unity that has for far too long characterized Darfur's rebel movements remain major obstacles to solving this crisis.

Throughout the first part of this volume we interspersed a visual essay by the accomplished Sudanese photographer Issam A. Abdel Hafiez and thematically divided his powerful images of Darfur, its landscape and its people, to complement as much as possible each of the five sections. Abdelhafiez's gripping photographs, which capture the sorrow, resilience, and hope of Darfurians, perhaps best symbolize our commitment to bringing a human face to the conflict by showing Darfurians in the full complexity of their lives, rather than as a monolithic entity whose victimization is the only salient component of their identities, as is often the case in the widely circulated existing visual images of the conflict. With few exceptions, the typical Western media representation of Darfur and its people has shifted between what has come to be known in current discourses of visual anthropology as a "pornography of violence" on the one hand, and "miserablism" on the other. The focus has been on the victimization, grotesqueness, and horror of the war, with an emphasis on showing victims when they are at their most vulnerable. We are not in any way suggesting that such images should be censored or hidden. However, the oversaturation of such images runs the risk of having a numbing effect on the public, who are bombarded by such imagery, and in the process normalizing the victim's pain and suffering. They also reinforce the stereotype of Africa as the "heart of darkness," where violence becomes a normalized aspect of the state of nature associated with the so-called primitive natives.

Part Two reproduces an array of primary documents and secondary sources, giving readers access to otherwise hard-to-find documents that chart and explicate critical moments in the history of the war in Darfur and the still unfolding efforts to resolve the conflict. These documents include manifestos and proposals by the major Darfurian resistance movements, as well as position papers by the SPLM/A and Sudanese Communist Party. Also included are a review of *The Black Book: Imbalance of Power and Wealth in Sudan*, along with the first part of *The Black Book* and documents of The Arab Gathering, accompanied by commentary by Abdullahi Osman El-Tom. We have also included major UN documents and resolutions pertaining to the conflict in Darfur. For the benefit of readers, a comprehensive bibliography of all referenced works in the book is accompanied by a selected bibliography by Eric Kofi Acree, the librarian of the John Henrick Clarke Africana Library at Cornell University. The volume concludes with the biographies of the contributing authors and an index.

The completion of this volume coincided with the dramatic development of the referral of President Omar Al Bashir to the ICC by Louis Moreno Ocampo in July 2008, the first-ever application for the arrest of a sitting president. This episode is proof of the speed with which Darfur-related events are moving – a rate faster than can be fully addressed and accommodated in this volume. For this reason we have included, as appendix N, the ICC Prosecutor's "Application for Warrant of Arrest under Article 58 Against Omar Hassan Ahmad Al Bashir: Summary of the Case," dated July 14, 2008.

Concluding Remarks

Despite the diversity of their perspectives, the essays in this volume by and large lead to the same conclusions: First, the conflict in Darfur is part and parcel of the larger crisis of governance in Sudan and must therefore be viewed holistically, rather than in isolation. Second, like its predecessor in the South, and long-brewing conflicts in the East, which have all witnessed rebellions against the central government, the war in Darfur must be understood as a derivative of the tension and inequality between the center and the margin. Finally, the onus is on the center to restructure power and address injustices within a truly democratic structure. The essays do, however, offer a diversity of opinion about how to resolve the conflict. For instance, there are those who advocate for a robust international intervention, such as Abdullahi Osman El-Tom and Abaker Mohamed Abuelbashar, while others like Mahmood Mamdani argue that if such a move is implemented without a clear mandate it may pave the way for a far more permanent occupation.

While the contributors to this volume agree that the essence of the conflict in Darfur is not religious, in that all Darfurians are Muslims, religion has emerged as a factor, albeit a subtle one.[9] While Darfurians are widely regarded as particularly pious and devout Muslims by the majority of Sudanese, contributors such as Fahima Hashim, Karen Willemse, and Abdullahi Osman El-Tom point to the negative rhetoric of NIF ideologues' about Darfurians, which casts them as less authentically Muslim from an orthodox perspective. This rhetoric has been especially visible in the discourse deployed by some of the regime's defenders to deny the existence of gender-based violence and the deliberate use of rape as a weapon of war against Darfurian women. The religious-cum-sexual piety of Darfurian women has been called into question by the regime's defenders and allies in Darfur, such as Musa Hilal,[10] in order to portray these women as willing participants rather than what they are: victims of rape and sexual violence. Thus, we also want to signal our awareness of the subtle ways in which religion is being used and/or abused in the context of the crisis in Darfur.

The process of editing this volume on Darfur, like the conference that preceded it, raises a fundamental question concerning our personal, moral, and political stand in relation to our responsibility as academics engaged in seeking a reasonable level of scholarly objectivity and truth. We realized from the beginning the need for rigorous analysis and understanding of the root causes of the violence in Darfur. However, we are also very clear that our objective is not to engage in an endless intellectual exercise that may help deconstruct the crisis but stops short of taking a clear stand on the issues at stake. Rather, we believe that such an exercise coupled with a clear moral and political stand on issues of injustice is the first step toward a lasting solution to the problem.

There is no doubt in our minds that the conflict in Darfur is about resistance to the injustices inflicted upon the people of Darfur, rooted in a state-sanctioned policy of marginalization, compounded by years of neglect and disregard for Darfurians' right to access their share of national wealth, to partake in the development of their region, and to share power at every level of governance. This has been exacerbated by the NIF government, which, instead of righting the wrongs, has resorted to a set of horrific counterinsurgency policies, including scorched-earth tactics, murder, rape, and other forms of gender-based violence, which in addition to their immediate impact has led to the massive displacement of millions of Darfurians and the destruction of their livelihoods over the last five years.

As in the case of apartheid South Africa, one does not need to live in Darfur to realize the horrific crimes against humanity and ethnic cleansing that Darfurians of specific ethnicities have been subjected to. In Darfur, justice has been delayed for too long. Justice needs to be served. As such, our engagement is motivated by a search for the truth in service of justice by engaging Sudanese voices, and more specifically the voices of Darfurians. Accordingly, in soliciting contributions to this book we tried our best to involve a diverse array of Sudanese scholars and civil society activists. Avoiding the pitfalls of a naïve authenticity, we engaged other scholars beyond Sudan whose experience and knowledge of Darfur and Sudanese affairs has further strengthened the volume's contents.

Finally, we tried as much as possible not to interfere with the contents of the essays, including instances in which we disagreed with some of the views expressed by our contributors. In the end, we must emphasize that the opinions expressed in this volume are the contributing authors' responsibility and not ours, except of course our own texts.

Notes

[1] See Nancy Scheper-Hughes and Philippe Bourgios, *Violence in Peace and War: An Anthology* (Oxford: Blackwell Publishing, 2004), p.1.

[2] Alexander de Waal and Julie Flint, *Darfur: A Short History of a Long War* (London: Zed Books, 2005), Alexander de Waal, *War in Darfur and the Search for Peace* (Cambridge, MA: Harvard University Press, 2007). Also see his classic work, *Famine That Kills: Darfur, Sudan*, Rev. ed., Oxford Studies in African Affairs (Oxford: Oxford University Press, 2005). M. W. Daly, *Darfur's Sorrow: A History of Destruction and Genocide* (Cambridge: Cambridge University Press, 2007). Abdel Ghaffar M. Ahmed and Leif Manger, eds., *Understanding the Crisis in Darfur: Listening to Sudanese Voices* (University of Bergen: Centre for Development Wa-Al-Hawiyah, First ed. (London: Cambridge Publishing House, 2004). Sulayman Hamid, *Darfur: Wadh' Al-Niqat 'Ala Al-Huruf* (Khartoum: Midan Books, 2004). Douglas Johnson, *The Root Causes of Sudan's Civil Wars* (Bloomington: Indiana University Press, 2003). Mahmood Madani, *Saviors and Survivors: Darfur, Politics, and the War on Terror* (New York: Pantheon, 2009). For other note-worthy literature that contributes to understanding the history and evolution of the conflict in Darfur please see the selected bibliography prepared by Eric Kofi Acree, which appears at the end of this volume.

[3] For a more detailed interrogation of the concept "tribe," see the article entitled "Talking about Tribe: Moving from Stereotype to Analysis," which appears in *Africa Action's* website: http://www.africaaction.org/bp/ethall.htm. This essay was part of a teaching resource produced by the Washington-based *Africa Policy Information Center* (APIC, now *Africa Action*), which advocates for the use of more suitable and less racist terminology in classroom discussions about Africa and its people.

[4] Archie Mafeje, "The Ideology of 'Tribalism'," *The Journal of Modern African Studies*, Vol. 9, No. 2 (Aug., 1971), pp. 253–261.

[5] Mohamed Suliman, "Ethnicity from Perception to Cause of Violent Conflicts: The Case of the Fur and Nuba Conflicts in Western Sudan" (paper presented at the CONTICI International Workshop, Bern, Switzerland, July 8–11, 1997 1997). Suliman's essay can also be located at http://www.ifaanet.org/ifaapr/ethnicity_inversion.htm.

[6] Alex de Waal, "Tragedy in Darfur: On Understanding and Ending the Horror," *Boston Review*, Volume 29, Number 5, October–November 2004.

[7] Here we would like to note that another alternative to the misleading term *Arab* is, as Alex de Waal advocates in his essay, *Sudanized*. While we understand de Waal's rationale we have refrained from using *Sudanized* because to do so risks accepting on some level the hegemonic project of identity formation that the riverian ruling elites have embarked upon.

[8] See Alex de Waal's essay in this volume, "Who Are the Darfurians? Arab and African Identities, Violence, and External Engagement."

[9] Religion has always been a factor in Sudanese politics since independence. There are many examples of this, ranging from the specter of the Islamic constitution proposed at different times by the Islamist movement in alliance with conservative elements within the traditional sectarian parties, such as Umma and DUP, in their efforts to curb the influence of the left, secular political forces, and civil society during democratic periods, to the use of religion by the Islamists in their anti-communist propaganda. With the introduction of *shari'a* law in 1983 and the eventual ascendency of the NIF to power in 1989, religion has, however, intersected with the state in an unprecedented manner.

[10] Musa Hilal has been widely cited in the media saying that Darfurian women had brought rape upon themselves by being sexually promiscuous.

Entrance to Kalmah Camp
Nyala, 2006

Part 1
Essays

Section One
Origins and Evolution of the Conflict

1 Darfur:
A Problem within a Wider Problem

Mansour Khalid

Background

The Darfur conflict, on which the attention of the world has been riveted since 2003, has a vintage pedigree and, consequently, deeper causes than what analysts and commentators are currently proffering. Political, socioeconomic, cultural, and geographic factors interlaced to produce this seemingly unending conflict. One may also add a historical dimension that makes the Darfur region, compared to other regions in Sudan, unique. Since the nineteenth century, successive Sudanese rulers have never ceased to cast covetous eyes on Darfur; indeed, some of them gave their all to bring it under their jurisdiction. That greed for territorial aggrandizement was mutual, for while Khartoum rulers (Turks, Mahdists, British) were intent on conquering Darfur, Darfurian rulers, on their side, pulled out all the stops to extend their jurisdiction up to the banks of the Nile and eventually succeeded in incorporating Kordofan and parts of the Funj kingdom into the Darfur Sultanate.

The Sultanate, however, remained autonomous under its own sovereign rulers up to 1917. In effect, neither did France incorporate Darfur into neighboring French Central Africa (present-day Chad), nor did the British seek to absorb it in 1899 into the Anglo-Egyptian Sudan. Amazingly, that was the case even though Darfur was previously subjugated by the Turkish administration with the help of Zubeir Pasha and remained, thereafter, as part of the Sudanese state under the Mahdist. The Anglo-Egyptian condominium, in point of fact, rather than assimilating Darfur into the Anglo-Egyptian Sudan, decided to recognize de jure its autonomous status.

Furthermore, the sovereign Sultanate of Darfur, unlike other regions in Sudan, conducted its own foreign policy. For example, in 1799, Sultan Abdel Rahman al Rasheed established relations with Napoleon after his defeat of the Mamluks in Egypt and dispatched, in response to Napoleon's request, a contingent of Darfurian fighters to join the French army that was being prepared to invade the Near East. A successor of al Rasheed, Sultan al Fadl, aligned himself with the Sultan of Turkey during World War I alongside Germany in its war against Britain and France. That was an adventure into high international politics that led to the undoing of the Sultanate's sovereign status; the British did not hesitate in the face of this faux pas to conquer Darfur and annex it to Sudan in 1917.

The Root Causes

That said, the root causes of the Darfur conflict are to be found in policy omissions or commissions by the successive "national" governments that ruled Sudan since independence. Even so, those causes are essentially no different than those that have bedeviled other peripheral areas of Sudan. They may be summarized in two parts: first, hegemony by an omnipotent and omniscient Khartoum-based central government over the rest of Sudan; and second, the perpetuation of the economic development paradigm established by British rulers to serve their colonial interests.

I call the first the "Wingatesque" system of rule – the system of rule established by Reginald Wingate Pasha, the second Governor General of Sudan, to whom the establishment of Sudan's colonial administration was attributed. Be that as it may, the modern Sudanese state predates the British colonial system; it goes back to the Turkish rule. In effect, it was the Turks who artificially created that state by bringing together antagonistic local kingdoms without trying to reconcile their inherent antipathies. The colonial economic development regime was religiously followed by successive national governments even after it became obvious that that regime was both dysfunctional and detrimental to the public good in an independent Sudan.

For those two phenomena (i.e., inapposite system of rule and disadvantageous mode of economic management and development) to stay alive half a century after independence is not only regrettable but also a clear indicator of the failure of the post-independence Sudanese state to address the issue of nation building. As nationalist romantics, Northern Sudanese political analysts may be circumspect in subscribing to this condemnatory judgment on the "fathers of the nation," but any serious analyst who rigorously uses scientific tools of analysis has no alternative but to conclude that those leaders, at least as regards creating an enabling environment for Sudan's unity, do not deserve more than a below-average grade.

Was that because those leaders were evil or callous? Of course not. The leaders in question, especially in the early years of independence, comprised an array of proficient public officers and high-minded leaders. However, theirs was a Sudan writ small: an Arabo-Islamic country with no past before the coming of the Arabs to the land of Sudan and the conversion of its indigenous peoples to Islam. With this type of perception there shall be no future for the sons and daughters of Sudan who do not share this characterization of the country. Obviously, there is something more serious about this perception of the Sudanese reality. The perception not only reflects misapprehension of historical and contemporary realities of life in the Sudan but also often betrays complete obliviousness to those realities. In effect, it demonstrated a lack of vision of how to unite a country suffering from or, depending on the way you look at it, endowed with multiple diversities. Diversity can either be a running spring of mutual enrichment or perpetual strife. By *vision* here we mean the perceptiveness and insight that had enabled, for example, the Indian Fathers of the Nation to keep their country intact through appropriate constitutional architecture and pertinent economic, social, and institutional measures. India is a country that is beleaguered by religious, social, ethnic, and cultural heterogeneities much more complex than those encountered by Sudan.

This lack of vision is surprisingly revealed in the way Sudan's ruling class approached constitution making. In the fifty-two years that have elapsed since independence, that ruling class has failed to devise a permanent constitution for the country that responded to the aspirations of all its sons and daughters and was flexible enough to consolidate commonalities and harmonize conflictual differences rather than heightening them.

Consequent to this inadequacy in devising a supreme law acceptable to all, national governments settled for minor and formal modifications on the constitution designed by the colonial regime in 1953 for the sole purpose of administering Sudan during the self-government period (1953–1955). This was the case not only when

Sudan's ruling class inherited power from the British (January 1956) but also when they wrested power from two military regimes (October 1964 from Abboud and April 1985 from Numeiri). If that was the measure of the inadequacy of those regimes in addressing the most rudimentary task of a ruler – laying the foundation for governance – then little wonder that they underperformed in scaling down the size of the nation's crisis.

The Writing on the Wall

Why then have the people of Darfur, together with other politically or economically disadvantaged areas in Sudan's geographic north, continued to suffer their affliction in silence, while southerners, without ceasing, persevered in their struggle against what they perceived to be political marginalization and economic neglect? Sectarian affiliation, especially in the case of Darfur, had something to do with it. In reality, affiliation to the two major Islamic sects (Ansar and Khatmiya) was so staunch in Kordofan and Darfur, in the west, as it was in the Red Sea and Kassala in eastern Sudan, that those regions became the main bastions of support for the two sectarian-based political parties (Umma and National Unionist). The two parties ruled the Sudan during successive multiparty regimes and throughout their rule sought to maintain the political status quo and ensure acquiescence to it by their supporters in those regions. The assumed docility of those regions must have persuaded the two parties that nothing was the matter with the status quo when, indeed, something quite serious was the matter.

Effectively, when the chickens came home to roost, the sectarian hold began to wane. For example, from the late 1950s and especially since the mid-1960s, protest movements proliferated in West, East, and Central Sudan. Those movements called, collectively and individually, for the eradication of what they described as historical injustices. At the heart of those injustices was the real or perceived excessive control and unfair sharing of national power and wealth by the central authority, which was detectably colonized by northerners: those in senior ministerial posts, higher ranks and echelons in the army and civil service, top managers in banks and public corporations, and others of similar social rank. The protest movements in question comprised the Beja Congress (1958), Nuba Mountains General Union (1965), and Darfur Development Front (1964). The writing has thus been on the wall since the mid-1960s.

Cooperation among those groups climaxed in the formation of a joint parliamentary caucus that threatened, for the first time, the hegemony of northern traditional parties over national politics. Indeed, that caucus eventually encompassed southern Sudanese parties despite efforts by the ruling class to dissuade regional groups from cooperation with southern "infidels." The northern ruling class not only failed to address legitimate claims by politically aggrieved and economically marginalized Sudanese but also chose to sow the seeds of hatred among citizens of the same country based on ethnic and religious variations. Furthermore, despite sundry efforts to revise Sudan's constitution and system of rule with a view to addressing the sociocultural particularities of southern Sudan, those that relate to other peripheral states in the geographic north, including Darfur, were never on the table. The apotheosis of this oblivious, if not biased, policy was reached with

Darfur: A Problem within a Wider Problem

the ascendancy of Al Ingaz to power by the end of June 1989 and the launching of its Islamiscization program. That program covered all walks of life, including politics and war, resulting in the transformation of Sudan's civil war into a holy war. This pushed Sudan's polarization to extremes.

All the same, given the religious zeal of its people, Darfur became one of the strongholds of the new Islamic regime. However, religious devotion was not the sole reason for the rallying of Darfurians to the National Islamic Front (NIF); there was also the arduous work of Dr. Hassan Turabi, the Secretary-General of NIF, to build up support for the Islamist cause long before the emergence of NIF. During Numeiri's era, Turabi was the Darfur Political Overseer on behalf of the Sudanese Socialist Union (SSU), the ruling party at the time. Rather than using that position for the promotion of the SSU, Turabi furtively used it to lay the foundation for his future party, the NIF.

Explosion of a Myth

The emergence of the Sudan People's Liberation Movement/Army (SPLM/A) under the leadership of John Garang De Mabior in 1983 and his call for the restructuring of the Sudanese state through armed and other means of struggle ushered in a new era in Sudan's political history. The aim of the SPLM's multifaceted struggle was to end historical injustices and lay the foundation for a new Sudan based on justice for all, recognition of the country's multiple diversities, and empowerment of disadvantaged areas and groups. This agenda captured the imagination of many Sudanese, especially those in marginalized groups. Eventually, it produced a sea change in Sudan's political landscape, as evidenced by the impassioned manner in which Garang was received in Khartoum.

In reality, John Garang saw the "Southern problem" as a facet of a wider problem: that of Sudan. Without resolving the national issue, he opined, it would be well nigh impossible to resolve localized issues. To achieve that end, Garang made clear that the SPLM did not intend to fight wars on behalf of other Sudanese aggrieved regions and groups. Nonetheless, considering the common cause that united those groups with the SPLM, Garang pledged to do everything within his movement's power to channel the anger of the aggrieved groups and enhance their capacity to sustain struggle for change. Garang also asserted that Sudan's unity could never be predicated on substructures that were not commonly shared, no matter how hallowed those substructures were. In a country of multiple diversities, he maintained, any attempt to selectively choose one variable of those diversities as a badge of national identification would backfire. Only the status of joint citizenship and equality among all citizens irrespective of religion, culture, gender, or ethnic origin will keep Sudan and Sudanese people together.

Darfurian political activists were among the first to apprehend Garang's argument and respond to his call. Among those were dyed-in-wool NIF cadres like Yahia Dawood Bolad. The failure of the Islamist agenda to respond to what Darfurians, like Bolad, considered existential demands proved the fragility of the claim that religion, to the exclusion of all other factors, shall be a panacea for all Sudanese ills such as national disunity and conflict among people of different religions and cultures. Truly, man cannot live by bread alone, but it is equally true that without bread, religion shall not sustain man. In effect, much as religion failed to bring together Sindis and Bengalis in Pakistan, a state that was built on the brick and mortar of Islam, efforts to hold the Sudanese together by the glue of religion will not succeed either.

The cogency of the SPLM vision continued to attract other Darfurians, of whom Abdel Wahid M. Nur was one. In effect, Nur adopted, for his movement, the name of Sudanese Liberation Movement (SLM) and sought support for it from its namesake: SPLM. Another example of a Darfurian political activist who parted ways with NIF is Khalil Ibrahim, who was earlier involved in jihad against the "infidels" of Southern Sudan. Khalil established his own Justice and Equality Movement (JEM) and also sought support from his erstwhile foe, "the infidel" SPLM. To my mind, however, Khalil was also induced by the success of the SPLM in winning hearts and minds in Northern Sudan as well as in eventually concluding the landmark Comprehensive Peace Agreement (CPA) in 2005. The impact of those achievements clearly left their mark on Khalil, the jihadist, and on a large number of his onetime fellow Islamists.

The agreement in question called for total restructuring of the Sudanese state, effecting, for the first time since independence, a paradigm shift in the colonial development pattern through the Wealth-Sharing Protocol, radical decentralization of government via the Power-Sharing Protocol, and recognition of Sudan's cultural diversities, in which value was given to all local languages and cultures, and the redressing of imbalances in the civil, diplomatic, and security services. Even though the third measure concerned only Southern Sudan, it also provided a model to be applied by others. Those were enough factors to put fire under Khalil. It is, therefore, not a coincidence that the present phase of conflict in Darfur coincided with the first indications that there was a breakthrough in the peace negotiations between SPLM and the government of Sudan. If the South could achieve all those gains through armed struggle, Darfurian leaders must have asked themselves, why shouldn't we follow suit?

Intra- and Interstate Dimension of Conflict
It is obvious from the preceding that the Sudanese ruling class has, for one, failed to preempt conflict by devising appropriate political, economic, and constitutional measures. And rather than seriously engaging disaffected and malcontent groups in meaningful dialogues aimed at addressing the root causes of disaffection, they chose to destabilize those groups through the tactic of divide and rule, and sometimes, divide and destroy. That destabilization was based first on creating splits within the groups with a view to swallowing or destroying them. As a part of that destabilization stratagem, the centralizing government, especially during NIF rule, settled on creating barons in the periphery to rule on its behalf and, in exchange, gave those barons a free hand in satisfying their own agendas. Moreover, as a prize for protecting the centralizing state from the heat of war, these barons were allowed to loot the areas under their control with impunity. Prime examples of these tactics were also exemplified, in the case of Southern Sudan, by militias recruited from southern ethnic groups to destabilize the SPLM within the South, or from self-styled "friendly forces" drawn from Northern "Arab" tribes in the North–South border

Darfur: A Problem within a Wider Problem

region. The role of the border forces was to hem in SPLA. As for Darfur, that was the basic role entrusted to the so-called *Janjawid* by the government, especially before the international community focused its binoculars on the region.

Rebel movements swiftly responded in kind to the government's tactics. The SPLM, for example, rather than getting embroiled in Northern conflicts (i.e., Eastern Sudan and Darfur) provided advice and material support to Northern warriors. Sure enough, that support was invariably commensurate with the support provided by the government to its allied forces, who were entrusted with incapacitating the SPLM. This is the context within which the dynamics of internal destabilization need to be seen.

However, the interstate spillover of the Darfur conflict is equally a self-inflicted impairment, and Sudanese governments, in general, are not without blemish in this regard. Darfur borders three countries: Libya, Chad, and Central African Republic, the last of which also shares borders with Southern Sudan and played a negligible role in the conflict. However, since independence in 1956, Sudan's relations with Libya, and then with Chad, after it gained independence in 1960, were cordial and remained so until the 1970s. Muammar Qaddafi's rise to power (September 1969) and his activist policy to Arabicize Africa caused commotion in the region. Qaddafi, especially after the death of Nasser, set his sights on extending the Arab Empire, not only from the Atlantic Ocean to the Persian Gulf as Nasser was dreaming, but also into the African Sahel. Accordingly, Darfur became a pawn in a game of other people's making. That game was characterized by continual duels between Libya and successive Chadian regimes on the one hand, and between Libya and successive Khartoum governments on the other hand. All of those governments, of their own volition, factored Libya's concerns and ambitions into their foreign policy decisions, irrespective of the harmful effect that this may have had on peace within Darfur. In fact, the Sudanese governments' position in that period oscillated between supporting Chad (under Numeiri and Tombalbaye) or Libya (in the early years of Numeiri's rule and throughout the post-Numeiri era). The latter phase witnessed the escalation of encroachments by nomadic camel owners into farms traditionally owned by sedentary "African" farmers. Those nomadic tribes (dubbed "Arabs") were sponsored by Libya in its war against the Chadian government at the time, while Khartoum governments benignly overlooked that spectacle irrespective of its egregious effects on Darfur.

The terms *Arab* and *African* are dubious, not in their historical or cultural context, but in their present contrived contextualization. Sudan, with more than 300 spoken languages and nearly 400 ethnic groups, is one of the most ethnically diverse countries in the world. Darfur itself, with its 35 ethnic groups, is one of the most ethnically diverse regions in Sudan. In fact, if any fair commentator wants to detect a common thread that binds all those groups together, be it in Darfur or Sudan at large, that thread is neither Arabism (racially defined), Africanity (culturally defined), nor religion, be it Islam or Christianity. Large communities in Sudan adhere to traditional belief systems, which Sudan's 1973 Constitution designated "noble belief systems." Consequently, the Sudanese need to settle for a simple reality: They are all Sudanese of different ethnic origins, with diverse cultures and adhering to manifold religions. And while each group within this mixed bag of entities has every right to take pride in its distinctive culture, religion, or language, allowing any one to assume the preponderance of its culture, language, or religion over those espoused by other citizens will create discord and antagonism among Sudanese people. What I describe here is not a thesis I am advancing, but a clause enshrined in the constitution born out of the CPA. Clearly, it took Sudan half a century to come to this self-evident truth.

All the same, world media continue to define the conflict in Darfur as a clash between Arabs and Africans. This is a gross misreading of a complex situation in which geography, history, politics, and cultural proclivities all play a part. Worse still is the attempt by the media to present this flawed view as the only viable basis for decision making by the international community.

The misrepresentation of the Darfur crisis did not stop with the media's specious shorthand. Of late, environmental factors characterized by competition over an ever-decreasing natural resource base by an ever-increasing human and animal population have also been presented as the prime cause of the conflict. This view has progressively gathered currency following the statement made by UN Secretary-General Ban Ki-Moon after his visit to Darfur in September 2007. Environmental factors, as well as those emanating from inter- and intrastate spillovers of the conflict to which I alluded earlier, should only be treated as multipliers, not causes, of conflict. Suffice it to say that environmental degradation neither produces armies nor furnishes arms to combatants. Men do.

The writing was also on the wall on this score as early as the mid-1980s. Threats to the natural environment besetting Africa from the Horn and across the Sahel to the Atlantic were well known. This area of Africa suffered cyclical droughts in 1984–1985 and 1989–1990 and 1997, which upset the balance between agriculture and grazing. The governments of those regions drew up action plans, created sub-regional institutions, of which IGAD was one, and assigned roles to member states for the implementation of those plans. Sudan's government, among others in the region, failed to effectively carry out those plans. By attributing the Darfur conflict mainly to environmental origins, one may end up absolving the Sudanese governments' wrongheaded policies that have incrementally aggravated that conflict, indeed, offering an escape route for the perpetrators of those policies.

Obviously, the Darfur crisis is not one to which the world can turn a blind eye. Let us remember that, after only five years of war, Darfur is now in a much graver situation than the one in which the South was after two decades of war. According to UNHCR, there are today 2.4 million Darfurian displaced persons and 240,000 refugees compared, respectively, to 2.7 million and 255,000 from Southern Sudan. The deployment of African Union (AU) and UN Security Council resources in April 2004 and March 2005, respectively, was prompted by the size of the catastrophe.

But peace in Darfur cannot be achieved solely through the deployment of a 26,000-strong peacekeeping force. The crisis is political and should primarily be resolved by the Sudanese themselves. To ensure this, a domestic environment conducive to peacemaking must be created. This environment presupposes:

1. Genuine commitment by all parties to pacific settlement of conflict and unconditional engagement to partake in peace talks.

2. Cessation of hostilities by all parties and regional (AU) and international (UN) supervision of related arrangements.
3. Articulation of a common position by all Darfurian factions, especially insofar as the legitimate demands of Darfurians and future peace-building efforts are concerned.
4. Ascertaining the views of Darfurian civil society, including traditional leaders as important constituents of the peacemaking process.

Within the broader national context, it is imperative that the democratization and the national reconciliation processes called for by the CPA and enshrined in Sudan's interim constitution be concluded. For comprehensive peace agreements to be sustained, they must be comprehensively owned. This requires, on the side of the government, a demonstration of the same spirit that made the CPA possible. On the part of the Darfurian factions, it requires, as alluded to earlier, focus on and proper articulation of legitimate claims around which the people of Darfur would coalesce and the world would willingly and with conviction come forward to support. Current efforts by the SPLM to bring Darfurians together aim at achieving this end.[1] As for the regional and international community, the issue that should prey on their minds must be, first and foremost, peacemaking.

Notes

[1] In November 2007, the efforts of the SPLM to unify several of the Darfur rebel factions in Juba succeeded in bringing many of them together under two major groups that declared themselves ready to negotiate with the Khartoum government. As reported by the *Sudan Tribune* website on Friday November 30, 2007, "The Juba Declaration of Unity comes into force from November 14th 2007 and consented to by Sudan Liberation Movement (SLM) led by Haydar Galu Kuma, Sudan Liberation Movement (SLM) Field Command Abdel Aziz Ahmad Omer, United Revolutionary Forces Front led by Alhadi Adam Ajab Aldoar, National Movement for Development and Reforms (MNRD) led by Hassan Khamis Jarou, Justice and Equality Movement of Collective Leadership (JEM-CL) led by Tajadine Beshir Niam." http://www.sudantribune.com.spip.php?article24965

2   Ideological Expansionist Movements versus Historical Indigenous Rights in the Darfur Region of Sudan:
From Actual Homicide to Potential Genocide

Atta El-Battahani

Reports on Darfur have different characterizations of the situation – "ethnic-cleansing," "slaughter ... more than just a conflict," and "genocide." These views are perpetuated by the actions of government troops, rebel groups, and tribal militias, the most notorious of which are the *Janjawid*. Efforts by the government of Sudan, the African Union (AU), the United Nations (UN), and other members of the international community to put an end to this conflict have contributed to the further deterioration of the security situation. In recent years it has been reported that the Khartoum government resettled alien nomads of "Arab" origin in areas of Darfur from which the indigenous populations of "African" origin were forcibly displaced and moved to other, less fertile areas.

The ferocity of the conflict is indicative of the desperate positions that rival groups are locked into. Arab tribes believe that "Zurqa," or non-Arab tribes, mainly Fur, Masaliet, and Zaghawa, are harboring secessionist tendencies aimed at establishing an independent state to drive the Arabs out. "Zurqa" believe that Arab tribes are using the Islamic central government to marginalize them and grab more of their land. Smaller tribes, most likely with the connivance of the Khartoum government, were drawn into the conflicts, forming paramilitary and militias such as the Janjawid, whose atrocities were displayed on TV news programs all over the world. Other factors also count and are closely related to Darfur conflicts, such as the Islamic-expansionist movement's exploitation of the collapse and failure of state institutions and political manipulation of ethnic/tribal elites as pawns or instruments for its own grand designs.

At the root of the conflict is an unequal relationship between a predominantly Arab-Muslim center of power and the peripheral regions in Sudan – a relationship that has always been tense. Since the 1980s, both the central government and peripheral regions have been at war. These conflicts include a renewal of civil war in the South, violent tribal and ethnic conflicts in Darfur, and the deteriorating situation in East Sudan. The escalation of conflicts in Darfur is a manifestation of the failure of the national political ruling class to lead and to establish itself as hegemonic power bloc, in the Gramscian integrative sense of hegemony.

For the dominant faction within the ruling class, Darfur is too close to heart to give away; given the present power configuration, Darfur lays at the center of the debate on legitimacy, identity, and access to strategic resources (e.g., land, animal wealth, and political power). Hence, conflict between "Arab" nomads and "Zurqa" sedentary farmers in Darfur over land is misconstrued as "Arabs" versus "Africans" in Sudan at large. Playing on perceived or real fears combined with their failure to lead, Northern Arabized leaders rehearsed the politics of the past and drew historical parallels with the fate of Arabs after the 1495 collapse of the Muslim empire in Spain and the massacre of Arab and Indian Zanzibaris in the wake of the Zanzibar revolution of 1964, and in apocalyptic terms, heightened "existential concerns" in the extreme. The Arab Gathering's slogan about the "critical future existence of Arabs" in Darfur draws upon these fears as a means of drumming up support both internally and externally vis-à-vis a perceived enemy of the people of Sudan. Ironically, the signing of the Comprehensive Peace Agreement (CPA) in 2005 amplified identity politics and paved the way for an alliance between the center and land-hungry tribes in Darfur, who played the identity-demography card to the tune of the center. Conflict in Darfur is best understood via a *typology* of conflicts and a *periodization* schema, bringing out the specificity of Darfur's relation to the center of power.

This essay starts with a brief overview of the history and evolution of the Darfur region, followed by a survey of the wide range of factors behind the conflict in Darfur. Such factors are used as a foundation for suggesting a typology of conflict in Darfur, as a means of capturing the complexity of the current war. This is further explored in chronological order leading up to a set of conclusions, which should guide the way to a just and lasting resolution of the unfolding catastrophe in Darfur.

Darfur Region: The Land, Population, and Conflict

The Darfur region lies in Western Sudan and is approximately 490,000 square kilometers, about the size of France. The region covers the territorial area that now comprises the three states of Northern Darfur, Southern Darfur, and Western Darfur, with their capitals being El Fasher, Nyala, and El Geneina, respectively. The region borders three neighboring countries: Central Africa and Chad to the west and the Libyan Arab Jamahiria to the north. It also borders the three Sudanese states of Northern and Western Kordofan to the east and the state of Bahr El-Ghazal to the south. The population of the region is approximately 3,093,699. Of this total, 15 percent are nomads, 14 percent urban dwellers, and 71 percent are rural sedentaries. An observable population increase over the 1993 census figure and high population mobility are accounted for by migrations and displacement from neighboring areas, deterioration of economic conditions, and tribal conflicts.[1]

The region comprises three states – North, West, and South Darfur – and is divided into nineteen locality councils (*mahaliyas*). The states and the mahaliyas stand as corporate bodies, with the state run by a governor (*wali*) and the *mahaliya* by a commissioner (*mutamad*). Under this setup, there is the native administration system; parallel to these structures, there exist the judiciary, the police, and the army.

There are about fifty major tribes/ethnic groups and fifty smaller ones, identified as Arab and non-Arab ("Zurqa") groups. In Northern Darfur, the Arabs and Zaghawa (non-Arabs) are predominantly pastoral camel nomads (*abbala*). The central zones are inhabited by non-Arab sedentary groups such as the Fur, Masalit, and others, who are mainly engaged in farming. In Southern Darfur the predominantly Arabic-speaking *Baggara*, cattle owners, live side by side with non-Arab groups, sedentarists, and seminomads.

In Darfur, as in other parts of the country, land is divided into tribal domains known as *dars*. This, combined with the region's pastoralism, which entails the seasonal crossing of other tribal dars, has resulted in conflicts over resources that have intensified during the last three decades. With the exception of lands where urban centers are established, there is no piece of land that is not claimed by a particular tribe/ethnic group. Historical processes of tribal land acquisition differ from one tribe to the next. Some tribes acquired their landholdings by conquest, others by mere occupation of virgin lands, and others still by charters issued by Fur sultans. However, more important is the fact that it was the colonial government that effectively tribalized the land in the region now known as Darfur. "Tribal" consciousness and local patriotism were encouraged by the colonial administration to counteract the formation of nationalism. This was generally recognized as the policy of Indirect Rule, which mandated the appointment of tribal chiefs who would be in charge of their respective tribes and respective landholdings. Local administrative boundaries were drawn coterminously to tribal presence. However, the Indirect Rule model gave preferential treatment to larger tribes. Minority tribes were sometimes incorporated into the chieftainship of majority tribes, apparently against their will. Later on, desires for independence by such minority tribes and resistance by majority tribes constituted one form of tribal conflict.

The economy of the region largely depends on subsistence rain-fed agriculture and livestock raising. Agricultural production is characterized by dependence on erratic rainfall, lack of or minimal use of innovated inputs, poor technologies, and underdeveloped marketing infrastructures. Livestock production is predominantly migratory, suffering from a high prevalence of disease, poor husbandry practices, opportunistic use of the range, and again, undeveloped marketing infrastructures. The once-existing balance between the natural resource base and the needs of the population has been toppled by the annual rainfall variability, the long-term decline in rainfall, and the drought cycles, followed by drastic land-use changes, which are manifested in land and environmental degradation, frequent crop failure, food shortages, and range deterioration, with consequences of massive population movements and conflict over resources.[2]

A complex interplay of multiple factors contributed to the region's lack of security and widespread violent conflicts. Conflicts in greater Darfur stem from one or a combination of the following: local intertribal/interethnic conflicts; regional conflicts; and/or conflicts with the central government, over the distribution of national wealth and power, with all levels of conflict reflecting an underlying pattern of denying access to resources. Since the 1970s, recurring droughts and famine, along with the region's shrinking resource base among other things, triggered violent conflicts in which the widespread use of a variety of homemade and modern weapons resulted in colossal damage to property and human life.

The Range of Conflicts

A range of structural factors and catalyst factors all contributed to conflict and aggravation of confict in Darfur. These range from land, water points, *masarat* and *maraheel* (migratory pathways), drought and environmental degradation, tribal/ethnic rivalries, collapsed infrastructure, armed robbery, population movements, power struggle by educated elites, lack of basic social services, central government's ineffective administrative machinery in the region, deterioration and spillover of regional conflicts making weapons available and fomenting ethnic support, and the scramble by international powers over the riches of the region.

With regard to Darfur's ethnic-cum-racial composition, Harold MacMichael, a well-known British historian of Sudan, classified the regional population into three groups: the Arabs, the Non-Arabs, and the West Africans.[3] The West Africans have been fully integrated in regional communities identifying themselves as Arabs or non-Arabs. This integration was made possible because many tribal entities in the region have relatives of kin in neighboring Chad (e.g., the Masalît, the Zaghawa, the Bargo, the Borno, and almost all camel and cattle Arab nomads). The cattle nomads, otherwise known as the Baggara, occupy the rich savanna belt along latitude 12. They make seasonal movements to the south during the dry seasons and the north during the rainy seasons. Some are increasingly becoming transhumant, combining farming with livestock raising. Seasonal movements of the cattle nomads bring them occasionally into conflict with Bahr El-Ghazal population and farmers to the north of the savanna belt. The camel nomads, who are mostly Arabs, occupy the northern portion of the region amid the Zaghawa population, who also raise camels, but are largely engaged in cultivation whenever adequate rain is received in their semidesert country.

The drought of the African Sahelian belt, which started during the early 1970s, resulted in southward movements for both the Zaghawa and the camel nomads, and brought them into conflict with almost all sedentary populations to the south. Not only the camel Arabs and the Zaghawa are found in this semidesert land. There are also the *Midob* in the northeastern corner and the *Mellit Berti* to the south of the Midob. The strip of land between the two extreme zones – the semidesert and savanna – is the one with a sedentary population engaged in rain-fed agriculture. Major non-Arab tribes are to be found in this ecological belt – the Masalît, to the extreme west, the Fur, around Jebel Merra, the Birgid to the east of Jebel Merra, and the Berti of the eastern portion of northern Darfur State. There are also numerous other tribal entities living in bigger tribes' homelands (i.e., dars) or in their own smaller dars.

Deterioration of the natural environment and the lack of sustainable development programs in the Darfur region as a whole, and in the marginal areas in particular, disturb the equilibirium and mutual benefits of nomadism and subsistence agriculture. Consequently, movement to other dars and the lack of respect for the traditional system of organizing this movement led to confrontation. *Masarat* or *Marheel* are long-standing arrangements for land use to regulate peaceful coexistence between farmers and herders. The nomads in their customary annual movements usually use *Masarat* or migratory routes. Recently, as a consequence of environmental decline and mechanized schemes, farmers moved into the masarat zone and sometimes closed the assigned migratory routes. Then the herders open these routes by force, contributing to insecurity and violent conflict. The recent armed conflict has caused much insecurity in the area. This feeling of insecurity forced both farmers and nomads to arm themselves. As in the Mahriyya – Bani Halba conflict (1978) and the Masalît – Arabs conflict (1996), almost all conflicting tribes now have their own militia trained by tribesmen retired from the military or police services. These militias are well equipped with modern firearms, which make contemporary tribal conflicts so deadly.[4]

Section One: Origins and Evolution of the Conflict

Modern firearms were obtained initially from defeated or retreating Chadian factions, but later the region became a marketplace for firearms smuggled from different sources. The Chadian connection added another dimension: war culture. After engaging in a protracted civil war, the Chadians regarded the use of firearms as normal. Many warring factions in Darfur have relatives of kin across the Sudan – Chadian border (e.g., the Masalit, the Zaghawa, and almost all Arab subtribes). Conflicting parties accuse one another of receiving support from their Chadian brethren. The influence of external factors, such as the Libyan and Chadian conflicts, and the vested interest of the Sudanese political parties to win elections and get allies also aggravated tribal conflict by supporting one tribe against the others.

The rise of power-hungry, urban-based "elite" groups among each tribe made the elite of the smaller tribes resent the traditional divisions of dars and categorization of citizens according to their ascribed status of owners or affiliates. Hence, the conflict over power and resources contributed to many tribal conflicts. It is a contra-dictory situation between the rule of the constitution, in which all citizens are equal, and that of tradition, which divides resources unequally. In their pursuit of power, Darfur's ethnic tribal elites often seek support not only from Khartoum elites but also from neighboring states, such as Chad and Libya. In many cases, tribal zeal for political power is not limited to the tribe's own dar. Some tribes are known for their unlimited political ambition to extend their authority beyond their territiorial boundaries. Many observers perceive the Zaghawa as having such a zeal for political power. As mentioned earlier and for the same reason, the Zaghawa have conflicted with almost all tribes among whom they sought settlement (e.g., the Mîma, the Birgid, the Mararît, the Maaliya). This type of conflict involves one of the most contro-versial issues in the region: constitutional rights versus customary tribal rights. The diverging views about these rights bring parties into conflict. A Zaghawa delegate in Daein, for instance, argued persuasively that they were entitled to economic resources and political leadership by virtue of being Sudanese. The Rezaigat resist the Zaghawa's claims based on their own presumed tribal dar rights. Sometimes cases of border disputes (Rezaigat-Humr and Rezaigat-Habbania) and grazing rights (Rezaigat-Dinka) can also be subsumed under this category of conflict.

Toward a Typology of Conflict in Darfur

A typology is proposed here by way of capturing the complexity underlying the conflict in Darfur. Though it is my contention that this typology does not do justice to the complexity of the real and/or perceived situation on the ground in Darfur, it nonetheless provides us with an approach that can help in understanding some dynamics of the current conflict situation there.

Accordingly, five types of conflict are identified in the region: (A) local, (B) subnational, (C) national, (D) regional, and (E) international. These are interrelated, interdependent, and overlapping conflicts. Types A, B, and C are conflicts within the territorial boundaries of Sudan, while types D and E are conflicts operating at regional and national levels, but with significant impact on Sudan. While involving somewhat different actors pursuing different issues, all types of conflict have had, more or less, mutual feedback effects. Issues and causes of these conflicts are inter-dependent, yet each type of conflict is defined by a core conflict arena that may, at certain times, trigger further developments spanning over it and taking it beyond its analytically defined "boundaries." It is important to stress that these types of conflicts are not mutually exclusive; indeed, issues/sources of conflicts at different levels are mutually supportive.

Table 1. **A Typology of Conflicts in Darfur**

	Issues/Causes of Conflict	Actors Involved	Level of Conflict
Type A	Land ownership, water points Pasture	Clans, groups within and between	Local
Type B	Local council, province	Arabs versus "Zurqa"	Subnational
Type C	Wealth and power sharing	All Darfurians versus central government	National
Type D	Regional power struggle, terrritorial expansion	Neighboring states, IGAD, S+S	Regional
Type E	Humanitarian assistance and resouces	Superpowers, international community	International

Category A: Intertribal Conflict within the Region

The primary cause of fighting in this category is access to land and natural resources. As is the case in most other regions, land in Darfur has been divided into tribal homelands locally known as dars. So there are the Masalit dar, the Fur dar (from where the name of the region comes: "Darfur," or "land of the Fur"), the Zaghawa dar, the Rezaigat dar, the Taaisha dar, etc. Administrative boundaries were drawn coterminously with tribal chieftainships and at the top of each tribal administrative structure stands the *Nazier* (chief), who has extensive authority over both land and people. A tribe without land has no authority, no existence. Minority tribes were incorporated into these large tribal dars, sometimes without their consent. Without claims to land ownership, minority tribes stand no chance of having separate administrative entities; in most cases, they do not even qualify to stand up for election or appointment to local administrative posts. Hence, minority tribes struggled to have tribal independence, which was resisted by majority tribes and constituted one form of tribal conflict to be found in the region. The Maaliga – Rezaigat conflict (1966) and the Salamat – Taaisha conflict (1981) are cases in point.

According to Badri and El Zein, this system leads to the categorization of the region's inhabitants into two main categories. The first contains first-class citizens, the tribesmen who have the right to use the land and other resources, the right to own resources in the area, and the right to rule and run for administrative and political office within the traditional administration.[5] Within this category, the tribes-men who own the dar are subdivided into the rulers and followers. Political and administrative office is basically hereditary in a few families who are descendents of the first family that led other tribesmen to the dar. They also claim high status due to their wealth and advanced educational level. Thus the tribe is made up of elites and followers. The second category is composed of nontribesmen who came to live in the dar. They are considered second-class citizens and are given access to use the resources but not the right of ownership. They might be delegated to an administration, but they do not exercise politically autonomous power or equal power. The newcomers may choose to be fully affiliated and assimilated into the dominant tribe of the dar.

Within tribal dars, contestation over leadership creates both intra- and inter-tribal conflicts. Such leadership roles include traditional leadership positions commonly known as "native administration" (NA) and modern leadership positions with representation in local, regional, or national institutions. Tribes in charge of dars regard such positions as prerogatives; when newcomers contest them, another source of tribal conflict arises. The Rezaigat–Zaghawa conflict clearly represents this type of tribal conflict. Here, the notion of a tribal dar is also related to border disputes among neighboring tribes. The Rezaigat–Humr (both perceived as Arabs) dispute (1981 and 1983), the Rezaigat–Habbaniya (both perceived as Arabs) disputes (1955 and 1985), and the Fellata–Gimr (both perceived to be of non-Arab origin) dispute (1981) are cases in point.

Rezaigat–Zaghawa Conflict

This case involves one of the most controversial issues in the region: constitutional rights versus customary tribal rights. The diverging views about these rights bring parties into conflict. The Zaghawa argued persuasively that they were entitled to economic resources and political leadership by virtue of being Sudanese. The Rezaigat resist the Zaghawa's claims based on presumed dar rights. Both tribes have a warlike disposition, a considerable number of tribal militia equipped with modern firearms, and a widespread population of tribesmen not only in the Sudan but also in neighboring Chad. They also have connections with central government.

The Rezaigat tribe is regarded as one of the most populous in the region, estimated at more than 400,000 by the 1993 census. They live in the extreme south-eastern corner of the region with the Humr tribe (Arab) of Western Kordofan to the east, the Dinka tribes (non-Arab) of Bahr el-Gazal to the south, the Habbaniya (Arab) to the west, the Maaliya (Arab) to the northeast, and several sedentary tribes, including the Zaghawa (non-Arab), to the north. Another section of the Rezaigat tribe occupies part of Northern Darfur, neighbors to the Zaghawa.

At different times the Rezaigat have engaged in fights with nearly every neighboring tribe. Three factors seem to account for this rather unusual Rezaigat involvement in tribal fights: (1) the notion of a tribal dar – Rezaigat have a large homeland to which they are emotionally attached; (2) their mode of living as mostly cattle-nomads moves them in almost all directions of their dar in search of water and pasture for their livestock, but chiefly southward during dry seasons; and (3) their warlike disposition and use of their abundant supply of horses in tribal raids, which made it impossible for even the Fur sultans to bring them completely under their control.[6]

The Rezaigat camel-nomads of the north are generally of a lighter complexion in comparison to neighboring groups and more closely resemble the stereotype of an Arab as far as skin color and features are concerned. The Rezaigat of the south, who have become cattle-nomads, represent all the possible shades of skin color.

MacMichael attributes their darker skin to their having intermixed with indigenous African groups, chiefly the Dinka, Mandala, and Shatt.[7] The Rezaigat have one of the most important tribal chiefs, called the *nazir*. Under him are thirty-five *omdas* that represent the internal tribal sections. Some of the *omdas* are not Rezaigat. They represent tribes that moved to the area, settled for good, and regard themselves as part of the Rezaigat, including the Zaghawa, who were granted an *'umudiyya* (chieftenship) post rather recently, as the ensuing discussion will illustrate.

The Zaghawa are a mixture of Arab and non-Arab groups, who in the classical anthropological literature are often referred to as a mixture of "Hamitic, Tibbu, and Negro groups, with Libyo–Berber affinities." Their native tongue is a dialect of Tibbu, but most Zaghawa can now speak Arabic. They are described as being a lithe, stalwart, incontinent, and active folk who are "addicted to raiding and blood feuds."[8] Their original homeland is the whole of the northernmost part of Darfur that extends along the same latitude in Wadai – now Chad. Although this country is very spacious, it is largely desert or semidesert and capable of supporting very limited agricultural production. In the past, the Zaghawa were described as nomads or seminomads who owned considerable herds of camel. Their tribal dar is subdivided into smaller dars that correspond to their main tribal sections.

The Zaghawas' movements from their original homeland might be traced back to the early eighteenth century, when some of them made their settlement in Kagmar in Northern Kordofan State. They are now indistinguishable from the Kababish Arabs among whom they live. Another batch moved to Southern Darfur, possibly during the same time, and live to the east of Nyala town among the Rezaigat. They have forgotten their mother tongue and for practical purposes regard themselves as part of the host tribes among whom they live. Movements southward, individually or in small batches, have continued ever since without creating serious complications. Land was in abundance and tribal customs were observed by both migrant and host tribes. Since the early 1970s, however, new developments have taken place, and Zaghawa movements have become a source of tribal conflict. First, the entire region and particularly the Zaghawa country has been considerably affected by the drought and desertification that hit the African Sahelian belt. Zaghawa movements have become an exodus, furthering competition with host tribes over meager resources.

Second, traditional tribal customs have ceased to be respected chiefly because tribal leadership, known as native administration, has been politicized and undermined by the radical governments that took office in Khartoum between 1964 and 1969. Third, migrants normally move without being accompanied by their leaders, making them unaccountable to their authority figures. Fourth, a new tribal elite, which emerged in the postindependence era, has made tribal entities the basis upon which political and economic power is attained and this phenomenon has intensified over the last two decades. Fifth, the possession of modern firearms was made possible as a by-product of the Chadian civil war. Pressured by the continuing drought and desertification, the Zaghawa made their way almost to all tribal dars, but chiefly to the *goz* belt that stretches from El-Fasher in Northern Darfur to the savanna belt of Southern Darfur. Their settlement in this belt brought them into conflict with almost all dar owners (e.g., with the Maaliya, the Mararît, the Mîma, and the Birgid in 1991). With the Rezaigat, high tension was reached in 1986, but thanks to tribal and official endeavors, fighting was averted. Tension mounted again in 1966, leading to one of the most devastating tribal fights.

This is not the place to chronicle the history and give a detailed account of Rezaigat–Zaghawa conflicts. Both A and B categories of conflict are involved here: Driven by waves of drought in the 1970s and 1980s, the Zaghawa moved southward to the Rezaigat area with their unrivaled determination and an aggressive and industrious attitude. To make things worse, they were able in a few years to amass considerable wealth, and with wealth came political ambitions, even though they were not in their own dar.

Tensions between the two tribes came to a head in 1986 and 1996. The 1986 confrontation was averted, thanks to a concerted effort by the government and tribal institutions. The last confrontation, in 1996, developed into actual tribal fights that left many persons dead or injured and caused considerable damage to and loss of property. The underlying causes seem to rest with the political and economic power struggles between the two tribes, especially as the Rezaigat saw the Zaghawa becoming wealthy and aspiring for political power in their own tribal dar. Two distinct sad events stood out in this struggle: the rampage through shopping areas in Daein, the capital of the Rezaigat region, and the Black Tuesday massacre, in which many Zaghawa were brutally killed by armed Rezaigat men.

Categoy B: "Arab" versus "Zurqa" Regional Conflict

As mentioned earlier, certain factors, such as land tenure or the tribal landholding system, underlie all three types of conflict. When a particular type of conflict is generated by a certain factor, other factors remain dormant, while others can become more relevant and eventually subsume the catalyst factor or reinforce it by giving it more momentum. For example, a small-scale conflict over land may invite tribal or ethnic solidarity, which may come into play and further exacerbate conflicts, transforming them from one type of conflict to another. In fact, all conflicts of type B have their seeds sown, more or less, in type A.

Historians have stressed not only the tribal, ethnic identity of groups inhabiting the region but also their conflicting patterns of social organization and value systems.[9] Though a sense of togetherness and common identity may be forged by living in the same environment and sharing from different vantage points the natural calamities of drought and famine, and the historical experience of colonialism and national independence, for the most part preexisting loyalties are still dominant, and the people identify themselves as Arabs and non-Arabs.

Until recently, however, ethnic identification in Darfur did not manifest itself in the ethnic animosities characteristic of the national Southern–Northern conflict. Instead, peaceful coexistence among Arabs and non-Arabs has been the rule rather than the exception.[10] Several factors help to explain this phenomenon. First, intermarriages between tribes are widespread, including marriages between Arabs and non-Arabs. Second, the bulk of the Arabs are cattle nomads who intermixed with neighboring Africans to the south, which resulted in their acquisition of what are perceived to be stereotypical African features, including darker skin. Third, being chiefly nomads, the Arabs were not concerned with power struggles until fairly recently. Rather, their history reveals their relentless effort to avoid being taxed by the central authority. But dramatic changes have taken place, and the Arabs have become interested in power sharing both regionally and nationally. Central to these changes is the emergence of the nomad elites who received modern education or came into contact with other change-producing agents.[11]

Non-Arabs were far ahead of the Arabs in political consciousness and organization in Darfur. It is during the May Regime (1969–1985) that Arab political consciousness manifested itself. It started in the Southern Darfur province (1974), where the Arabs form a sizable number. The political dichotomy was between the Arabs and the "Zurqa" (i.e., blacks). However, the dichotomy was an organizational mechanism intended to wield the political support of tribesmen/ethnic groups during election times rather than a social stigma.

When a regional government system designed for northern Sudanese regions was implemented in Darfur (1980), ethnic rivalry to control the office of the regional governor led to heightened ethnic political tensions. After a brief celebration of a presumed victory of all Darfurians against the central government and the appointment of Ahmed Ibrahim Diraige as the first governor to be drawn from the region, ethnic politics dominated the scene. Diraige was then looked upon as a Fur affiliate rather than a regional native. Relations became strained at the grassroots level. Simple intertribal conflicts acquired an ethnic dimension. The Arab–Fur conflicts (1982–1989) and the Arab–Masalît conflict (1996) certainly revealed this ethnic dimension. In each case, more than thirty distinct Arab tribes are said to have fought against the Fur and against the Masalît.[12]

A more overt action on the part of the Arabs related to regional and national power sharing is the formation of the so-called Arab Gathering (Al-Tajammu' al-'Arabi). The emergence of the movement was documented in a memorandum presented to the Prime Minister of Sudan at the time, al Sadig al Mahdi (1988). Based on the proportional representation of Arabs in the region, their sizable educated cadre, and their relative wealth, the Arab Gathering demanded that they deserved to be granted their due leadership positions both regionally and nationally. Nothing was more effective in touching off ethnic consciousness throughout the region than the revelation of that memorandum. On their part, the non-Arabs are also said to have held meetings, particularly in Southern Darfur, to counter the effects of the Arab Gathering and the memorandum. The high tension between the two groups was certainly responsible for the escalation of the Fur–Arab conflict, particularly during 1988 and 1989. It once again affected the deadly Masalit–Arab war of 1996. Ethnic rivalry remains simmering under the surface and can be ignited when other factors bring Arab/non-Arab conflicts to a head.

In Category B, conflict over administrative and political resources between two emerging collectivities, "Zurqa" and "Arab," came out to be more important, even though the origins of these conflicts go back to competition over land, water, and pastures. According to Mohammed Suliman, the traditional assumption that violent conflicts in Africa emanate from ethnic/tribal, religious, and/or cultural differences is seriously limited. Except for "old" traditional conflicts, ethnic dichotomies appear to be a consequence of violent conflicts rather than a cause of them. Nonetheless, ethnic, religious, and cultural dichotomies potently shape people's perceptions of violent conflicts, especially those of fighters on both sides of the conflict divide, but as root causes of "new" conflicts they are weak or nonexistent. However, the longer a conflict persists, the more these ethnic, religious, and cultural factors come into play. In an old conflict, when even the initial causes have petered out or died away, that "abstract," ideological ethnicity becomes an active material and social force.[13] Markakis correctly notes:

> Of all ideological weapons used in African warfare: nationalism, socialism, religion, and ethnicity, the latter proved by far the more superior as a principle of political solidarity and mobilisation as well as a dominant political force.[14]

In the Darfur region, ethnic conflict between "Zurqa" and Arabs gradually grew out of type A conflicts. For some time ethnicity per se was never a serious problem in the region. The Arabs and non-Arabs had been living in peace for centuries at the grassroots level. However, new developments have awakened ethnic consciousness, and ethnicity has become a factor exacerbating if not generating conflicts. The deadly Fur–Arab conflicts (1982–1989) and the Masalît–Arab conflict (1996) were sparked by competition over land ownership and land uses, but the ethnic factor has greatly intensified the conflict.

Unfortunately, interethnic rivalries between "Zurqa" and Arab in Darfur have been escalating rather than declining due to intense competition over administrative and political resorces and also due to the emergence of Islamic fundamentalism in Central Sudan and the ensuing alliances and confrontations between center and periphery.

Efforts by the central government to peacefully resolve conflict between "Zurqa" and "Arab" elites failed. At one point, some tribal and ethnic elites were behind the idea of peacefully resolving the region's ethnic conflict by convening a Grand Regional Conference for building peace among the regional inhabitants. Had it not been for the meddling of Khartoum governments in the ethnic politics of the region, these peacemaking attempts, particularly the Nyala Comprehensive Peace Conference, could have been cited as a clear example of successful citizen-based peace building. The idea of a grand conference for popular reconciliation goes back to 1990, when a small group of different tribal affiliations first articulated the idea.[15]

In the periodization section below, reference will be made to the Khartoum government's intervention in the ethnic affairs of the region in a way that was perceived as favoring "Arabs" against the "Zurqa."

Category C: Regional – National Conflict

In Category C, conflict between the people of Darfur as a whole versus the people of the center in Sudan over power- and wealth-sharing in the country subsumed other types of conflicts (types A and B) and came to be of overriding significance, even though the origins of the conflicts were, in a special way, anchored to the Darfur people's own conflicts over land, water, and pasture, and to competition over administrative and political resources between rival groups in Darfur.

Darfur's political history is now a source of pride for Darfur rebels who demand more political autonomy from the center. Until 1916, Darfur was ruled as an independent Sultanate, and during British colonial rule, Darfur, like many regions, was ruled by the British through the Native Administration system, in which traditional chiefs were reinstated as rulers of their tribes.

Darfur's recent political history has known politicians of different political and ideological stances. Traditional political parties, mainly the Umma Party, and to a lesser degree the Democratic Unionist Party (DUP), have maintained strong holds in the region since 1956. Other radical political parties had some presence as well – the Islamists nominated candidates in the 1980 and 1986 elections, but they did not win the constituency, and the Communists had some presence, but they were not as effective as other political parties.

Educated elites were disillusioned by the failure of both multiparty and one-party political regimes to offer anything of use to their area. Mainly relying on patron-client networks for mobilizing support, politicians from traditional political parties show up only during election time. In the 1980s, traditional political parties supplied their clients in the area with sugar and tea to trade for votes. Unlike the traditional political parties, one-party military regimes relied on repression, thus denying people civil and political rights.

When the present Islamist military regime came to power in 1989, the educated class in Darfur reached a tacit understanding that enough was enough: "It is time to leave behind us political and ideological conflicts and focus on local issues and interests of our area," said one of my key informants. In fact, Darfur has a history of a "kind of" civic movement and vibrant civic environment for local level political democracy and quasi-sophisticated networks of social clubs, sport clubs, cooperatives, sandouks, women's groups, and zakat committees.[16]

To many observers, it seemed that the problems of Darfur could have been resolved had the postindependence government in Khartoum adopted the relevant political formulae. But it appeared that successive Khartoum governments were more interested in control than in good governance and development. For example, in the mid-1990s, the region was torn by armed robbery activities, and the government seemed to have an earnest desire to quell banditry. A series of peace conferences was convened representing social and political groups in Darfur, but then government affiliates were bent on manipulating conference proceedings.

It was clear that the representatives of Darfurian groups on the one hand, and the central government on the other, had different perspectives and interests. For the government, the popular gathering was an opportunity to receive allegiance and sealed covenants and to demonstrate its ability for peace restoration in the region. To achieve the latter objective, the whole region, in addition to the state of neighboring northern Kordofan, were put under martial law because they were riddled with banditry. On their part, Darfurian elites and representatives in the conference succeeded in passing numerous resolutions calculated to be conducive to peace building. It was at this time that calls for a political solution cropped up, calling for national wealth to be allocated in accordance with relative population ratios of regions. This was an alternative to a more extreme demand made by Southern Darfur delegates and rejected by the conference that the region be treated like southern Sudan and be given the post of a vice president and a coordinating council headed by one enjoying the status of a vice president.[17] Khartoum politicians did not at all like to listen to such calls, since they point to a picture of another South, where an armed rebellion had been taking place since 1956, except for a lull during 1972–1983.

That Darfur is underdeveloped compared to other regions is well documented. In 1971, an International Labor Organization (ILO) commission was invited to visit the Sudan and propose a future development plan that would take into account the requirements of development, employment, and equity. The commission found that Sudan was characterized by uneven regional development, with both economic and social services being concentrated in the triangle of Khartoum–Kosti–Gedarif. This is the region where agriculture is either irrigated or mechanized rain-fed. The rest of the regions (chiefly western Sudan and the south) were labeled by the commission as the traditional agricultural sector with rain-fed agriculture and livestock raising as the main sources of livelihood. Although in its 1976 report the ILO called for the traditional agriculture sector to be given "the lion's share" of development projects in order to redress uneven development and regional disparities. Despite this, subsequent development plans continued to concentrate on development and social services in the same advantaged regions.

It will be shown that Khartoum governments during Islamist rule (1989–2004) not only reinforced the Center's dismissive attitudes toward Darfur but also, perhaps even more seriously, seemed to have been more involved and directly implicated in the Darfur conflict by siding with one group against the other. Since the Islamist military regime of Al Bashir assumed power in June 1989, the Islamists, represented by their National Islamic Front (the ruling party known now as the National Congress Party), have come to be perceived as taking part in type A and B conflicts; that is to say, the Khartoum government has intervened in local matters (such as control of land and pastures) without regard to local customs, history, or tradition. As a result, the current regime in Khartoum is perceived as supporting one tribe against another, one ethnic group against another. This development has had serious implications for Darfur's conflict and its escalation.

In many cases the policies of the central government even prior to the 1989 military coup added to conflict transformation. First, a Land Registration Ordinance was passed in 1970 rendering all unregistered lands as government lands. This created a chaotic situation with regard to tribal landholdings (a contrast between a de jure and a de facto land ownership). Second, after revolutionary elements came to power in 1964 and 1969, in 1971 the paramount tribal chiefs were unseated by the then-revolutionary government, culminating in a policy of anti-Native Administration. The consequence for Darfur was devastating, as tribesmen resorted to taking the law into their own hands to resolve their tribal disputes.

The region had been brought under the effective control of the colonial government in the year 1916, when its last sultan, Ali Dinar, was defeated, and the colonial government was more able to pacify all regional tribes, some of whom the Sultanate had been unable to control.

A unified administration was established, with its headquarters in El-Fasher, and lasted as such up to the year 1974 when the region was redivided into the two separate provinces of Northern Darfur, with El-Fasher as its capital, and Southern Darfur, with its headquarters in Nyala. Then the region was divided again in 1994 to create three states, still with El-Fasher and Nyala as capitals for the Northern and Southern Darfur states, respectively, and El-Geneina as a capital for the newly founded state of Western Darfur.

Category D: Regional Conflict

Protracted conflicts and territorial expansionist tendencies among regional powers (mainly Libya) and the political instability in Chad (and its spillover in the region of Darfur in Sudan and Central African Republic) on the one hand, and the rivalry and scramble of international powers (United States, France, China, Britain, Russia) on the other, have transformed the region and given it a distinct character as one of the "security threat regions," not only of the African continent but also of the world at large. Roaming nomad tribes from West Africa cross Sahelian countries, such as Mali, Niger, Chad, and Sudan, further adding to the region's complexity and giving conflicts additional supranational dimensions.

Category E: International Conflict

Worldwide humanitarian relief operations since the 1980s, spillover of regional conflicts, and reports about the richness of the region's minerals have paved the way for and fed into the internationalization of the Darfur conflict. The bulk of humanitarian operations are concentrated in Darfur, drawing hundreds of international nongovernmental organizations (INGOs), national NGOs, and networks channeling food, tents, and medical and educational equipment to the displaced people in Darfur and refugees on the Sudanese–Chadian borders. Recently, the visible role played by China in the oil economy of Sudan, combined with diplomatic and military support to the Khartoum government, have raised the fears of both the United States and France, who seem to be embroiled in a power contest over western and central sub-Saharan Africa.

Periodization Schema of Darfur Conflicts

Having identified the sources of conflict and broadly categorized types of conflicts in Darfur, it is now time to look at how actors played out their roles in Darfur's recent history. I propose to do this by way of a periodization schema, indicating phases or turning points in the course of conflict in Darfur. Periods or phases are not definitively separated from one another in a clear-cut fashion, but in most cases periods may overlap, and one period's traits may carry over to another. Traits carried over from one period to another, however, will be subordinated to the dominant nature of the period/phase in question. For example, during the relatively tranquil period, when conflicts were confined to land issues within the Darfur region, and the major players were local actors, issues of conflict other than land – those characteristics of other periods – were present in a dormant/embryonic form and had not yet taken shape. The recent history of conflict in Darfur is divided up into different periods according to a combination of categories and issues of conflict together with actors, weapons used, and level of conflict.

Table 2. **Phases of Conflict in Darfur**

	Categories of Conflict	Actors	Weapons and Scale of Violence	Level of Conflict
1956–1983, relative tranquillity	Combination of C, A, and B	Local tribal groups	Traditional weapons	Local level
1983–1994, escalation and containment	Combination of A, B, and C	Tribal/ethnic gatherings Chadian groups, central government	Modern arms	Local and regional levels
1994–2002, ethnic polarization and political Islam	Combination of A, B, and C	Polarization: Arabs and government versus SPLM and non-Arabs	Modern arms, massive causalities	Regional and national levels
2003, fragile peace and war by proxy	All types of conflicts, with D	SLM, JEM versus government and Arab militia	Modern arms, large-scale casualties	National and international levels

Colonial Leviathan and Control: 1898–1956

The region has been the homeland for three successive Sultanates: the Daju, the Tunjur, and the Fur. However, it is only the last Sultanate that has been adequately documented. The Fur Sultanate was established around 1650 and dominated by the Fur people. Unlike its contemporary, the Funj Sultanate, which was largely a loosely knit confederation of tribes, the Fur Sultanate was able to establish a central authority that exerted a reasonable command over its sedentary tribes and made a relentless effort to subdue nomadic tribes.[18] With open frontier to the West and East, the region has been receiving migrants from West Africa as well as riverians from Central Sudan. The two movements have had considerable impact on the cultural and demographic formation of the region.

While the Darfur Sultanate was historically dominated by the Fur people, it was ruled by a title-holding elite recruited from all the major ethnic groups. Under the Sultan, the settled peoples, basically non-Arabs, were able to control or keep out the nomads. The Sultan even went so far as to use heavy cavalry attacks to drive them away. After Ali Dinar restored the Sultanate in 1898, he spent most of his reign driving the nomads back, until the British killed him in 1916. The British then discovered that they had no alternative but to continue his policy.[19] They also kept the old ruling elite intact, and many of today's educated Darfurians are descended from that elite.

Relative Tranquility and Regional Politics: 1956–1983

From 1916 to 1956, Darfur was an interior backwater ruled by British officials presiding over the Native Administrative system. After Sudan obtained independence, political and economic structures were in the hands of predominantly Arab-Muslim Northerners, or a Riverian Arab-Muslim Power Bloc (RAMP). It was only in the mid-1960s that Darfurians, both Arab and non-Arab, began to enter the national political arena and assert their own identity. Though Darfurians took pride in their political history, they were nonetheless marginally incorporated into dominant power structures and only fully woke up to their political rights in the mid-1960s. The RAMP's ability to incorporate, co-opt, and contain enabled the soft pacification of the 1960s Darfurian political awakening. Prominent politicians and elites in Darfur, like Ahmed Ibrahim Drieg, a symbol of the Darfurian elite, were integrated into the Umma Party as leaders of parliamentary opposition in the 1960s.

Following the overthrow of the Abboud Military regime in 1964, Darfur intellectuals formed a regional pressure group, called the Darfur Renaissance Front (DRF), with Ahmed Ibrahim Diraige as its leader. Its overriding concern was Darfur's underdevelopment compared to the northern regions. The DRF called for an equitable distribution of national wealth and power positions. Other Darfurian organizations propagating the cause of the Darfur people, albeit in a more radical form, were Sunni and al Lahib al Ahmar (Red Flame). However, these radical organizations did not win wide support among the intellectuals who, at that time, were more inclined to use peaceful, constitutional means to further the interests of Darfur.

In the second half of the 1970s Jabhat Nahdat Darfur (Darfur Development Front) was founded, thus signaling the beginning of a new phase in which Darfurians were bent on making their mark on national politics. Indeed, many politicians and elites from Darfur were reportedly implicated in the 1973, 1975, and 1976 attempts to topple the military regime of Ja'far Numeiri who, to placate these pressures, introduced Regional Rule in 1980, allowing a degree of decentralization and some autonomy for the regions in governing themselves.

As far as the conflicts in the region were concerned, between 1956 and 1980 – that is, between political independence of the country and the institution of regional governments in 1980 – tribal and ethnic conflict (more of type A and less of type B) occurred, either because groups were competing for natural productive resources, pasture, and water, or because of mutual raiding of livestock. But, most of the conflicts remained under the control of government agencies and were, in most cases, settled by tribal reconciliation conferences supported by the district or provincial authorities with *ajawid* or *joudiyya* (indigenous conflict resolution mechanisms) bringing the two hostile parties to the conflict into agreement. The government authorities usually played the role of a neutral go-between and later the guarantors for the fulfillment of the terms of such agreements.[20] In other words, political frictions within Darfurian elites did not show up during this period, and conflict between farmers and pastoralists (mainly type A conflict) was largely resolved by resort to joudiyya/ajawid.[21]

Underlying the conflict with the central government is a conflict of interest and mistrust between oligarchic, "national," Arab-Muslim elites and regional, Darfurian elites. The former perceives the latter as secessionist, while the latter view the behavior of the former as racist. Ironically, however, the official Sudanese media dubs regional elites, who call for more participation and sharing of power and resources, as racist. The attitude of the ruling oligarchs and "national" elites is endorsed by some of the leaders and members of some of Darfur's Arab tribes, as has been shown in the tribal-ethnic conflict in the region.

Popular radicalism, however, was not lost to the people of Darfur, who in 1981 staged a regional popular uprising, forcing the central government to appoint a regional native (Ahmed Ibrahim Diraige) as the Regional Governor in place of El-Tayib El-Mardi, who was a native of Kordofan, Darfur's immediate regional neighbor. They also rejected an earlier attempt at combining Darfur and Kordofan into one region with its headquarters being in El-obeid.

The changes occurring in Darfur were by the late 1970s and early 1980s given further impetus by a combination of factors, including severe drought-induced famine in Darfur in 1983 and 1984; a raging Chadian civil war and cross-border movements of fighting groups; Libyan meddling in the affairs of both Chad and Darfur; West African tribes flocking in large numbers toward Darfur and Sudan; and easy access to modern weapons. All of these factors combined to contribute to political instability in Sudan and to bringing the politics of Darfur into a new phase.

Escalation and Uneasy Containment: 1983–1994

According to Harir, after the institution of a regional government and the installation of Darfurians as regional governors, ministers, and commissioners, the conflict situation changed dramatically.[22] People who shared tribal and ethnic affinities with parties to conflict held the reins of power. While taking sides does not necessarily follow from this fact, unfortunately, as time went on, many, though not all, government employees started taking sides in local ethnic conflicts. Very early in 1981, officeholders in the Darfur government started identifying their opponents in such categorical terms. It was at this stage that the two opposing political alliances crystallized: the Zaghawa, the nomadic Arab groups, and the doctrinaire Muslim Brotherhood on one side; and the Fur, Tunjur, and elements within the urban Darfur elite on the other side.

These developments coincided with worsening environmental conditions already affecting, to an unprecedented degree, the northern half of the Darfur region. This caused a massive movement of population groups and livestock into the farming belts of central Dar Fur, the heartland of the Fur, and of other Darfur ethnic groups, which have a long tradition of settled rain-fed cultivation, based upon land-tenure systems that exclude nonmembers (the *haykura* system). As mentioned above, the haykura system is based upon lands allocated by the Fur sultans to leaders of specified ethnic or family groups for the common use of the members of those groups. In each locality, as the practice was among the Fur, a headman allocated usufruct land rights to the members of a diffusely constituted, ambilineal descent group.[23] While strangers and individual nonmembers can be allocated land on usufructuary terms in return for remitting one-tenth of the produce at harvest, a massive influx of nonmembers created a number of problems. While individuals or a few migrant families were always granted temporary land-use rights and were in due time incorporated into the local system, an influx of whole tribal groups created problems regarding the availability of arable land resources and also raised questions regarding the system of political authority. Animal theft across ethnic borders was also rife and, though localized, nonetheless gave rise to serious and frequent interethnic conflicts.[24]

The influx of non-Fur ethnic groups into the Fur area, which took place in the early 1970s and 1980s, was, however, of a completely different character. Fleeing from drought-stricken areas and hunger, the displaced groups were there to stay on a more permanent basis. To forward their interests, they opted for a different concept of access to natural productive resources. They were to be seen as Sudanese nationals who had inalienable and equal rights to all productive resources available. The difference between this new concept and the customary haykura system of land tenure prevalent among the Fur was bridged by various ethnic wars.[25] Each position was backed by a different ideological rationalization that was racist in content. In tandem with this development, war broke out again in Southern Sudan, led by the Sudan Peoples Liberation Movement/Army (SPLM/A). This would radically change the nature of politics in Darfur as well as in the country as a whole in the 1990s and after.

As stressed earlier, this process (of change in politics), which was initiated by a cluster of factors in the early 1980s, assumed its full momentum during the 1990s with the advent of a new Islamist regime in the country in 1989. Each group overplayed its cultural differences from the other and hence justified culturally the call for a separate administration – not on a geographical basis, but on ethnic grounds. A fragile federal structure of government in the 1990s and a central government in Khartoum bent on utilizing these differences for political gain has greatly contributed to inflaming an already precarious security situation in the region.

To reiterate, one of the root causes of the present crisis goes back to the 1980s, when prolonged droughts accelerated the desertification of northern and central Darfur and led to pressure on water and grazing resources as the camel nomads were forced to move southward. Conflicts over wells – conflicts that in earlier times had been settled with spears or mediation – became much more intractable in an era awash with guns. The situation disintegrated with the decision of Sadiq al-Mahdi, Sudan's prime minister in the mid-1980s, to give arms to the Arabic-speaking cattle nomads, the Baggara of Southern Darfur, ostensibly to defend themselves against the SPLA. Later, no one was surprised when these *Murahalin*, now called *Janjawid*, started to turn their guns on their northern neighbors, the Fur, Masalit, and others. How did this come about?

The Rise of the Arab Gathering

Heightened tensions and conflict over resources led major ethnic groups to organize in separate blocs. According to Rabah, the Arab Gathering first made itself known in a letter to Prime Minister al-Mahdi, whose power base in Darfur is mainly drawn from Arab tribes.[26] Twenty-three Darfur leaders of Arab extraction, a mix of mainstream intellectuals, tribal figures, and senior officials, attributed to the "Arab race" the "creation of civilization in this region … in the areas of governance, religion, and language."

As mentioned in the memo of the Arab Gathering, the "Arabs" in Darfur comprise about 70 percent of the population, spread over 55 percent of the Darfur region, contribute to the national income of the country by 15 percent, and comprise 40 percent of Darfur's educated elite. Despite all of this, they have only fourteen members in the national parliament.[27] Different estimates, however, are given in Table 3.

Table 3. **Population and Access to Resource among the Tribes/Ethnic Groups of Darfur**

Tribe	Population	Education	Economic Resources	Animal Wealth	Armament
Zaghawa	10%	50%	60%	10%	15%
Arab tribes	25%	10%	57%	70%	68%
Fur	40%	25%	23%	18%	14%
Masalit and other tribes	20%	15%	10%	2%	3%

Source: Nazik Rabah, 1998

Whatever the truth, the Arabs in Darfur complained of underrepresentation in local, regional, and national governments and demanded a 50 percent share for Arabs at all three levels in recognition of their demographic weight, contribution to the generation of wealth and knowledge in the region, and their historic role as "civilization bearers." They concluded with a thinly disguised threat: "We fear that if this neglect of the participation of the Arab race continued things will break loose from the hands of the wise men to those of the ignorant, leading to matters of grave consequence."[28]

To date, the Arab Gathering remains a Darfur phenomenon, but its destructive ideology could as easily spread throughout Sudan's diverse communities, where there are groups that view themselves as racially and culturally superior to others. In this regard, Darfur is not much different from other places in Sudan and beyond, where tensions exist among ethnic, regional, or religious groups. These occasionally turn into violent confrontations, and the triggering factor is often the political and economic ambitions of unscrupulous individuals who can manipulate the collective fears and aspirations of their communities to their personal advantage. The Arab Gathering's supremacist ideology clearly shares responsibility for enabling the "ignorant" people alluded to in their letter to kill, loot, and rape fellow Darfurians while believing their victims are lesser people.[29]

The emergence of the Arab Gathering deeply alarmed non-Arab Darfurians. The intermittent surfacing of what non-Arab activists believed were internal memorandums far less reserved than the first public document seemed to confirm fears of a detailed plan, including deals with foreign nomadic elements, to engineer the forced replacement of sedentary non-Arab tribes on Darfur lands with Arab tribes. One document attributed to the Arab Gathering purported to record the minutes of a secret meeting alleged to have taken place in mid-1988, following the appointment of Tigani Sese, a Fur, as governor of Darfur by al-Mahdi. It called upon members to

> obstruct the reform programs of the regional government; paralyze the service sectors in areas inhabited by the Zurqa [sic] to persuade the population of the government's inability to provide basic needs; destabilize security, stop production and liquidate leaders in these areas; and encourage disputes among the Zurqa [sic] tribes to keep them disunited.

The document further called for "gathering members in executive posts … to commit to the following: concentrate services in areas of the Gathering as far as possible; avoid appointing Zurqa [sic] sons in positions of importance and create … obstacles for those among them occupying administrative and executive positions; and use all means possible to destabilize schooling in Zurqa [sic] areas."[30]

The outbreak of the current rebellion extended ethnic polarization to new political and military extremes. A mobilization of non-Arabs is now undeniably in progress, spurred by fears of the strategic designs attributed to the Arab Gathering and the indiscriminate nature of the government's counterinsurgency campaign. Moderate leaders of Arab and non-Arab groups alike are said to be greatly alarmed by these developments because of their potential for threatening the long-term coexistence of Darfur's peoples.

The ruling regime in Khartoum has received anguished appeals from within the Darfur establishment and traditional chiefdoms across the ethnic divide warning of full-scale ethnic war. In a disturbing incident largely unreported in Sudan and internationally, twenty-one Darfur tribal leaders accused unnamed members of the ruling National Congress Party in South Darfur State of having toured as a political coordination committee to propagate Arab Gathering ideology. They attached to their statement six allegedly internal documents in order to "demonstrate the Gathering's heinous project and show … that the predicament of Darfur beginning with armed robbery and tribal wars and ending with the atrocities of the Janjaweed [sic] have in fact resulted from … the continuous thrust of an organization known as The Arab Gathering."[31]

They claimed the documents proved the "racist tribal organization" existed and had "specialized committees tasked with implementing … well-defined and calibrated strategies"; it was using "the institutions and capacities of the state and the ruling party"; and its mission "did not limit itself to the destabilization of Darfur … but its activities have gone beyond the boundaries of Darfur and Sudan to neighboring countries."[32]

The allegations gained considerable credibility when, nine days later, some 111 members of the NCP's South Darfur chapter, including state and national parliament members, addressed a memorandum to the chairman and secretary of the NCP warning of the efforts of some members of the party to achieve the objectives of an unnamed "racist organization" advocating the division of Darfur region along racial lines, thereby undermining NCP cohesion and its national credibility and threatening the unity of the whole country.[33]

These protests by senior NCP members and other concerned leaders in South Darfur coincided with the visit to Nyala of a high-level NCP delegation. Upon returning to Khartoum, al-Haj Atta al-Manan, the delegation leader and NCP secretary in Khartoum State, warned that the situation was threatening to become an ethnic conflict between the Arab and non-Arab tribes.[34] However, the ruling party remained focused on military victory. In a December 31, 2003, President Al Bashir claimed in a televised speech to the nation that "part of a tribe" was responsible for the insurgency. The reference was obviously to the Zaghawa, whom the government was seeking to isolate from the Fur, the Massaleit, the Meidoub, and other groups that were in revolt. While manipulating ethnic realities for short-term military gains, the government nonetheless launched a campaign in the last quarter of 2003 to "stitch the social fabric together again" in Darfur. This relied on mobilizing tribal leaders under the umbrella of the ruling party and the legislative and executive branches of the government to preach peaceful coexistence. At the same time, the government effectively froze diplomacy. The purpose of this approach was to gain time for a military victory that would avoid the need to negotiate with the armed Darfur rebel groups

Ethnic Polarization and Political Islam: 1994–2003

As a divine creed, Islam is a call for people of all races and ethnic and tribal groups across the world. In Sudan, political parties that adopted Islam, in one way or another, as a political ideology opened its membership to people of all racial, ethnic, and tribal backgrounds and affiliations. Traditional religious political parties such as Umma and DUP derive their broad mass support from religious sects, namely the Ansar and Khatmiyya, respectively. Modern religious political parties like the National Islamic Front have also attracted members from both Arab and non-Arab groups in Sudan. In fact, at one time the NIF boasted that in its leadership ranks it had more non-Arab politicians from the South, West, and East Sudan than other political parties. But the fact remains that the top NIF leadership has always been from the riverian areas largely dominated by Arabs and as such is susceptible to the perceived or actual influence of Arab-Muslim culture/centricity.

To reiterate, the process of change in politics in Darfur, which was initiated by a cluster of factors in the mid-1970s to early 1980s, assumed its full momentum during the 1990s with the advent of a new Islamist regime in the country in 1989. Since then, the ethnicization and racialization of the conflict has grown more rapidly since the military coup in 1989 that brought to power the regime of Omar Al Bashir, which is not only Islamist but also Arabo-centric. This has injected an ideological and racist dimension to the conflict, with the sides defining themselves as Arabs or Africans. O'Fahey, a well-known historian and Sudanist, believes that many of the racist attitudes traditionally directed toward slaves have now been redirected toward sedentary non-Arab communities.[35]

To a large extent, the Khartoum Islamist government is responsible for the high ethnic tension that has characterized life in the region ever since 1989. Most of the top state posts in state/regional governments in Darfur were given to trustees of Khartoum who were of Arab origin. Unlike previous Khartoum governments, the Islamists in Khartoum did not hesitate to intervene and meddle with tribal matters without regard to local customs if this intervention served their grand Islamic designs in Darfur and in Sudan. Much to the admiration of Islamist ideologues, organizations bearing the names and symbols of Arab genealogy (such as Quraish 1 and Quraish 2) came to the fore in Darfur. Along with this, vehement attempts were undertaken to win non-Arab tribes.[36] Reports had it that the Khartoum government adopted a carrot-and-stick strategy toward the Fur with the intention of clearing the land stretching from Fasher, Kabkabiya, to Guneina in the far west of Darfur. In line with this policy, in 1994 the wali (governor) of Darfur State issued decrees *Islamizing* native administration in West Darfur, the area of the Masaleet tribe. As a result, structures, titles, and symbols of indigenous administration were replaced by Arab titles and entitlements. On the ground of being Muslim and Sudanese, Arab tribes could now claim ownership rights to the land of indigenous tribes in Darfur. Repressive state power and armed militia (Janjawid) were used against tribes that refused to abide by the new policies.

The racist dimension comes to the fore in reports of rape and mass killings, cynically supported by the Khartoum government, which is determined to retain control over the area. The reason, according to some press reports, is simple: a possible oil pipeline through Darfur, not to mention Darfur's riches in minerals and animal wealth.

Fragile Peace and War by Proxy: 2003–2008

Feeling that enough is enough, the Fur came out in early 2003 with the Darfur Liberation Army. Subsequently, when joined by the Zaghawa, the name was changed to Sudan Liberation Army (SLM). Shortly after, another group called the Justice and Equality Movement (JEM) came into being as an armed rebel movement in Darfur. Both the SLM and JEM were predominantly "Zurqa" (non-Arab) organizations, and the military strikes of both organizations against government troops won the admiration and support of the "Zurqa" population in Darfur.

Fearing that the signing of Peace Protocols between the government of Sudan and the SPLM in the South in 2002 would provoke drastic changes in the power structure in the whole country, powerful Arab groups in Darfur moved to exploit their alliance with hard-liners in the Islamist government of Khartoum in order to settle once and for all a long-standing conflict over land with the "Zurqa" in Darfur. The powerful Arab groups in Darfur and hard-liner Islamists in Khartoum both resemble what is left of an ideological expansionists' movement of Political Islam in Sudan, the dreams of which were shattered with the dismal performance, failure, and eventual collapse of the Islamists in Sudan. This eventuality has strengthened the alliance between the Islamist government and Arab militia in Darfur. Both are wings of an ideological expansionist movement against historical indigenous rights in land claimed by non-Arab tribes in Darfur. Khartoum's ruling Islamists are using "Arab" militias to defeat Darfur's rebel movements and stall the peace process with the SPLM/SPLA. At the same time, Darfur's Arab tribes have found in these events a unique chance to settle, once and for all, the land question by physically removing non-Arabs from their historically claimed lands and settling there. It is a situation of actual homicide and potential genocide.

Conclusion

Sudan's government troops and their allies are reckoned to have killed approximately 250,000 civilians, burned about 3,000 villages, and displaced almost 1.5 million people in Darfur, many of whom eventually fled into neighboring Chad, where they were attacked again by Sudanese troops in cross-border raids, worsening regional security problems.[37] Government troops and their allied militia (Janjawid) are using an ethnic cleansing strategy, developing in the process a racist ideology and a warrior culture with weapons and plenty of horses and camels – still the easiest way to get around Darfur. They have forced a million civilians from their homes by bombing, burning, and mass rape, and have corralled the survivors into refugee camps. A UN official reported that the only difference between Rwanda, scene of ethnic slaughter by Hutus in 1994, and Darfur was the number of casualties. He added that this was not simply a war but an "organized attempt to do away" with ethnically defined groups of people.[38]

According to the ideological Islamist faction in the government of Sudan, the CPA has given the South more than they deserve, and this "mistake" of giving to rebels should not be repeated in Darfur or in the East of Sudan. In a way, the tortuous north–south peace negotiations have given the Sudanese government enough respite from the SPLM/A rebels in the south to redirect its military force against rebel groups in Darfur. The Khartoum government saw in Darfur's rebel movements the specter of African peripheries marching against the Arab-Muslim center. Closely connected to the ruling circles, Islamist ideologues organized the North Peace Forum (NPF) to rally the support of Arabs inside and outside the country, warning of the imminent danger to which the Arabs in Sudan are exposed, and recalling cases of expulsion of Arabs from Spain and Africa. When a powerful minority behaves like a beleaguered minority, surely this is a situation of potential genocide.[39]

So bad are the conditions in Darfur that the normally cautious former UN Secretary-General, Kofi Annan, during his tenure said: "The international community must be prepared to take action … by action I mean a continuum of steps that may include military action."[40] His remarks were made in 2004 on the tenth anniversary of the start of the Rwandan genocide, which claimed 800,000 lives.

Strictly speaking, where race is concerned there are few Arabs in Darfur. More generally, the Arabs in Darfur are those who speak Arabic as a home language, and sometimes those who are nomadic in lifestyle. In this sense, many have become Arabs, as many have become Africans. Both identities are fluid at their borders, but adversaries use tribal/ethnic/racial identification in an exclusive sense in the field fighting each other. In the political sense, the term *Arab*, or for that matter *Arab-Muslim*, refers to a political identity called Arab that RAMP, the ruling group in Khartoum, has elevated as an exclusive index of identity and leverage to power and wealth of the Sudanese nation.

Darfur was a stronghold of Ansar religious sects of the Mahdist movement, whose troops defeated and killed the British Army General Gordon leading a Turko-Egyptian army a little more than a century ago. Since then, Darfur has been the power base of the Umma Party, currently led by the grandson of the Mahdi, Sadiq al-Mahdi. In the 1980s, Sadiq al-Mahidi, the Prime Minister then, was perceived to have treaded on a thin line and placated the Arab Gathering of Arab tribes in Darfur without alienating the "Zurqa" tribes in Darfur. Changes in politics in Darfur, particularly with the introduction of Islam as a political identity, soon made maneuvering all too difficult.

It is important to emphasize that *Islam*, as a cultural as well as political identity, refers to "Muslims" who are believers and for whom Islam means individual worshipping of God (Allah), whereas *Islamist* refers to political activists who use Islam as an exclusive index of political identity and leverage to power and wealth. Mahdist thought is based on the Sufi belief system and therefore its followers, the Ansar, are Muslims but not Islamist in the orthodox sense. In contrast to sectarian, traditional Muslim political parties of Umma Party of Sadiq al-Mahdi and DUP of al-Mirghani stand the radical, militant, modernist, and international type of Political Islam championed by Hassan Al-Turabi of the National Islamic Front (NIF), a predominantly middle-class, urban-based, cadre-led, vanguard party bent on assuming power by any means. An NIF alliance with a faction in the Sudanese Army fulfilled their political dream, and NIF has been in power in Sudan since 1989. But a recent split within the ruling Islamists of Sudan prompted Turabi to seek support not from the more urban, central parts of Sudan (typically identified as being the preserve of President Al Bashir), but from Darfur. Political schisms within the ranks of Islamists in Sudan forced both leaders to retreat to a narrower political support and identity.

With the rise of SPLM/SPLA, the identity of "African" was given a new political dimension. The term *African* came to have a much more powerful political connotation and identity. The SPLM/SPLA promised to unite the Africans in Sudan against the historically powerful Arab-Muslim Center of Khartoum (RAMP) and called for the non-Arab tribes in Darfur to rise against the Arabs. Now, one of the two major rebel movements in Darfur, the SLM, is a member of the National Democratic Alliance, an umbrella opposition movement, comprising SPLM/SPLA and Northern groups.

Protagonists have in their ranks members of "other" ethnic categories. Both rebel groups now fighting the Khartoum government in Darfur are not purely ethnic in their composition. The Khartoum government has in its ranks members belonging to the Fur, Masalit, and Zaghawa, whom the government was reportedly bent on destructing. Therefore, both the anti- and the pro-government militia have outside sponsors, but they cannot just be dismissed as external creations. Khartoum rulers, it was reported, organized local militias in Darfur and other regions in the 1980s, using them both to fight the SPLM/A in the south and to contain the expansion of the Southern rebellion to the west. At the beginning, the militias were Arabs, but later non-Arab tribes organized their own militias and found support from the central government, particularly in the 1990s.

When the Islamists split in 1999 between the Turabi and the Bashir groups, many of the Darfur militia suspected of supporting Turabi were purged. Those who were not, like the Berti, retained a measure of local support. This is why it is wrong to think of the Janjawid as a single organization under a unified command, even though the Khartoum government is known for supplying these militias with arms and logistics.

That the militias have no central command, however, does not absolve the government of Sudan from its responsibility for the atrocities committed by the Janjawid, which it continues to supply. In Mamdani's words (2004), "the patron must be held responsible for the actions of the proxy."

The Khartoum ruling Islamists have used Arab militia Janjawid to defeat Darfur armed opposition movements suspected of receiving support from other major opposition groups such as the SPLM/A, NDA, and Turabi Islamists. They also want to stall the peace process with the SPLM/A, since a hawkish faction in the Islamist government in Khartoum believe that they have already given too many concessions to the Southern rebels. In addition, the aim of the Islamists is also to rally Arab and Muslim support all around the world on the belief that Arabs in Sudan are at risk of being exterminated by the Africans.[41] Arab tribes found in these events a unique chance to settle, once and for all, the land question by physically removing non-Arabs from their historically claimed lands and settling there. It is a situation of actual homicide and potential genocide.

Notes

[1] Mohamed O. El-Sammani, et al., *A Strategy for Development Project in Darfur*, (Khartoum: UNDP, 2004).

[2] Ibid.

[3] Harold A. MacMichael, *A History of the Arabs in the Sudan* vol. 1 (London: Frank Cass & Co. Ltd., 1967).

[4] Nazik E. Rabbah, "The Role of National Government and Native Administration in Conflict Resolution in Darfur Region," M.Sc. Thesis, Faculty of Economics and Social Studies, University of Khartoum, 1998.

[5] Balghis Badri and Adam El Zein Mohammed, *The Rezeigat – Zaghawa Conflict in Darfur Region*, A Fund for Peace Report, Washington, 2000.

[6] Rabbah, 1998.

[7] MacMichael, 1967.

[8] Ibid.

[9] MacMichael, 1967; R. S. O'Fahey, "A Complex Ethnic Reality with a Long History," *International Herald Tribune*, Saturday, May 15, 2004.

[10] Badri and Mohammed 2000

[11] Rabah 1998.

[12] Ibid.; Mona Mohammed Taha Ayoub, *Resolution Conference Between Fur and Arabs as an Example of Tribal Conflict Resolution in Sudan*, M.Sc. Thesis, Afro-Asian Institute, University of Khartoum, 1992.

[13] Mohammed Suliman, *al-Sudan: Hiroub al-Mawarid Wa al-Hawiya* (Sudan: Resources, Identity, and War), London: Cambridge Academic Press, 2000.

[14] Mohammed Suliman, *War in Darfur*, London: IFAA Publications, 1994.

[15] Badri and Mohammed 2000.

[16] *Sandouk (Sanduq)*, which literally means "saving box" in Arabic, is part of a well-known tradition of self-reliance and self-managed financial networks that operate outside the official banking system. It is based on a group of people, mostly women (in a village or city neighborhood), pulling their resources together. Each member contributes a monthly fee with the lump sum going to one person each month as a loan. These payments normally rotate until each member is paid, which signals the end of one round and the beginning of a new one. *Zakat* is a system of alms giving which constitutes one of the five pillars of Islam, and zakat committees operate as social welfare agencies by collecting zakats from able Muslims and distributing them to the less fortunate.

[17] Rabah 1998; Badri and Mohammed 2000.

[18] John Howell, *Local Government and Politics in the Sudan*, Khartoum: Khartoum University Press, 1974.

[19] O'Fahey 2004.

[20] Sharif Harir, "Arab Belt Versus African Belt: Ethno-Political Conflict in Darfur and the Regional Cultural Factors," in Sharif Harir and Terje Tvedt, *Short-Cut to Decay, the Case of the Sudan* (Uppsala: Nordiska Afrikainstitutet, 1994), 144–185.

[21] Atta El-Battahani, *Tribal Peace Conferences in Sudan: The Role of Joudiyya Institution in Darfur*, Zurich: ECOMAN, 1999.

[22] Harir 1994.

[23] Ibid.

[24] Ibid.

[25] Ibid.

[26] Rabah 1998.

[27] Arab Gathering, Foundation Statement (*Bayan Assasi*), October 1987. Excerpts from this document are reproduced in the Appendix of this volume.

[28] International Crisis Group, "Darfur Rising: Sudan's New Crisis," *Africa Report* No. 76, March 25, 2004.

[29] Ibid.

[30] Ibid.

[31] Ibid.

[32] Ibid.

[33] Ibid.

[34] al-Hayat 2004.

[35] O'Fahey 2004.

[36] Guraish is known as the tribe of the Prophet Muhammad in Mekka.

[37] Al-Arabiya, 17/10/2004.

[38] Mukesh Kapila, Un report on the situaton in Darfru, Khartoum: UNDP, 2005.

[39] Mahmood Mamdani, "The Politics of Naming: Genocide, Civil War, Insurgency," *London Review of Books*, 8 March 2007.

[40] UN Reports.

[41] North Peace Forum 2004.

Ideological Expansionist Movements versus Historical Indigenous Rights in the Darfur Region of Sudan

3 Marginalization and War:
From the South to Darfur

Benaiah Yongo-Bure

The War in Darfur in Perspective

Although the conflict in Darfur came to the surface in February 2003, conflict in the region had been simmering for decades. Although ecological and "racial" factors cannot be ignored in explaining the conflict, these factors in and of themselves are not the primary causes. The underlying cause can best be located in the political economy of postcolonial Sudan. The consolidation of power by a minority to the exclusion of most Sudanese, especially those from outside "Hamdi's Privileged Triangle," and the consequent concentration of economic development in that triangle to the neglect of the rest of the country are the underlying causes of virtually all the wars in Sudan, whether it be war in the South, Nuba Mountains, Blue Nile, the East, and now Darfur.[1] But because of the racial and religious diversity of the country, the ruling clique mobilizes support along the religious, ethnic, and "racial" faults. Because the South is non-Arab and non-Islamic, the wars there have been described as being between the Arab-Islamic North and the African-Christian South. Since most Darfurians are Muslims but not all identify themselves as Arabs, the mobilization in Darfur is often portrayed as African versus Arab. However, it must be remembered that many countries are diverse culturally, racially, linguistically, and even ecologically, yet most have not been involved in prolonged vicious civil wars, as has been the case for Sudan.

This essay argues that the marginalization of most Sudanese through exclusion from political participation and the neglect of the socioeconomic development and cultures of the majority of Sudanese best explain Sudan's wars. Without restructuring power and redirecting the economic, cultural, and social policies of the country, the protracted conflicts in Sudan cannot be permanently resolved.

Background

Sudan has been at war with itself since it attained self-government in 1953. The first war broke out in August 1955, just a few months before the country was formally granted independence on January 1, 1956. This first civil war lasted for seventeen years and was ended with the Addis Ababa Agreement in March 1972. The second war, which broke out in May 1983, was concluded with the Comprehensive Peace Agreement (CPA), signed in Nairobi on January 9, 2005. While the first civil war was virtually limited to Southern Sudan, the second war extended to parts of Northern Sudan such as Southern Kordofan, Southern Blue Nile, and Eastern Sudan. The Sudan People's Liberation SPLM/A Movement/Army (SPLM/A) made a brief incursion into Darfur in 1991, but it did not establish a permanent presence there.

The issues that triggered the first war were the refusal of the Arabist- and Islamist-dominated government in Khartoum to accept the demand of the South for a federal system of rule. In the course of the war, most Southerners came to demand a separate country of Southern Sudan. The Addis Ababa Agreement that ended the first North–South civil war was abrogated in 1983, and Islamic Law (*shari'a*) was decreed as the law of the whole country by the military regime of Ja'far Numeiri (1969–1985). Oil was discovered in the region of Bentiu, in Bahr El-Ghazal, Southern Sudan in 1978, and conflict over its development added to the tension between Southern Sudan and the Khartoum establishment.[2]

When the SPLM/A started the second war in the South, its leadership declared that the objectives of the movement were to fight for a New Sudan of equality, inclusiveness, and prosperity for all, regardless of their religion, language, race, ethnicity, gender, or other attributes.[3] As the SPLM/A was declared to be a national movement, and not just a Southern movement, its goals appealed to many marginalized communities in Northern Sudan. Hence, many Northerners joined the SPLM/A, including a few from Darfur. The majority of the Northerners who joined the SPLM/A were from the Nuba Mountains and the Fung of the (Southern) Blue Nile.[4]

Also, the SPLM/A, unlike the Islamist military regime or earlier Sudanese governments, did not kill its prisoners of war. Instead, it reeducated them about the basic problems of Sudan from which even the prisoners of war were suffering, as a lot of the foot soldiers in the Sudanese Army are from Darfur and other marginalized areas. This problem, according to the SPLM/A, is the marginalization of the majority of Sudanese by a minority group in Khartoum, who oppress the Sudanese people through divide-and-rule policies. The reeducated soldiers were redeployed to their regions to champion the cause for a New Sudan of opportunities for everyone regardless of their individual characteristics. This more scientific diagnosis of the problem of Sudan by the SPLM/A attracted support for the movement from Northern Sudan and greatly contributed to the spread of the war beyond the borders of Southern Sudan.

Correlation of Wars with Marginalization

The colonial government concentrated educational and economic development along the Nile, north and south of Khartoum, especially on the Gezira plains between the Blue Nile and White Nile. The rest of the country was neglected, except for central Kordofan, where gum arabic was extracted, and parts of Eastern Sudan. These areas contained the major agricultural schemes and benefited most from the spread of education and health services. Significant urban development occurred in these parts of the country. This uneven development led to interprovincial migration, with people drifting from the neglected to the favored areas in search of work. This led to interpersonal stratification in the areas of migration along ethnic/racial lines, which reinforced the regional disparities. Moreover, trade in the poorer regions was and is dominated by merchants from the richer regions. The postcolonial governments continued to reinforce the colonial pattern of development instead of transforming it for the benefit of all regions and peoples of Sudan. These disparities are in all aspects of Sudanese national life: political, cultural, social, and economic.

Volume 1 of the *Black Book*,[5] whose authorship is attributed to some Darfurian intellectuals, catalogs the political marginalization of the warring regions of Sudan, namely, Eastern, Southern, and Western (including Darfur) Sudan. Using the population census of 1993, which was undertaken during the peak of the war in the South, the Nuba Mountains, and the Blue Nile, the *Black Book* puts the regional populations as 12.2 percent in the East, 5.3 in the North, 35.4 percent in the Center, 31.4 percent in the West, and 11.4 percent in the South. The distribution of ministerial positions in the various Sudanese central governments, from self-government in 1954 to the split of the National Islamic Front (NIF) into National Congress Party (NCP) and Popular Congress (PC) in 1999, is shown in Table 1.[6]

Table 1. **Regional Distribution of Ministerial Posts in the Central Governments of Sudan**

Region	Percentage of Positions by Region						
	1954–1964	1964–1969	1969–1985	1985–1986	1986–1989	1989–1999	1999
Eastern	1.4	2.1	2.5	0.0	2.6	3.0	3.3
Northern	79.0	67.9	68.7	70.0	47.4	59.4	60.1
Central	2.0	6.2	16.5	10.0	14.7	8.9	6.6
Southern	16.0	17.3	7.8	16.7	12.9	14.9	13.3
Western	0.0	6.2	3.5	3.3	22.4	13.8	16.7

Source: Justice and Equality Movement, *The Black Book: Imbalance of Power and Wealth in Sudan, Part I and II.* English Translation (UK: JEM, 2004).

At independence, Sudan consisted of nine provinces: Northern, Eastern (Kassala), Central (Blue Nile), Khartoum, Kordofan, Darfur, Bahr el Ghazal, Upper Nile, and Equatoria. In the *Black Book*, Khartoum is included in the central region. The Western region consists of Darfur and Kordofan, while the Southern region is made up of Bahr el Ghazal, Equatoria, and Upper Nile. The twenty-five states existing in 2008 resulted from subdivisions of the original eight states except for Khartoum.

Given that there has never been any reliable population census of Sudan, representation and distribution of public development activities could have been based on administrative units. In this case, each of the original nine provinces would have 11.1 percent of the positions in the central government. On regional basis, this would have meant 11.1 percent for each of Eastern, Northern, Central, and Khartoum regions, 22.2 percent for the West, and 33.3 percent for the South. If the Central and Khartoum regions were combined, as in the *Black Book*, their joint share would have been 22.2 percent.

These appointments reflect the decisions of presidents and prime ministers (civilian and military), all of whom hail from the Northern Region. In fact, many of the ministers from the Eastern and the Central regions have the same ethnicities as those from the North because they are from the Northern Region. Furthermore, most ministers from the marginalized regions are usually handpicked by the establishment as "good boys," and, hence, do not really represent their people. They are just window-dressings, co-opted to try to portray a "national face." Also, members of the civil service, where policy analyses and recommendations are made, are predominantly from the Northern and Central Regions, and are mainly children of the establishment who have no knowledge of the marginalized areas. A more diversified, genuinely representative cabinet and civil service would have better knowledge of the whole country and would be in a better position to take into account the interests of the diverse Sudanese population.

Examples of the effects of ineffective and superficial representations in the center were demonstrated during the droughts of the mid-1980s and the floods of the late 1980s. Most of the relief supplies for the drought victims in the west (Darfur and Kordofan) did not reach them but instead were consumed in Khartoum. Many of the victims had to trek from the west to the cities along the Nile to receive relief. Many perished en route to the Nile valley. The relief convoys bypassed the Beja, who were equally affected by the drought and through whose territory the Port Sudan–Khartoum highway passes, as their plight remained unnoticed. Only after they moved to the highway did they receive some relief, but by then many of them had perished in their remote settlements or while en route to the highway. However, when Khartoum and the Northern Region were flooded, businessmen and other elites in Khartoum mobilized aid for relieving their kinsmen. Even the University of Khartoum was closed so that students could travel home to participate in the relief effort.

In the media, the cultures and the languages of the marginalized are seldom used. Arabic and Islamic programs monopolize national radio and television, as though Sudan were monolingual and monoreligious. Educational, health, and development programs and projects are concentrated in the irrigated and mechanized agricultural subsectors, which are dominated by traders, retired senior military officers, and civil servants from the establishment. Since the regions or original provinces reflect the ethnic/racial distribution of the Sudanese population, we will illustrate the marginalization of the majority of the Sudanese through regional or provincial distribution of economic and social services. Darfur and the other marginalized regions/provinces are highlighted in the tables.

Table 2. **Regional Distribution of Health Facilities**

Province	Colonial Period (1953)			Eve of the Second Civil War (1980)				
	Population (thousands)	Hospital Beds	Dispensary Beds	Population (thousands)	Hospital Beds	Health Centers	Dispensaries	Dressing Stations
Central	1,841	1,098	67	4,026	4,129	74	259	624
Darfur	1,006	382	256	3,111	1,005	17	62	92
Eastern	788	691	141	2,208	2,008	24	119	185
Khartoum	486	1,311	6	1,802	3,528	35	57	68
Kordofan	1,672	710	484	3,091	1,657	24	116	195
Northern	716	649	12	1,083	1,583	41	156	187
Bahr el Ghazal	771	385	264	2,271	1,077	1	36	85
Equatoria	633	989	330	1,408	1,266	1	54	137
Upper Nile	852	345	229	1,595	952	3	28	46
Total	8,764	6,560	1,789	20,594	17,205	220	887	1,619

Source: Southern Development Investigation Team, 1954, p. 146; Department of Statistics, *Third Population Census, 1983*, Khartoum.

Table 2 illustrates the inequitable distribution of health services. This unequal distribution of health services reflects the colonial policy of inequitable development, which has been continued in the postcolonial era. Central and Khartoum provinces had the largest number of facilities, while Eastern, Equatoria, Kordofan, and Northern provinces were moderately supplied. Among the Northern provinces, Darfur had the fewest facilities during both periods. After independence, Equatoria's rank sank to the lower end.

This pattern of unequal development of health facilities is repeated in the field of education. Darfur, rural Eastern Sudan, Southern Kordofan, and rural Southern Blue Nile are the most neglected regions in Northern Sudan. The situation in the South (Bahr el Ghazal, Equatoria, and Upper Nile) is by far worse than that in any province in the North.

The Central, Northern, and Khartoum provinces have the most privileged positions, even though the Northern Province is among the least-populated areas of the country. Availability of both health and educational opportunities tends to correlate with the distribution of political power in the country, as illustrated in Tables 2 and 3.

But even within the relatively well-supplied provinces, the facilities were unevenly distributed. For example, most of the facilities in the Eastern province were concentrated in the large urban areas of Port Sudan, Kassala, and Gaderif, later to be joined with Khashm el Girba.

Table 3. **Regional Distribution of Pupils and Teachers in Sudan, 1980–1981**

	Primary		Intermediate		Secondary	
Province	Pupils	Teachers	Pupils	Teachers	Pupils	Teachers
Central	456,494	13,870	89,903	4,337	36,663	1,311
Darfur	137,310	4,486	17,797	957	5,816	277
Eastern	141,486	4,792	27,321	1,144	11,039	518
Khartoum	214,051	4,310	50,791	1,669	32,813	906
Kordofan	218,496	5,369	25,902	1,329	10,149	344
Northern	181,273	6,361	45,535	1,974	18,355	662
Bahr el Ghazal	32,491	949	4,741	177	1,869	NA
Equatoria	77,676	1,419	13,385	430	2,195	NA
Upper Nile	32,431	1,064	5,282	306	2,448	NA
Total	1,491,704	42,620	280,657	12,323	121,347	4,243

NA = Not available separately. Total of 225 secondary teachers for Southern Sudan.
Source: Department of Statistics, *Statistical Abstract* (1983), 39–43.

In the Central province, most facilities were concentrated in what are today Gezira and Sennar States. The present Blue Nile state of the Funj/Ingessina shared little from the facilities. The facilities of Kordofan have been concentrated in the El Obeid area of central Kordofan. The Nuba Mountains of Southern Kordofan have shared little in the development.

Exclusion in Development Programs

The simultaneous creation of a privileged few and the exclusion of the majority of Sudanese from development opportunities can be clearly seen through tracing the history of public development programs and policies since the end of World War II. The pursuance of such development policies reinforced the colonial pattern of marked regional and interpersonal inequalities, as summarized in Map 1.

The government of Sudan implemented three public investment programs between 1946 and 1961 and three comprehensive development plans from 1961/1962 to 1977/1978 before reverting back to public investment programs.[7] Most of the investments were concentrated in central, eastern, and northern Sudan. The first program (1946–1951) focused on the improvement and development of transport and communications in the areas of colonial concentration of development. Irrigated agriculture in the Gezira Scheme was the main focus of the directly productive sector. In the field of education, the University of Khartoum was developed from the Gordon Memorial College and the Kitchener College. Since these colleges had concentrated their intakes from central and northern Sudan, it was obvious that these areas were to be the beneficiaries of higher education. The second program continued with projects of the first program, but new projects were also initiated in transport, communications, public utilities, and irrigation schemes. The new large projects in the third program (1956/1957–1960/1961) included the Managil Extension of the Gezira Scheme, Sennar Hydro-Electric Project, Gunied Sugar Scheme, and mechanized farming. The embarkation on mechanized agriculture was to intensify in the 1960s, leading to major encroachment on Beja grazing land. The Beja, the indigenous inhabitants of Eastern Sudan, have been excluded from the major developments in the region, from the Baraka and Gash flood irrigation schemes to the allocation of land for mechanized farming schemes, and the creation of the Khashm el Girba Resettlement Scheme for the Nubians displaced by the building of the Aswan Dam.

The 1960s were dominated by the implementation of the Ten-Year Plan (1961/1962–1970/1971) in the North and war in the South. The major projects of the Ten-Year Plan included projects continued from the 1950s and new power and irrigation schemes. The projects continued from the 1950s included the Managil Extension of the Gezira Schemes, the Sennar Hydro-Electric Project, and the Guneid Sugar Scheme. The two largest new projects of the Ten-Year Plan were the Roseires (Damazin) Dam and the Khashm el Girba Dam with consequent irrigation works.

The completion of the major schemes would provide more irrigation water for the Blue Nile and White Nile pump schemes as well as those along the Atbara River. Private-sector investment in transportation and distribution would also be encouraged in the neighborhood of these major development projects.

Because of deterioration in existing projects, the original Five-Year Plan (1970/1971–1974/1975) emphasized capacity utilization of existing schemes. However, with the availability of Arab petrodollars and Western technology for a friendly Sudanese regime, the Five-Year Plan was amended and extended to 1976/1977. Emphasis shifted to new projects. Major irrigation projects were embarked upon. These included the El Suki, Rahad, and Kenana irrigation schemes, which are all located in central Sudan. Sudan was to be turned into the breadbasket of the Arab

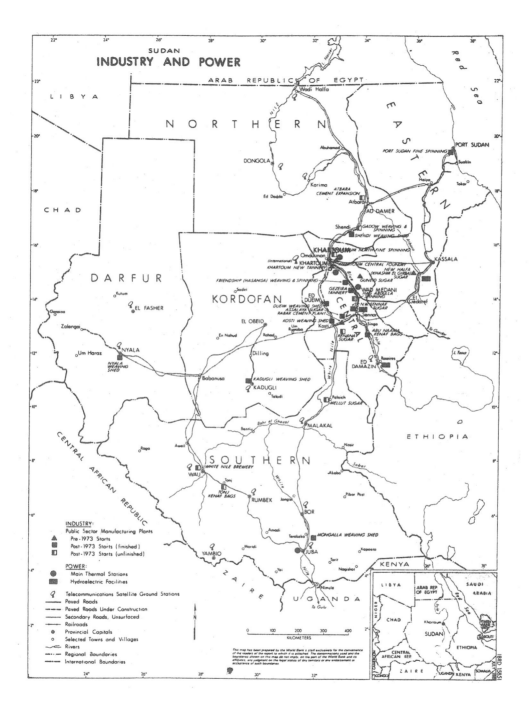

Map1: Regional Development Disparities in Sudan
Source: IBRD, Sudan Investing for Economic Stabilazation and Structural Change
(Washington, D.C., 1982), Annex 2, Map 3.

world. There was further expansion of mechanized farming in Gaderief (Beja land), Damazin (Funj/Ingessena land), Habila (Nuba land), and Renk (the South). The owners of the mechanized schemes are from the ruling elites of Sudan. They are usually absentee landlords, mainly merchants, retired senior military, and civil servants. The land was allocated by the Khartoum-located Mechanized Farming Corporation and financed by the Agricultural Bank of Sudan (ABS). Mechanized farming, through use of tractors and indiscriminate uprooting of trees, greatly contributed to desertification and the famine of the 1980s. The Sudan Development Corporation was established in the 1970s and concentrated its activities in central Sudan and along the Nile north of Kosti and Sennar/Singa.

Some sugar and textile projects were also started. A number of them were thrown to the marginalized regions as political tokens. Since there were no proper feasibility studies on these projects, most did not materialize. The rise of wages in the Gulf Region because of high oil prices led to many Sudanese professionals and technicians to migrate for petrodollars. This emigration, coupled with corruption, deterioration in old schemes and of infrastructure, and uncompleted new projects led to economic crisis. However, the government was unaware of these major negative developments in the economy. Hence, it embarked on an ambitious Six-Year Plan (1977/1978–1982/1983). Most of the breadbasket projects were to be implemented during the Six-Year Plan.[8] However, because of the major structural imbalances in the economy, the Six-Year Plan could not be implemented beyond its first year. Hence, from 1978/1979, the government scaled back its plans and began to implement three Three-Year Rolling Public Investment Programs under the supervision of the World Bank and the International Monetary Fund (IMF). The privatization started under the World Bank and the Islamist government in the 1990s and beyond voluntarily continued IMF programs. These programs have favored elites from the establishment and have greatly reinforced their economic and political weight.

But even the rolling rehabilitation programs favored the old schemes, and there was nothing new for the marginalized. The programs aimed primarily at rehabilitating the irrigation schemes. The basic aims of these programs were the provision of spare parts and of machinery needed to reverse the deterioration of the capital equipment, the allocation of more foreign exchange to finance needed inputs, policy reform, and a revision of the incentive system in irrigated agriculture to stimulate production. Funds were allocated to the existing irrigated agriculture, power, port, and transport. Overall, for the whole of the twentieth century, the peasant subsector of Sudan's economy was left out of all aspects of Sudanese development policy, including provision of credit.

As the marginalized regions are basically populated by subsistence farmers and pastoralists, the neglect of the peasant subsector means they have been excluded from participating in the development of the country, and have therefore continued to live in abject poverty. This is best illustrated by the activities of the ABS, which was established to promote the development of all agricultural subsectors, but instead came to concentrate its activities on the mechanized and irrigated subsectors at the expense of the peasant subsector.

Marginalization of Peasant Agriculture

In 2001, total lending to the agricultural sector in Sudan amounted to SD44 billion ($1 US = SD260). The irrigated schemes received about 60 percent, the mechanized schemes got about 39 percent, and the peasant subsector received only about 1 percent.[9] In that year the ABS, the main vehicle for agricultural credit, distributed its credit as follows: 58.8 percent for mechanized farming, 31.4 percent for irrigated schemes, and only 9.8 percent for peasant farming.[10]

The ABS was established in 1957 with the following lofty objectives:
1. To achieve self-sufficiency in the production of basic food crops and the need to transcend the self-sufficiency stage to export production.
2. To increase per capita output and income, and the consequent improvement in the standard of living for the small-scale farming community, who comprise the vast majority of the rural poor.
3. To achieve a substantial increase of per capita income in real terms through the development and expansion of agricultural production in the modern as well as traditional subsectors, with the ultimate aim of giving a push to the growth of the economy using the agricultural sector as the dynamic sector.
4. To improve and enhance the employment opportunities in the rural areas in order to reduce the influx of people from the rural areas to the urban centers.
5. To bring about a balance in the distribution of national resources through equal allocation of agricultural investment among various regions of the Sudan.
6. To provide the necessary funds to acquire agricultural inputs for the development and improvement of agricultural productivity as well as providing storage and marketing facilities for storage and sale of surplus crops.[11]

The ABS was to be the main source of public sector credit for agricultural development and started operations in 1959 with a capital of LS5 million. The capital was raised to LS15 million in 1976, and to LS50 million in1983. In addition to its capital, the ABS also received loans and grants from many other sources. The Bank of Sudan extended short-term loans to the ABS. The ABS, through the government of Sudan, also obtained funding from external organizations such as the World Bank, the African Development Bank, and the International Fund for Agricultural Development. Some of the bilateral foreign aid to the government of Sudan is allocated to the ABS.

However, over time, the activities of the ABS came to deviate greatly from what it was meant to do. The irrigated and mechanized agricultural subsectors became the main beneficiaries, while the peasants, most of them from the peripheries, received almost no service from it. Yet, together with nomadic pastoralists, the peasant subsector sustains more than 80 percent of the Sudanese population. This figure was even higher when the ABS was established at the end of the 1950s. The ABS hardly played any role in attempting to remove any of the constraints on peasant development. Instead, it added to the enhancement of rural stratification and environmental degradation with tragic consequences for the rural population around the mechanized schemes.

To qualify for a loan, the applicant must submit land, buildings, crops to be harvested or in stores, letters of credit from a bank, bonds, or shares as guarantees for loan repayments. But the authorities know very well that peasant farmers do not possess registered land titles, permanent buildings, and letters of credit, shares, or bonds. Hence, it was not by accident that the bank came to concentrate its activities on aiding established farmers, traders, politicians, and retired civil and military officers.

From its inception, the ABS concentrated on funding the private sector Blue Nile and White Nile cotton pump schemes. They were the beneficiaries of the irrigation water provided by the Jebel Aulia Dam on the White Nile, and the Sennar and Rosaries (Damazin) dams on the Blue Nile. There was a direct correlation between the political developments of the 1950s and 1960s and the rapid growth in private pump schemes. "[H]uge schemes [were] ... allocated to individuals with close connections to ministers and the Prime Minister himself."[12] The ABS continued to supervise and finance the cotton pump schemes until the Numeiri coup of May 1969, when these schemes were taken over by the government and the Agricultural Reform Corporation was set up to run them. The Agricultural Reform Corporation obtained its financing directly from the Bank of Sudan (the Central Bank). The ABS was to concentrate its resources on financing the private sector only.

The ABS divided the country into three operational regions: (1) the North/East Region consisting of Eastern and Northern Provinces; (2) the Central Region consisting of Blue Nile, Gezira, Khartoum, and White Nile Provinces; and (3) the South/West Region consisting of Bahr el Ghazal, Darfur, Equatoria, Kordofan, and Upper Nile Provinces.

The regional distribution of ABS branches in about thirty years of its operation is illustrated in Figure 1. ABS loans were concentrated in the North/East and the Central regions. The bank opened branches in Dongala, Merowe, and Shendi in the Northern province; Gedaref and New Halfa in Eastern Sudan; Dueim, Khartoum, Kosti, Sennar, and Wad Medani in the bank's Central region. Zelingi was the only branch in Darfur, while the bank had no branch in Kordofan and Upper Nile until the 1970s. The Juba (Equatoria) and Wau (Bahr el Ghazal) branches of the ABS were opened in mid-1981. They were opened due to political pressure on President Numeiri. In 1980, the Southern Farmers Association petitioned Numeiri during one of his visits to the South. On his return to Khartoum, Numeiri ordered for the immediate opening of ABS branches in Juba and Wau.

In the1978/1979 season, the ABS opened its first branch in Upper Nile at Renk. Most of the ABS credit extended in the South goes to the mechanized farms of Renk. For example, between 1982 and 1984 the total agricultural credit extended by the ABS was LS72 million.[13] The share that was extended to the South was LS9.6 million. Renk disbursed 82 percent of the ABS credit in the South for the period 1982–1984; Wau, 17.7 percent, and Juba, 0.3 percent.

The irrigated cotton pump schemes of the White Nile were extended from Kosti to Renk in northern Upper Nile in 1953.[14] These schemes were managed from Kosti where the owners resided. They were nationalized by the Nimeiri regime in 1969.

Private capital extended mechanized rain-fed farming to the northern Upper Nile, from Kosti, in 1964. In 1969, the White Nile Agricultural Corporation (WNAC), which was charged with running the nationalized pump schemes, established a pilot scheme in the Renk area. In 1978, a state farm was established for experimental purposes. More businessmen from the cities and towns of central Sudan acquired

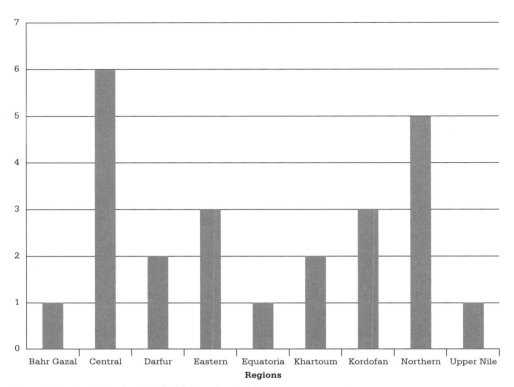

Figure 1. **Regional Distribution of ABS Branches, 1988**

farms in northern Upper Nile.[15] After the end of the first war, the Southern Regional Government distributed land to Southern returnees, but these recipients did not qualify for loans from the ABS because their plots were not allocated by the Khartoum-located Mechanized Farming Corporation. To qualify for allocation by the Mechanized Farming Corporation, one must be able to meet at least a quarter of the cost of operations. This requirement limited the clients of the bank to merchants, politicians, and retired senior military and civil servants hailing from the ruling clique in Sudan.

However, despite the extension of the activities to other regions, the peasant subsector continued to be neglected. Table 4 shows the overall picture of ABS loans in a period when some attention was paid to the peasant subsector.

Table 4. **Subsectoral Distribution of Credit from the ABS, 1982–1984 (LS million)**

Region	Irrigated	Mechanized	Peasant	Total
Central	9.0	5.0	0.0	14.0
North/East	8.0	29.0	0.0	37.0
South/West	0.0	17.0	5.0	22.0
Total	17.0	51.0	5.0	73.0

Source: Abalgak Them Madut, *Regional Distribution of Public Agricultural Credit in the Sudan* (Development Studies and Research, University of Khartoum, 1986), p. 63.

The LS17.0 million extended to mechanized farming in the South/West region went largely to the Habila Scheme in the Nuba Mountains. Apart from small-scale financing of a few crops such as sorghum, groundnuts, and sesame, the major operations of the ABS in the West started in the 1970s with the opening of the Habila Scheme. As usual with such schemes in Sudan, the beneficiaries of this scheme have not been the Nuba peasants, but the dominant merchants of Sudan. The demarcation of land involved displacement of peasants as their land was allocated for large-scale mechanization. The Nuba peasants were left to continue with their simple tools for land clearing, digging, weeding, and harvesting. The wages the peasants earned working in the schemes were insufficient for their maintenance. Hence, they seasonally migrated between the schemes and their traditional farms. The simultaneous abandonment of mechanized schemes that have lost their fertility and the allocation of new land cost the local inhabitants considerably, in terms of availability of fertile virgin land, and degraded the environment.[16] Rural stratification and conflict increased.

The ABS opened an office in El Obeid, working with a limited number of cooperatives and horticultural producers around the city. But the clients of such operations are not peasants.

Another cooperative credit project at El Nahud, in Khordofan, did not benefit the peasants. This project was aimed at rehabilitating the area from the drought of the mid-1980s. The people were to be organized into cooperatives to be eligible for credit. A sum of $13 million was committed in foreign exchange and $3.7 million from the ABS.[17] The ABS was entrusted with credit delivery to the cooperatives, as well as supervision and monitoring of the project, through its branches in the area. The project centered on extending seasonal credit to eligible members of cooperatives for meeting seasonal expenditures, largely labor costs and procurement of seeds. Since most small-scale farming operations basically depend on family labor, such cooperative farms that hire nonfamily labor are limited to a few local elites. Hence, this project was surely not designed for most of the farmers in the area.

The Um Ruwaba branch, again in Kordofan, initially provided loans for cultivation costs. Later, credit became available for harvesting and marketing.[18] Originally, it provided loans to cooperatives only. The offices of cooperative, extension, and protection services of the Ministry of Agriculture were involved in the activities of the branch. The branch also involved heads of villages to determine the credit-worthiness of its loan applicants. The branch extended financing to all stages of sesame and groundnut, and later, gum arabic production. The loan payments were made in installments that were phased to coincide with planting, weeding, and harvesting. After harvesting, the crops were transported to collection centers and then to stores rented from merchants at Um Ruwaba. The area financed by the bank in Um Ruwaba expanded from 5,000 *feddans*[19] in 1977/1978 to 30,000 feddans in 1981/1982. The number of cooperatives rose from two to twenty-one. Hence, where efforts were made to reach many farmers, the response was positive.

However, services to develop peasant agriculture should not be limited to extension of credit facilities. Some of the public-sector financing that was extended to large farmers could have been spent on improving the general rural infrastructure if it was not possible to directly channel it to peasant farming. For example, poor transportation and communication put considerable limits on rural production and marketing. Institutional support in essential areas such as research and development, repair and maintenance, and marketing and distribution can go a long way in relieving the constraints on peasant productivity and raise their output, incomes, and living standards. Other measures include ecologically specific research and development, marketing and storage facilities, supply of farm inputs and implements and higher yielding seeds, pricing policies, and radio programs in the languages of the peasants.

But in Sudan, the majority of peasants still depend overwhelmingly on simple hand tools and implements. Only small areas are cultivated with tractors or oxen. Generally, local blacksmiths make the hand tools from scrap, with negligible improvements, except for minor changes in shapes and sizes. There has been no attempt to create research institutions that can develop alternative farming tools with an emphasis on design development and modification.[20]

Shifting cultivation is practiced in all but the most densely populated rural areas. There have been no efforts made to encourage the nomadic pastoralists to become settled through the development of pastures, watering points, stocking routes, and drainage of swampy environments.

Sudanese policy makers do not realize that their narrow, selfish policies have stifled overall national development. It has not dawned on them that without raising the productivity and incomes of the majority of the population, who are peasants, the development of the whole economy will be held back as the overall productivity, income, and the size of the domestic market will remain low. Such a situation cannot support the diversification and industrialization of an economy. Instead, it fosters more rebellions by the marginalized majority. A diversified and industrialized economy can absorb a large portion of the rural labor force, including those from arid zones, thus reducing rural tensions over land.

Marginalization and Rebellion

The development of regional political, and eventually guerrilla, movements in Sudan is highly correlated with the marginalization of the regional populations. The Liberal Party, from Southern Sudan, that was championing the call for federation had started to form alliances with marginalized Northerners in the 1950s. In the 1960s, the Sudan African National Union (SANU), also from Southern Sudan, continued the policy of allying with marginalized Northerners to attempt to restructure the Sudanese political system. The results of all these alliances were the formation of the Beja Congress (BC) in 1958, and those of the Darfur Development Front (DDF) and the General Union of the Nuba (GUN) in 1965. These alliances led to the emergence of the New Forces Congress after the overthrow of the first military government of Ibrahim Abboud in 1964. Rural Solidarity was another alliance of the marginalized political organizations, born in 1985 after the overthrow of the second military regime of Ja'far Numeiri. Although a few individuals from the privileged regions joined the SPLM/A, most came from the marginalized regions of the Funj/Ingassena and the Nuba Mountains. The SPLM/A operated in Beja territory without problems from the local population. In the late 1980s, a leading ex-student Islamist movement leader from Darfur, Dawood Yahiya Boulad, joined the SPLM/A, but was captured by government forces in Darfur where he had been deployed for mobilization.

However, by the time Boulad joined the SPLM/A, there were already many anti-government forces in Darfur.

Darfur's open defiance of Khartoum became conspicuous as early as the beginning of the 1980s. In the early years of independence, Darfurians were even represented in Khartoum by Mahadists from the Nile Valley. However, in 1981, Darfurians rejected President Numeiri's appointed governor of Darfur, who originated from the North. They demanded the appointment of an indigenous Darfurian (Ahmed Ibrahim Diraige) as their governor, and Numeiri had to comply. Although President Al Bashir was able to force one of his regime's hard-liners as the governor of Darfur in the 1990s, he was not able to subdue the region. Instead, instability continued to intensify until the outbreak of the war in 2003.

Polarization of the Islamists in government on issues of regional development split them into *awalad al Gharib* (sons of the West) and *awalad al balad* (sons of those from the Nile Valley, predominantly from the Northern region). Soon after assuming power, the Islamists embarked on the beautification of Khartoum, development of the city's infrastructure, and construction of private housing for themselves. They allocated to themselves public assets through their privatization programs. In regional development, they embarked on constructing two highways to the Northern region, one on each bank of the Nile. An expensive private wheat project is also being developed in the Northern region. Two other major projects the *awalad al balad* Islamists are developing in the Northern Region are the Kajbar and Merowe hydroelectric projects and eventual irrigation works. While all these projects were being implemented, the future of the only major project for the west, the Western Road, became unclear. The Northern *awalad al balad* blamed prominent Islamists from the west for embezzling the funds meant for the Western Road project, while the Westerners blame the Northerners for diverting the money to the Wheat Project in the North. For the Westerners, this was another slap on their face by the *awalad al balad*, similar to the failure of the Sudan–Libya highway planned during the Numeiri regime. But while these events triggered the beginning of the rebellion, the response from the masses to join the struggle is a result of long-term accumulated grievances against Khartoum.

As happened in other regions of war in Sudan, the government has been able to take advantage of local conflicts to divide the Darfurians. But this polarization has resulted from the marked interpersonal inequalities being officially rationalized in the name of racial superiority. The use of Arabism and Islamism by the ruling elites has succeeded to divide most uncritical Sudanese. This is particularly so when privileges and access to power are highly correlated with those racial and religious classifications.

Concluding Remarks

Any long-term solution to the protracted conflicts in Sudan has to address the fundamental issue of the Sudanese political economy. This is the issue of political, cultural, and economic marginalization of the majority of the Sudanese. The concentration of power, wealth, and other privileges in Sudan in favor of those elites who claim "Arab-ness" has led to the African-versus-Arab divisions spreading in the North. These divisions can never be eliminated by mere appeals to nationalism or religious commonality, but only through the initiation of a credible program of political, legal, cultural, and socioeconomic restructuring of the existing establishment.

Restructuring requires effective decentralization and equal participation in the central government. The pseudo-federalism and pseudo-democracy of the past have to give way to new political, economic, social, and cultural structures. The central political, military, and civil services must mirror the diversity of the country at all levels. This requires a responsible, nonsectarian government in the center that represents all Sudanese.

The state and local authorities have to be really autonomous, with resources to promote their own independent development programs. There must be free education for the children of all peasants and the other poor. The rich should either directly pay fees for their children or pay an educational tax. A percentage of proceeds from natural resources, such as oil and gold, must be devoted to education, rural water supply, and health services. National universities should take an equal number of students from all states, while state universities in poor regions should have in-state intakes of 75 to 80 percent for the first ten years of their full establishment. The intakes to the universities, especially to the state universities, must be consistent with the human resource needs of the state and local governments.

Rural development will greatly raise incomes, reduce poverty, and create a large domestic market for an all-round self-sustaining economic development. The rural development programs should be devised at the local level and funded jointly by the central, state, and local governments. In addition to embarking on serious rural development, it is essential to devise a strategy of balanced regional industrial development. This requires the involvement of all levels of government and experts from all sectors of Sudanese societies.

Short of transforming the existing establishment, Sudan will continue to bleed and eventually disintegrate, regardless of whether a military or an elected sectarian government is in charge in Khartoum. These wars will continue as long as the marked inequities persist in the country, even if a miracle were to make Sudan a monocultural country.

Notes

[1] Hamdi is a senior member of the NIF/NCP. He was the Islamists' Minister of Finance in the 1990s. In a conference speech given in Khartoum after the signing of the CPA, Hamdi advised Khartoum to concentrate its resources on the development of the historically privileged area, which he defined as the triangle with its vertexes on the towns of Dongola, El Obeid, and Sennar.

[2] The oil-rich region of Abyie, which is historically part of Southern Sudan, has now become a disputed area between the current Islamist regime and its partner in the power-sharing government, the SPLM. This is in spite of the fact that the CPA in 2005 devised a clear road map to resolve the border issues between North and South, including Abyie. The current Islamist regime also carved out the oil-rich areas into a new state known as Unity State, which was historically part of the Upper Nile Province, as part of its administrative restructuring of Sudan in 1994.

[3] Sudan Peoples Liberation Movement/Army, *Manifesto*, Bilpam, 1983.

[4] After the signing of the CPA, the state of Southern Blue Nile changed its name to Blue Nile.

[5] See the appendixes of this volume for the full text of Part One of the *Black Book* and other related essays.

[6] The *Black Book* sources include government documents such as the Directory of Federal Rule, Presidential/Republican Decrees, Public Administration Regulations, National Fund for Social Insurance, Bank of Sudan, and People Councils Publications.

[7] Data and other information on the various government development plans are available in the various development plan documents listed in the references/bibliography.

[8] Hashim Awad, *Why the Bread Basket Is Empty*. Seminar Paper, Development Studies and Research Center, University of Khartoum, 1984.

9 International Monetary Fund (IMF), Sudan: Final Review under the Medium-Term Staff-Monitored Program and the 2002 Program, Washington, D.C. (June 2002): 36, 53.

10 Ibid., 36, 52.

11 Stephen Lomeling, et al., *The Agricultural Bank of Sudan: Twenty-Five Years of Agricultural Credit*, 1959–1984, Development Studies and Research Center, University of Khartoum, Group Research, 1985, 9–11.

12 Taisir Mohamed Ali, "The Road to Jouda," *Review of African Political Economy* vol. 10, no. 26 (Summer 1983): 5.

13 Abalgak Them Madut, *Regional Distribution of Agricultural Credit in Sudan*, Development Studies and Research Center, University of Khartoum, M.A. Thesis, 1986, 100.

14 Department of Statistics, *A Report on the Census of Pump Schemes* vol. 1, Khartoum, 1967.

15 Ayul Abwol Dak, *Who Benefits from the Agricultural Schemes of Northern Upper Nile?* Development Studies and Research Center, University of Khartoum, Post-Graduate Diploma Thesis, 1989.

16 Ibrahim Kursany, "Peasants of the Nuba Mountains Region." *Review of African Political Economy* vol. 10, no. 26 (1983): 15–34.

17 Babikir Osman Abdel Nour, *Financing Rural Development in Sudan*. Presented at Alternative Policies for Sudan conference, Cairo, Egypt, 2000, 19–20.

18 Stephen Lomeling, et al., *The Agricultural Bank of Sudan: Twenty-Five Years of Agricultural Credit*, 1959–1984. (Khartoum: Development Studies and Research Center, University of Khartoum, Group Research, 1985) p. 45.

19 A *feddan* is equivalent to 1.038 acres.

20 International Labor Office (ILO), "Appropriate Farm Equipment Technology for Small-Scale Traditional Sector: Synthesis Report," Addis Ababa, 1983.

4 Darfur People:
Too Black for the Arab-Islamic Project of Sudan

Abdullahi Osman El-Tom

The eminent Sudanese scholar Francis Deng once said: "What divides us is what we don't talk about." What we don't talk about is in effect a taboo that has stifled debate and prevented true discussion among past and current Sudanese scholars. This situation has made it impossible to debate certain issues whose examination is crucial to solving the most obstinate of Sudan's persistent problems.

In a way, that taboo has now been broken. A milestone in its destruction was the courageous publication of the *Black Book of Sudan*. With as many as 300,000 dead and four million displaced, and the numbers expected to rise, the Darfurians are left with no time for niceties, and certainly not for taboos.[1] As Martin Luther King expressed it, an abscess can only be cured if its ugly pus is fully exposed to the air. Let that be the mission of this essay.

Before we proceed, let me define where I stand with regard to the current crisis in Darfur. From the reader's perspective, discerning the author's label is crucial to buying into the goods. As a matter of principle and like many others the world over, I take the view that war is neither an ideal nor an effective way of conflict resolution, particularly if the conflict is primarily political in nature, as is the current problem in Darfur. As a matter of fact, most of us, from and in Darfur, have never been party to the decision to raise arms against the government of Khartoum. This is despite the fact that many Darfurians, including government supporters, concur with the grievances and the objectives of the Darfur rebels but do not condone raising arms to pursue these objectives.

However, once the armed struggle started, most Darfurians found themselves with little choice but to take a stand and only one stand. Let us Darfurians, and particularly those who are deemed "too African" for Sudan, face it: We simply cannot afford to let the armed movement fail. Fortunately, the objectives of the Darfur Movement need not be achieved entirely through armed struggle. It is not too late to lay down arms and continue the struggle through peaceful negotiation of the problem.

Darfur Problem

Scholars working on the current Darfur crisis have often looked inside the region in search of its causes. Not surprisingly, this approach reduces discussion of the problem to localized indices like drought, environmental degradation, conflicts over local resources, and tribalism. This essay departs from this approach for two reasons. First, Darfur is not an isolated region. It is part of a national structure in which the policies of Khartoum governments have played a great part. Second, Darfur is not in any way unique in its problems. Other regions in Sudan with which Darfur is intricately connected share its plight. Darfur should be seen as an indivisible part of a defective whole that is bedeviled by the hegemony of a favored segment over the rest of Sudan.

Darfur, Identity, and History

Darfur, the size of France, covers an area of 160,000 square miles. It has a population of six million and constitutes roughly a fifth of Sudan's current population. Numerous ethnic groups that are all Muslim inhabit Darfur. The majority of Darfur's population now classify themselves as Black African or simply "Zurqa" (Black). Some retain their own original languages, but Arabic is the *lingua franca*. Others have long lost their indigenous languages and have been speaking Arabic for centuries. Major ethnic groups in Darfur on the so-called Black African side are the Fur, the Massaleit, the Zaghawa, the Meidobe, and the Berti. On the Arab side are the Baggara, the Rizaigat, the Zayadia, the Maalia, and the Beni Halba. It must be noted that this list is not exhaustive and that division between one group and another is fluid, ideological, and subject to continuous change.

The population of Darfur is categorized in different ways, each time according to the purpose at hand. Sometimes, the division is based on language, whereby you have Arabic speakers versus non-Arabic speakers. Just as often you have distinctions based on mode of livelihood, whereby you have pastoralists, sedentary farmers, and urban dwellers. Yet another division stresses the extent of ideological claim to Arab identity or culture. A far less useful way is to use the ethnic boundary as a marker between one group and another, like the Fur, the Zaghawa, the Masaaleit, and so forth.[2]

The current crisis has simplified and rigidified these categories. It has precipitated a new dominant criterion that operates as an ideology that is consciously enacted on the ground in forging alliances among various ethnic groups. Darfur can now be primarily divided into two broad categories: Arabs, mostly but not all nomads, who have a strong claim to Arab culture and ancestry, and Black Africans ("Zurqa") who regard themselves as essentially non-Arab and African in origin. Surprisingly, many ethnic groups in the latter category speak Arabic as their mother tongue and, at least until a few years ago, courted both Arab ancestry and culture. But for many of these now, Africanism has finally superseded language, Islam, and the influence of Arab culture as a determining factor of identity. For them, Africanism connotes both historic belonging to the land and pride in their darker color and, above all, distinctiveness from their new Arab opponents.

Information on Darfur's history is still scant and hard to come by. From the fourteenth century right through to the nineteenth century, Darfur was dominated by three kingdoms, the Dajo between the thirteenth and sixteenth centuries; the Tunjur, who ruled Jebel Mara until the seventeenth century; and the Keira Dynasty, which was only partially defeated by the Turks in 1874. Hence Darfur was, to a great degree, a separate Sultanate until the British annexed it to the current Sudan in 1916. With the exception of a brief period of its history (1887–1898), Darfur stood as a separate kingdom whose borders encroached into Chad but occasionally moved east deep into the current Region of Kordofan.[3]

The paucity of knowledge of Darfur's history is not accidental. Rather, it is a logical outcome of the orchestrated state campaign to obliterate the history of non-Northern Sudanese. It is to be noted that since independence in 1956, the Sudan has been controlled by three Arabized ethnic groups that originate in the northern region of the Sudan to the detriment of all others, both in the northern region and other parts of the nation. The success of their campaign to undermine others is so spectacular that many of the target populations have accepted their banishment from history. In official Sudanese discourse, Darfur has always been presented as a region of no history in line with other marginalized areas in the Sudan. As a child growing up in western Darfur, I was taught to look beyond the Red Sea and explore my history as part of the Arab peninsula and its glorious Arab-Islamic Empire. When I was a young boy at El Fasher secondary school, our four classrooms were named after the famous four Islamic Khalifas, the successors of the Prophet Mohammed (Abu Bakr, Omer, Othman, and Ali).

When Arab-Islamic history gives way, it is often replaced by symbols from northern Sudan and rarely by those from the marginalized areas in the country. The hostels in both the intermediate and secondary schools that I attended bore the names of Sudanese historical figures like Tihraqa, Nijoomi, Abu Likailik, and Dinar, the last being the only Darfurian who was occasionally honored by this deliberate reinvention of history.

The onslaught on Darfur history was so overwhelming that the local people also participated in it. This brazen project to clear history of non-Arab elements is exemplified by an order of a then-fanatic Minister of Culture and Information (1980s) decreeing that all pre-Islamic symbols in the National Museum in Khartoum be removed and replaced by artifacts that reflected Islamic culture and history. Such a vision of history has now become evident among the marginalized, particularly in Darfur. My own District town of Umkeddada in North Darfur is now divided into four residential quarters officially known as Muzdalifa, Safa, Taqwa, and Alsalam. Two of these names refer to pilgrimage spots in Saudi Arabia, and the third (Taqwa) can simply be translated as Islamic "piety." Only one of the four chosen names (Alsalam) refers to a general human virtue, but that too equally resonates with Islamic philosophy, teaching, and thought. After all, the word *salam*, a derivative of the term *aslama* ("to become a Muslim"), is central to Islamic greeting formulae and is also used in Islamic prayers.

The evolution of a nation is a long and arduous process that cannot be pinned to a definite date in its history. Sudan as a nation is no exception, and its birth cannot be referenced by a single date. Nonetheless, there are certain landmarks in its history, and I will take the liberty of starting from just over a century ago. The Mahdist state in Sudan (1885–1898) was a landmark in the formation of the present official Sudanese national identity, but only if we leapfrog history and omit the golden era of Amara Dunqus, the king of the first Black Sultanate in central Sudan during the seventeenth century. The Mahdist era was important not only due to its ability to bring together a substantial territory of the current Sudan under one rule but also because it was appropriated by the colonial invaders and used as a basis for modern Sudan. The cleavage of that Mahdist state is central to our plight today. So much energy, historical revisionism, and national and Western scholastic endeavors have reduced that cleavage to simple religious differences. Hence you have northern Muslims versus Christian-cum-animist south, a division that is now reflected in the north–south civil war brought to an end by the accession of John Garang's party to power in Khartoum in July 2005. But the Mahdist state reflected the realities of Sudan differently, and this image might be a better base for analyzing current Sudan.

In the Mahdist reign the state witnessed intense struggle between two main groups: (1) the Ashraf of the northern Sudan that lies north of Khartoum (honorable descendents of the Prophet Mohammad), who identified with the Mahdi; and (2) the Gharraba (Westerners of Darfur and Kordofan), who sided with Khalifa Abdullahi, the architect of the Mahdi's regime. It is to be noted that Khalifa Abdullahi was Almadi's deputy but later became his successor, hence the title "khalifa" ("successor" in Arabic). In some ways, the seeds of what was to become the nucleus of Sudanese identity were sown. The Ashraf were to be staged as the core of that identity against the Gharraba, who occupied a position of inferiority in the new dispensation. Although the Mahdist movement was instigated by the ills of Turkish rule (1881–1885), which included slavery, the abolition of slavery was not central to Mahdist policies. In Mahdist policies, slavery was tolerated if not encouraged by the state. More damagingly, a slaving mentality was augmented during the Mahdist regime through the institutionalization of Arab hegemony during the reign of Khalifa Abdullahi, who ran the state after the Mahdi's death. Ironically, the Mahdi did little about slavery in the Sudan under the pretext that there was no clear statement regarding its abolition in the Koran. At the same time, he channeled considerable energy into banning the use and sale of tobacco, which did not feature in the Koran.[4]

It is possible to argue that Khalifa Abdullahi had no choice, as slavery was historically part and parcel of the Islamization of the Sudan. For example, the fourteenth-century intrusion of Islam into north Sudan was signaled by the Baqt Treaty, which was made conditional on the provision of slaves to the Islamic state in Egypt. The Turkish invasion of the Sudan itself was driven by several motives, one of which was to procure slaves. In line with the culture of the Arab slave traders who operated in the Sudan between the fourteenth and the nineteenth century, any (black) Sudanese was generally enslaveable. Since then, "black Sudanese" has become associated with "slave." It has to be conceded, however, that the association of blackness with slavery in the Arab mentality or in Arab mythology/history dates back much earlier.

Khalifa Adbullahi, the Mahdi's successor, found himself in an unenviable position. To begin with, he was a Fulani adopted into the Baggara Arabs of western Sudan. While the Baggara to this day profess their Arab ancestry, their intermixing with indigenous black Africans left them with a color that belied their claims to be regarded as true Arabs. Moreover, the Khalifa needed the support of many ethnic groups whom he rushed to Omdurman to back him against the northern Sudanese people, who openly declared themselves to be the rightful heirs of the Mahdi, who died a few months after the fall of Khartoum (1885). Not surprisingly, the Khalifa had to pursue a ruthless regime to remain in power. His legendary show of force was displayed every week in Omdurman in what was at the time a residential park that bears the name Alarda, the Display Park, to this day. In his quest to maintain power, the Khalifa committed several atrocities, the most infamous of which was his onslaught on Berber, a northern city that was accused of collaborating with the colonial invaders. The Khalifa has never been forgiven for his excesses, although the Mahdi had emerged almost untainted by all the ills of his state.

The legacy of the Mahdi is inseparable from the present Arab-Islamic Project and the construction of Sudanese identity. The Mahdi's credentials rested on two pillars. First, he was a theological scholar with a mission that afterward earned him sainthood. Second, he had "the right pedigree" connecting him directly with the Prophet Mohammed. While the Mahdi dedicated his short victorious life to discharging his *baraka* (blessings), it was the Khalifa who oversaw the mundane work of laying the foundation of the new state, the present Sudan. Despite his alleged Arab credentials, the so-called Asharaf constantly challenged the Khalifa. Claiming to be related to the Mahdi, the Asharaf saw themselves as a cut above others and the legitimate heirs of the Mahdi. For them to be dominated by Westerners in the guise of the Khalifa and his fellow countrymen was, in short, heretical. Although the Khalifa persevered, he left behind a nation that was nowhere near the melting-pot state that was accommodative of diverse populations. His own courtship of Arab ancestry allowed the slave-trade mentality that equated "blackness" with "slave" to prevail. His alienation of the northern ethnic groups paved the way for his overthrow, as those groups became the vanguards of the invading Anglo-Egyptian armies (1898).

As I mentioned before, the Khalifa retained the perils of the Mahdist rule, while the Mahdi, being a northerner, emerged as a national hero, worshipped to this day in Sudan's history and mythology. Why not? Because he was instrumental in entrenching the current Arab-Islamic monoculture. His fellow northern merchants known as *Jallaba* (procurers of goods – especially slaves in the past) were encouraged to retain their slave-trade mentality in return for their financial support of the Mahdist revolution. These Jallaba created a web of trade networks that spanned the whole country, but remained allied to their homeland along the Nile River in northern Sudan (hence, riverian Sudanese). The Jallaba continue to control national trade across the nation and finance northern-based politicians to this day.

The Anglo-Egyptian rule of the Sudan (1898–1956) also laid the foundation for modern Sudan, and equally for many of its present ills. Western commanders of the Khalifa's army retreated to form the last kingdom of Darfur under Sultan Ali Dinar. For those ethnic groups north of Khartoum, the new era was that of unlimited opportunity. Having lost faith in the Mahdist regime and its Western supporters, they flocked to welcome and fight for their new masters, the colonial invaders. The colonial regime rewarded them by making them their assistants and, later, their heirs.

In its pursuit of establishing a modern state with a modern civic society, the colonial regime also established regulated markets all over the country. The Jallaba of the northern Sudan were to play an important role in this sphere. Their early flight from excessive tax imposed by the Turkish Regime (1821–1885) had led to their exodus from northern Sudan to the areas far away from the Nile.[5] This dispersion proved worthwhile during and after the independence of the country. Northern traders in non-northern cities of the Sudan continue to operate as conduits to redirect wealth into the same clans of northern Sudan. These Jallabas monopolize both trade and parastatal agencies for their own enrichment.

The biggest benefit of the colonial regime to the hegemony of northern Sudan was yet to come. Colonialism rested on the monopoly of modernity that underpinned the philosophy of all modern European empires. Through this monopoly, colonial staff portrayed themselves as of superior standing in terms of rationality, science, order, discipline, and so forth. Flip the coin and you get the attributes that were associated with the natives. They were to accept their position as superstitious, chaotic, unruly, tribalistic, irrational, and barbaric.[6] This construct of social relations ran throughout every colonial institution and was part and parcel of the colonial machinery of legitimacy. With the demise of colonial rule, members of the northern region of the Sudan (the three northernmost provinces at the time) simply slotted themselves into the social relations vacuum left by their colonial masters. As colonial heirs, these northern Sudanese assumed the mantle of being the vanguards of modernity in Sudan, complete with its colonial attributes. They were to become the civilized, the rational, the scientific, the orderly, and so on. These attributes were central to northern Sudan's claim to legitimacy to rule the country and are part of a discourse that remains alive to this day. Non-northerners who were in the margins of power in the Sudan were portrayed as superstitious, primitive, and tribalistic – the same qualities that were once the preserve of all Sudanese nationals.

Darfur at a Crossroads

Since its independence in 1956, Sudan has been packaged to both insiders and outsiders as an outright Arab-Islamic country. Throughout its postindependence life, the Sudanese ruling elite has pursued this project with impeccable rigor, oblivious to its consequences. This Arab-Islamic project proceeded unhindered and survived irrespective of the democratic, socialist, military, or religious credentials of the government of the day. What is even more perplexing is that, had the ruling class been fully faithful to this project, Darfur would be facing fewer problems today. Darfur is 100 percent Muslim, a substantial proportion of the population has credible claim to "Arab ancestry," and all Black Darfurians use Arabic as a mother tongue or as a *lingua franca*. There is, however, another agenda behind this project that has taken many marginal Sudanese like the Darfurians several decades to comprehend.

The chosen Arab-Islamic identity is not solely a symbolic tag. Rather, it is a discourse through which the entire Sudan can be managed and ordered into specific social relations. More lethal than that, it is so elastic and flexible that it can pave, so to speak, different routes that lead to the same station, a "dead end," one might say. Hence, irrespective of the nature of the government that sits in Khartoum, the social relations seem to remain the same. The marginalized retain their marginality and the ruling elite of the north prevails with its power and privileges intact.

Islam was primarily spread by people of Arab culture. In many ways, it is hard to disentangle Islam from Arab culture. Wherever there are Muslims, the world over, one can observe substantial elements of Arab culture underpinning their practice of Islam. It is therefore not unreasonable to expect some confusion, if not outright interchangeability, between the process of Islamization and that of Arabization. The Sudan is certainly not unique in this regard. From North Africa to India to the Far East, many Muslim ethnic groups also claim to be Arabs. Nowhere is this phenomenon clearer than in the Sudan. In the local vernacular, Arabization and Islamization are seen as synonymous and interchangeable. For example, circumcision, which is seen as Islamic in Sudan, is referred to equally as Arabization (*taareeb*), or admittance into Sunna, the prophetic way of life (*idkhalhum filsunna*).[7] This understanding of the dual aspects of being a Muslim has had wide ramifications for ethnicity and its transformation over decades if not centuries in the Sudan.

At present, the Nubians of northern Sudan, like the Danagla, claim to be Arabs and so do the Beja of east Sudan and the Hawazma of Kordofan. In Darfur, many of the groups that are now classified by their Arab neighbors as Africans and hence dispossessed of their acquired Arab connections also make similar claims, but the situation is changing quickly. Some of these groups who profess Arab connections in Darfur still retain their African languages while others have lost theirs to Arabic in the last century or two. Groups who have lost their own languages include the Zaghawa, the Fur, the Berti, the Slamat, and the Meidobe, to mention but a few. Claims of these groups to Arab ancestry are often accompanied by written pedigrees codifying their ancestral link with either the Prophet Mohammed or with his close associates. Sometimes, these pedigrees bear authentication stamps bought in Saudi Arabia. Incredible as it may be, there are now commercial offices in Saudi Arabia trading on verification of these pedigrees.

As alluded to earlier, it was not the simple claim to Arab ancestry that elevated riverian Sudan to its hegemonic position in the country. Rather, it was their opportunistic monopolization of modernity that was once the preserve of British colonial staff. By appropriating modernity and becoming its overseers in the Sudan, they have succeeded in dislodging many other ethnic groups across the Sudan that can mobilize their claim to Arab ancestry. Nomadic groups like the Kababish, the Ziyadiya, the Rashaida, and the Zibaidiya can all profess Arab identity to an extent that cannot be matched by the current hegemonic groups in the country. However, in the current discourse of power, they are classified as essentially backward and at odds with modernity.

Why the Janjawid

The term *Janjawid*, which has now entered international lexicons, is new to most Sudanese, including the Darfurians. The term literally means "hordes" but has also taken descriptive connotations, hence other translations like "unruly men on horses," "Arab Militias," "jinn on horses," or even "horsemen brandishing JIM 3 machine guns" (Jawad = horse). The term became popular in the mid-1980s following assaults by Arab militias in west Darfur.

The formation of the Janjawid was neither spontaneous nor accidental. Rather, it was the result of planned actions by successive Khartoum governments. Ironically, if the Janjawid were to look for a god father in the apex of power in Khartoum, they can find it in the guise of none other than Sadiq Al Mahdi, reputed to have led the most flourishing democracy in postindependence Sudan (1986–1989). It was Al Mahdi, the grandson of the Mahdi, who signaled to the Arab groups that expanding their power base could go hand in hand with the national ideal of promoting Arab-Islamic culture; that they could massacre thousands and thousands in their search for new wealth in an ethnic-cleansing fashion without facing the law; and that their leaders could maintain respectability and associate freely with the ruling elite.

At a different level, the predominantly Christian south/Southern Region of Sudan has been fighting the Khartoum government, which represented the rest of the country, collectively referred to as "north" for several decades (1955–2005). Note that in this particular context, the term *north* does not refer to the area north of Khartoum, as it does in the rest of this essay. With the accession of John Garang to power in the south in 1983, the fortunes of the Sudanese army started to wane. Having lost faith in successive Khartoum governments, the marginalized areas in the country were no longer providing fresh recruits to the army. With extreme foolishness, the government turned to Arab groups and used them as instruments in its war against the south. The Arab groups obliged in return for provisions of arms and protection from the law. Thus, in 1987 the Al Mahdi government armed the Baggara Arabs of south Kordofan to provide a buffer zone against the rebels in the south. Enslavement, burning of villages, and cattle grabbing became the order of the day. Under the protection of the state, the Arabs prospered at the expense of the innocent ethnic groups that were deemed to be affiliated with the Sudanese People's Liberation Army (SPLA).

But the power base of the Arabs did not stop at the gate of the Southern Region. Darfur also saw orchestrated attacks on the Fur and the Masaaleit in an organized fashion. Africa Watch narrates how these attacks were preceded by a warning a day ahead by the nomads to the Black farmers ordering them to vacate their villages. The Janjawid war cry is frightening and explicit: "Whoever dies goes into martyrdom and whoever survives gets the wealth of the slaves" (*almat mat shaheed, wal hia yahil leeho mal al abeed*).[8]

There can be no doubt that the atrocities of the Janjawid proceeded with the blessings of Khartoum governments, past and present. In 1987, Al Mahdi met with what was called "The Arab Congregation," also known as the Arab Gathering. Their intention was – and still is – to create "an Arab balance" in Darfur favorable for Khartoum and its policy of mono Arab-Islamic culture. The aim of the Arab Congregation was spelled out very clearly in clandestine pamphlets issued in the mid-1980s. Released in two parts under the titles *Quraish 1* and *Quraish 2*, the pamphlets call for creating what is referred to as "an Arab Belt" spanning from central Sudan to the borders of Chad. The process involves removing all those who are classified as non-Arabs from this zone. The term *Quraish* is rich in Arab-Islamic symbolism and connotes the ethnic group of nobody other than the Prophet Mohammed himself. The Arab Congregation is still active, with branches in most Darfur towns, and has been vocal in several local elections, even during Al Bashir's government (1989 to date).

The free rein given to the Arabs to pillage, massacre, rape, and enslave those who were not fortunate enough to fit into the Khartoum racists' project was chillingly demonstrated in Al-Diein city, Darfur, during Al Mahdi's highly praised democracy (1986–1989). The Baggara massacred their once neighbors and workers in a Holocaust-style slaughter. One thousand were murdered, some burnt alive near a police station, and one thousand survivors were taken as slaves. The courageous writers Baldo and Ushari, who exposed this to the public, were castigated by Khartoum scholars for defects in their research methodology. The government of Al Mahdi remained faithful to its Arab allies. As Hashim put it in his breathtaking article: "If you want to kill a case – in Sudan – form a committee of investigation for it"; and that is what the Prime Minster did.[9] We are still waiting for the investigation report. And if Al Mahdi were to look for anything comforting in his response to that massacre, let me remind him of his government's participation in the mass burial of the victims. But that too was instigated by uncomfortable motives, for Al-Diein's people, including the killers, had to be spared the sight of rotten, mutilated, and charred bodies around them and the imminent outbreak of disease in the city.

The collaboration of the Janjawid has taken a much more lethal turn in the life of the present government. Their leaders are now promoted to the highest government positions in Dafur, ranging from heads of security to state governors. The convergence of the Khartoum government with the Janjawid is so bizarre that one of the Janjawid leaders is now among the government delegation to the UN/African Union Peace Negotiations on the Darfur Crisis.

What is obscene about the government's use of the Arab militia is that it has demonstrated its failure from day one. Yet the Arab militia continues to be mobilized. In 1987, the Arab militia proved to be no match for the SPLA, against whom they were launched in the first place. Instead, they redirected their lethal weapons against the innocent and clearly unarmed civilians with stunning brutality. They obliterated thousands of villages in the Abye area in the south Kordofan Region while carefully avoiding any contact with the SPLA.

The same chilling story is now repeated in Darfur. Neither the militia, now called Janjawid, nor the army can confront the so-called rebels in Darfur. Rather, the Janjawid's war, backed by heavy aerial bombardment, is mainly waged against innocent civilians.

The Black Book, the Hegemony of the North, and the Zapping of Darfur
Anyone who is interested in unveiling Darfur's grievances and hence the current rebellion doesn't need to go very far. The question of Darfur is well articulated in the well-known publication *The Black Book of Sudan: Imbalance of Wealth and Power in Sudan*. This mysterious book appeared in the streets of Khartoum in 2000. At that time its unknown authors wrote under the name "Seekers of Truth and Justice." We now know that most of these authors come from the current Darfur group Justice and Equality Movement (JEM).

The mystery of the *Black Book* was compounded by its impeccable method of distribution, which was executed with military precision. A one-off distribution of the book took place at Friday prayer in the capital to avoid tight government censorship. Within days the *Black Book* took on a life of its own. With no copyright attached, it has continued circulating through spontaneous photocopying. Most readers of the *Black Book* have not seen an original print of the document. Within days, the book became a topic of conversation at every grassroots venue in the Sudan. While the authors printed only 500 copies initially, the free duplication of the book led government security to estimate the number of copies in circulation at 10,000. Part Two of the *Black Book* was published four years later.[10]

In a nutshell, the *Black Book* (Parts I and II) claims that the Northern Region has controlled Sudan throughout its independent history, and that this control has remained the same irrespective of the nature of the government of the day. The Northern hegemony has prevailed through democratic, theocratic, socialist, and military governments alike. The domination of the North, which is thought to constitute only 5 percent of Sudan's population, is pervasive and has been maintained at a huge cost to the nation. This disparity of wealth and power created a deep sense of political grievance leading to the current crisis in the country. Let me now try to throw some light on this thesis. The claim is supported by an impressive array of statistics showing the regional origins of all key officeholders in the country: ministers, heads of Sudan Central Banks, prime ministers, heads of universities, and so on.

To begin with, all the presidents/prime ministers of the Sudan have come from the 5 percent of the Northern Region. Going through the ministerial positions dating from 1956 to 1989, a whopping 62 percent went to the North, while only 11 percent went to the Western Region, which includes both Darfur and Kordofan and which holds 33 percent of Sudan's population. During the first decade of the reign of the present government (Al Bashir's), the North controlled 60 percent of the national ministerial positions, while the share of Darfur with its 20 percent of Sudan's population was around 11 percent. The same pattern of government domination can also been seen in membership of the Revolutionary Command Council, where the North had 53 percent representation while Darfur had just 13 percent. Fifty percent of the presidential advisors also came from the North, as opposed to 10 percent from Darfur (Table 1).

State governors did not escape this Northern hegemony. During the same period, 40 percent of state governors came from the North, while the share of Darfur remained dismal at 15 percent (Table 1). The statistics of power sharing if not power holding are boringly similar throughout, leaving no hope for those whose fortunes destined them to have been born outside the ethnic groups of the Northern Region. The same pattern of high job allocation also occurs at other levels, including the positions of attorney general, heads of constitutional courts, national security, police force, ambassadors, bank managers, the Gezira Scheme, and the top public and semi-state companies (Table 1).

This unusual disparity in high job allocation left a clear deficit in the developmental fortunes of non-northern states. This is apparent in various developmental indices revealed in the Black Book. For example, primary school enrollment is 88 percent for the North, as opposed to 31 percent in Darfur. The rate of hospital beds per 100,000 is 151 in the Northern Region compared to 24.7 in Darfur. Again there are 13.4 doctors per 100,000 in the Northern Region compared to 1.9 in Darfur (see Table 2).[11] Using corroborative statistics from various sources, including the World Bank, the IMF, and the African Development Bank, Alex Cobham has this to say about the conclusions of the *Black Book*:

> The *Black Book of Sudan* ... sets out data showing the disproportionate access to power – since independence in 1956 – of the 5 percent of the population from the Northern states. It further makes the claim that this has led to distorted distribution of government resources and therefore of development opportunities. This paper has used the most recent reliable data, much of it provided by the current government itself, to explore this claim. The results offer overwhelming support.[12]

Table 1. **Regional Division of Key Offices in Sudan**

	Office/Item	Northern Region	Southern Region	Darfur Region
1	As Percentage of Sudan's Population	5%	16%	20%
2	Presidents 1956–present	All of Northern Origin	0%	0%
3	National Ministers 1989–2000	52%	13%	11%
4	Members of Revolutionary Command Council 1989–present	53%	20%	13%
5	Presidential Advisors 1994–2001	50%	0%	10%
6	State Governors excluding Southern States	40%	All from the South	15%
7	Attorney Generals 1989–2000	50%	0%	0%
8	Heads of Constitutional Court	74%	13%	13%
9	Heads of National Internal Security	50%	0%	0%
10	Heads of External National Security	100%	0%	0%
11	Sudan Intelligence System	100%	0%	0%
12	Heads of National Police Force	44%	0%	0%
13	Sudanese Ambassadors (2000)	66%	6%	2%
14	Sudan Consuls	47%	2%	0%
15	Presidents of Universities (56)	55%	0%	17%
16	Managers of Bank of Sudan 1988–2000	100%	0%	0%
17	Mangers of Other Banks and Financial Houses	67%	0%	1%
18	Managers of Gezira Scheme	100%	0%	0%
19	Major Public Companies (52)	73%	0%	0%

Table 2. **Human Development**

Item/Region	Northern Region	Southern Region	Darfur Region
Percentage of Sudan's Population	5%	16%	20%
Primary School Enrolment	88%	21%	31%
Hospitals per 100,000	3.9	1	0.4
Hospital beds per 100,000	151	68	24.7
Doctors per 100,000	13.4	2.8	1.5

The Tripartite Coalition of the Northern Region

When the British colonial government left the Sudan in 1956, nationals had to be promoted to fill their vacated posts. There were altogether 800 new civil service posts, of which 778 went to persons from the Northern Province, while the remaining eight provinces of the Sudan were left to haggle over the leftovers. The divine right of the North to rule Sudan was thus inscribed in no uncertain terms. But there was a problem. The divine right had to be safeguarded against subsequent change of governments: Some of these were democratic, but most were not. But there was no limit to the genius of our Northern leaders, and here lies the story of the tripartite coalition of the north (Kayan Alshimal, a.k.a. KASH). The term *KASH* can loosely be translated as "the Northern Entity," referring to a body that is entrusted with promoting the interests of the Northern Region. But membership in KASH is open only to elite ethnic groups, just in case other Northerners delude themselves, dreaming of being treated like "proper" Northerners. There is no place in KASH for "lowly nomads" like the Manaseer of the Northern Region who claim Arab ancestry, and it is equally out-of-bounds for those unfortunate enough to speak Nubian or one of the other African languages as a mother tongue. These non-Arabic languages are referred to as *rutanas*, which can simply be translated from Arabic as gibberish, incomprehensible, or simply "bird's talk." These rutanas are considered no good, and the sooner they vanish from the Sudan the better. Not surprisingly, Sudanese who "still" have a rutana are embarrassed to show it. Speaking it is taken to be vulgar in the company of others, and it is better to pretend not to have one at all. To have had one in the past is stigma enough, but to have one now is beyond forgiveness. Among other things, it means immediate exclusion from the Arab-Islamic club, and you lose your right to belong. The Mahas of the Northern Region now deny that they ever had a rutana even though living memory proves otherwise. Most of these rutana groups in the North have remained virtually unknown to the rest of the Sudan, with whom they share the fate of the marginalized majority. They are meant to remain nonexistent, invisible except to nosy anthropologists and archaeologists.

So who belongs to the club? Well, no prize for guessing; you only have to check the presidents and the prime ministers of the Sudan since independence, and you will work it out. If your memory cannot take you that far back, not to worry, just pay attention to Al Bashir and his close associates in Khartoum's Presidential Palace. KASH is an exclusive club, barely big enough for the three most formidable ethnic groups of the North. These are the Jallayeen (President Al Bashir's ethnic group), the Shaigiya (ex-President Sir Alkhatim and Current Deputy President Taha's ethnic group), and the Danagla (ex-Prime Minster Al Mahdi, ex-President Nimeiri, and ex-Deputy President Alzibair's ethnic group). So boringly uniform is this that it would be appropriate to rename the Presidential Palace in Khartoum as the KASH Palace, Northern Entity Palace, or simply to register it for the Jallayeen, the Shaigiya, and the Danagla. One does not need to have a sophisticated mind to conclude that this is no way to run a modern state. But this is precisely what has proved incomprehensible to our leaders to date.

What is the function of KASH? It is plain and simple: Irrespective of the nature of the government in Khartoum, democratic or otherwise, military or otherwise, fanatic or otherwise, socialist or otherwise, jobs must remain in the hands of "the boys," and wealth must flow into the Northern Region. Other ethnic groups from the Northern Region can be co-opted from time to time, but rarely to key posts. However, by virtue of sharing the North with the eminent members of KASH, they ultimately benefit in terms of flow of resources into the Northern Region. As far as the rest of the country is concerned, they are only used if they prove their worth to KASH and only until political uncertainty is brought under control and a more worthy member of one of the elite ethnic groups is found. Thus, when Turabi, who is of northern origin, was dislodged from power, a situation of extreme uncertainty arose in Khartoum. To deprive Turabi of any support from Darfur, Al Bashir rushed Ustaz Tigani Sirag, a Darfurian, to occupy his position. Barely three weeks later, there was no need for a Darfurian in such a prominent position. When the dust had finally settled and Turabi, the once formidable imam of the regime, turned out to be no more than a paper tiger, Ustaz Sirag was not even granted the honor of being notified about his dismissal. The disappearance of his official car from in front of his office was enough to remind him of his place and teach him about the divine right of the North to rule the country, a right that he happily and humbly accepted.

KASH became a formal organization following the abortive coup of Hasan Hesain in 1976. Although Al Mahdi's party orchestrated the attempt, a Darfurian-born combatant led it. That was too much for the North. When the Northerners topple an elected government in Khartoum, it is often assumed that it must be for the good of the nation. Not if the leaders of the coup happen to be from the marginalized people. Thus, Hesain's attempt at power was immediately dismissed as that of mercenaries. The Westerners who dared to challenge the northern hegemony were banished from the Sudan altogether. For a brief period, the state radio entity, Radio Omdurman, described them as "the Black Tigers" (*Alfuhoud al-soud*). The term was telling, as it implied that other Sudanese nationals, and particularly the rightful rulers, are something other than black. The term *Black Tigers* was subsequently replaced by the term *mercenaries*, a label that still freely and unashamedly circulates in popular Sudanese imagery. For days after the abortive coup, the media in Khartoum continued to broadcast interviews with captive coup leaders. Their poor command of Khartoum colloquial Arabic was mocked and interpreted as evidence of their not belonging to Sudan, hence the term *mercenaries*.

In January 2005, Al Bashir's ruling National Congress Party concluded a peace agreement with the southern rebels, the Sudanese People's Liberation Movement/Army, popularly known as SPLM/A. The agreement, officially referred to as the Comprehensive Peace Agreement (CPA), has been publicized as a model for all other African countries in similar circumstances; it is claimed that it guarantees a new Sudan of democracy, justice, and inclusiveness. Among its provisions, the CPA stipulates the formation of a new government of national unity along with a well-defined proportional division of all key national cabinet positions in the country. The government of national unity was formed in September 2005. Rather than reflecting the inclusiveness of Garang's vision of the New Sudan, the government of national unity appears to have been sabotaged by KASH and its insidious philosophy. According to the CPA, the Southern Region was to hold sixteen cabinet positions in the national government, leaving thirty-two positions for the remaining five Regions represented by the Khartoum government. The allocation of these thirty-two cabinet positions was astounding. Surprisingly or otherwise, twenty of the thirty-two positions are filled up with personnel ethnically affiliated to one Region only, and that is the Northern Region. Much worse, KASH's elite ethnic groups of the North, i.e., the Shaigiya, the Jallayeen, and the Danagla, control all the cabinet positions that went to the Northern Region. This is despite that fact that the Northern Region houses no fewer than seventeen indigenous ethnic groups (Tables 3 and 4).

Table 3. **Old Habits Die Hard**

Region	Number of Positions	Percentage of Population
Southern	16	16
Northern	20	5.4
Kordofan	6	12
Darfur	6	20
Eastern	0	11
Central	0	20

Table 4. **Ethnic Composition of Cabinet Members from Northern Region, Government of National Unity, September 2005, Excluding Southern Region**

Ethnic Group	Shaigiya	Jallayeen	Danagla	Others
No. of Positions	3	12 (*Al Bashir's ethnic group*)	5	0

Before I leave this section, I must emphasize that not every member of the ethnic groups that form the tripartite alliance approves of the selfish and shortsighted mission of KASH. Fortunately, these ethnic groups contain many citizens who are working hard and aspiring to build a just Sudan that is accommodative of all, irrespective of ethnic differences.

Khartoum, the "White" City, and Its Black Belt

1983 was the first time that Darfur had a Darfurian governor. The struggle to have just that was not easy. It took a formidable uprising that brought the regional capital, El Fasher, to a standstill. At the end, the dictator Numeiri had to concede and humiliatingly issued a presidential decree against his constitution and withdrew his handpicked puppet nominee in favor of one acceptable to the people. That was an important gain, but nowhere near enough to assuage the feelings of marginalization in the Sudan. Sadly, the media in Khartoum still thinks otherwise. For example, many Khartoum intellectuals still maintain that the South has long been ruled by southerners and should have shut up and stopped complaining. By continuing the fight for more positions in the central government, the SPLM must harbor other ills. The same "Home Rule" is now conceded to Darfur in the guise of federation or even regional autonomy. As far as Khartoum, the center of power, is concerned, it is to remain out-of-bounds for southerners and westerners alike.

Despite the existence of the Nile River, the Northern Region remains most inhospitable for human habitation with exceptionally low carrying capacity in comparison to many other Regions in the Sudan. Traditionally, the Northern Region has always been an area of out-migration. As the capital of a state and a seat of government dominated by Northerners, Khartoum became a favored destination for immigrants from the Northern Region. Their access to jobs has, over the years, remained exceptionally high and disproportionate to the size of their population. But Khartoum, too, has attracted others from all over the Sudan. Lack of development in other regions of the Sudan made Khartoum, by default, attractive, if only to avail of the meager services that it offered. Despite this, and oblivious to history, many Northerners seem to have extended their right to rule and treat Khartoum as a northern city. This view metamorphosed into a powerful ideology that holds that others like the Southerners and the Darfurians should forget about Khartoum and be content with ruling their own regions.

In his recent work on the current Sudan crisis, Mohammad Hashim maintains that the name *Khartoum*, traditionally pronounced as "Khertum," is of Dinka origin. Khartoum owes its name to the Dinka language, in which the words *ker tom* translates as "the river confluence."[13] It is to be noted that the term *Khartoum* has no Arabic origin. Earlier attempts to rewrite history by attributing the origin of the term *Khartoum* to the Arabic *khurtoum*, meaning "elephant's trunk," simply did not sell well in Sudanese schools. Moreover, and just 250 years ago, the White Nile area that extended north of Jabal Aulia on the outskirts of Khartoum was Shillukland.[14] For those readers who are not familiar with the lands of Sudanese ethnic groups, let me note that the Dinka and Shilluk come from the Southern Region of the Sudan and count among the Christian and animist supporters of Garang's SPLM.

As for Omdurman, it owes its name to Darfur. Traders from Darfur who were not well versed in Arabic referred to a female food seller as mother of Abdurahman (*umduraman*). Recent history shows that until the Mahdi's uprising (1885–1898), the city of Omdurman was nothing but a small market and a few scattered fishing hamlets.

The Northern ownership of Khartoum is not a simple dream. It is an ideology that successive governments have pursued with vigor. Reminiscent of the now-defunct South African apartheid system, and in the name of tackling fighting and loitering, those who were deemed too dark for Khartoum were often rounded up by the army and the police to be sent back to their various areas, which were impoverished by the Khartoum government. These raids were practiced throughout the reign of all governments that have ruled the Sudan since the 1970s. However, this practice has become much harsher during the reign of Al Bashir's government and particularly during the time in office of Deputy President Alzibair, whose hatred of the Gharraba, not to mention the Southerners, was legendary. Hashim says that those who were herded out did not understand the action and thought that their leaders at the top had lost their common sense.[15] But it gets even more bizarre, and you could be forgiven for confusing Khartoum for an all-white Afrikaner city. The racist philosopher of the current regime, Hasan Mekki, portrayed Khartoum as a city besieged by black people. For that, he coined the unfortunate term *Black Belt* (*alhizam Alaswad*), referring to those who live in the outskirts of Khartoum. These are impoverished sectors of the capital, and people from the Southern and Western Regions populate most, but not all of them. The eminent philosopher, or perhaps more accurately, bigot, described those "black people" as descending on Khartoum, filling it with flies during the day and spoiling its peace with night burglary. The Black Belt is responsible for messing up the otherwise tranquil life of the (certainly not black) Khartoumese people. The inability of members of KASH to accept the very plain fact that they, too, are black has culminated in a deep inferiority complex. This complex, described by Al-Baqir Al-Afif Mukhtar as an "identity crisis," is chillingly and no less embarrassingly revealed in the following words:

In 1990, a group of Northern Sudanese in Birmingham in Britain convened a meeting to discuss how to fill in the Local Council's Form, and especially the question about the social category. They felt they did not fit in any of the categories that include, among others, White, Afro-Caribbean, Asian, Black African, and others. It was clear to them to tick on "Others," but what was not clear was whether to specify as "Sudanese, Sudanese Arab or just Arab." There was a heated discussion before they finally settled on "Sudanese Arab." When the question why not to tick on the category of Black African was raised, the immediate response was that, "but we are not blacks."[16]

Khartoum certainly belongs to the Northern Region. But inasmuch as it does, it also belongs to other Sudanese irrespective of their shade of color, region, or religion. Ironically speaking, the common denominator of those described as black here is neither color nor religion or even regional origin. It is poverty that is responsible for their marginalization.

The Road to War in Darfur

It is legitimate to question the wisdom of taking up arms against the government of Khartoum and to assume that a peaceful way of addressing the problem would have been better. One thing, however, is sure in the case of Darfur. Arms were taken up only after the failure of Khartoum to listen to the voice of peace, which was raised on numerous occasions by Darfurian leaders. Bizarrely, Al Bashir is famous for repeating in his public speeches that he negotiates only with those who raise arms.

Callous dictators facing catastrophes often hide behind ignorance, blaming their advisers for not conveying to them the extent of imminent disasters until it is too late. With their strong control of the media, dictators always run the risk of forfeiting the use of so-called early-warning systems that could prompt them to act in timely fashion. Well, Al Bashir and his predecessors simply do not have the luxury of hiding behind ignorance. Despite his oppressive control over the media, Al Bashir's government knowingly sat and watched Darfur progress toward war. Instead of extinguishing the fire, he and his government added more fuel to it.

I cannot possibly match Harir's excellent documentation of the Janjawid atrocities in Darfur, which prevailed long before the current armed "rebellion." Harir shows how many opportunities were lost by reducing a clearly political problem to its military underpinnings.[17] Let us start the debate from a much later date in the history of Janjawid atrocities and government intransigence in Darfur.

January 1999 witnessed a colossal attack by the so-called Arabs on their African neighbors in West Darfur. The assault was orchestrated and assisted by the army and led to the deaths of more than a hundred unarmed civilians, the burning of one hundred villages, and the displacement of thousands of people, all for the sake of land and wealth. The crisis led to a well-publicized condemnation by all political parties, including the opposition parties. Al Bashir himself shed a few crocodile tears and sent his envoy to bring things under control.

Darfurians did not stand idly by. They engaged with the Presidential Palace, warning Al Bashir about the imminent disaster facing the country. The Memorandum of March 1999 was accompanied by 1,300 signatures of Darfurian dignitaries, including those of key figures in Al Bashir's government. The memorandum was very detailed and covered the cause of the problem as well as outlining ways toward its circumvention. Had the government paid attention to that memorandum and followed it to the letter, there would not be war now in Darfur. Instead, the government harassed those who signed the memorandum and declared the crisis as nothing but a subversive action premeditated by enemies of the government.[18]

The Darfur Armed Movements

There are currently two main armed movements operating in Darfur. The Sudan Liberation Movement/Army (SLM/A) is the biggest. It is an offshoot of an earlier movement led by Daud Bolad.[19] Bolad, a Darfurian himself, was a prominent member of the Muslim Brotherhood of the 1970s and 1980s. Following his defection from the Muslim Brotherhood, he resurfaced in Darfur leading an SPLA (of Garang) battalion in 1991. His battalion was defeated and he was captured and later killed by his captors.

The second Darfur Movement operates under the name Sudanese Justice and Equality Movement (JEM). It operated as a clandestine movement throughout the 1990s, but became known to most of us much later. JEM is famous for the publication of the *Black Book of Sudan*, although some of the fifty-four authors are now members of the SLM/A.[20] JEM is often portrayed as an affiliate of Turabi's Popular Congress Party (not to be confused with the National Congress Party of Al Bashir), where many of its current leaders learned the ABCs of politics. Al Bashir's government has overemphasized this alleged connection with the Popular Congress Party of Turabi in an attempt to galvanize the Sudanese public against JEM. The success of Abashir in defaming JEM with such an alleged connection was so spectacular that several circles in the international community, as well as international official bodies, also believed it. Views, however, are now changing regarding the possible affiliation of JEM to the "Islamist" Popular Congress Party of Turabi. During the Sixth Round of Abuja Talks on Darfur, Roger Winter, the U.S. Special Representative for Sudan, declared to this author that "the United States no longer maintains that JEM is affiliated to Turabi's Party." Julie Flint and Alex de Waal also express the same view in their recent book on Darfur.[21]

Both SLM and JEM are broad organizations that accommodate many who are unified by broader objectives and a common enemy. The objectives of both movements boil down to establishing a Sudan that is free of ethnic, color, cultural, religious, or regional marginalization.[22]

By the late 1980s, the government of Khartoum was fighting for its survival following numerous defeats in the south. It found new allies among the Janjawid, who were enticed by the promise of expanding their land and wealth base. It was a lethal marriage, exploited by certain "Arab" groups to enrich themselves at the expense of other indigenous Darfurians. By 2002, the indigenous Darfurians, referred to as "Zurqa" (Blacks), could not take it anymore. A perfect environment for armed insurgence ensued.

In February 2003, the movements of Darfur began their assaults. It was clear from the beginning that it was an armed rebellion and not simply armed robberies as the government wanted to maintain. Darfurian people in and out of the government approached the Khartoum authorities to move immediately and accept that the rebellion was instigated by political grievances that could not be reduced to military operations. Khartoum listened and participated in the selection of a committee of eighty prominent people representing all stakeholders in Darfur. It was a wise course of action, and the committee soon moved into a positive debate with the so-called new rebels of Darfur. But Khartoum had another vision. For many at the top echelons, the members of the movements were no more than amateur boys who could easily be crushed by the army. In April 2003, Al Bashir convened a Dual Summit with Idris Deby, the President of Chad. The summit worked out a plan to annihilate the armed movement and this intention was declared in no uncertain terms. Days after the summit, Darfur witnessed its most intensive aerial bombardment. The attack was brutal and indiscriminate and devoid of any strategy of targeting the rebels or sparing unarmed civilians. The assault continued nonstop for five days. The message to the rebels was crystal clear: Attack the government troops and we will bomb your innocent people. This strategy still underlies Khartoum's military operations in Darfur.

The response of the rebels was impeccable and swift. Even before the government's bombardment was over, "the amateur boys" hit back. They attacked El Fasher, the capital of the region and the seat of the army headquarters, burning six airplanes, killing thirty-two army members, and taking the army's commander captive (he was later released unharmed). The rebels entered the army headquarters and emptied it of its weapons and vehicles. Then they marched into the city center for a rally and a speech before they withdrew with the loss of twenty men. Documenting this incident, Abu Khalid narrates that rebels had no interest in harming civilians, including top government officials. They ordered many of them to leave their offices and go to their homes. The head of the Popular Defense Force, clearly a target given the circumstances, was included among those officials.[23]

The successful attack on El Fasher was devastating for the government of Khartoum. Their new enemy proved to be more than a bunch of disorganized adventurers. As described by a top Sudanese army general, their attack combined elements of military surprise, accurate timing, clear targeting, and swift entry and exit with minimal casualties, a dream of every military commander.

As for the rebels, the attack on El Fasher was a turning point in their movement. It clearly catapulted them into a force that cannot be taken for granted. Their attempts to avoid civilian casualties won them much praise in the city. It was clearly at odds with the normal behavior of the Sudanese army, in peace or in combat. Through their public rally, the rebels were able to present their case and counteract government propaganda. Not surprisingly, the movements have never since then run short of volunteers to go to the battlefield.

The predicament of Khartoum's government is getting worse. The marginalization thesis has now reached every corner in the Sudan and is likely to lead to other similar rebellions. At least two other new movements have already declared war against Khartoum and in June 2007 they formed alliances with Darfur's movements. These are the Shahama (Pride) Movement of the Misairia Arabs of Kordofan and the Maalia Arabs of Abkarinka in Darfur. The armed rebels in the East, Red Lions and Beja Front, and numerous Arab groups have also signed a memorandum with the Darfur Movement. With that, it is clear that Khartoum's dilemma is now taking a different twist. In Khartoum's lexicon, these groups do not figure among the "Zurqa" (Blacks) of Sudan. Rather, they are Arabs and hence part of the pool that has traditionally allied itself with the Khartoum government. Perhaps receiving Garang's SPLM in Khartoum is after all not that bad. It is a lesser evil. At least Khartoum's rulers can still count on the Islamic card that can be raised to keep "Christian" SPLM at arm's length and to rally others against them. That cannot be done with the Gharraba (Westerners). They may prove to be too close for comfort and a much harder nut to crack.

Notes

Originally published in *Irish Journal of Anthropology* vol. 9, 1 (2006): 5–18

1   United Nations High Commissioner for Refugees (UNHCR), "Darfur Situation Deteriorating," http://www.sudaneseonline.com/enews2005/oct30–65143.shtml. Agence France-Presse (AFP) 2005. "US extends sanctions on Sudan, presses for peace results," posted November 1, 2005.

2   See M.A. Abdul-Jalil, "The Dynamics of Ethnic Identification in Northern Darfur," in *The Sudan, Ethnicity and National Cohesion*, M. O. Beshir, ed. (Bayreuth: University of Bayreuth, 1984); A. M. Ahmedand S. Harir, "Sudanese Rural Society: Its Development and Dynamism," *Development Studies and Research Centre (DSRC)* (Khartoum: University of Khartoum Press, 1982) (in Arabic); F. Ibrahim, "Ecological Imbalance in the Republic of Sudan," *Bayreuther Geowissenschaftliche Abreiten*, no. 6 (1984): 215; F. Ibrahim, "Ideas on the Background of the Present Conflict in Darfur: Discussion Paper" (University of Bayreuth, Germany, 2004); R.S. O'Fahey, *State and Society in Darfur* (London: C. Hurst and Company, 1980); M. Sulaiman, "Civil War in the Sudan: From Ethnic to Ecological Conflict," *The Ecologist* 23, no. 3 (1993).

3   See Ibrahim, 2004; R.S. O'Fahey, "Religion and Trade in the Keira Sultanate of Dar Fur," *Sudan in Africa*, Y. F. Hassan, ed. (Khartoum: KUP, 1969); O'Fahey, 1980; A.B. Theobold, *Ali Dinar: Last Sultan of Dar Fur 1898–1916* (London: Longman, 1956).

4   Mohammad Jalal Hashim, To Be or Not to Be: Sudan at Crossroads. http://www.sudanjem.com/sudan-alt/english/books/TOBEORNOTTOBE/20040418_books_TOBEORNOTTOBE.htm, (2004): 12.

5   K. Beck, "Tribesmen, Townsmen and the Struggle about a Proper Life-style in Northern Kordofan," in *Kordofan Invaded: Peripheral Incorporation and Social Transformation in Islamic Africa*, M. Kevane and E. Stiansen, ed. (Leiden: Brill, 1997).

6   Victoria Bernal, "Colonial Moral Economy and the Discipline of Development: The Gezira Scheme and Modern Sudan," *Cultural Anthropology* 12, no. 4 (1997): 447–79.

7   See Abdullahi El-Tom, "Female Circumcision and Ethnic Identity in Sudan with Special Reference to the Berti of Darfur," *GeoJournal* 46, no. 2 (1998): 163–70 and "Islam and Ethnic Identity among the Berti of Darfur, Sudan," *GeoJournal* 46, no. 2 (1998): 155–62.

8   See Africa Watch, *The Forgotten War in Darfur Flares Again. A Report.* London, 1990; M. Sulaiman, "War in Darfur or the Desert Versus the Oasis Syndrome,"

Sudan Programme Paper No. 3. (UK: Institute for African Alternative, 1994): 26; Ibrahim Yahia Abdulrahman, "Root Causes of the Genocide in Darfur, Sudan," unpublished paper, 2005.

9   Hashim, 29.

10 See Justice and Equality Movement, *The Black Book: Imbalance of Power and Wealth in Sudan, Part I and II.* English Translation. (UK: JEM, 2004), and Abdullahi El-Tom, "The Black Book of Sudan: Imbalance of Power and Wealth in Sudan," *Journal of African International Affairs* 1, no. 2 (2003): 25–35. Also in *Review of African Political Economy* 30, no. 97 (2003): 501–511 (Joint authorship with M.A. Salih).

11 See F. Ibrahim, "Ideas on the Background of the Present Conflict in Darfur: Discussion Paper" (Germany: University of Bayreuth, 2004); Darfur Forum for Dialogue and Peaceful Co-Existence (DFDPC), Economic and Developmental Axes: Darfur Working Document, Khartoum (2005); Elzain Adam et al. Development Is Key for Peace in Darfur (Khartoum: Friedrich Ebert Stiftung, 2003).

12 Alex Cobham, *Causes of Conflict in Sudan: Testing the Black Book*, QEH Working Paper Series No. 121 (Oxford: University of Oxford, 2005), 9.

13 Hashim, 41.

14 Ibid.

15 Ibid.

16 Al-Baqir Al-Afif Mukhtar, "The Crisis of Identity in Northern Sudan: A Dilemma of a Black People with a White Culture," in *Race and Identity in the Nile Valley: Ancient and Modern Perspectives*, ed. C. Fluehr-Lobban and K. Rhodes (Trenton, NJ: The Red Sea Press, 2005), 6.

17 See S. Harir, "Militarization of the Conflict, Displacement and the Legitimacy of the State: A Case from Darfur, Western Sudan," paper presented to Center for Development Studies, University of Bergen, Norway, 1992, and "Racism in Islamic Discourse! Retreating nationalism and Upsurging Ethnicity in Dar Fur, Sudan," paper presented to Center for Development Studies, University of Bergen, Norway, 1993.

18 See the excellent documentation by Abu Ahmed, Khalid, "Darfur, Watergate and the Politics of Lies," http://www.sudanjem.com, 2004.

19 Harir, 1993.

20 El-Tom, 2003.

21 Julie Flint and Alex de Waal, *Darfur: A Short History of a Long War* (London: Zed Books, 2005).

22 Justice and Equality Movement (JEM), "A Proposal for Change: Towards a Sudan of Justice and Equality," UK: JEM, 2005.

23 Abu Ahmed, p. 16.

5   The Darfur Conflict:
A Natural Process or War by Design?

Ali B. Ali-Dinar

Stemming from political, ecological, and regional factors, the current conflict in Darfur is one of many conflicts that have plagued the region over the past several decades. The causes of such conflicts have evolved over the years and become more complex than the manner in which they have been analyzed and represented in the press and the academy. Many still argue that competition between "Arab" nomads and "African" sedentary farmers over increasingly scarce natural resources is the major cause of the current conflict in Darfur. This essay argues that the war in Darfur, which started in 2003, is a major departure from earlier conflicts that have plagued the region since the precolonial period, and more specifically, especially in its root causes and manifestations at the political, social, and global levels. Therefore, it is important to examine the factors that led to the current globally publicized conflict in comparison to previous ones. This will help to identify its nature and map the most appropriate way in which the conflict can be resolved in a just and lasting manner.

Darfur Conflicts in Historical Perspective

Historical references to conflicts in Darfur date back to the formation of this independent entity as a seventeenth-century Sultanate in the (1650–1916).[1] Most of the reported conflicts in Darfur between the eighteenth and nineteenth centuries involved either intra-Darfur rivalries or conflicts with the Sultanate's contemporaries, such as the Kingdom of Sennar in eastern Sudan and the Kingdom of Wadai, its western neighbor. In 1786, after the defeat of Sultan Hashim of Musba'at in Kordofan, Sultan Teirab of Darfur followed the army to present-day Omdurman only to stop when he fell ill and later died on his journey back to Darfur.[2] Kordofan remained part of Darfur until Turko-Egyptian forces annexed it in 1821.

Westward, the Fur sultans at times exerted greater influence upon the Kingdom of Wadai by aiding their favorites in ascending to the throne, and this led to a number of wars between the two states with their shared ethnic groups. Settling the boundaries between Darfur and Wadai was an important factor, which was used by the French government in pressuring the British administration in the Sudan to occupy Darfur.[3] In this process of diplomatic negotiation between the two colonial powers, many areas that were historically part of Darfur became part of present-day Chad.[4] According to Darfur's indigenous system of administration, tribal entities maintained political and administrative powers on behalf of Darfur's sultans.[5] In order to retain the loyalty of these tribal entities, Darfur's sultans made sure to have wives from various ethnic groups. Symbols of material wealth acquired through long-distance trade in forms of cloth, fabric, perfumes, swords, and other exotic merchandise were also used as gifts to maintain allegiance.[6]

Ethnic conflicts during this period were mainly between the sultans and some nomadic Arabs and resulted from failure or delay in paying taxes to the Sultan's agents, or competition with the sultans over trade. During the reign of Sultan Mohammad Al Fadul, several Arab sheikhs were executed as a punitive measure.[7] During the reign of Sultan Ali Dinar, several Arab groups fled to Kordofan, where they sued him through the Anglo-Egyptian administration and later aided in the invasion of Darfur by the condominium forces.[8]

Aside from periodic conflicts between the Fur sultans and some disobedient ethnic groups, the region had witnessed periods of collective revolts in which the whole population has revolted against oppressive national or foreign policies. In Darfur's history, such revolts took place during the Turkish rule of Darfur between 1874–1882, led mainly by Fur shadow sultans against the occupation; during the Mahdist rule in Darfur, as represented in the Abujimaiza revolt[9]; and later the Suheini revolt during the Anglo-Egyptian rule in 1921.

Ethnicity, as a powerful force for intimidation and divide-and-rule policies, was cleverly used by the British administration during their preparation for the invasion of Darfur in 1915. British policies at the time involved arming Arab groups in the borders between Darfur and Kordofan and using Arab militias to track Sultan Ali Dinar in Jebel Marra, which resulted in his murder in 1916.[10] In Darfur, this was the first time in which ethnically based Arab militias were recruited by an invading army against the rulers of Darfur.

Unlike the current situation in Darfur, in which land ownership is one of the reasons behind the ongoing carnage, in the past Darfur Sultans encouraged the migration of people to populate the region; these people were later granted land charters legalizing their presence and their land ownership.[11] The acceptance of foreigners also included Darfur Sultans calling for learned men (Muslim clerics) to take up residency in Darfur.

However, the peaceful coexistence of the various ethnic groups in Darfur was later disrupted by the incorporation of Darfur into a national framework with unjust structural policies. After the independence of the Sudan in 1956, the surge in ethnic violence can be ascribed to two interrelated factors: political factors at the domestic, national, and regional levels; and ecological factors related to desertification and drought, which have negatively impacted the environment and water resources.

Political Factors: Domestic, National, and Regional
Following the incorporation of Darfur into the rest of Sudan in 1915, little has changed outside the urban centers, where the traditional system of administration was embraced in harmony with the British policy of indirect rule. Since the British administration was not keen, from the beginning, on annexing Darfur to the rest of the Sudan, it was less enthusiastic in pursuing long-term policies for inclusion of Darfur and economic development in the region. A lack of basic governmental services in Darfur, compared to other regions (particularly those in the North), has led to widespread discontent in Darfur. The absence of education, transportation, and political-representation development projects are characteristic of this region, because its budget does not correspond to the size of its population. This situation pushed many Darfurians to migrate, mainly to Libya, while others engaged in trade with neighboring countries.[12] Goods from Libya, Chad, and Nigeria have enriched the local markets in Darfur, and some of these goods found their way to other parts of Sudan, including Khartoum. But Darfur was also affected by political unrest in Chad and Libya, including the Chadian–Libyan wars

(1978–1987), and the long-term showdown between Libya and the west.[13] The conflict between Sudanese and Libyan political interests in deciding who rules Chad has contributed to flooding Darfur with arms and armed groups whose entry into Darfur has prompted strong tendencies toward the use of arms to settle ethnic disputes. The ease with which these arms were acquired and smuggled into Darfur has had a direct impact on the conflicts that are currently ravaging Darfur. The Chadian–Libyan conflict coincided with a time in which Libya was obsessed with Arabism, a sentiment that was slowly adopted by certain groups in Darfur and served as a catalyst for future ethnic intimidation against its non-Arab inhabitants.[14]

Under the pretext of regional autonomy, which was introduced to Sudan in 1981 during the military rule of Ja'far Numeiri, the central government relegated many of its responsibilities to the newly created states, which were staffed by the citizens of each state. In Darfur, some politicians started to consider ethnicity as a factor in the acquisition of jobs and political power. This process of ethnically based demands for power culminated in the division of Darfur into three states. This division has benefited many elites and allowed the central government to shift its responsibilities to the cash-strapped states.

Environmental Factors: Desertification, Successive Droughts, and Their Sociopolitical Implications

Since the early 1970s, Darfur has witnessed waves of climatic change that have internally displaced many ethnic groups within the region and into urban areas nationally.[15] Hence, Zaghawa moved from their homeland (Dar Zaghawa) to different places inside Darfur. Their presence was not limited to one area; they settled in lands traditionally belonging to various ethnic groups – Fur, Arabs, Masalit, Birged – and in many urban centers in Darfur and beyond.[16] This earlier phase of gradual migration was done without reported incident and without government assistance. The same could be said for the movement of nomadic Arabs looking for water and pastures for their livestock. Throughout the years land ownership and ethnic boundaries were amicably respected by these groups, who for centuries settled their disputes through traditional means of mediation (*ajawid/mu'atamarat al sulh*). Ideally, under this mechanism, all mediation and conference decisions are honored and respected, while the government stays neutral and serves as a facilitator and rarely enforces its own vision of peace. With the existence of ethnic conflicts in Darfur in the past, the neutrality of the government has prevented these conflicts from spreading to other areas.[17]

The aforementioned formulas for settling conflicts, however, changed with the military tactics developed to fight the Sudan People's Liberation Movement/Army (SPLM/A) in southern Sudan. Although conflict over pastures and other resources tended to be resolved amicably between the Baggara/Misseiriya and the Dinka, with the infiltration of the SPLM/A in the Nuba Mountains, the Sudanese government created the *Murahaleen* militias, which fought parallel to the Sudanese government army.[18] The creation of these militias has resulted in polarizing the neighbors in the conflict, and by arming the Baggara/Misseiriya the government has poisoned the relationship between groups that for the most part have managed to peacefully coexist and intermarry for decades. It is also amid this atmosphere that the Ed Dein Massacre of 1986, committed by the Rizeigat against the Dinka took place,[19] which was followed by the creation of the Arab Gathering during the time of the democratically elected government of Sadiq Al Mahdi. In its founding declaration, the Arab Gathering criticized the marginalization of Arab groups in Darfur and called for more representation of them in the government regionally and nationally.[20] There was no condemnation of the Arab Gathering and its ethnically chauvinist rhetoric, and some of those who signed that document have held highly esteemed positions within the upper echelons of the National Islamic Front (NIF).

Ethnic Conflicts Prior to 2003

The period prior to 2003 witnessed many conflicts in the Darfur region. These conflicts date back to the early 1980s; the most important were the conflicts between the Fur and their Arab nomadic neighbors in Jebel Marrah, which ended in 1989.[21] Fur–Arab conflict has followed a clear pattern of destruction, including the looting and burning of properties and people. This conflict has gradually intensified the ethnic tension between the two warring groups. What has happened in Jebel Marrah also took place in Dar Masalit between the Masalit and the newly arrived Arab nomadic groups. With the central government backing the newly arrived Arab nomads, by granting them land rights in Dar Masalit, and at the same time reducing the powers of the Masalit Sultan, such policies have fueled the violence between the two groups.[22] In both areas of conflict, the local government administration and the army sided with the Arab groups against the Fur and the Masalit. During the course of these conflicts, the groups' natural resources were exhausted and depleted; and it proved that the longer the conflict, the more time is needed to reach a consensus in settling it. During the conflicts in Jebel Marrah and Dar Masalit, reports by many activists from these regions documented the scale of the destruction of individuals and villages. Rather than attempting to control these conflicts, the central government aggravated the situation by ignoring all calls for intervention and provision of security. Later, the government started a wave of military campaigns in Dar Zaghawa, accusing them of being the main source behind the violence and banditry in Darfur. Using the sheer power of the army to fight banditry is regarded by some as a disguised government policy to target certain ethnic groups, and the real motive behind the violence in Darfur.

History of the Current Conflict: 2003–Present

The sudden appearance of the Sudan Liberation Army (SLA) in Darfur was not a complete surprise within the context of the aggravated violence committed against civilians and the sporadic attacks against the army and top government officials. It was under these circumstances and the ensuing chaos that a conference was held in El Fasher in February 2003 to discuss ways of deescalating the violence and improving security. The conferees sent representatives to contact the main ethnic groups involved in the conflict to state their demands and explain their grievances. A considerable and daring development that emerged during the course of these events was the initiation of contact with the SLA fighters, who disclosed their nascent political demands. Their main demand was for the government to stop attacking their bases. However, the government forces did attack their bases, and the SLA response was the swift and costly counterattack on El Fasher, Maleit, and Kutum. The government showed less interest when a group of Darfurian ministers and parliamentarians met with the SLA and listened to their demands and came to Khartoum to announce them at a well-publicized press conference, which was abruptly canceled by the government. With the SLA's capture of large numbers of government troops, a cease-fire was signed in Abeche, Chad, between the Sudan government and SLA, and according to which both sides agreed to curb the activities of the *Janjawid* (armed militia), release war prisoners, and deliver aid to affected parties. In April 2004, another cease-fire agreement between these groups and the government was signed in N'djamena. However, the atrocities against civilians, which included heavy aerial bombardment, burning of villages, bombing of water sources, destruction of farms, arbitrary arrests, the widespread use of torture, and the systematic raping of women and girls, have not ended, and in many cases they have intensified.

It was only after the visit to the region by Kofi Annan, the UN Secretary-General, and U.S. Secretary of State Colin Powell to Darfur in July 2004 that more pressure was placed on the government regarding the atrocities in Darfur. Rather than addressing the real issue of curbing the Janjawid, the government continued to absorb them into the army and police forces, under the pretext of deploying more troops to provide security in Darfur, which was the main call from the inhabitants to the central government prior to the appearance of the Sudan Liberation Army (SLA) and Justice and Equality Movement (JEM).

Characteristics of the Current Conflict

Unlike previous ethnic conflicts, the recent conflict in Darfur is considerably different for the following reasons:

1. The extent of government involvement. While in past ethnic conflicts the involvement of government troops was limited to the geographical location of the conflict, the current conflict engulfed wider areas, which necessitates more troops in Darfur now than during previous conflicts.
2. Size and nature of destruction. Unlike past ethnic conflicts, destruction resulting from the current conflict covers wider areas than in the past, and methods such as rape, burning of mosques, and poisoning of wells, previously unheard of in Darfur's history.
3. Ethnically based militias terrorizing civilians as a counterinsurgency tactic. The widespread use of Janjawid militias is unprecedented, especially in light of their government-sanctioned impunity and the government's defiance of all calls from the international community to disband them.
4. Use of aerial bombardment. The use of gunship helicopters and bombers against civilians on a large scale is one of the basic characteristics of the current conflict.
5. Regional and international concerns: This conflict has received considerable coverage in the Western media, and human rights campaigns have focused their attention on Darfur to the exclusion of many other serious conflicts. The extent of global activism around Darfur is unprecedented, as is the number of involved organizations.

Ethnic conflicts that ravaged Darfur prior to the current one were characterized by:

1. Prevalence of conflicts between neighboring groups regardless of their race.
2. Involvement of only the residents of specific geographical locations.
3. Result of environmental factors.
4. Likley resolution by the traditional system of mediation and compensation.

Regardless of the uniqueness of each period, there are common denominators in both types of conflicts:
1. Darfurians are both the victims and the aggressors.
2. The central government shows partiality by taking sides.
3. All conflicts occur within a context of an underdeveloped region that lacks basic services.

Why the Government Is Waging War in Darfur

There are several reasons for the National Islamic Front government's war in Darfur. It is partly explained by the nature of the regime, which, since it came to power, has used widespread repression, emergency laws, forcible conscription, and arbitrary dismissal from work, as well as a *jihad* (typically defined in this context as "holy war") in the south and the Nuba Mountains, to tighten its grip on power.

The eruption of the war in Darfur at time when the NIF government was negotiating with the SPLM/A to end the war in the South enticed the government to use all its military might to avoid another military confrontation, opening up the possibility of another protracted war. The NIF regime feared the potential of the Darfur armed resistance to become a substitute for its costly war in the south, which it was seeking to end. Additional factors that have likely influenced the NIF regime's handling of the conflict in Darfur are taken up next.

Considering the historical role of the national army in postcolonial Africa and the Arab world, the only potential internal threat to the NIF's rule could have come from the government army itself; hence, the war in Darfur keeps it preoccupied, thereby avoiding a possible coup d'etat. Moreover, the Darfur war provided a pretext for the extension of emergency laws and other repressive polices implemented by the NIF regime at the national level and most specifically in urban areas where the threat of a popular uprising, such as those that occurred in October 1964 and April 1985, could lead to the end of the NIF and its oppressive rule. The war in Darfur might also serve as an excuse for delaying the elections required by the Comprehensive Peace Agreement (CPA) and the eventual referendum on self-determination for the South, which may eventually lead to its secession from Sudan. Ironically, the war in Darfur has enriched the NIF elites and their cronies in the security forces, and with the signing of the CPA, a new source of profiteering regarding the war in Darfur has been good for many. Other motives behind the war include the need to take revenge for what was destroyed by the Darfur rebels in their 2003 attack. The government's perceived, albeit momentary, victory has also been viewed as compensating for the loss of the war and the eventual defeat of the NIF regime in southern Sudan. It is also a known fact that a large percentage of government soldiers are from western Sudan, so it is in the NIF regime's interest to continue creating divisions among them as one group, and weakening the historical loyalties among non-Arab Darfurians to traditional sectarian-based parties such as the Umma Party, and in the process generate support for the NIF from individuals and groups who have benefited from the war. Finally, the war was perceived as a means of creating new alliances with Arabized nomadic groups that own livestock – a significant source of wealth – as future strategic partners, and thus shifting the radius of the NIF's ideological expansion westward, after its defeat southward.

The involvement of the government in the current war in Darfur, siding with some groups against others, has certainly shattered the basis of peaceful coexistence among Darfurians. Peace in Darfur is necessary for stabilizing the surrounding regions and nations – which include southern Sudan, Chad, and the Central African Republic – and for preventing the conflict from spreading outward. There is no doubt that the future of the whole region is at stake.

Conclusion

It is important to acknowledge that Darfur, like other regions of Sudan, is not immune to ethnic conflicts, which have existed since precolonial times and occurred even when the government army was militarily involved in the war in southern Sudan. However, as explained in this essay, the current conflict in Darfur is qualitatively different from earlier ones in its primary causes and in its magnitude and the scale of horror that has come to define it. While earlier conflicts could be attributed to interethnic competition over land and natural resources – conflicts intensified by environmental degradation and successive droughts – the current war in Darfur is largely defined by the central government's use of its military might and security apparatus to execute a punitive war in which counterinsurgency and manipulation of ethnic loyalties have played a major role. Darfur's disunited opposition forces do not pose an immediate threat to the NIF government's existence. One of the fundamental roles of government is to provide protection and peace to its citizens, but the current NIF regime has failed to do so. In such a case, it is important to differentiate between conflicts that exist between neighboring ethnic groups and a conflict that the state orchestrates by pitting one group against another in order to secure its own interest. The war could have been avoided earlier on, but knowing the current regime and its policy of staying in power at all costs, the war will end only when the regime's survival is at stake.

Notes

[1] R. S. O'Fahey and J. L. Spaulding, *Kingdoms of the Sudan* (London: Methuen & Co. Ltd., 1974), 111.

[2] Ibid., 137.

[3] Alan Buchan Theobald, *Ali Dinar, Last Sultan of Darfur, 1898–1916* (London: Longmans, 1965), 118.

[4] Ibid., 222.

[5] R. S. O'Fahey, *State and Society in Dar Fur* (London: C. Hurst & Company, 1980), 69.

[6] Lidwien Kapteijns and Jay Spaulding, *After the Millennium: Diplomatic Correspondence from Wadai and Dar Fur on the Eve of Colonial Conquest, 1885–1916* (Lansing: Michigan State University, 1988), 29.

[7] O'Fahey and Spaulding, 111.

[8] Theobald, 174.

[9] Lidwien Kapteijns, *Mahdist Faith and Sudanic Tradition: History of Dar Masalit, 1870–1930* (London; Boston: Kegan Paul International, 1985), 84.

[10] Theobald, 204.

[11] O'Fahey, 120.

[12] Julie Flint, "Darfur's Armed Movements," in *War in Darfur and the Search for Peace*, Alex de Waal, ed. (Cambridge, MA: Harvard University Press, 2007), 180.

[13] J. Millard Burr and R. O. Collins, *Darfur: The Long Road to Disaster* (Princeton: Markus Wiener Publishers, 2008), 82.

[14] Alex De Waal and Julie Flint, *Darfur: A Short History of a Long War* (New York: Zed Books, 2005), 49.

[15] Musa Adam Abdul-Jalil, "Some Political Aspects of Zaghawa Migration and Resettlement," in *Rural – Urban Migration and Identity Change Case Studies from the Sudan*, ed. Fouad N. Ibrahim and Helmut Ruppert (Bayreuth: Druckhaus Bayreuth, Verlagsgesellchaft, 1988), 24.

[16] Jerome Tubiana, "Darfur: A War for Land?" in *War in Darfur and the Search for Peace*, ed. Alex de Waal (Cambridge, MA: Harvard University Press, 2007), 89.

[17] Sharif Harir, "Arab Belt versus African Belt: Ethno-Political Conflict in Dar Fur and the Regional Factors," in *Short-Cut to Decay: The Case of the Sudan*, ed. Sharif Harir and Terje Tvedt (Uppsala: Nordiska Afrikainstitutet, 1994), 182.

[18] Douglas Johnson, "Nationalism, Independence, and the First Civil War 1942–1972," in *The Root Causes of Sudan's Civil Wars*, by Douglas Johnson (Oxford: James Curry, 2003), 82.

[19] Johnson, 82.

[20] De Waal and Flint 2005, 49.

[21] Harir, 144.

[22] De Waal and Flint 2005, 57.

Fire in Bindisi
Bindisi, 2006

Kalmah Camp
Nyala, 2006

Fire in Bindisi
Bindisi, 2006

Fire in Bindisi
Bindisi, 2006

Horse Riders Soldier and Local Man
Bindisi, 2006

Two Young Boys Kalmah Camp
Nyala, 2006

Section Two
Representations of the War in Dafur

6 Who Are the Darfurians?
Arab and African Identities, Violence, and External Engagement

Alex de Waal

This essay is an attempt to explain the processes of identity formation that have taken place in Darfur over the last four centuries. The basic story is of four overlapping processes of identity formation, each of them primarily associated with a different period in the region's history. The four are the "Sudanic identities" associated with the Dar Fur Sultanate, Islamic identities, the administrative tribalism associated with the twentieth-century Sudanese state, and the recent polarization of "Arab" and "African" identities, associated with new forms of external intrusion and internal violence. It is a story that emphasizes the much neglected east–west axis of Sudanese identity, arguably as important as the north–south axis, and redeems the neglect of Darfur as a separate and important locus for state formation in Sudan, paralleling and competing with the Nile Valley. It focuses on the incapacity of both the modern Sudanese state and international actors to comprehend the singularities of Darfur, accusing much Sudanese historiography of "Nilocentrism," namely, the use of analytical terms derived from the experience of the Nile Valley to apply to Darfur.

The term *Darfurian* is awkward. *Darfur* refers, strictly speaking, to "domain of the Fur." As I shall argue, *Fur* is historically an ethno-political term, but nonetheless at any historical point has referred only to a minority of the region's population, which includes many ethnicities and tribes.[1] However, from the Middle Ages to the early twentieth century, there was a continuous history of state formation in the region, and as Sean O'Fahey remarks, there is a striking acceptance of Darfur as a single entity over this period.[2] Certainly, while I was living in Darfur in the 1980s and traveling to most parts of the region, the sense of regional identity was palpable. This does not mean there is agreement over the identity or destiny of Darfur. There are, as I shall argue, different and conflicting "moral geographies." But what binds Darfurians together is as great as what divides them.

Identity formation in Darfur has often been associated with violence and external engagement. One of the themes of this essay is that today's events have many historic precursors. However, they are also unique in the ideologically polarized nature of the identities currently in formation, and the nature of external intrusion into Darfur. The essay concludes with a brief discussion of the implications of the U.S. determination that genocide is occurring in Darfur. There is a danger that the language of genocide and ideologically polarized identities will contribute to making the conflict more intractable.

While primarily an exercise in academic social history, this essay also has a political purpose. It is my contention that, for almost a century, Darfurians have been unable to make their history on their own terms, and one reason for that is the absence of a coherent debate on the question, "Who are the Darfurians?" By helping to generate such a debate, I hope it will be possible for the many peoples for whom Darfur is a common home to discover their collective identity.

Sudanic Identities

The first of the processes of identity formation is the "Sudanic model" associated with indigenous state formation. In this respect, it is crucial to note that *Dar Fur* (the term I will use for the independent Sultanate, which existed from circa 1600 to 1916, with a break from 1874 to 1898) was a separate center of state formation from the Nile Valley, which was at times more powerful than its riverian competitors. Indeed, Dar Fur ruled Kordofan from about 1791 to 1821 and at times had dominion over parts of the Nile Valley, and for much of its life the Mahdist state was dominated by Darfurians. Before the twentieth century, only once in recorded history did a state based on the Nile rule Darfur, and then only briefly and incompletely (1874–1882). This has been grossly neglected in the "Nilocentric" historiography of Sudan. Rather than the "two Sudans" familiar to scholars and politicians, representing North and South, we should consider "three Sudans," and include Dar Fur as well.

The Keira Sultanate followed on from a Tunjur kingdom, with a very similarly placed core in northern Jebel Marra (and there are many continuities between the two states, notably in the governance of the northern province) and a Daju state, based in the south of the mountain. Under the Sultanate, we have an overall model of identity formation with a core Fur-Keira identity, surrounded by an "absorbed" set of identities that can be glossed as Fur-Kunjara (with the Tunjur ethnicity, the historic state-forming predecessor of the Fur-Keira enjoying similarly privileged status immediately to the north). *Kunjara* itself means "gathered together." This is a pattern of ethno-political absorption familiar to scholars of states, including imperial Ethiopia, the Funj, Kanem-Borno, and other Sudanic entities. Analyzing this allows us to begin to address some of the enduring puzzles of Fur ethnography and linguistics, namely, the different political structures of the different Fur clans and the failure to classify the Fur language, which appears to have been creolized as it spread from its core communities. However, the ethnography and history of the Fur remain desperately understudied and underdocumented.

Surrounding this are subjugated groups. In the north are both nomadic Bedouins (important because camel ownership and long-distance trade were crucial to the wealth of the Sultan) and settled groups. Of the latter, the Zaghawa are the most important. In the eighteenth century, the Zaghawa were closely associated with the state. Zaghawa clans married into the ruling Keira family, and they provided administrators and soldiers to the court. To the south are more independent groups, some of which "became Fur" by becoming absorbed into the Fur polity, and others of which retain a strong impulse for political independence, notably the Baggara Arabs. As in all such states, the king used violence unsparingly to subordinate these peripheral peoples.

To the far south is Dar Fertit, the term *Fertit* signifying the enslaveable peoples of the forest zone. This is where the intrinsically violent nature of the Fur state is apparent. The state reproduced itself through dispatching its armies to the south, obtaining slaves and other plunder, and exporting them northward to Egypt and the Mediterranean. This nexus of soldiers, slaves, and traders is familiar from the historiography of Sudanic states, where "wars without end" were essential to ensure the wealth and power of the rulers.[3] O'Fahey describes the slaving party as the state in miniature.[4] This in turn arose because of the geopolitical position of the Sultanate on the periphery of the Mediterranean world, consumer of slaves, ivory, and other plunder-related commodities. During the eighteenth and nineteenth centuries, the Forty Days Road to Asyut was Egypt's main source of slaves and other sub-Saharan commodities.[5] When Napoleon Bonaparte occupied Egypt, he exchanged letters and gifts with the Sultan of Dar Fur.

All the major groups in Darfur are patrilineal, with identity inherited through the male line. One implication of this is that identity change can occur through the immigration of powerful males, who were in a position to marry into leading families or displace the indigenous men. Historically, the exception may have been some groups classed as Fertit, which were matrilineal. A combination of defensive identity formation under external onslaught and Islamization appears to have made matri-lineality no more than a historical fragment. This, however, only reinforces the point that identity change is a struggle to control women's bodies. With the exception of privileged women at court, women are almost wholly absent from the historical record. But, knowing the sexual violence that has accompanied recent conflicts, we can surmise that rape and abduction were likely to have been mechanisms for identity change on the southern frontier.

Identity formation in the Sultanate changed over the centuries, from a process tightly focused on the Fur identity (from about 1600 to the later 1700s) to a more secular process in which the state lost its ideologically ethnic character and ruled through an administrative hierarchy (up to 1916). It is also important to note the role of claims to Arab genealogy in the legitimation and the institutions of the state. The founding myth of the Sultanate includes Arab descent, traceable to the Prophet Mohammed. This is again familiar from all Sudanic states (Ethiopia having the variant of the Solomonic myth). Arabic was important because it brought a literate tradition, the possibility of co-opting traders and teachers from the Arab world, and above all because of the role of Islam as the state religion.

The state's indigenous Arab population was meanwhile "Arab" chiefly in the archaic sense, used by Ibn Khaldun and others, of "Bedouin." This is a sense still used widely, and it is interesting that the Libyan government (one of three Bedouin states, the others being Saudi Arabia and Mauritania) has regarded Tuaregs and other Saharan peoples as "Arab."

This model of identity formation can be represented in the "moral geography" illustrated in Figure 1.

The significance of this becomes apparent when we map the categories onto the Turko-Egyptian state in the middle Nile Valley, 1821–1874. For this state – which is essentially the direct predecessor of what we have today – the core identity is "Arab," focused on the three tribes: Shaigiya, Jaaliyiin, and Danagla. (The first and second are particularly dominant in the current regime. The last is "Nubian," illustrating just how conditional the term *Arab* can be.) The other identity pole was originally *Sudanese*, the term used for enslaveable black populations from the South in the nineteenth and early twentieth centuries, but which by a curious process of label migration came by the 1980s to refer to the ruling elite, the three tribes themselves. Meanwhile, Southerners had adopted the term *African* to assert their identity, contributing to a vibrant debate among Sudanese intellectuals as to Sudan's relative positions in the Arab and African worlds.[6] From the viewpoint of Southern

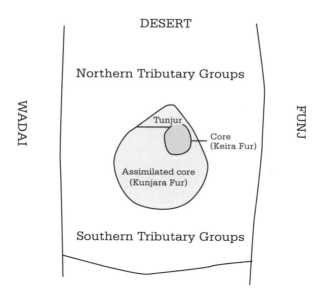

DESERT

Northern Tributary Groups

WADAI

FUNJ

Tunjur

Core
(Keira Fur)

Assimilated core
(Kunjara Fur)

Southern Tributary Groups

FERTIT

Figure 1. **Moral Geography of the Dar Fur Sultanate as Seen from the Center**

Sudan (and indeed east Africa), *African* and *Arab* are polar opposites. From the viewpoint of Darfur and its "Sudanic" orientation, *Arab* is merely one subset of *African*. Darfurians had no difficulty with multiple identities, and indeed would have defined their African kingdom as encompassing indigenous Arabs, both Bedouins and cultural-literate Arabs.

The transfer of the term *African* from Southern Sudan to Darfur and its use, not to encompass the Fertit groups but to embrace the state-forming Fur and Tunjur, and the similarly historically privileged Zaghawa, Masalit, Daju, and Borgu, is therefore an interesting and anthropologically naïve category transfer. *African* should have rather different meanings in Darfur.

Dar Fur's downfall came in the 1870s because it lost out to its competitor, the Turko-Egyptian regime and its client Khartoum traders, over the struggle for the slaving/raiding monopoly in the southern hinterland. The current boundaries of Sudan are largely defined by the points that the Khedive's agents had reached at the time their predatory expansion was halted by the Mahdist revolution. Their commerce and raiding inflicted immense violence on the peoples it conquered, subjecting them to famine and, in some cases, complete dissolution and genocide. Historians have managed to reconstruct some of the societies that preexisted this onslaught, but others live on in memory only, and others have disappeared without a trace.[7]

Islamic Identities

The second model is the "Islamic model." This substantially overlaps with the "Sudanic model" and complements it, but also has distinctive differences, which came to a head with the Sudanese Mahdiya (1883–1898). Let us begin with the overlaps.

Islam was a state cult in Dar Fur from the seventeenth century. Most likely, Islam came to Dar Fur from the west, because the region was part of the medieval Kanem-Bornu empire, which was formally Islamic from the eleventh century if not earlier. Nilocentric historians have tended to assume that Islam reached Dar Fur from the Nile Valley, but there is much evidence to suggest that it is not the case. For example, the dominant Sufi orders in Darfur are West African in origin (notably the Tijaniya), and the script used was the Andalusian-Saharan script, not the classic Arab handwriting of the Nile Valley.

The majority of Darfur's Arab tribes migrated into the Sultanate from the west in the middle of the eighteenth century.[8] They trace their genealogy to the Juheiyna group, and ultimately to the Prophet (in common with all ruling lineages, Arab or non-Arab). During the eighteenth century, they exhibited a general south and east- ward drift. At all times they were cultivators and herders of both camels and cattle, but as they moved east and south, cattle herding came to predominate and they became known collectively as the Baggara. Most of the tribal names they now have emerged in the eighteenth, nineteenth, or twentieth centuries, in some cases as they merged into new political units. An interesting and important example is the Rizeigat, a vast confederation of clans and sections, that migrated east and south, with three powerful sections (Nawaiba, Mahamid, and Mahriya) converging to create the Rizeigat of ed Daien in south-eastern Darfur. But they also left substantial sections to the north and west, historic remnants of this migration. These sections have a troubled and uncertain relationship with their larger southern cousins, alternately claiming kinship and independence. Whereas the southern Baggara and Rizeigat were awarded a territory by the Fur Sultan (who had not subjugated the area where they chose to live), the northern clans continued a primarily nomadic existence on the desert edge, without a specific place they could call home. When sections did settle (and many did), they were subject to the administrative authority of the Sultan's provincial governor of the northern region, Dar Takanawi or Dar el Rih. For historic reasons, this was an area in which administration was relatively detribalized, so the northern Bedouins were integrated into the Sultanate more as subjects than as quasi-autonomous tribal units.

The same process explains why we have a large Beni Halba Baggara group, with territorial jurisdiction, in southern Darfur, and a small Abbala group farther to the north, and also similarly for the Misiriya whose main territories lie in south Kordofan, but who have remnant sections in northwest Darfur and Chad. Meanwhile, the Zayadiya and Ma'aliya are not Juheiyna at all, did not migrate in the same manner, and had different (though not necessarily easier) historic relations with the Sultanate.

The Hausa and Fulani migrations that occurred in the nineteenth and twentieth centuries also have important parallels. They also populated substantial territories in Darfur (and also further east), and included remnant and more purely pastoral sections (such as the Um Bororo) that continued the eastward migration well into the late twentieth century. An important component of the eastward drift is the influence of the Haj (many see themselves as "permanent pilgrims," seeking to move toward Mecca), and Mahdist tradition that emphasizes eastward migration.[9]

As we shall see, militant Mahdism is itself an import into Sudan from West Africa, brought with these migrants. There are other significant groups with origins to the west, such as the Borgu and Birgid, both of them sedentary Sudanic peoples. We should not see eastward migration as exclusively a phenomenon of politically Islamized groups, pastoralists or Arabs.

The Juheiyna groups brought with them their own distinctive "moral geography," one familiar to pastoral nomadic groups across the central Sudan and Sahelian regions. This sees all land as belonging to Allah, with right of use and settlement belonging to those who happen upon it. It sees Darfur as a checkerboard of different localities, some belonging to farmers and others to herders, with the two groups in a mutually advantageous exchange relationship. It is also open-ended, especially toward the east. (The extent to which this is coterminous with the moral geography of a Muslim pilgrim, exemplified by the West African migrants in Sudan, is an interesting question.)

This is represented in Figure 2, which was drawn for me in outline by one of the most eminent Abbala Sheikhs, Hilal Musa of the Um Jalul Rizeigat, in 1985.

Several legacies of this are evident today. Most of the "Arab" groups involved in militia activities, including land grabbing, are what we might call the Abbala remnants, with weak historic claims to tribally defined territories, and traditions of migration and settlement to the east and south. Meanwhile, the majority of the Baggara Arabs of south Darfur are uninvolved in the current conflict.

Three other elements in the Islamic identity formation process warrant comment. One is Mahdism, which arrived in Darfur from the west, and has clear intellectual and social origins in the Mahdist state founded by Osman Dan Fodio in what is now northern Nigeria. Unlike the Nile Valley, where the Mahdist tradition

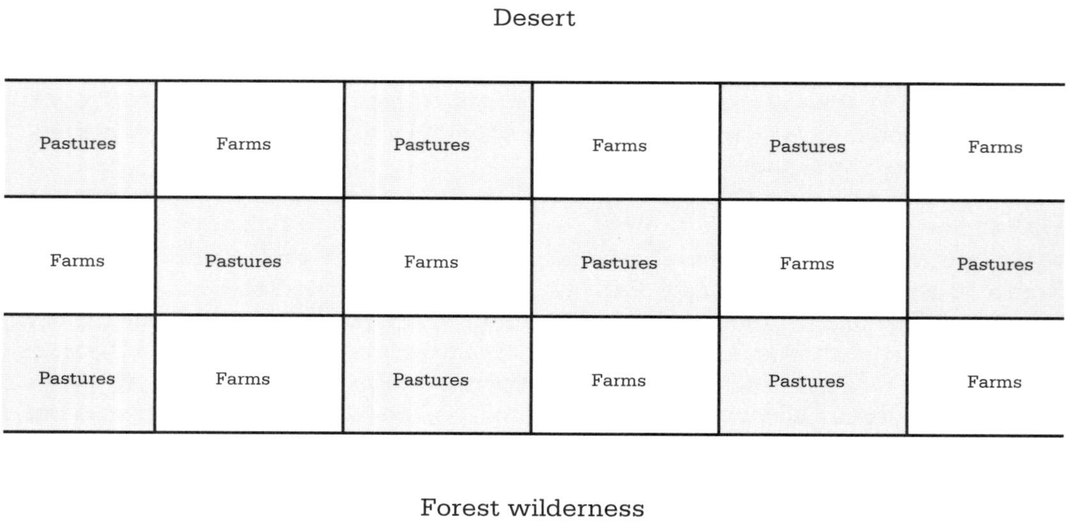

Desert

Pastures	Farms	Pastures	Farms	Pastures	Farms
Farms	Pastures	Farms	Pastures	Farms	Pastures
Pastures	Farms	Pastures	Farms	Pastures	Farms

Forest wilderness

Figure 2. **The "Moral Geography" of Darfur, from a Camel Pastoralist Viewpoint**

was weak, in the West African savannas it was strong and well articulated. Dan Fodio wrote ten treatises on Mahdism, plus more than 480 vernacular poems, and insisted that the Mahdi had to bear the name Mohamed Ahmed (which ruled him out).[10] The first Mahdist in nineteenth-century Sudan was Abdullahi al Ta'aishi, grandson of a wandering Tijani Sufi scholar from somewhere in West Africa, who met the Dongolawi holy militant Mohamed Ahmed in 1881 and proclaimed him the Mahdi, in turn becoming his Khalifa. The majority of the Mahdist armies derived from the Baggara of Darfur and Kordofan, and for most of its existence the Mahdist state in Omdurman was ruled by the Khalifa and his Ta'aisha kinsmen. In fulfillment of Mahdist prophecy and to support his power base, the Khalifa ordered the mass and forced migration of western peoples to Omdurman. The Mahdiya was, to a significant extent, a Darfurian enterprise. And it involved extreme violence, though of a radically different kind to that on which the Dar Fur Sultanate was founded. This was religious, messianic jihad, including population transfers on a scale not seen before or since.

Such is the stubborn Nilocentrism of Sudanese historiography that the influence of West African and Darfurian forms of Islam on this pivotal episode in Sudanese history are consistently underestimated. It was the collision between the heterodox Mahdist Jihadism of the west, including the egalitarian ideology of the Tijaniya, and the more orthodox and hierarchical (though also Sufist) Islam of the Nile Valley that created the Mahdiya.

The Mahdist period is remembered even today in the cultural archive as a time of extraordinary turmoil and upheaval. It was a time of war, pillage, and mass displacement. In 1984/1985, people looked back to the drought of 1913/1914 as their historical point of reference. One wonders if the current historic reference point is the famine of 1888/1889, known as "Sanat Sita" because it occurred in the year six (1306 Islamic calendar), and which seems to have surpassed the Darfurians' otherwise inventive capacity for naming tragedy.

Beyond that historic precedent, I do not want to suggest that there are parallels between the Mahdiya and contemporary or recent political Islam in Sudan, which has had its own manifestations of extreme violence and jihadism. On the contrary, I would argue that it is the failure of Sudan's recent Islamist project that has contributed to the war in Darfur. This arises from the last important theme of Islamic identity, namely, Hassan al Turabi's alliance-building across the east–west axis of Sudanese identities.

Among the many intellectual and practical innovations in Turabi's Islamism was an opening to African Muslims as individuals and African Islam as a tradition. The National Islamic Front recognized that Darfur represented a major constituency of devout Muslims that could be mobilized. It made significant openings to Darfur and to the substantial Fellata communities across Sudan.[11] It promised that Islam could be a route to enfranchisement as citizens of an Islamic state. In doing so, Turabi and his followers moved away from the traditional focus of the political Islamists on the more orthodox Islam of the Nile Valley, and its close association with the Arab world. It was, unfortunately, a false promise: The Sudanese state is the inheritor of the exclusivist project of the nineteenth-century Khartoum traders and sought only to enlist the Darfurians and Fellata as foot soldiers in this enterprise. For the Fellata it had a quick win: It could grant them citizenship, correcting a long-standing anomaly of nationality policy. And it has gained the loyalty of many Fellata leaders as a result. But for Darfurians, the best it offered was relative neutrality in the emergent conflicts between Darfur's Arabs and non-Arabs, and increasingly, not even that. Darfur was marginal even to the Islamists' philanthropic projects in the 1990s, which at least provided basic services and food relief to many remote rural communities. Perhaps because the Islamists took the region for granted, and certainly because the ruling groups were focused on the threats from the South, Nuba, and Blue Nile, Darfur was neglected in the series of Islamist projects aimed at social transformation.

When the Islamist movement split in 1999, most Darfurian Islamists went into opposition. By an accident of fate, the most powerful Darfurian in the security apparatus was an air force general from the Abbala Rizeigat, and members of those sections were rapidly put in place as leaders of the Popular Defence Force in critical locations, removing men whom the government suspected of having sympathies with the Turabi faction. Thus was created a set of militias popularly known as *Janjawid*, adopting a term first used to refer to Chadian Abbala militias that used western Darfur as a rear base in the mid-1980s, and who armed some of their Abbala brethren and helped instigate major clashes in 1987–1990. The Darfur war is, in a significant way, a fight over the ruins of the Sudanese Islamist movement, by two groups, both of which seem to have abandoned any faith that the Islamist project will deliver anything other than power.

The third note of significance concerns the position of women. In the Tijaniyya sect, with its far more egalitarian tradition than the Sufis of the Nile, women can achieve the status of sheikh or teacher. This reflects both the religious traditions of the Sudanic region and the relatively higher socioeconomic status of women in savanna societies, where they could own their own fields and engage in trade in their own right. Darfurian ethnographies repeatedly note the economic independence enjoyed by women among non-Arab and Arab groups alike. The subsequent spread of Islamic orthodoxy, described in more detail later in this essay, contributed to a regression in women's status.

Administrative Tribalism and "Becoming Sudanese"
The British conquest of Dar Fur in 1916, and the incorporation of the then-independent Sultanate of Dar Masalit in 1922–1923, represented a clear break with the past. Darfur was ruled by an external Leviathan that had no economic interest in the region and no ideological ambition other than staving off trouble. Darfur was annexed when the basic determinants of British policies in Sudan had already been established, and the main decisions (e.g., the adoption of Native Administration after 1920, the expulsion of Egyptian civil servants after 1924, the embrace of neo-Mahdism and the Khatmiya, the adoption of the Famine Regulations in the 1930s, the Sudanization of the civil service, and the moves toward independence) were all taken with scant reference to Darfur.

The key concern in Darfur in the decade after the conquest was security, and specifically the prevention of Mahdist uprisings. An attack on Nyala in 1921 was among the most serious threats the new rulers faced, and the last significant uprising was in 1927. In riverian Sudan, the British faced a more immediate danger, in the form of revolutionary nationalism, on the slogan of unity of the Nile Valley, among the educated elite and detribalized elements, especially Sudanese soldiers. To suppress both, and to ensure the utmost economy in rural administration, the British chose a policy of "Native Administration." This was not "Indirect Rule" as practiced in the Nigerian Emirates or Buganda (except in the case of the Sultanate of Dar Masalit, where the British officer was a Resident). Rather, it was the creation of a new hierarchy of tribal administrators, with the significant innovation of the 'omda, the administrative chief intermediate between the paramount chief (nazir for Arab tribes) and the village sheikh. 'Omda was an Egyptian office specially imported for the purpose.[12]

In a series of ordinances, the British regularized the status of tribal authorities. A particularly important act was to grant judicial powers to chiefs, in addition to their executive powers. This was a means of setting the tribal leaders to police their subjects, to keep an eye on both millenarian preachers and discontented graduates. (It is interesting that the leader of the 1924 nationalist revolt, Ali Al Latif, as a detribalized Southerner, or "Sudanese" in the parlance of the day, having no tribal leader to whom he could become subject, was kept in jail in Sudan long beyond his prison term and then exiled to Egypt.) Along with this came the "Closed Districts Ordinance," much criticized for shutting off the South and Nuba Mountains from external influences, but used in Darfur to keep an eye on wandering preachers and West African immigrants.

But the most significant corollary of Native Administration was tidying up the confusion of ethnic identities and tribal allegiances that existed across Sudan. This was an administrative necessity more than an ideological cleaning-up.

The colonial archives from the 1920s and 1930s are filled with exchanges of letters on how to organize the ethnic chaos encountered in rural Sudan.[13] In Darfur, the most significant question was the administration of the Rizeigat, which included shoring up the authority of the pro-British Nazir, Madibbu, regulating the shared pastures on the Bahr el Arab river, also grazed by the Dinka, and deciding the status of the Abbala Rizeigat (initially subject to Nazir Ibrahim Madibbu, then with their own deputy Nazir, finally with their own full Nazir). Other activities included grouping the two sections of the Beni Hussein together and providing them with land in northwestern Darfur (a very rare instance of a wholesale tribal relocation, albeit one done with the consent of the section that needed to be relocated), administratively uniting the two parts of the Beni Halba, finding means of appointing a chief for the Birgid, and grouping the miscellaneous sections living in an area called "Dar Erenga" together to form one tribe. A lot of attention was paid to the Fertit groups living on Darfur's southern frontier, including a brave but futile attempt to move them into Southern Sudan and create a cordon sanitaire between Muslims and non-Muslims. But that was an anomaly: The basic approach was "live and let live."

Native Administration was reformed in the 1940s and 1960s (when chiefs were stripped of most of their judicial powers) and formally abolished in 1971, although many people elected to Rural People's Councils were former native administrators.

Along with the regularizing of tribal administration came the formalizing of boundaries. The British stuck with the fourfold division of the Dar Fur Sultanate into provinces and demarcated tribal territories for the Baggara in south Darfur (following the Sultan's practice). Elsewhere, the allocation of tribal dars was some-what haphazard. The creation of Dar Beni Hussein in the western part of north Darfur was anomalous: When a group did not present a problem, it was left to be. However, the de facto recognition of the legality of a tribal dar in south Darfur began to build a legacy.[14] Beforehand, the term *dar* had been used in many different senses, ranging from a specific location or administrative unit, to the specific territory of an ethnic group, to the whole Sultanate, to an abstract region such as Dar Fertit. But, by constant usage, twinned with a tribally based administrative system with judicial powers, the term *dar* came primarily to refer to an ethnic territory in which the dominant group had legal jurisdiction. By the 1970s, Sudan's leading land law scholar could conclude that tribes have become "almost the owners of their home-lands."[15] During most of the twentieth century, this had no significant political repercussions, as it coincided nicely with the customary practice of a settler adopting the legal code of one's hosts. There was sufficient free land, and a strong enough tradition of hospitality to settlers, that by the 1970s all dars in south Darfur were ethnically mixed, some of them with very substantial settler populations from the drought-stricken north.

Let us not overemphasize the implications of tribal administration for identity formation. It undoubtedly slowed and even froze processes of identity formation. But it was lightly implemented. Many district officers in Darfur reveled in the myriad forms of ethnic identity and chieftanship they found, documenting the intermediate identities of the Kaitinga (part Tunjur/Fur, part Zaghawa), the Jebel Si Arabs, the Dar Fongoro Fur, and numerous others; also allowing Darfurian administrators to keep their wonderful array of traditional titles, including Sultan, Mek, Dimangawi, Shartay, Amir, and Nazir. Given that there were no significant economic interests in Darfur, no project for social change or modernization, and no land alienation, we must recognize the limits of imperial social engineering. It had a very light hand, both for good and ill.

Indeed, in the 1960s and 1970s, Darfur became something of a textbook case for identity change. During the preparatory studies for establishing the Jebel Marra Rural Development Project, a number of eminent social anthropologists were employed to study social change in Darfur.[16] Among their writings are a number of studies on how sedentary Fur farmers, on acquiring sufficient cattle, would "become Baggara" in stages, to the extent of teaching their children the Arabic language and adopting many sociocultural traits of the pastoralists they moved with. This was a remarkable reversal of the previous pattern whereby communities "became Fur" for political reasons; now individuals might "become Baggara" for economic ones. There were also studies of the sedenterization of nomads, underlining how the nomad/farmer distinction is an extremely blurred one. Sadly, there were no comparable studies in northern Darfur.

Most proposals for a settlement of Darfur's conflict include the revival of Native Administration in some form, both for the resolution of intercommunal conflicts (including settling land disputes) and for local administration.[17] Whether or not the important role of chiefs' courts will be reestablished is far less clear. However, the context of the early twenty-first century is very different from that of the 1920s. This is clear from a brief examination of the role played by the tribal leaders in the resolution of the 1987–89 conflict and the revived Native Administration Council after 1994.

The first major conflict in Darfur of recent times occurred in 1987–1989 and had many elements that prefigure today's war, not least the fact that the major protagonists were Fur militia and Abbala Arab fighters known as "Janjawid." Belatedly, a peace conference was called, including tribal leaders on both sides, some of whom sought to reestablish their authority over younger militant leaders, and some who sought for advancement of their own positions. Assisted by the fact that the NIF coup occurred while the conference was in session – allowing both sides to make compromises without losing face – an agreement was reached. But it was not implemented; fighting broke out again, and another conference was held in early 1990, which came with similar recommendations, which again were not properly implemented. The key lesson from this is that Native Administration is not a solution in itself, but rather a component of finding and implementing a solution. Control of armed groups, payment of compensation, and measures to deal with the causes of dispute are all necessary.

A form of Native Administration Council was established in 1994, a measure that coincided with the division of Darfur into three states and renewed conflict in western Darfur. There are two ways in which the NAC is implicated in the conflict. First, the government saw the award of chieftancies (usually called *Emirates*) as a means of rewarding its followers and undermining the power of the Umma Party, which retained the allegiance of many of the older generation of sheikhs. Second, the positions were awarded with a new, simplified, and more administratively powerful view of ethnicity. The very rationale for creating the new entities was to reinforce the power of a central authority (a party as much as, or more than, a state). In a militarized environment, with no services delivered by party or state, the reward for the new chiefs was the power to allocate land and guns within his jurisdiction. It was a recipe for local-level ethnic cleansing, which duly occurred in several places.

During the colonial period – less than four decades for Darfur, scarcely three for Dar Masalit – and the first decades of independence, Darfur was subject to a state in Khartoum that knew little, and cared less, about this faraway region. Little changed with independence. The entire debate over Sudanese independence was conducted in Nilocentric terms: The dual questions were whether Sudan should be united with Egypt, and what should be the status of the South.[18] The position of Darfur was almost wholly absent from this discourse, and remained a footnote in ongoing debates on Sudanese national identity. For example, perhaps the most eloquent analyst of the dilemmas of Sudanese identity, writing in the format of fiction that allows him to explore more explicitly the unstated realities of Sudanese racism, treats Darfurian identity wholly within the North–South framework.[19]

The state that ensued was a clear successor to the Turko-Egyptian colonial state. It was, and remains, a merchant-soldier state, espousing Arabism, using Arabic as a language of instruction in schools and in the media, and promoting Islam as a state ideology. Its political discourse is almost wholly Nilocentric: The key debates leading up to independence concerned whether Sudan would opt for unity with Egypt under the slogan of "unity of the Nile Valley," and subsequent debates on national identity have been framed along the North–South axis of whether Sudan is part of the Arab or African world. There were brave attempts by scholars and activists to assert that Sudan is at once Arab and African, and that the two are fully compatible. These efforts came from all parts of the political spectrum: It is particularly interesting to see the Islamists' arguments on this score.[20] Some of the academic historians who engaged in this debate worked on Sudan's westward links. They, however, were both academically a minority and found no political reverberations for their writings. Whether polarizing or attempting bridging, the discourse was overwhelmingly North–South. And, within Northern Sudan especially, we see the relentless progress of absorption into the culture of the administrative and merchant elite.

What we see is a process that has been called many names, of which I prefer "Sudanization," following Paul Doornbos, who produced a series of superb if underreferenced studies of this phenomenon in Dar Masalit in the early 1980s.[21] "Arabization" is not adequate because Darfur's indigenous Bedouin Arabs were also subject to the same process, and because it did not result in people who were culturally "Arab." Rather, individuals came to belong to a category of Sudanese who spoke Arabic, wore the jellabiya or thoub, prayed publicly, used paper money, and abandoned tribal dancing and drinking millet beer. Doubtless, the newly Sudanized were at social and financial disadvantage when dealing with the established elites. But they were not expropriated of land or identity, and most of them straddled both the "Sudanized" and local identities, and gained from it.

One of the most marked aspects of Sudanization is a change in the status of women. The Darfurian Sudanized women is (ideally) circumcised, secluded at home, economically dependent on her husband, meek in her behavior, and dressed in the thoub. The spread of female circumcision in Darfur in the 1970s and 1980s, at a time when the Sudanese metropolitan elite was moving to abandon the practice, is perhaps the most striking physical manifestation of this process, and yet another illustration of how identity change is marked on women's bodies. It is also an illustration of the recency of a "traditional" practice.

What is remarkable about these processes of identity change is not that they occurred or that they were subject to the arbitrary impositions of a state, but that they were almost entirely nonviolent (with the significant exception of genital mutilation). This is an important contrast with the South and the Nuba Mountains.

Incorporation into a Sudanese polity did bring with it a clear element of racism, based on color of skin and facial characteristics. Although both the Sudanic and Islamic processes of identity formation could not avoid a racial tinge, it was with Egyptian dominance and the successor Sudanese state that this became prevalent. The Egyptian or Mediterranean littoral "moral geography" of Dar Fur can be charted as early as 1800, when the Arab trader Mohamed al Tunisi lived there: He graded the land and its inhabitants according to the color of skin, the beauty of women, and their sexual mores.[22] A broadly similar racist classification became evident in Egyptian occupation of the Nile Valley in the mid-nineteenth century and remains essentially unchanged today.

A particularly important difference between Darfur and other parts of Sudan is the significance of land and labor. Under the British and independent governments, very substantial agricultural schemes were established along the Nile and in eastern

Sudan, and subsequently in south Kordofan. These involved widespread land alienation and the transformation of a rural peasantry into a wage labor force, much of it seasonally migrant.[23] In Darfur there was no land alienation to speak of, and seasonal labor migration is almost entirely within the region, to work on locally owned smallholdings (some of which are large by Darfur standards, but do not match the huge registered schemes of the eastern savannas). The violent depredation and dispossession inflicted by the Sudanese state in the 1980s and 1990s on the Nuba, Blue Nile peoples, and adjacent areas of Upper Nile, creating mass internal displacement with the twin economic aims of creating mechanized farms owned by a Khartoum elite and creating a disadvantaged labor force to work them, has no parallel in Darfur. To a significant degree, Darfur has served as a labor reserve for Gezira and Gedaref, but because of the distances involved, the migration is long-term and not seasonal.[24] And the Darfurian labor reserve has never been of strategic economic significance, such that national economic policies have been geared to sustaining it. Male out-migration has left the poorest parts of Darfur with a gender imbalance and a preponderance of female-headed households.[25]

Labor migration has had implications for the way in with the riverian elite regards westerners. In the 1920s, landowners were reported as saying that just as God (or the British) had taken away their slaves, he/they had brought the Fellata. The lowly status of this devout Muslim pilgrim group is closely associated with their low-status laboring occupations, and much the same holds for the Darfurians (of all ethnicities). The term *abid* was often applied to them all, indiscriminately, reflecting both racism and their laboring status.[26] It is arguable that racist attitudes followed economic stratification, rather than vice versa. In either case, there is a clear association between status and skin color.

Incorporation into a Sudanese national state also, simultaneously, represented incorporation into a wider regional identity schema, in which the three attributes of skin color, economic status, and Arab identification all served to categorize populations. Mohamed al Tunisi would feel at home in the contemporary moral geography of Sudan, almost two centuries after his travels.

Militarized and Ideological "Arab" and "African" Identities

The complex history of identity formation in Darfur provides rich material for the creation of new ethnic identities. What has happened is that as Darfur has been further incorporated into national Sudanese processes, wider African and Middle Eastern processes, and political globalization, Darfur's complex identities have been radically and traumatically simplified, creating a polarized "Arab versus African" dichotomy that is historically bogus, but disturbingly powerful. The ideological construction of these polarized identities has gone hand-in-hand with the militarization of Darfur, first through the spread of small arms, then through the organization of militia, and finally through full-scale war. The combination of fear and violence is a particularly potent combination for forging simplified and polarized identities, and such labels are likely to persist as long as the war continues. The U.S. government's determination that the atrocities in Darfur amount to "genocide" and the popular use of the terms *Arab* and *African* by journalists, aid agencies, and diplomats have further entrenched this polarization, to the degree that community leaders for whom the term *African* would have been alien even a decade ago now readily identify themselves as such when dealing with international interlocutors.

Internally, this polarization began with some of Darfur's Arabs. Exposed to the Islamist-Arabism of Khartoum, drawing upon the Arab lineage ideology latent in their Juheiyna identities, and often closely involved in Colonel Muammar Qaddafi's ideologically Arabist enterprises in the 1970s and 1980s, these men adopted an Arab supremacist ideology. This seems to have been nurtured by Qaddafi's dreams of an Arab homeland across the Sahara and Sahel (notwithstanding the Libyan leader's expansive definition of *Arab*, which, true to his own Bedouin roots, includes groups such as the Tuareg), and by competition for posts in Darfur's regional government in the 1980s. In 1987, a group of Darfurian Arabs wrote a now-famous letter to Prime Minister Sadiq Al Mahdi, demanding a better deal for Darfur's Arabs. They appealed to him as "one of their own." At one level this was simply a legitimate demand for better political representation and better services. But within it lurked an agenda of Arab supremacism. Subsequently, it has become very difficult to separate the ambitious agenda of a Darfurian Arab homeland from wider and more modest goals, and to identify which documents are real and which are not. But there is no doubt that, twinned with similar ambitions among the Chadian Juheiyna Arabs, a political and territorial agenda was emerging. This helps explain why some of the first and fiercest clashes of 1987 were in the highland Jebel Marra area of Gulu, a territory that would be clearly indentified as a "Fur" heartland on any moral geography of the region, including that of Sheikh Hilal, reproduced in Figure 2, whose son Musa has since become infamous as commander of a major PDF brigade. The attacks on Gulu in 1987 and again in 2002 and 2004 represent a symbolic strike at the heart of Fur identity and legitimacy, as well as a tactical assault on a Fur resistance stronghold.

This newly politicized Arab identity was also militarized. Three overlapping strands of militarization can be seen. One is the Ansar, the core followers of the Mahdi, who are historically a political, religious, and military movement. Between 1970 and 1977, the Ansar leadership was in exile in Libya, planning its return to power, which it tried in 1976 and failed. Many returned to Sudan in 1977 as part of the "National Reconciliation" between Al Mahdi and Numeiri, but were not, as they had hoped, absorbed into the national army. Instead, they were settled on farming schemes. Disproportionately drawn from the Baggara tribes, former Ansar fighters were instrumental in the creation of the first Baggara militias in the mid-1980s. A second group of Ansar returned in 1985–1986, following the fall of Numeiri.[27] While in Libya, the Ansar had been organized, trained, and armed alongside Qaddafi's Islamic Legion, which drew recruits from across the Sahelian countries.[28] This is the second contributor to the militarization of the Bedouin. The Islamic Legion was disbanded after its defeat in Ouadi Doum in 1987, but its legacy remained. The third contributor was the formation of Arab militias in Chad, which used Darfur as a rear base for their persistent but unsuccessful attempts to take state power. The different political, tribal, and ideological strands of this story have yet to be teased apart. Clearly there are important differences within these groups, including a competition for the allegiance of the Ansar fighters between the Umma leadership and the NIF. Qaddafi was also quite capable of dealing with non-Arab groups such as the Zaghawa when it suited him, and was quick to recognize the government of Idris Deby when it took power in late 1990. Although Deby had been a commander of the forces that defeated the Libyan army and Islamic Legion a few years earlier, Qaddafi's main quarrel was with Hissene Habre.

While there is a definite strain of Arab supremacism, the significance of "Arab" identity must not be overstated. The groups involved in the current conflict are overwhelmingly Juheiyna Abbala (excluding, for example, the Zayadiya), with relatively few Baggara groups (notably including one part of the Beni Halba, many of whom were armed and mobilized in 1991 to counter the SPLA incursion into Darfur). This means that the largest and most influential of Darfur's Arabs are not involved, including the Baggara Rizeigat, the Habbaniya, the Maaliya, and most of the Taaisha. As the conflict continues to spread and escalate, this may change, and there are clear attempts by some in government to bring in all Arab groups (especially the Rizeigat) on their sides, and attempts by some on the rebel sides to provoke them. The character of Arab supremacism is manifest in a racist vocabulary and in sexual violence. The term *zurug* [plural form is "Zurqa"] has long been used in the casual racism of Arabs in Darfur, despite – or perhaps because of – the absence of any discernible differences in skin color. Attributions of female beauty or lack thereof are similarly made, again despite or because of the lack of noticeable difference. The term *abid*, which has long been used by the riverian elites to refer to all Darfurians, has been adopted by some Arab supremacists to refer to non-Arab Darfurians, despite – or because of – its lack of historical precedent. And widespread rape itself is a means of identity destruction or transformation, particularly salient and invasive for Muslim communities. In the early 1990s Nuba Mountains counterinsurgency campaigns, there is ample documentation that rape was used systematically and deliberately for this purpose.[29]

The creation of "Africanism" is more recent than the ascent of Arab suprem-acism. It owes much to the SPLA, whose leader, the late John Garang, began to speak of an "African majority" in Sudan to counter the Islamist government's claim that Sudan should be an Islamic state because it had a majority Muslim population. Garang reached out to the Nuba and peoples of southern Blue Nile, for whom "African" was an identity with which they could readily identify. For example, the Nuba clandestine political and cultural organization of the 1970s and early 1980s, known as Komolo, asserted the Nuba's right to their own cultural heritage, which they identified as distinctively "African." Under the leadership of Yousif Kuwa, Komolo activist and SPLA governor of the Nuba Mountains, the Nuba witnessed a revival of traditional dancing, music, and religion.[30]

Trapped in a set of identity markers derived from the historical experience of the Nile Valley, a number of educated Darfurian non-Arabs chose "African" as the best ticket to political alliancebuilding. The veteran Darfurian politician Ahmed Diraige had tried to do this in the 1960s, making alliances with the Nuba and Southerners, but had then switched to trying to bring Darfur's non-Arabs into the Umma Party, hoping thereby to broaden and secularize that party. Daud Bolad, a Fur and a prominent Islamist student leader, switched from one political extreme to the other and joined the SPLA, leading a poorly planned and militarily disastrous SPLA expedition into Darfur in 1991. Sharif Harir, a professor of social anthropology and as such inherently distrustful of such labels, was one of the first Darfurian intellectuals to recognize the danger posed by the new Arab Alliance, and has ended up reluctantly donning the "African" label. He is now one of the political leaders of Darfur's Sudan Liberation Movement (SLM).

The influence of the SPLA on the Darfurian opposition should be acknowledged. What was originally a peasant *jacquerie* was given political ambition with the assistance of the SPLA. Indeed, the Darfur Liberation Front was renamed the Sudan Liberation Army (SLA) under SPLA influence and it adopted Garang's philosophy of the "New Sudan," perhaps more seriously than its mentor.

It is a commonplace of ethnographic history that communal violence powerfully helps constitute identity. In times of fear and insecurity, people's ambit of trust and reciprocity contracts and identity markers that emphasize difference between warring groups are emphasized. Where sexual violence is widespread, markers of race and lineage are salient. Much anecdotal evidence indicates that this is happening today and that the civilian communities most exposed to the conflict are insisting on the "African" label. We can speculate that it serves as a marker of difference from the government and its militia, an expression of hope for solidarity from outside, and – perhaps most significant in the context of forced displacement and threats of further dispossession – a claim to indigeneity and residence rights. For whatever reason, identity markers that had little salience in the past are extremely powerful today, and the overwhelming reason for this is the appalling violence inflicted on people.

From the point of view of the SLA leadership, including the leadership of the communities most seriously affected by atrocity and forced displacement, the term *African* has served them well. It is scarcely an exaggeration to say that the depiction of "Arabs" killing "Africans" in Darfur conjures up, in the mind of a non-Sudanese (including many people in sub-Saharan Africa), a picture of bands of light-skinned Arabs marauding among villages of peaceable black-skinned people, of indeterminate religion. In the current context in which "Arabs" are identified, in the popular Western and sub-Saharan African press, with the instigators of terrorism, it readily labels Darfur's non-Arabs as victims.

From the point of view of the government in Khartoum, the labels are also tactically useful. While insisting that the conflict is tribal and local, it turns the moral loading of the term "Arab" to its advantage, by appealing to fellow members of the Arab League, that Darfur represents another attempt by the West (and in particular the United States) to demonize the Arab world. In turn this unlocks a regional alliance, for which Darfur stands as proxy for Iraq and Palestine. Looking more widely than Darfur, the term *Arab* implies global victimhood.

The U.S. categorization of the situation in Darfur as genocide plays directly into this polarizing scenario. It is easy for self-identified Arab intellectuals in Khartoum (and elsewhere) to see this finding as (yet another) selective and unfair denigration of Arabs. If, in the confrontation between the Arabs and the Israelis and Americans, Arabs are cast as "terrorists," warranting preemptive military action and a range of other restrictions on their rights, now in the context of Africa, they are cast as "genocidaires" and similarly cast beyond the moral pale and rendered subject to military intervention and criminal tribunals. Arab editorialists are thus driven both to deny genocide and to accuse the United States of double standards, asking why killings in (for example) Congo are not similarly labeled.

In fact, the U.S. State Department was reluctant to conclude that the situation in Darfur counted as genocide, and the Secretary of State insisted, almost in the same breath that he announced "genocide," that it would not change U.S. policy. The impetus for the genocide finding did not come from Washington's neocons, but rather from liberal human rights activists and members of the religious right. The origins of this coalition lie both in genuine outrage at the conditions of life in Sudan and also in the politics of support for the SPLA (with the Israeli lobby as a discreet marriage broker), which intersected with influence trading in Congress, specifically finding an issue (slavery in Southern Sudan) that brings together the Black Caucus, the Israeli lobby, the religious right (for whom Sudan is a crusade), and the human rights groups (who began campaigning on this long before the others). Several of these groups were frustrated that the State Department, under the Republicans, had switched from a policy of regime change in Khartoum to a pursuit of a negotiated peace for Southern Sudan. The war in Darfur was a vindication of their thesis that no business could be done with Khartoum's evildoers. The atrocities were sufficiently swift and graphic and coincided with the tenth anniversary of the preventable genocide in Rwanda, giving remarkable salience to the genocide claim. Congress passed a resolution, and the State Department prevaricated by sending an investigative team, confident that because there was no evident intent at complete extermination of the target groups that their lawyers would find some appropriately indeterminate language to express severe outrage, short of moral excommunication of Khartoum (with which the State Department was still negotiating) and military intervention. What the State Department had not counted on was that the definition of genocide in the 1948 Convention is wider than the lay definition and customary international usage, and includes actions that fall short of a credible attempt at the absolute annihilation of an ethnic or racial group. The State Department's lawyers, faithful to the much-neglected letter of the law, duly found genocide, and the Secretary of State, doubtless judging that it would be more damaging to ignore his lawyers' public advice, duly made the announcement, and then said that this would not affect U.S. policy.

Arrived at without grand design other than faithfulness to the facts as reported, the genocide finding has a number of implications. One is that it divides the United States from its allies in Europe and Africa. Given that the Sudan peace process is a rare contemporary example of multilateralism (albeit ad hoc) and rare example of a success in U.S. foreign policy (albeit incomplete), it is important that this unity is not fully sundered. At present, it appears that the State Department has succeeded in keeping its policy on track, despite being outflanked by the militants in Washington. (Had the Democrats won in November 2004, we might have faced the ironic situation of a more aggressive U.S. policy.)

Second, the broader interpretation of the Genocide Convention, while legally correct, is one that diplomats have been avoiding for decades, precisely because it creates a vast and indeterminate grey area of atrocity, in which intervention is licensed. A tacit consensus had developed to set the bar higher. Now the United States has lowered it, and Arab critics are correct: If the situation in Darfur is genocide, then so are the situations in Congo, Burundi, Uganda, Nigeria, and a host of others. The neocons do indeed have another weapon in their armory of unilateral inter- vention. Arguably, they didn't need it, already having sufficient reason to intervene on the basis of the September 2002 U.S. National Security doctrine.

And third, for Darfur, the genocide finding is being internalized into the politics of the region. This is occurring in the context of considerable external dependence by Darfur's political organizations and communities. The political organizations have centered their strategies around external engagement. The Islamists in the Justice and Equality Movement (JEM) have a strategy for regime change: using the atrocities in Darfur to delegitimize the Khartoum government internationally, thereby bringing it down. The SLA, representing a broad coalition of communities in arms, has yet to develop a full political program, and is instead largely reacting to events, especially the escalating atrocities since late 2003.[31] It seeks international intervention as a best option, and international monitoring and guarantees as a second best. The communities it represents, many of them either receiving or seeking international assistance, are also orienting their self-representation to the inter- national audience. They have been provided with a simple and powerful language with which to make their case.

The other lenses for analyzing Darfurian identities are too subtle and complex to be of much use for journalists and aid workers. So we are stuck with a polarizing set of ideologically constructed identities, mutually antagonistic. If, as seems likely, these labels become strongly attached, they will hugely complicate the task of reconstructing the social fabric of Darfur or, given the impossibility of returning to the recent past – they will obstruct the construction of a new Darfurian identity that stresses the common history of the region and the interdependence of its peoples.

Conclusion

Let me conclude this essay with two main observations:

First, who are the Darfurians? I argue that Darfur has had a remarkably stable continuous identity as a locus for state formation over several centuries, and it is a recognizable political unit in a way that is relatively uncommon in Africa. But the incorporation of Darfur into Sudan, almost as an afterthought, has led to not only the economic and political marginalization of Darfurians but also the near-total neglect of their unique history and identity. Just as damaging for Darfurians as their socio- political marginalization has been the way in which they have been forced to become Sudanese, on terms that are alien to them. To overcome this, we must move to acknowledging a politics of three Sudans: North, South, and West. It is probably a naïve hope, but recognizing the unique contribution of Darfurians and the inclusive nature of African identity in Darfur could provide a way out of Sudan's national predicament of undecided identity. Short of this ambition, it is important for Darfurians to identify what they have in common and undertake the hard intellectual labor of establishing their common identity.

Second, what we see is the gradual but seemingly inexorable simplification, polarization, and cementing of identities in a Manichean model. Within four generations, a set of negotiable identities have become fixed and magnetized. We should not idealize the past: While ethnic assimilation and the administration of the

Sultanate may have been relatively benevolent at the center, at the southern periphery it was extremely and systematically violent. Similarly, while Sufism is generally and correctly regarded as a tolerant and pacific set of faiths, it also gave birth to Mahdism, which inflicted a period of exceptional turmoil and bloodshed on Sudan, including Darfur. Violence has shaped identity formation in the past in Darfur, just as it is doing today. Also, from the days of the Sultanate, external economic and ideological linkages shaped the nature of state power and fed its centralizing and predatory nature. Today, the sources and nature of those external influences are different. A "global war on terror" and its correlates influences the political and ideological landscape in which Darfur's conflict is located, including the very language used to describe the adversaries and what they are doing to one another and the unfortunate civilians who are in the line of fire. The humanitarians and human rights activists, as much as the counterterrorists and diplomats, are part of the process whereby Darfurian identities are traumatically transformed once again. Hopefully, there will be a counterprocess that allows for Darfurians to carve out a space in which to reflect on their unique history, identify what they share, and create processes whereby identities are not formed by violence.

Notes

[1] The use of the label *tribe* is controversial. But when we are dealing with the subgroups of the Darfurian Arabs, who are ethnically indistinguishable but politically distinct, the term correlates with popular usage and is useful. Hence, *tribe* is used in the sense of a political or administrative ethnically based unit. See Abdel Ghaffar M. Ahmed, *Anthropology in the Sudan: Reflections by a Sudanese Anthropologist* (Utrecht: International Books, 2002).

[2] R. S. O'Fahey, *State and Society in Dar Fur* (London: Hurst, 1980).

[3] See S. P. Reyna, *Wars without End: The Political Economy of a Precolonial African State* (Hanover: University Press of New England, 1990); Lidwien Kapteijns, *Mahdist Faith and Sudanic Tradition: A History of the Dar Masalit Sultanate 1870–1930*, (London: Kegan Paul, 1985); Janet J. Ewald, *Soldiers, Traders and Slaves: State Formation and Economic Transformation in the Greater Nile Valley, 1700–1885* (Madison: University of Wisconsin Press, 1990). The phrase *wars without end* was used by the nineteenth-century traveler Gustav Nachtigal with specific reference to the central Sudanic state of Bagirimi.

[4] R. S. O'Fahey, 1980.

[5] In the late eighteenth century, Egypt's trade with Dar Fur was five times larger than with Sinnar.

[6] For the seminal debates on this issue, see Yusuf Fadl Hasan, *Sudan in Africa* (Khartoum: University Press, 1971).

[7] Dennis D. Cordell, "The Savanna Belt of North-Central Africa," in *History of Central Africa*, David Birmingham and Phyllis M. Martin, eds. (London and New York: Longman, 1983); Stefano Santandrea, *A Tribal History of the Western Bahr el Ghazal* (Bologna: Nigrizia, 1964).

[8] H. A. MacMichael, *A History of the Arabs in the Sudan* (Cambridge: Cambridge University Press, 1922); Ian Cunnison, *Baggara Arabs: Power and the Lineage in a Sudanese Nomad Tribe* (Oxford: Clarendon Press, 1966).

[9] C. Bawa Yamba, *Permanent Pilgrims: The Role of Pilgrimage in the Lives of West African Muslims in Sudan* (Washington D.C.: Smithsonian Press, 1995).

[10] Ahmed Mohammed Kani, *The Intellectual Origin of Islamic Jihad in Nigeria* (London: Al Hoda, 1988).

[11] Awad Al-Sid Al-Karsani, "Beyond Sufism: The Case of Millennial Islam in the Sudan." In *Muslim Identity and Social Change in Sub-Saharan Africa*, Louis Brenner, ed. (Bloomington: Indiana University Press, 1993).

[12] The Turko-Egyptian regime had also used administrative tribalism and had created the position of "sheikh al mashayikh" as paramount chieftancies of the riverain tribes. In the 1860s, this title was changed to "nazir." The sultans of Dar Fur tried similar mechanisms from the late eighteenth century, awarding copper drums to appointees.

[13] This discussion derives chiefly from the author's notes from research in the Sudan National Archives in 1988. For simplicity, specific files are not referenced.

[14] The real drive for the recognition of tribal territories was elsewhere in Sudan, where ethnic territorialization was less complex and administration denser.

[15] Saeed Mohamed El-Mahdi, *Introduction to Land Law of the Sudan* (Khartoum: Khartoum University Press, 1979), 2. In southern Darfur, there was a strong push by the regional authorities and development projects to recognize tribal dars in the 1980s. See Mechtild Rünger, *Land Law and Land Use Control in Western Sudan: The Case of Southern Darfur* (London: Ithaca Press, 1987).

[16] Frederik Barth, "Economic Spheres in Darfur." In *Themes in Economic Anthropology*, Raymond Firth, ed. (London: Tavistock, 1967); Gunnar Haaland, "Economic Determinants in Ethnic Processes." In *Ethnic Groups and Boundaries*, ed. Frederik Barth (London: Allen and Unwin, 1969).

[17] James Morton, *The Poverty of Nations* (London: British Academic Press, 1994).

[18] See Gabriel R. Warburg, *Historical Discord in the Nile Valley* (Evanston, IL: Northwestern University Press, 1993).

19   See Francis M. Deng, *The Cry of the Owl* (New York: Lilian Barber Press, 1989). In this novelistic exploration of Sudanese identities, the main protagonist, who is a Southerner, meets a Fur merchant on a train. The encounter reveals that anti-Southern racist feeling exists among Darfurians, while Darfurians themselves are marginalized, exploited, and racially discriminated against by the ruling riverain elites.

20   Muddathir Abd al-Rahim, "Arabism, Africanism and Self-Identification in the Sudan," in Y. F. Hasan, *Sudan in Africa* (Khartoum: Khartoum University Press, 1971).

21   Paul Doornbos, "On Becoming Sudanese." In *Sudan: State, Capital, and Transformation*, T. Barnett and A. Abdelkarim, eds. (London: Croom Helm, 1988).

22   Eve Troutt Powell, *A Different Shade of Colonialism: Egypt, Great Britain and the Mastery of the Sudan* (Berkeley: University of California Press, 2003). Powell shows convincingly how similar attitudes informed Egyptian attitudes toward Sudan into the twentieth century.

23   Ahmad Alawad Sikainga, *Slaves into Workers: Emancipation and Labor in Colonial Sudan* (Austin: University of Texas, 1996).

24   Darfurian migrant labor is remarkably under-researched in comparison with the Nuba and West Africans. In the modest literature, see Dennis Tully, "The Decision to Migrate in Sudan," *Cultural Survival Quarterly* 7.4 (1983): 17–18.

25   See, for example, my discussion of Jebel Si in *Famine that Kills: Darfur, Sudan* (New York: Oxford University Press, 2004).

26   Mark Duffield, *Maiurno: Capitalism and Rural Life in Sudan.* (London: Ithaca Press, 1981); C. Bawa Yamba, *Permanent Pilgrims: The Role of Pilgrimage in the Lives of West African Muslims in Sudan* (Washington D.C.: Smithsonian Press, 1995).

27   Alex de Waal, "Some Comments on Militias in Contemporary Sudan" In *Civil War in the Sudan*, M. Daly and A. A. Sikainga, eds. (London: Taurus, 1994).

28   Qaddafi's African policy has not been well documented by journalists and scholars.

29   African Rights, *Facing Genocide: The Nuba of Sudan* (London: African Rights, 1995).

30   The Nuba's "African" identity is well documented. The best treatment is Yusuf Kuwa's own memoir, "Things Would No Longer Be the Same," in *The Right to Be Nuba: The Story of a Sudanese People's Struggle for Survival*, S. Rahhal, ed. (Trenton, NJ: Red Sea Press, 2002).

31   Editor's note: Since this essay was first published in 2005, the SLA has fragmented into a number of different movements; most prominent among them are the SLM-Abdul Wahid (SLM/AW), the SLA-Minnawi (SLA/MM), SLA-Unity, SLA-Abdesh-Shafi factions. Prior to the splintering of the SLA/M in 2005 their objective, as stated by Minni Minnawi, was "to create a united democratic Sudan."

7   The Politics of Naming:
Genocide, Civil War, Insurgency

Mahmood Mamdani

The similarities between Iraq and Darfur are remarkable. The estimate of the number of civilians killed over the past three years is roughly similar. The killers are mostly paramilitaries, closely linked to the official military, which is said to be their main source of arms. The victims, too, are by and large identified as members of groups, rather than targeted as individuals. But the violence in the two places is named differently. In Iraq, it is said to be a cycle of insurgency and counterinsurgency; in Darfur, it is called genocide. Why the difference? Who does the naming? Who is being named? What difference does it make?

The most powerful mobilization in New York City is in relation to Darfur, not Iraq. One would expect the reverse, for no other reason than that most New Yorkers are American citizens and so should feel directly responsible for the violence in occupied Iraq. But Iraq is a messy place in the American imagination, a place with messy politics. Americans worry about what their government should do in Iraq. Should it withdraw? What would happen if it did? In contrast, for most Americans, there is nothing messy about Darfur. It is a place without history and without politics, simply a site where perpetrators clearly identifiable as "Arabs" confront victims clearly identifiable as "Africans."

A full-page advertisement has appeared several times a week in the *New York Times* calling for intervention in Darfur now. It wants the intervening forces to be placed under "a chain of command allowing necessary and timely military action without approval from distant political or civilian personnel." That intervention in Darfur should not be subject to "political or civilian" considerations and that the intervening forces should have the right to shoot – to kill – without permission from distant places: These are said to be "humanitarian" demands. In the same vein, a *New Republic* editorial on Darfur has called for "force as a first-resort response." What makes the situation even more puzzling is that some of those who are calling for an end to intervention in Iraq are demanding an intervention in Darfur; as the slogan goes, "Out of Iraq and into Darfur."

What would happen if we thought of Darfur as we do of Iraq, as a place with a history and politics – a messy politics of insurgency and counterinsurgency? Why should an intervention in Darfur not turn out to be a trigger that escalates rather than reduces the level of violence as intervention in Iraq has done? Why might it not create the actual possibility of genocide, not just rhetorically but in reality? Morally, there is no doubt about the horrific nature of the violence against civilians in Darfur. The ambiguity lies in the politics of the violence, whose sources include both a state-connected counterinsurgency and an organized insurgency, very much like the violence in Iraq.

The insurgency and counterinsurgency in Darfur began in 2003. Both were driven by an intermeshing of domestic tensions in the context of a peace-averse international environment defined by the War on Terror. On the one hand, there was a struggle for power within the political class in Sudan, with more marginal interests in the west (following those in the south and in the east) calling for reform at the center. On the other, there was a community-level split inside Darfur, between nomads and settled farmers, who had earlier forged a way of sharing the use of semi-arid land in the dry season. With the drought that set in toward the late 1970s, cooperation turned into an intense struggle over diminishing resources.

As the insurgency took root among the prospering peasant tribes of Darfur, the government trained and armed the poorer nomads and formed a militia – the Janjawid – that became the vanguard of the unfolding counterinsurgency. The worst violence came from the Janjawid, but the insurgent movements were also accused of gross violations. Anyone wanting to end the spiraling violence would have to bring about power sharing at the state level and resource sharing at the community level, land being the key resource.

Since its onset, two official verdicts have been delivered on the violence, the first from the United States the second from the United Nations. The American verdict was unambiguous: Darfur was the site of an ongoing genocide. The chain of events leading to Washington's proclamation began with "a genocide alert" from the Management Committee of the Washington Holocaust Memorial Museum. According to the *Jerusalem Post*, the alert was "the first ever of its kind, issued by the U.S. Holocaust Museum." The House of Representatives followed unanimously on June 24, 2004. The last to join the chorus was Colin Powell.

The UN Commission on Darfur was created in the aftermath of the American verdict and in response to American pressure. It was more ambiguous. In September 2004, the Nigerian president Olusegun Obasanjo, then the chair of the African Union, visited UN headquarters in New York. Darfur had been the focal point of discussion in the African Union. All concerned were alert to the extreme political sensitivity of the issue. At a press conference at the UN on September 23, Obasanjo was asked to pronounce on the violence in Darfur: Was it genocide or not? His response was very clear:

> Before you can say that this is genocide or ethnic cleansing, we will have to have a definite decision and plan and programme of a government to wipe out a particular group of people, then we will be talking about genocide, ethnic cleansing. What we know is not that. What we know is that there was an uprising, rebellion, and the government armed another group of people to stop that rebellion. That's what we know. That does not amount to genocide from our own reckoning. It amounts to of course conflict. It amounts to violence.

By October, the Security Council had established a five-person commission of inquiry on Darfur and asked it to report within three months on "violations of international humanitarian law and human rights law in Darfur by all parties," and specifically to determine "whether or not acts of genocide have occurred." Among the members of the commission was the chief prosecutor of South Africa's Truth and Reconciliation Commission (TRC), Dumisa Ntsebeza. In its report, submitted on January 25, 2005, the commission concluded that "the Government of the Sudan has not pursued a policy of genocide ... directly or through the militias under its control." But the commission did find that the government's violence was "deliberately and indiscriminately directed against civilians." Indeed, "even where rebels may have been present in villages, the impact of attacks on civilians shows that the use of military force was manifestly disproportionate to any threat posed by the rebels." These acts, the commission concluded, "were conducted on a widespread and systematic basis, and therefore may amount to *crimes against humanity*" (my emphasis). Yet, the commission insisted, they did not amount to acts of genocide: "The crucial element of genocidal intent appears to be missing ... it would seem that those who planned and organized attacks on villages pursued the intent to drive the victims from their homes, primarily for purposes of counter-insurgency warfare."

At the same time, the commission assigned secondary responsibility to rebel forces – namely, members of the Sudan Liberation Army and the Justice and Equality Movement – which it held "responsible for serious violations of international human rights and humanitarian law which may amount to *war crimes*" (my emphasis). If the government stood accused of "crimes against humanity," rebel movements were accused of "war crimes." Finally, the commission identified individual perpetrators and presented the UN Secretary-General with a sealed list that included "officials of the government of Sudan, members of militia forces, members of rebel groups and certain foreign army officers acting in their personal capacity." The list named fifty-one individuals.

The commission's findings highlighted three violations of international law: disproportionate response, conducted on a widespread and systematic basis, targeting entire groups (as opposed to identifiable individuals) but without the intention to eliminate them as groups. It is for this last reason that the commission ruled out the finding of genocide. Its less grave findings of "crimes against humanity" and "war crimes" are not unique to Darfur, but fit several other situations of extreme violence: in particular, the U.S. occupation of Iraq, the Hema-Lendu violence in eastern Congo, and the Israeli invasion of Lebanon. Among those in the counterinsurgency accused of war crimes were the "foreign army officers acting in their personal capacity," in other words, mercenaries, presumably recruited from armed forces outside Sudan. The involvement of mercenaries in perpetrating gross violence also fits the occupation in Iraq, where some of them go by the name of "contractors."

The journalist in the U.S. most closely identified with consciousness-raising on Darfur is the *New York Times* op-ed columnist Nicholas Kristof, often identified as a lone crusader on the issue. To peruse Kristof's Darfur columns over the past three years is to see the reduction of a complex political context to a morality tale unfolding in a world populated by villains and victims who never trade places and so can always and easily be identified. It is a world where atrocities mount geometrically, the perpetrators so evil and the victims so helpless that the only possibility of relief is a rescue mission from the outside, preferably in the form of a military intervention.

Kristof made six highly publicized trips to Darfur, the first in March 2004 and the sixth two years later. He began by writing of it as a case of "ethnic cleansing": "Sudan's Arab rulers" had "forced 700,000 black African Sudanese to flee their villages" (March 24, 2004). Only three days later, he upped the ante: This was no longer ethnic cleansing, but genocide. "Right now," he wrote on March 27, "the government of Sudan is engaged in genocide against three large African tribes in its Darfur region." He continued: "The killings are being orchestrated by the Arab-dominated Sudanese government" and "the victims are non-Arabs: blacks in the Zaghawa, Massalliet and Fur tribes." He estimated the death toll at a thousand a week. Two months later, on May 29, he revised the estimates dramatically upward, citing predictions from the U.S. Agency for International Development to the effect that, at best, "only" one hundred thousand people will die in Darfur this year of malnutrition and disease," but "if things go badly, half a million will die."

The UN commission's report was released on February 25, 2005. It confirmed "massive displacement" of persons ("more than a million" internally displaced and "more than 200,000" refugees in Chad) and the destruction of "several hundred" villages and hamlets as "irrefutable facts"; but it gave no confirmed numbers for those killed. Instead, it noted rebel claims that government-allied forces had "allegedly killed over seventy thousand persons." Following the publication of the report, Kristof began to scale down his estimates. For the first time, on February 23, 2005, he admitted that "the numbers are fuzzy." Rather than the usual single total, he went on to give a range of figures, from a low of seventy thousand, which he dismissed as "a UN estimate," to "independent estimates [that] exceed 220,000." A warning followed: "and the number is rising by about ten thousand a month."

The publication of the commission's report had considerable effect. Internationally, it raised doubts about whether what was going on in Darfur could be termed genocide. Even U.S. officials were unwilling to go along with the high estimates propagated by the broad alliance of organizations that subscribe to the Save Darfur campaign. The effect on American diplomacy was discernible. Three months later, on May 3, Kristof noted with dismay that not only had "Deputy Secretary of State Robert Zoellick pointedly refused to repeat the administration's past judgment that the killings amount to genocide," he had "also cited an absurdly low estimate of Darfur's total death toll: 60,000 to 160,000." As an alternative, Kristof cited the latest estimate of deaths from the Coalition for International Justice as "nearly 400,000, and rising by 500 a day." In three months, Kristof's estimates had gone up from 10,000 to 15,000 a month. Six months later, on November 27, Kristof warned that "if aid groups pull out ... the death toll could then rise to 100,000 a month." Anyone keeping a tally of the death toll in Darfur as reported in the Kristof columns would find the rise, fall and rise again very bewildering. First he projected the number of dead at 320,000 for 2004 (June 16, 2004) but then gave a scaled-down estimate of between seventy thousand and 220,000 (February 23, 2005). The number began once more to climb to "nearly 400,000" (May 3, 2005), only to come down yet again to 300,000 (April 23, 2006). Each time figures were given with equal confidence but with no attempt to explain their basis. Did the numbers reflect an actual decline in the scale of killing in Darfur, or was Kristof simply making an adjustment to the changing mood internationally?

In the April 23, 2006, column, Kristof expanded the list of perpetrators to include an external power: "China is now underwriting its second genocide in three decades. The first was in Pol Pot's Cambodia, and the second is in Darfur, Sudan. Chinese oil purchases have financed Sudan's pillage of Darfur, Chinese-made AK-47s have been the main weapons used to slaughter several hundred thousand people in Darfur so far and China has protected Sudan in the UN Security Council." In the Kristof columns, there is one area of deafening silence, to do with the fact that what is happening in Darfur is a civil war. Hardly a word is said about the insurgency, about the civilian deaths insurgents mete out, about acts that the commission characterized as "war crimes." Would the logic of his April 23 column not lead one to think that those with connections to the insurgency, some of them active in the international campaign to declare Darfur the site of genocide, were also guilty of "underwriting" war crimes in Darfur?

Newspaper writing on Darfur has sketched a pornography of violence. It seems fascinated by and fixated on the gory details, describing the worst of the atrocities in gruesome detail and chronicling the rise in the number of them. The implication is that the motivation of the perpetrators lies in biology ("race") and, if not that, certainly in "culture." This voyeuristic approach accompanies a moralistic discourse whose effect is both to obscure the politics of the violence and position the reader as a virtuous, not just a concerned, observer.

Journalism gives us a simple moral world, where a group of perpetrators face a group of victims, but where neither history nor motivation is thinkable because both are outside history and context. Even when newspapers highlight violence as a social phenomenon, they fail to understand the forces that shape the agency of the perpetrator. Instead, they look for a clear and uncomplicated moral that describes the victim as untainted and the perpetrator as simply evil. Where yesterday's victims are today's perpetrators, where victims have turned perpetrators, this attempt to find an African replay of the Holocaust not only does not work but also has perverse consequences. Whatever its analytical weaknesses, the depoliticization of violence has given its proponents distinct political advantages.

The conflict in Darfur is highly politicized, and so is the international campaign. One of the campaign's constant refrains has been that the ongoing genocide is racial: "Arabs" are trying to eliminate "Africans." But both *Arab* and *African* have several meanings in Sudan. There have been at least three meanings of *Arab*. Locally, Arab was a pejorative reference to the lifestyle of the nomad as uncouth. Regionally, it referred to someone whose primary language was Arabic. In this sense, a group could become "Arab" over time. This process, known as *Arabization*, was not an anomaly in the region: There was Amharization in Ethiopia and Swahilization on the East African coast. The third meaning of *Arab* was "privileged and exclusive"; it was the claim of the riverian political aristocracy who had ruled Sudan since independence, and who equated Arabization with the spread of civilization and being Arab with descent.

African, in this context, was a subaltern identity that also had the potential of being either exclusive or inclusive. The two meanings were not only contradictory but also came from the experience of two different insurgencies. The inclusive meaning was more political than racial or even cultural (linguistic), in the sense that an "African" was anyone determined to make a future within Africa. It was pioneered by John Garang, the leader of the Sudan People's Liberation Army (SPLA) in the south, as a way of holding together the New Sudan he hoped to see. In contrast, its exclusive meaning came in two versions, one hard (racial) and the other soft (linguistic) – "African" as Bantu and "African" as the identity of anyone who spoke a language indigenous to Africa. The racial meaning came to take a strong hold in both the counterinsurgency and the insurgency in Darfur. The Save Darfur campaign's characterization of the violence as "Arab" against "African" obscured both the fact that the violence was not one-sided and the contest over the meaning of "Arab" and "African": a contest that was critical precisely because it was ultimately about who belonged and who did not in the political community called Sudan. The depoliticization, naturalization, and, ultimately, demonization of the notion "Arab," as against "African," has been the deadliest effect, whether intended or not, of the Save Darfur campaign.

The depoliticization of the conflict gave campaigners three advantages. First, they were able to occupy the moral high ground. The campaign presented itself as apolitical but moral, its concern limited only to saving lives. Second, only a single-issue campaign could bring together in a unified chorus forces that are otherwise ranged as adversaries on most important issues of the day: at one end, the Christian right and the Zionist lobby; at the other, a mainly school- and university-based peace movement. Nat Hentoff of the *Village Voice* wrote of the Save Darfur Coalition as "an alliance of more than 515 faith-based, humanitarian, and human rights organizations"; among the organizers of their Rally to Stop the Genocide in Washington last year were groups as diverse as the American Jewish World Service, the American Society for Muslim Advancement, the National Association of Evangelicals, the U.S. Conference of Catholic Bishops, the U.S. Holocaust Memorial Museum, the American Anti-Slavery Group, Amnesty International, Christian Solidarity International, Physicians for Human Rights, and the National Black Church Initiative. Surely, such a wide coalition would cease to hold together if the issue shifted to, say, Iraq.

To understand the third advantage, we have to return to the question I asked earlier: How could it be that many of those calling for an end to the American and British intervention in Iraq are demanding an intervention in Darfur? It's tempting to think that the advantage of Darfur lies in its being a small, faraway place where those who drive the War on Terror do not have a vested interest. That this is hardly the case is evident if one compares the American response to Darfur to its non-response to Congo, even though the dimensions of the conflict in Congo seem to give it a mega-Darfur quality: The numbers killed are estimated in the millions rather than the hundreds of thousands; the bulk of the killing, particularly in Kivu, is done by paramilitaries trained, organized, and armed by neighboring governments; and the victims on both sides – Hema and Lendu – are framed in collective rather than individual terms, to the point that one influential version defines both as racial identities and the conflict between the two as a replay of the Rwandan genocide. Given all this, how does one explain the fact that the focus of the most widespread and ambitious humanitarian movement in the United States is on Darfur and not on Kivu?

Nicholas Kristof was asked this very question by a university audience: "When I spoke at Cornell University recently, a woman asked why I always harp on Darfur. It's a fair question. The number of people killed in Darfur so far is modest in global terms: estimates range from 200,000 to more than 500,000. In contrast, four million people have died since 1998 as a result of the fighting in Congo, the most lethal conflict since World War Two." But instead of answering the question, Kristof – now writing his column rather than facing the questioner at Cornell – moved on:

"And malaria annually kills one million to three million people – meaning that three years' deaths in Darfur are within the margin of error of the annual global toll from malaria." And from there he went on to compare the deaths in Darfur to the deaths from malaria, rather than from the conflict in Congo: "We have a moral compass within us and its needle is moved not only by human suffering but also by human evil. That's what makes genocide special – not just the number of deaths but the government policy behind them. And that in turn is why stopping genocide should be an even higher priority than saving lives from AIDS or malaria." That did not explain the relative silence on Congo. Could the reason be that in the case of Congo, Hema, and Lendu militias – many of them no more than child soldiers – were trained by America's allies in the region, Rwanda and Uganda? Is that why the violence in Darfur – but not the violence in Kivu – is named as a genocide?

It seems that genocide has become a label to be stuck on your worst enemy, a perverse version of the Nobel Prize, part of a rhetorical arsenal that helps you vilify your adversaries while ensuring impunity for your allies. In Kristof's words, the point is not so much "human suffering" as "human evil." Unlike Kivu, Darfur can be neatly integrated into the War on Terror, for Darfur gives the Warriors on Terror a valuable asset with which to demonize an enemy: a genocide perpetrated by Arabs. This was the third and most valuable advantage that Save Darfur gained from depoliticizing the conflict. The more thoroughly Darfur was integrated into the War on Terror, the more the depoliticized violence in Darfur acquired a racial description, as a genocide of "Arabs" killing "Africans." Racial difference purportedly constituted the motive force behind the mass killings. The irony of Kristof's columns is that they mirror the ideology of Arab supremacism in Sudan by demonizing entire communities.[1]

Kristof chides Arab peoples and the Arab press for not having the moral fiber to respond to this Muslim-on-Muslim violence, presumably because it is a violence inflicted by Arab Muslims on African Muslims. In one of his early columns in 2004, he was outraged by the silence of Muslim leaders: "Do they care about dead Muslims only when the killers are Israelis or Americans?" Two years later he asked: "And where is the Arab press? Isn't the murder of 300,000 or more Muslims almost as offensive as a Danish cartoon?" Six months later, Kristof pursued this line on NBC's *Today Show*. Elaborating on the "real blind spot" in the Muslim world, he said: "You are beginning to get some voices in the Muslim world ... saying it's appalling that you have evangelical Christians and American Jews leading an effort to protect Muslims in Sudan and in Chad."

If many of the leading lights in the Darfur campaign are fired by moral indignation, this derives from two events: the Nazi Holocaust and the Rwandan genocide. After all, the seeds of the Save Darfur campaign lie in the tenth-anniversary commemoration of what happened in Rwanda. Darfur is today a metaphor for senseless violence in politics, as indeed Rwanda was a decade before. Most writing on the Rwandan genocide in the U.S. was also done by journalists. In *We Wish to Inform You that Tomorrow We Will Be Killed with Our Families*, the most widely read book on the genocide, Philip Gourevitch envisaged Rwanda as a replay of the Holocaust, with Hutu cast as perpetrators and Tutsi as victims. Again, the encounter between the two seemed to take place outside any context, as part of an eternal encounter between evil and innocence. Many of the journalists who write about

The Politics of Naming

Darfur have Rwanda very much in the back of their minds. In December 2004, Kristof recalled the lessons of Rwanda: "Early in his presidency, Mr Bush read a report about Bill Clinton's paralysis during the Rwandan genocide and scrawled in the margin: 'Not on my watch.' But in fact the same thing is happening on his watch, and I find that heartbreaking and baffling."

With very few exceptions, the Save Darfur campaign has drawn a single lesson from Rwanda: The problem was the U.S. failure to intervene to stop the genocide. Rwanda is the guilt that America must expiate, and to do so it must be ready to intervene, for good and against evil, even globally. That lesson is inscribed at the heart of Samantha Power's book *A Problem from Hell: America and the Age of Genocide*. But it is the wrong lesson. The Rwandan genocide was born of a civil war that intensified when the settlement to contain it broke down. The settlement, reached at the Arusha Conference, broke down because neither the Hutu Power tendency nor the Tutsi-dominated Rwanda Patriotic Front (RPF) had any interest in observing the power-sharing arrangement at the core of the settlement; the former because it was excluded from the settlement, and the latter because it was unwilling to share power in any meaningful way.

What the humanitarian intervention lobby fails to see is that the United States did intervene in Rwanda, through a proxy. That proxy was the RPF, backed up by entire units from the Uganda Army. The green light was given to the RPF, whose commanding officer, Paul Kagame, had recently returned from training in the United States, just as it was lately given to the Ethiopian army in Somalia. Instead of using its resources and influence to bring about a political solution to the civil war, and then strengthen it, the United States signaled to one of the parties that it could pursue victory with impunity. This unilateralism was part of what led to the disaster, and that is the real lesson of Rwanda. Applied to Darfur and Sudan, it is sobering. It means recognizing that Darfur is not yet another Rwanda. Nurturing hopes of an external military intervention among those in the insurgency who aspire to victory and reinforcing the fears of those in the counterinsurgency who see it as a prelude to defeat are precisely the ways to ensure that it becomes a Rwanda. Strengthening those on both sides who stand for a political settlement to the civil war is the only realistic approach. Solidarity, not intervention, is what will bring peace to Darfur.

The dynamic of civil war in Sudan has fed on multiple sources. First, the post-independence monopoly of power is enjoyed by a tiny Arabized elite from the riverian north of Khartoum, a monopoly that has bred growing resistance among the majority, marginalized populations in the south, east, and west of the country. Second, the rebel movements have, in their turn, bred ambitious leaders unwilling to enter into power-sharing arrangements as a prelude to peace. Finally, external forces continue to encourage those who are interested in retaining or obtaining a monopoly of power.

The dynamic of peace, by contrast, has fed on a series of power-sharing arrangements, first in the south and then in the east. This process has been inter-mittent in Darfur. African Union–organized negotiations have been successful in forging a power-sharing arrangement, but only for that arrangement to fall apart time and again. A large part of the explanation, as I suggested earlier, lies in the international context of the War on Terror, which favors parties who are averse to taking risks for peace. To reinforce the peace process must be the first commitment of all those interested in Darfur.

The camp of peace needs to come to a second realization: Peace cannot be built on humanitarian intervention, which is the language of big powers. The history of colonialism should teach us that every major intervention has been justified as humanitarian, a "civilizing mission." Nor was it mere idiosyncrasy that inspired the devotion with which many colonial officers and archivists recorded the details of barbarity among the colonized – *sati*, the ban on widow marriage or the practice of child marriage in India, or slavery and female genital mutilation in Africa. I am not suggesting that this was all invention. I mean only to point out that the chronicling of atrocities had a practical purpose: It provided the moral pretext for intervention. Now, as then, imperial interventions claim to have a dual purpose: on the one hand, to rescue minority victims of ongoing barbarities and, on the other, to quarantine majority perpetrators with the stated aim of civilizing them. Iraq should act as a warning on this score. The worst thing for Darfur would be an Iraq-style intervention. That would almost certainly spread the civil war to other parts of Sudan, unraveling the peace process in the east and south and dragging the whole country into the global War on Terror.

Notes

[1] Contrast this with the UN commission's painstaking effort to make sense of the identities "Arab" and "African." The commission's report concentrated on three related points. First, the claim that the Darfur conflict pitted "Arab" against "African" was facile. "In fact, the commission found that many Arabs in Darfur are opposed to the Janjawid, and some Arabs are fighting with the rebels, such as certain Arab commanders and their men from the Misseriya and Rizeigat tribes. At the same time, many non-Arabs are supporting the government and serving in its army." Second, it has never been easy to sort different tribes into the categories "Arab" and "African": "The various tribes that have been the object of attacks and killings (chiefly the Fur, Massalit, and Zeghawa tribes) do not appear to make up ethnic groups distinct from the ethnic groups to which persons or militias that attack them belong. They speak the same language (Arabic) and embrace the same religion (Muslim). In addition, also due to the high measure of intermarriage, they can hardly be distinguished in their outward physical appearance from the members of tribes that allegedly attacked them. *Apparently, the sedentary and nomadic character of the groups constitutes one of the main distinctions between them*" (emphasis mine). Finally, the commission put forward the view that political developments are driving the rapidly growing distinction between "Arab" and "African." On the one hand, "Arab" and "African" seem to have become political identities: "Those tribes in Darfur who support rebels have increasingly come to be identified as 'African' and those supporting the government as the 'Arabs.' A good example to illustrate this is that of the Gimmer, a pro-government African tribe that is seen by the African tribes opposed to the government as having been 'Arabised.'" On the other hand, this development was being promoted from the outside: "The Arab-African divide has also been fanned by the growing insistence on such divide in some circles and in the media."

8   Naming the Conflict:
Darfur and the Crisis of Governance in Sudan

Salah M. Hassan

Existentially speaking, I am one of those diasporic Sudanese who has lived in the United States for more than twenty years, and like many of them I remain connected to my native land through long-distance networks that have ensured stable levels of engagement with its political, social, and cultural developments. This enduring contact has inevitably highlighted the disjuncture between my experiences abroad and the experiences of those who remained inside the country, in the thick of things. While in no way romanticizing exile and migration, the experience of living between two cultures and occupying a precarious space of "otherness" and "in-between-ness" allows one to look at issues from both sides of the divide: the "West" and the "Rest," "diaspora" and "homeland." Moreover, in today's world – with increased globalization and technological advances in communication – most political theorists would acknowledge the importance of what Benedict Anderson calls "long distance nationalism" and the role diasporic communities play in shaping political crisis at home and affecting their evolution and final settlements. No single case in the recent history of conflicts in Sudan demonstrates these connections and disjunctures, as well as their effects, better than the crisis of Darfur.

I am deeply concerned and terribly saddened by the tragedy in Darfur. Yet, I am also disturbed by the nature of activism around Africa-related crises and issues, and more specifically the Save Darfur movement and the damage it has done not only in its representation of the conflict in Darfur, but also to the prospects for a final and just solution to the current crisis in Sudan. A lasting solution, as I argue in this essay, can only materialize within a Sudan that is secular, democratic, and united, a place within which all people will have equal access to power, wealth, and natural resources, irrespective of their ethnicity, race, class, or gender. What follows are my own reflections on the current crisis in Darfur and the prospects for a meaningful resolution to it.

Before delving into the root causes of the current crisis in Sudan, I would like to reflect on the nature of activism around Darfur in the post-9/11 world, in comparison to an earlier moment of engagement with Africa that energized university campuses in the United States in similar ways two decades ago – that is the anti-apartheid movement of the 1980s. Major differences come to mind between these two moments of activism. First, the anti-apartheid movement of the 1980s was by and large guided by the voice of the African National Congress (ANC) and the agenda of the resistance movement inside South Africa. The ANC played the leading role in rendering anti-apartheid activism more effective and in accordance with the vision and priorities of the South African people. Second, the anti-apartheid movement of the 1980s was conspicuously progressive, internationalist, anti-imperialist, and anti-racist in its vision. Its membership was forged through an alliance of progressive and leftist forces that succeeded in cutting across the racial divide by involving a wide range of movements including labor unions. It was consistent in its agenda and internationalist in both its discourse and scope. For example, the same groups that joined forces to protest the apartheid policies in South Africa also protested racism in the United States and its imperialist wars and interventions in places such as Nicaragua and El Salvador, stood firmly against injustices abroad such as the Israeli occupation of Palestine, and expressed sincere solidarity with other oppressed peoples and their movements.

In comparison to the anti-apartheid movement several contrasting features characterize Save Darfur and the other major issue-focused groups involved in protesting the atrocities in Darfur. First, there is a stark absence of articulate Sudanese voices in the leadership of these groups and among the faces that represent them in the media.[1] In the few cases where Sudanese have been involved, their presence has been marginal and in most cases secondary to those of their Western counterparts and experts. The dominant voice has been that of NGO representatives, and as is generally the case in Africa-related advocacy, the discourse has been dominated by Western celebrity activists, aid workers, and other self-appointed experts and spokespersons, thus reconfiguring the "White Man's Burden" in a significant way. The agendas of these movements are dictated by their ideological concerns and the self-interest of their leadership, with little concern for any discourse inside Sudan or interest in the views of Sudanese on both sides of the conflict. Among the leading voices of such groups and their allies in the popular press there continues to be a glaring disregard for Sudanese voices and visions.[2] In the few cases where the press or other media have chosen to involve Sudanese in general or Darfurians in particular, they have selected victimized people whose trauma only serves as a backdrop to Western heroism. In many ways this is reminiscent of the media's fascination with the story of the "lost boys," which came out of the North/South civil war.

A typical example of Darfur advocacy and coverage in the media is the documentary "Searching for Jacob" featured on CBS's *60 Minutes* program, where the victim's voice was marginal to the arduous efforts and journey of the reporter, Scott Pelley, and his companion, a western NGO expert/advocate. Rather than providing a platform for the victim, whose real name is Ya'qub, not Jacob, to tell his own story, the program is fixated on their grueling search for him, from the Museum of Tolerance in Los Angeles to a remote and inaccessible internally displaced persons (IDP) camp in Darfur.[3] This phenomena is of course deeply rooted in the Western media's representation of Africans, and non-Western people in general as helpless, inarticulate, and unable to voice their own concerns, hence the need for the Westerner as the "ventriloquist-savior" to speak on their behalves. Moreover, in a country such as Sudan, known for its vibrant civil society and the visible presence of highly articulate intellectuals and activists (academics, lawyers, economists, and so forth) within the leadership of the Darfur resistance movements, there is no justification for refusing to allow Sudanese to speak for themselves. Intimately related to this issue is the visual representation of Darfur, its people, and its landscape in the Western media, which has projected Darfurians as victims with no regard for their perseverance, resilience and resourcefulness. This propensity, however, has been challenged by the visually compelling humane representation of Darfur and its people in the work of the Sudanese photographer Issam Abdelhafiez, whose images are included in this volume.

The media's racialization of the Darfur conflict as "Arabs" against "Africans," – with Arabs cast as aggressors and Africans as victims – has further consolidated the negative stereotypes of Arabs that have been widely circulating in the West. In the process the root causes of the conflict have been mystified and the main culprit, the National Islamic Front (NIF) government, has been exculpated from its direct responsibility in using so-called Arabs to fight its dirty war against the Darfur resistance movement. In reality, both victim and aggressor are victims of the government's counterinsurgency tactics, which will have far-reaching consequences on the region, its demographics, and future development.

However, one must acknowledge that the aforementioned picture is gradually changing. A rising number of interventions – in writing and in public forums – by several Sudanese and, more specifically, Darfurians with long established track records of scholarship and activism, such as Salih Mahmud Osman, Abdullahi Osman El Tom, Sharif Harir, Munzoul Assal, and Eltigani Seisi M. Ateem, are challenging these perspectives and influencing the agenda in progressive circles and the alternative media. In addition, as of 2006 a number of well-researched books and articles written by Sudanese and other experts have shed more light on the complexity of the Darfur crisis and the need to address it in the context of the larger crisis of governance in Sudan and regional politics.[4]

The contributions of those who have experiential knowledge derived from their lives and work in Sudan supply unique perspectives on the various processes contributing to the crisis. To my mind, their analytical and descriptive frameworks are not only valuable for what they tell us concretely about the issues at hand, but also because they provide a unique opportunity to learn something about how Sudanese read their own society in times of immense political turmoil and conflict. My own effort to amplify Sudanese views on a subject of great political complexity is a task that has occupied me both as a scholar and a citizen. My emphasis on the imperatives of the production of indigenous knowledge underscores my concern with foregrounding our understanding of the crisis of governance in Darfur in Sudanese terms. Not only will this interrogation contribute to a better understanding of the specificity of this crisis, it will also articulate homegrown strategies for sustainable solutions proposed by those whose lives have been most affected by the pervasive political practices and the "violence of representation" that infuses much of what we hear about Darfur from non-Sudanese writers and commentators.

Second, Save Darfur and other related movements are partially influenced by the agenda of right-wing groups associated with the Christian right and the pro-Israeli lobby in the United States and Europe. By focusing on the Darfur crisis, those who wield tremendous influence within these groups found a means of diverting the attention of the mainstream media from American atrocities in Iraq and Afghanistan, and from Israel's brutal oppression of the Palestinians and their occupation of Gaza and the West Bank. This is by no means to suggest that everyone who has joined Save Darfur in cities, towns, and university campuses across the United States adheres to a right-wing and anti-Arab or Islamo-phobic agenda. Many, if not most, of Save Darfur's members are genuinely concerned with the brutality of the ruling NIF regime in Darfur and have found a means of expressing their solidarity with the people of Darfur, as they work to stop the slaughter, rape, and devastation of their communities. Yet, the lack of interest among members of Darfur advocacy groups in other causes closer to home, such as the American war in Iraq and Afghanistan, is bewildering and contradictory to say the least. I shall return to this critique later in this essay.

African-American political leaders and public personalities have also joined in the mobilization against the war in Darfur, albeit with caution. While many within this constituency view the mainstream's perspective on the war in Darfur with suspicion, their concern with Darfur signals a shift in attitude that recalls the activism against the apartheid regime in South Africa and the influential role played by African-American lobby groups, such as Trans-Africa, in protesting it. This role will positively impact global solidarity with the people of Darfur by broadening the base of the movement and challenging the media's problematic representation of the conflict.

One may wish to genuinely ask what difference does it make having a "progressive activism" in the context of a horrific tragedy, involving crimes against humanity and genocide, as is the case in Darfur? Shouldn't we be grateful for the attention given to Darfur by Western celebrities and spokespersons when thousands of people have perished and thousands more continue to languish in refugee camps? My straightforward response is that an effective activism requires an informed activism, and that the role of solidarity groups and responsible public intellectuals should be to foreground the voices of the oppressed in their most articulate manifestations. This was the legacy of progressive anti-apartheid activism during the 1960s through the 1980s when the voices of the oppressed were represented by the leaders of the ANC and other liberation movements, including formidable intellectuals and highly thoughtful activists, who were able to advance the dialogue on apartheid beyond one of victimhood, to encompass the political, social, and economic agenda of a highly organized network of political organizations that was pushing for the complete transformation of South African society into a multiracial democracy.

It is imperative, moreover, for us, as academics and public intellectuals, to address the root causes of the crisis instead of pushing for patchwork solutions, such as a swift military intervention that still leaves the main culprits in power (Al Bashir's regime) and Darfurian refugees languishing in endless encampments. We must also advocate for radical and lasting solutions as articulated by Darfurians themselves and by leaders of the Sudanese civil society at large. This is precisely the rationale behind the thrust of my arguments in this essay and the larger conceptualization of the project within which it is framed.

Accordingly, the title of this essay best expresses my conviction about the nature of the conflict in Sudan and how it should be addressed. The war in Darfur is part of a larger crisis of governance in Sudan and is intricately related to how the ruling classes have managed ethnic, religious, and cultural diversity within Sudan as a nation-state since independence. Sudan, as a nation-state, has been and continues to be scarred by the monopoly of power by a minority of Arabized elites from the central and northern Sudan at the expense of the marginalization of people from other regions, including Darfur and western Sudan, the south, the east, and a large sector of the north itself.

I opted not to focus in this essay on the root causes and history of the current crisis in Darfur as they have already been sufficiently addressed by several Sudanese and non-Sudanese scholars.[5] The solid foundation laid by these groundbreaking publications enables me to delve into a focused examination of the "politics of naming," critiquing the conflict from *within* Sudan as a base for identifying a final and just resolution to the conflict in Darfur.

My main objective is to read the issue of Darfur within the context of the crisis of governance in Sudan by paying special attention to the views and analysis of what came to be known as the "Modern Forces" in the lexicon of contemporary Sudanese political discourse.[6] This loose alliance of diverse groups includes non-sectarian political parties, such as the Sudanese Communist Party and its allies, the Sudan People's Liberation Movement/Sudan People's Liberation Army (SPLM/A), civil society groups such as trade unions, the women's movement, professional associations, and urban-based ethnic (tribal) associations, including the rebel movements in Darfur. The broad vision of these groups was popularized and crystallized by the SPLM/A under the leadership of the late John Garang through his idea of "The New Sudan," which in turn translates into a vision of a united secular and democratic Sudan that calls for the separation of religion and the state, respect for diversity, equal access to national wealth, and power sharing among all groups.[7] This broad alliance of political forces shares several common views of the war in Darfur.

First, the war is perceived as a "counter-insurgency on the cheap," to borrow Alex de Waal's insightful term, in which nomadic groups (the so-called Arabs) are trained, armed, and used by the NIF government to fight sedentary communities, such as *Fur, Zaghawa*, and *Masalit* (the so-called Africans), with whom these nomads have, for hundreds of years, shared a peaceful co-existence that was intermittently disrupted by episodes of conflict over grazing land and natural resources. Over the last several decades these conflicts have gradually intensified as a result of a combination of natural environmental crises, such as draught and desertification, and the side effects of internal conflicts and regional wars in neighboring countries such as Chad, Libya, and the Central African Republic.

Second, while the war in Darfur is a modern one, it has been fought with a "pre-modern" ideology and orchestrated by the NIF government in attempt to speedily crush an armed rebellion that started in 2003, the same year the government signed the Naifasha Protocols, which led to the CPA of 2005. It is a "modern war" because it is central to a conflict over control of power and resources and distribution of wealth within a postcolonial nation-state ruled by a regime that is bent on staying in control at all costs. It is not in anyway a primeval "tribal" war rooted in an endless primordial animosity between "tribes" or "races" that are not capable of mutual co-existence. Yet, it is "pre-modern" in its ideological outlook because it is a war that is based on evoking pre-modern traditions and values of warfare among nomadic groups to serve as "counterinsurgents" in executing the government's war against the Darfur rebel movements and their population base, the mostly sedentary Fur, Zaghawa, and Masalit.

Darfur: The Politics of Naming Inside/Out
In his article on the politics of naming featured in this volume, Mahmood Mamdani offers an insightful analysis of the U.S.-based Save Darfur movement and its alliance

of strange bedfellows from disparate ideological and political orientations.[8] He highlights the contradictions in the Save Darfur movement by analyzing the politics of naming vis-à-vis the idea/label of "genocide," and by contrasting the attitudes of the concerned public in the United States toward the wars in Darfur and Iraq – the latter of which is similar if not larger in the scale of horror and human fatalities than Darfur. As Mamdani eloquently states:

> The similarities between Iraq and Darfur are remarkable. The estimate of the number of civilians killed over the past three years is roughly similar. The killers are mostly paramilitaries, closely linked to the official military, which is said to be their main source of arms. The victims too are by and large identified as members of groups, rather than targeted as individuals. But the violence in the two places is named differently. In Iraq, it is said to be a cycle of insurgency and counter-insurgency; in Darfur, it is called genocide. Why the difference? Who does the naming? Who is being named? What difference does it make?

Mamdani further elaborates:

> The most powerful mobilization in New York City is in relation to Darfur, not Iraq. One would expect the reverse, for no other reason than that most New Yorkers are American citizens and so should feel directly responsible for the violence in occupied Iraq. But Iraq is a messy place in the American imagination, a place with messy politics. Americans worry about what their government should do in Iraq. Should it withdraw? What would happen if it did? In contrast, there is nothing messy about Darfur. It is a place without history and without politics; simply a site where perpetrators clearly identifiable as "Arabs" confront victims clearly identifiable as "Africans."

Mamdani argues that the war in Darfur is like other conflicts all over the world: It is a "man-made crisis subject to man-made solutions." He also contends that contrary to popular perception, Darfur is a place with history and, as such, the current crisis must be looked at within this context. Equally, its implications and intersections must also be understood nationally, regionally, and globally. In this respect, Mamdani argues that the Darfur crisis is as messy and complex as any other crises, whether in Iraq, Afghanistan, or Ireland. His is a call for an honest intellectual engagement to deconstruct the war in Darfur and to investigate the origins and evolution and the unspoken role of the international community, including the Western-based support groups, in deepening the crisis rather than resolving it. However, what Mamdani does not fully address is the role of the state and more specifically the NIF government and its security apparatus in the creation and perpetuation of the current crisis. He also does not fully address the obscene imbalance of power within Sudan between the state's military might and its powerful security apparatus on the one hand, and the Darfur rebels on the other, with the state having the upper hand in dictating its will to crush the hopes and aspirations of the people of Darfur. What Mamdani leaves out most importantly is addressing the politics of naming from within Sudan and the discourse on Darfur among Sudanese civil society groups and resistance movements. No one can expect Mamdani to address all these issues in one essay, and I am in no way suggesting that he failed to do so deliberately.

Mamdani's analysis with respect to the politics of naming requires further explication. The elaboration of the multiple uses, appropriations, and particularities of how the politics of naming are mobilized in given contexts is critiqued here. In order to do so, it is necessary to recall another set of contradictions from within Sudan, namely, the politics of naming vis-à-vis the older North-South conflict, which resulted in Africa's most protracted civil war that lasted nearly 50 years. Furthermore, the comparison between the two highlights the machinated politics of naming and the tendency of Western scholars and mainstream media to describe conflicts in Sudan and Africa more generally in binary terms that reference religion, ethnicity, and race. These descriptions often obfuscate the complex origins and histories of these conflicts and result in artificial dichotomies and oversimplifications. In so doing, this argument interrogates the easy binaries that have plagued representations of and modes of thinking about Sudanese sociopolitical and historical realities.

Before Darfur: Lessons from the South Sudan

Sudan is typical of many postcolonial nation-states in Africa that are home to multiethnic, multicultural, and multireligious societies. It is an example of a pluralistic society formed by people whose notions of belonging and national identity differ markedly. As in other African countries, the Sudanese condition is shaped to a large extent by prevalent power inequalities, unequal development, and differential access to resources and opportunities. The outcome has been a constant crisis of governance, civil war, ethnic cleansing, famine, and other man-made disasters that have gripped the country since independence, but whose roots were formed during the colonial period. Differing visions for the future of the country have been contested. At one extreme is the vision of separation (fragmentation of the country into several states), at the other, the preservation of the status quo by any means, including violent ones (the military solution), which ultimately means the continuation of inequalities within a "united" country. Various political groups have at times propagated proposals to decentralize state power through a federal system that provides an autonomy for regions such as the South, and other disenfranchised areas, and guarantees the right to self-determination for their people.

The protracted war in the South began in 1955 at the dawn of Sudan's independence from British colonialism and was a logical outcome of the inequalities and imbalance in power sharing that characterized the colonial period. The war was also a consequence of the failure, typical of postcolonial regimes since 1956, to seriously address these inequalities. By all accounts the scale of horror and loss of human life over the stretch of fifty years of the civil war between the South, represented first by the Anya-Nya (1955–1971) and SPLM/A (1983–2003) on the one hand and the government army on the other, was equally if not more devastating than the current conflict in Darfur. Most important, there are many significant similarities between the manner in which the war was conducted by the government in the South and in Darfur, with respect to the political discourse, ideological justification, and military tactics adopted by successive governments since independence in resolving regional conflicts and civil wars, including the use of paramilitary militias as counterinsurgents. Similar to the case of the *Janjawid* in Darfur, the practice of recruiting Arabized nomads to fight the SPLM/A in areas bordering the South can be traced to Numeiri's regime (1969–1985). The continued mobilization of paramilitary groups known as *Murahaleen* formed by recruits from the Baggara nomads – the *Misayriyyah* – was carried out well into the democratically elected government of Sadiq Al Mahdi. The *Misayriyyah* wrought painful devastation and undertook mass killings in the south among the Dinka communities in Northern Bahr Al Ghazal. In many ways this served as a rehearsal of the *Janjawid* attacks against the Fur, Masalit, and Zaghawa, who at present form the social base and ground support for the guerrilla warfare waged by the Darfur resistance movements.

The comparison, which I draw here with the South–North civil war becomes even more compelling and enlightening in the case of Darfur, when we examine the intersections between the two conflicts. Both in turn have serious bearings on their final resolution for the following interconnected reasons.

First, the Darfur armed rebellion is a direct offshoot of its Southern counterpart and the rise of the SPLM/A as an important political force on the national scene. As a matter of fact, the earlier incarnation of the rebel movement in Darfur – not to underestimate its autochthonous causes and legitimacy – was directly linked to the political vision of the SPLM/A's efforts to build a national movement based on alliances of the oppressed and marginalized people of the Sudan. A case in point is the Darfur-based SPLM/A battalion led by Dawood Bolad, himself a former NIF member and student activist in the Muslim Brotherhood, which was brutally crushed by the NIF government's armed and security forces in 1992.

Second, the CPA, which ended the North–South armed conflict, has simultaneously created both a model and a ceiling for expectations about what might be envisioned or agreed upon as a resolution to the Darfur crisis. It is a model because the CPA provided the means to address issues of self-governance, inequality, and access to power. It also made available resources for postconflict rebuilding of affected communities. On the other hand, it is a ceiling because the CPA's provisions for power sharing and representation at both the executive and legislative branches of government, including the security organs, have given the two signatories (SPLM/A and NCP) a disproportionate advantage over the rest of the country's political powers, which constitute the majority of the Sudanese civil society and constituencies, including Darfurians. Third, the rise of the insurgency in Darfur was directly linked to the timing of the signing of the protocols of the Naivasha Agreement in 2003, which ended the war in the South in a clear victory for the SPLM/A. Encouraged by this victory, it is not a secret that the timing of the Darfur rebels' 2003 attack on the military base near El Fasher signaled the beginning of the war in Darfur, which was intended to deliver a strong message to the government that their legitimate demands could not be ignored.

Before Darfur, the conflict in Sudan has been commonly perceived as North (Arab, Muslim) against South (African, Christian, and Animist). Accordingly, the war was portrayed in both racial and religious terms, while in the case of Darfur the conflict has been represented in racialized rather than religious terms – that is as "Arab" versus "Black African" – since both groups are Muslims. The racialization of the war has shaped the involvement of right-wing evangelists and the more conservative segments of the international community with devastating effects on both the production of knowledge around Darfur and the overall formulations of foreign policy vis-à-vis a population in distress. This propensity to racialize the war not only dominates the discourse of the Western media, it has also further perpetuated internalized racialization among certain elements on both sides of various conflicts within Sudan. These include constituencies within the northern Arabized ruling elites and within the Southern and Darfur resistance movements. The former hoped to exploit the religious feeling and emotions of the northern masses and to gain the backing of Arab and Muslim states in furthering their local agenda. The latter, justified by decades of exploitation, discrimination, and broken promises by the ruling classes, have found a convenient way to describe the conflict and to draw the sympathy of the outside world. Though it contains an unfortunate element of truth, this racial and religious perception of the Sudanese crisis is both misleading and simplistic as it tends to conceal a far more complex and ever-changing dynamic political and cultural scene.

Closely linked to this is the shifting nature of identity and racial identification among Dafurians, especially diaspora Darfurian communities in Europe and the United States. Many Darfurians in the past have identified as Muslims and many of their intellectuals who are now formidable rebel leaders were members of the Islamist movement that brought the NIF regime to power. In the past many embraced its jihadist discourse and practices against non-Muslims, a position that has since been renounced.[9] Their past affiliations, orientations, and sympathies to the pan-Islamist and pan-Arabist projects were established facts. The shift toward an "African" identity is largely shaped by a Darfurian diasporic discourse that aims at creating new ideologies of race and belonging. Not to be understated is the fact that this shift should be attributed to the ugly realities on the ground where the ideology of Arab chauvinism has been deployed by the NIF regime to mobilize the Janjawid and other paramilitary militias who have had a devastating impact on Darfurian societies. This situationality in identification is not unique to Darfurians, considering the fluid nature of identity and race as constructions shaped by sociopolitical realities.[10] The role of diasporic Darfurians in influencing patterns of identification on the basis of the prevailing concepts of race in their host societies, especially in the context of the United States, is a subject I have touched upon to varying degrees in this essay, but nonetheless warrants furthers investigation in a separate study examining diasporic community formations, linkages between exile and host societies, and exile vis-à-vis homeland politics.

There has been a rising awareness, especially among the modern forces inside Sudan, that the civil war in the South, and now in Darfur and the East, should be ascribed to the conflict between a "center" – north and central Sudan – controlled by the established economic interests of a ruling group dominated by northern and central Arabized elites, and the "periphery," which is dominated and exploited by this center. This center is more developed than the peripheries. However, this perception should be viewed with some caution, as it tends to assume a homogeneity of interests among Northern groups and does not pay attention to specific historical developments and cultural differences within regions labeled as peripheries. Among the peripheries, the South is the most underdeveloped economically and most

Section Two: Representations of the War in Darfur

controlled by the center, although there is a tremendous potential for change in the current state of affairs. Yet, it is not radically different from other peripheral regions such as Darfur, the Nuba Mountains, and the Red Sea Hills in the eastern Sudan. That is to say, if the war did not start in the South, it would have started elsewhere in the disadvantaged regions or the North's own localities.[11] Here too I find it crucial to interrogate the oversimplified binary of center and periphery as absolute social, economic, and political formations. The interface of race and class identities is bound to recast this dichotomy by elucidating its complexity and multiplicity.

The fact that the war could have started somewhere else other than the South is exemplified by the rise of ethnically based political resistance movements in those regions that at one point or another called for armed struggle against the government. As witnessed during the years of the conflict between 1985–2003, certain elements from regions, such as Darfur, the Eastern front, the Nuba mountains, and even the North, have joined the SPLM/A or formed their own battalions as affiliates to the movement.

Historically, by and large, this second perception is the view of the modern forces within the Sudan, including the SPLM/A and most of the Darfur armed resistance movements today. Inside Sudan, this view is gaining acceptance and has become the starting point for the current national dialogue on the on-going crisis and the future of the country.

In light of Sudan's historical and geopolitical circumstances, I argue that the current crisis of governance in Sudan is explained by two major factors.

First, the policy of unequal development between the center (mainly the areas of Northern and Central Sudan) and the peripheries (more specifically in the south, east, and west of Sudan), created by colonial policies and perpetuated by the dominant postcolonial ruling class. The power structure, represented by the different vital state institutions, such as the economy, the army, the civil service, and security apparatus, are controlled and monopolized by a minority of Arabized Muslim Sudanese from the relatively developed areas of the Central and Northern Riverian Sudan. Not to be discounted is the alliance of politically mobilized self-interested individuals and groups from marginalized areas such as Southern Sudan and Darfur who worked hand-in-glove with repressive governments to the detriment of their own populations.

Second, all the successive postcolonial governments have consistently perpetuated the racist policy of Arabization and Islamization of the South. Starting with the first military dictatorship in the late 1950s and early 1960s, this policy has violently repressed the Southern rebellion and efforts to address the injustices and policies that afflicted their communities for decades.

At this juncture important distinctions must be clearly drawn. While the reality of the North–South conflict was not religious, religious bigotry coupled with racial and sectarian manipulations of political loyalties have always been the inflaming factors. The introduction of Islamic law (shari'a) in September 1983 meant that the conflict was increasingly reformulated in religious terms. The injection of religion into Sudanese politics has now reached its climax with the policies of the NIF regime, which present a serious threat to the unity of the country. Accordingly, the conflict is increasingly perceived as one between the NIF government on one side, and the secular Sudanese modern forces all over the country on the other.

Certain dangerous developments have added to the complexity of the Sudanese crisis. It bears repeating that the policy of forming and arming paramilitary tribal militias was initiated by the Numeiri regime and further consolidated by Sadiq Al Mahdi in 1986 under the pretext of defending civilian populations against SPLM/A attacks. This policy, with its devastating effect of the militarization of rural areas, has been taken to its extreme by the NIF government's incorporation of these militias into a paramilitary fundamentalist army known as the Popular Defense Forces (PDF), established by a government decree. In the case of Darfur this resulted in the creation of the *Janjawid*.

The tragic consequences of this policy have been the worst human rights violations and massacres committed in the history of Sudan against civilians, including Southerners and now against the people of Darfur. Earlier on, these cases included the infamous massacres of El Jabalain (1989) and El Dien (1986). In addition to Southerners, the tragic policy of ethnic cleansing pursued by the NIF junta has targeted certain non-Arabized Islamic groups like the Nuba and Fur. This racist policy is now being pursued to its extreme in the case of Darfur, leading to massive displacements of Darfurians, destruction of their environment, cultures, and their social and economic wellbeing.

Moving Beyond the Vicious Circle: A Plea for Optimism
As I have argued thus far, the rise of armed resistance movements in the South, and in other similarly disenfranchised parts of the country such as Darfur, is both a reaction and a genuine reply to the central government's long-standing policy of marginalizing and viciously repressing the "periphery" in Sudan. This resistance, especially in its armed incarnation, should be linked to the lack of true democracy, greed, and narrow hegemonic interests of a minority of Arabized elites (military and civilians), who have controlled power since independence. Even democratically elected leaders have at one point or another resorted to curbing democratic rights, including freedom of expression, and clamping down on civic and political organizations. They have also chosen violence to counteract the legitimate demands and genuine grievances of the marginalized regions. All have adhered to the concept of a Sudan assumed to be predominantly Arabo-Islamic in both culture and outlook. This orientation constitutes the base for government's policies on education, information, cultural planning, and foreign relations.

Yet, Sudan, I would passionately argue, is one case where it is possible, by virtue of its unique history, the complexity of its situation, and certain developments before and after independence, to become a model for creative answers to questions about the crisis of nation-states in postcolonial Africa. These solutions are envisaged in the context of a unity that preserves and respects diversity within a pluralistic democratic system. The country can also provide creative perspectives on democratization in Africa as a whole. One lesson to be drawn from the modern political history of the Sudan is that a lack of democracy and the guarantee of basic rights endanger unity, the real base of which can only be negotiated under democratic rule. To some extent, unity in Sudan has been the logical outcome of certain objective historical developments.

It is true that the current borders of Sudan were drawn after the Turko-Egyptian colonial occupation in the nineteenth century. The same borders have produced a

Section Two: Representations of the War in Dafur

history of relations necessitated by the nature of the land, the flow of its rivers and water resources, population movements and internal migrations, ancient trade routes, and other mutual benefits between the inhabitants of its various regions. Centralized states from the days of Kush and Meroe had been established in different parts of the country. Although none of these states succeeded in controlling the whole area known as Sudan today, economic exchange, social, and cultural influences flourished beyond their centers to include the whole country. In Sudan, where reciprocity has been central to society and culture, these values will no doubt come to play an instrumental role in conflict resolution and peace promotion. The relationships between the different regions of the Sudan have been marked by exchange and interdependency in economic development and security, as well as in social and cultural systems. Despite the current malaise and crisis, this interdependency and exchange would benefit the different regions more than exchange between each region and neighboring countries.

Sudan's borders have remained intact despite Europe's scramble for Africa, the Mahdist revolution and other anti-colonial uprisings, postindependence civil wars, and the upsurge in ethnic violence. Unity has prevailed in spite of British colonial policies that led to the current state of unequal development and the imbalance in power relations between the center and the peripheries. The colonial separatist scheme was first defeated in the Juba Conference of 1947, when Northerners as well as Southerners agreed on an independent unified country. Sudan gained its independence in 1956 with approximately the same borders. This was not a gift from the British or any other foreign power, but a consequence of the nationalistic struggle of the Sudanese people. In spite of continuous challenges and crises, Sudan has managed to preserve its unity and territorial integrity as a country.

The democratic struggle for the preservation of unity is exemplified by several positive landmarks in the history of the Sudan: the Charter of the October 24th 1964 Revolution; the Round Table Conference of 1965; the Declaration of the 9th of June 1969; the establishment of the SPLM/A in 1983; the Charter of April 1985 Uprising; the Koka Dam Declaration of 1986; the Peace Initiative of 1988; the Interim Program of the National Government formed after the events of December 1988; the spirit of the Armed Forces Memorandum of February 1989; the signing of the Charter of the National Democratic Alliance in 1989 and the amendments added to it when the SPLM/A became a signatory to the NDA Charter in 1990; and most recently the CPA and its success in bringing peace to the South and opening up room for a resurgence of civil society and creating openings for greater civil liberties and freedom of expression.

However, Sudan continues to live through a tragic crisis of governance, engulfed in a vicious cycle that starts with a popular uprising, followed by parliamentary rule, which is overthrown by a military coup d'état. The civil war in the south raged intermittently for five decades, lasting through three military and three civilian democratically elected governments. Within this bleak political landscape a democratic option capable of affecting a just and lasting peace was impossible to institutionalize. Furthermore, democratic ideas have not been able to establish themselves within institutions that are capable of protecting and defending themselves.

The source of my optimism is that Sudan has a long history of "people's power," which managed to topple two military governments, in October 1964 and

March–April 1985, through nonviolent means, including popular uprisings, civil disobedience, and general strikes. Sudan was one of the first democracies in the region, as it started its political life after independence as a multiparty democracy. Unlike many African countries, Sudan has a strong civil society base in terms of powerful trade unions, well-organized professional associations, and political parties. Despite the troubling history of military rule aborting short-lived democratic experiments, which has plagued its political life since independence, Sudan has continued to have one of the most powerful grass roots democratic movements in Africa.

A major cause of democracy's failure in Sudan is that the modern forces, known for being the main instigators and architects of the uprisings and revolutionary change, always fail to retain power during the transitional period of democratic rule. While these periods always involve enacting electoral rules, these very rules intentionally curb the representation of the modern forces in the parliament and the government at large, and thus deprive democracy of its social power base. Consequently, power flows into the hands of the traditional sectarian forces known for their betrayal of the people's basic needs and demands. The consequence of the exclusion of the modern forces from power – in addition to other flaws in democratic practice, corruption, and lack of seriousness in providing a solution to the basic problems facing the country – has been a total sense of desperation and chronic crisis. The new election laws passed in 2008 in the transitional parliament and signed by the two ruling parties to pave the way for the national elections scheduled in 2009 pose new challenges and point to new forms of exclusion of women and other smaller parties classified within the modern forces.

Breaking this vicious cycle by ensuring the participation of three major political forces – the political parties, the Modern Forces, and the military – at all levels of the government (judicial, executive, and legislative) to ensure a smooth transition to working democarcy is the only way out of this crisis. This point and other basic demands have been consistently stated in revolutionary charters signed prior to popular uprisings (October 1964, April 1985, and October 1989) led by the Modern Forces. It is important to remember that out of the fifty-two years of Sudan's independent rule, multiparty democracy has ruled for only eleven years (1956–1958, 1964–1969, and 1985–1989). Forty-one years have been under military rule. Perhaps because of their short-lived rule, democratic regimes have failed to redress these shortcomings.

The struggle for democracy continues vigorously in the Sudan, despite the brutality and the unprecedented oppressive policies of the current NIF military regime, which came to power in June 1989. This struggle culminated in several positive developments. The first one is the appearance of the SPLM/A as an important political force on the national scene with a progressive vision and inclusive agenda for the whole country. This has been a great departure from the Anya-Nya movement, which espoused both separatist and reactionary visions in its political and social agenda. The rise of the SPLM/A has broadened and strengthened the role of the modern forces as a foundation for a transformative and democratic politics in Sudan. The SPLM/A objective of a "New Sudan" builds on the struggle of the modern forces to subvert the hegemony of sectarian politics and cycles of military rule in establishing a democratic society. The second positive development was the formation of the National Democratic Alliance (NDA), a pro-democracy coalition of opposition groups that signed a major charter in 1989, offering the hope of an alliance between different political groups. Although it is almost defunct now, and despite its troubling history, the rise of the NDA has enriched the public discourse on politics by offering the hope of an alliance between different political parties and civil society groups to agree on national programs and a detailed agenda for the transition to a multiparty democracy. The NDA offers a feasible plan of action to counteract the NIF's monopoly of power. Furthermore, it solidified measures for a national transitional government and advocacy of a constitution that is crucial to the rebuilding of multiparty democratic rule.

It is true that the signing of the CPA in 2005 between the NIF government and the SPLM/SPLA, which is a member of the NDA, to the exclusion of all other political forces, has complicated the possibility of a more comprehensive national reconciliation that could have paved the way for a national constitutional conference with the aim of restoring a true democracy to the whole country as suggested by the NDA charter a decade earlier. At this juncture, it is imperative to identify the real obstacles thwarting the establishment of democratic and good governance in the Sudan. Major issues, which represent frontiers of democratization in Sudan, should be addressed, taking stock of the burning issues pertaining to civil wars, political violence, burgeoning militarism, and the role of religion in politics.

This is exceptionally relevant in light of the NIF government's articulation of the relationship between religion and the state. Although *Shari'a* was introduced first by Numeiri in 1983, the ascension of the Islamist military government to power in 1989 signaled a new phase in the reinforcement of the relationship between religion (Islam) and the state as it conforms to NIF's infamous Islamic civilizing project. However, most serious is the resurgence of separatism as an ideology in the political public sphere, which envisions the fragmentation of Sudan into several states. The option of the separation of South Sudan is already embedded in and legitimized by the CPA through the referendum that allows Southerners to vote for or against secession in 2011. The exclusionary and repressive politics of the ruling NCP do not make unity a desirable option, and all indicators point to separation as the most preferred scenario for the Southern public. Although the post-CPA governance structure necessitated the formation of a government of a national unity, the commitment of the NCP to the future of a unified Sudan is questionable.

Toward a Lasting Peace in Darfur

In light of the arguments I have tried to advance throughout this essay, the true challenge has become that any subsequent government embarking on democratizing the country must face these issues. Moreover, recent regional and international developments must be taken into consideration in our analyses. First are the complications of the post-CPA government in Sudan, which represents a monopoly of power between two ruling parties (NCP and the SPLM/A). Most importantly, within this context, the NCP's exclusionary practices toward all other political forces outside the government and even toward its partner in the government of national unity, the SPLM, continue to stall the implementation of the CPA. For example, if unchallenged, the conflict over Abeyie and the drawing of borders between the

North and South, the monopoly of oil revenues, and the appalling lack of transparency with regard to their distribution will have disastrous consequences for the future of democratization in Sudan. Second, the insistence of the NCP on a military solution in Darfur, despite its empty rhetoric of peaceful negotiation, has opened the door to the possibility of a permanent foreign military intervention, which may lead to a de facto fragmentation of the country. With the latest development of the possible indictment of President Al Bashir by the International Criminal Court (ICC), the first ever against a sitting head of state, and the lack of cooperation of the NIF regime with the ICC and the absence of serious efforts to prosecute crimes against humanity in the region, the future of Sudan as a viable democratic and united entity has become gloomier than ever before.

The only way out of this impasse is embodied in the demands advanced by the most active elements of the civil society and political parties, including the SPLM. These steps include the convening of a national conference, with the participation of all component parts of the civil society and political parties, including all the Darfur rebel groups. This should help set up a framework for lasting and just peace, for security throughout the country, for the strengthening of national unity and a united democratic Sudan by settling questions of identity; promoting development and the sharing of power and wealth; specifying the relationship between state and religion; and then drafting a permanent constitution in light of decisions taken by the conference.

Second, the most urgent task is to put an end to the Darfur crisis through a serious national effort that involves all concerned entities. This includes addressing the heinous crimes committed by the government against Darfur and the persecution of all criminals at all levels, by collaborating with the ICC and other international entities involved in the Darfur crisis. This effort should include an inter-Darfur dialogue leading to a final settlement that involves all the parties to the conflict and addresses the regional and international dimensions of the issues in question.

Finding a way out cannot happen without the acceleration of the serious democratic transformation that is embedded in the CPA even with all its limitations. This means moving forward with implementing all agreements and instituting a national mechanism that will ensure its effectiveness. As stated above, involving all political parties and civil society organizations is key to ensuring basic democratic liberties and freedom of expression and the total lifting of the NCP's control over security and the freedom of the press. Seriousness on part of the NCP in dealing with these wide-ranging concerns is the only way to bring any credibility to the current government's effort to resolve the Darfur crisis and convince local, national, and international communities of its intentions. Finding a sustainable solution to the predicament of governance lies at the heart of Sudanese political conflict. Such a solution will not come to full fruition without serious engagement with the CPA's provisions on democratization. Notwithstanding the flaws of the CPA, there is no doubt that it offers the road map for the implementation of useful mechanisms for restructuring the extant power hierarchies.

Notes

1. Here I refer to the preference on the part of the Western media to feature narratives of victimization and suffering over more analytical reflections by Darfurians on the nature of the Darfur crisis that reflect the ability of local activists to effect tangible change.

2. By using the term "indigenous" I do not mean to imply certain hierarchies or homogeneity among Sudanese. Instead, I wish to highlight the originality of Sudanese ideas about their predicaments.

3. This segment was originally broadcast on Oct. 22, 2006. It was updated on July 16, 2008. See: http://www.cbsnews.com/stories/2006/10/20/60minutes/main2111909.shtml *Ya'qub* is the Arabic name for *Jacob*, the biblical prophet whose prophecy is central to the story of the dispersal of the Jews and the idea of return to the homeland. The decision to use the non-Arabic version of the victim's real name is, I contend, deliberate in terms of its appeal to the Western imagination, and by extension, its sympathy.

4. See the titles of books and other works I pointed to earlier in this essay.

5. In addition to the essays by Mansour Khalid, Atta El-Battahani, Benaiah Yongo-Bure, Abdullahi Osman El-Tom, and Ali B. Ali Dinar, which appear in this volume, other important scholarship cited in the introduction to this volume include Muhammad Sulieman's *Darfur: The War over Natural Resources and the Conflict of Identities*; the literature of Sudanese political parties, most especially the Communist Party document included in the appendices of this volume, along with the position papers issued by the SPLM/A and the Darfur resistance movements; Alex de Waal's *The Famine that Kills*, and his co-authored work with Julie Flint, *Darfur: A Short History of A Long War*; Martin Daly's historical overview *Darfur's Sorrow: A History of Destruction and Genocide*;

and Abdel Ghaffar M. Ahmed and Leif Manger's edited volume *Understanding the Crisis in Darfur: Listening to Sudanese Voices*.

6. The Modern Forces are defined here broadly to include the left, the Sudanese Communist Party and its allies, and other elements of the secular democratic movements in Sudan. It is a term that was first introduced through the literature of the Sudanese Communist Party, which remains influential in shaping Sudanese politics and public intellectual life in Sudan.

7. It is important to mention that the concept of the "New Sudan" is rooted in the idea of the Modern Sudan or the Modern Forces propagated decades earlier by the Sudanese Communist Party and in the writings of its charismatic leader, the late Abdul Khaliq Mahjub (Abdel Khalig Mahgoub).

8. Mahmood Mamdani's article, "The Politics of Naming: Genocide, Civil War, Insurgency," first appeared in the *London Review of Books*, 8 March, 2007. Reprinted in this book (Chapter 7).

9. To be fair, starting with the late Dawood Bolad and ending with Dr. Khalil Ibrahim, many of the Darfur rebel leaders who were NIF members have renounced their earlier positions vis-à-vis the South and issues of marginalization in general.

10. See Alex de Waal, "Who Are the Darfurians? Arab and African Identities, Violence, and External Engagement," *African Affairs* 104, no. 415 (2005):181–205. Reprinted in this book (Chapter Six).

11. By "localities," I mean to include poor and oppressed northerners suffering from government neglect and discriminations, such as the people who suffered in the aftermath of the Kajbar Dam massacre and also in the flooded zones of Merowe Dam among other incalculable losses and dispossessions visited upon them by the state.

9 Darfur in the African Press

Carina E. Ray

The international media's coverage of the war in Darfur has often drawn attention to the gap between rhetoric and action, highlighting how governments around the world have failed to respond appropriately. Western governments have come under fire for failing to follow their loud condemnations of the Sudanese regime's brutality with meaningful action.[1] The media has also roundly condemned Arab governments for their silence on Darfur.[2] And so too have African governments and the African Union (AU) been criticized for not being more forceful in bringing an end to the Sudanese government's human rights atrocities in Darfur.[3] Indeed, at the state level, African governments, along with their counterparts in the Arab world, have rarely been forceful in their public condemnations of the Al Bashir regime's assault on Darfur. Where internal affairs are concerned, the widespread failure of governments to vigorously criticize or condemn the actions of another sovereign state is a common feature of global diplomatic practice.[4]

In the case of Africa, this tendency can be further understood as a legacy of the former Organization of African Unity's (OAU) policy of nonintervention in the internal affairs of its member states.[5] With the birth of the African Union in 2002 the organization has shifted away from its predecessor's strict noninterventionist protocol. Yet, the lingering tension between these two positions is evident in the Constitutive Act of the African Union, which simultaneously provides for the "The right of the Union to intervene in a Member State pursuant to a decision of the Assembly in respect of grave circumstances, namely war crimes, genocide and crimes against humanity," while also upholding the principle of "non-interference by any Member State in the internal affairs of another."[6] Perhaps more important than constitutive acts, however, are the diplomatic imperatives that still structure the way in which the AU goes about addressing thorny issues such as electoral fraud, human rights abuses, and civil war.[7] Accordingly, the African Union's response to the crisis in Darfur is perhaps best judged through its actions rather than the dearth of its public statements condemning the Al Bashir regime. To date the AU has been a major sponsor of several rounds of peace talks, including those held in Abuja between 2004 and 2006, and it has taken the lead in deploying peacekeeping troops to the region.

If individual African states have been quiet on the issue of Darfur for diplomatic reasons or because they believe the African Union is better suited to deal with the issue, a different picture emerges when looking at the African press. Just as it is widely acknowledged that the press in America and Europe has forcefully kept Darfur on the international agenda, so too has the African press kept the issue of Darfur alive. Since the first major escalation of the war in 2004, African newspapers have increasingly featured news and commentary on Darfur. Indeed, Africans all over the continent have been writing and reading about Darfur on a regular and increasingly frequent basis. This essay analyzes how Darfur has been discussed and represented in various African newspapers and what the African press can tell us about African understandings, opinions, and concerns in relation to Darfur. It draws on this analysis to highlight the differences and similarities in the reportage on Darfur within Africa and between Africa, on one hand, and Europe and America, on the other hand.

First, a word about methodology is in order. A wide cross-section of English-language newspapers was searched by using the Factiva search engine, which culled the allAfrica database for newspaper articles with the single word *Darfur* in them. AllAfrica Global Media, a multimedia content service provider, is the largest electronic distributor of African news and information worldwide. Its website, allAfrica.com, posts more than one thousand stories daily in English and French and has a massive searchable archive, which includes the Africa News Service's archive dating from 1997. AllAfrica is partnered with more than 130 African news organizations; hence using their database was the most effective way of searching African newspapers. Here it is important to note, in allAfrica's own words, that its content providers "include government and opposition-controlled newspapers, as well as the growing number of independent, professional news publications across the continent."[8] As such, using this particular database had the built-in advantage of being able to search a wide cross-section of differently oriented news sources. A caveat to this is that they publish articles exclusively in English and French; the search undertaken in preparation for this article was limited to English-language articles. Moreover, not all major African newspapers are partnered with allAfrica – for instance, the prominent English-language Egyptian newspaper *Al Ahram Weekly* is not featured in their database, which made it necessary to search *Al Ahram Weekly's* database separately.[9] Finally, it must be noted that with the exception of *Al Ahram Weekly*, restricting my search to English-language newspapers available through the allAfrica database necessarily leaves out a range of different perspectives. The Arabic- and French-language African press, as well as the multitude of newspapers that are published in various African languages along with other English-language newspapers not partnered with allAfrica, would certainly yield a broader and more diverse picture than the one I will sketch herein. While both time constraints and language limitations necessitated limiting my research in this way, the sources I was able to review were nonetheless rich and varied enough to substantiate the consistent and impassioned, if at times problematic, ways in which Africans across the continent have engaged the question of Darfur. Indeed, the search turned up more than 1,500 articles published between early 2004 and December 2007 in African (English-language) newspapers. These articles range from coverage of the war itself and events related to the war to local, national, and international responses to the war as well as commentary pieces, including editorials and opinion pieces. In addition, many of these newspapers published essays and analytical pieces on Darfur written by scholars, activists, and political figures from within and outside the African continent.

Several major themes are readily discernable in the reportage on Darfur appearing in the African press. The dominant thread is the tendency to report on issues that are linked to national interests; as a result, Darfur features most prominently in newspapers in countries like Nigeria and Rwanda, which have been directly involved in peacekeeping efforts in Darfur. This of course is not unusual, given that newspapers tend to prioritize news of local importance. One can also see a pattern of reportage based on both national and regional interests in Egypt's *Al Ahram Weekly* newspaper. The proximity of Egypt to Sudan, the historical linkages, and the important political and security ties between the two countries help to explain why Darfur has featured so prominently in this newspaper.

A second theme running through the reportage was the tendency to report on the violence in an oversimplified racialized way that often reveals an anti-Arab bias. Very few reports addressed the complex identity politics at work in the violence, and in this way mirrored much of the reportage in Western news sources. In fact, it was only in commentary and analysis pieces that one could find attention being paid to the Darfur region's complicated identity politics, as well as to the politics behind the violence and the way it has been constructed as "Arab" against "Black African." Third, the war in Darfur is typically reported on in isolation from the larger crisis of governance in Sudan, which includes the ruling government's strategy of marginalization as well as the glass ceiling for power sharing that was created by the recently negotiated 2005 Comprehensive Peace Agreement (CPA), which brought an end to the long-standing North–South civil war, but is itself now in peril. A final trend that deserves attention is the stark absence of reportage on the particularly devastating effect the war is having on women. The widespread rape of women and other forms of gender-based violence, which have become a chronic feature of the attacks on civilian populations in Darfur, are generally mentioned only in passing to describe the violence rather than to analyze it. Indeed, search results only turned up four substantive articles on sexual violence against women in the context of the conflict in Darfur. This contrasts sharply with Western reportage, which, dating back to 2004, has drawn attention to the way in which sexual assault against women and girls has become an integral component of the violence associated with the war.[10]

An analysis of these four major trends forms the first part of this essay. Commentary and analysis pieces are examined in the second half of the essay in order to highlight and evaluate the wide range of African opinions on the Darfur crisis. While an array of topics has been covered in the editorial and opinion pages of various African newspapers, several issues in particular were the subjects of lively debate. These include AU action/inaction on Darfur; the pros and cons of African peacekeeping efforts and the advisability of deploying an AU/UN hybrid force; and the racial and geopolitics behind the conflict. Finally, it should be noted that inasmuch as this essay is intended to give an overview of Darfur in the African press, it is also intended to be a resource for those who are interested in looking at the coverage themselves. Accordingly, I have provided extensive citations in the endnotes for articles that correspond to the various themes I discuss in the text.

Part One: Covering Darfur in Nigeria, Rwanda, Ethiopia, and Egypt

English-language newspapers from Nigeria, Rwanda, Ethiopia, and Egypt featured the most extensive coverage of the war in Darfur. Each of these countries has a specific set of ties to the conflict in Darfur in particular or to Sudan more generally and this factor likely accounts for the more frequent domestic coverage given to war.

Darfur features prominently in the surveyed Nigerian newspapers largely as the result of two main factors: the peace talks held in the Nigerian capital, Abuja, between 2004 and 2006 and the deployment of Nigerian troops as part of the AU peacekeeping force. In addition to being one of Africa's largest countries, Nigeria is the continent's most populous nation and has a large newspaper industry, both in print and online, fuelled by thousands of on-the-ground reporters. Papers such as the *Vanguard* (popular Lagos-based Nigerian daily), *This Day* (Nigeria's Lagos-based major independent daily), and *Daily Trust* (Abuja-based, nationwide, daily newspaper), in addition to others, reported regularly on the progress of the Abuja peace talks, paying particularly close attention to the breakthrough moments when various security and humanitarian protocols were signed, as well as reporting on all related public statements made by former President Obasanjo, who was not only in power during the duration of the Abuja peace talks, but was also chairman of the African Union for part of the talks.[11] Obasanjo's role in the peace talks as a mediator between the Justice and Equality Movement (JEM), Sudan Liberation Movement/Army (SLM/A) and the government of Sudan was often highlighted.[12]

Nigerian newspapers have also followed closely the deployment of Nigerian troops to Darfur, as well as the appointment and progress of the former Nigerian Chief of Defence Staff, General Martin Luther Agwai, as the commander of the joint UN/AU peacekeeping force in Darfur.[13] A spike in coverage occurred in early October 2007 when seven Nigerian peacekeepers (along with five other African peacekeepers) were killed in an attack on an AU army base in Haskanita.[14] In addition to reporting on the attack itself, local newspapers covered the contentious senate debates that followed the attack in which Nigeria's role as a provider of peacekeepers was scrutinized.[15] This was followed by a spate of articles covering the deployment of more Nigerian troops in the wake of the strike on Haskanita; all of the articles emphasized that Nigeria's commitment to ending the conflict in Darfur had not been diminished by the violence.[16] It is worth noting here that in countries like Botswana, where reportage on Darfur was comparatively scant, an event such as the attack on the AU base was reported on because one of the peacekeepers killed was a member of the Botswana Defence Force (BDF).[17] Returning to Nigeria, reportage based on national interest issues can also be seen in articles such as a December 2004 *This Day* article that reported on the possible threat to the Nigerian economy posed by the influx of refugees from Darfur into the country and a September 2007 article in the *Vanguard* that reported on the pressure being applied by Nigerian nongovernmental organizations on the government to unequivocally condemn the violence in Darfur.[18]

While beyond the scope of this paper, there are two points of comparison that could yield interesting insights into how Darfur plays out in the Nigerian press. The first would be to compare the privately owned dailies that I surveyed with state-owned papers, such as the *Daily Times* and *New Nigerian*, neither of which are searchable through the allAfrica database. Given the government's leading role in trying to resolve the crisis in Darfur, did state-owned newspapers downplay the stalled negotiations that characterized the Abuja peace talks? Were they more reluctant to publicize the fatal attack on Haskanita, along with the contentious senate debates that followed it and the subsequent troop deployments to Darfur? Second, given that northern Nigeria is predominantly Muslim and has closer ties with Sudan and Darfur because of Islam and linked migration patterns, did the coverage in the region's Hausa-language newspapers reflect these connections and differ considerably from the Lagos and Abuja-based English-language newspapers that were surveyed? This question serves as an important reminder that we must bear in mind how geography and the location of newspapers within individual African countries and their proximity to Sudan shape their coverage on Darfur.

Rwanda's first daily paper, *The New Times*, was the only Rwandan English-language newspaper that was searchable through the allAfrica database. The paper was established in 1995, a year after the 1994 genocide, and while it is privately owned, it is printed by the *Office Rwandais d'Information*, the country's public media parastatal, and in effect functions as a state-run paper. Moreover, the Rwandan government, under Paul Kagame's leadership, is regarded as severely restricting press freedom.[19] Thus, *The New Times*'s coverage of Darfur must be situated within the context of its relationship with the Rwandan state and the Rwandan state's contentious attitude toward press freedom. As was the case with newspapers in Nigeria, *The New Times* focused its attention primarily on Rwanda's involvement in efforts to bring an end to the Darfur crisis. It reported almost exclusively on the deployment of troops from the Rwanda Defense Forces (RDF) to Darfur, which dates back to 2004, when Rwanda along with Nigeria were the first to pledge soldiers for the AU's peacekeeping mission.[20] Over the years, as the number of Rwandan troops rose to approximately 2,500, coverage has become more intense and has often praised the performance of Rwandan peacekeepers.[21] Coverage has also scrutinized the obstacles that RDF troops have faced as a result of logistical problems within the AU mission, as well as other dangers.[22] Similar to the way in which the attack on AU forces in Haskanita prompted a spike in coverage in the Nigerian press, the deaths of RDF peacekeepers in Darfur have been widely reported on in Rwanda.[23] Notably, the 1994 Rwandan genocide rarely featured as a backdrop to the reportage on the war in Darfur and Rwanda's extensive involvement in the AU and AU/UN peacekeeping missions.[24]

The Ethiopian newspapers surveyed fall outside of the trend of reporting on Darfur as it relates to issues of domestic national interest. Rather, the extensive reportage on Darfur in the English-language Ethiopian press appears to be the result of the location of the African Union's headquarters in Addis Ababa. Papers such as the *Addis Tribune* and *Daily Monitor* (both privately owned papers published in Addis Ababa) as well as the government-owned *Ethioipian Herald* reported on significant developments in the AU's handling of the conflict.[25] As such, the reportage tended to be about political, military, and diplomatic initiatives within the African Union and between the African Union and other international actors, rather than about events on the ground in Darfur, or about the intersection between Darfur and Ethiopian domestic national interests, as was the case in Nigeria and Rwanda.[26] For those familiar with the complex and intense nature of Ethiopian–Sudanese relations, this trend in the reportage on Darfur will likely be perplexing because Ethiopia's interests have always been closely tied to Sudan and it has been a major player in Sudanese conflicts, just as Sudan has been major a player in inter-Ethiopian and Ethiopian–Eritrean conflicts. Besides being weary of the Islamist agenda inside

Sudan and the role it could play in spreading Islamic fundamentalism in the region, Ethiopia is undoubtedly worried about Eritrea's influence on the Darfur liberation movements, several of which have at one time or another been headquartered in Asmara. Given Ethiopia's very real domestic national interests in Sudan, how can we explain the paucity of coverage on the Darfur crisis outside the AU paradigm? The first and most obvious answer is that only a fraction of the Ethiopian press was surveyed for this essay. Perhaps other English-language newspapers not included in the allAfrica database had more to say about the crisis in Darfur in relationship to Ethiopian national interests. Amharic-language newspapers might have been more revealing, and perhaps more critical on this account as well. The second possible answer is that increasingly draconian restrictions on the freedom of the press in Ethiopia may account for why reportage is typically limited to the AU's Darfur-related activities.[27] English-language private dailies and Amharic-language papers, like the *Addis Zemen*, might offer more critical perspectives on these issues were it not for the fact that the Ethiopian government has relentlessly retaliated against those among them that have been critical of the government.

As indicated in the introduction, the allAfrica database does not include any Egyptian newspapers, and more generally only contains a few newspapers from other North African countries. There are, however, several English-language newspapers published in Egypt, including *Daily News Egypt* (Egypt's only independent English-language daily newspaper), *Egyptian Gazette* (the Middle East's oldest English-language newspaper, published in Cairo), and *Al-Ahram Weekly* (government-affiliated leading Egyptian newspaper). While the *Egyptian Gazette* was not searchable, both the *Daily News Egypt* and *Al-Ahram Weekly* have online searchable databases, which yielded considerable coverage on the crisis in Darfur and Egyptian as well as international efforts to address the problem. Of the two papers, *Al-Ahram Weekly* offered the most sophisticated and in-depth analysis of the crisis; in fact, *Al-Ahram Weekly* offered the most comprehensive, consistent, and nuanced coverage of all the reviewed English-language African newspapers. This is in large part due to *Al-Ahram*'s Gamal Nkrumah, who reported on the full scope of Darfur-related events, as they pertained to Sudan itself, to Egypt, to Africa, and the world. In this sense, *Al-Ahram*'s coverage also departed from the pattern visible in other countries, such as Rwanda and Nigeria, where national interests primarily drove Darfur-related news.

Nkrumah was one of the earliest journalists on the continent to signal that while the Comprehensive Peace Agreement (CPA), which brokered an end to the long-running North/South civil war, was finally nearing consolidation, tensions in Darfur were reaching their breaking point.[28] Since 2003, Nkrumah has followed events in Darfur closely and has provided the most holistic reportage as he has consistently framed the conflict within the larger context of the crisis of governance in Sudan and the government's relentless campaign of marginalization.[29] In addition to covering the major diplomatic initiatives to bring the crisis to an end, Nkrumah, along with other *Al Ahram* contributors, has also provided readers with a sense of the lived realities of Darfurians themselves.[30] Nkrumah's reporting is characterized by balanced yet critical assessments of the major players, and his familiarity with Sudan's history; internal, regional, and international politics; and developments within the various rebel movements set him apart as the most authoritative journalistic voice on Darfur.[31] Here it is worth noting that Nkrumah, the son of Pan-African giant and Ghana's independence leader, Kwame Nkrumah, and an Egyptian woman, Fathia Nkrumah, has a particularly unique vantage point from which he reports on African affairs. In the same way that his parent's marital union was meant to symbolize the unity of Africa and to transcend the so-called Arab–African divide, Nkrumah brings a holistic approach to his reportage on Africa. There are perhaps few others outside Sudan that can understand the complex identity politics at work in the Darfur crisis better than Nkrumah. Additionally, because his familiarity with Sudan predates the war in Darfur he has a far more substantial framework for analyzing recent events than most journalists. Fortunately, for those interested in a firsthand review of Nkrumah's reportage, the *Al-Ahram Weekly's* web-based archive contains all of Nkrumah's articles on Darfur dating back to the outbreak of the conflict in 2003.

The second major theme coming out of the reportage on Darfur in African newspapers is the tendency to describe the conflict in oversimplified racialized terms that reveal an anti-Arab bias, often constructing Darfur's so-called Arabs as foreigners. Other essays in this volume unpack the complex identity politics involved in the conflict and how the "politics of naming" have been mobilized from within and from outside; the point here is to highlight the way in which this complexity has been largely reduced, in the pages of many African newspapers, to a narrative of good versus evil/African versus Arab by drawing attention to the language used to describe the war. Strikingly, the racial labels that have been used to demarcate the fault lines in this conflict are often the same as those used by the Western media.

Typical of much of the reportage on the violence in Darfur is the following description found in a 2004 *New Vision* (government-owned daily newspaper in Uganda) article: "... thousands have been killed and more than a million *black Africans* have fled attacks by *Arab militiamen* [emphasis added]."[32] While the article's focus is on various AU, UN, and U.S. pronouncements on Darfur, the only causal factor given to explain the violence is racial difference. This point is reiterated later when we are informed that "U.N. officials and human rights groups have accused Sudan of backing the *Arab militias*, engaged in a campaign to expel *African farmers* [emphasis added]."[33] Given the absence of any other explanatory tools for understanding the multiple sources of the violence, and most especially (as others have already pointed out elsewhere in this volume) the central government's long-standing practices of marginalization, underdevelopment, and neglect of its "peripheries," the reader is left to conclude that what is occurring in Darfur is a race war perpetrated by "Arabs" against "black Africans." Racial antipathy is therefore posited as the reason why groups that historically lived, traded, intermarried, and interacted with one another, for the most part, in a synergistic fashion are now in the midst of a deadly war. Ironically, this dichotomy, which implicitly relies on the old trope of a geographically-cum-racially divided Africa (Northern Africa/Sub-Saharan or Black Africa), is being used to describe a conflict in the African country that perhaps best defies, indeed obliterates, the idea of two distinct Africas. This should not be taken as a denial of Sudan's heterogeneity. After all, it is one of Africa's most linguistically, religiously, ethnically, and racially diverse countries; rather, it is precisely this intense heterogeneity that flies in the face of the idea that Sudan is inhabited by two distinct geographically bounded racial groups.[34]

What is all the more striking about the application of this formulation to Darfur is that it absolves the government of its leading role in the conflict. Khartoum is regarded as a supporting actor: "backing" Arab militias, but not directing them. For instance, an article in Nigeria's *Daily Champion* argued that Darfur would not be in such a "grim situation" had the Sudanese government "not given full support to the Arab militias called the janjaweed [*sic*], who have taken free rein to rape, rob and kill the black Africans ..."[35] This places the cart before the horse. Accordingly, the government is often accused of not doing enough to reel in the renegade *Janjawid*, instead of being held responsible for empowering and financing the Janjawid to do its bidding in Darfur.[36] Indicative of the preoccupation with the Janjawid at the expense of holding the government accountable for the totality of its devastating actions is the fact that the government's use of its own officially recognized troops and military equipment in perpetrating the violence is rarely mentioned.[37]

With regard to the anti-Arab tone of much of the reportage in the Lagos and Abuja-based Nigerian newspapers surveyed, it may be helpful to contextualize this trend within Nigeria's own internal religious tensions. The division between Muslims and Christians has long been a marker of national politics in Nigeria and it is not inconceivable that the tone of reportage in the predominantly Christian south, as well as the demographically more balanced middle belt, reflects local anxieties about the continued growth of Islam within Nigeria. It would almost seem as though the contours of the deadly violence that has characterized clashes between Christians and Muslims in Nigeria is being mapped onto the conflict in Darfur, with Nigeria's Christian population being represented by Darfur's so-called Black Africans and Nigeria's Muslim population represented by Darfur's so-called Arabs. The racialization of the war, which is so apparent in the language used to describe the conflict, enables this transference because it elides the fact that in reality both parties involved in the conflict are Muslim.

In short, the de facto reliance on "Arab versus Black African" as the basis for understanding the fault lines of the conflict is reflective of the profoundly reductive nature of much of the reportage on Darfur and what amounts to an almost willful denial of the relationships and overlaps between Darfur's so-called Arabs and Africans.[38] Indeed, "Arab" and "African" are falsely constructed as mutually exclusive categories – once someone is labeled "Arab" he/she ceases being African and vice versa. Based on this formulation there is, moreover, almost no recognition of "Arab" indigenity; rather, those who are defined as "Arab" are conceptually relegated to being permanent outsiders and usurpers of the land, while those labeled "African" are conceptually defined by a static and timeless rendering of history in which their ties to the land are primordial rather than shaped by patterns of migration, state building, and ecological change. One need only look at photos of the so-called Arab Janjawid and the so-called Black African rebels to see how these categories cloud rather than clarify our understanding of how identity factors into the war in Darfur. The deceptive power of these labels is made possible, simultaneously, by the fallacy of race and the steadfastness with which people invest in racial categories as explanatory tools. Yet, we must also acknowledge the very real role that local actors have played in the internal racialization of this conflict. The government has both invoked and evoked Arab supremacy in its efforts to garner regional support and to mobilize the Janjawid to carry out its dirty war. Members of the Janjawid, for a number of different reasons outlined elsewhere in this volume, have willingly bought into this ideology as a means of securing their own interests in a time of increased competition over diminishing resources. So too has the Africanization of Darfurian identities among the rebel movements and their citizenry emerged as a powerful means of coalition building within Sudan, especially among the SPLM/A and its broad base of supporters. It has also been an effective strategy for eliciting support within Africa and from the international community in the context of the current conflict. Beyond this, however, we must ask about the wider political agendas that are being promoted through the constant deployment of such problematic and obfuscating categories as the primary lens through which the violence is explained. Fortunately, many of the essays in this volume shed light on this question, including those by Munzoul Assal, Salah Hassan, Mahmood Mamdani, and Alex de Waal.

The third major theme that emerges from a reading of African newspapers' reportage on Darfur is the tendency to analyze and report on the war in isolation from other important and clearly interrelated factors, including the much larger crisis of governance in Sudan; central governments' long-standing strategy of marginalizing "peripheral" areas as a means of securing its own localized interests and brutally repressing those who challenge the state's power, regardless of their race, ethnicity, or religion[39]; other arenas of potential and actual armed conflict; and perhaps most importantly the ever-fragile North–South peace agreement (CPA).[40]

In many ways the isolated nature of the reportage on Darfur has much to do with the second theme discussed above. Because the conflict is often stripped of its complexity and presented at its most basic level as a "race war" it is typically reported on as a local phenomenon, which is delinked from larger national issues.[41] As indicated earlier, the center only comes in as a factor in much of the reportage as a support apparatus to the Janjawid, rather than the other way around.

The fourth theme that stood out was the way in which many reports glossed over the rampant sexual violence against women in the context of the war in Darfur, which has formed an integral part of the politics of fear and the regime of violence against civilians in the wake of the 2003 rebellion. Other contributions to this volume, especially those by Fahima Hashim and Adrienne Fricke and Amira Khair, shed light on the extent of gender-based violence and why it has been so difficult for survivors of sexual violence to seek justice. The point to be made here is that widespread rape and other forms of gender-based violence, rather than forming a subject of analysis in and of itself, appear in the press as only one category in a range of many used to index violence in Darfur. Typical of this kind of reportage was a line appearing in the *Accra Mail*, a popular Ghanaian daily newspaper, which stated, "Thousands of Africans are being killed, raped, kidnapped, bombed, displaced, starved and burnt alive."[42] While not offering more comprehensive analysis, some articles managed to specify that rape has become a weapon of war in Darfur and that women have become particularly vulnerable to sexual assault as a result of the daily activities they must undertake in order to survive, including collecting firewood and water in outlying areas.[43] Strikingly, the database searched for this article contained only four articles that substantively treated the question of rape, other forms of gender-based violence, and the plight of women as they attempt to improve their situations.[44] As indicated earlier, this contrasts sharply with the reportage on Darfur and Africa more generally in the European and American press, both of which have reported extensively on sexual violence in the context of African conflicts. While we must interrogate the Western press for its near fetishization of sexual violence in Africa, we must also ask tough questions about the reluctance of the African press to confront this very real and troubling phenomenon head on.

Part Two: Editorial and Analytical Approaches to Darfur

Darfur featured prominently in the editorial, analysis, and opinion pages of various African newspapers. It is in these articles that one begins to get a sense of the wide range of African opinions on Darfur, as well as more critical and nuanced approaches to understanding the conflict. The year 2004 witnessed the arrival of Darfur in Africa's opinion and editorial pages, with two main themes being discussed, often together: (1) the categorization of the violence in Darfur as genocide, and tied to this are the racial politics surrounding the violence; and (2) responses to African and world action/ inaction on Darfur. An excellent example of the way in which these two themes are often discussed together comes from an August 2004 opinion piece that appeared in Uganda's popular privately owned daily, *The Monitor*, under the title "It's Genocide in Darfur." Muniini K. Mulera, the article's author, expressed disbelief at the world's failure to call the violence in Darfur genocide, and paralleled this with similar debates over the use of the term *genocide* in the context of Rwanda and shortly thereafter the Democratic Republic of Congo, implicitly raising the question of why when black lives are being taken, it is not called genocide and consequently the international community fails to respond appropriately.[45]

Other opinion pieces expressed the view that the root of the violence was to be found, as one title put it, in the fact that "Bigotry Still Assaults Black Africans."[46] The most extreme example of this trend appeared in 2004 in the popular Lagos-based Nigerian daily newspaper *This Day*, under the title "Genocide in Sudan." In the course of criticizing "Black African nations" for reelecting a Sudanese government delegate to represent Africa on the U.N. Commission on Human Rights, author B.A. Akwiwu described the perpetrators of violence in Darfur as "rabid Arab militias" and "murderous Arabs," and the victims as "Black Africans." The author concluded his lament with the following assertion: "It is bad enough that the black nations have not done anything to defend their people in Sudan but that we should be locked in a cozy embrace with these Arabs who have turned our people into hunting game is soul destroying."[47] Even if other opinion pieces were less extreme in their characterizations, like much of the news reportage on Darfur, there still emerged the sense that many perceive the conflict in Darfur as being primarily motivated by anti-African racism on the part of "Arabs."[48]

Another series of editorials and opinion pieces appearing in Kenyan, Ugandan, Sierra Leonean, Botswanan, and Nigerian papers called for different forms of intervention in Darfur and critiqued the shortcomings of the various initiatives under-taken thus far. L. Muthoni Wanyeki, writing in *The East African*, a Nairobi-based business-oriented regional weekly, called for Africans to be allowed to sort out the

Darfur crisis, while also making a strident critique of international aid organizations, which by the very nature of their infrastructure and staffing policies prevent Africans from solving their own problems.[49] Representatives of the Sudanese government did not shy away from using the opinion pages in the African press to express their insistence on an all-Africa force for Darfur. In 2006, Mr. Mohammed Eisa Ismail Dahab, Sudan's Charge D'Affairs in Kampala, authored an opinion piece in Uganda's *New Vision* in which he not only decried the West's "antagonistic propaganda" against Sudan, but also lauded those African leaders who espoused the mantra of "African solutions for African problems."[50] Conversely, the veteran Sierra Leonean academic and journalist Lansana Gberie took the view that while the AU was prepared to continue deploying peacekeepers to Darfur and "steadily but quietly putting pressure on the Sudanese government" to stop the atrocities, it lacks both the "leverage of the [UN] Security Council and its permanent members" and the resources to mount an effective humanitarian intervention. Gberie, therefore, suggested that the UN "robustly back the AU in both its peace-making efforts, and its efforts to provide protection to civilians" and that a Security Council member, perhaps Britain, "should consider deploying troops alongside the AU raising the necessary donor support to sustain the entire operation."[51] In short, he argued that Darfur is a clear-cut test case for *international* (rather than just regional) intervention.

Meanwhile, writers in Botswana and Nigeria, respectively, blasted the African Union for "play[ing] the fiddle while Sudan burns" and "playing the ostrich."[52] Writing in *This Day*, Okey Ifionu criticized the African Union for neglecting to act in a timely and forceful enough manner to bring the crisis to an end. Ifionu further contended, "It took the international outrage that came in the wake of United Nation's Secretary-General's comments on Darfur [in June 2004] to arouse the African Union into the current diplomatic efforts to find a solution to the tragedy." Expressing a similar feeling of frustration in the opinion page of the Botswanan daily, *Mmegi*, Patrick Van Rensberg noted that the BBC, Colin Powell (then U.S. Secretary of State), and Kofi Annan (then UN Secretary-General) had all expressed concern over the atrocities occurring in Darfur, while the African Union had come last in line and refused to call the crisis genocide.

Three years later, in 2007, the African Union was still coming under fire for its Darfur policy decisions. Writing in Kenya's *The Nation*, Okiya Okoiti criticized the African Union for deciding to "whittle down the United Nations–AU peacekeeping operation in Darfur to an African troops–only affair." In doing so, Okoiti contended that the African Union was, in effect, doing more to protect the Al Bashir regime than the beleaguered citizens of Darfur. According to Okoiti, "Insisting on an all-African deployment, whose very limited investigative and other capabilities are well known, is their [Al Bashir's regime] way of protecting themselves."[53] If most opinion writers agreed that not enough was being done to solve the crisis in Darfur, there were a few who argued that Darfur is receiving too much attention, while other important issues have been neglected. In late 2004, Peter Mwaura argued, as the title of his opinion piece put it, that "Darfur [is] Attracting 'Undue' Attention." Mwaura contended that the nature of the Darfur conflict "lends itself well to drama-tization" and consequently attracts considerable media attention, but in the process, southern Sudan has been sorely neglected.[54] Indeed, he was one of the earliest to recognize that the prospects for peace in the south would suffer because the international community only seemed to have eyes for Darfur. Similarly, Zachary Ochieng, writing in the *East African*, warned that conflicts in the east, Kordofan, and the far north of Sudan all require attention lest they go the way of Darfur.[55] Here it should be noted that African commentators took the lead in expressing this concern – only recently has Nicolas Kristoff, *The New York Times* journalist, who has written the most extensively about Darfur in America, started to acknowledge the potentially devastating effects that the world's preoccupation with Darfur could have on South Sudan.[56]

The year 2004 witnessed some important analytical and editorial interventions in the prevailing discourse on the conflict in Darfur. Pan-Africanist scholar and activist Abdul Raheem Tajudeen published a piece entitled "The Root of Chaos in Darfur," which identified the imbalance of power within the Sudanese state and the failure of democratic governance as the primary causes of the conflict.[57] As such, Tajudeen's piece was one of the first to look holistically at the conflict. Indeed, Tajudeen extended the scope of his focus beyond the government to include the Darfur rebel movements, stating "… as we rightly criticize the Government of Sudan for abdicating its responsibility to defend all its citizens and maintain the rule of law, we should also look critically at the rebels, their promises, their actions and what alternative vision of society beyond becoming the 'new bosses' they are offering." These were sage words of advice, but unfortunately they were not heeded; the rebel factions have largely been unable to overcome their own divisions in order to unite on behalf of the Darfurian people. Finally, Tajudeen's piece was one of only two that deliberately framed the violence as Africans killing Africans, rather than Arabs killing Africans.[58] To dismiss this as an ideological outcome of his Pan-Africanism, however, would be a serious mistake, because it offers an alternative paradigm for thinking through the violence in Darfur, which is free from the politics of fear and other baggage that accompanies the label "Arab" in the post-9/11 world. Tajudeen's writing and analysis, along with that of Gamal Nkrumah discussed earlier, provide two clear examples of the important role that the personal, ideological, and political biographies of individual authors play in shaping reportage and opinion pieces on Darfur and highlight the key work that African activists, journalists, and intellectuals are doing to push back against some of the more dangerous trends that characterize how Africa is reported on in both the West and in Africa itself. Both come from a progressive political background rooted in the 1960s and 1970s tradition of Pan-Africanism, in which progressive political mobilization across the African continent transcended localized ethnic politics, was generally nonracialized, and was based on an anti-imperialist agenda that unified national and international solidarity movements.

African newspapers also welcomed analytical interventions from outside the continent. In August 2004 Alex de Waal, the noted British scholar of Darfur, published "Racism and Nature: Roots of Darfur Crisis" in Uganda's *New Vision*.[59] Therein he uncovered the complex and complicated realities, especially those related to the environment and identity politics, which have been obscured by the characterization of the Darfur war as "Arabs" versus "Africans." Importantly, de Waal provided a nuanced and differentiated analysis of the multiple Arab communities in Sudan in order to disrupt the common assumption that the Arabic-speaking nomads of Darfur are the kith and kin of Khartoum's riverian elites. De Waal also drew attention to the way in which the Darfurian rebel movements, and many of the citizens they represent, have adopted the label "African" in order to further their solidarity with the SPLM, and to tap into existing strands of Western sympathy.

If many of the opinion, analysis, and editorial pieces cited here appeared during 2004, when the world's attention was just beginning to focus on Darfur, there has certainly been no letup since. By 2007 the number of editorials appearing in Africa's newspapers had only increased, as have the range of topics covered. These include the plight of the AU forces in Darfur;[60] the legitimacy of the AU in relationship to Darfur;[61] and the internationalization of the war with UN forces, China, and the United States increasingly taking on more prominent roles, as well as Chad and Libya's mounting investments in the war.[62] African newspapers have also continued to provide space in their editorial and opinion pages for people from outside the continent to express their concerns and thoughts.[63]

Taken as a whole, the articles reviewed in this essay, as well as all those that could not be referenced due to both space constraints and research limitations, unequivocally demonstrate that Africans have not remained silent about what is going on in Darfur. On the contrary, they have vigorously discussed and passionately written about the conflict since its inception and by all indications will continue to do so until a just and lasting resolution has been put into place. Equally so, the surveyed reportage demonstrates that the African press has not been immune to some of the pitfalls that have characterized Western reportage on Darfur, particularly as it relates to positing race as the primary causal factor of the war and reporting on the war in isolation from the larger crisis of governance in Sudan. In seeking to understand the trends in reportage on Darfur in the African press, we must bear in mind that in many countries across Africa restrictions on the freedom of the press play a significant role in determining what ends up in print. The independent press often labors under threat of closure and individual journalists are often the targets of government reprisals. Undoubtedly the underground press and the fledgling independent papers that circulate locally in various African countries would provide another set of critical vantage points from which we might think through how the war in Darfur is being read and understood by millions of Africans. And, as indicated earlier, so too would the myriad non-English-language newspapers that thrive all across Africa add additional insights into the questions posed herein. Thus, in as much as I have been able to say something about the newspapers surveyed for this essay, it is equally clear that there is much more to know.

Notes

1   London's *The Independent* online criticized Western governments for wringing "their hands in horror at the sufferings of the poor people of Darfur," while doing "practically nothing concrete to help them." Similarly a *New York Times* editorial accused the international leaders of writing the epitaphs of Darfur's embattled population with their "fine words and empty deeds." *The Boston Globe* urged its readers "to demand action to save their brothers and sisters in Darfur because nation-states have no conscience." See in respective order: "The deafening silence," *The Independent*, http://www.independent.co.uk/opinion/leading-articles/ leading-article-the-deafening-silence-794426.html, March 12, 2008; "Talking Darfur to Death," *The New York Times*, http://www.nytimes.com/2007/03/31/opinion/ 31sat1.html, March 31, 2007; "Ending the Darfur silence," *The Boston Globe*, http://www.boston.com/news/globe/editorial_opinion/ editorials/articles/2006/04/30/ending_the_darfur_silence, April 30, 2006.

2   For example see Joseph Britt, "Arab Genocide, Arab Silence," *The Washington Post* (July 13, 2005): A21; Steven Stalinsky, "The Arab Silence on Darfur," www.frontpagemag.com/Articles/Read.aspx?GUID=CF02

6FD7–6530–46F4–8891–2CF66295E617, October 21, 2005; "Arabian Shame," *The Washington Post* (August 12, 2005): A18. Gamal Nkrumah has also argued that Arab civil society organizations have responded slowly to the Darfur crisis. Gamal Nkrumah, "Dragging feet over Darfur," http://weekly.ahram.org.eg/2004/704/fr3.htm, August 19–25, 2004.

3 For example, see George Haley, Chinua Akukwe, and Sidi Jammeh, "Darfur: A Defining Moment for African Leaders," http://www.worldpress.org/Africa/1954.cfm, October 13, 2004. While the African Union is widely recognized as leading the effort to resolve the crisis, prior to the formation in 2007 of the African Union/ United Nations Hybrid operation in Darfur (UNAMID), the African Union came under fire for its pursuit of an "Africans-only solution," which did not support the deployment of non-African troops to Darfur. The United States' former assistant secretary of state for African Affairs, Susan Rice, suggested in 2005 that the African Union was reluctant to beef up its peacekeeping mission with non-African soldiers because it was fearful of "antagonizing the Sudanese government with the prospect of Western intervention." Susan Rice, "Why Darfur Can't Be Left to Africa," http://www.washingtonpost.com/wp-dyn/content/article/2005/08/05/AR2005080501988.html, August 7, 2005. Also see, Paul D. Williams, "The Crisis in Darfur: Why 'African Solutions' Are Not Enough," http://www.yes-dk.dk/YES/index.php?option=content&task=view&id=288&Itemid=173 (cited June 16, 2008).

4 There are of course exceptions to this. A notable one, in the context of Africa, is Zimbabwe, whose president, Robert Mugabe, has since the early 2000s been widely criticized by Britain and the United States. For many observers, however, Western criticism of Mugabe is cited as an example of the tendency on the part of Britain and the United States to demonize only those leaders who threaten Western interests, while those with even worst records are ignored and even embraced provided they toe the West's line.

5 *The Charter of the Organization of African Unity*, Article 3, paragraph 2. http://www.africa-union.org/root/au/Documents/Treaties/text/OAU_Charter_1963.pdf. The Arab League's original 1945 charter also stipulates that every member state "shall respect the form of government obtaining in the other States of the League... and shall pledge itself not to take any action tending to change that form." *Pact of the League of Arab States*, Article 8. U.N. doc. A/C. 6/L.111 (also in U.N. Treaty Series, vol. LXX, pp. 237–263).

6 *Constitutive Act of the African Union*, Article 4, principles G and H. http://www.africa-union.org/root/au/AboutAU/Constitutive_Act_en.htm

7 Returning to the example of Zimbabwe, its neighbors in the Southern African Development Community (SADC), and especially South Africa under the leadership of President Thabo Mbeki, have opted to pursue a policy of "quiet diplomacy" in dealing with Robert Mugabe. It has only been since the failed presidential and parliamentary elections of March 2008 that SADC members have been more forceful in their critiques of Mugabe's lack of electoral transparency and oppression of the opposition.

8 "Content Providers," http://allafrica.com/publishers.html?language=en, cited on June 26, 2008.

9 With regard to *Al Ahram Weekly* it should also be noted that its Arabic-language counterpart, known simply as *Al Ahram*, is a daily newspaper. Moreover, the content of the two papers is thought to differ widely, with the English-language edition being geared toward a more international audience, while the Arabic version is geared more specifically to an Egyptian, North African, and Middle Eastern audience. The varying contents of the two papers is often attributed to the Egyptian government's desire to control information internally, while simultaneously projecting a democratic image to the outside world. According to this theory, the English version tends to offer more critical analysis of Egyptian and other Arab governments' actions, and as such one might expect softer coverage on Darfur in the daily Arabic-language *Al Ahram* and harder coverage in the English-language *Al Ahram Weekly*. While I do not have any definitive pronouncements on this, since I am not an Arabic reader and am therefore unable to read the daily Arabic version, my sense is that the tough and consistent coverage on Darfur appearing in the *Al Ahram Weekly* is best attributed to the paper's writer who has most closely covered Darfur since 2004, Gamal Nkrumah.

10 From the BBC, alone, see the following: "UN attacks Darfur 'fear and rape,'" http://news.bbc.co.uk/2/hi/africa/3690232.stm, September 25, 2004; "UN accuses Sudan over Darfur rape," http://news.bbc.co.uk/2/hi/africa/4728231.stm, July 29, 2005. "Aid agency warns on Darfur rapes," http://news.bbc.co.uk/2/hi/africa/5280286.stm, August 24, 2006; "Women demand end to Darfur rapes," http://news.bbc.co.uk/2/hi/africa/6165017.stm, December 10, 2006; Amber Henshaw, "Sudan rape laws 'need overhaul,'" http://news.bbc.co.uk/2/hi/africa/6252620.stm, June 29, 2007.

11 For Nigeria's role as host of the Abuja peace talks, as well as the progress of the talks, see Andrew Ahiante, "Sudan: AU Meets in Abuja, Aug 23," *This Day*, August 12, 2004; "Sudan Govt, Rebls Adopt African Union Agenda for Peace," *Vanguard*, August 25, 2004; "Sudanese Parties Sign Security and Humanitarian Protocol," *Nigeria First*, November 10, 2004; Josephine Lohor, "Final Meeting on Darfur for Abuja Soon," *This Day*, May 18, 2005; "Darfur Peace Talks Resume in Abuja," *Nigeria First*, June 13, 2005; "Sudanese Govt, Darfur Rebels Sign Peace Accord in Abuja," *Nigeria First*, July 6, 2005; Jibrin Abubakar, "Darfur Peace Talks Postponed," *Daily Trust*, August 25, 2005; "Sudanese Officials, Darfur Rebels in Talks," *Business Day*, October 4, 2005; Elkanah Chawai, "Darfur: How Far Can Abuja Talks Go?," *Daily Trust*, October 10, 2005; Iyefu Adoba, "Darfur: Peace Talks Kick off with Consultations in Abuja," *This Day*, October 23, 2004; "Darfur: Parties Unite on Peace Resolution," *Daily Trust*, December 1, 2005; Charles Onunaiju, "Darfur Talks: Commission on Power Sharing Holds First Session," *Daily Trust*, December 2, 2005. On Obasanjo and Darfur see, Abiodun Adelaja and Lere Ojedokun, "AU'll Resolve Darfur Crisis – President," *Daily Champion*, August 18, 2004; "Darfur Peace Talks: Obasanjo Urges Cooperation," *Nigeria First*, September 15, 2004; Lere Ojedokun, "EU Team Visits Obasanjo over Darfur Crisis," *Daily Champion*, October 16, 2004; "Obasanjo in Libya for Darfur Talks," *Nigeria First*, October 19, 2004; "Obasanjo Hopeful on Resolution of Sudan Conflict," *Nigeria First*, November 22, 2004; Charles Ozoemena and Habib Yacoob, "Sudan's Peace Talks Adopt 4-Point Agenda on Darfur," *Vanguard*, August 25, 2004; "Obasanjo Confers on Darfur, Leaves for US," *Nigeria First*, December 2, 2004; "Obasanjo Tours War-Ravaged Darfur," *Nigeria First*, January 10, 2005.

12 Josephine Lohor, "Darfur: Obasanjo Meets Parties to Peace Talks," *This Day*, August 21, 2004; Kingsely Omonobi, "155 Soldiers for Darfur Peace Mission," *Vanguard*, August 31, 2004; Andrew Ahiante, "Sudan:

AU Meets in Abuja, Aug 23," *This Day*, August 12, 2004; "President Mediates at Darfur Peace Talks," *Nigeria First*, August 24, 20004; Paul Ibe, "Darfur: Confab Raises Panel to Harmonise Govt., Rebel's Position," *This Day*, August 27, 2004; Josephine Lohor, "Obasanjo, El Bashir Meet to End Darfur Crises," *This Day*, July 21, 2006.

[13] See, for example, Kola Ologbondiyan, "Darfur: Senate Okays Obasanjo's Troops Deployment," *This Day*, August 20, 2004; Nnamdi Duru, "Nigerian Troops Leave for Sudan," *This Day*, August 31, 2004; Olawale Olaleye, "Darfur – 'Nigerian Soldiers Are Outstanding,'" *This Day*, November 5, 2007; On Agwai and the joint AU/UN force see, "UN Okays Hybrid Force for Darfur," *This Day*, November 17, 2006; "Agwai Appointed Darfur Force Commander by AU," *This Day*, May 25, 2007; Juliana Taiwo, "Political Will Panacea to Darfur Crisis – Agwai," *This Day*, September 24, 2007; Tunji Ajibade, "Darfur and Martin Agwai's Many Challenges," *Daily Trust*, September 24, 2007.

[14] See, for example, Gboyega Akinsanmi, "7 Local Soldiers Killed in Darfur," *This Day*, October 1, 2007; G. Akinsanmi, "Darfur – 10 Soldiers Missing," *This Day*, October 2, 2007; Kingsley Omonobi, "7 Soldiers Killed, 10 Missing in Darfur," *Vanguard*, October 2, 2007; Kenneth Ehigiator, "Darfur – Nwachukwu Tasks FG," *Vanguard*, October 3, 2007; Sufuyan Ojeifo and Juliana Taiwo, "Darfur – FG Sends Azazi to Assess Situation," *This Day*, October 3, 2007; Juliana Taiwo, "Darfur – Dead Soldiers for Burial Tomorrow," *This Day*, October 4, 2007; Kingsley Omonobi and Umoru Henry, "Darfur – Corpses of Slain Soldiers Arrive for Burial Today," *Vanguard*, October 5, 2007; Juliana Taiwo, "Tears as Soldiers Killed in Darfur Get Heroic Burial," *This Day*, October 6, 2007.

[15] Abdul-Rahman Abubakar, "Darfur – Senate Summons Yayale, Agwai," *Daily Trust*, October 3, 2007; Cosmas Ekpunobi, Daniel Idonor and Yabolisa Ofoka, "Tension in Senate over Darfur Killings," *Daily Champion*, October 3, 2007; Samuel Odaudu, "AU, Darfur Killing and the Price of Peace-Keeping," *Leadership*, October 15, 2007.

[16] Kenneth Ehigiator, "200 Soldiers Leave for Darfur," *Vanguard*, October 8, 2007; Chinedu Eze, "Nigeria Sends More Soldiers to Darfur," *This Day*, October 8, 2007; Chris Ochayi, "Fresh 680 Troops Leave for Darfur," *Vanguard*, October 9, 2007; Juliana Taiwo, "680 Soldiers Head for Darfur," *This Day*, October 9, 2007. For the Nigerian government's reaction to soldiers' refusal to be deployed to Darfur in the wake of the Haskanita attack, see George Oji, "Darfur – Reject Deployment, Be Sanctioned, Soldiers Warned," *This Day*, October 11, 2007.

[17] "The Darfur Crisis – BDF's Major Tiro Dies on Darfur Mission," *The Voice*, October 9, 2007. Similarly, what coverage there was of Darfur in the Botswana press tended to be dominated by the activities of the BDF vis-à-vis Darfur. See, for example, Bame Piet, "BDF to Send Troops to Darfur," *Mmegi*, February 6, 2006; Bame Piet, "Botswana to Airlift Troops to Darfur," *Mmegi*, March 15, 2006; "Change of Guard in BDF Darfur Mission," *Mmegi*, August 7, 2006.

[18] Toba Suleiman, "UNHCR Raises Alarm on Refugee Influx," *This Day*, December 14, 2004. On Nigerian NGO activism on Darfur see "IAP, Serap Task Yar'Adua on Darfur," *Vanguard*, September 15, 2007; Babajide Komolafe and Clifford Amuzuo, "Darfur – Time for AU to Act, Say Serap, IAP," *Vanguard*, September 18, 2007; "Darfur – AU, FG, Tasked on Human Rights," *This Day*, September 19, 2007; Elkanah Chawai and Idris Ahmed, "Abuja Joins in Global Rally for Darfur," *Daily Trust*, September 18, 2006; "Abuja Hosts Rally for Darfur," *This Day*, September 17, 2006.

[19] International Press Institute, "World Press Freedom Review 2007: Rwanda," http://www.freemedia.at/cms/ipi/freedom_detail.html?country=/KW0001/KW0006/KW0204/, accessed on June 23, 2008.

[20] John Bayingana, "2,000 More RDF Set for Darfur," *The New Times*, June 29, 2005; Eleneus Akanga, "More RDF Soldiers for Troubled Darfur," *The New Times*, February 13, 2006; "RDF to Send More Troops to Darfur," *The New Times*, June 18, 2006; Magnus K. Mazimpaka, "Over 600 RDF Return from Darfur," *The New Times*, February 22, 2007; Felly Kimenyi, "Brown Extols Rwanda on Growth, Darfur," *The New Times*, October 8, 2007; Felly Kimenyi, "New RDF Battalion for Darfur This Month," October 10, 2007.

[21] See, for example, Patrick Bigabo, "AU Awards Pioneer Darfur-RDF Troops," *New Times*, August 10, 2005; Patrick Bigabo, "Gen. Kabarebe Lauds RDF on Darfur," *The New Times*, October 6, 2005; Steven Baguma, "Police Hailed over Darfur Mission," *The New Times*, February 23, 2006; George Kagame, "Sudan Envoy Commends RDF in Darfur," *The New Times*, January 25, 2007; Alphonse Rutazigwa, "Senate Hails Darfur Peacekeepers," *The New Times*, July 2, 2007.

[22] See, for example, Steven Baguma, "Kabarebe Speak Out on UN Darfur Mission," *The New Times*, April 27, 2006; "RDF Could Leave Darfur," *The New Times*, September 5, 2006; James Munyaneza, "Rwanda Almost Pulled Out of Darfur," *The New Times*, December 13, 2006; James Munyaneza, "Rwanda May Withdraw from Darfur – Kagame," *The New Times*, March 14, 2007; Felly Kimenyi, "Gov't, U.S. Discuss Darfur," *The New Times*, March 17, 2007; Robert Mukombozi and Edwin Musoni, "Darfur – Worry over 'Pullout,'" *The New Times*, March 23, 2007; Robert Mukombozi, "Government, AU in Talks over Darfur," *The New Times*, May 4, 2007; James Munyaneza, "Bin Laden Calls for Jihad Against Darfur Peacekeepers," *The New Times*, October 26, 2007.

[23] Magnus K. Mazimpaka, "Another RDF Soldier Dies in Darfur," *The New Times*, April 12, 2007; Edwin Musoni, "Fallen Darfur Peacekeepers' Bodies Flown in," *The New Times*, November 1, 2007; "Fallen RDF Darfur Peacekeepers Buried," *The New Times*, November 4, 2007.

[24] For a few exceptions to this pattern see Patrick Bigabo, "Genocide in Darfur, Says Rice," *The New Times*, July 22, 2005; Gasheegu Muramila, "Govt Affirms Darfur Loyalty," *The New Times*, August 22, 2007; James Munyaneza, "General Karake Takes Up Darfur Hybrid Force Post," *The New Times*, September 17, 2007.

[25] See, for example, "PSC Adopts Communique on Darfur Crisis," *Addis Tribune*, August 13, 2004; "The Chairperson of AU Expresses Concerns over Violation of Accord," *Addis Tribune*, April 30, 2004; "Proposals Submitted for a Cease-Fire Commission," *Addis Tribune*, May 7, 2004; "Greece Gives 100,000 Euro to AU for Humanitarian Support," *Daily Monitor*, September 16, 2004; "Konare Expresses Concern over Deteriorating Situation," *Addis Tribune*, December 30, 2004; "UN Diplomats to Hold Darfur Talks with Sudan and African Union," *The Ethiopian Herald*, November 12, 2006; "Konare Appoints Darfur Force Commander," *Ethiopian Herald*, May 25, 2007; Dagnachew Teklu, "UN, AU Start Serious Consultation on Darfur Issue," *Daily Monitor*, June 12, 2007; Dagnachew Teklu, "Sudan Accepts Hybrid Force for Darfur – AU," *Daily Monitor*, June 13, 2007. Less obvious headlines, such as the *Daily Monitor's* "France Calls for Speedy Deployment of Darfur Force," on July 30, 2007, still referenced AU business taking place in Addis Ababa – this time the French Foreign Affairs Minister Bernard Kouchner met with AU Chair-

person, Alpha Konare, to discuss expediting the deployment of the hybrid AU/UN force to Darfur.

26 Exceptions to this general pattern include a December 2006 *Daily Monitor* article, which reported on a non-AU meeting between Ethiopian Prime Minister Meles Zenawi and former U.S. Secretary of State Madeleine Albright to discuss Darfur and Somalia. "Premier, Albright Hold Talks on Somalia, Darfur," *The Daily Monitor*, December 4, 2006. Also see "Emi Release 'Voices for Darfur' DVD," *The Ethiopian Herald*, September 7, 2005.

27 Committee to Protect Journalists, "Backsliders: The 10 countries where press freedom has most deteriorated," http://www.cpj.org/backsliders/index.html, May 2, 2007.

28 On this point see, "Home to roost," in which Nkrumah alerted readers to the fact that Darfur and other marginalized areas were not finding that their grievances were being adequately addressed by the central government in Khartoum and were therefore resorting to armed rebellion, following the South's lead. Gamal Nkrumah, "Home to roost," http://weekly.ahram.org.eg/2003/631/re2.htm, March 27–April 2, 2003 (Issue No. 631). Also see "Talking heads, Sudanese style," http://weekly.ahram.org.eg/2003/637/re11.htm, May 8–14, 2003 (Issue No. 637) and "Principles and Personalities," http://weekly.ahram.org.eg/2003/670/re8.htm, December 25–31, 2003 (Issue No. 670). In the following year Nkrumah again focused attention on the disparity between the progress being made on concluding the North/South civil war and the escalating violence in Darfur. See Gamal Nkrumah, "Now to Darfur," http://weekly.ahram.org.eg/2004/695/re8.htm, June 17–23, 2004 (Issue No. 695) and "Pinning hopes on peace," http://weekly.ahram.org.eg/2004/718/re7.htm, November 2–December 1, 2004 (Issue No. 718); "Darfur on the backburner," http://weekly.ahram.org.eg/2005/729/re4.htm, February 10–16, 2005 (Issue No. 729). It should be noted that in addition to Nkrumah, others writing in *Al-Ahram Weekly* also drew attention to this issue. See, Eva Dadrian, "Good and bad news," http://weekly.ahram.org.eg/2004/675/re12.htm, January 29–February 4, 2004 (Issue No. 675). So too did Kenya's leading private daily, *The Nation*, in its July 29, 2004, article, "Darfur: A Deadly Paradox."

29 See, for example, Gamal Nkrumah, "Sudan in the crucible," http://weekly.ahram.org.eg/2004/710/fr1.htm, September 30–October 6, 2004 (Issue No. 710); "Rectitude for Darfur," http://weekly.ahram.org.eg/2005/736/re6.htm, March 31–April 6, 2005 (Issue No. 736); "Clutching at Straws," http://weekly.ahram.org.eg/2006/792/re4.htm, April 27–May 3, 2006 (Issue No. 792); "Dying for Darfur," http://weekly.ahram.org.eg/2006/805/re113.htm, July 27–August 2, 2006 (Issue No. 805); "Yesterday's men and tomorrow's," http://weekly.ahram.org.eg/2005/747/re3.htm, June 16–22, 2005 (Issue No. 747); "Khartoum's bare knuckle," http://weekly.ahram.org.eg/2006/778/re9.htm, January 19–26, 2006 (Issue No. 778); "Open to Abuse," http://weekly.ahram.org.eg/2007/867/re93.htm, October 18–24, 2007 (Issue No. 867); "Sudanese spats," http://weekly.ahram.org.eg/2007/877/reg202.htm, December 27, 2007–January 2, 2008 (Issue No. 877). Nkrumah has also focused attention on the environmental degradation and competition over increasingly scarce resources that has fueled the conflict as well. See "The land question," http://weekly.ahram.org.eg/2006/794/sc21.htm, May 11–17, 2006 (Issue No. 794).

30 On Nkrumah's coverage of the diplomatic initiatives undertaken to bring an end to the crisis see: "Dateline Darfur," http://weekly.ahram.org.eg/2004/697/fr2.htm, July 1–7, 2004 (Issue No. 697); "Deadlocked,"

http://weekly.ahram.org.eg/2004/707/re6.htm, September 9–15, 2004 (Issue No. 707); "Tripoli treat," May 19–25, 2005 (Issue No. 743); "Foot-dragging forebodes Darfur peace," http://weekly.ahram.org.eg/2005/771/re8.htm, December 1–7, 2005 (Issue No. 771); "Uneasy peace," http://weekly.ahram.org.eg/2006/794/re4.htm, May 11–17, 2006 (Issue No. 794); "Who's scuttling Sirte?," November 1–7, 2007 (Issue No. 869). On the plight of Darfurians see, Ahmed Reda, "Human disaster in Darfur," http://weekly.ahram.org.eg/2004/696/re7.htm, June 24–30, 2004 (Issue No. 696); "Down and out in Darfur," http://weekly.ahram.org.eg/2004/698/re71.htm, July 8–14, 2004 (Issue No. 698); Yasmine Fathi, "To be alive," http://weekly.ahram.org.eg/2004/704/fe2.htm, August 19–25, 2004 (Issue No. 704); Gamal Nkrumah, "Testimonies: Sudan," http://weekly.ahram.org.eg/2004/723/sc20.htm, December 30, 2004 – January 5, 2005 (Issue No. 723); Gamal Nkrumah, "Here today, gone tomorrow," http://weekly.ahram.org.eg/2007/856/eg9.htm, August 2–8, 2007.

31 An excellent example of Nkrumah's command of the intricate and complex factional, local, regional, national, and international politics behind the Darfur crisis can be seen in "Sudan at the crossroads," http://weekly.ahram.org.eg/2004/713/re4.htm, October 21–27, 2004 (Issue No. 713). Along these lines, also see "The horrors of Darfur," http://weekly.ahram.org.eg/2004/698/re72.htm, July 8–4, 2004 (Issue No. 698); "Turning the tables," http://weekly.ahram.org.eg/2005/775/re182.htm, December 29, 2005 – January 4, 2006 (Issue No. 775). For Nkrumah's detailed knowledge of the major actors in the government and the rebel movements see "Winning the west," http://weekly.ahram.org.eg/2003/636/re5.htm, May 1–7, 2003 (Issue No. 636); "Talks about talks," http://weekly.ahram.org.eg/2004/678/re6.htm, February 19–24, 2004 (Issue No. 678); "Divisive Darfur," http://weekly.ahram.org.eg/2005/770/re102.htm, November 24–30, 2005 (Issue No. 770); "An unequal Sudan," http://weekly.ahram.org.eg/2006/797/re64.htm, June 1–7, 2006 (Issue No. 797); "Raging rivalries," http://weekly.ahram.org.eg/2006/804/re3.htm, July 20–26, 2006 (Issue No. 804).

32 "AU Summit Opens Today," *New Vision*, July 6, 2004.

33 *New Vision* is by no means alone in its use of these labels to describe the violence in Darfur. Other examples of the standard reliance on the Arab versus Black African (or sometimes Arab versus African) include "Sudan to Disarm Arab Militias," *This Day*, July 5, 2004; "Annan Seeks to Evade Sudan Blame," *Addis Tribune*, June 25, 2004; "Saving Darfur," *Daily Champion*, August 10, 2004. Although fewer in comparison, some articles eschewed the label "African," in favor of using the names of specific ethnic groups (i.e., Fur and Masalit). The same ethnic specificity, however, is not given to the so-called Arabs, who are either referred to as "Arab" or "Janjawid." See, for example, "Sudan Accused of 'Ethnic Cleansing,'" *The East African*, May 10, 2004.

34 An excellent example of the way in which Sudan's heterogeneous population often gets characterized as if it is bifurcated into two distinct groups (Arab and African) can be seen in the following sentence from *The East African Standard*: "Sudan, the bridge between black and Arab Africa, should lead in rewriting the historical script between the two peoples." What this fails to miss is that the historical script was rewritten long ago when Arabs and Africans in the Sudan first came into contact with one another and began inter-mixing. The idea that Sudan's "Arabs" are not "Africans"

and that its "Africans" are not also, in many cases, "Arab" is what is in need of being rewritten. Makau Mutua, "Racism at the Root of Darfur Crisis," *The East African Standard*, July 26, 2004.

[35] "Saving Darfur," *Daily Champion*, August 10, 2004. For a similar example see Sophia Morris-Jones, "Amnesty Demonstrates for Citizens in Darfur," *Ghanaian Chronicle*, September 19, 2007, wherein Morris-Jones states that the Sudanese government's "support of the Janjaweed with arms has resulted in mass killings of ethnic Africans …"

[36] There are exceptions to this general trend. For example, see "China and Darfur," *Daily Champion*, April 5, 2007, in which the author states that despite the Sudanese government's denials, its response to the SLM and JEM led rebellions "was to arm and unleash an Arab militia, a bunch of gangsters known as Janjaweed." Also see Chege Mbitiru, "Darfur the Loser as Row Rages," *The Nation*, September 11, 2006.

[37] For a rare exception to this pattern, see "Sudan Strives to Keep Darfur Pledges" (August 12, 2004) in the Namibian government–owned daily *New Era*, which specifies that raids are not only being carried out by "Arab militiamen" but also by "Sudanese forces." Indeed, the article went on to note the possibility that the Janjawid were being incorporated into the government's security forces. Also see "Sudan Accused of 'Ethnic Cleansing,'" *The East African*, May 10, 2004.

[38] For examples of the standard reliance on the Arab versus Black African (or sometimes Arab versus African) dichotomy see "Annan Seeks to Evade Sudan Blame," *Addis Tribune*, June 25, 2004; "Saving Darfur," *Daily Champion*, August 10, 2004. Although fewer in comparison, some articles eschewed the labels "Arab" and "African," replacing them respectively with "Janjawid" and the names of specific ethnic groups (i.e., Fur and Masalit). See, for example, "Sudan Accused of 'Ethnic Cleansing,'" *The East African*, May 10, 2004.

[39] While much of the reportage acknowledges that the Darfurian rebels launched their uprising in order to protest the region's marginalization, the government's response is explained in terms of racial politics, rather than also through the politics of marginalization and the kinds of brutally repressive tactics that the state has developed in order to maintain its domination over the periphery. A succinct example of this can be found in an article from *The East African Standard* in which the conflict is explained in the following way: "Rebels launched their uprising in the vast desert region in early 2003 against what they said was marginalization by the federal government. Khartoum responded by backing Arab militia to drive non-Arabs from their villages." "Army Arrests Darfur Rebels as New Peace Talks Resume," *The East African Standard*, June 13, 2005. Also see, "Festering War in Darfur," *Daily Champion*, March 10, 2006 and "China and Darfur Crisis," *Daily Champion*, April 5, 2007.

[40] For a rare example of an article that considers the relationship between the conflict in Darfur and the North–South civil war see Fred Oluoch, "How the Conflict Is Affecting Prospects of Peace in S. Sudan," *The East African*, September 15, 2004. Also see "Festering War in Darfur," *Daily Champion*, March 10, 2006, and "Darfur Peacekeeping Row Divides Sudan," *The Herald*, July 3, 2006.

[41] See, for example, "Sudan Accused of 'Ethnic Cleansing,'" *The East African*, May 10, 2004; "CPP Joins Protests Against the Murder of Africans," *Accra Mail*, July 23, 2004; Gitau Wa Njenga, "Kenyans in UK Protest over Killings," *The East African Standard*, June 1, 2004.

[42] "CPP Joins Protests Against the Murder of Africans," *Accra Mail*, July 23, 2004. For other examples of the way in which rape appears as only a category in a larger index of violence see "Sudan Accused of 'Ethnic Cleansing,'" *The East African*, May 13, 2004; Abubaker Mukose, "Sudan Bishops Decry Deaths," *New Vision*, August 30, 2004; Tony Okerafor, "Will the UN Enter Darfur," *Daily Champion*, September 8, 2006; Ambibola Akosile, "Darfur – Amnesty Urges UN on Civilians' Safety," *This Day*, November 1, 2006; Gamal Nkrumah, "Old Dogs, New Tricks," http://weekly.ahram.org.eg/2006/822/re72.htm, November 30–December 6, 2006 (Issue No. 822); Richard Goldstone, "A Dangerous Silence as Darfur Screams," *Business Day*, December 11, 2006; Dominic Odipo, "State Silence over Darfur Says a Lot About Itself," *The East African Standard*, April 2, 2007; Is'haq Modibbo Kawu, "Darfur – On the Margins of the AU Summit," *Daily Trust*, August 13, 2007; Dina Ezzat, "Conditional Solidarity," http://weekly.ahram.org.eg/2008/907/re3.htm, July 24–30, 2008 (Issue No. 907).

[43] See Bruck Shewareged, "Will the Darfur Peace Hold?," *The Reporter*, September 2, 2006; Abimbola Akosile, "Darfur – Falana Tasks FG, AU on Sanctions," *This Day*, May 2, 2007, and Sophia Morris-Jones, "Amnesty Demonstrates for Citizens in Darfur," *Ghanaian Chronicle*, September 19, 2007.

[44] Elias Biryabarema, "NGO Accuses Sudan of Darfur Rapes," *The Monitor*, July 20, 2004; "Female IDP's Raped and Beaten in Darfur," *Media Institute of Southern African*, December 9, 2004; Joyce Mulama, "Rights – Sudan: Women Boost Darfur Talks," *Inter Press Service*, December 22, 2005; Asha Hagi Elmi, et al., "Give Women of Darfur and Chad a Hearing," *East African*, September 11, 2007.

[45] Muniini K. Mulera, "It's Genocide in Darfur," *The Monitor*, August 9, 2004. Also see Oscar Kimanuka, "Darfur's Plight Is Like Rwanda's," *East African*, October 9, 2007.

[46] Kintu Nyago, "Bigotry Still Assaults Black African," *The Monitor*, August 5, 2004.

[47] B.A. Akwiwu, "Genocide in Sudan," *This Day*, May 14, 2004.

[48] See, for example, Makau Mutua, "Racism at the Root of Darfur Crisis," *The East African Standard*, July 26, 2004; Ambrose Murunga, "Darfur in Burning as We Fiddle," *The Nation*, September 16, 2006; "Ray of Light in Darfur?," *The Nation*, June 14, 2007; Okiya Okoiti, "AU Decision on Darfur Misguided," *The Nation*, August 27, 2007.

[49] L. Muthoni Wanyeki, "Yes, Let Africans Sort Out Darfur Crisis," *The East African*, August 24, 2004.

[50] Mohammed Eisa Ismail Dahab, "Darfur – Solution Must Come from Africans," *New Vision*, October 1, 2006.

[51] Lansana Gberie, "A Test Case for Humanitarian Intervention," *Concord Times*, October 1, 2004. For a similar viewpoint see Gitau Muthuma, "The Darfur Crisis: Are Accords Enough?," *The New Times*, March 14, 2005.

[52] Patrick Van Rensberg, "African Leaders Play the Fiddle While Sudan Burns," *Mmegi*, July 16, 2004, and Okey Ifionu, "Darfur as Another Blooodstain," *This Day*, August 12, 2004.

[53] Okiya Okoiti, "AU Decision on Darfur Misguided," *The Nation*, August 27, 2007. For a similar viewpoint see E. Ablorh-Odjidja, "The All African Darfur Force," *Accra Mail*, August 22, 2007 and Chege Mbitiru, "Darfur Attack Confirms Old Fears," *The Nation*, October 8, 2007.

[54] Peter Mwaura, "Darfur Attracting 'Undue' Attention," *The Nation*, November 19, 2004.

55 Zachary Ochieng, "Darfur Crisis Blanks Out Many
    Unresolved Conflicts," *East African*, August 7, 2007.
56 Abdul Raheem Tajudeen, "The Root of Chaos in Darfur,"
    New Vision, August 12, 2004.
57 The other piece was Joel Gure, "Understanding the
    Darfur Conflict," *Vanguard*, August 19, 2004.
58 Alex de Waal, "Racism and Nature: Roots of Darfur
    Crisis," *New Vision*, August 2, 2004.
59 Tunji Ajibade, "Darfur and Martin Agwai's Many
    Challenges," *Daily Trust*, September 24, 2007; Samuel
    Odaudu, "AU, Darfur and the Price of Peace-Keeping,"
    Leadership, October 15, 2007; E. Ablorh-Odjidja, "It Is
    Darfur Again and the Misery Goes On," *Accra Mail*,
    October 8, 2007; "Nigerian Soldier in Darfur," *Daily
    Champion*, October 8, 2007.
60 Tanonoka Joseph Whande, "Darfur Disgraces the
    African Union," *Mmegi*, February 26, 2007; Is'haq
    Modibbo Kawu, "Darfur – On the Margins of the
    AU Summit," *Daily Trust*, August 13, 2007; "Free
    Darfur – Or Forget About African Union," *Accra Mail*,
    August 20, 2007; "Deadly Lesson for the AU,"
    The Nation, October 1, 2007.
61 Mahmood Mamdani, "Darfur Crisis," *New Vision*, March
    19, 2007; Kenro Oshidari and Felix Bamezon, "Darfur
    Crisis Snowballing Across Central Africa," *The East
    African*, April 3, 2007; "China and Darfur Crisis," *Daily
    Champion*, April 5, 2007; "Darfur – Galvanise the Hybrid
    Force," *This Day*, June 28, 2007; "Ending Darfur Crisis,"
    The Daily Observer, July 10, 2007; Reason Wafawarova,
    "Darfur, AU and Global Politics," *The Herald*, October 31,
    2007; Fred Oluoch, "Gadaffi Blows Hot and Cold on
    Darfur Issue," *The East African*, November 12, 2007.
62 Ban Ki-Moon, "The Real Work Begins in Darfur," *The
    Reporter*, June 25, 2007; Ban Ki-Moon, "The Conflict
    in Darfur Beyond What We Think," *New Times*,
    September 19, 2007; Ban Ki-Moon, "Darfur Crisis Defies
    Easy Solutions," *The Nation*, September 20, 2007;
    John Prendergast and Colin Thomas-Jensen, "Echoes
    of Genocide in Darfur, Eastern Chad," *East African*,
    September 25, 2007.

Woman Kalmah Camp
Nyala, 2006

Man from near Bindisi Bindisi Market
Bindisi, 2006

Scene from Bindisi Market
Bindisi, 2006

Young woman Bindisi Market
Bindisi, 2006

Woman Kalmah Camp
Nyala, 2006

Section Three
Gender, War, and Violence

10 Competing Masculinities:
Probing Political Disputes as Acts of Violence against Women from Southern Sudan and Darfur

Rogaia Mustafa Abusharaf

Everyone, as a member of society, has the right to social security and is entitled to realization, through national effort and international co-operation and in accordance with the organization and resources of each state, of the economic, social, and cultural rights indispensable for his dignity and the free development of his personality.

The Universal Declaration of Human Rights (Article 22)

This essay identifies the major forces militating against the promotion of women's rights in the Sudan. These factors are intimately linked to the country's multiple political disputes, including those in Darfur and southern Sudan. The effects of political violence are elaborated through a detailed examination of women's political, economic, and cultural rights. The essay concludes by identifying the promotion of good governance and democratization as fundamental prerequisites for advancing human rights and sustainable peace in the war-torn nation.

The Sudan, Africa's largest country in area, is a territory with incredible historical and political importance. The land and its location at the crossroads of Africa and the Middle East have influenced the course of its history and politics in a dramatic fashion. The country is the birthplace of numerous ethnolinguistic groups, all with distinctive outlooks on life, culture, faith traditions, cosmology, and experiential knowledge. This remarkable variety is in itself not a cause for clash and fragmentation. However, ethnic differences coupled with widespread competition over scarce resources and systematic marginalization presented grounds for conflict and hostility rather than providing a basis for concord and tranquillity as group differences became increasingly politicized under successive military regimes.

One observer astutely pointed out that the Sudan is a country at war with itself, and in so being, it infringes upon numerous conventions, including the International Covenant on Civil and Political Rights, which declares that, "In those states in which ethnic, religious, or linguistic minorities exist, persons belonging to such minorities should not be denied the right, in community with the other members of their group, to enjoy their own culture, to profess and practice their own religion, or to use their own language."[1] Indeed, the Sudan's past and present civil wars contradict every feature set forth in this covenant, working against human rights, in general, and women's rights, in particular, in devastating ways. First, these conflicts violate the rights of indigenous people of southern Sudan and Darfur in general by undermining the functioning of their communities to live in security critical to human welfare. Second, these wars led to substantial population displacement, forcing people to flee to locations where they become subjected to laws and regulations that ignore their rights to culture and self-determination and dismiss the legitimacy and sound-ness of their indigenous associations and modes of knowing. The Qanoon El-Nizzam El-Amm, or Public Order Law, in Khartoum, for instance, is a case in point. This law has been demoralizing to displaced Sudanese people by restricting their mobility and participation in some labor-force occupations viewed illicit by the Islamic State.

In this essay, I comment on the effects of the multiple civil wars in the Sudan on women's rights from the regions of southern Sudan and Darfur. I will bring into play material gathered in various Sudanese shantytowns in order to illuminate the specificity of gender-based violence in Sudan's political disputes. I will then advance to provide particular examples on the breach of cultural, social, and economic rights in those locations. I end by highlighting the emergent sense of political subjectivity and agency among displaced women as the unintended consequences of these fierce disputes. It should be stated at the outset, however, that highlighting individual rights and self-determination, in this case, should not be understood as mere advocacy of a liberal tradition that has no roots in Sudanese society. Defenders of the liberal traditions of human rights would argue that "While we are right to be concerned about the cultural health of minority communities, this gives us insufficient reason to abandon, modify, or reinterpret liberalism. Far from being indifferent to claims of minorities, liberalism puts concern for minorities at the forefront."[2] For the purposes of this essay, pointing out the pervasive contraventions of the rights of Sudanese indigenous people problematizes and interrogates the institutionalized state power over minorities, especially defenseless populations such as displaced women from southern Sudan and Darfur.

Case 1: Southern Sudan
Elsewhere I have argued that the Sudan is a perfect illustration of an African country unable to achieve nationhood despite a successful struggle for independence. As a result, the southern Sudanese people, in general, and women, in particular, have been enduring the wrath of the longest-running civil strife in Africa's postcolonial history. A report titled "Follow the Women and the Cows," by the U.S. Committee on Refugees, stated that the death toll of southern Sudanese is larger than the combined fatalities suffered in recent wars in Bosnia, Kosovo, Chechnya, Somalia, and Algeria.[3] Since the civil war started, an estimated 1.9 million Southerners have died, 2.5 million are famine afflicted, and 350,000 crossed the borders to neighboring countries. This war continues to expose the South to widespread instability, forced capture and slavery, destruction of physical and natural environment, disturbance of cultural life and social cohesiveness, death, and displacement. Approximately four million people have been forced to flee their homes in the southern provinces of Equatoria, Bahr Elghazal, and Upper Nile. Joyce Yatta, a Christian Fujulu from Yei, explained what war displacement has meant to her:

> I arrived from Juba in 1993. I have very fond memories of prewar days and before I was forced to move. I am very sad and stressed about the thoughts of what happened to my family back home and in Khartoum. I pray that peace will come back so that we can return to our land and enjoy life in the same way as we did before war displacement.

Yatta's story resonates with the stories of millions of others and speaks forcefully to how war has undermined the rights of Sudan's indigenous peoples to live peacefully in their home villages.

Largely cast in religious terms, the conflict has embodied the ideals of Arabization and Islamization of the Sudanese populations, irrespective of their indigenous affiliations. In this regard, the war exemplified an uncompromising effort on the country to manufacture one national identity against the wishes of ethnic and religious minorities. As Michael Ignatieff argues, nationalism in this respect can be seen as "the claim that while men and women have many identities, it is the nation that provides them with their primary form of belonging."[4] According to Ali Mazrui, Arabization and Islamization have been transforming North Africans' identities since the seventeenth century. Although the effort to create one national identity is by no means recent, it was introduced in the Sudanese political scene by former President Ja'far Muhammad Numeiri and strictly enforced by Omar Al Bashir, another military commander, who came to power in 1989.

This forced assimilation process, deeply embedded in the forging of a monolithic Sudanese national identity, did not go unchallenged. "Faced with the assimilative excesses of the ruling classes in the North," writes Mansour Khalid, "the South has experimented with the entire spectrum of resistance, from a political crusade to be recognized as having their own authenticity and rights as citizens of the Sudan, to carrying arms."[5]

In diagnosing the root causes of war, some observers have suggested that British colonial policies planted the seeds of disunion in the Sudan, a country with extraordinary ethnic diversity, pitting North against South, Muslims against Christians, and Arabs against Africans. In the process, the policies enhanced the development and security of one group at the expense of another. But upon closer inspection, we find that colonial history, memories of the slave trade, unequal development, and other abuses of political, economic, and cultural rights undermined the trust upon which a peaceful environment could have been founded. To concentrate on the culpability of history, though important, not only oversimplifies the agency of violators who infringe upon conventions and rules, but also absolves them from their responsibility in shaping policies that made Sudan's civil war the longest in Africa's twentieth-century history. Colonial history notwithstanding, since the country attained its independence from Britain in 1956, millions of southern Sudanese have been left dead or displaced as competing masculinities continue to undercut human security and welfare.

Let us take a look for example at the crimes against humanity that were committed by former President Numeiri (1969–1984), whose own military record in southern Sudan in 1965, before his coming to power, not only earned him the derision of many Southerners, but also attests to egregious forms of violence against innocent civilians as evidenced in the document released by Anya-nya Movement in 1971 titled "What Nemeriy [sic] Did":

It should be noted that Major General [Ja'far Muhammad Numeiri] was the Garrison Commander in Torit. He was responsible for Eastern Equatoria that is Torit and Kapoeta Districts. Before he went to Khartoum to take the government by the usual military coup d'etat, the following villages were burnt according to his orders:

- Obira with a population of about 500
- Ilen with a population of 3000
- Galamini with a population of 300
- Oronyo with the population of about 3000
- Lohuto with a population of about 700
- Mura-Hatiha with a population of 500
- Tirrangore with a population of 1500
- Burung with a population of 200[6]

Numeiri's adoption of Islamic *shari'a* laws in September 1983 contributed significantly to the reactivation of civil war. This not only imperiled individual and collective security, which has been acknowledged in international conventions as a basic inalienable right, but also infringed on cultural, economic, and political rights deemed fundamental more than five decades ago by the United Nations in the Universal Declaration of Human Rights. Unquestionably, the devastation of the villages enumerated above should supply strong justification for bringing perpetrators like Numeiri before an international criminal tribunal. Alas, Numeiri's crimes against humanity continue to go unpunished after he received clemency from Khartoum's regime. As a young southern Sudanese student points out, "There is no accountability in the Sudan. If people like [Numeiri] are punished, others will be afraid to commit murders and steal the wealth of the country. But it seems that no one cares."

Case 2: Darfur

To the readers of Samantha Power's compelling report "Dying in Darfur: Can Ethnic Cleansing in Sudan Be Stopped?," which appeared in *The New Yorker*, history has repeated itself yet again in the most dreadful and rancorous manner.[7] Examining the Darfur crises through the lenses of a personal story of Amina Abaker Mohammed, Power illuminates the multiple ways in which the *Janjawid* ("evil horsemen") have perpetrated acts of ethnic violence and genocide against a defenseless, immobilized population. Notwithstanding, stories like those of Amina Abaker Mohammed were common among a group of a recently displaced Darfurian women in Khartoum, who reiterated trials and travails markedly similar to those noted in Power's essay, among many important reports on the crises like those of Jennifer Leaning, Amnesty International, and other local and international NGOs. For example, in the words of Asha Ali, whom I interviewed in Khartoum on August 14, 2004:

> Our situation is a real catastrophe. When the fighting started we all tried to run away with our children. The men fled after seeing others get killed and beaten by the Janjawid. These people acted like devils. They don't have good hearts. They burnt villages, attacked and kidnapped women and caused a lot of pain and misery. We fled on foot in a very difficult terrain.
>
> Now we are staying with people from home who came to Khartoum long time ago. Like us they don't have a lot, but they allowed us to stay with them in these small houses. We don't have money to buy food. We are also very

worried about work. We cannot find work since this place is very far. Now the rainy season created added problems because this area is flooded. We depend only on Allah to change our situation. Our children are in danger too. Our situation is extremely terrible. We don't know what had happened to other relatives and neighbors. We hope that they are still alive. We are also worried that we will not be able to go back. We have no hope that we will get assistance. Not in this place anyway.

These stories, which are originating from the western region of Darfur, bear witness to the worst humanitarian crises in the world today.[8] The total death toll resulting from these crises is estimated at 50,000 in the entire region. In the words of David Nabarro, head of crisis operations for the World Health Organization, "These figures are higher than those we had from East Timor, higher than the figures we had from Iraq in 1991, comparable to what we had in Rwanda in the bad times."[9] This conflict exploded in early 2003 when two main rebel groups, the Sudan Liberation Movement/Army (SLM/A) and the Justice and Equality Movement (JEM), decided to strike military installations with the intention of sending a hard-hitting message of resentment and bitterness toward the region's unremitting sociopolitical and economic exclusion and marginality. The International Crisis Group has also reported that:

> The rebels … also took arms to protect their communities against a twenty-year campaign by government-backed militias recruited among groups of Arab extraction in Darfur and Chad. These Janjawid militias have over the past year received greatly increased government support to clear civilians from areas considered disloyal. Militia attacks and a scorched-earth government offensive have led to massive displacement, indiscriminate killings, looting and mass rape, all in contravention of Common Article 3 of the 1949 Geneva Conventions that prohibits attacks on civilians.[10]

While multiple rounds of peace negotiations have been undertaken, many Darfurian refugees and internally displaced people continue to be particularly skeptical about the prospect of peace and repatriation. According to a compelling study by Suleiman Hamid, the Islamic movement, which was led by Hassan El-Turabi, perpetuated an ideology of creating an Arab-Muslim state in spite of the country's ethno-religious differences. The government reinforced this project even after El-Turabi's marginalization by continuing its mission with incredible zeal. Darfur, in light of this analysis, was seen as part and parcel of this endeavor. Therefore, the characterization of the conflict as ethnic cleansing has a particularly strong resonance as far as the targeted groups (Zaghawa, Massaleet, and Fur) are concerned.

Women's Rights to Physical Integrity
Perhaps the biggest concern that plagues women dealing with the civil war in the Sudan, as well as other ethno-religious antagonisms around the world, is the grueling abuses they face as sexed bodies. Catherine MacKinnon sees the underlying principle behind this glaring lapse as follows:

What is done to women is either too specific to women to be seen as human or too generic to human beings to be seen as specific to women. Atrocities committed against women are either too human to fit the notion of female or too female to fit the notion of human. "Human" and "female" are mutually exclusive by definition; you cannot be a woman and a human being at the same time.[11]

Although displacement is harrowing for everyone involved, it is far worse for women and girls who are the most likely victims of sexual violence and torture, as the Darfur crisis makes abundantly clear. Displaced women are confronted with sexual violence experienced before, during, and after flight and arrival in new communities and are left to deal with significant physical and psychological effects of this victimization. Christina Dudu, a displaced Southern woman living in Khartoum, outlined the gendered forms of exploitation that accompanied the mass flight of women and girls, but were absent at home in the South before the renewal of the civil war, including sexual abuse, prostitution, and harassment.[12] This wide constellation of sexual abuses contravenes the right to bodily integrity as a fundamental right, which includes sexual and reproductive rights. These rights signify the capability of women and men to exert control over matters concerning their sexuality and reproductive freedom. Alas, these entitlements have proved to be the most widely violated rights during wartime.

Consider the striking similarities in two reports released by Amnesty International on the topic of rape and other violence against women during the civil war in Sudan and during the Darfur crisis, respectively. The first report on South Sudan covered the period of January to December 2000 and stated that:

Violence against women by combatants on all sides, long a feature of the conflict in Sudan, intensified during the year. There were widespread reports of sexual abuse, including sexual slavery, rape and forced pregnancies. Rape was used as a tactic of war by both government and opposition forces to dehumanize and humiliate civilians in the conflict zone. However, because of the taboos and stigma attached to rape, reports were rare and impunity for the rapist was the rule.[13]

Contrast this report with a 2004 statement regarding sexual violence against women in Darfur. This statement is based on testimonies from refugee women in Chad in the camps of Goz Amer, Kounoungo, and Mile:

The organization was able to collect the names of 250 women who have been raped in the context of the conflict in Darfur and to collect information concerning an estimated 250 further rapes. This information was collected from testimonies of individuals who represent only a fragment of those displaced by the conflict. Other human rights violations which have significantly targeted women and girls are: abductions, sexual slavery, torture and forced displacement.[14]

The violation of women's rights to bodily and sexual integrity is compounded by the victims' reluctance to report rape for fear of shame and community ostracism. What makes rape an exceptionally alarming affront are the widely held beliefs regarding sex and sexuality in the region. Attitudes toward sexuality and reproduction are positioned at the heart of significant cultural and religious beliefs among the Sudanese. Open discussion of matters pertaining to sexuality is extremely proscribed by these beliefs. To a great extent, this interdiction is intimately linked to how society views sexuality in the first place: It is largely seen as an ominous threat that looms largely over one's purity and morality if left unchecked. As a result, social and physical regulation of sexuality is aggressively pursued.

Among large segments of Darfur populations, female circumcision is one of the most important vehicles for dulling women's sexuality. Violations of these taboos embody an insult on the community's codes of morality and honor, a factor that produces significant fears of speaking about and reporting rape crimes. A displaced woman echoed this fear when she explained the situation to me:

> Many women who have been attacked and raped are afraid to report the incidents. When we were talking about this issue, some people said el-kalam da aib, this talk is shameful. That is why many preferred to suffer in silence. We are a religious people and this crime has brought dishonor and humiliation. It could have been better to kill than to rape. Our only hope is that Allah will punish the criminals.

Closely linked to the abuses of women's bodily integrity is the violations of their rights to health as they become exposed to HIV/AIDS and other STDs, among other diseases. It is therefore imperative that the international community should urge state and nonstate actors to investigate the full extent of the infringements on women's right to physical integrity and health.

Cultural Rights

One of the most salient features of Arabization and Islamization is embodied in what came to be known as the Public Order Law, or El-Nizam El-Aam, for Khartoum State of 1996. This law, which is emblematic of the politicization of ethno-religious identities, is also an authoritative commentary on the status of "minority cultures" of people living under Shari'a. This law was passed by the government to curb practices that government officials labeled as "un-Islamic." Those who do not comply with its codes were brought to court. This law, which is extensive in scope, deals with a wide range of issues. It limits the length and duration of wedding parties. It affects women's employment and Islamic dress, or *hijab*. It mandates gender segregation on public transportation.[15] The law even prohibits people from bathing naked or half-naked in the Nile, a practice accepted by previous governments.

To ensure the enforcement of this law, the government expanded the Criminal Procedures Act of 1991 and vested the Supreme Court, Courts of Appeal, General Criminal Courts, and People's Criminal Courts with full authority to imprison, fine, whip, confiscate, and enforce any punishment they see fit on noncompliants. The law was hailed as the right arm of Arabization and Islamization. Indeed its infringement on the rights on religious and ethnic minorities did not seem to warrant its modification. According to a report put out by the Sudan Council of Churches Unit of Advocacy and Communication, "The Public Order Police are not bound by any geographical jurisdiction. Any of the units may make a campaign of searches kasha in any place even if it falls within a jurisdiction of another unit. This makes it very difficult to know the jurisdiction to which the arrested persons are taken." The report points out that the targets of the Public Order Police are primarily displaced persons, especially women held by authorities in Omdurman Women Prison for charges ranging from prostitution to alcohol brewing, the latter made a crime under the law. The law also made Islamic dress mandatory among women irrespective of their religious affiliation.

As Susan Sered correctly argues, this imposition reflects the thinking of "[an] authoritarian institution with a large stake in women's bodies."[16] Emelide Kiden, a 45-year-old Kuku Christian from Bahr-El-Jebel, told me: "I came to Khartoum in 1995. Ever since I was not able to wear my traditional dress and I felt forced by law to cover my whole body. I am also afraid to brew." Other women echo the same sentiments. For many, alcohol brewing is about a way of making a living, and has many uses in numerous ceremonial practices, ranging from birth to marriage to death.

Cultural rights, as numerous conversations with displaced women have demonstrated, are among the most obvious casualties of war. The link between cultural rights and human rights was strengthened through the 1966 International Covenant on Economic, Social, and Cultural Rights, although the covenant does not attempt to define cultural rights, per se. The covenant's preamble recognizes that the "ideal of free human beings enjoying freedom from fear and want can only be achieved if conditions are created whereby everyone may enjoy his economic, social, and cultural rights, as well as his civil and political rights." Boutros Boutros-Ghali argued, "By the right of an individual to culture, it is to be understood that every man (or woman) has the right to access to knowledge, to the arts and literatures of all peoples, to take part in scientific advancement and to enjoy its benefits, to make his (or her) contribution toward the enrichment of cultural life."[17]

As can be expected during war, human distress multiplies and takes on different forms of individual and collective trauma. Selfhood and personhood also undergo dramatic shifts. Since personhood is a highly differentiated experience, the systematic destruction of a community's physical safety and cultural life intersected to strike at its foundations in profound ways. The loss of community has meant that people are reconsidered afresh. Everyday experience, which emerges from dislocation, prompts a serious deliberation of the dialectal relationship between person and community and self and the world in roundabout ways. The sense of solidarity and the fear of losing it were explained in Francis Deng's analysis of attitudes toward moving away from home: "To a Dinka, his country, with all its deprivations and troubles, is the best in the world. Until very recently, going to foreign lands was not only a rarity, but also a shame. For a Dinka, to threaten his relatives of leaving Dinkaland, was seen as little short of suicide. What a lot to give up, and for what?"[18] In the context of war, violence, and forced migration, assimilation into the Arabo-Islamic practices of host communities in the North means annihilation of an "unambiguously" African world that is itself far from monolithic.

Section Three: Gender, War, and Violence

The effect of war on self-perception and sense of security is distilled in Eisenbrush's notion of "cultural bereavement." This bereavement is attributed to the loss of shelter as well as vanishing security. Eisenbruch's notion of bereavement receives ample validation from the testimony of Theodora Poni, a Kuku Christian from Equatoria, who has lived in Khartoum since 1984. "Sometimes I say to myself, it is better to die rather than live in the conditions I am living in right now," she says. "I desperately want to reunite with my family members, from whom I have been separated twenty years ago. I cannot stop thinking about them. I hope to be able to go back to the South so that these feelings could get resolved."

Forced migration, as shown in Poni's story and many others, affects collective and self-perception, representations of self and others, and national and ethnic culture, as well as material and economic security. Consider, for example, the migration biography of Cecilia Joseph Wani:

Wani, a 39-year-old Christian Nilo-Hamite, moved to Khartoum from Kajokeji in 1979. A widow with five children and one dependent, and whose husband died in Khartoum, Wani now works as a cleaner in St. Phillip Health Center. Wani's husband came to Khartoum to look for work, and before the war, she describes life as "very good," her lifestyle as normal, and the youth as decent. When the war started, life changed in Khartoum. Wani describes an influx of relatives, the changing lifestyle of youth, market changes, and her inability to afford rent for a house, which resulted in her move to a displaced location. During this move, her husband died, and she had to sell all her assets to maintain her children. She resides in an area where other relatives live, as they joined her after departure. Aspects of cultural life that she has been able to maintain include her food, and her language, Bari, but she notes that her children refuse to learn it. As a result, she cannot teach, or tell, her children the folktales that she considers to be valuable. She is not able to maintain her folk dances, traditional dress, and folktales. These folk dances are hard to maintain because they are not allowed, and she is prevented from maintaining her traditional dress due to laws requiring the Islamic lawful dress, or tobe. She has no interaction with Northerners, but knows that their cultural practices include "henna," circumcision, the prohibition of young girls from attending the market, dressing "tobe," etc. She is not prepared to embrace any of these practices except for dress, which is required, and is repulsed by female circumcision, which she describes as "dangerous" and wrong. Since her husband has died, she is responsible for the decisions in her household. Life for her, she says, is difficult, and will be more difficult, both economically and socially, as long as there is a war. Besides that, her most pressing concern is that her children will forget her culture.[19]

Wani's biography effectively illuminates the ways in which bereavement becomes associated with vulnerability, an emotion that is also powerfully depicted in the story of Nora Mule below:

Mule is 60 years old and has been separated from her husband since she departed Kopoeta in 1989 with her son. She works as a housekeeper, but relies on her grown children for support. She described life before the war as much better, but feels better being in Khartoum, away from the sounds of guns in Kapoeta. She lives far from other friends of relatives, but has been able to maintain her culture through food and occasional folk dances. She has given up alcoholic drinks, however, due to her commitment to Christianity. Since she was separated from her husband, she has maintained decision-making authority in her household, which she feels has given her a better life. She was, as she puts it, "at peace with [her husband]." Although she feels that her life has no pressing conditions, she misses her children who are working in the army, and makes do with the photos she has of them. When asked for an acceptable solution to the problems facing herself and others, she reflected that, although peace would bring some joy, death might be the only solution.

Stories like those of Nora Mule prompt the question, how are loss and bereavement to be understood in the southern Sudanese milieu? In the words of Margaret Mondong, who arrived in Khartoum in 1996:

> I am concerned that continued residence in Khartoum would lead my people to abandon or lose contact with their culture. Although we try to teach our children our culture, we often find it impossible to compete with Arab and Islamic culture taught to them in school. I feel that my problems are the problems of all displaced people; we are drinking in the same pot. The only acceptable solution to these complicated issues is peace.

Displaced women's experiences show that as family forms and kinship systems disintegrate as a result of war, violence, identity, and belonging take on complex meanings, new memories are made. One existential condition that prompts the negotiation of self and community is residential patterns. The need to find shelter, wherever that may be, is more immediate for displaced people than the need to live among relatives. Also important to note is that the kinship "vacuum" that results from displacement does not go unfilled. Neighbors in the host communities step up to fill the role as fictive kin, both ready and willing to enter into a new chain of exchanges and conversations. In spite of the importance of these new relationships, cultural loss remains a powerful force that contributes to the reshaping of ideas and values.

Loss of cultural rights in both their ideational and phenomenal dimensions are therefore of special importance to non-Muslim Southerners. If we are to assess the meaning of cultural rights in southern Sudanese cosmology, we will be confronted with an impressive overabundance of cultural expressions and rules that govern every aspect of one's existence from the cradle to the grave. The fact that the very foundation of village societies has been blasted to bits has meant that whatever notions and significances people attached to their practices are being shattered. These include many "traditional structures": age classes, clan classifications, childbirth rituals, kinship rules, betrothal and marriage, laws regulating inheritance and property ownership, rules of compensation of injury, distribution of resources, totems, magic, oath taking, rainmaking and sacrifice, supreme beings and guardian spirits, initiation, burial, and stories told around the evening fire.

Philister Baya, a southern Sudanese woman living in Khartoum, explained the extent to which displacement in Khartoum destabilized their cultural life:

When we organize for social occasions such as marriages, funerals, and rites which are to continue late at night, we should get permission from the local authorities, namely El-Nizam El-Aam, to conduct such occasions. In most cases El-Nizam El-Aam go into houses and interrupt the occasions without good reasons. Christians are ordered to close their shops on Fridays during Jumma prayers by the same governmental body. On refusal, the southern displaced women are struggling to maintain their living, are dragged to the Public Order Court to be fined.[20]

In Sudanese shantytowns and camps for the internally displaced, people repeat analogous concerns, showing the enormous pressure of the Public Order law on their economic rights, to which I turn next.

Economic Rights

Contraventions of cultural rights, notwithstanding the consequences of the Public Order Law outlined earlier, have been immeasurable in the economic realm as they restricted women's involvement in certain occupations. According to Susie Pito, a Mikaya Christian who arrived at Khartoum in 1996: "I am no longer able to make alcoholic drinks because of shari'a law. I am troubled by being viewed as an infidel under shari'a." Since little work is available for women who struggle against urban poverty, in desperation they turn to sex work and alcohol brewing. Yahya el-Hassan, a PANA correspondent, described the forbidding reality:

Once in the north, (women) are forced to live in cramped camps around the big cities that lack all conditions of a decent living. This situation forces women to compete for the very limited opportunity available, such as washers and maids. The rest opt for the brewing of local gin (araqi), or prostitution, two lucrative but dangerous businesses if the women are caught by the police. If convicted, the women are moved to an all-female prison. A recent UN research has found that over eighty percent of the inmates of Omdurman women prison in Khartoum were women from the South convicted of trafficking in araqi or prostitution.

Obviously, the Public Order Law has had deleterious effects on southern Sudanese displaced women's economic rights by abrogating their right to work and earn a living in a secure environment. This problem was addressed by Christina Dudu:

The other major problem facing Southern displaced women is unequal job opportunities. If one makes a survey, one will find that there are many Southern women and men who are highly educated graduates but are jobless. Southern women in government and non-government institutions are accommodated within the domestic labor force. They are sweepers, cleaners, or messengers. Southern women have to accept [this] as they had no other options for survival.[21]

As for women from Darfur who do not necessarily engage in beer brewing for religious considerations, displacement violated their economic rights by undercutting their access to adequate standards of living, which "encompasses several more rights, including the right to food, the right to health, the right to water, the right to necessary social services, the right to clothing, and the right to housing."[22] Khadijia Yagoub, who arrived at Khartoum in May 2004, explains:

> We used to farm back home in our village. We did not extend our hands or begged for food or anything else. The poverty and want we saw in Khartoum is causing us a lot of worries and stress. We have to think about the little children because at least the adults are strong enough to bear hunger. Our life in the village was merciful. Here in Khartoum there is no assistance. We are here in this faraway place where we cannot move to find work, especially the majority of women who have little children. There is no food and our hosts are struggling and are themselves in trouble. This fighting destroyed our life there and caused us humiliation and hunger here. I don't know what the future holds. Now, I have no hope.

Political Futures

In this essay, I tried to demonstrate the ways in which Sudan's multiple conflicts have led to serious violations of economic, social, and cultural rights. These infringements have certainly had far more damaging effects on women and girls, since they are denied the opportunity to live in an environment in which they could take part in decisions vital to their safety and well being. The perpetuation of gender-based violence before, during, and after the conflicts has positively sharpened women's consciousness about themselves as first and foremost political subjects.

Furthermore, it refined their views on their political futures as they ponder new roles in peacemaking and the reconstitution of communities. In contemplating the role of women in southern Sudan and Darfur as the major stakeholders in peaceful settlements in their respective communities, we have to take into consideration their experiences as displaced women. Without romanticizing forced migration, we can concede that it created avenues for women to express agency and create avenues for self-empowerment in ways previously unknown.

Nowhere has this been so powerfully demonstrated than in Mary Hillary Wani's compelling paper "Women's Agenda for Peace," which she delivered at the Sudanese Women's Peace Forum held in October 29, 2001. Relying on an indigenous conceptualization of peace, Wani writes:

> For the purposes of drawing a women's agenda for peace I have opted to consider the definition as projected by the majority of the displaced women. In simple terms they defined peace to mean having security; peace means the right to move without restrictions; peace means love, unity and solidarity; peace is justice, freedom and absence of all forms of discrimination; peace means having a house, a job and land to cultivate, having enough food and being free from diseases; peace means the right to education for our children; peace means freedom of worship; peace means the right to our historical heritage, peace means participation in decisions and plans that affect our lives.[23]

Section Three: Gender, War, and Violence

As much as gender-based violence, war, and displacement have combined to create a legion of challenges and struggles, they generate new spaces within which women can participate on equal footing with men in decisions vital to their lives. The renegotiation of these roles was made clear in two accounts from a Southerner and a Darfurian, respectively.

In the words of Olga Odera, a Christian Acholi who moved to Khartoum from Torit in 1993:

> Men are used to making decisions in my community of origin. Women accepted that as a natural thing.
> Since I came here alone, I feel free to make my own decisions. Long time ago, I used to ask my husband to tell me what to do about many things. Now I am in control of my life and I support myself. This situation gave me the chance to have a say on many issues.
> I no longer think that women should follow men obediently. They can use their experience in Khartoum to influence decisions outside the home as well."

Views like those of Olga Odera abound, as becomes obvious from the narrative of Sakina Adam from Darfur.

> When the fighting started in my village, all the women started to run all over. We fled to Kas before coming to Khartoum. The journey with the children took us very long days. It was the most difficult journey. We started to talk about why the men were preying on us. What did we do to them? We understood that after they burnt villages, looted animals from many people including Haboba (a woman who was sitting next to Sakina during the interview), that men were using us to hurt the men in our family and village. They wanted to cause a lot of pain by attacking the women. The whole village fled fearing for their lives. Some beautiful women were abducted and others were beaten and humiliated. Now we understand that we are here because the men wanted to degrade the community. For this reason we cannot not go back until we are assured that we will not be hurt again. We need security and we need every-one outside to know that without providing safety we cannot take this big risk. We will remain in Khartoum and see about peace. Peace will help but the damage has been done. We need women to be able to protect themselves because some back home did their best to protect their families.

This view corroborates Amartya Sen's most commanding observations on women's agency:

> The active agency of women cannot, in any serious way, ignore the urgency of rectifying many inequities that blight the well being of women and subject them to unequal treatment. Thus the agency role must be much concerned with women's well being also. Similarly, coming from the other end, any practical attempt at enhancing the well-being of women cannot but draw on the agency of women themselves in bringing about such change."[24]

Drawing on the experiences of Sudanese women from the South and Darfur will help formulate strategies for gender equity in postconflict Sudan. This approach will depend fundamentally, however, on the state and nonstate actors' capability to uphold peace and fortify security measures so that war-displaced women can help rebuild their shattered lives. In light of this political context, women as the main stakeholders in the reconstitution of their communities have undoubtedly earned their right to equitable participation. In the meantime, for those women who still live in shantytowns and camps, fulfillment of the Guiding Principles on Internal Displacement as has been brilliantly articulated by Sergi Vieira de Mello is fundamental. According to de Mello, "Internally displace persons shall enjoy in full equality, the same rights and freedoms under international and domestic law as do other persons in their country. They shall not be discriminated against in the enjoyment of any rights and freedoms on the ground that they are internally displaced."[25]

Acknowledgments

I would like to acknowledge the Royal Anthropological Institute's support of my ethnographic research in the Sudan. I also want to thank Leni Silverstein and Sheila Dauer for inviting me to the Northwestern University workshop on Human Rights in Africa.

Notes

[1] UNESCO, *Cultural Rights as Human Rights*, Paris: UNESCO, 1970.

[2] Chandran Kukathas, "Are There Any Cultural Rights?" *Political Theory* 20, no. 1 (1992): 105–139.

[3] U.S. Committee on Refugees, *Follow the Women and the Crows: Personal Stories of Sudan's Uprooted People*, Washington, D.C., 2000.

[4] Michael Ignatieff, *Blood and Belonging* (New York: Farrar, Straus, and Giroux, 1994).

[5] Mansour Khalid, *War and Peace in Sudan: The Tale of Two Countries* (London: Kegan Paul, 2003).

[6] Mario C-Lye-Labu, "What Nemeriy [Numeiri] Did" (Anya-Nya Movement Publication, 1971:3).

[7] August 30, 2004.

[8] August 25th has been designated by the Committee on Consciousness of the United States Holocaust Memorial Museum a national day of conscience for Darfur (July 26, 2004).

[9] Associated Press, Boston Edition September 14, 2004: 1.

[10] International Crisis Group, "Crisis in Dafur," www.crisisweb.org, 2004.

[11] Catharine MacKinnon, "Rape, Genocide, and Women's Human Rights." In *Violence Against Women: Philosophical Perspectives*, Stanley French et al., ed. (Ithaca: Cornell University Press, 1998) pp. 43–57.

[12] C. Dudu, "Southern Sudanese Displaced Women: Losses and Gains" In *The Tragedy of Reality: Southern Sudanese Women Appeal for Peace*, M. Elsanosi, ed. (Khartoum: Sudan Open Learning Organization, 1999).

[13] Amnesty International, *Sudan Report*, 2001, www.amnesty.org.

[14] Amnesty International, *Sudan: Darfur: Rape as a Weapon of War: Sexual Violence and Its Consequences* (New York: Amnesty International 2004).

[15] Recent months have witnessed a relaxation of this law. Strong economic realities mitigated against the implementation of law as far as sexual segregation is concerned.

[16] Susan Sared, *What Makes Women Sick? Maternity, Modesty and Militarism in Israeli Society* (Hanover: University Press of New England, 2000).

[17] UNESCO, *Cultural Rights as Human Rights* (Paris: UNESCO, 1970).

[18] Deng, 1972, 6.

[19] E. Morawska, "Intended and Unintended Consequences of Forced Migrations: A Neglected Aspect of East Europe's Twentieth Century History," *International Migration Review* 34, no. 4 (2000): 1049–1087.

[20] Philister Baya, "Seeking a Refuge or Being a Displaced: Analysis of a Southern Woman's Personal Experience" In *The Tragedy of Reality: Southern Sudanese Women Appeal for Peace*, M. Elsanousi, ed. (Khartoum: Open Learning Organization, 1999).

[21] Dudu, 1999.

[22] www.cesr.org.

[23] Wani, 2.

[24] Amartya Sen, *Development as Freedom* (New York: Knopf, 1999).

[25] Posted on United Nations Office for the Coordinator of Humanitarian Affairs at www.reliefweb.int.

11 The Darfur War:
Masculinity and the Construction of a Sudanese National Identity [1]

Karin Willemse

Since February 2003, Darfur has been the site of mounting violence, which has led the United Nations to repeatedly describe the conflict as "the world's worst humanitarian crisis."[2] The U.S. Congress even labeled the conflict "genocide." In Darfur, diverse ethnic groups as well as the government were engaged in violence in the 1980s and 1990s; however, the violence has reached a new dimension in the recent war since 2003, when racism has become the main legitimating discourse of the conflict. This construction of the war as racial is, thus, a recent phenomenon. In this article I will analyze the extent to which this discursive shift can be related not just to local conflicts, but also to the Sudanese government's project of constructing a Sudanese identity in its own terms.

In the 1990s, when I was conducting anthropological research in the town of Kebkabiya, both the locals and the government saw the violence in Darfur as the result of ethnic conflicts or ethnic clashes. The shift from a discourse of ethnicity to one of race to legitimize the violence in Darfur occurred around 2003 and coincided with an "outbreak" of violence in Darfur that was marked by a shift in the scale and scope of the fighting.[3] These shifts were accompanied by a third shift: from a government fighting "rebels" in Southern Sudan to a government fighting those in Darfur. The fact that the Sudanese government's discourse shifted from labeling the rebels in the South "black" to the "opposition forces in Darfur" is particularly significant. *Black* is hereby used to refer to the "enemy" of "the Sudanese" and discursively related to both "non-Muslims" and "slaves," terms that do not relate to any person, since all Darfur groups engaged in the conflict are Muslims. In order to critically examine the discursive strategy by which the Sudanese government legitimizes the violence against its own citizens, I will in this article argue that the war in Darfur should be considered part of the Sudanese government's political project to construct a "Sudanese" national identity, rather than a localized conflict over resources, or "a fight over a camel," as Muammar Qaddafi put it at the opening of the Darfur peace talks in Sirte, Libya.[4] I will show that the construction of the Darfur opposition forces as "blacks," as well as the shift of the civil war from the South to Darfur, fit into a pattern that connects both to the issue of Muslim masculinity and the struggle over citizenship on a national level.

Without a doubt, economic, social, cultural, political, and other forms of marginalization of Darfur within the Sudanese nation-state have been determining factors in the conflict, which account for the scale and frequency of the violence.[5] To say anything definitive on the nature or sources of the current Darfur war is, however, at this moment premature. The Darfur conflict – like most conflicts – can hardly be explained in terms of one underlying aspect and my analysis will therefore necessarily be partial. At the same time, "ethnicity" and, since 2003, "race"[6] have become major explanatory labels to account for the violence and this has led to an exoticizing of the conflict. Particularly problematic in using the terms *ethnicity* and *race* as shorthand for, if not the main denominators of the source of the conflict, is that it leads to an oversimplification of the causes of, the current war. I maintain that if the ethnic and racial labels used in context of the Darfur war are not qualified, the users of these labels are complicit in propagating the discourse that continues to be used by the current Islamist government of Sudan to legitimize this civil war.

I will in my analysis focus on how ethnicity and race have become part of the construction of diverse, intersecting identities. I will in the first place analyze the Darfur war in relation to the problematic construction of masculinity by young men. Next, I will relate the recent shift in the legitimizing discourse of perpetrators from ethnicity to race and the "masculinity-in-crisis" to the construction of a Sudanese national identity. I will start, however, by giving a brief outline of the war in Darfur and refer to some important moments, or key shifts,[7] in Darfur history in which ethnicity became intersected in particular ways with other identities, marking positions of power and authority in specific contexts.

Ethnicity in Some Key Shifts in Darfur History

The war in Darfur has attracted ample media attention as well as international political concern. In the current conflict the Fur, Masalit, and Zaghawa ethnic groups are cast as "Black African farmers," while both the Abbala camel and Baggara cattle nomads are labeled "Arabs." While a few notable articles appearing in both popular and academic publications have attempted to deconstruct this binary opposition, it is misleadingly presented as self-evidently constituting the basis of the current conflict in Darfur.[8] It is the relationship between ethnic groups and religious identity in relation to the distinction between "African" and "Arab" that needs scrutiny in order to understand the dynamics of the war in Darfur.

To start with, the dichotomy of "Arabs" versus "Black Africans," which is based on "named" ethnic groups, constructs ethnic identity as fixed, homogeneous, self-evident, and thus easy to distinguish. I take the view that ethnicity is fluid, nuanced, and context bound. In addition, ethnicity, as an important marker of identity, always intersects with social, economic, political, and cultural contexts.[9] In this respect, ethnicity must be viewed as only one aspect of a complex of intersecting identities, which may shift according to context. I will briefly outline some of the arguments that underscore the flexibility of ethnicity. This overview, however, is by no means exhaustive, nor is it meant to give a neat chronology of events.

The construction of the conflict as one of "Arab Muslim nomads" against "Black African farmers" implicitly casts the latter as non-Muslims and even slaves, and in the process glosses over the fact that the parties involved are all Muslims who are linked with each other by a long history of exchange, intermarriage, and even lifestyle. Already in 1969, Haaland described how the shift from farming to nomadism by fortunate Fur farmers also meant a shift from a Fur to a Baggara identity: the so-called "Fur al-Baggara" as de Waal refers to them.[10] Although the newcomer was not readily accepted as "one of us" by the Baggara, the reason they gave Haaland for this was the lack of respect shown to visitors by not keeping to the cultural codes of hospitality (i.e., offering tea and food) and not the act of taking up nomadism in itself.[11] The reverse was also true: Whenever a person settled among sedentary farmers, the granting of land by the community leader meant that one could become part of that community within one generation.[12]

The links between ethnic identity, location, livelihood, and land dates back to an even further-removed past, when the Muslim Sultanate was founded. The myth of origin of Dar Fur as an Islamic Sultanate refers to Suleiman Solondungo (Fur for "the Arab"), son of a Muslim "stranger," Ahmad al-Ma'qur, and a non-Muslim royal woman of the Keira, the then-ruling Fur clan in the sixteenth century.[13] From that time on, inhabitants of the Sultanate were considered to be Muslims.[14] Most inhabitants retained their language and culture alongside or intertwined with the Arabic language and incoming Islamic traditions. The process of Islamization was influenced to a large extent by traders and pilgrims who traveled through Darfur to and from West Africa to either Cairo or, via Central Sudan, on to the Red Sea coast in order to go to Mecca, and back again. The well-educated preachers were attracted to the court of the Sultan of the Darfur Sultanate,[15] while the less-educated religious men would teach their less-informed interpretation of Islamic principles to the rural population of Darfur.

Allegedly, those Fur who did not want to become Muslim were forced to migrate south. In due time, these "ex-Fur" became "Fertit," an ethnic group whose name signified their non-Islamic status and thus their potential for being raided as slaves.[16] In the process, ethnic identity merged with religious identity as well as with political identity, locality, and livelihood: Being "Fur" meant that one lived within the boundaries of the Fur Sultanate ruled and protected by a Fur sultan who, since the seventeenth century, adhered to Islam.[17] A Fur ethnic identity thus represented "citizenship" within the Fur Sultanate.[18]

National and regional politics have been an important cause of the solidification of ethnic identities in the more recent past. The Anglo-Egyptian colonial government used ethnicity as a means to "divide and rule" by literally partitioning the former Fur Sultanate into more or less fixed *dars*, administrative areas under the control of appointed tribal leaders under the Native Administration system set up in the 1920s. Already under the Sultan, most Baggara, or cattle nomads, were awarded land grants or *hakuras* in the area south of Jebel Marra, while most of the Abbala or camel nomads in the North did not receive any territory they could claim as their own.[19] The colonial government built on this land division, which led in particular in North Darfur to clearly demarcated "homelands" related to fixed ethnic identities. This fixedness was expressed in the names of these tribal areas, like "Dar Zaghawa," that were placed under the rule of officially appointed "tribal leaders," who represented the ethnic group to the government and vice versa. Those nomadic Arab groups that did not receive a "homeland" of their own also had no one to represent them.[20] Although the tribal leaders never lost complete power, in 1994 the Native Administration Council was "reinvented" under the new Islamist military government in order to govern the area through local leaders "on the cheap."[21] Their reestablished power over land allocations directly led to renewed conflicts in the far west of Darfur.[22]

I do not want to suggest that ethnicity in the seventeenth century has remained unaltered over the last three centuries that followed, or that there are strict analogies between "being a Fur" during the period of the Fur Sultanate or the colonial era and the experiences of those who consider themselves to be Fur by the end of the twentieth century.[23] On the contrary, since ethnic identity has historically intersected with other identifications such as religion, location, means of survival, etc., shifting meaning in changing socioeconomic and political contexts, it cannot be taken as an identity in and of itself.

My brief outline is, therefore, meant to caution that one should be clear about the context in which ethnicity is given meaning and look for other important identities that intersect with ethnicity. As the late Claude Aké remarked, "ethnic groups do not exist."[24] Here Aké was referring to the fact that ethnicity only makes sense when analyzed as intersected with other social, economic, political, and cultural identities. Fredrik Barth, one of the first anthropologists who wrote about the Fur,[25] maintained that ethnic identity is constructed mainly at the "boundaries" between cultural groups,[26] instead of considering it to be primarily based on a core identity. In his view, ethnic identities are articulated most clearly when members of one cultural group meet those of another. This "meeting" both requires one to identify oneself and may trigger interethnic competition in situations of scarce resources. In other words, ethnic identity marks a difference between self and other and should, rather than being innate, be taken to be a constructed, contextualized, and performed identity. The confrontation with other cultural groups may or may not make ethnicity a viable aspect of differentiation and competition, depending on what is at stake. Considering a saying from the people of Dor in Northern Darfur, as quoted by Flint and de Waal, "Conflict defines origins,"[27] I maintain that it is the nature of the conflict that is of importance for understanding how ethnicity is articulated and validated. This requires precision as to how meanings of ethnicity were historically and contextually constructed.[28]

An important context to the ethnic conflicts in Darfur is the ongoing desertification in the postcolonial era. Camel nomads and seminomadic groups who had been allotted dars by the colonial government in the far north of Darfur, or none at all, suffered most from the deteriorating environmental conditions.[29] In particular, after the droughts of the 1970s and 1980s, they would more frequently and earlier in the season come down from the desert in the north and northwest with their camels that trampled, ate, or otherwise destroyed the not-yet-harvested crops of the local farmers and threatened to deplete the local water resources.

In addition, recent political developments have solidified ethnic identities even further. In 1981, Darfur was the last region to get a governor from the same area he was to rule under the 1972 Regional Autonomy Act. However, the installation of Ahmed Diraige, a Fur, as governor turned out to be a bone of contention. Intellectuals claiming Arab descent organized themselves in the Arab Congregation or Gathering (*Altajamu' Al 'Arabi*). As a direct consequence, raids by Arab *fursan* (knights) and Fur *malishyat* (militia) were quite problematically cast as an ethnic conflict waged between the "Arab belt" and the "African belt." The Fur felt that the Arabs aimed at destroying their ancestral rights to the land, while Arabs claimed that the Fur threatened to oust them under the slogan "Darfur for the Fur." The influx of high-tech weapons in the same period due to the war between Libya and Chad, the donations of arms by diverse national political parties to their respective constituencies during and after the democratic elections, and the arming of militia by consecutive national governments has fuelled this conflict.[30]

In 2003, the Opposition Forces constituted by the the Sudan Liberation Movement/Army (SLM/A), formerly the Darfur Liberation Front, led by Abdel Wahid Mohammed Al-Nur) together with the Justice and Equality Movement (JEM, led by Khalil Ibrahim, a former member of the National Islamic Front) attacked government forces and installations in Darfur.[31] Despite their differences, the SLM/A came forth from the Darfur Liberation Front and connected with the SPLM/A in the South, while the JEM was an offshoot of the NIF splinter group (under the leadership of Hassan El-Turabi, the prominent spiritual and political leader of the Islamist movement in Sudan) that had been part of the Islamist government in Khartoum since 1989. The groups were united in their cause: They accused the government of neglecting the huge economic problems in Darfur while doing nothing about the increasing insecurity and lawlessness related to the continuous influx of high-tech arms into the region. To support their claims they referred to a book distributed mainly in Khartoum in May 2000 titled *The Black Book: Imbalance of Power and Wealth in the Sudan*[32] in which a group calling themselves "The Seekers of Truth and Justice," who would later found JEM, formulated their grievances about the socioeconomic and political marginalization of Darfur.[33]

The opposition movement is thought to be made up of mainly three ethnic groups, the Fur, the Masalit, and the Zaghawa, who have been collectively cast by perpetrators and in the international media as "Black African farmers." As I indicated earlier, the label "black" has been used in the history of Sudan by those in positions of power for non-Muslims, which in the past marked these groups as "enslaveable." In other words, there is in Sudanese dominant discourse a direct relation between the labels "black," "slave," and "non-Muslim." Interestingly, while the Fur and Masalit are indeed farmers, the Zaghawa are seminomads, which makes the distinction between "farmers" and "nomads" contingent. The clustering of these groups as "African" is related to the fact that they have retained their local African language, alongside Arabic, which is not only the lingua franca but also considered the "holy" language of Islam. The label of "black farmers," "*Zurqa*," or "*Zuruq*," which in Arabic literally means "blue," therefore seems to be part of the government's political rhetoric that uses race in order to cast the opposition forces as one unified enemy.

The so-called Janjawid, the other party to the conflict, are usually characterized as Muslim "Arab" nomads. They are seen as the perpetrators of the violence enacted upon the sedentary population, supported by Sudanese soldiers and the Sudanese Air Force and arms supplied by the Sudanese government, operating with total impunity.

Thus far I have problematized a seemingly self-evident but misleading dichotomy based on ethnicity and race. As I have shown, in Darfur ethnicity became solidified when it intersected with political identities, whether under the Sultanate, as part of the colonial politics of indirect rule, or after independence as part of national politics. At the same time, my argument does not seem to be able to escape the notion of ethnic identity as a main aspect of understanding the current war. This points to an heuristic problem: When one starts an analysis from the perspective of ethnicity, one will always end up considering ethnic identity. A critical reflection on the dynamics of the war that goes beyond ethnicity therefore requires me to start somewhere else. As an anthropologist, I think that any reflection on the war should be based on the experiences and views of the Darfur people who have lived through it, which so far I have not been able to access in a comprehensive and ongoing manner. I can, however, go back to the anthropological research I conducted in Jebel Marra in the 1980s and in the town of Kebkabiya, North Darfur, in the 1990s, before the outbreak of the war to shed light on issues of ethnicity and ethnic identities as I have experienced them.

Darfur: Local Youth, Arms, and the Construction of a Social Self[34]

After the attacks in Darfur by the Darfur opposition rebel forces in 2002 and 2003, the government was caught by surprise. As it distrusted its own army, which largely consisted of soldiers of Darfur origin, its response was to mount a campaign of aerial bombardment and military intelligence, supporting ground attacks by an "Arab" militia. This militia, the Janjawid, was recruited from local ethnic groups and armed by the government.[35]

In the early 1990s, when I conducted anthropological research in Kebkabiya, a town that has been recently under heavy siege, conflicts over scarce resources such as land and water concerned predominantly Fur and Zaghawa, groups that have now become allies in the Opposition Forces. The failure of traditional negotiation and peacekeeping mechanisms, such as tribal reconciliation conferences, was due to not only the politicization of ethnic identities but also the unwillingness of the government to enforce peace treaties.

Of critical importance as well was the growing discontent within the region's ethnic groups. In particular, young males increasingly contested the authority of tribal leaders and elderly men in general. For example, during my stay in Kebkabiya in 1991, one of the Zaghawa representatives who had attended a reconciliation conference inside the town of Kebkabiya was ambushed when returning home. It turned out that he was killed by youngsters from his own constituency because they felt their rights were being thwarted and their needs were neglected by the agreement he had signed.[36]

The general neglect of Darfur in national development plans left young men with few possibilities for establishing themselves as heads of families and thus of becoming "men" in sociocultural terms. They had difficulties paying for the bride-price and wedding arrangements that mark the transition to manhood and adult social status. Even when they did marry, young nomads could hardly provide for their families. For their part, many young sedentary farmers had to migrate to towns for some extended period of time in order to earn the money necessary to raise a family. Moreover, despite the high expectations placed on education, educated young men, even when employed as white-collar workers, barely had the means and ability to provide for their families.[37]

In most farming communities in Darfur, women, aided by their daughters, are the main cultivators, while single young men are often redundant. Formerly, boys would wander, sometimes from the age of eight, from one Qur'anic school to the next, or engage in odd jobs in order to survive, at the same time building networks and acquiring skills as well as the Arabic language as part of "becoming a man." In times of drought, young men would be the first to migrate out of the community in order to fend for themselves, followed by married men, while women, children, and the elderly would leave only when cultivation was no longer possible. Women were de facto "keepers of the land" despite the fact that entitlement and land-ownership were male affairs.[38]

Among nomadic groups, however, single young men were most important for herding camels. In times of drought, only young men would tend to the smaller herds, temporarily leaving behind women, children, and the elderly in small settlements near sedentary peoples. This process of settling by female nomads coupled with male out-migration among sedentary farmers has created communities that consist of predominantly female-headed households of both sedentary and nomadic backgrounds. These engage with increasing frequency and scale in interethnic exchange, sharecropping, and intermarriage. Although there are "no true nomads in Darfur," as "most of the people who are described as such are in fact seminomadic or transhumant,"[39] even the seminomadic lifestyle is increasingly difficult to maintain. Temporary nomadic settlements have become more permanent and, moreover, now host an increasing number of young male nomads, which might mean that the nomadic lifestyle has even become extinct.[40] The result of this radical change is insecurity and anxiety among the settled nomadic communities. Moreover, in order to survive, the new settlers needed access to land, water, labor, money, and know-ledge, thus competing more directly over exactly the same resources that sedentary farmers used in these transition zones for their survival.[41] Not surprisingly, these are the areas where most of the outbursts of violence have taken place.

In these deteriorating conditions of deprivation and despair among nomadic and sedentary young men "without a future," weapons may form an easy and immediate satisfaction in the quest for respect, self-identity, and a sense of control. Musa Hilal, a high-profile warlord and leader of some of the Janjawid groups in North and West Darfur, exemplifies this generational shift.[42] In 1986 he took over rule from his father, Sheikh Hilal Mohammed Abdalla, who is depicted by Flint and de Waal as a tribal leader of the Um Jalul camel nomads whose court was sought after by a diversity of ethnic groups, both nomads and farmers, for settling disputes in the "old way." By the end of Sheikh Hilal Abdalla's life, Kalashnikovs were easy to come by and cheap. Musa Hilal took advantage of this situation. As Flint and de Waal point out: "Young men with guns were not only able to terrify the population at large, but were free of the control of their elders."[43]

Due to the large numbers of young disenfranchised men who are experiencing a "masculinity-in-crisis" on both sides of the conflict, the war has taken on an especially troubling gender dimension. Women are systematically verbally and physically abused, raped, mutilated, and their relatives killed in front of their eyes, while young men of "battle age" are targeted for mass killings. This so-called "gendercide"[44] is symptomatic not only of the Darfur war but also of many recent conflicts in Africa and elsewhere, such as the Congo, Liberian, and Bosnian civil wars.[45]

The illusion of ethnic homogeneity among the Janjawid has become part of the political-ideological project of those who cast themselves as the "Arabs" in Darfur. It is not clear whether the Janjawid were indeed as ethnically homogeneous as has been claimed. For example, when discussing the Janjawid, Flint and de Waal note how "one young Zaghawa volunteer ran away on being told that Arabs would attack civilian targets – villages – while non-Arabs like him would be sent to fight the rebels, their ethnic kin."[46] Moreover, support for Khartoum came not only from "Arab" tribes but also, for example, from Fellata, Birgid, and Daju, whose recruits joined the government-founded Janjawid forces.[47] The fact that that Musa Hilal, the leader of some of the Janjawid, made a point of "purifying" the ranks of his militia from "African" elements points to the same conclusion: "Non-Arabs" were originally members of the Janjawid.

Even so, the ideology of the Janjawid's "Arab purity" has become the mainstay of a regional discourse of ethnic and religious superiority. At the same time, even these "Arabs" are composed of a diversity of groups with different backgrounds, like those formerly serving in the Sudanese Popular Defence Forces (PDF) in Dar Masalit, who, in turn, had been trained by the *Quwat al Islam*, a militia under the control of the Northern Sudanese General Dabi in South Kordofan; recently migrated "Arabs" from Chad and Libya; and Abbala and Baggara "Arabs" from different parts of Darfur, who are constructed as the descendants of the *Quraysh*, Prophet Mohammed's ethnic group, who migrated in a far removed past from the Arabian Peninsula looking for "new pastures." In addition, after the race riots in Libya in 2000, 250 black migrants were killed and thousands expelled. Those "African Arab" migrants who had been in Libya under the umbrella of the Arab Gathering came to North Darfur to military training camps, some of which were headed by Musa Hilal.[48]

Although the Sudanese government denied allegations of supporting the Janjawid militia – calling them "thieves and gangsters" – the conflict in Darfur has become part of national politics, and thereby it has been burdened with a new political meaning. In response to the rebellion of 2003, the Sudanese government has actively "adopted, spread, and intensified Janjawiidism, so that in many instances the armed forces and security institutions of the state have become indistinguishable from the Janjawiid."[49] Musa Hilal, himself, claimed he was waging a "holy war" under the direction of the Sudanese government,[50] "burning, looting and killing 'of intellectuals and youths who may join the rebels in fighting.'"[51]

The strategy of turning "Arab" nomads into a militia is, however, not novel – it is a policy that was applied by consecutive regimes in the civil war with southern Sudan prior to the Darfur war. Both the democratic regime (1985–1989) under the leadership of Sadiq Al Mahdi and the current Islamist regime had armed Arab nomads from Kordofan and Darfur and turned them into so-called *Murahalin*.[52] The recent deployment of similar counterinsurgency tactics in Darfur suggests that the conflict represents a "southern Sudan speeded up" rather than a new "Rwanda in slow motion."[53]

Apart from fighting tactics and the application of a "scorched-earth" policy, the racial rhetoric used to justify the violence also bears similarities with the war in the south Sudan. This suggests that the current religious-racial discourse of Islamic superiority used in the war in Darfur is part of an ongoing national "project" of inclusion and exclusion. Moreover, although the Sudanese government's Arabized elites from Central Sudan have allied with the Arab nomads in the current war in Darfur, the meaning of *Arab* given to each of these groups carries different connotations of class and culture. The notion of "Arab" that is used for the nomadic peoples in Darfur is used in the sense of Bedouin and indicates backwardness and marginality.[54] Alternatively, members of the educated Arabized elites residing in the Nile Valley have constructed themselves as "*Awlad al-Arab*" and "*Awlad al-Balad*," or the children (sons) of Arabs and inheritors of the land. They were instrumental in founding political Arab nationalism and claimed the Sudanese nation-state as theirs. By constructing Sudan both as Islamic and as Arab, they excluded not only Southerners but also other marginal groups of Muslims such as the Fur, the Beja, and the Nubians in the west, east, and north of the country, respectively.

In other words, the militarization of the Janjawid was closely related to national politics and, in some contexts, seemed to override ethnic difference. At the same time "Arabism" seems to be an ideology used to support the illusion that the Darfur war is a local or regional conflict rather than a national one.[55] Arabism has only recently been introduced to legitimize the government's involvement in the Darfur war. When the current military regime, backed by the Islamist National Islamic Front, took power in 1989, it proclaimed Darfur the "least Islamized region after the South."[56] This stigma concerned all Darfurians, nomads and sedentary farmers alike. Although it casts the Darfur population as lesser Muslims, it did not divide them along racial lines. In order to understand this shift, I will go back to the period before the onset of the Darfur war.

The Islamist Government and the Discourse on Religion in Darfur

When the Islamists took power in 1989, the government's elites considered that the Sudan was not properly Islamized everywhere. It instigated what it called *al-mashru' al-hadari*, or the "Islamist Civilization Project."[57] In general, the project focused on the conduct and appearance of women in public; both upper- and middle- class professional women and female street vendors were targeted specifically in "street cleaning" campaigns.[58] As articulated in speeches and other public addresses by government representatives, Darfur also constituted one of the targets of its re-Islamization offensive.[59] The government accused the population of Darfur of incorrectly practicing Islam because it intersected with local customs, and thus cast Darfuris as lesser Muslims, as inferior and backward. In speeches given by a touring *al-Lagna al-sha'abia*, or the Popular Committee, which I taped in December 1990, Darfur men in particular were called upon to return to the "right way," as the head of the Popular Committee pointed out at the end of several speeches on the correct Islamic behavior:

> My family, *assalaamu 'alaikum,* I want to talk to you about the *hadith* and the Qur'an of our prophet Mohammed, peace be upon him [...] We want to continue on the Islam and on Qura'nic behavior [...] The duties of the popular committees are to collect the traditional habits and customs of the communities and to encourage those that follow Islam [...] Now we have permission from the government to report about bad customs and bad behavior and to send it to the popular committees so they can decide on what to do about it quickly [...] We are not united for a bad cause, we only want to stimulate good behavior and create good Muslims [...][60]

In other words, despite the low status of Darfurians as Muslims, they were at that time considered Muslims who could be redeemed, their ways amended, and their souls saved so that they might be included into the community of righteous believers once they mended their conduct and became better ("proper") believers. According to this logic Darfurians could potentially become faithful members of the *umma* (the Muslim Nation), which meant that they were not only addressed as Muslims, but also as potential Sudanese citizens.[61] In the same capacity, they were reprimanded for what were called ethnic clashes and/or armed robberies:

> There is also no end to the armed robberies even if Omar Al-Bashir[62] brought planes and heavy guns to fight them […] And we say that we are Muslims and we kill among ourselves? Did God create us to fight and harm each other? He created a lot of tribes and nations for us, to get to know one another and to understand each other, not to fight […] Now we have become divided amongst ourselves: Arabs, Fur, Tunjur, Zaghawa, Gimr, all tribes on their own, killing each other […][63]

Even though this might never have been a seriously inclusive project of the government, at that time Darfur was discursively constructed as part of the Muslim north, and, therefore, the government called upon all the Darfur ethnic groups to stop emphasizing ethnic difference in favor of Muslim unity. It only needed some re-Islamization in order for the Darfur population at large to become included in the Sudanese Muslim nation state. This "inclusive" discourse of inferiority has changed since 2003, when the war broke out in Darfur.

In the current discourse, the Darfur population are cast not as fellow Muslims whose ways must be redeemed, but as blacks and thus as non-Islamic, enemies who, as non-Arabs, do not have a right to live on Muslim soil. This view is propagated by the Arab Gathering, acted upon by the Janjawid, and condoned by the Sudanese government, which, by extension, is complicit in this rhetoric.[64] The war in Darfur can therefore indeed be seen as a "Southern Sudan" revisited. It is important to note that "black" does not refer to skin color in any determined way. The Central Sudanese elite as well as the Darfur population, both sedentary and nomadic peoples, consists of peoples with different shades of skin color. Thus, it is very difficult to judge from the skin color whether a person is an "Arab" or an "African," a "nomad," "farmer" or a "member of the riverian elites." This is even evident when looking at those Sudanese who are members of parliament.

The term "black" is not novel in Darfur: Fur and Masalit were cast as "*zuruq*" (plural form of the singular "Zurqa"),[65] from *azrag* ("blue"), even before the onset of the current conflict. During my stay in Kebkabiya, color was not an important way that people were categorized, although occasionally people would ask me what color I thought their skin was. As it turned out, all shades of color were given, like *akhdar* ("green"), *ahmar* ("red"), shades of *asmar* ("brown"), and *azrag* ("blue"). When I asked about *aswad* ("black"), it was denied that this color existed in Darfur society since it referred to non-Muslims, and thus to slaves. Rather, it was the color of the Southern, non-Muslim, groups.[66] Other authors point out that in the Nile Valley, for example, in due time *aswad* ("black") and *azrag* ("blue") have become synonymous.[67] This process of conflation seems also to have taken place in Darfur: Those that were, and still are, referred to as "zuruq" have become classified as "aswad," formerly reserved for southern Sudanese, and in the process they have gone from "redeemable Muslims" to "enslaveable non-Muslims."[68] The notion of "black" seems to be, rather, a rhetorical device in a discursive struggle over political power and the legitimacy to rule.

From the above, it may be clear that this shift in discourse took place about the same time that the Janjawid were recruited and organized as a government-supported militia. The discursive shift, therefore, is to be sought not in a local history of the conflict, but in shifts in national politics.

The "Other" and the Construction of a Sudanese National Identity

As I stated in the introduction, the war in Darfur is related to a series of interconnected shifts. These include the government's legitimizing discourse in the Darfur war, and the shift in the use of the label "black non-Muslims" from being applied to Southern Sudanese to those in Darfur, not only after the eruption of violence in Darfur, but also after the peace negotiations between the Sudanese government and the Sudan People Liberation Army/Movement in Machakos in 2002. In other words, the position of the "Other," and thus as noncitizens, relative to the Sudanese government, shifted from the South to Darfur.

The Sudanese government's need to construct an "other" is related to the fact that the elites at the center of the Sudanese nation-state, literally and figuratively, do not constitute the homogeneous unity they suggest to be. On the contrary, since the economic crisis of the 1970s and 1980s, the supremacy of the Central Sudanese elite has been at stake. The question is why provincial war is a precondition for the maintenance of the "dominant but factionalized core."[69] De Waal suggests that Sudan is a "turbulent state" for which "provincial war and destabilization is the habitual *modus operandi* of the Khartoum elites [...] its balance achieved at the price of deadly disorder in its peripheries."[70] In short, the Sudanese elites' "factionalized core" makes provincial war, and thus the construction of an "other," a precondition for survival. For the sake of my argument, it is, therefore, necessary to give a brief history of the Sudanese elite in Central Sudan.

The process of Islamization in the Nile Valley differed considerably from the process of Islamization in Darfur. The replacement of the nobility of the Funj Sultanate on the Nile, by a middle class of merchants, administrators, army, and police, which took place in the seventeenth and eighteenth centuries, was accelerated after the Turko-Egyptian conquest of 1821. Turko-Egyptian rule, or *Turkiyya*, established a mercantile economy, which revolved around the slave trade. The emergent urban administrative and mercantile class that had established itself in the Nile Valley in the preceding centuries turned to Islam for a new legal and commercial code. The new elite used a stricter Islamic code of conduct, a specific lifestyle, and their position in the administration and trade as a means of distancing itself from the local, tribal religious elite. When the Anglo-Egyptian Condominium came to power in the Sudan in 1899, the new colonial government made use of this powerful indigenous administrative class to rule the colony for them.[71]

Thus, within the new colonial government, formal education and a white-collar position became new assets by which the new urban administrative elite differentiated itself from local elites and the amorphous "nonelite other." However, the need for junior administrators created the possibility of upward mobility, especially for boys from the rural areas outside the Nile Valley.[72] By acquiring formal education in the newly established government schools in the vicinity of the capital, these boys had the chance to enter into this white-collar class. There they acquired, apart from formal education, training in the culture of the riverian elite, by means of language, dress codes, mores of hospitality, and so forth. They were taught to perform a specific elite lifestyle – in short, a new code of conduct, of thinking, and of constructing themselves as persons. In this process, the boarding house played an important role, as it allowed for disciplining the aspirant-elite members according to elite norms while they were cut loose from their rural backgrounds and their ethnic and kin identities.[73] The young recruits thereby invested in the construction of a new, imagined community[74] of Sudanese nationals, engaging in both "detribal-ization" and "Sudanization."[75] When these educated aspirant-elites acquired positions as government officials reference to a local identity was by definition taboo as the government elite considered itself to represent the ideal image of the typical Sudanese citizen, which meant enacting a national identity and negating a local identity.

In the postcolonial era, formal education coupled with a government position became the hallmark of the new ruling class, which referred to itself as Sudanese, thus claiming to represent a national identity without any ethnic differentiation. Citizenship open to all Sudanese subjects was, however, never part of the nationalist project. The riverian elite used its Nile valley culture, with its specific history of Islamization and Arabization, to legitimize their prerogative of political power, based on its superiority and privilege as *Awlad al-Balad*, "the legitimate sons of the land," and *Awlad al-Arab*, "sons of Arabs."[76] Thus Islam and its "twin component, the Arab culture"[77] became the main aspects of a unifying, and supposedly "detribalized," national identity. This culture-cum-location-cum-class difference subsequently marked the difference between the "Sudanese" and the "othered non-Sudanese" population. This created a paradox: While education was originally used as part of a strategy of exclusion by the riverian elite, it created a process of inclusion of nonriverian aspirant-elite members into the national elite, which ultimately caused cracks in the surface of the Sudanese national identity.

The process of Sudanization and detribalization of aspirant-elite members was frustrated by the liberal educational policy under the military regime of Numeiri in the 1970s.[78] His liberalization of education led to the establishment of primary schools in remote areas and an increase of secondary high schools in regional capitals. This facilitated access to education for rural children, both boys and girls, and at the same time made a stay in boardinghouses less necessary. Pupils retained their relations with their kin and local culture. This prevented the early and intense socialization of aspirant-elite members into the Nile Valley elite culture, as was previously the case. This process was accelerated by the economic crisis in the 1970s, which led to an increase in the number of men, especially the highly educated, who migrated to the oil-states or to the West.[79]

The subsequent demand for educated white-collar workers not only allowed women into the government service but also led to the inclusion of regional secondary high schools into the government ranks. As these junior administrators and teachers, among others, were not sufficiently trained, they had to make do with lower qualifications, salaries, and social status than their predecessors. Male aspirant-elite members, who were "insufficiently detribalized" to start with, came from the countryside with their diplomas and high hopes of obtaining a position in the government. Even if they did get a position, the wages were so low that they could hardly pay for the high bride-prices and other wedding costs, let alone afford the expenses of keeping up an elite status. This meant that the economic crises of the 1970s and 1980s stimulated the new generation of elite members to stay in contact with their family in local areas, even after they entered the government service.

Consequently, the educated government elite has grown in numbers, but has thereby lost control over its "core culture." It has had to admit educated men and women as members to its ranks despite the fact that these new members retain characteristics of "other," nonelite classes, which defy the construction of a national identity that is expected to escape local, parochial identities even though this national identity is itself based on a local identity – the Nile valley of the riverian elites.[80]

In other words, recent processes of economic, social, and cultural change have led to a contestation of the dominant Sudanese identity and its middle-class notion of the ideal family from within its own ranks. Though the national ruling elite had to construct boundaries to differentiate themselves from the "nonelite" in order to safeguard its privileged position, it was this increasing heterogeneity within the elite itself that posed the largest threat to the moral and political dominance of the government. The administrative elite of the Nile valley had never been as homo-geneous as it professed to be. However, it now had to incorporate large numbers of aspirant members that had not been "properly Sudanized" and consequently suffered a loss of social status that also reflected on the elite as a whole. It was precisely this problem of permeable boundaries of the elite and the problematic status of male government elite members, within their families and the society at large, which the Islamist government that came to power in 1989 addressed in its moral discourse. No doubt mindful of the fact that Numeiri had been toppled by strikes in the towns of Central Sudan by intellectuals and government employees, the new government had to deal with the discontent among this affluent part of its constituency who were also to be the main implementers of the Islamist policy.

Contested Dominant Masculinity: Boundaries and Others
As I indicated earlier, the Islamist government's Civilization Project focused its moral policy first on women. It concentrated on women's conduct in the public sphere, which was directed by speeches, circulars, and decrees and controlled by vigilantes and special public security police. Their roles as wives and mothers have been emphasized as the most important duties of proper female Muslims. As I have argued elsewhere, when the boundaries of a group are threatened, it is the conduct of women in general and, interestingly, the women of one's own class in particular, that is addressed in reconstructions of group identities. Women, therefore, constitute the "other within." This strategy meant that men from diverse backgrounds proved

they could, however temporarily, overcome their internal differences and close their ranks with respect to the one issue they could all agree on, which is the control of the behavior of "Muslim" women as mothers.[81] Charlton, Everett, and Staudt see this as a more general feature of state building:

> State elites have discovered that promoting male domination contributes to the maintenance of social order in a period of state formation […]. A common solution involves offering a bargain to (some) men: in return for ceding control over political power and social resources to the state, they gain increased control over their families. Not only does this solution promote male domination, but it also establishes or strengthens a distinction between public and private spheres, and subordinates the private sphere to the public.[82]

Indeed, as Pettman argues, "nationality and citizenship, like race and ethnicity, are unstable categories of contested identities. They are all gendered identities and the construction of 'women,' inside and outside their borders, are part of the process of identity formation."[83] This boundary maintenance is important because the notion of a national identity, in general, is necessarily ambiguous, vague, and continuously changing as it has to incorporate diverse peoples in ways that allow them to believe the illusion that they are all equal citizens within the same nation-state. Thus, rather than resting on a common core, the construction of a unifying national identity needs a common "other" against whom to define itself.

A national identity is therefore based on exclusion, and may refer to class, ethnicity, race, location, or education in order to draw its boundaries, as we have seen with respect to Sudanese national identity. In any case, as Pettman indicates, a national identity is gendered. However, although women constitute an obvious "other," they do not constitute the only, or primary, means of marking the boundary of belonging. According to Donaldson:

> Through hegemonic masculinity most men benefit from having control of women; for a very few men, it delivers control of other men. To put it another way, the crucial difference between hegemonic masculinity and other masculinities is not the control of women, but the control of men […].[84]

This dominant masculinity, like citizenship, must seem attainable, in principle, for all male subjects of a nation-state. Accordingly, it lacks a well-defined core identity, and instead relies on the existence of categories of "others" against whom to construct its boundaries.[85] In other words, since dominant masculinity – as part of a national identity – is derivative, relational, and oppositional it needs "significant others" in order to define itself. Apart from women, "subordinate" or "lesser" men constitute the point of reference for constructing a form of restrictive citizenship and the "proper" national identity.[86]

The Islamists' Civilization Project can be considered an attempt to construct a modern Sudanese "Muslim" national identity. This is a continuous project and related to the construction of a Sudanese hegemonic (or dominant) masculinity. This dominant masculinity needs particular significant "others" in order to attain an exclusivist citizenship. In the case of the Islamist government of Sudan, these others are women and "lesser-men" who are defined in relation to restricted notions of "proper Islam." Citizens were only equal under the Islamic law when the Islamist government came to power. The search for citizenship was, therefore, marked by a process of securing the boundaries of the Sudanese national identity whereby, apart from women, "black non-Muslims" were constructed as the "lesser males," which used to refer more specifically to the Southern Sudanese "subjects." The notion of "black" did not so much refer to skin color, but to status – the status of those who, as non-Muslims, are considered as potential "slaves" to constitute this new imagined "other." This status not only refers back to historical times when slave raids were actually carried out in southern parts of contemporary Sudan, including southern part of Darfur Region, it also constructs the "other" as inferior in contemporary Sudanese society and serves to define a supposedly unified "Sudanese self" as superior, whether in terms of culture, language, or religion.[87] This strategy, however, was not the prerogative of the Islamist government, but has been the mainstay of the Sudanese governing elites in general since independence.

Conclusion

The use of women and "other lesser" males as markers of the boundaries of national identity and belonging is a recurrent theme in secular nation-state building projects, and not only confined to Islamic societies. Masculinity does not necessarily refer to real men, but rather to features that a nation-state tries to use as a means to assert an image of respect and strength. The image of a strong nation-state is related to, for example, a large army, a winning sports team, a strong leader, or a severe national discourse on citizenship. Thereby some categories of men are, implicitly or explicitly, referred to as constituting the dominant masculine ideal, and others as its denial.

In the case of the Sudanese nation-state, this notion of the "other" has historically been cast in ethnic-cum-racial and religious terms. "Black" refers to the inferior subject within state boundaries who, because of a fallacy in terms of ethnicity-cum-race, also fails to live up to the religious, class, and cultural standards of a "real" Sudanese. It may be obvious from the preceding that this idea of Darfurian African black farmers is a construction, an illusionary category. As Salih and Harir point out:

> Hence, even though the national political arena is dominated by debate over the values and ideology of the state, Islam and Christianity have never entered the realm of local politics nor have they provided the main source of antagonism at the village level.[88]

The Darfur population consists of only Muslims and the label *black* does not refer to actual skin color but, rather, is used by the government and those attacking local Darfur communities as a discursive device. From the perspective of the center, it means that "blacks" are not entitled to full citizenship, and as noncitizens they are a liability to state stability and thus it is legitimate to fight them.[89]

In short, Darfurian young men deal with a masculinity-in-crisis by claiming respect, power, and a form of manhood by force of arms. According to Salih and

Harir, this strategy may even be considered an extension of local notions of warrior-hood, since "governments are unable to offer citizens the minimum condition of individual security." This has forced local communities to resort "to ways familiar to their social organizations and value systems in order to protect their lives and property."[90] According to these authors, local modes of self-defense can be "transformed from traditional to modern military combat, albeit with considerable modification."[91] Whether the participation in the Darfur war by mainly young men is indeed a transformation of a local warrior tradition needs more investigation; it does suggest, however, that young men turning into militia has a widespread local history and that "Janjawidism" cannot be taken as a feature of only the "Arab" nomads.

For their part, the Sudanese government deals with the masculinity-in-crisis closer to home, by legitimizing its involvement in the violence in its peripheries in discursive terms – of the eternal clash between righteous Sudanese Arab Muslims against African non-Muslim others. By constructing this far-off common "other," the riverian elite may attain closure of their contingent boundaries. Despite their internal differences, based on economic, social, religious, political, and cultural difference, they at least can thus agree on the threat of those amorphous, unknown, and thus uncontrollable others to the status quo. This facilitates its illusion of a unified identity, as de Waal maintains:

> Sudan's elites possess a cultural cohesion that belies its political fragmentation. For this group, Sudan's crisis has become a way of life ... and implies that Sudan will most probably continue to function in the fashion of a deadly gyro-scope, its balance achieved at the price of deadly disorder in its peripheries.[92]

Violence by the Sudanese government seems to be the ultimate consequence of the search for a means to mark the boundaries of an exclusionary form of citizenship. This is not just specific to Sudan, but works also in other contexts, as De Vries and Weber, who in their foreword to the volume *Violence, Identity and Self-Determination*, state:

> It becomes more difficult to consider violence to be an act perpetrated by others when in an increasing number of cases it is being practiced in the name of self-determination. Determination of the Self now reveals itself to be what it probably always has been: determination of the Other.[93]

This is not to say that the application of violence by the Sudanese government, in order to (re-)construct a national self, is thereby made understandable or justifiable. It does mean, however, that a more radical shift in thought and practice is needed for breaking with this past of constructing otherness by reference to the notion of "black" in order to attain a more inclusive notion of citizenship. This is first and foremost a matter of balanced socioeconomic, political, and cultural development. However, I agree with Amir Idris when he states that:

> The legitimising function of the apparatus of truth in the Sudan is the official denial of race as a source of conflict. By abolishing racial otherness as a socially

relevant frame of reference, the dominant discourse in the Sudan removed the critical issue of ethnic and racial hegemony and discrimination from the realm of legitimate debate [...] Contemporary scholars of Sudan's civil war thus need to seek an alternative discourse of history that can be used to understand the root causes of the tragedy.[94]

We, as contemporary scholars of Sudan's civil war, thus need to take some of the responsibility to find such an "alternative discourse" that is inclusive, rather than exclusive. We have to acknowledge the differences and diversity in local histories and trajectories of transformation in order to be able to write a more inclusive Sudanese national history as a means of finding alternative roads to change.

Notes

1   Portions of this essay are taken from my article "Darfur in War: The Politicisation of Ethnic Identities?" which appeared in ISIM Review 15, Spring (2005): 14–15.
2   "UN Coordinator Mukesh Kapila calls Darfur 'the world's worst humanitarian crisis' and makes a comparison to Rwanda," stated in the entry "March 2004" of the "Chronology," in War in Darfur, and the Search for Peace, Alex de Waal, ed. (Cambridge, MA: Harvard University Press,2007): xvi.
3   Generally 2003 is referred to as the start of the rebellion, as the SLA and JEM announced their existence early that year. Political as well as armed resistance against the government had been building for a longer period 2001, as an important date for the start of organized resistance, when "rebels" attacked a police station in Golo, the district headquarters of Jebel Marra; or June 2002 when a group calling themselves the "Darfur Liberation Front" officially claimed this attack on Golo. See Alexander de Waal and Julie Flint, Darfur: A Short History of a Long War (London: Zed Books, 2005) p. 76.
4   See, for example, "Darfur Rebels May Unite but Talks Still Tough," Sudan Tribune, Tuesday November 13, 2007, http://www.sudantribune.com/spip.php?page=imprimable&id_article=24712 (accessed April 9, 2008).
5   Scholars, such as Ali Dinar, even state that the watershed that the war is thought to represent is exaggerated as violence, poverty, and the neglect by the government are symptomatic for Darfur. In this respect I agree with him. Here I will argue, however, that the way the violence has been legitimized does make a difference. I would like to thank Ali Dinar for his critical remarks on a paper I presented at the Twenty-Fifth Anniversary of the Sudan Studies Association, Bergen, Norway, April 6–8, 2006.
6   While race is officially not a sociological or biological category, it has become part of the war's legitimizing discourses and shapes people's experiences and is thus a phenomenon to be analyzed in this context.
7   After Foucault; see Sara Mills, Discourse (London and New York: Routledge, 1997) p. 26.
8   See, for example, Mahmood Mamdani, "The Politics of Naming: Genocide, Civil War, Insurgency," London Review of Books, 8 March 2007, http://www.lrb.co.uk/v29/no5/mamd01_.html, (accessed April 20, 2007).
9   I consider identity not as a property of a person, but as performative and thus contingent, ambiguous, and transformative. See Judith Butler, Gender Trouble: Feminism on the Subversion of Identity (New York and London: Routledge, 1990) pp. 70–90; also see Rachel

Alsop, Annette Fitzsimons, and Kathleen Lennon, eds., Theorizing Gender (Cambridge: Polity, 2003) p. 103.
10 Alexander de Wall, Famine That Kills, Darfur, Sudan, 1984–1985 (Oxford: Clarendon Press, 1989) p. 50.
11 Gunnar Haaland, "Nomadization as an Economic Career among the Sedentaries in the Sudan Savannah Belt," in Essays in Sudan Ethnography, I. Cunnison and W. Jones, eds. (London: Hurst, 1972) pp. 49–172. See also Gunnar Haaland, "Economic Determinants in Ethnic Processes," in Ethnic Groups and Boundaries: The Social Organization of Culture Difference, Fredrik Barth, eds. (Oslo: Scandinavian University Press, 1969) pp. 58–74.
12 de Waal, 1989, pp. 48–49.
13 This myth might be a transformation of earlier versions of the coming of a "Wise Stranger" used to explain the founding of Sultanates of the Sudanic Belt at large, of which Darfur was the easternmost Sultanate. This visitor was "not particularly a Muslim figure." Originally, al-Maq'ur was seen as the one who introduced more civilized traditions to the long-standing Sultanate of Darfur, such as table manners. Only in later versions has the "bringing of Islam" been ascribed to Maq'ur's arrival, lending the Sultanate, with his son Solongdungo as its "founder," a Muslim pedigree [R.S. O'Fahey State and Society in Darfur (London: Hurst & Company, 1980) pp. 123].
14 Apart from Fur, there were other groups living within the boundaries of the Sultanate, like Tunjur, Berti, Bergid, Masalit, and Zaghawa (e.g., see Flint and de Waal, 2005, p. 9).
15 The most affluent Islamic teachers were attracted to the court receiving large plots of land or hakuras, which were exempted from taxation by the Sultan. Its inhabitants were seen as subjects of the person with the land grant, rather than of the Sultan [e.g., see Lidwien Kapteijns, Mahdist Faith and Sudanic Tradition: The History of the Masalit Sultanate 1870–1930 (London: Kegan Paul International Series, 1985); G. Michael La Rue "Land and Social Stratification in Darfur, 1785–1875: The Hakura System," in The State and the Market: Studies in the Economic and Social History of the Third World, Clive Dewey, ed. (New Delhi: Manohar, 1987); O'Fahey, 1980, pp. 24–44].
16 See O'Fahey, 1980, pp. 9–10, 122 and "Fur and Fartit: The History of a Frontier," in Culture History in the Southern Sudan: Archaeology, Linguistics and Ethnohistory, John Mack and Peter Robertshaw, eds. Memoir number eight (Nairobi: The British Institute

in Eastern Africa, 1982), pp. 75–89.

17 Darfur was located strategically on the caravan route between West Africa and Egypt, the so-called *darb al-arba'in*, or forty-days road, and on the route to Mecca in the east. Quite a number of traders and pilgrims settled in North Darfur, at the crossroads of peoples and cultures.

18 Apart from being a Muslim, a full subject of the Sultanate would, for example, accept the rights and duties, such as paying taxes and levies, and receiving protection from slave raids, which came with belonging to a certain locality. See Lidwien Kapteijns, *Mahdist Faith and Sudanic Tradition: The History of the Masalit Sultanate 1870–1930* (London: Kegan Paul International Series, 1985); O'Fahey, 1980; and de Waal, 1989, p. 48.

19 Flint and de Waal, 2005, p. 9; de Waal 2007, p. 9.

20 The British retained some of the already existing titles and invented others to construct a viable administrative hierarchy. They did not succeed everywhere to control the local leaders, however. The Rizeigat Arab, on the other hand, did not get land rights, only *damra* or temporary settlements. They also did not get their own paramount chief. See Flint and de Waal, 2005, pp. 13–15, 41–46; De Waal, 2007, pp. 29–31; Jérôme Tubiana, "Darfur: A War for Land?" in *War in Darfur, and the Search for Peace*, Alex de Waal, ed. (Cambridge, MA: Harvard University Press, 2007), pp. 73–75.

21 See Alex de Waal, "Counter-insurgency on the Cheap," *London Review of Books* 26, no. 15 (5 August 2004, http://www.lrb.co.uk/v26/n15/waal01_.html, accessed April 20, 2007). The Islamist government invented new leadership positions, like *amir*, which were almost all given to diverse groups of Arabs that previously held no land rights (Flint and de Waal, 2005, pp. 57–59).

22 Ibid.; Flint and de Waal 2005, 12–13, 58–59; and Sharif Harir, "Arab Belt Versus 'African Belt' Ethno-Political Conflict in Dar Fur and the Regional Cultural Factors," in *Short-Cut to Decay: The Case of the Sudan*, Sharif Harir and Terje Tvedt, eds. (Uppsala: Nordiska Afrikainstitutet, 1994), pp. 178–184.

23 Douglas H. Johnson, *The Root Causes of Sudan's Civil Wars* (Oxford: James Currey, 2003), p. 4.

24 Professor Claude Aké stated this in an hour-long television interview in the series *In My Father's House* hosted by the Netherlands anthropologist Anil Ramdas. He pointed out that it is theoretically problematic to think "ethnic groups" or "ethnic conflict," and that in situations where ethnic consciousness is called upon, issues of power and survival are at stake. As he put it, the fact that one likes one's culture, one's dishes, and one's customs is in itself not a reason to fight each other. See also his article "What Is the Problem with Ethnicity in Africa?" *Transformation*, no. 22 (1993): pp. 1–14.

25 "Economic Spheres in Darfur," in *Themes in Economic Anthropology*, Raymond Firth, ed. (London: Tavistock, 1970), pp. 49–179; *Human Resources: Social and Cultural Features of the Jebel Marra Project Area*, FAO Report: Rome, 1967; *The Fur of Jebel Marra: An Outline of Society*, Khartoum: Department of Anthropology of the University of Khartoum, 1964.

26 Barth, 1969, pp. 9–38.

27 Flint and de Waal, 2005, p. 7.

28 Amir H. Idris, *Sudan's Civil War: Slavery, Race and Formational Identities* (Lewiston, NY: Edwin Mellen Press, 2001), pp. 57.

29 See Fouad Ibrahim, *Desertification in North Darfur* (Hamburg: Hamburger Geographisher Studien 35, 1980).

30 See Flint and de Waal, 2005. p. 51; Harir, 1994, pp. 160–184.

31 The SLM is considered to be associated with the Fur and Masalit, while the JEM is associated with the Zaghawa of northern Darfur. See Flint and de Waal, 2005, pp. 26, 89, 95; Flint, "Darfur's Armed Movements," pp. 148–150 and Dawit Toga, "The African Union Mediation and the Abuja Peace Talks," p. 214, both in *War in Darfur, and the Search for Peace*, Alex de Waal, ed. (Cambridge, MA: Harvard University Press, 2007).

32 See Appendix I of this book for detailed excerpts of *The Black Book*.

33 Flint and de Waal, 2005, pp. 17–18.

34 Parts of this section appeared in Willemse, 2005, pp. 14–15.

35 The label "Janjawid," used to refer to the Arab nomadic militia, has been dissected into "devil" (*jaan*), "horse-men" (*jawid*), or "devils" (*jiin*) riding horses, carrying *jim*, Arabic for GM-3 rifles. However, prior to the recent conflict, the term was used more generally to refer to "rabble," "hordes," or "outlaws," in particular in cases of banditry and camel theft committed predominantly by young men. It is this reference to young men that is crucial to my argument.

36 The last large conference was held to settle a war between Fur and Arabs in 1989. Some months after the signing of the agreement, attacks again took place. See Harir, 1994, pp. 171–173.

37 Information from a talk with one of the Zaghawa negotiators from Kebkabiya Town, present at this conference.

38 Harir, 1994, p. 170; Karin Willemse, "On Globalization, Gender and the Nation-State. Muslim Masculinity and the Urban Middle-Class Family in Islamist Sudan," in *The Gender Question in Globalization: Changing Perspectives and Practices*, Tine Davids and Francien van Driel, eds. (Burlington, VT: Ashgate Publishers, 2005), pp. 159–179.

39 See also Barth, 1970; Grawert, Elke, *Impacts of Male Out-Migration on Women: A Case Study of Kutum, Northern Darfur, Sudan* (Bremen: University of Bremen, 1992); and Elke Grawert, *Making a Living in Rural Sudan: Production of Women, Labour Migration of Men, and Policies for Peasants' Needs* (New York: St. Martin's Press, 1998).

40 de Waal, 1989, p. 50.

41 For example, see Tubiana, 2007, pp. 87–89.

42 See Flint and de Waal, 2005, pp. 46–48.

43 In December 2007 Musa Hilal has been appointed special advisor for the Ministry of Federal Affairs by President Omar Al Bashir; for example, see *Sudan Tribune*, Wednesday 09 April 2008 Edition: "Profile: Musa Hilal from a convicted felon to a government official," Tuesday 22 January 2008, http://www.sudantribune.com/spip.php?article25660, accessed April 4, 2008.

44 Flint and de Waal, 2005, pp. 35–36, 63; the quotation, ibid., p. 35. Sheikh Hilal himself, however, had relocated his ethnic group, the Mahamid Arabs, to the Amu region in 1976 after he acquired the land, originally owned by farmers, through forgery and bribing a local official: http://www.sudantribune.com/spip.php?article25660, accessed April 4, 2008.

45 See Gendercide Watch: http://www.gendercide.org/what_is_gendercide.html, accessed 18–11–2004.

46 In Darfur, where ethnic affiliation is traced patrilinially, intermarriage results in women begetting children of a different ethnic background than their own. This means that the involvement of women in ethnic politics differs from those of men who have a more unified ethnic identity. Even in ethnically more homogenous communities women and children of diverse ethnicities have in fact been caught similarly in the crossfire between

Section Three: Gender, War, and Violence

rebels, government, and bandits.

47 Flint and de Waal, 2005, p. 41. Other authors argue that the Janjawid have always been comprised of Arabs. For example, see Haggar, 2007, p. 114 and Tubiana, 2007, p. 69. This may be a particularity of a certain region rather than a general feature of the Janjawid militia.

48 For example, see Haggar, 2007, pp. 129, 139, who points out how the government recruited both Arab and non-Arab tribes, who were then considered part of one and the same military organization: the Janjawid.

49 See Haggar, 2007, p. 139.

50 Flint and de Waal, 2005, p. 61. Significantly, there are also Arab nomads who refused to join this "Arab Gathering," or "Congregation," such as the Bagarra Rizeigat under Saeed Mahmoud Ibrahim Musa Madibu south of Jebel Marra. See Haggar, 2007, pp. 129–130. See also Flint and de Waal, 2005, pp. 122–125.

51 See Flint and de Waal, 2005, pp. 33–65 and Harir, 1994b, p. 161.

52 Document dated August 16, 2004, quoted in Flint and de Waal, 2005, pp. 106, 144 n. 19.

53 Johnson, 2003, p. 170.

54 For example, see John Ryle, "Disaster in Darfur," *The New York Review of Books* (51, no. 13 (August 12, 2004). See also Flint and de Waal, 2005.

55 The Arab nomadic groups that have come from Libya and Chad perceive this difference differently. They claim ancestry with the Qureish, the nomadic group of the Prophet Mohammed. They see themselves therefore as the "true custodians of Islam" and therefore entitled to rule Muslim lands. Adherents regard Sudan's riverian elite as "half-caste" Nubian-Egyptians (Flint and de Waal, 2005, p. 53) and thus not entitled to rule the Sudan. Historically, however, the riverian elite are at the center of political and socioeconomic power and thus of notions of Sudanese citizenship. I will return to this issue later.

56 For example, see De Waal, 2007, pp. 11–38, for the strategy of the Sudanese government to construct war in its peripheries as "tribal" and thus of local rather than national importance.

57 As articulated in speeches on television and those delivered in Darfur. For parts of these speeches see Willemse Karin, *"One Foot in Heaven": Narratives on Gender and Islam in Darfur, West-Sudan* (Leiden: Brill Publishers, 2007), pp. 91–131.

58 Hala Abdel Magid, al-Ahmadi, *Globalisations, Islamism and Gender: Women's Political Organisations in the Sudan*. Ph.D. Dissertation, Catholic University of Nijmegen (2003): 28.

59 See Al-Ahmadi, 2003, pp. 50–52; Willemse, 2007.

60 Willemse, 2007 and "'In My Father's House,' Gender, Islam and the Construction of a Gendered Public Sphere in Darfur, Sudan," *Journal for Islamic Studies* Special Issue: "Islam and African Muslim Publics" 27 (2007): 72–113.

61 Ahmed Yussuf, representative of the provincial Department of Religious Affairs of Kutum, member of the popular committee addressing the Kebkabiya town's population on December 12, 1991. See for a more extensive representation and analysis of the speeches Willemse 2007, pp. 71–90.

62 Men, in particular, were addressed in these parts of the speeches. For a more elaborate analysis of the way women were addressed see Karin Willemse, "'A Room of One's Own.' Single Female Teachers Negotiating Alternative Gender Roles," *Northeast African Studies Journal*, Special Issue 'Women in the Horn of Africa' VIII, no. 3 (2006). Back issue 2001 and 2007: 71–90.

63 The captain who led the military coup on June 30, 1989,

64 *Faqih* (religious teacher) a member of the visiting popular committee addressing the Kebkabiya town's population on December 12, 1991. The last part of this quotation refers to a Qur'anic text (49:13 "O Men, We created you from male and female and made you peoples and tribes that you may know one another (not that you may despise each other)." http://www.islamic-world.net/islamic-state/evidence.htm (accessed April 7, 2008).

65 See Flint and de Waal, 2005, pp. 33–65, 97–117; Haggar, 2007, pp. 126–139, the latter reference includes the Qureish manifestos, which openly propagated Arab supremacy.

66 "Zuruq" is used predominantly to refer to Fur, Zaghawa, and Masalit, the groups that formerly were the leaders in the former Sultanate. Cailliaud, a French traveller at the beginning of the nineteenth century, who described the Funj Sultanate, or Sultanate al-Azrag, pointed out that blue referred to the position of indigenous rulers rather than skin color. See F. Cailliaud, 1823, *Voyage à Meroé, au Fleuve Blanc*, Paris, 4 volumes, in *Kingdoms of the Sudan*, R.S. O'Fahey, and Jay Spaulding, eds. (London: Methuen & Co., 1974): pp. 30–31. It is of course highly problematic to transpose this meaning to contemporary times, and would need more research. See for usage of "color" in a contemporary setting: Al-Baqir al-Afif Mukhtar, 1999, "The Crisis of Identity in Northern Sudan: A Dilemma of a Black People with a White Culture," Paper Presented at the *CODESRIA African Humanities Institute*, Published by the Program of African Studies (Evanston: Northwestern University), 14–19; Janice Boddy, *Wombs and Alien Spirits. Women, Men and the Zar Cult in Northern Sudan*, (Madison: University of Wisconsin Press, 1989), p. 64; in the context of Egypt: Anita Fabos, "Resisting 'Blackness': Muslim Arab Sudanese in the Diaspora," *ISIM Review*, no. 21 (Spring 2008): 24–25.

67 This diversity of colors is similar as those given to Boddy when she was conducting research in the 1980s in a small village along the Nile in North Sudan (Boddy, 1989 p. 64).

68 Ahmed Al-Shahi, "Proverbs and Social Values in a Northern Sudanese Village," in *Essays in Sudan Ethnography*, Ian Cunnison and Wendy James eds. (London: Hurst & Co., 1972), p. 97; Al-Baqir al-Afif Mukhtar, 1999, pp. 14–19.

69 Many witness accounts of survivors of attacks by Janjawid refer also to this relationship between blackness, religion, and the position of a slave.

70 De Waal, 2007, p. 36.

71 De Waal, 2007, pp. 37–38.

72 See Kapteijns, 1985, pp. 55, 66–67; Jay Spaulding, *The Heroic Age in Sinnar*, Ethiopian Series Monograph no. 15 (East Lansing: Michigan State University, 1985), pp. xviii–xix, 150, 178–198, 238; O'Fahey, 1980, pp. 115, 131–145. The Turkiyya was overthrown by the Mahdi, an indigenous Muslim charismatic leader who established an Islamic state, the Mahdiyya, in 1885. In 1898 Sudan became a British-Egyptian Condominium.

73 Paul Doornbos, "On Becoming Sudanese," in *Sudan: State, Capital and Transformation*, Tony Barnett and Abbas Abdelkarim, eds. (London: Croom Helm, 1986), pp. 99–120; Mansour Khalid, *The Government They Deserve: The Role of the Elite in Sudan's Political Evolution* (London: Kegan Paul International, 1990), pp. 54–115; and Tim Niblock, *Class and Power in Sudan: The Dynamics of Sudanese Politics, 1898–1985* (Hampshire: Macmillan Press, 1987), pp. 160–203.

74 See for the importance of the boardinghouse for female

pupils and teachers Willemse, 2007, pp. 72–113.

75 The term comes from Benedict Anderson *Imagined Communities: Reflections on the Origin and Spread of Nationalism*, (London: Verso, [1983] 1991).

76 Doornbos (1986, pp. 99–120) coined this term and stated that in this case *Sudanization* also meant "Arabization."

77 See Kurt Beck, "Tribesmen, Townsmen and the Struggle over a Proper Lifestyle in Northern Kordofan," in *Kordofan Invaded: Peripheral Incorporation and Social Transformation in Islamic Africa*, Endre Stiansen and Michael Kevane, eds. (Leiden: Brill, 1998), 267; Harir, 1994, "Recycling the Past in the Sudan," in *Short-Cut to Decay: The Case of the Sudan*, Sharif Harir and Terje Tvedt, eds. (Uppsala: Nordiska Afrikainstitutet, 1994), pp. 27–33; Johnson 2003, pp. 4–7.

78 Ali Bob, "Islam, the State and Politics in the Sudan," *Northeast African Studies* 12, no. 2–3 (1990): pp. 201–219.

79 Numeiri ruled from 1969 until 1985. At the beginning he opted for a predominantly socialist course, but he gradually shifted to an increasingly Islamist ideology.

80 Richard Brown, *Public Debt and Private Wealth. Debt, Capital Flight and the IMF in Sudan* (Basingstoke, The Hague: Institute of Social Studies, 1990); Richard P. C. Brown, *Sudan's Other Economy. Migrants' Remittances, Capital Flight and Their Policy Implications*. ISS Working Paper, Sub-Series on Money and Finance and Development 31 (The Hague: Institute of Social Studies, 1990).

81 See Willemse, 2007, pp. 417–449.

82 See Willemse 2005, pp. 170–179; 2007, pp. 417–449. This phenomenon has also been argued for colonial elites, using women to construct a *cordon sanitaire* around the powerful but very heterogeneous colonial elite, for example, Ann Stoler, "Carnal knowledge and imperial power. Gender, race, and morality in colonial Asia," in *Gender at the Crossroads of Knowledge: Feminist Anthropology in the Postmodern Era*, ed. Micaela di Leonardo (Berkeley: University of California Press, 1991).

83 Charlton, Everett and Staudt, 1989, p. 180; quoted in: E. Sanasarian, "The politics of gender and development in the Islamic Republic of Iran," in: *Women and Develop-*

ments in the Middle East and North Africa*, Joseph G. Jabbra and Nancy W. Jabbra, eds. (Leiden: Brill, 1992), p. 58.

84 Pettman 1996 quoted in Wilford, Rick, "Women, Ethnicity and Nationalism: Surveying the Ground," in *Women, Ethnicity and Nationalism: The Politics of Transition*, Rick Wilford and Robert L. Miller, eds. (London and New York: Routledge, 1998), p. 16.

85 Donaldson, 1993, p. 655, cited in Hooper, 2000, p. 70.

86 See C. Hooper, *Manly States: Masculinities, International Relations, and Gender Politics* (New York: Columbia University Press, 2000); G. Sahgal and Nira Yuval-Davis, eds. *Refusing Holy Orders Women and Fundamentalism in Britain* (London: Virago, 1992); Nira Yuval-Davis, "Gender and Nation," in Wilford and Miller, 1998, pp. 23–36; and Wilford, 1998, pp. 1–23.

87 See for an analysis of the excelsior of females and "lesser males" in Habermas's notion of civil society, Willemse 2007, pp. 74–77.

88 This is not to say that the Central Sudanese population is to "blame" for racism. Rather, it has been part of the way national identity has been constructed, and thus has become part of a discourse of power and privilege, which is related to the history of slavery. Central Sudan became a booming center of slave trade while ruling both the areas where the administrative elite resided and the slave-raiding areas. This past has become part of Sudan's national present.

89 M.A. Mohamed and Sharif Harir, "The Genesis of National Disintegration," in *Short-Cut to Decay: The Case of the Sudan*, ed. Sharif Harir and Terje Tvedt (Uppsala: Nordiska Afrikainstitutet, 1994), p. 188.

90 See also De Waal, 2007, pp. 31–38.

91 Salih and Harir, 1994, pp. 199.

92 Salih and Harir, 1994, p. 201

93 De Waal, 2007, pp. 36, 38.

94 Hent de Vries, and Samuel Weber, eds., *Violence, Identity and Self-Determination* (Stanford, CA: Stanford University Press, 1997), pp. 1–2.

95 Idris, 2001, pp. 26–28, 136.

12 Sudanese Civil Society Strategizing to End Sexual Violence against Women in Darfur

Fahima A. Hashim

This essay focuses on the roles and challenges facing Sudanese civil society as it works to end the sexual violence against women now occurring in Darfur. I shall therefore start by briefly addressing the history and the causes of the conflict, followed by a general perspective on the state of violence against women in Sudan, then highlight the findings of several reports that have documented sexual violence in Darfur. I will also address how the Sudanese government's denial of the existing crisis has shaped how victims of these crimes are treated. Finally, a brief history of the formation of civil society in Sudan will be followed by an analysis of how Sudanese civil society organizations deal with sexual violence in Darfur, the obstacles and challenges put in their path, and how they can devise strategies to overcome these problems.

To underline how Sudanese civil society organizations are acting and strategizing to work in the area of sexual violence in Darfur, some issues and challenges need to be emphasized, such as the consequences of sexual violence for Darfurian women; the problematic definition of rape in its legal context; the impact of sexual violence on women's dignity and integrity; and civil society maneuver to end women sexual violence.

The primary causes of the present armed conflict in Darfur are complex and multifaceted. Briefly, such causes include the unjust policies of the Northern ruling elites since independence, and most specifically the current government's policies toward the marginalized regions and sectors of the country. This has been complicated further by the failure of the traditional management system for the allocation of natural resources in the region between nomads and sedentary farmers. This failure is also aggravated by a combination of ecological changes and government manipulation. Over the years local communities have been less able to cope with decades of drought and famine, and the capacity of the traditional system of conflict resolution has been diminished by the rapidity with which resources have become scarce.[1] The Libyan–Chadian war during the 1980s also accelerated the pace of the crisis in Darfur by making the region a depot of sophisticated weaponry and guns; the absence of the central government increased insecurity, and owning a gun became vital for survival. This has resulted in the spread of arms all over the region and the concomitant suffering of civilians and the devastation of lives. The whole society is held in division: "Arabs versus Africans." The long-term implications of this polarization are difficult to pinpoint, but to be certain the damage inflicted on the social fabric of Darfur is serious. The international media has not only exposed the crimes committed against civilians, including sexual violence against women in the region, it has also contributed to the formation of strong international opinion on the Darfur crisis.[2]

However, violence against women (VAW) is not unique to the war in Dafur and has been practiced in different forms and patterns of behaviors elsewhere in Sudan. Some of these forms are accepted and socially endorsed, such as female genital mutilation (FGM) and early marriage. In 2002–2003 the Gender Centre for Research and Training, a Khartoum-based nongovernmental organization (NGO), conducted the first survey on violence against women (in Khartoum State). This study was crucial for the women's rights movement to understand how women perceive violence and the different forms that afflict Sudanese women. The research outcome not only confirmed the existence of violence, but it actually substantiated the discrimination, humiliation, tyranny, oppression, and injustice practiced at different levels (i.e., cultural violence, domestic violence, class violence, street violence and harassment, sexual violence, psychological violence, legal violence, economic and political violence, and violence against women in armed conflict).[3]

Patterns of Rape and Unjust Laws: Facts and Women's Strategies

At the beginning of the armed conflict in Darfur – basically the period from late 2003 to the beginning of 2005 – mass rape was, according to Amnesty International (AI), systematic, and it was used as a weapon of war. Victims' testimonials bear witness to this fact. A woman refugee from Disa (Masalit village, West Darfur) interviewed by AI in Goz Amer camp in Chad, May 2004, stated:

> I was sleeping when the attack took place. I was taken away by the attackers in khaki and in civilian clothes, along with dozens of other girls, and had to walk for three hours. During the day, we were beaten and the *Janjawid* they told us: "you, the black women, we will exterminate you; you have no God." We were taken to a place in the bush [where] the Janjawid raped us several times at night. For three days, we did not receive food and almost no water.

Reporting and documenting violence against women in Darfur was tackled mostly by international nongovernmental organizations (INGOs), thus most of the reports examined herein are selected INGO reports. Fortunately, many of these international reports have made their way into the public domain. These include the Darfur Assessment Mission Consortium report in September 2004 titled "Assessment of Conflict Affected Populations in Kabkabiya & Kutum Localities, North Darfur State," which proved the existence of rape and sexual violence. It also documented police-registered cases in both localities, as well as registered cases in hospitals for women seeking medical treatment and assistance for sexual crimes.

In March 2005, *Medecins Sans Frontieres* (MSF) Holland published their first report on the widespread sexual violence in Darfur faced by hundreds of women and girls seeking medical care. MSF Holland then highlighted the immediate need to stop sexual violence in May 2005. The government of Sudan, in reaction to the report, arrested two of the MSF senior staff, accusing the organization of publishing false information, undermining Sudanese society, and spying. The international humanitarian actors demanded that the charges should be dropped since they were without foundation. The government authorities under pressure subsequently dropped the charges against MSF Holland staff members and released them on June 20, 2006.

Human Rights Watch's April 2005 report "Sexual Violence and Its Consequences among Displaced Persons in Darfur and Chad" not only provided statistical information on the issue but also highlighted the social and psychological implications of sexual violence. The report confirmed that:

> Many of the victims of rape and other sexual violence are deeply traumatized, as are many of their family members. Rape, when used as a weapon of war, is specifically aimed at terrorizing and subjugating entire communities, and affects the social fabric of the communities. In the conservative culture of Darfur, the stigma of rape is difficult to overcome: as one Fur woman remarked, "no one would accept to marry a raped woman."[4]

Pregnancy as a result of rape was another important issue identified in the report. The victims are sometimes blamed for disgracing their families, and as a result they are sometimes abandoned by their husbands. Furthermore, the report also highlights the medical consequences of sexual violence, including internal bleeding, fistulas, incontinence, and sexually transmitted diseases (STDs), among other health problems. Treatments include treating injuries that occur in the course of sexual violence, preventive treatment for STDs, testing for HIV/AIDS and hepatitis B and C, termination of unwanted pregnancies, and counseling to address the emotional and psychological impact of sexual violence.[5]

Another report issued by Amnesty International in 2004 provided information on human rights violations and sexual violence in Internally Displaced Persons (IDP) camps in Chad and Darfur. This report laid out comprehensive statistical information on rape and sexual violence and provided testimonies of both women and men. These testimonies showed the different kinds of violations that have occurred during the armed conflict and the systematic crimes committed by the Janjawid militias, such as gang rape of women and girls; sexual slavery; abduction and trafficking; torture, killing, and looting of men, women, and children; and burning of villages, property, and cattle. It also highlighted the causes and consequences of sexual violence against women and their communities, including social stigmatization, negative mental and physical health consequences, and debilitating economic and political implications for women. Moreover, Amnesty International looked at the legal aspects of the violence, including the impunity with which perpetrators violate international legal standards and human rights conventions and treaties.[6]

Refugees International's (RI) June 2007 report "Laws without Justice" comprehensively covered different aspects of the circumstances of rape in Darfur and systematically documented the obstacles that rape survivors face in seeking justice as a result of both the government's denial of rape and the legal system's flawed approach to prosecuting rape claims.[7] The findings of this report are reproduced in Adrienne Fricke and Amira Khair's contribution to this volume and I will accordingly not elaborate any further on them here. Suffice it to say that RI's report, along with the others previously mentioned, underscore that rape and other forms of sexual violence in Darfur are not only acts of sexual violence, they also expose women (victims) to extensive psychological and social harm. Indeed, the extent to which violence has been woven into the everyday fabric of life in Darfur

Sudanese Civil Society Strategizing to End Sexual Violence against Women in Darfur is poignantly underscored in the following statement by a North Darfurian woman, "When we leave the camp to look for firewood or other needed items we prefer to go as women rather than sending our men. When we women go we only get raped, but when our men go they get killed, so we would rather get raped and come back, than letting our men go and they never come back again."[8]

Despite the continuous denial of the government of Sudan's different institutions and official statements, rape and sexual violence in Darfur are used as systematic weapons of war. This was confirmed in August 2006 by UNMIS staff in Nyala.[9] In that same month the Al Amel Centre against Torture won the first rape court case in Nyala.[10]

The tactics used to deny the existence of sexual violence will be addressed in the following section.

The Government's Standpoint on Sexual Violence in Darfur: Women and the Hard Way to Justice

The government of Sudan has barely acknowledged rape as a major problem in Darfur. In the late Magzoub Al Khalifa's[11] disturbing statement on the alleged sexual promiscuity of Darfuri women in the printed media, he stated that "there are now more than 376 cases of pregnancy in the IDP camps which proved to be outside marriage," and he continued by saying, "Darfuri women are known for being promiscuous, and shameless."[12] This statement is problematic on a number of different levels: First, it shows the government of Sudan's refusal to accept that sexual violence is rampant in Darfur. Second, it blames the victims for the crimes perpetrated against them and in the process it disrespects and humiliates the women of Darfur and Darfur society in general. Al Khalifa's position violates article 28 of the 2005 Interim Constitution's Bill of Rights, which states that "Every human being has the inherent right to life, dignity, and the integrity of his/her person, which shall be protected by law; no one shall arbitrarily be deprived of his/her life."[13] Al Khalifa is, however, by no means alone in taking such a stand. In March 2007 Sudanese President Omar Hassan Al Bashir was quoted as saying, "it is not in the Sudanese culture or in the culture of the people of Darfur to rape. It doesn't exist."[14] This denial is compounded by the fact that prosecuting rape cases in Sudan is exceedingly difficult to do and places a greater burden of proof on women than on men. For example, many judges will accept the testimony of a man who swears on the Qur'an that he did not commit rape, but will not accept a contrary testimony from a woman that she was indeed raped."[15]

Al-Khalifa's and President Al Bashir's statements, as well as the rulings of some of the judges, are no doubt related to the prejudices of many Northern Arabized Sudanese from the center toward gender relations in Darfur, which differ considerably from those in Northern and Central Sudan, especially when it comes to the economic and sociocultural position of women. In Northern and Central Sudan, Darfur women are cast as hard workers who move freely in the public domain, and are therefore also considered to have an inferior sense of morality. It is therefore relevant to pinpoint what this prejudice is based on. Darfurian women are known for their significant economic contributions and their participation in market and agricultural economies, particularly as sellers of handicrafts, food, and so on. Women

Section Three: Gender, War, and Violence

are the major economic providers in many parts of Darfur. They are supposed to feed their children and therefore have larger fields on which they grow staple crops (millet or sorghum) and larger grain storage rooms than their husbands.[16] Men have to provide only the amount of grain they need for their own consumption. This allows them to grow cash crops, such as irrigated citrus fruits, to trade, or to engage in wage labor, since they are expected to pay for anything that costs money (taxes, clothing, utensils, etc). In order to earn this money, men spend a great deal of time outside their villages, while women take care of daily life inside the village – women are the de facto "keepers of the land."[17]

In practice, women need to have some income, as men are not always around when the need for money arises, and they do not always earn a sufficient enough income to cater for their family's needs. This has led to the misconception among men from Northern and Central Sudan, especially the ruling elites, that men in Darfur are lazy and can easily marry four women who work on the land for the upkeep of his children. By extension, Fur women are seen as "loose" and promiscuous, since they are quite self-assured with daily decision-making and taking skills, and they move in public spaces quite easily. More important, in the eyes of the Northern and Central Sudanese elite, men are not around to control the conduct of their women, wives, daughters, or sisters. The male members of the elite in Darfur predominantly act as bureaucratic civil servants, or hold positions in the official army, and constitute the "face" of the government. In dealings with local issues, especially in cases of sexual violence, this prejudice looms large and influences the decisions they take on behalf of the government they represent. It is precisely this prejudice that also directs the perspective taken in the current issue of sexual violence and rape under war conditions.[18]

In short, the notion that Darfur people are improper Muslims, which the Islamist government has propagated since it came to power in 1989, consists of different layers of moral condemnations, which makes the tackling of issues of sexual violence and rape very complicated. In fact, the Darfur population and its culture in general, and the women who are raped in particular, are blamed for the sexual violence perpetrated against them. Despite the Sudanese government's public denial that sexual violence is part of the war in Darfur, it has not reacted to international pressure on the issue. Thus, when the Security Council Resolution 1593 (2005) for Darfur was issued to end the impunity of war crimes against humanity, it also included people who commit sexual violence and rape against women of Darfur, whether the Army or the militias (the Janjawid).

However, the government of Sudan, in response to the international pressure on this issue, created the Violence against Women Unit under the Ministry of Justice's responsibility in 2005. The VAW unit formed three committees at the state level to deal with gender-based violence (GBV) in Darfur (committees were established in West, North, and South Darfur). In South Darfur, the *wali* (governor) endorsed the GBV issue under his responsibility and named it the Wali Committee. These committees organized weekly meetings with UN agencies, INGOs, and civil society working in the area of GBV to follow up on the services provided to survivors of sexual violence. They also provided awareness workshops for legal staff to address the complicated legal procedure for proving rape under the law and for the police on the usage of Form 8.[19] The VAW Unit partnered with UNFPA and AMIS to organize training sessions with lawyers, health workers, UN police, and UN staff. The Unit hired twenty female police and has deployed them to IDP camps in North and South Darfur. The unit, however, has not been supported by the government of Sudan to meet its objectives. Instead they had to seek donor funding, which confirms the Sudanese government's lack of commitment to tackling the matter. Moreover, while these committees are functioning, they are not genuinely interested in addressing the issue of sexual violence in Darfur.[20]

Even though, implicitly, these government institutions seem to acknowledge that the problem of sexual violence as part of the war is serious enough to take into account, it also proves that women's rights in general have not been considered by those in power in the Sudanese government. Examples of the government's disinterest in women's rights include the continuing refusal to ratify CEDAW, the lack of implementation of the Security Council Resolution 1325 for women in conflict and postconflict situations, and the complete silence around the African Protocol for Women's Rights, to mention a few. The lack of interest in such important issues can only be attributed to the specific Islamist ideology of those in control of the Sudanese state and its security organs and institutions.

Civil Society: A Brief History

Until the 1980s, Sudan had a relatively strong and well-developed civil society based primarily in the northern part of the country. However, civil society organizations (CSOs), like trade unions engaged in politics, have progressively been restricted by the state or dislocated by new welfare-based or issue-based organizations, influenced by the regime or the international development and relief agencies. These newly formed organizations neither have the political role nor the power that was held by the trade unions; accordingly their capacity for influencing Sudan's peace process or democratic transformation has been relatively weak. Sudan's civil society segment now faces significant challenges in fulfilling a peace-building role in the wake of the Comprehensive Peace Agreement (CPA).[21]

Abdel Aatti sums up the decline of the independent civil society sector as follows:

> After 1985, the political parties that had benefited from the trade unions' revolutionary spirit turned their back on the unions, thereby exposing democratic rule to further military coups. A new generation of civil society organizations started to emerge in response to drought, famine, the large-scale displacement and destitution caused by the renewal of the war in the south, as well as the large numbers of INGOs and relief agencies that arrived. This contributed to the marked increase in modern intermediary NGOs (intermediaries between donors and target groups) that direct their efforts to serving the victims of famine and war. Government inability to address the situation contributed to a short period (1985–1989) of cooperation, encourage-ment, and some state support of national voluntary organizations and the creation of a favorable environment for INGOs operating in the country. Most of these national organizations, however, were Khartoum-based, largely

nonpolitical, service-oriented, and dependent on external funding from INGOs and UN agencies, a characteristic that has remained constant ever since."[22]

Following the 1989 coup, the new regime dissolved all political parties and trade unions, and NGOs were required to reregister on new conditions that prohibited political engagement. The coordinating agency for voluntary work (COVA), later named the Humanitarian Aid Commission (HAC), was transformed into a security organ, imposing heavy restrictions on NGOs (national and international). The government prohibited NGOs from engaging in political issues like human and civil rights and governance and restricted their activities to service delivery. Yet, the National Islamic Front (NIF), which was behind the new regime, had been one of the first political parties to invest in and work through civil society for its own ends. It started by winning control of student unions in schools and universities and gradually infiltrated certain trade unions and created a base in the army. In power, it replaced freely formed unions with organs associated with the one-party system and interfered directly in selecting the leadership of independent organizations, ranging from sporting clubs to the Sudanese Red Crescent Committee. This strategy was designed by NIF to preempt the functions of existing independent organizations, supplanting them with its own bodies. Several "Islamic" organizations were formed, supported by the state and primarily funded by charity organizations close to the ruling groups in the Arabian Gulf's Emirates, Kuwait, and Saudi Arabia. Sudan's support of Saddam Hussein in the Gulf War halted most of the funding from the Gulf states, including the Arab Emirates and Kuwiat, and only the strongest and most heavily state-supported survived, such as the Zubeir Charity Foundation and El-Shaheed Organization. But given the utility of CSOs as a vehicle for receiving donor money, the number of registered organizations was reduced as Sudan's international isolation began to recede after 2002, most of them nonetheless still linked to the state and the ruling party.[23]

In the 1990s, the Islamist government continued to restrict the independent civil society sector. This resulted in transferring its social and economic responsibility for groups such as displaced persons, children, and the urban poor to national and international NGOs. Amidst Sudan's isolation, the consequences of natural disaster, growing violent conflicts, and the short-term negative impact of economic liberalization policies, NGOs were left to address the gap left by the ten-year ban on political parties and the weakness of state governments. Meanwhile, their agenda was being reshaped by increased interaction with international organizations, precipitating new visions and methods of civic action, and the spread of new development concepts like grassroots empowerment, participation, and peace building.[24]

During the course of the preparation for the UN Fourth World Conference on Women held in Beijing in 1995, Sudanese women started to organize themselves. From their inception in 1990 the Mutawinat Group, a Khartoum-based women's organization, for example, has worked in the area of legal aid to women in prison and women's rights education. The Almanar Group, founded in 1992–1993, focused on women's rights and paralegal training for women. In subsequent years, both the Gender Centre for Research and Training and the Salmmah Women's Resource Centre have worked in the area of research, training, and documentation, while the AZZA Women Association has worked to promote entrepreneurship and small-business ownership for women and others. However, it was during the last quarter of 2000 and the beginning of 2001 that a more substantial opening for civil society contributions in the area of peace building and women's rights issues occurred. Even still, working in the area of violence against women remains problematic – the Gender Centre was closed by security in 2003, the staff of the Khartoum Centre for Human Rights and Environmental Development, and its partner Amel Centre Against People's Torture, were interrogated, and some arrested, by the security forces. In May 2006, the Director of Salmmah Women's Resource Centre was also interrogated for conducting a series of workshops in the area of violence against women and for the organization's work on highlighting the sexual violence and rape in Darfur.[25]

Sudanese Civil Society: The Impossibility of Addressing Sexual Violence in Darfur

The government of Sudan has restricted the ability of civil society to gather and disseminate information relating to rape and sexual violence, abduction, and other violations of the rights of women, especially in the case of Darfur. In February 2006, the Sudan government enacted a law for humanitarian and voluntary work, which imposes severe restrictions on NGOs and gives the government excessive discretionary and regulatory powers over their work. The new law, however, required new registration for all NGOs under the Humanitarian Aid Commission (HAC), including the already registered NGOs. Amnesty International and other human rights organizations, as well as the Sudanese civil society in Khartoum, have condemned the legislation and noted that it violates the right to freedom of association contained in the international human rights treaties to which Sudan is a party.

Despite these condemnations, the Islamist government has developed a powerful strategy that disrupts the work of the existing civil society groups in Darfur by closing their organizations, arresting their staff, and confiscating office equipment. Civil society organizations that have been subject to such treatment include Sudan Social Development Organization (SUDO); Khartoum Centre for Human Rights and Environmental Development; Al Amel Centre for Treatment and Rehabilitation of Victims of Torture; and Strategic Initiative in the Horn of Africa (SIHA).

The Sudan Social Development Organization (SUDO) established its head-quarters in Khartoum in April 2001 and registered itself as a national NGO with HAC. It is a rights-based organization working toward achieving "justice for all." They have two programming approaches, which comprise both practical intervention (such as relief, recovery, and development) and human rights protection, under which all programs are designed. Their human rights activities include protection, peace-building, psychosocial services, awareness raising, empowerment, organizing people, and advocacy. SUDO is currently working in Darfur through five suboffices in Nyala, Al Fashir, Al Ginina, Al Dein, and Zalingi.

The Khartoum Centre for Human Rights and Environmental Development was established in 2001. Registered at HAC as a national NGO, they started working in Darfur, and since 2003 they have provided legal aid and paralegal training. Regarding sexual violence and other violations of human rights, they provide free legal support and follow-up for court cases, and they have good lobbying and advocacy skills.

They work in partnership with Al Amel Centre for the Treatment and Rehabilitation of Victims of Torture[26] and the Sudan Organization against Torture (SOAT). They have a strategic plan to support victims of torture in all Darfur states, and have thus far opened branches in Nyala and El Fasher in 2005. They operate with ten other network groups of lawyers in other parts of the Darfur region. When starting their work in Darfur, these organizations did not have the full capacity to work in conflict areas – they said that they "learned by doing." Nevertheless, these organizations remained strong, while at the same time the unstable situation was well-utilized by the Sudan government. Moreover, the government of Sudan instigated new legal procedures and policies for UN agencies and INGOs working in Darfur (these are not written policies, but were implemented on an ad hoc basis). In order for these organizations to operate in Darfur, they must follow many restrictive policies. For example, they are not allowed to report on all issues of human rights violations, and face specific restrictions on reporting on rape and gender-based violence issues. Additionally, the recruitment procedures for local staff have to be finalized by HAC for both INGOs and local NGOs alike. NGO leaders report that, among other things, this legislation restricts the ability of NGOs to receive funds by making it contingent upon permission from the HAC; the law also allows HAC to veto the nomination of individuals to serve on NGO boards.[27]

Consistent restrictions on funding and recruitment procedures, and other forms of harassment, have created a vacuum by depriving the subsistence of local organizations that opt to work in Darfur. As mentioned earlier, the government of Sudan benefited from the situation, and it filled the vacuum with government-created NGOs, the so-called "GONGOs,"[28] which are well funded and capable of supporting the government agenda. Still, registration of local NGOs remains a complex process, yet there are 2,180 organizations registered at the national level to work in Darfur, in addition to 1,500 organizations registered at the state level, which highlights the government's intention to hamper the operation and ability of local and international NGOs and civil society organizations to address critical issues in Sudanese society by creating its own organizations.[29] Indeed, any local organization based in Khartoum and operating or trying to work in Darfur is not viable without security and HAC intervention; therefore, building alliances and networking in Darfur was made impossible.[30] This has been especially the case with regards to alliance building around the question of sexual violence:

> ... rape survivors are also negatively impacted by the draconian legal regime governing the operation and activities of NGOs, including those that provide vital services to victims of sexual violence. The regime does so through a powerful government entity called HAC that is charged with enforcing laws concerning the composition and operation of local and International NGOs, as well as UN and other multilateral aid agencies."[31]

Civil Society: Challenges and Strategies

It is very clear that ending sexual violence in Darfur is not an easy task for the Sudanese civil society organizations, with their limited resources, skills, and the government's restrictions. Nonetheless, Sudanese civil society is strategizing to overcome these challenges to end sexual violence in Darfur, and in this context several NGOs are shedding light on the Darfur crisis and building alliances and partnerships, albeit slowly. There is a great need for capacity building among Sudanese civil society organizations' (CSO) staff, to enable them work in crisis situations with their limited resources, with the great lack of financial support for institution building and the need for fund-raising and reporting expertise. There is growing realization of the great need for legal reform as required by the CPA and the Interim Constitution of 2005, and the need for building a women's rights defenders network. It is important to note that despite HAC restrictions on civil society operational activities, different methods have been created to defeat the system and to provide services and conduct various activities such as psychosocial and trauma counseling; reporting rape cases; paralegal training and legal aid; and awareness raising in the area of transitional justice and the International Criminal Court procedures. I will highlight the challenges for selected organizations that are known for their genuine work and commitment to ending human rights violations in Darfur, such as Al Amel Centre for Treatment and Rehabilitation of Victims of Torture, Khartoum Centre for Human Rights and Environmental Development, and their partner, Sudan Organization against Torture (SOAT), Sudan Social Development Organization (SUDO), and finally Strategic Initiative for the Women in the Horn of Africa (SIHA).

Amel Centre for the Treatment and Rehabilitation of Victims of Torture was established in Khartoum in 2001, as well as the Khartoum Centre for Human Rights and Environmental Development, both registered as national NGOs, in collaboration with Sudan Organization against Torture.[32] In 2003, with the growing conflict in Darfur, they started to plan strategically to work in partnership to prevent human rights violations in Darfur. However, in 2004, in response to the alarming deterioration of human rights in the Region, Al Amel Centre and Khartoum Centre for Human Rights and Environmental Development were able to create two branches to work in Nyala (South Darfur), followed by another branch in El Fasher (North Darfur) in 2005. Now they have about ten small branches all over the three states in the region working through a network of lawyers. They provide legal aid, paralegal training, trauma counseling, medical treatment by the Amel Centre, lobbying, and advocacy. SUDO also provides humanitarian aid and legal aid, and they work in collaboration with Al Amel Centre and Khartoum Centre for Human Rights and Environmental Development.

SIHA is a regional network that operates in the Horn of Africa; they work in Sudan, Ethiopia, Eritrea, Somaliland, Somalia, and Djibouti. This initiative is aimed at supporting civil society organizations in the Horn of Africa region to enable them to address gender equality and violence against women. SIHA started working in Darfur in 2004 as a response to the prevalence of gender-based violence. Due to the limited number of women-focused organizations, SIHA intervention in Darfur was very crucial, and accordingly they recognized and planned two main forms of intervention: to reduce violence against women generally, and violence against women in conflict situations in particular. They provide medical, psychosocial, legal, and economic support for women. The second area is prevention, which includes interventions to reduce the risks that women face at different levels, as well as advocacy campaigns. SIHA operates in Nyala and El Fasher.

The prevention strategy was based on the formation of a platform for national and community-based organizations operating in North and South Darfur. They formed fifteen organizations in South Darfur and seven organizations in North Darfur and have a clear memorandum of understanding in partnership with them. In addition to training and capacity-building for community-based organizations in the area of project objectives and strategies, they also provide gender-based violence training, and preventive and responsive strategies for sexual abuse. They have also increased their capacity to facilitate the mainstreaming of gender-based violence training in their work. Finally, SIHA created a women's centre in Bilbil Camp South Darfur and another in Al Salam Camp North Darfur. These centers were created to provide safe environments for women survivors of violence, while providing counseling and education.[33]

Conclusion

Civil society organizations represent the main national forces working with communities to counter the impact of war, mismanagement of resources, and poor policies. Their resources for peace building include external links and extensive experience in negotiation over the last two decades, which have enabled them to survive in a hostile environment. Yet CSOs in Sudan are faced with challenges relating to government restrictions, internal failings, and external conditionality. [34]

The government continues to try to curtail the independence of CSOs. It uses its own parallel organizations to undermine existing CSOs, especially those working on human rights and women/gender issues. New legal restrictions on CSOs include the Organization of Humanitarian and Voluntary Work Act (2006), which requires HAC's approval of all CSO proposals before they are submitted to donors. The ministry can also ban any person from voluntary work. The dependence on foreign funding and a lack of specialization among CSOs has undermined the formation of effective networks, making them competitive rather than cooperative. Donor conditionality is sometimes imposed in favor of their own policies and agendas.

Finally, the donors need to recognize the importance of civil society's role in uplifting women in Darfur and lobby the Sudan government to allow NGOs and civil-society initiatives, including Darfur- and Khartoum-based organizations, especially women and human rights organizations, to work in Darfur. Khartoum-based organizations are generally well equipped and led by highly experienced women and other professionals and activists who have been working on those issues since the early 1990s. More to the point, they are able to work more independently of the government than civil society organizations based in Darfur, who come under heavy government scrutiny.

Notes

1. Munzoul Assal, "National and International Responses to the Crisis of Darfur," *The Ahfad Journal: Women and Change*, 24 (1). See also: http://sudaninstitute.org/Assal.pdf
2. Ibid.
3. Asha Elkarib, et al., Violence against Women Survey, unpublished research, Gender Centre for Research and Training, May 2003.
4. Amnesty International report, "Sudan, Darfur Rape as a Weapon of War: Sexual Violence and Its Consequences," July 2004.
5. Darfur Assessment Mission Consortium report, "Assessment of Conflict Affected Populations in Kabkabiya & Kutum Localities, North Darfur State, September, 2004.
6. MSF Holland Report, "Crushing the Burden of Rape: Sexual Violence in Darfur, Sudan," 2005.
7. Human Rights Watch Report, "Sexual Violence and Its Consequences among Displaced Persons in Darfur and Chad," April 2005.
8. Ibid.
9. Amnesty International Report, "Sudan, Darfur Rape as a Weapon of War: Sexual Violence and its Consequences," July 2004.
10. These legal obstacles include the conflation of rape with *zina* (adultery) in Sudanese legal codes governing the prosecution of rape cases, such that if a woman is unable to prove that she was raped she can be charged with adultery. For further information see this volume's Appendix O: Sudanese Law Related to Rape from Section 15 of the Criminal Act of 1991.
11. An interview with IDP women in Abu-Shok Camp, El Fasher, 2004.
12. An interview with UNMIS GBV staff, Nyala, South Darfur, August 2006.
13. Director Amel Centre for the Treatment and Rehabilitation of Victims of Torture, August 2006.
14. Dr. Magzoub Al Khalifa, the former Wali of Khartoum from the late 1990s until 2000, former Mininster of Agriculture, and the peace leader of Abuja Peace Talks, died in 2006.
15. *Akhir Lahza*, daily newspaper, no. 27 (August 2006): 3.
16. The Interim National Constitution of the Republic of Sudan, Article 28 "Life and Human Dignity," the Bill of Rights, Ministry of Justice, 2005.
17. Refugees International, *Laws without Justice: An Assessment of Sudanese Laws Affecting Survivors of Rape*, 2007.
18. Ibid.
19. Fredrik Barth, "Economic Sphere in Darfur," in *Themes in Economic Anthropology*, ed. Raymond Firth, London: Tavistock, 1970. And Elke Grawert, *Making a Living in Rural Sudan: Production of Women Labour Migration of Men*, and *Politics for Peasants' Needs*, Basingstoke: MacMillan; New York, St. Martin Press, 1998. Karin Willemse, *One Foot in Heaven: Narratives on Gender and Islam in Darfur, West Sudan*, Leiden: Brill Publishers, 2007.
20. Willemse, 2007.
21. Elke Grawert, 1998.
22. Willemse, 2007.
23. Dr. Atiyat Mustafa presentation, www.unfpa.org/emergencies/symposium06/docs/daytwosessionfiveeattiat.ppt
24. For more on Form 8 see the contribution to this volume by Fricke and Khair.
25. Fahima Hashim, "Sudanese Women Acting to End Sexual Violence," in *Forced Migration Review* 27 (2007): 44.
26. Hassan Abdel Atti, "Civil Society in Sudan," http://www.c-r.org/our-work/Accord/Sudan/civilsociety
27. Ibid.
28. Ibid.
29. Ibid.
30. Fahima A. Hashim, the Director of Salmmah Women Resource Centre, was summoned to meet with NGOs Department of the National Security and Intelligence body of the Sudan government on Tuesday May 2, 2006.
31. Amnesty International report, "Sudan, Darfur Rape as a Weapon of War: Sexual Violence and Its Consequences," July 2004.
32. Amel Centre for Treatment and Rehabilitation of Victims of Torture.
33. An interview with Khartoum Centre staff, March 2008.
34. "GONGOs" are government-operated NGOs, which may have been set up by governments to look like NGOs in order to qualify for outside aid and promote the interest of governments, http://en.wikipedia.org/wiki/GONGO.
35. An interview with Khartoum Center for Human Rights and Enviornmental Development.
36. An Interview with Khartoum Centre staff, Khartoum, March, 2008.
37. Frank and Khair, 2007.
38. SOAT (Sudanese Organization Against Torture), established in 1993, works in Sudan and the UK. The primary objective of SOAT is to prevent torture and challenge impunity, http://www.soatsudan.org.
39. http://www.Sianet.org/Darfur_Programme.html.
40. Abdel Atti, Hassan, "Civil Society in Sudan, http://www.c-r.org/our-work/Accord/Sudan/civil society.

Men on Top of a Lorry
Nyala, 2006

Scene from Bindisi Market
Bindisi, 2006

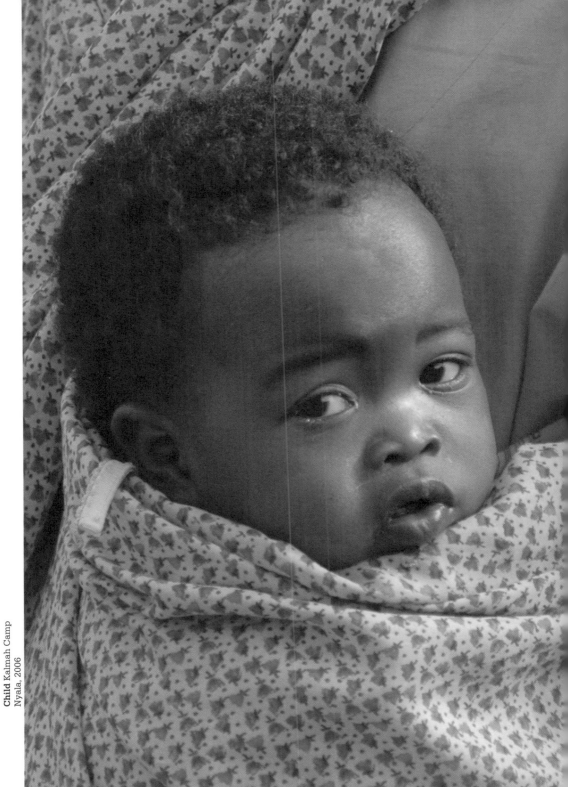

Child Kalmah Camp
Nyala, 2006

African Union Soldiers
Mukjar, 2006

Scene from Kalmah Camp
Nyala, 2006

Section Four
Darfur: Law, Human Rights, and Prosecution

13 The Erroneous Confrontation:
The Dialectics of Law, Politics and the Prosecution of War Crimes in Darfur

Kamal El-Gizouli

Translated from Arabic by Mustafa Adam

This essay addresses what I have deemed "the erroneous confrontation" between the government of Sudan (GOS) and the International Criminal Court (ICC) in The Hague. This confrontation is rooted in the conflict between the GOS and the international, albeit mostly Western community, and is somewhat divided in its strategy of pursuing a just settlement of the Darfur crisis, which the GOS and its allied *Janjawid* militia have been promulgating for the past six years. This confrontation is partially complicated by the double standard of the international community toward the prosecution of war crimes in other places such as in Palestine and Iraq, and the failure of the most powerful Western nations, specifically the United States, to recognize the ICC as a legal entity out of fear that its citizens may face similar indictments for war crimes in the future. Thus, elucidating the dialectics of law and politics around Darfur war crimes is a matter that I tackle by chronicling the referral process and the proceedings of the Office of the Prosecutor of the ICC and the Pre-Trial Chamber as a framework for understanding of the conflict between the GOS and the ICC. The best example of this dilemma is Al Bashir's presidential decision revoking the Sudanese Public Prosecutor's decision to reopen the investigation of Ahmed Harun, Sudan's Minister of State for Humanitarian Affairs, when the ICC declared him to be responsible for criminal activity in the region. Al Bashir intervened to protect his minister and to put an end to the dispute by declaring in public that "Harun will not be surrendered; will not surrender himself and will never be subjected to any sort of investigation."[1]

Analyzing such a confrontation necessitates the illumination of the national legal and judicial contexts of the crisis and their lingering effects on international and national politics, a task that I address in the discussion to follow.

The Legal and Judicial National Context of the Crisis

From the start, the GOS was both unable and unwilling to apprehend the perpetrators of Darfur crimes in ways that meet the standards of international justice as enshrined in the Rome Statute. In 2004, pursuant to the Sudanese Inquiry Commissions' Act of 1954, a national Inquiry Commission on Darfur, known as Daffalla's Commission, was formed. Subsequently, the report delivered by this commission was similar to the one issued later by the Cassese's International Commission of Inquiry (ICI) as to the enumeration of violations committed in Darfur. Later on, the findings and recommendations of Dafalla's Commission led to the establishment of three Special Criminal Courts in Darfur by the Sudanese Chief Justice on June 7 and 11, 2005, and on November 16 and 18, 2005, respectively.

The first court, known as "Abkam's Court," after the President of the High Court Justice Mahmoud Saeed Abkam, was not immune to criticism when compared to the ICC, at least with regard to three basic points.

First, the ICC is a permanent judicial authority that was established after significant international demands for a competent, impartial judicial system, surpassing those of Nuremburg, Tokyo, Yugoslavia, and Arusha, to mention a few. However, the first special national court for Darfur is an ad hoc court and the pretext of its establishment can only be understood within the context of the conflict between the Sudanese regime and the institutions of the international community. It is the GOS's attempt to defend its position in spite of its failure to secure justice within the workings of an effective judicial system that would grant the arrest and prosecution of perpetrators of crimes in Darfur.

Second, the ICC exercises its jurisdiction over individuals for the most dangerous crimes of international concern as referred to in the Rome Statute article number 1, which classifies these crimes following article number 5/1 as genocide under article number 6, crimes against humanity under article number 7, and war crimes under article number 8. The fundamental elements in these crimes are identified as follows:

A.1: To be committed in situations of wars or local or international armed conflicts.
A.2: Characterized by extensive range and of methodical nature.[2]

Within this framework, exploring the broader legal and judicial context reveals the marked shortcomings of the first Darfur Special Court, which, pursuant to article number 5 of the decree of its establishment, is limited to actions punishable by the provisions of the Sudanese Criminal Code and other criminal acts. These provisions do not involve the elements of the International Criminal law. The Sudanese Criminal Code includes provisions that punish actions like the misuse of detention powers and torture (articles numbers 89 and 90 of the Sudanese Criminal Code of 1991, and article number 4/d of the Criminal Procedures' Act of 1991). It also incriminates and punishes murder (article number 130), rape (article number 149), banditry (article number 175), and property damage (article number 182). The National Security Forces Act of 1999 also renders illegal and punishes actions committed by members of the National Security and Intelligence Organ (NSIO) who misuse their jurisdiction, with the intention of causing harm to others (article number 47). However, these provisions stipulate the prohibition and punishment of these crimes as crimes committed within ordinary circumstances and for ordinary criminal motives, but not as war crimes, crimes against humanity, or genocide, which generally represent "the most dangerous crimes" by international standards. It is possible, then, to equate "honor murders" committed in ordinary circumstances or rape committed for mere satisfaction of sexual desire with mass killing and rape committed widely and methodically during armed conflicts as a means of liquidating the enemy or causing physical and psychological injury. These limitations led the international commission to consider the Sudanese state unable and unwilling to prohibit impunity.

Third, the Rome Statute on international cooperation curtails the excessive use of immunity as a defensive shield against criminal liability. The decree of the establishment of the first Darfur Special Court was lacking in provisions dealing with these immunities that protect government officials from being subject to the provisions of the law, as much as the law itself lacks such provisions. The members of the NSIO enjoy a special status with respect to the range of authority and immunities entitled to them under the National Security Forces Act of 1999, even though it contradicts the 2005 interim constitution that renders this Act unconstitutional. It provides that the tasks of the NSIO are to be limited to the gathering and analyzing of information and providing advice to the designated authorities. It is important to note here that in a press conference on May 5, 2006, former UN High Commissioner for Human Rights Louise Arbour expressed her concerns about the Security Forces that commit grave violations of human rights, including abusive detention and torture in secret places belonging to the NSIO. Such practices, Arbour continued, call for immediate action to reestablish and reform this body because it does not comply with the international standards of human rights, as they comprise cases of impunity on the part of government officials. Furthermore, Arbour reiterated that the NSIO enjoys undeserved privileges and that the law governing the state of emergency should be revised to adhere to the aspirations of preserving human rights. There is also an urgent need, she added, to change the whole organizational structure of the National Security authority.

Above all, the International Commission, headed by Judge Cassese, has also observed that the Sudanese criminal laws involve provisions that effectively impede taking legal action against government officials. As mentioned before, Article number 33 of the National Security and Intelligence Forces Act of 1999 gives vast immunities to members and collaborators of these Forces. It prohibits forcing any of them to testify on any activities they were acquainted with as part of their job. No civil or criminal lawsuit is to be raised against any such persons on any of their actions related to their work without the prior permission of the director of the NSIO. Although only the director could allow taking action against those persons, they retain the right for compensation from the state. Even if the director grants such permission, they are to be brought before an unordinary and closed court session within the NSIO itself. The International Commission correctly regarded such provisions as contrary to the international standards of upholding justice. It is, in particular, against the provisions of article number 41/1 of the International Convention for Civil and Political Rights.

When confronted with this issue, General Salah Goush, the Director of the NSIO, attributed the whole problem to the incorrect English translation of the text. It behooved the International Commission to secure an accurate translation, and in so doing concluded that article number 33 practically stipulates enabling any member of the NSIO to torture a suspect – or even kill him – and get away with such an action, as it is considered part of the overall immunity these officers enjoy. The International Commission has put forward a recommendation to write off this law with an eye to the consequences of its application and the ongoing cases of impunity. It is paradoxical to realize that the Sudanese legislator, just a couple of months before establishing Abbkam's court and seven months before establishing the other two special courts, introduced two major amendments to the law. These amendments were issued by a temporary presidential decree on October 4, 2005. The first amendment was to the Criminal Procedures Act of 1991 and the second to the

Peoples' Armed Forces Act of 1986. Obviously, the purpose of these two amendments is to enable police and armed forces to enjoy impunity by providing immunity against all kinds of criminal liability arising from murder of unarmed civilians. The punishment for such acts is a mere payment of blood money, which the state is to pay on behalf of the perpetrator as provided by the new amended article number 73/3 of the Criminal Procedures Act and article number 79/a/3 of the Armed Forces Act.

The fact that the National Assembly did not endorse these two amendments will neither make up for the immunity they provided when the amended laws were enforced by the power of the temporary presidential decrees, nor will it prevent the state from resorting to exceptional authority to grant impunity by way of immunity to its affiliates in the future.

For the assessment of the overall performance of the Special Darfur Courts, a closer examination of the statement made by the Sudan Minister of Justice is necessary. He contended that these national courts have started practicing their judicial mandate to prosecute the perpetrators in the incidents that have occurred in Darfur, noting that:

> As has previously been stated, in addition to the "Abbkam's court" established in El Fasher on June 7 and 11, 2005, the Chief Justice issued two other decrees, numbers 1128 and 1129 on November 16 and 18, 2005, respectively, that involved the formation of two other special criminal courts in the region; the first in Nyala presided by Supreme Court Judge Jar Al-Nabi Gism-Al-Seid, and another in El-Gineina, presided by Supreme Court Judge Ahmed Abu Zaid.[11]

The criticism against the first Special Court is also applicable to the two other courts. However, there is a paradox here: The first Special Court's jurisdiction is limited to actions punishable by the provisions of the Sudanese Criminal Code and other criminal acts, pursuant to article number 5/1 of the decree of its establishment. Yet, knowing that these provisions do not involve the elements of the International Criminal law, article number 5/1 of the decree establishing the two other courts, allows them to decide on actions comprising crimes following "International humanitarian law." This situation gives rise to two main objections.

First, the wisdom necessitating the inclusion of a provision stipulating that the new Nyala and Al-Gineina courts be competent in prosecuting crimes against International Humanitarian Law should have also be applied to the first Abbkam Court in El Fasher, by amending article number 5/1 of the latter's decree of establishment. However, because such an amendment did not take place, a bizarre paradox takes shape here: The two other courts seem to operate within a degree of competence larger than the first Abbkam court, even though all three are supposed to have been established within the same degree of competence and for the same purpose.

The second objection is that the international conventions and treaties, of which the Sudan is a state party, comprise what is generally known as judicial notice, pursuant to the provisions of article number 14/3/d of the 1993 Sudan Evidence Act, which reads: "The court takes judicial notice relating to the following matter ... (d) each state recognized by the Sudan, and for that matter, all international and political affairs related to Sudan foreign affairs." Yet, the mechanism of judicially incorporating international treaties practically calls for including them, initially within national legislation, especially when concerned with criminal questions and particularly the punitive part of these treaties. It is not conceivable to envisage a criminal court judge deriving provisions for war crimes or crimes against humanity from the mere judicial notice of the four Geneva Conventions issued on December 18, 1949. Even if such a judge existed, how would it be possible for him or her to decide on appropriate punishments for such crimes? This is the job of the legislator, not the judge.

Whatever the case might be, the performance of the three courts during the last two years provides practical evidence of their glaring failure to comply with the requirements of international criminal justice at the levels of both practice and enforcement, a reality that contributes to the continuation of Darfur's atrocities with terrible tenacity. Witness the chaos that has surrounded the most notorious perpetrators of Darfur crimes and the overall response to the investigation that yielded their names. Instead of backing the Public Prosecutor, who decided to reopen the investigation with Minister Ahmed Harun, the Minister of Justice, aligned with the president, said that he could not find any evidence justifying or supporting the case of the ICC against Minister Ahmed Harun.[3] It is understandable that the only way to verify the existence of such evidence, within the framework of national criminal justice, is simply to carry out the ruling of the Sudanese Public Prosecutor to subject Minister Ahmed Harun to investigation, which was rendered impossible by the intervention of the President of the Republic. Hence, trying high-status perpetrators in Darfur before the national judiciary hinges solely on the willpower of the ruling political authority rather than on the competence of the judges presiding over the three Special Criminal Courts. This political willpower is conspicuously absent, notwithstanding the government's dismissal of the ICC.

The failure of the government to address the question of Darfur crimes has continued over an extended period of time and in all contexts within the judicial and legal frames. For instance, it went on from the date of the issuance of the UNSC resolution number 1593 on March 5, 2005, up to the decision of the Pre-Trial Chamber attesting to the admissibility of the case and the evidence brought forward, on February 5, 2007. President Omar Al Bashir has already barred the way to bring Minister Ahmad Harun to justice by revoking the decision of the Public Prosecutor to subject Harun to investigation. Attempts to bring perpetrators to justice are ultimately futile because the most significant element required to ensure the integrity of the national courts is altogether missing. In effect, these perpetrators are actually protected from being brought before an impartial and internationally accepted court of justice in compliance with article number 17/3 of the Rome Statute. This was clearly evident as the government did not actually name any of the so-called defendants and was satisfied by declaring that more than 150 people were going to be brought before the national courts of justice. Such a swift, uncalculated decision gives rise to suspicion of resorting to a sort of preemptive measure enabling them to claim that the investigation is already opened with whatever name that might crop up in any list of accused persons disclosed by the ICC at any time in the future. Within this ambiguous national judicial context, referral of the case to the ICC seemed like the next logical step, a topic to which I now turn.

The Referral

On October 1, 2004, and as requested by the United Nations Security Council, former UN Secretary-General Kofi Annan formed an International Commission of Inquiry (ICI) headed by the honorable Italian Judge Antonio Kassesse to investigate the events that have occurred in Darfur since July 1, 2002. In January 2005, the commission submitted its report to the Secretary-General, wherein it concluded that there is ample evidence to believe that crimes against humanity and war crimes were thought to have been committed in Darfur by Sudanese government troops, the Janjawid, and some elements of the Darfur liberation groups fighting against the government. Fifty-one suspects were named. Although the commission recommended the referral of the case to the ICC, it excluded the possibility of describing the criminal acts as genocide, as far as it was doubtful with regard to the existence of the *mens rea* or the nonmaterial element for carrying out this crime.

On March 31, 2005, and relying on this recommendation, the UNSC issued the referral resolution number 1593 (2005), under the provisions of chapter 7 of the UN Charter, and in conjunction with article number 13/b of the Rome Statute 1998, upon whose provisions the ICC was established. The resolution considered the case to be a threat to international peace and security and persuaded all member states to cooperate with the ICC. Therein, the referral decision involved reference to some of the provisions of the Rome Statute, including the following articles:

1. Article number 1, which stipulates that the court shall exercise its jurisdiction over persons, as complementary to national criminal jurisdiction, only when the concerned state is proven unable or unwilling to exercise its jurisdiction therein.
2. Article number 16, which stipulates that no investigation or prosecution may be commenced or proceeded with, under the provisions of this statute for a period of 12 months after the Security Council, in a resolution adopted under chapter 7 of the UN Charter, has requested the court to that effect; that request may be renewed by the council under the same conditions.
3. Article number 75, which provides for the reparations for victims.
4. Article number 79, which stipulates for the establishment of a trust fund.
5. Article number 98/2, which provides for conditions for cooperation with respect to waiver and consent to surrender.

It should be noted that a heated debate ensued within the Security Council with regard to whether genocide was committed in Darfur, as contended by a number of member states led by the United States and Britain. The council left the issue to the discretion of the ICC as suggested in the commission report and declared by Juan Mendez, UN Special Adviser on the Prevention of Genocide.[4]

Proceedings of the Office of the Prosecutor and the Pre-trial Chamber

On receiving the document archive from the UN Secretary-General, the General Prosecutor of the ICC, Luis Moreno-Ocampo, declared the commencement of an independent inquiry that would not be bound by the findings of either the commission or the previously prepared list of the fifty-one perpetrators. This inquiry was conducted over a span of eighteen months, during which the prosecutor submitted periodic reports to the UN Security Council, including those submitted on December

13, 2005, and June 14, 2006, respectively. He disclosed in the first report the findings of a visit of ICC delegates to the Sudan to gather information on the proceedings within the national courts to ensure that international standards considered by the Rome Statute are fully observed. He informed the council that the special court established in El Fasher, in Northern Darfur, convicted only 13 out of 160 suspects, and only one suspect was convicted of manslaughter.[5] The report stated that the independence of the ICC complements the local national judiciaries and is indeed what renders it an important tool for seeking justice for victims around the world. Its independence allows it to conduct necessary and effective investigations, successful arrest operations, improve interactions with victims and address their interests, and establish forms of cooperation with states and organizations to maximize the office's commitment to ending impunity.

Toward the end of November 2006, as part of the fifth session of the Assembly of States Parties, the prosecutor announced the completion and submission of Darfur's file to the ICC Pre-Trial Chamber comprising three judges who decided the admissibility of the case. On February 27, 2007, he informed the media that his office's investigations involved seventeen countries and collected more than one hundred testimonies from witnesses. The office has also studied the report filed and submitted by the National Commission of Inquiry formed by the Sudanese government, together with testimonies from government officials, including the Minister of Defense. Two names were disclosed as perpetrators, together with the evidence leading to the decision. The two culprits are Ahmad Harun, Sudan's former Minister of State for the Interior, and Ali Muhammad Ali Abd-Al-Rahman (Kushayb), a Janjawid leader. Based on evidence collected during the period from August 2003 to March 2004, as part of government attacks against the armed rebels within a regional armed conflict, the prosecution has concluded that there are reasonable grounds to believe that the two said culprits bear criminal responsibility in relation to fifty-one counts of alleged crimes against humanity and war crimes such as sexual violence, killings, torture, pillaging and looting of residences and marketplaces, and displacement. These findings led the prosecutor to conclude that there is solid evidence to decide that the two individuals bear criminal responsibility for most of the war crimes and the crimes against humanity in Darfur. He called into question the competency and will of the government to bring these perpetrators to justice. On February 5, 2007, the Pre-Trial Chamber decided that the case and the prosecutor's evidence are admissible and issued arrest warrants against the two officials, emphasizing that the Security Council resolution number 1593 obliges the Sudanese government and concerned parties to collaborate with the court proceedings.[6] On the issuance of the resolution, the prosecutor urged the government to comply, as the Sudan is the culprits' country of domicile, as well as appealed to member states and regional and international bodies to cooperate fully in seeking arrests and surrender.

The Erroneous Option of Confrontation

As signatory to the UN Charter and the Rome Statute declaration, the Sudan is obliged to comply with all the resolutions and provisions for international legitimacy. Contrary to the government's reservations about the ICC being an instrument of intervention in national affairs, compliance does not conflict with principles of sovereignty in any way. In addition, the discretionary power to decide upon this matter falls entirely upon the UN Security Council to decide what measures to take to eliminate threats to international peace and security as enshrined in article 39 of the charter. The GOS had to decide whether to cooperate with the court proceedings or to stand against it within an unfavorable national and regional political climate. With respect to the second option, the consequences are truly grave, as it will jeopardize the whole country in an uncalculated confrontation with the provisions of chapter 7 of the UN Charter, the most obvious outcome of which is international isolation. Alas, the GOS opted for this course of action by failing to satisfy the conditions of the existence of will and ability to prevent impunity.

From the start, the government denied any commitment or obligation on its part toward the ICC, relying entirely upon the fallacy of not being a signatory to the Rome Statute. When it appeared easy to prove that Sudan did sign the Statute on August 9, 2000, the GOS tried to argue that it had not ratified that signature yet. By saying this, the GOS absolutely ignored another fact, that it is a party to the Vienna Convention for International Treaties of 1969, Article 19, which obliges all its parties, until ratifying, not to obstruct the implementation of whatever agreement they might sign. Most important, and on top of what has already been stated herein, there is still the fact that the referral of the Darfur case from the UN Security Council to the ICC was carried out under chapter 7, and accepted by the court under article 13(b). Such measures do not necessarily require a ratification, or even being a signatory to the Rome Statute, on the part of the territorial state, contrary to the issue of whether the case falls within the jurisdiction of the ICC under articles 13(a) and 13(c), which stipulate the consent of the territorial state as a prerequisite.

Thus, and by relying on such ill arguments, the GOS's positions were, actually, fraught with confusion and contradiction, and lost the initiative to resolving the conflict in a just manner. All that is needed from the GOS is to show that it has enough "will" and "ability" to prevent impunity. Thus, it could have done it either legally, by requesting the issuance of a decision from the ICC Pre-Trial Chamber maintaining the lack of admissibility of the case, pursuant of article 17/a of the Statute, or, at least, politically, by convincing the Security Council to ask the court to postpone the proceedings pursuant to Article 16. But it is obvious that both ways require the GOS's recognition of the court and its statute, and this, by its turn, could have been possible only if the GOS was capable of doing it as part of the solution rather than being part of the dispute.

As soon as the government realized the built-in weaknesses of its arguments vis-à-vis the ICC, its rhetoric took a drastic turn as it shifted to denouncing the ICC as an arm of the infidels' dominance and desire to undermine national sovereignty. This stance reflects the serious dismissal of the enormous campaigns crafted by millions of people, political parties, civil society organizations, independent media, and intellectuals worldwide that combined in the making of the court. Charges of the ICC contravention of sovereignty are, moreover, ill-founded from an international legal perspective that challenges the state's institutionalized transgression of its citizens. In the West Valia Conference of 1648, the national states admitted each other's absolute rights on their territories, wealth, and peoples. But, in accordance with the development of the public international law, the individual state now is compelled to comply with certain commitments toward its own subjects. Failing to do so provokes international intervention.[7] Therefore, sovereignty is no longer applicable to the Darfur situation, since the national state no longer enjoys the absolute right to act freely with regard to the rights of its citizens, and since the lack of "will" and "ability" to prevent impunity is clear on the part of the GOS. In order to prove this, one need only consider the following grave statement by the Sudanese Minister of Justice: "the government is not able to even know the whereabouts of the perpetrators of serious Crimes against Humanity, let alone tracking, arresting, and punishing them."[8]

The perpetuated legal and political confusion on the part of the GOS pushed the situation deep into muddy waters of ethical confusion. There are many examples.

First, while dealing with the ICC is supposed to be open and transparent, the GOS, despite its public denunciation of the ICC, tried to resort to iniquitous under-cover play, which completely lacks legal transparency or justification. The General Prosecutor of the ICC revealed, in his regular report to an open session of the UN Security Council held on December 13, 2005, that the Sudanese government commendably cooperated with him, during the period before the report was compiled. The GOS also agreed, within that framework, to receive a delegation from his office in February 2006 to inspect the procedures adopted by the national courts to find out if they meet international standards and provisions of the Rome Statute. Accordingly, he stated that he was looking forward to more positive cooperation from the GOS.[9] Only after that, the government hastily issued a statement praising the report, despite their previously declared negative responses. The Sudan Mission to the UN described the report as "balanced and professional because there are real attempts on the part of the government to enforce justice and put an end to impunity."[10] The Minister of Justice of Sudan also described the report as objective and fair to the GOS. He even went further by agreeing to allow the visit revealed by Ocampo in the report. A delegation from Ocampo's office actually visited the Sudan on November 17, 2005, without being publicly announced and conducted the proposed inspection of the ministries concerned. The minister also admitted that the government revealed the steps taken to intensify the investigations, to activate the public prosecution offices, and to revitalize the court proceedings. But all those statements were soon retracted, and the previous aggressive tone was again adopted. The minister suddenly turned to describe the aforementioned report as "an exemplification of the ICC's hidden agenda." Those new statements went on to claim that the government "will never allow the investigators of the ICC permission to visit Darfur," that "they do not have judicial authority within the Sudan," and that "their investigation bears no significance whatsoever." Hence, and in response to those very aggressive statements, the ICC General Prosecutor immediately retaliated by refusing to specify the range of cooperation proposed by the GOS with regard to the investigation into the Darfur crimes and withdrawing his previous candid statement. Kofi Annan, the former UN Secretary-General, followed suit to restate that it was premature to decide if the GOS was really cooperating with the ICC with regard to the investigations on the violations of international law in Darfur.[11] Falling in line with this, the British UN Envoy took the opportunity to push the matter further by saying that there is a central government overseeing the violations of international law taking place in Darfur, and the officials will be followed, in order to track down those responsible for giving orders to the perpetrators.[12] This is quite understandable if we are to remember that Britain has reservedly cautioned the UN Security Council against the commendation of the government's cooperation.

Following the sudden aggravation of conflict between the government and the ICC, the Minister of Justice went back on his previous aggressive statements to welcome the visit of the ICC delegation, scheduled for February 2006, and expressed the government's determination to collaborate. He was even prepared to go as far as to suggest the possibility of what he called the *integration* between the ICC and the national courts already set up in Darfur to institute legal proceedings against the perpetrators. The term *integration*, suggested by the minister, is void of any definitive legal significance. The ICC does not *integrate* with national courts, but acquires *complementary* cognizance and jurisdiction only when it verifies that the concerned state is neither *able* nor *willing* to effect justice. Therefore, the serious-minded application of justice, along international standards, is a legitimate reason to rule out the condition of "inability" or "lack of will" on the part of that particular state. But, contrary to this rule, the GOS assumes that its actions should be fully endorsed by the ICC as meeting the international requirements of instituting justice, though it does not satisfy the logical conditions to be met.[13] However, there are but three possibilities in the case of the Darfur violations. The first is that justice is to be instituted internally by the national government in good faith and in line with international criteria. The second is that, if the national state fails to institute justice, the ICC takes over. Finally, the third possibility is that the national state adopts a procrastinating attitude by neither prosecuting the perpetrators nor letting the ICC do its job, knowing that following the route leading to this third possibility, as the government of Sudan evidently prefers, will eventually lead the whole country into the trap of international intervention according to the provisions of chapter 7 of the UN Charter, as well as the dictates of the international community, a tune that the GOS shall never be able to dance to.

The second example is that, although it candidly refused to cooperate with the ICC on many occasions, the GOS signed an agreement of cooperation with the Ugandan government in November 2005 to "implement" the warrant of arrest issued by the one and same ICC against Joseph Kony, the leader of the Lord's Resistance Army, and three of his aides, as claimed by the Kenyan daily paper, *The Daily Nation*.[14]

The third example is that the GOS never missed participating actively in the general assembly of the states members' regular sessions of the ICC.

The examples recounted here, among many others, establish a political and ethical argument preventing the government from reiterating denial of recognition of the ICC and its statute. This denial is clearly indicated by the words of the Sudanese Minister of Justice commenting on the Prosecutor's declaration on February 27, 2007, concerning the depositing of prosecution evidence against Harun and Kushayb before the Pre-Trial Chamber Court for deciding on the admissibility of the case. The minister said, "The prosecutor may, if he chooses so, soak it in water and drink,"[15] as the Sudanese proverb goes for describing useless written documents. Later on, the government reverted to its obstinate attitude by refusing to cooperate with the ICC on several occasions. Space limitations, however, militate against recounting them at length.

Concluding Remarks

Several considerations could guide the way for circumventing the predicament of the Darfur crisis as it relates to national governance and international justice-seeking mechanisms.

First, the transitional constitution of 2005, derived from the CPA ratified on January 9, 2005, is the point of reference for governance in the present Sudan. Undoubtedly, its main goal is to accomplish two dialectically intertwined tasks during a transitional period of six years (2005–2011): to achieve comprehensive peace, and to ease the way toward democratic transformation and radical restructuring of power, a fundamental element of which is the solidification of transitional justice. The concept of "transitional justice" refers to a field of activity and inquiry focused on how societies address legacies of past human rights abuses, mass atrocity, or other forms of severe social trauma, including genocide or civil war, in order to build a more democratic, just, or peaceful future. It is commonly understood as a framework for confronting past abuse as a component of a major political transformation.

It is a costly illusion to envisage the process of democratic transformation as a mere option to be adopted or otherwise ignored. Sudan is not new to democratic governance, as the fight for independence was originally linked to the struggle for the democratic structuring of the state. The effort to build a democratically run state has since become one of the milestones of Sudanese revolutionary thought. Yet long spells of dictatorship have largely contributed to the relative fragility of the social structure, allowing excessive religious fundamentalism to take root, weakening the mechanisms for struggling against coercion and consecrating free-market values over those of social cooperation and solidarity. This is clearly manifest in the performance of Al Bashir's government, which fakes an illusory nominal acceptance of the concept of democratic transformation without delivering the essential building blocks to achieving this goal. This acceptance is nominal because it was a reaction to international pressures rather than a genuine response to internal developments.

The requirements for democratic transformation in Sudan entail enforcing "transitional justice" while the government prefers "reconciliation." It also entails fighting against the marginalization of women, non-Arabs, and non-Muslims, resolving the false antagonism between democracy and religion at the level of general social consciousness accomplishing the political and legislative reforms necessary for such a project and acknowledging the agency of the Sudanese people to participate in generating solutions to their own experiences of victimization and suffering. Yet, we should consider the fact that the issues pertaining to democratic transformation in our country are inseparably interlaced within the fabric of international movements. The communication revolution enables us to inaugurate an alternative globalization, which is indefatigably and persistently taking shape in the face of the imperialist globalization. The number of international civil organizations founded on the principles of mutual exchange and concerned with issues of human rights and self-determination for marginalized populations is on the rise. These organizations include, among many other respectful entities, thousands of national societies and regional and international federations, syndicates, and caucuses. The international Coalition for the International Criminal Court (CICC), whose main goal is to bring more states to endorse the Rome Statute, is actively involved in this worldwide alternative movement.

Therefore, it would be a grave error to consider the term "transitional justice," inevitably linked with the concept of democratic transformation, a mere linguistic term to be interpreted according to individual whims. "Transitional justice" is a precise concept whose semiotic designation was contributed to through powerful experiences worldwide. It has become evident that any step taken toward genuine democratic transformation is conditioned by stipulating provisions of "transitional justice" as a prerequisite for cementing the processes of transformation as the ultimate solution to the crisis of governance and sustainable peace.

Applying what is said above to the Sudanese question in general, and the Darfur situation in particular, must derive lessons from Morocco's Equity and Reconciliation Commission, and South Africa's Truth and Reconciliation Commission, not to mention more than forty other experiences worldwide.

In conclusion, the sum total of expertise gained from all the aforementioned experiences of "transitional justice" can be summarized in the following point: The international community's discourse of human rights has shifted from theoretically addressing only what is known as access to justice, during the 1970s and 1980s, to embracing, as of the early 1990s, a more practical and firm insistence on what is known as "disallowing impunity." This is a process of transformation that Sudan in general and Darfur in particular desperately need for rematerializing a more equitable state and society that is committed to repudiating the politics of vengeance and violence in a country under siege.

Epilogue

Since the completion of this essay, new developments have taken place with regard to the erroneous confrontation between the ICC and the government of Sudan, which merit an update and deserves close analysis. On July 14, 2008, the chief prosecutor of the ICC, Luis Moreno-Ocampo, asked the court to indict the President of Sudan, Omar Hassan Al Bashir, on charges of genocide, crimes against humanity, and war crimes committed in Darfur. Such a move, the first of its kind that may result in the indictment of a sitting president, is certainly a historic moment in international justice. With such a move, the confrontation between the ICC and the government of Sudan has entered a completely new phase, which has serious implications for not only the prospects for resolving the conflict in Darfur and the peace process, but also for the peace agreements that have already been signed by the government, such as the CPA with the SPLM, the agreements with some other internal political and armed fronts, and most especially on the constitutionality of the current government and the future of the country as a whole.

For more details on these developments, the editors wish to refer readers to Appendix N in this volume: International Criminal Court, The Office of the Prosecutor: Situation in Darfur, the Sudan, Prosecutor's Application for Warrant of Arrest under Article 58 against Omar Hassan Ahmad Al Bashir.

Notes

1 *Al-Sudani*, March 26, 2007.
2 Rome Statute of The International Criminal Court; http://untreaty.un.org/cod/icc/STATUTE/99_corr/cstatute.htm.
3 *Al-Sahafa*, April 5, 2007.
4 *Al-Ayam*, September 27, 2005.
5 *Al-Sahafa*, December 14, 2005.
6 *Al-Sudani*, March 5, 2007.
7 Ibid., March 5, 2007.
8 Ibid., March 5, 2007.
9 Ibid., March 5, 2007.
10 Ibid. See also Second of the Prosecutor of the International Criminal Court, Mr. Luis Moreno Ocampo, to the Security Council Pursuant to UNSCR 1593 (2005), December 13, 2005.
11 *Al-Sahafa*, December 15, 2005.
12 Ibid., December 14, 2005.
13 Rome Statute of The International Criminal Court; http://untreaty.un.org/cod/icc/STATUTE/99_corr/cstatute.htm
14 See http://www.nationmedia.com/dailynation/nmgindex.asp
15 Well-known statement by the Minister, which was also repeated by President Al Bashir in a statement broadcast on SudanTV and cited in the press.

14 Sudan's Legal System and the Lack of Access to Justice for Survivors of Sexual Violence in Darfur

Adrienne L. Fricke and Amira Khair

Rape on a mass scale is one of the hallmarks of the conflict in the Darfur region of Sudan. Compounding the terrible physical and psychological trauma is an almost complete lack of access to justice for victims. There is a manifest absence of political will to prosecute or investigate rape on the part of the government of Sudan, which almost invariably uses immunity laws to shield government-affiliated alleged perpetrators from prosecution. This climate of impunity is matched by fundamental flaws in the legal system, which labors under an inadequate definition of rape, unclear and deficient evidentiary standards, and a system of justice that perversely forces victims to expose themselves to a real risk of prosecution for crimes related to sexual morality. Furthermore, although the government has gestured at reform of policies affecting access to medical treatment, both rape victims and medical service providers remain at risk of harassment by the authorities. The government further obstructs victims' access to essential services through onerous laws regulating nongovernmental organizations (NGOs) and frequent intimidation of their members.

The inadequacy of Sudan's rape laws can only fully be understood in the context of the prolonged armed conflict in the Darfur region. In 2003, rebel movements, organized along ethnic lines, rebelled against the Arab-dominated central government located in Khartoum to protest long-standing economic, social, and political marginalization. The government responded with massive violence targeted not only against the rebel military forces, but also against civilian groups perceived as supporting them. In this campaign, the government has made extensive use of irregular forces, often referred to as *Janjawid*, drawn primarily from nomadic "Arab" groups in Darfur, and now integrated into the "Popular Defense Forces" (PDF).[1] Frequently operating in concert, the Sudanese military and Janjawid have systematically destroyed villages and harmed or killed their inhabitants. An important aspect of the pattern of attack has been the mass rape of women and girls. It is impossible to provide accurate numbers of rape victims because of the government of Sudan's practice of harassing and even detaining members of organizations who try to report such statistics. In this hostile climate, few survivors are willing to come forward to report the trauma. Many survivors of these attacks have moved into camps for internally displaced persons (IDPs), yet women remain at risk even in the camps. When they leave their confines to seek firewood or other sources of income, women and girls are often attacked and subjected to sexual violence.

Obstacles to Reporting Rape

Rape is among the most underreported violent crimes in many societies.[2] Many in Darfur view rape as a serious stigma; as a result, Darfurian women, like most women from conservative cultures, are often extremely reluctant to report they have been raped. Sudanese NGOs working within the camps have implemented valuable education and awareness programs that are helping these communities to cope with the problem of mass rape, but even when women would be otherwise willing to report their assaults, important structural impediments impact their ability and willingness to do so.

One such problem concerns the entanglement of medical services for rape victims with criminal procedure documentation requirements. Article 48(1)(c) of the Criminal Procedure Act of 1991 is designed to make sure the police collect all standard evidence during their investigations. In cases involving death or severe bodily injury, the law requires the police to "take the necessary steps to call a competent physician to examine the body or the injured person" and to transport the injured person to the nearest hospital. The law requires police to provide all seriously injured persons, including rape victims, with a document called a "Form 8" in order to record the findings of the medical examination, and to serve as evidence. When widespread rape first became a major problem in Darfur, rape victims were required by law to fill out and file Form 8 at the police station before they could legally receive medical treatment.[3] Doctors who treated rape victims before they had filed a Form 8 faced arrest or harassment.[4] In the face of pressure from the international community, including Refugees International, the Minister of Justice issued a circular on August 11, 2004 (Criminal Circular 1/2004), that referenced the conflict in Darfur and stated that where urgently needed, medical treatment can be provided prior to completing a Form 8.[5] A later circular in December 2004 (Criminal Circular 2/2004) elaborates on the procedures to be followed.[6] The governor of South Darfur then issued a statement saying that victims of rape should be allowed to receive treatment without first completing the form, though the victim remained obligated to complete the form after being treated if pursuing a legal claim.[7]

Despite this modest improvement, Form 8 remains a serious problem because of ongoing confusion surrounding its use and value in criminal prosecutions. First, the form suffers from important deficiencies as a means for documenting evidence of rape: It records only limited information, such as whether there has been a recent loss of virginity, bleeding, or presence of sperm, and it does not provide for a comprehensive medical report.[8] Yet, under Sudanese law, Form 8 takes the place of medical documentation for purposes of criminal prosecutions.[9] A physician familiar with rape-related issues said, "The law needs to be changed so that medical tests and reports can be admissible as evidence without the Form 8, which doesn't provide a lot of documentation about the rape."[10]

A closely related problem is that the forensic procedures for documenting rape fall far short of international best practices; there are no established protocols for collecting and identifying biological material such as semen, and even when such samples are obtained, the only laboratories capable of performing DNA analysis are in the capital city of Khartoum. Moreover, if a woman has waited several days before seeking treatment or has filed a claim without having received treatment, she will often be unable to substantiate her claims.

In the current political climate, medical professionals are unsure if they are supposed to determine rape has occurred (as opposed to simply describing a rape victim's medical condition). For instance, a physician with extensive experience treating rape victims in Darfur reported that "With the current law, doctors are supposed to fill out a Form 8, but it isn't clear how much information we are supposed to provide or whether we are supposed to determine whether a woman was raped."[11] This confusion is compounded by the fact that law enforcement officials have rejected rape charges on the basis that insufficient medical evidence was recorded on the Form 8.[12] Physicians who treat rape victims claim it is not clear whether they may legally provide emergency contraception or terminate a pregnancy in these cases.

Doctors and health personnel who provide medical treatment to raped women also face harassment and intimidation. One physician explained that given the regime's suppression of the problem of rape in Darfur, "Doctors are scared to mention [on a Form 8] that a woman's injuries are consistent with rape because we have no protection from National Security."[13]

Important socioeconomic factors also cause raped women to be reluctant to file claims, even when their community would support them. The overwhelming majority of internally displaced women come from rural backgrounds with little or no formal education. As a result, they need assistance filing claims with the police, which is often lacking. This problem is compounded by the fact that human rights workers report that the police are frequently unhelpful, poorly trained in handling gender-based violence, and verbally abusive. Even when a rape victim presents the police with a completed Form 8, reports suggest that women are often unable to convince the police to open a criminal file against the perpetrator. Although the police claim they cannot investigate reported rapes, many advocates working in Darfur disagree. The general reluctance of women to report rape is also compounded by the perception among the displaced that the government is behind the attacks. As noted above, their perception is often accurate, given the high incidence of rape among Sudanese government forces.

Since raped women know how few perpetrators are brought to justice, and that victims themselves can be accused of illegal sexual activity, there are few incentives to pursue justice and powerful disincentives to speak out.[14] The lack of security in Darfur means that women expose themselves to further sexual violence when they choose to pursue their claims, as this requires them to travel to the city centers in which the courts are located. Because of the time and effort involved in filing official reports and legal claims, which often involves traveling long distances at great personal risk, there are major social and economic costs for women who choose to pursue redress. Time and energy spent preparing for a legal proceeding necessarily reduces the amount of time a woman can pursue income-generating activities.

Flaws in the Legal Regime Governing Rape

Sudan's laws governing rape suffer from significant infirmities that contribute to a denial of access to justice. As one practicing human rights attorney said, "The problem in Darfur is that the criminal system is not capable of bringing [rapists] to justice. The police and the judiciary have issues, but they are not the main problem. The law itself is the main problem."

As an initial matter, the rape laws expose the victim to potentially devastating consequences by intertwining the law of adultery with rape. Articles 145–152 of the

Criminal Code codify Islamic jurisprudence regarding crimes of sexual immorality. Rape is defined in Article 149 as the offense of *zina* – often translated as "adultery," but more precisely meaning intercourse between a man and a woman who are not married to one another – that is performed without consent.[15] The relevant clause states: "There shall be deemed to commit the offence of rape, whoever conducts sexual intercourse by way of adultery (zina) or sodomy with any person without his consent."[16/17] Defining rape as zina without consent has potentially dire repercussions for a woman alleging she has been raped. Proving rape requires the rape victim to admit that she engaged in sexual penetration outside of marriage. Where a woman is subsequently unable to prove that she did not consent to such intercourse, she becomes at risk for being charged with the crime of zina (fornication or adultery) because she has confessed to sexual penetration outside of marriage.

Rape victims have strong reasons not to subject themselves to even the possibility of being charged with zina, since the penalties for this crime are extraordinarily harsh. Unmarried women convicted of zina receive one hundred lashes; married women are sentenced to death by stoning.[18] Such sentences are not merely theoretical but a very real possibility. For instance, on February 13, 2007, a court in Gazeera state sentenced a 22-year old Darfurian woman to death by stoning for committing adultery. On March 6, 2007, a second Darfurian woman, age 23 and also a resident of Gazeera state, was likewise charged with adultery and received the same sentence.[19] Fortunately, these sentences were later overturned on appeal[20]; however, the fact that they were imposed at all reflects the reality that Sudanese judges feel free to punish women accused of adultery with death.

Lawyers and other activists working with victims of gender-based violence stress the negative impact of the law's conflation of rape and adultery. As noted by one person familiar with the challenges of rape prosecutions, "The problem with article 149 is that the definition of rape and adultery are up to the person trying the case. In several cases raped women were then charged with adultery." As a result, according to this expert, "The definitions of rape and adultery need to be separated from one another."

Defining rape in terms of zina also often creates insurmountable evidentiary obstacles. Zina is one of the *hudud* crimes under Islamic law, that is, a crime designated by the Qur'an and thus especially serious and requiring a heightened standard of proof. Article 62 of the Evidence Law of 1994 (law number 31 of 1994) provides the evidentiary requirements for establishing rape.[21] The law reflects the Qur'anic requirement that a conviction for zina requires the sexual act to have been witnessed by four competent men (Qur'an 24:4).[22] It is all but impossible to obtain four male witnesses to testify on behalf of a rape victim. As a result, where the judge imposes this evidentiary requirement, a prosecution for rape has essentially no chance of success. This evidentiary requirement is subject to frequent complaints. An established human rights attorney explained, "The problem with article 149 is that it mixes up the crimes of adultery and rape," which is "why the judges use the standard of four witnesses to prove it. Where there is strong evidence of sexual violence, we shouldn't have to meet the evidentiary burden for adultery."

Although some judges do not impose this next-to-impossible standard of proof, even the more flexible courts often employ flawed and discriminatory means of weighing evidence when determining whether intercourse was consensual. For example, many judges will accept the testimony of a man who swears on the Qur'an that he did not commit rape, but will not accept contrary testimony from a woman that she was indeed raped. Moreover, many judges use untrustworthy indicators to decide whether the sex was consensual, such as whether the victim wore underwear. "Judges decide rape cases along their own biases, sometimes judging a woman based on the way she is dressed," a human rights activist complained. There is also a general lack of sensitivity and understanding of gender-based violence, and a prevailing notion that women who have survived gender-based violence are untrustworthy. This attitude has been expressed by militia leader Musa Hilal, who asked, "Why would you want to rape these women? They're disgusting; rape is shameful. We have honour, but our men wouldn't need to use force. These things hold no shame for these women."[23] In addition, members of the Sudanese government are reported to have privately expressed the belief that women in Darfur are "sexually generous," and that since sex is "a part of their culture," rape is not a significant issue.

Another major flaw in Sudan's rape law is that it does not encompass penetration with inanimate objects. Thus, a perpetrator who rapes a woman with a gun barrel would likely be found not guilty under the existing definition of rape. Nor does the definition of rape adequately account for sexual coercion. Although, on occasion, where the elements of rape cannot be proven, the court has found the perpetrator guilty of "gross indecency" under article 151, this article does not sufficiently address the weight of sexual and gender-based crimes against women in Darfur. As a politician familiar with the work of Parliament's Human Rights Committee explained, "Cases aren't being reported as rapes, because the definition of rape is too hard to meet. Since 2004 the majority of rape cases have been officially reported as incidences of adultery or gross indecency."

The statute of limitations provides an additional impediment. Under the applicable statute of limitations, a rape prosecution must commence within three years of the offense, and there is no provision for this period to be "tolled," or temporarily suspended. As a result, a rape victim who is unable to file a claim within three years, for any reason – including the prevailing lack of security and resources or being in a refugee camp in Chad – forever loses the right to have her assailant prosecuted. This makes it functionally impossible for many refugees and internally displaced people to even try to seek justice.

Many in the legal and human rights communities recognize the need to address the serious deficiencies in Sudan's rape laws. Sudanese judges themselves have called for reform of the rape law to address, among other things, the problems of defining rape in terms of zina and the corresponding evidentiary problems. The rapes in Darfur have also mobilized many in Sudanese civil society to consider the problems in articles 145–152 of the Criminal Code of 1991. For example, in July 2006 prominent Sudanese NGOs collaborated with the UN Mission in Sudan (UNMIS) in holding a workshop on legal reforms necessary to protect victims of rape and other sexual violence.[24] The resulting recommendations to the government included policy matters, such as the adoption of practical measures to prevent rape in Darfur, as well as measures to protect victims of rape and sexual violence; the establishment of a clear policy on sexual violence for judges to follow; training police on human rights and sexual violence; and the appointment of more women police officers in Darfur to assist victims in reporting rape claims. Recommended legal reforms included adjusting the definition of rape found in the 1991 Criminal Code to avoid confusion with zina; revision of the Evidence Law of 1994; and the adoption of decisive measures to prevent a rape victim from being accused of zina where there is insufficient evidence to establish she was raped.[25]

Although the government of Sudan has not adopted any of these recommendations, one promising development is a concept paper on reforms to the rape laws that, as of March 2007, was being circulated in parliament. This paper addresses many of these reform proposals. It remains unclear, however, whether the government will allow formal discussion of the proposed amendments.

Sudan's Granting of Immunity to Government-Affiliated Perpetrators and Other Deficiencies in the Legal Regime

Even where survivors of sexual violence have strong evidence of a perpetrator's guilt, prosecution is often functionally impossible because Sudan grants immunity to individuals with government affiliations. This immunity can generally only be waived by the alleged perpetrator's superior officer, who almost never consents to a waiver. As a result, members of the military, security services, police, border guards, and the PDF, which include many members of the Janjawid, are invariably exempt from prosecution.

For instance, article 33 of the National Security Forces Act (1998) provides that "no civil or criminal proceedings shall be instituted against a member or collaborator for any act connected with the official work of the [National Security] member, save upon approval of the Director." Article 46 of the Police Forces Act (1999) provides that "no criminal procedure will be taken against any police officer for a crime committed while executing his official duty or as a consequence of those official duties without permission of the Minister of the Interior." Similarly, the People's Armed Forces Act (1986) states in article 8 that when the armed forces are tasked with providing internal security, they shall enjoy the same powers and legal immunity granted to all other internal security forces. Sudan amended this last law by a presidential decree on August 4, 2005, which provides that "There shall not be taken any procedures against any officer, ranker [sic] or soldier who committed an act that may constitute a crime done during or for the reason of the execution of his duties or any lawful order made to him in this capacity and he shall not be tried except by the permission of the General Commander or whoever authorized by him."[26] This amendment has been used to shield perpetrators of rape from prosecution since the crime occurred ostensibly "during the execution of his duties" as a member of the PDF.

Since members of the armed forces and other government militias perpetrate the majority of the gender-based violence occurring in Darfur, Sudan's immunity laws create, in all but the rarest cases, an insurmountable obstacle for their prosecution. Human rights workers told of numerous instances where women could provide compelling evidence of a rapist's guilt, but a prosecution could not proceed because of the perpetrator's immunity. "Even where a woman has very good evidence, it is difficult to convince the military legal advisor to lift immunity and allow the case to go forward," said a human rights advocate with experience monitoring rape cases.

Another human rights worker recalled a case in North Darfur in which two married women and a girl had been raped. Although "there was strong evidence and witnesses," the "perpetrators belonged to the Border Guard. Even when the Judge ordered the commander to hand over the perpetrators, he refused, saying they were covered by the immunity laws."[27] A human rights attorney who follows the issue closely observed that "The decision to lift immunity should not be made by the authorities the alleged perpetrator is working for, because those authorities aren't neutral. Immunity should be automatically lifted where there is *prima facie* evidence of rape or any other crime." Some activists note that officers and Janjawid understand they will never be held to justice for committing rape and other gender-based violence, and that they take advantage of this impunity, which portends badly for the future of women in Darfur.

Sudanese human rights advocates also cite other serious structural flaws in the judicial system as important obstacles to achieving justice for victims of sexual violence. First, the plethora of different courts creates confusion regarding which court is the correct venue for bringing a claim. In addition to the statutory courts created by the Interim National Constitution, the government has instituted by decree various other courts for criminal activities in Darfur. These include the so-called Special Courts established by the Chief Justice in 2001 under the Emergency and Public Safety Act (1997), which were replaced by "Specialized Courts" in 2003. The crimes over which the Specialized Courts have jurisdiction include, among other things, matters "considered a crime by the *wali* or head of state or head of the judiciary."[28] Further adding to the confusion, on June 7, 2005, the Chief Justice created a Special Criminal Court for the Events in Darfur (SCCED), which has jurisdiction over any act contained in the Sudanese penal code, any charges arising from the National Committee of Inquiry on Darfur, and international humanitarian law. Since the regular statutory courts, the Specialized Courts, and the SCCED all appear to have jurisdiction over rape, advocates complain that it is unclear where they should file cases. A senior opposition politician observed, "The Special Court for Darfur isn't working. People don't have enough legal information to file cases properly."

A significant deficiency in the staffing and training of court personnel, including judges, is another problem that affects the quality of justice in Darfur. Not only are the courts chronically understaffed, local human rights activists have raised serious concerns about the qualifications of judges sitting on the Specialized Courts, who they report have little legal training and have been recruited from the military. Although the judges on the SCCED are generally viewed with higher regard, this court has proven almost entirely ineffective, having heard very few cases and delivered even fewer judgments.[29] A senior academic who focuses on gender-based violence in Darfur said, "I don't know what the judges are doing to stay busy, sitting out there [in El Fasher]. They don't have any cases to hear, because women won't bring claims forward since they consider the government itself as a perpetrator."

Even where judges in Darfur are properly trained and courts are adequately staffed, the lack of independence of the judiciary in Sudan means that justice often is still denied. This is particularly true in cases brought by rape survivors, since the law suffers from crucial structural flaws that disadvantage rape victims. A person familiar with the judiciary reported that judges who believe the existing laws are unfair to women feel no choice but to apply them. "We have a very weak judiciary," an attorney noted. "Judges don't have to be experienced or well-trained; they just have to be followers." Under Sudanese law, Chief Justice Jalal el Din Mohammed Osman has the power to "nominate and discard" judges, and there has reportedly been an "exodus of strong Sudanese judges" since the beginning of the Bashir regime. The ongoing conflict in Darfur means it is even harder to attract strong and competent members of the judiciary. Moreover, because the courts often sit far from the IDP camps, access to justice is further limited by geography. In a cruel irony, a woman who leaves her camp to travel to court faces the very real threat of gender-based violence while in transit. "Traveling is a risk for the women," one activist said, "and the people they are going to file reports with are often the same people who are committing the crimes."

Harassment of NGOs Working on Issues of Sexual Violence

Rape survivors are also negatively impacted by the draconian legal regime governing the operation and activities of NGOs, including those that provide vital services to victims of sexual violence. The regime does so through a powerful government entity called the Humanitarian Aid Commission (HAC), which is charged with enforcing laws concerning the composition and operation of local and international NGOs, as well as UN and other multilateral aid agencies.

One of the principal laws the HAC is responsible for enforcing is the recently enacted Humanitarian and Voluntary Work Act of 2006. NGO leaders report that, among other things, this legislation restricts the ability of NGOs to receive funds by making it contingent upon permission from the HAC. They also report that the Act also allows the HAC to veto the nomination of individuals to serve on an NGO's board. In addition, the law requires NGOs to publish the names of its current executive members, and requires the organizations to hold yearly general assemblies, in which a new executive board must be chosen. The annual general assembly must be public, and each organization is required to give the HAC prior written notice, which is then publicly posted, stating the time and location of the meeting. The HAC is reported to dispatch government-affiliated individuals and organizations to attend these meetings to influence their policies and report to the HAC about discussions of sensitive topics, such as rape. This technique has been used to undermine NGOs that address gender-based violence.

In no small measure because of the government's strategy for infiltrating otherwise independent NGOs, many victims of sexual violence are deeply suspicious of such organizations and are therefore reluctant to report rapes or pursue legal remedies through them. Their hesitancy is accentuated by the regime's creation of pseudo-NGOs that outwardly appear committed to human rights, but in actuality are fronts for the government. In the climate of fear and suspicion that prevails in Darfur, many survivors of sexual violence choose not to avail themselves of the medical, legal, and psychosocial services offered by legitimate national and international NGOs.

Another technique employed by the government to prevent NGOs from providing much-needed services is simply ordering them by decree to cease operation. For example, in March 2007, the HAC announced the closure of fifty-eight organizations in South Darfur State.[30] Although the government cited a variety of alleged reasons for the closures, NGO workers report that the real reason was to prevent internally displaced persons from receiving the direct services they provide and to limit the NGOs' ability to report on conditions to the international community. Although the government claimed the closure would be "temporary," nearly three months later the regime still had not permitted their activities to resume. As a result, many of the organizations most active in providing services to rape victims cannot function. Many NGO workers believe that the disruption is so serious that numerous NGOs will be forced to close permanently even if the regime allows them to reopen.

In tandem with its outwardly legal mechanisms to restrict the activities of NGOs, the regime also employs extra-legal techniques. NGO workers are often subject to threats and intimidation. For instance, on January 19, 2007, aid workers as well as UN staff and African Union peacekeepers attending a social event were arrested and assaulted by local police and security officials, resulting in serious injuries. Other forms of harassment include threatening phone calls and harassment of women for improper dress, especially focusing on "correct" wearing of headscarves.

Conclusion

Current laws and procedures for documenting rape are in dire need of revision, a fact recognized by members of the judiciary as well as human rights activists. The definition of rape and related evidentiary rules make it functionally impossible to prosecute successfully; significantly, almost all convictions have resulted from confessions by perpetrators. Immunity laws must also be changed to combat the climate of impunity that prevails for rape in Darfur. The government's attempts to undermine and harass NGOs providing direct services to raped women must be addressed immediately. In addition, negative attitudes and stereotypes about victims of rape must be confronted, so that women are not blamed for the very crime that has been committed against them. As a senior activist observed, "Changing the laws would help, but we can't focus on that alone. We must encourage people to speak about the problem of rape, so that women who have been raped feel supported."

It is vital to note that there is nothing inherently Islamic about the way Sudan's rape law is constructed.[31] In fact, Pakistan, a country that imposes Islamic law, changed its rape law in 2006, allowing rape to be considered a crime distinct from zina.[32] Similarly, in 2006 the Republic of the Maldives took steps to reform its laws by commissioning a draft penal law and sentencing guidelines that, though based on Islamic law, still comply with international norms.[33] The government of Sudan must act immediately to prevent rape from occurring in Darfur and, like other Islamic countries seeking to improve justice for women who have been raped, to revise the harmful laws that penalize both rape victims and those who support them.

Notes

1. A version of this essay was previously published by Refugees International (RI) as Laws Without Justice: An Assessment of Laws Affecting Survivors of Rape (June 2007). The authors thank RI for their generous permission to use this material as the basis for this essay.

2. As the U.N. International Commission of Inquiry explains, "For operational purposes, the Sudanese armed forces can be supplemented by the mobilization of civilians or reservists into the Popular Defence Forces (PDF)." The PDF derives its legal status from the Popular Defence Forces Act of 1989, which defines the PDF as "para-military forces" made up of Sudanese citizens who meet certain criteria. For more information, see International Commission of Inquiry on Darfur, Report of the International Commission of Inquiry on Darfur to the United Nations Secretary-General, January 25, 2005, p. 28.

3. For a review of issues related to underreporting of rape, see, e.g., McGregor et al., "Why Don't More Women Report Sexual Assault to the Police?" Canadian Medical Association 162, no. 5 (2000): 659; Swiss et al., "Violence Against Women During the Liberian Civil Conflict," Journal of the American Medical Association 279, no. 8 (1998): 625–629; Miller et al., "Victim Costs of Violent Crime and Resulting Injuries," Health Affairs 12, no. 4 (1993): 186–97; Soeken, et al., "Randomized Response Technique: Applications to Research on Rape," Psychology of Women Quarterly 10, no. 2 (1986): 119 ("Authorities agree that rape is probably the most underreported serious crime," citing U.S. Federal Bureau of Investigation statistics [1974]: 14–15).

4. UNHCR, "Access to Justice for Victims of Sexual Violence," July 29, 2005, pp. 26–29, available at http://www.ohchr.org/english/press/docs/20050729Darfurreport.pdf (hereinafter "Access to Justice"). See also Refugees International, "Sudan: Inform Rape Survivors of Right to Seek Life-Saving Treatment," December 21, 2006 (analyzing the problems in disseminating the changes in Form 8 laws); Refugees International, "Sudan: For Raped Women in Darfur, Access to Reproductive Health Services Limited," October 26, 2004 ("Some NGOs say that they do not advertise services to rape survivors because Sudanese law (Article 48) prevents doctors from treating rape victims without a referral from the police department").

5. Access to Justice, p. 30.

6. Access to Justice, p. 27.

7. Ibid.

8. Decree Number 17 (on file with RI). The decree also established protections for doctor-patient confidentiality and instructed the police not to forcibly enter medical facilities. See also Refugees International, "Sudan: Inform Rape Survivors of Right to Seek Life-Saving Treatment," December 21, 2006, for further analysis of problems related to implementation of changes in Form 8 laws.

9. Access to Justice, 15.

10. Ibid.

11. In light of the inadequacies of Form 8, some international NGOs that provide medical services are reported to be supplementing the form with more extensive medical documentation.

12. Due to the extremely sensitive political nature of the subject of rape in Darfur and the inadequacy of the legal system for dealing with this problem, the sources we interviewed are not identified in this essay by name.

13. Access to Justice, p. 19.

14. In a case reported in March 2005, in Nyala, police arrested a rape victim who had sought treatment at an NGO clinic prior to completing a Form 8 and forced her to be reexamined at a state hospital. The police charged the doctors who treated her with "furnishing false information" under article 97 of the Criminal Procedure Act, a crime that may be punished with up to a year of imprisonment, a fine, or both. Access to Justice, 29.

15. Women in Darfur, like all rape victims, must be supported in whatever decision they reach after being informed of their rights to pursue prosecution. One activist emphasized that "The choice to report a rape is the woman's, and she should never be forced to do it. Already she has been traumatized, and we must not traumatize her again."

16. For discussion of zina, see Peters, R. "Zina or Zina' (a.)," Encyclopedia of Islam, P. Bearman, Th. Bianquis, C.E. Bosworth, E. van Donzel and W.P. Heinrichs, eds. (Leiden: Brill, 2007).

17. "There shall be deemed to commit the offence of rape, whoever conducts sexual intercourse by way of adultery (zina) or sodomy with any person without his consent." Report of the High Level Mission on the situation of human rights in Darfur pursuant to Human Rights Council decision S-4/101, A/HRC/4/80, March 7, 2007, fn 18, p. 15.

18. Under article 146 (a) of Sudan's 1991 Penal Code, "whoever commits the offence of adultery shall be punished with: a) execution by stoning when the offender is married (Muhsan); b) one hundred lashes when the offender is not married (non-Muhsan)."

19. See "Sentencing to Death by Stoning of Two Women on Adultery Charges," World Organization Against Torture, Geneva, March 9, 2007, available at http://www.omct.org/index.php?id=EQL&lang=eng&actualPageNumber=1&articleSet=Appeal&articleId=6911&PHPSESSID=2c740df6f87caeff97ae9d65851825e9.

20. Personal communication with a Sudanese activist, July 2007.

21. Article 62 of the Evidence Law of 1994 (Law No. 31 of 1994) provides the evidentiary requirements for establishing rape. The law was first published October 13, 1993, but was later published in Official Gazette 1580 on January 5, 1994. See Qawanin As-Sudan 1901–2003, issued June 2005, Ministry of Justice: Khartoum (digital copy); see also SOAT Press Release, Man Convicted of Rape in Darfur, August 8, 2006, for a discussion of article 62 of the Evidence Act of 1994 in the context of Darfur.

22. See article 62(b) of the Evidence Law of 1994.

23. Ann McFerran, "Curse of the Janjaweed," The Sunday Times, September 23, 2007.

24. See the Report of the Workshop on Legal Reform of Rape and Other Sexual Violence, 5 July 2006, Khartoum, Arabic version on file with RI.

25. Report of the Workshop, p. 4. The workshop participants also declared Sudanese civil society should serve as interlocutors with the government by monitoring rapes and supporting women in filing rape claims through providing assistance and encouragement.

26. Temporary Decree, People's Armed Forces Act 1986, Amendment 2005, "Seeking Permission to Institute Criminal Procedures Against Any Officer, Ranker or Soldier," August 4, 2005, as cited in Human Rights Watch, Lack of Conviction:The Special Criminal Court on the Events in Darfur, available at http://www.hrw.org/backgrounder/ij/sudan0606/3.htm.

27. The disregard of the armed forces for civilian courts is well documented by UNMIS workers. For example,

a briefing note on accountability for crime in Darfur explains, "The administrative procedure of granting civilian jurisdiction by a supervisory official in some cases has led to delays of many months. However, even after jurisdiction is accorded to the civilian courts, there have been instances of substantial delay in presentation of the accused either by the concerned security force or due to the non-appearance of the accused ... [a] sense of accountability to the civilian courts appears problematic for some security forces members." El Geneina Human Rights Unit, *Briefing Note for Sub-JIM on Human Rights*, June 2006, at 1, on file with RI.

[28] The Specialized Courts, like the Special Courts before them, also have jurisdiction over crimes of particular interest to the state, including offences against the state, including espionage, robbery, banditry, killing, and the unlicensed possession of firearms.

[29] A Supreme Court Judge and two Appellate Judges sit on the SCCED, including one female judge. The members of the SCCED, who are appointed by the Chief Justice, are President Justice Mr. Mahmoud Mohammed Saeed Abkam, of the Supreme Court; Madam Justice Inshirah Ahmed Mukhtar, of the Appeals Court; and Justice Awad el Karim Osman Mohammed, also of the Appeals Court. *See* Press Release, Embassy of the Sudan in London, June 7, 2005, available at http://www.sudan-embassy.co.uk/display.php?id=129.

[30] South Darfur State Decree of March 18, 2007, signed by Jamal Yousef Idris, issued under article 18 of the Humanitarian and Voluntary Work Act of 2006, on file with RI.

[31] For an argument that some states use religious law to permit violence against women, see Lisa Hajjar, "Religion, State Power, and Domestic Violence in Muslim Societies: A Framework for Comparative Analysis," *Law & Social Inquiry* 29, no. 1 (Winter 2004). Hajjar, however, remains attentive to the variations in the uses and interpretations of *shari'a* that show a lack of consensus among Muslims and consequently warns that over-generalizing about Islam should be avoided.

[32] Associated Press, "Pakistan Leader Amends Rape Law," *The Washington Post*, December 1, 2006. While many activists have criticized the law for doing too little to protect women who have been raped, it is significant that Pakistan has chosen to allow for the separation of rape from *zina*.

[33] Robinson, Paul H., et al. "Codifying Shari'a: International Norms, Legality & the Freedom to Invent New Forms" (November 3, 2006), University of Pennsylvania Law School, Public Law Working Paper no. 06–26, available at SSRN: SSRN _ID 942304_code615352.pdf. At the time of writing, the draft code awaits action by the Parliament.

15 Locating Responsibilities:
National and International Responses to the Crisis in Darfur

Munzoul A.M. Assal

There is no doubt that the crisis in Darfur represents one of the worst humanitarian tragedies that followed the 1990s crises in Rwanda and the Balkans. The Rwandan genocide took place under the gaze of the whole world, and it was already too late by the time the international community intervened. One lesson drawn from that crisis was that the international community should not wait until genocide is committed. But has that lesson been learned? Unfortunately, the Balkan and the Darfur crises show that it has not. It took a long time before the international community led by NATO forces intervened and stopped the atrocities in the Balkans. NATO also intervened against former Yugoslavia and averted a possible genocide against Kosovo Albanians. Approximately one decade after the Rwandan and Balkan crises in the mid-1990s, the Darfur crisis unfolded and represented a glaring challenge to both Sudan and the international community. The response of the Sudan government has been dodgy throughout the crisis, and continues to be so. Lack of seriousness, denials, and belittling the crisis in Darfur are the main responses of the government to the crisis. It was only when conditions on the ground could no longer be kept hidden that the government acquiesced to the mounting pressure and acknowledged that indeed there is a serious problem. The response of the international community was mainly brought about by the appalling images of burned villages and debris, which were one of the main characteristics of the conflict. Both national and international responses to the crisis in Darfur are, at best, flawed and, at worse, complacent.

The half-hearted engagement of the Sudan government and the confused intervention of the international community resulted in the signing of the Abuja agreement (also known as the Darfur Peace Agreement, or DPA) in March 2006. The agreement has not brought positive changes to the lives of people in Darfur, as it fell short of addressing the root causes of the problem and did not satisfy the aspirations of internally displaced persons and refugees. On the contrary, it led to further divisions within Darfur, with one rebel faction signing and others staying out.

This essay attempts to provide an explanation as to why both responses are flawed and/or complacent. Since the crisis has already received a lot of scholarly attention, particularly with regard to the causes that underlie it, I will not say much about it here.[1] I will, instead, focus mainly on how and in what ways national and international responses fail to address the situation and, hence, further escalate it. Before engaging with this, however, a brief note that provides a glimpse of the underlying causes of the crisis is necessary here.

The underlying cause of the present disaster in Darfur is the failure of traditional systems for the allocation of land and water resources and the mediation of conflict.[2] This failure is aggravated by a combination of ecological changes and government manipulation. The ability of local communities to cope with drought and famine has dwindled over the last couple of decades, and the capacity of their traditional systems of conflict mediation over rapidly diminishing resources became overwhelmed. It is difficult to separate or rank these underlying and aggravating causes, as they tend to interact with and reinforce each other, sometimes linking to broader or very local factors. In all this, however, the role of the central government is central in aggravating the situation.[3] But the crisis in Darfur certainly has historical roots. Failure of traditional systems can be traced back to when British colonial administrators resurrected native administration in the Sudan, whereby so-called paramount tribal chiefs had jurisdiction over specific territory and its population, including the power to allocate land. This system undermined the fluidity and flexibility of traditional land tenure and informal conflict mediation systems.

After independence, national governments continued discredited colonial policies or imposed their own misguided and authoritarian models. As control over allocation of land changed, and with growing armament and the polarization of ethnic identities (Arabs versus Africans), traditional conflicts acquired drastically different dimensions and scale.

The image of the crisis in Darfur is familiar throughout postcolonial Africa, but the scale of the crisis is probably second to none in recent history due to protracted instability, endemic proclivity for destructive power struggles among politicians, and a lethargic Darfurian political elite that has historically allied with the central government. The manner in which the central government reacted to the problem has indeed been one of the aggravating factors. Inaccurate characterization of the crisis, tampering with the complex ethnic makeup of Darfur, and the use of excessive force are the main features of Khartoum's reaction. This warrants the argument that the Darfur crisis also reflects the paradox of the postcolonial state in Africa: asserting the prerogatives of sovereignty without fulfilling its responsibilities toward its citizens.[4]

Other regional factors have indeed contributed to scaling up the crisis. The Libyan-Chadian war during the 1980s resulted in making Darfur a depot of sophisticated weaponry that includes automatic rifles and submachine guns. Due to the absence of the government and the generalized state of insecurity, owning a gun became vital for survival. The result is the spread of arms all over the region. Apart from the suffering of civilians and the devastation of life in the region, the whole society is held in polarity: "Arabs" versus "Africans." The long-term implications of this polarization are difficult to pinpoint, but to be certain the damage inflicted on the social fabric of Darfur is serious. Such polarization is also likely to persist as long as war continues.[5] The attempts undertaken so far to deal with the crisis have not matched the gravity of the situation. The absence of goodwill, from both the government and those who are carrying arms, and the lack of knowledge and goodwill on the part of the international community, thwart attempts to conclude a just and peaceful solution to the crisis. To be certain, however, the various Sudanese governments have historically adopted similar policies when dealing with problems in peripheral regions. Therefore, before dealing with the response of the incumbent government, a brief historical overview is necessary here.

The National Response I: It Is about History Repeating Itself

The strange way the government in Khartoum reacted to and dealt with the crisis in Darfur is not something new. In fact, there were many historical precedents that are akin to the current national response to the crisis in Darfur. It thus becomes imperative to historicize the conflict, particularly the ways different government regimes dealt with problems in Darfur in recent Sudanese history. To start with, it is important to note that throughout the history of Darfur, there has been a sort of cliental relationship between the dominant ruling groups and their subordinate followers. This existed even during the reign of the Fur, where there has been a contradiction between the dominant position of the Fur and the cliental position of the Baggara to the south and the Zaghawa and Meidoub to the north; a contradiction that had marked the Fur Sultanate.[6] Through its policy of pacification and other measures that followed the annexation of Darfur in 1916, British colonial rule succeeded in removing this contradiction. However, the manipulation of Darfur by the center in the way it is happening today can intelligibly be traced back to Turko-Egyptian rule in Darfur (1874–1888) and the Mahdist period (1885–1898).[7] During the reign of these two regimes, the use of excessive force against foes and the policy of divide and rule represented the main markers of the center's intervention in the affairs of the periphery, Darfur in this case.

Both Turko-Egyptian rule in Darfur (1874–1888) and the Mahadist State (1883–1898) adopted similar policies when dealing with the different insurgent groups in Darfur. Until the Turko-Egyptian forces occupied it in 1874, the Kira, a Fur dynasty whose descendants claim to have an Arab origin, ruled Darfur. Historians show that Fur rule goes back to 1640 when Suleiman Solong[8] managed to subject and rule over the different tribal groups in the region.[9] The Kira dynasty ruled Darfur from 1640 to 1874, when the Turko-Egyptian troops, led by Al-Zubair Pasha (a famous Sudanese warlord and slave trader), defeated their Sultan, Ibrahim Qarad. Rudolf von Slatin, an Austrian national, was appointed by the Turko-Egyptian government to run Darfur. The office of Slatin was characterized by chaos and recurrent insurgencies and intertribal wars, until he surrendered to the victorious Mahdist troops in 1888.[10] Slatin spent most of his time in the region confronting the Fur and other Arab groups that often defied his rule. In dealing with the different insurgents, he used the policy of divide and rule, of supporting different groups to fight each other.

The Mahdist rule in Darfur (1883–1899) was also a chaotic period. Many wars were fought between the different tribes and against the Mahdist state, too. In its attempts to pacify Darfur, the Mahdist state adopted many intrigues and waged war against the Zaghawa, the Fur, the Masalit, Rezeigat, Habbaniya, and Meidoub. Members from almost all tribes in the region were forcibly conscripted to confront the threats of the Abyssinians in the east, the Anglo-Egyptians in the north, and the Ashraf (the Mahdi's kinsmen who refused to recognize the Khalifa's authority) in Omdurman, the national capital of the Mahdist state. What is taking place in Darfur at the present time bears resemblance to the chaos and overwhelming instability that prevailed during the Mahdist rule over the region.[11]

British colonial rule adopted a policy that went into a different track than that of its predecessors. The British policy was one of pacification and regularization of ethnic and tribal groups (Beck 1996).[12] The basic concerns of the British in Darfur during the few years that followed conquest in 1916 were security and the prevention of Mahdist revival. To that end, the British went for native administration. Through the issuance of ordinances, they regularized the status of tribal chiefs. Such chiefs were given a wide range of powers that included tax collection and judicial responsibilities. According to de Waal,[13] "this was a means of setting the tribal leaders to police their subjects, to keep an eye on both millenarian preachers and discontented graduates. Along with these came the 'Closed Districts Ordinance' used in Darfur to keep an eye on wandering preachers and West African immigrants." Moreover, the British also regularized boundaries through the formalization of tribal *dars* or *hawakir*. These measures certainly succeeded in curbing the rampant cross-tribal feuds and provided stability in Darfur. Tribal leaders could solve disputes that fell within their jurisdiction and resorted to the colonial office only in serious cases that they failed to address. But the colonial policies had negative long-term implications for the stability of Darfur, to the extent that all national regimes subsequent to independence in 1956 followed some of the discredited colonial policies. One thing that policy makers take for granted is the role of native administration. Although things have changed significantly, tribal leaders are still viewed through the same lens that the British used almost a century ago. One cannot help but argue that when the state fails to confront head-on challenges of its own creation, it resorts to proxies. In fact, this seems to be the case in most postcolonial African states.[14] In the Darfurian context, one really wonders whether native administration can play any positive or constructive role the way it allegedly did previously. This argument is based on my belief that things in Darfur changed dramatically and, in fact, the dramatic unfolding of the crisis was in itself an indicator of the inability of native administration to avert it. Gone are the days when native administrators could play both judicial and administrative roles. Perhaps it is time to look for a different modality. The following section deals with the response of the incumbent government to the present crisis.

The National Response II: 2003 and Beyond

A dominant feature of the government's response to the crisis in Darfur since 2003 and beyond has been the absence of a proper characterization of the conflict.[15] Building on a legacy of environmental degradation and armed robbery, the war in Darfur has been dubbed by the government as representing a violent competition between farmers and nomads and a culmination of crimes committed by armed gangs and robbers. This characterization continued for a long time before it became obvious that it could no longer be sustained. The conspicuous (international) media coverage of the conflict in Darfur resulted not only in the exposure of heinous crimes committed against civilians, but also contributed to building up a strong international opinion against what is taking place in the region. Demonstrations and campaigns of support have been organized in Europe and the United States. Against this conspicuous international media coverage, the national media's behavior is, to say the least, bizarre. While appalling pictures of burnt and destroyed villages occupied pages in the foreign press and on TV screens, these images hardly appear in local media outlets. But perhaps one should be cautious in criticizing local media and the press. The government has a strong control on local newspapers, radio, and TV. Censorship of the media has crippled any objective engagement with the Darfur crisis. Even relatively independent newspapers could not touch the issue in a meaningful manner. Their coverage thus resonated with the official position. In 2003, just after the SLA attacked El Fasher, the author of this essay sent a commentary on the incident to the independent *Khartoum Monitor*. The response of the editor was: "we are instructed not to talk about or publish any article relating to Darfur."[16]

The absence of a proper characterization of the conflict led to interventions that further escalated the situation in Darfur. The government was not ready to listen to some wise voices that had a different view about the situation. The then-governor of Northern Darfur, General Ibrahim Suliman, was among a few members of the ruling party who advised the government to adopt a more flexible and open political approach to the problem. As early as 2002, he led a delegation that met with the rebels in Jebel Marra and listened to their demands. Nonetheless, the security framework adopted by the government thwarted his efforts and, following the attack on El Fasher in March 2003, Ibrahim Suliman was sacked. What followed the attack on El Fasher was a military campaign that escalated the situation and with the appearance of the *Janjawid* things got out of hand. Both the government and the armed groups were determined to defeat each other militarily. But both failed, and the only thing they achieved was the destruction of the social fabric and the creation of one of the most horrendous humanitarian crisis in the continent.

A third characterization, which is a corollary of the above two, is a lack of interest on the part of the government in negotiating a peaceful settlement to the crisis. This lack of interest is predicated on the mischaracterization of the conflict and the arrogant outlook that has historically shaped how Khartoum responds to problems in peripheral regions.[17] The characterization of the conflict as "tribal" underlies, in part, the government's lack of interest in addressing the conflict in scrupulous manner. What is more, labeling the conflict as "tribal" constituted the ground for an ugly polarization of the entire society in Darfur into "Arabs" and "Africans." Contrary to the widely held belief that the polarization of the society into Arab and African blocs was the creation of a biased and skewed international media, I would argue that international media just appropriated terms that were already in use; terms that the government helped to create through its alliances with and support of certain tribal groups in Darfur long before the present crisis (Harir 1994).[18]

It is in the context of this polarization that the term *Janjawid* appeared and became a defining feature of the crisis. Janjawid is a very mysterious group that is yet to be thoroughly studied and understood. Easy explanations characterize members of this group as veiled Arab militiamen armed with AK-47s, mounting horses, killing innocent civilians, burning villages, looting, and raping women.[19] Certainly, some elements of this description are correct. What remains unclear, however, is whether or not all the Janjawid are Arabs. Another thing that is unclear is the relationship between Khartoum and the Janjawid. Khartoum has consistently denied that it arms the Janjawid, and describes them as "undisciplined groups." It is, however, extremely difficult to give Khartoum the benefit of the doubt: Even if we accept its denial, one cannot help but argue that it has condoned the actions of the Janjawid. Since the Janjawid are enemies of the armed groups (the SLA and JEM), they must be friends of Khartoum. This being said, it must be stressed that the regional dimension of the crisis in Darfur should not be underestimated. Some groups of the Janjawid are cross-border tribes that traverse the boundaries among Sudan, Chad, and the Central Africa Republic.

The lack of humane action in the national context is not something that is uniquely a governmental trend. Part of the national inaction relates to the behavior of the society at large, represented by trade unions and civil society organizations. The miseries of people in Darfur did not catch the attention of ordinary Sudanese people, particularly in Khartoum, the national capital. Through demonstrations, Khartoum is famous for its response to problems in the Middle East and the Muslim world at large, but this was absent in the case of Darfur. To be certain, a repressive environment is a key element here and like the case with the press, the government would repress any group that seeks to publicly denounce the atrocities in Darfur. Nonetheless, even within the dim margin of freedom that exists, civil society organizations failed to show a noticeable concern over Darfur. It is only when the process of negotiation began that some civil society organizations started to talk about the importance of engaging with the crisis. Their absence from the scene contributed to the weaknesses of the Abuja agreement.

The Abuja agreement (a.k.a. the Darfur Peace Agreement, or DPA), brokered in May 2006, again reflected the government's lack of interest in addressing the underlying causes of the crisis. When negotiations dragged for a long time, the international community lacked patience and was therefore pushing for any deal that would stop the war in Darfur. Instead of solving the problem, the agreement created other serious problems, chief of which is the rift between the different armed groups. It was also very frustrating to the displaced and refugee persons whose cause was not properly addressed by the agreement. The formation of the National Redemption Front (*jabhat alkhals alwatani*) is in fact one consequence of the agreement. Two key features of the DPA can be identified. First, as just mentioned, the agreement led to rifts within the SLM. While Minni Minnawi signed (under the pressure of the mediators), Abdelwahid Nour refused. The Justice and Equality Movement (JEM) also refused to sign. In effect, the agreement was born weak. Second, as bad and weak as it was, the agreement exposed the hypocrisy and lack of will of the government in Khartoum. More than two years since the agreement was signed, its implementation is lethally slow. This led to frustration among Minnawi's group and its allies. Minnawi, who is currently senior assistant to the President, is seen by the Darfurians as a lame duck.

The way the government reacted to and engaged with the crisis in Darfur appears to be one in which the state monopolized coercive power to inflict suffering on civilians. It is tempting thus to describe the Sudanese state as strong, insofar as it was able to use force in its response to the crisis, and insofar as the government has been trying in vain to convince the international community that it is able to deal with the crisis in Darfur. Yet, there are certain features that stand against the image of a strong state. These include, first, the central government in Khartoum's loss of effective control over vast territories in Darfur. Rebel movements were able over a short period of time to control vast areas in the countryside. Second, violence has been rampant – all parties to the conflict were engaged in this violence. Third, the level of human suffering in Darfur has been appalling. Whether these features constitute the ground for labeling Sudan as a failed state or not is debatable. But certainly they present too many conundrums. Such conundrums make it extremely difficult for the international community to engage in a meaningful and constructive way in its efforts to address the crisis. But this is not to say that the international community is conundrum-free. In the following section I shall discuss the ways in which the international community engages with the crisis in Darfur.

The Response of the International Community

Whatever response the international community has had to Darfur, it was basically the result of the appalling images brought by media coverage. The images coming out of Darfur put the region on the world's agenda. But years after the escalation of the problem into full war, there was no concrete response. With the international community unwilling to act, the African Union came forward to try to stop the violence in its own region. After helping to negotiate the April 2004 cease-fire between the armed movements and the government, the African Union deployed several hundred unarmed observers to monitor it. When the fighting continued, the African Union deployed armed peacekeepers to protect the monitors and then expanded the numbers to be sent in and the mandate itself so that its police and troops could increase security for IDP camps and IDP returnees, and protect civilians under imminent threat. The first African troops were represented by the Rwandan contingent that arrived in August 2004, followed in the subsequent months by Nigerian and other African troops.[20] But the African presence in Darfur was not robust, and the presence of these troops did not stop the atrocities as the war became more ferocious.

Being on the world agenda has not yet led to meaningful steps to end the fighting or even adequately to address the needs of those uprooted. So what is it that has impeded the international response? This question can be answered at two levels: legal and practical. First, the lack of a meaningful engagement is predicated on the competing characterizations of the conflict. Since its onset, two verdicts were delivered on Darfur, the first from the United States, the second from the United Nations. According to Mamdani, "the American verdict was unambiguous: Darfur was the site of an ongoing genocide."[21] In contrast to the U.S. position, the United Nations was ambiguous. In its report of 25 January 2005 on Darfur, the UN Commission on Darfur concluded: "the government of the Sudan has not pursued a policy of genocide ... directly or through the militias under its control."[22] Nonetheless, the UN report stated that the government's violence was deliberately and indiscriminately directed against civilians. These contradictory verdicts have certainly affected the way the crisis is dealt with at the international level. It is as though genocide must happen before the international community could intervene. The lesson of the Rwandan case has not yet been learned.

Second, at the practical level, "one reason the international community finds the Darfur problem difficult to address is that state reliance on excessive force against ethnic or racial groups seeking greater autonomy is not unique to Sudan."[23] Another reason for the lack of a strong international response is the absence of tools and structures available to the international community to address internal crises. For these reasons, the international community is faced with formidable challenges.

This is because most of the instruments available to the international community for intervening in crisis situations depend on the existence of an effective state. In the case of Darfur, the state has no effective or meaningful presence since the armed movements control vast areas in the region. Under such circumstances the international community does not really know who should be put under pressure: the government or the rebel movements. So far the pressure has been on the government, with predictably little outcome. In situations where security is deteriorating, any meaningful presence of the international community would have to be backed by force. But the use of force cannot be a panacea, and may in itself complicate the situation.

The continuation of atrocities and human suffering led the African Union and the international community to press for a negotiated settlement of the crisis. After long months of negotiations between the government and the armed movements, a peace deal was brokered in Abuja in May 2006. To many people, the DPA reflected the need of the international community to end the misery in Darfur, rather than to address the underlying causes of the crisis. This is reflected in the following two observations. First, the United Nations, United States, United Kingdom, and other key players were pushing too hard to reach a deal by putting pressure on both the government and the armed movements. Second, the pressure, although it succeeded in getting the agreement, led to the split of the movements and caused the Justice and Equality Movement (JEM) and a faction of the Sudan Liberation Army (SLA) to reject the deal. Efforts to convince the dissenting voices have failed so far. But the most serious implication of the DPA is that it created a rift between people in Darfur: Some look at it as a bad deal that did not really address their concerns, while others cautiously welcome it. Based on the increase of violence in the immediate aftermath of the agreement, one can argue that the DPA did not win the hearts and support of local communities in Darfur.

The escalation of violence in Darfur prompted the United Nations to start consultations to deploy troops in Darfur, to help enforce the agreement, and mandate these troops to take all necessary measures to protect UN personnel and disarm illegally armed groups. The government of Sudan completely rejected any role for the United Nations in Darfur. Efforts to convince the government to let in UN troops failed, and until the UN resolution 1706 was passed on August 31, 2006, there was no sign that the government would rescind its decision. The resolution states in its first article: "the UN Security Council invites the *consent* of the government of national unity for the deployment of UN troops in Darfur."

The UN Security Council's Resolution 1706 was not unanimous, and it lacked the appropriate mechanism to enforce it. The weaknesses of the resolution were the result of a number of reasons: First, the word *consent* is too ambiguous to be specific and it is not clear from the resolution whether this consent is necessary or not. Second, in light of the Sudan government's rejection of resolution 1706, it is doubtful whether member states will pledge troops knowing that these troops would be in great danger. Third, if the United Nations ignores this issue of consent and sends in troops, such troops will be fighting for a totally different cause. This will increase human suffering in Darfur. Fourth, the African Union and those who brokered the DPA pledged to impose sanctions on those who refuse to sign, but nothing of that sort is happening. In fact, those who declined to sign are currently active in the war in Darfur. The credibility of the international community is indeed at risk, and actually there are too many examples that devalue UN military engagement.

Precisely one year after resolution 1706 was passed, the UN Security Council passed resolution 1769 on July 31, 2007. Unlike its predecessor, the Security Council unanimously adopted resolution 1769, and the government in Khartoum accepted it. The resolution authorized the deployment of a 26,000-strong joint United Nations–African Union force, "in an attempt to quell the violence in Sudan's western Darfur region, where fighting between pro-government militias and rebel guerrillas has killed more than 250,000 people since 2003." The UN "hybrid force" (a combination of UN forces and AU forces already in Darfur, known as UNAMID "will have up to 19,555 military personnel, including 360 military observers and liaison officers, a civilian component including up to 3,772 international police, and 19 special police units with up to 2,660 officers." One of the important provisions in the resolution states that the Council, acting under Chapter VII of the United Nations Charter, authorized UNAMID to take the necessary action to support implementation of the Darfur Peace Agreement, as well as to protect its personnel and civilians "without prejudice to the responsibility of the Government of Sudan."

Although robust and unanimous, resolution 1769 has some problems. First, the resolution states that UNAMID is authorized to take the necessary action to support the implementation of the Darfur Peace Agreement. To my mind, this is yet another mistake the international community will commit. First, the DPA did not win the hearts of people in Darfur and led to rifts between and among the armed groups. Since many factions were not signatories to the DPA, one wonders how it can be implemented. Furthermore, the United Nations, in 2005, threatened to take action against anyone who impedes the implementation of the DPA, but nothing of the sort has happened thus far. The UN will have to seek a unity of purpose among the different rebel factions before talking about supporting the implementation of the DPA. The Arusha meeting of August 2007 was certainly one step toward the unification of the different armed groups, but more needs to be done.

Second, with regard to the UNAMID mission, there are also some problems related to coordination between the new arriving forces and the AU troops that are already stationed in Darfur. Command structures and logistical issues are also among the questions that will likely complicate and slow the full deployment of the forces.[24]

Third, while Sudan accepted the hybrid forces in principle, the government still insists that it will only accept troops from African countries. Interestingly, the AU leadership is backing the Sudanese position. These cracks are part of the overall lack of clarity in the position of the international community with regard to the crisis in Darfur. Apart from this, UNAMID might get sucked into the circles of violence in Darfur, and instead of being a peacekeeping mission it might come under attack and end up trying to protect its own personnel. An early indication of the likelihood of this scenario occurred in July 2008 when UNAMID forces were attacked in North Darfur by gunmen whose affiliation has yet to be confirmed, but who are widely suspected to be Janjawid militiamen.

Fourth, and finally, in dealing with the government of Sudan, the international community is holding the stick in the middle. On the one hand, the Sudan government is seen as a "rogue" regime that supports terrorism and violates the human rights of its own citizens. On the other, the Sudan government is an incumbent government with which the international community must do business. Adopting these two contradictory positions is like shooting yourself in the foot. Additionally, such ambiguity allows the government to manipulate international politics and buy time for its tactics, not only with regard to the crisis in Darfur, but also with regard to the question of consolidating the Comprehensive Peace Agreement (CPA), which brought the long-standing North–South civil war to an end, and democratic transformation.

The Armed Groups: A Revolutionary Force Turned into Its Antithesis?

Part of the responsibility for the escalation of the crisis and stalemate in the peace process rests with the different armed groups in Darfur. This is for a number of reasons that will be discussed shortly. Here, however, it is necessary to note that the armed struggle in Darfur is linked to two main armed groups: The Sudan Liberation Army/Movement (SLA/M) and the Justice and Equality Movement (JEM). In the beginning, the leadership and the rank and file in both movements were Zaghawa and Fur, but later their membership expanded to include people from other tribes, including the so-called Arabs. The political manifestos of both movements address injustices, marginalization, and inequity in the sharing of wealth and power in the Sudan. Their project was thus a national one. But instead of confronting the central government, these two movements were trapped in fighting the Janjawid, who are no less marginalized, but are considered government allies. The revolutionary strength of these two movements is therefore turned into its antithesis: a destructive force that is contributing to the creation of the region's humanitarian crisis. This trap detracted from the main issue, which is the fight for equality and justice.

Subsequent to the N'djamena cease-fire agreement in 2004, cracks appeared within the armed movements. The first splinter group was the so-called National Movement for Development and Reform (NMDR), which was an offshoot of JEM. But the main crack happened during the Haskanita Convention in 2004, in which Minni Minnawi was elected as SLA leader, thus effectively ousting Abdelwahid Nour. SLA suffered further cracks in the aftermath of the Darfur Peace Agreement, which was signed only by Minnawi's faction. Subsequently, both factions (Minnawi's and Nour) suffered splintering. It is difficult to know exactly how many factions exist at the present time. Suffice it to note that JEM also suffered. Its leader, Khalil Ibrahim, has been accused of nepotism, despotism, and the propagation of kinship clientele within the movement.

It is tempting to put the blame on the government in Khartoum, which has long been playing a game of "divide and rule." But then it is also true that many leaders of these different factions and splinter groups do not really know what they want or what they stand for. They are unclear about their mission, and they lack a vision. If all these different factions are fighting for the cause of Darfur, why is it so difficult for them to forge a unity of purpose? Why is it so difficult to unify their agenda and put it on the negotiating table? Factionalism among the armed groups is certainly one contributing factor in the increasing human suffering in the region.

Concluding Remarks

Government cynicism, international confusion (and lack of will), and complex local dynamics contributed to the escalation of the crisis in Darfur. The same factors are also effectively present when peaceful settlement initiatives are attempted. While civil society organizations, human rights activists, and columnists worldwide do their utmost to bring the attention of the world to what is happening in Darfur, it is unfortunate that much of the effort is counterproductive. This is because the Darfur crisis, a complex political crisis, is being reduced to "a morality tale," to use Mamadani's phrase, unfolding in a world populated by villains and victims.[25] The villains are so evil and the victims are so helpless that the only possibility is a rescue mission, preferably in the form of a military intervention. This view amounts to a dangerous reductionism. Darfur has a long history of conflict, of competition between the different constituent forces. Such a long and complex history must not be forgotten while attempting to deal with the crisis.

The international community, represented by the UN, has been repeating mistakes when dealing with the crisis in Darfur. The first mistake was made when too much pressure was put on Minnawi to sign the DPA. When that happened, the UN went public and declared that it would punish anybody who stands against the implementation of the agreement. But nothing of the sort happened, even though most groups have stood against the DPA since day one. The second mistake was committed in resolution 1769, which stated in its opening that the hybrid force, UNAMID, will have the power to take all necessary measures to ensure the imple-mentation of the DPA. This means that no peace will be achieved soon in Darfur. It appears that deploying the hybrid forces is the last chance for the international community to bring peace to Darfur. The question that needs to be asked is: Do we have reasons to believe that UNAMID will be successful?

The incumbent government in Sudan is still playing its tactical games with cynicism. The government is not open to deal sincerely with the root causes of the crisis. Questions of equitable distribution of political power and economic resources and just development are some of the issues that the government is not really willing to discuss. The stalemate in the already standing three peace agreements (the CPA, DPA, and ESPA) indicates that the government – the National Congress Party – is not serious about implementing agreements it signs. It also indicates that any future peace talks on Darfur might just be another instance of public relations diplomacy. A key element in forcing the government to be serious is the unification of the armed groups in Darfur. Perhaps this is where the international community should focus its efforts.

Notes

1. An earlier version of this essay appeared under the title "National and International Responses to the Crisis of Darfur" in The Ahfad Journal: Women and Change, 24 (1) and at http://sudaninstitute.org/Assal.pdf.
2. See A. Mohamed, et al., *Development is the Key for Peace in Darfur* (Khartoum: Centre for Development and Peace Studies (Juba)/Fredrich Ebert Stiftung, 2003); A. Mohamed and Belgis Bedri, *Inter-Communal Conflicts in Sudan Cases, Resolution Mechanisms and Transformation: A Case Study of Darfur Region* (Omdurman: Ahfad University, 2005); and A. G. Ahmed and L. Manger, *Understanding the Crisis in Darfur: Listening to Darfur Voices* (Bergen: Bric, 2006).
3. This paragraph and the following two ones are based on Assal, 2005, pp. 4–5.
4. M. Assal, "It Is All about History Repeating Itself: The State and the Involution of Conflict in Darfur," *Journal of Darfurian Studies* 1 (2006): 6–22 (sample copy); M. Assal, *Darfur: An Annotated Bibliography of Social Research* (Bergen: Bric/The University of Bergen, 2005).
5. A. An-Naim, *Causes and Solutions for Darfur*, unpublished paper, August 2003.
6. A. De Waal, "Briefing: Darfur, Sudan: prospects for peace," *African Affairs*, 104 (414): 127–135.
7. S. Harir, "Arab Belt versus African Belt: Ethno-Political Conflict in Darfur and the Regional Cultural Factors." In *Short Cut to Decay: The Case of the Sudan*, T. Tvedt and Sharif Harir, eds. (Uppsala: The Nordic Africa Institute, 1994), 154.
8. M. Al-Mubarak (second edition) *Tarikh Darfur al-syasi* (*The Political History of Darfur*) (Khartoum: Khartoum University Press, 1995).
9. *Solong* means "Arab" in the Fur language.
10. S. R. O'Fahey, *State and Society in Darfur* (London: Hurst and Co., 1980).
11. Y. Takana, "A Report on Tribal Conflict in Darfur" (in Arabic), a paper presented to the deliberations of the Tribal Reconciliation Conference in Nyala town, December 25–30, 1997.
12. For more on the Mahadist policies on Darfur, see Al-Mubarak, 1995, and Assal, 2006, pp. 8–10).
13. K. Beck, "Nomads of Northern Kordufan and the State: From Violence to Pacification," *Nomadic Peoples* 38 (1996): 73–98.
14. A. De Waal, "Who Are the Darfurians? Arab and African Identities, Violence and External Engagement," *African Affairs*, 104 (415): 192.
15. M. Mamdani, "Preliminary Thoughts on the Congo Crisis," *Social Text* 17, no. 3 (1999): 53–62.
16. Assal, 2006.
17. Personal communication with the editor of *Khartoum Monitor Daily*, April 2003.
18. A. El-Battahani, "The Relationship between the Region and the Centre: The Status of Darfur Region in Light of Naivasha Protocols, conference paper, 2004.
19. Harir, 1994.
20. The "African" and "Arab" divide in Darfur is certainly one complicating factor in the crisis. Despite the striking focus on these labels, they are basically political constructions. The UN Commission on Darfur (2004) found that "many Arabs in Darfur are opposed to the *Janjawid*, and some Arabs are fighting with the rebels, such as certain Arab commanders and their men from the Messeriya and Rezeigat tribes. At the same time, many non-Arabs are supporting the government and serving in its army." Arabs and non-Arabs can hardly be distinguished in their outward physical appearance. The UN Commission concludes: "apparently, the sedentary and nomadic character of the groups constitutes one of the main distinctions between them."
21. R. Cohen, "The International Response to Darfur," *Forced Migration Review* 23 (2005): 7–9.
22. Mamdani, 2007.
23. United Nations, "Report of the International Commission on Inquiry on Darfur to the United Nations Secretary-General," January 25, 2005, p. 4.
24. Cohen, 2005, p. 7.
25. Personal communication with the Head of Civilian Protection Unit, UNAMIS, Khartoum, May 2007.
26. Mamdani, 2007.

Scene of a burnt Village
Near Bindisi, 2006

African Union Mission Camp
Mukjar, 2006

African Union Soldiers
Mukjar, 2006

Scene from Kalmah Camp
Nyala, 2006

Scene from Kalmah Camp
Nyala, 2006

Scene near Bindisi Market
Bindisi, 2006

UNITED STATES AG

USAID

INTERNATIONAL DEVELOP

U S A

ROM THE AMERICAN P

Sack for USAID Food Aid Kalmah Camp
Nyala, 2006

Section Five

Sudanese Civil Society, the State, and the Struggle for Peace in Darfur

16 The End of Violence:
Against Civil Society

Grant Farred

With their rights respected, and generous and sustained international involvement to oversee a return to the rule of law, the people of Darfur can still live a decent life together within their common home
Julie Flint and Alex de Waal, *Darfur: A Short History of a Long War*

Civil society is the gift of peace. It is the act of living together in political tolerance, of being able to live with difference without violence. In civil society, the politics of identity – à la Rwanda (ca. 1990s) or Kenya (ca. 2007/2008) or as Darfur has for years now been cast – does not equal death. It is worth remembering, however, that civil society is never the place of pure friendship. On the contrary, it is celebrated as the place of the nonviolent dissensual. The civil, broadly understood as the conglomeration of social entities (civic organizations, community groups, non-governmental organizations, the guarantee of public forums, or even trade unions, although their "civic credentials" may be more difficult to assert) that stand outside of the state's political but insist on their right to practice "politics," is that place where conflict, difference, and disagreement can be accommodated. With, of course, the foundational proviso that the civil be constructed as that space where there is no threat of the retreat into violence. Civil society is, in this formulation, the place of nonextreme partisanship – partisanship without the threat to life or the threat of death. Politics without fear. The politics for life, life – in its most basic and elaborate form – as the absolute precondition for politics.

  The civil stands, not to put too fine a point on it, in contradistinction to the Schmittian political. For Carl Schmitt, the political is the "most intense and extreme antagonism, and every concrete antagonism becomes that much more political the closer it approaches the most extreme point, that of the friend–enemy grouping."[1] Read against Schmitt's "intense political," what civil society demands – what it imagines itself to be, the political that is simultaneously outside the political, the "political" that is, precisely for its externality, the nonpolitical – is politically impossible. It is the demand of and for peace as the first condition of politics that provokes the question of the political: Might the gift of life, so critical, so fundamental to our and any thinking of Darfur, also be, ironically, the gift of political death? After all, as Kant reminds us in his famous joke about death, there is only one true peace – that of the graveyard. How, you might ask, dare I speak so casually, so rhetorically, so philosophically of death? I dare not, of course, and yet I must – I must speak of death because, after all, the final word on Darfur is death. Every speaking of Darfur is today a necropolitical enunciation evoking the specter of the dead or, at best, invoking the ongoing horror of the "IDPs" – internally displaced persons, those still alive, those who survived the violence to live in the camps.

I speak of death not to trivialize it or to reduce its importance – one cannot, in any case, do that when there is such carnage taking place in Darfur – or to suggest that the desire for the civil can or should be dismissed out of hand. I speak of violence in relation to the civil because violence – the sovereign state's monopoly on violence, violence first and foremost – can easily put an end to the civil. Violence can put an end to the civil; only rarely can the civil put an end to violence – and almost never without a violence of its own. The civil stands not, as its proponents might claim, against the sovereign, but, always, as subject to the sovereign. The sovereign tolerates the civil – gives it conditional life – only because it has, and can, authorize it. The state has sovereignty over the civil so that it can, if it chooses to (and has done so in many places), found governmental nongovernmental organizations (GONGOs) in opposition to NGOs. GONGOs represent both a paradox and the extension of sovereignty. That the state should establish GONGOs is at once a recognition of the ideological work done by NGOs, the state understanding the need to articulate itself in a politically distinct way, and a clear demonstration of the power of sovereignty: Nothing is outside the power of the sovereign. Everything is political, in Schmitt's sense, so that the civil is in no way exempt from that "most extreme antagonism." The state can, in a single stroke, found a GONGO to counteract the NGO and bring the intensity of the friend–enemy antagonism to civil society. Or, the state of Omar Al Bashir can, as it did in the event of an NGO report that was critical of sexual violence against women in Darfur, simply ignore or amend the report.

No form of politics can exist outside of the purview of sovereignty so that, hyperbolically phrased, we might say that GONGOs (or NGO reports) represent the "failure" of civil society to "insulate" itself from the political because it cannot stay the "intrusion" of the sovereign into the affairs of the civil. The GONGO, properly speaking, represents the ubiquity of sovereignty, the infinite capacity of the sovereign to extend itself. The sovereign alone decides not only the exception – that is, when the normative functioning of the state is suspended upon the word of the sovereign – but also the terrain and the "im-possibilities" of the civil. The GONGO reminds the citizen of the nondelimitation of the political. There is no end to the sovereign. The civil, first and finally, has no sovereignty. That is precisely why civil society is so committed to the preservation of (nonpolitical) difference. Difference, *sans* (the threat of) violence, is the very *raison d'etre* of the civil – it is what distinguishes the civil from the political. For the political, it is the inscription of difference that ensures conflict. One of the key features of the political is its insistence upon the right to conflict – not simply to difference but to violent disagreement. The political under-stands, and indeed thrives, because difference is infinite and, as such, inherently a political issue. Difference is a condition that civil society tries to, in vain, at best, ameliorate, at worst, endure through liberal accommodation and the political embraces as constitutive.

When the civil overwhelms the state, as it has in countless places, but, most recently, in the slew of "color revolutions" that swept former Moscow satellites such as Georgia (the "Rose revolution," 2003) or Ukraine (the "Orange revolution," 2004) that is the moment that we know, definitively, that we are confronting more than simply a failed, un-sovereign or soon-to-be "re-sovereignized" state. We can be sure that we are, precipitously, hopefully, on the doorstep of a new sovereign. The state always precedes the civil. The state always comes before the civil so that the civil is a sign of the sovereign, a guarantee that the state's sovereign power is operative. Within it, the civil contains what Slavoj Žižek might term the "perverse core" of a new political – a new political imagined out of the idealistic nonpolitical of the civil. However, it is a political that can only be achieved through sovereignty. The sovereign authorizes the civil to be civil and intrudes upon it – politically – when it aspires to the political. Civil society is, for this reason, the sign that political life is always, must of necessity be, political. Political life cannot be diffused away from the state or usurped by the civil. The political can only be contested politically, only rarely civilly (and then only as an incipient sovereignty).

The In-civility of the Name

> **If there were no eternal consciousness in a man, if at the bottom of everything there were only a wild ferment, a power that twisting in dark passions produced everything great or inconsequential; if an unfathomable, insatiable emptiness lay hid beneath everything, what then would life be but despair?**
> Søren Kierkegaard, *Fear and Trembling*

> **Political subjects exist in the interval between different names of subjects.**
> Jacques Rancière, *Hatred of Democracy*

The issue of the name, the "meaning" of the name *Darfur*, the political that is "Darfur," raises more than the question – the question of disorder, the question of violence, the question of rebellion, the question of genocide – for Sudanese sovereignty. Or, some might say, for the issue of sovereignty in and for the North. That is why today the "political subjects" of Darfur, be they the Fur or the Masalit, or, for that matter, the *Janjawid*, "exist in the interval": in the time between sovereignty and its violent articulation; or, as the time of violent sovereign articulation. In the time between sovereignty and rebellion there is the moment for the other names: "victims" of the violence, "survivors," "IDPs," names that resonate with judgment – the condemnation of the Al Bashir government by the West – and power – Khartoum's capacity to impose itself in the Darfur region. The subject of the "Darfurian political," which must be distinguished from the more general designation "Sudanese subject," demonstrates how subjectivation – the making of the political subject, if you will – can only be understood in and through the workings of sovereignty.

The subject of the Darfurian political, which can be said to exist only precariously, not only emerges from within the bloodiness of conflict, from within the plethora of names ("genocide," "state-sponsored violence," and so on), but through its existence it "names" the sovereign itself. Because there is such intimacy between sovereign violence and rebellion, because the "intervals" – such as they are – between "violence" and "peace" are truncated and perilous, because peace treaties can neither be effectively agreed upon or enforced (*Abuja* is one such unsuccessful name), *Darfur* comes to stand as the only name that matters politically. Because of what is happening in Darfur, the sovereign – both Sudan and Al Bashir – come to stand in the shadow of sovereign violence. Not simply indicted internationally, but the sovereign is undone by its own violence. The sovereign being made, as it were, subject to (the condemnation of) other sovereigns – the United States, Britain, France, (even) the nonsovereign United Nations.

In our moment, among other appendings, *Darfur* is the very name of incivility. Darfur is Conradian in its spectral power. There is, of course, "the horror, the horror" of the Janajwid, the sovereign shadow of Omar Hassan Ahmad Al Bashir and his National Congress Party (in Arabic, *al-Mu'tamar al-Watan*).[2] Not only is there the historic hegemony of the North, executed by Khartoum's violent treatment of the South, but this is also a horror tinged with heartfelt loss – in some quarters, over the passing of former SPLM/A rebel commander and Sudanese vice president John Garang (July 2005), of the memory of the Addis Ababa Accords (1972), marking the end of the First Sudanese Civil War (1955–1972). There is the massive carnage that was the Second Civil War (1983–2005), Anyanya II, fought mainly in the South in which 1.9 million people were killed and some four million displaced; there is the broken promise of Naivasha, the Comprehensive Peace Agreement (CPA) signed between the SPLM/A and the Khartoum government at Naivasha, Kenya, in 2005 that has turned out not to be "comprehensive" after all. And who is not troubled by the names of first vice president Ali Osman Taha and Janjawid leader Musa Hilal?[3]

Omar Al Bashir, Ali Osman Taha, and Musa Hilal are names that evoke, in Kierkegaard's terms, "dark passions." These are men whose actions have caused the people of Darfur to, literally, live while trembling with fear. These are names, we might suggest, which Colonel Kurtz himself might fear. *Darfur* is the political term that marks the death of civility – the death of peace; or "peace" as the Kantian joke – among the Masalit, the Fur, and the Zaghawa, to mention only three groups,or "political constituencies"; "Darfur" marks the death of Darfur's communal living. Darfur is no longer the place that can accommodate ethnic difference, the difference that is also the marker of sociopolitical difference – the Arab nomads and the black African farmers, insofar as one can invoke such reductive descriptors. Darfur can no longer live with its own history of difference – which is to say, with the history of migration, of international crisscrossings among the Sudan and Chad, the Sudan and Libya or Egypt. When the only (remaining) enunciation of difference is conflict, when difference demands its proper speaking, conflict, that is the precise location at which the civil is superseded – invalidated – by the political. The war in Darfur is, in this way, the "eruption" of the political – the coming into the political, which produces the deconstruction of the material – the existing but no longer tenable arrangements that enabled the nomadic groups to move freely, to tether, feed, graze, and water their camels on "African" land, that enabled farmers and nomads to trade and barter with each other, to coexist on the land. Beyond the tragedy of the Darfur situation (the destruction of a long-standing mode of political life), what Martin Daly calls "Darfur's sorrow," there is one unmistakable recognition: All difference is, ultimately and necessarily, political.

At issue, then, is not difference per se, but the matter of how conflict is decided politically. Whose rights, those of the farmer or those of the nomad, are upheld? Can both constituencies be allowed to make mutually respected claims upon the land? These issues have to be decided. The "pre-Darfur" Darfur situation – where coexistence and cooperation were the (finally, unsustainable) order of the day –

made it possible to suspend, if not abolish, the need for the decision. The "Darfur" conjuncture demands the decision – Who belongs? Who has rights? At what expense are those rights granted and secured? – through the political articulation of the conflict. What needs to be understood is that conflict – the conflict that makes imperative the decision – is the normative, not the exceptional, mode of the political. As William Rasch argues, "politics preserves the ability to initiate and the ability to put a halt to conflict, the ability to recognize and determine the difference between conflict and peace."[4] And, to account for the conflict – which means, of necessity, to acknowledge that peace is, at this moment, impossible. The conflict must be thought – it cannot remain unreflected upon or go unacknowledged; a conflict must be thought in order to apprehend the violence, the ongoing, still-operative, violence of the decision. In the midst of violence, of a long-running civil war, the political project becomes: How can the civil – the civility of Darfurian life – be restored? There is only one answer: sovereignty. If conflict is the only basis of the political, then the Darfur violence can only be terminated – not, in liberal terms, "resolved" – by sovereign decision.

The destruction of the civil is the consequence of sovereignty. It is because the state, based in, but not restricted to, the power of Khartoum and the North, has long now underwritten the kind of violence that has been destroying civil life in Darfur. The state has armed, encouraged, funded, provided ideological sustenance for the Janjawid and Musa Hilal's paramilitary brigades. The (Northern) Sudanese state, in both its postcolonial and colonial formations, engendered the current violence through studious neglect, itself a deliberate political decision. Al Bashir's government's policy worked through its reliance on the *hakura*, through its dependence upon a system of rough self-governance for the people of Darfur. And this is why we must, philosophically, think of death – rather than of "peace," "peace" as a discourse sans political purchase – because the Al Bashir state has decided upon death – even as Khartoum committed itself to "peace" in Abuja – as the political (policy) for Darfur. The sovereign has no (natural) inclination toward peace. The sovereign will only decide upon peace when its own life – the sovereignty, the sustainability of the state – is put at risk.

Conflict

In a world where conflict has been outlawed, how is opposition to be staged?
William Rasch, *Sovereignty and its Discontents*

The civil is the place of first vulnerability. The civil is always dependent upon the political. The civil, in order to endure, to continue to live, must be subject to the political. It is not enough for the civil to coexist with the political; the civil must understand its place in the relation of sovereignty. The civil can challenge the sovereign, as it has in Sudan on two occasions: in the October 21 revolution of 1964 when civil society activists, led by trade unionists, workers, and so on ousted the military regime of General Aboud after minimal violence and replaced it with a civilian government – this was undone by the Free Officers Movement, led by Ja'far Numeiri, who seized power in a coup on May 25, 1969, overthrowing the civilian government of Ismail al-Azhari.[5] Again, in April 1985, a civilian uprising, in which the Trade Unions Alliance

(TUA) played a crucial role, displaced the Numieri regime before itself being usurped by the military dictatorship of Al Bashir. Still in office today, Al Bashir took power following the coup d'etat of June 30, 1989. It is, of course, precisely the exception that proves the rule – that reveals the rule of sovereignty – so that we understand that while civil society can oppose, sometimes successfully, sovereignty, civil society can never displace or supercede it. Neither the second (1964–1969) nor third (1985–1989) experiment with Sudanese democracy lasted very long.

That is why it is necessary, in order to sustain civil society, to argue for the political as a life-and-death struggle over the everyday life – and as such a prohibition against the death – of the Darfurian people. It is the political alone that gives life, that can protect and maintain it. As long as there is a political, there is sovereignty, and at the very core of sovereignty is the inalienable right of the state to violence: the right over life and death, the Schmittian/Al Bashirian division of Darfur into a region, in the most biopolitically crude terms, of "friends" – Hilal and the Janjawid – and "enemies" – the "rebels," in itself a name that inscribes the challenge to Khartoum's sovereignty. What Al Bashir and his allies are doing (and the Janjawid and their ilk do not, as is the nature of clients who are also rogues, always follow Khartoum's bidding) in Darfur is insisting upon the right to dispense with life in the name of the state.

Because of the complicated relationship between the state's *de jure* and its proxy forces in Darfur, because of Khartoum's difficult relationship to the region itself, it is plausible to argue that Darfur instantiates – metonymically – the Sudan as failed or failing state. Darfur marks the inability of the state to implement the law and yet to insist, through expropriated and outsourced violence, on its right to the Law. Al Bashir has declared that those who oppose the National Congress government in Darfur are engaged in an unlawful act (even as he symbolically negotiates "peace treaties" with the rebels in Abuja), that the rebels are, in that age-old red herring, "enemies of the state." Having learned the lesson of Anyanya II (the Second Civil War in the South; today, of course, the SPLM/A continues to harbor its own desires for sovereignty), to refuse the disarticulation of "Sudan," Al Bashir's government is skilled in the rhetoric that critiques the "extreme partisanship" that goes by the name of "rebels" – the "enemy" of, and therefore the threat to, Khartoum. The threat of the uncurtailed, rampant rebel – the Sudan Liberation Army, the Justice and Equality Movement, the Darfur Liberation Movement, the *Black Book: Imbalance of Power and Wealth in Sudan*, the *akadas* – is intolerable to the Al Bashir government.

There can, then, not in the Sudan or anywhere else, ever be a politics without violence. Civil society's claim to live in peace, to conduct nonpolitical life civilly is, finally, unsustainable. That is because civil society is an expression of the desire – a legitimate desire, to be sure, but an unfulfillable one, in the end – to live politically without the threat of sovereign violence – to live without difference as conflict. This claim, issued from and by the civil, is one that no state, which reserves to itself the right of sovereign violence, can permit. The state that concedes its monopoly upon violence is the state that will, sooner rather than later, cease to exist.

Because the political is always violent, it is also a critique of any notion of return – "return" here marking both a temporal thinking, as in "turning back to the moment before, the moment that is passed, and a "Palestinian" articulation, the

right of access to land, property, and, dare one say, a history that was violently
sundered. There can only be a "return" to civil life, there can in fact only be civil life,
indeed, life, in Darfur if there is a new political – which is at the core of the argument
about the "New Sudan" as reinaugurated by John Garang in 1983 – that, first,
permits it, and, second, sustains it: no life without sovereignty.[6] Garang's vision
of a "New Sudan," motivated as he was by his critique of Khartoum's Islamicization
(Garang was a non-Muslim Southern Sudanese former military officer and scholar
who did not do politics in the name of his faith but certainly did organize his SPLM/A
troops against the North's Islamicization project, especially the declaration of shari'a
in September 1983), is not precisely consistent with the struggle confronting the Fur,
the Masalit, and the Zaghawa today in the very place named Darfur. What is valuable
about Garang for the contemporary conjuncture is that he did understand that the
North had to be, and could be, politically reoriented through violent opposition.
For Garang the Southern politician and solider, there could be, as it were, no return
to either the failures of the Numieri era or to the ongoing disenfranchisement of
the South and other marginalized regions of Sudan.

Garang grasped the fundamental terms of the Sudanese political: It functioned
through (protracted) conflict. This is instructive for a Darfurian region that, with
its indistinct, porous borders, its itinerant, nomadic peoples, its settled farmers,
its itinerants, the "incursionaries" from Chad, its migrants, with its collective and
singular histories that speak of its own in-civility, of the conflicts between and among
these various communities, understands the politics of the Western Sudanese land.
To offer such an evaluation of "pre-Darfur" Darfur life is neither to exaggerate nor
undermine the conflict of Darfurian life.

It is, instead, to raise a question that is pertinent to not only Darfur but also
our political moment: the question of the migrant, more specifically, the question
of who the migrant is, who the migrant is if not the stranger (in Christian religious
thought, Christ as the – unexpected – stranger). Of, in the specific terms of Darfur's
history, of the neighbor as "stranger" – of the neighbor, more precisely, the erstwhile
neighbor, the now-displaced neighbor, the one-time neighbor who now lives in the
camp under the categorical name "IDP." Of, in Levinas's terms, the "stranger" – the
Other who is not truly a stranger because the "stranger" is known, historically
knowable as a neighbor, so that the "stranger" cannot but haunt, in/through its very
face, the Self – who is also, at once, the Self, of the stranger who makes the (political
transgressions of the) Self visible to the Self.[7] The stranger as the incarnation of the
Sudanese political. It is in the violence done to the "stranger" that it becomes possible
to recognize the politics of division – not only the constituencies of Darfur, but the
schisms between North and South, Muslim and animist – as the politics of naming.
It is to ask, "Who is my neighbor?" And to answer: "My neighbor must have a
political name." For any subject of the African (or diasporic) political, it is to know –
tragically – the politics of the Kenyan poor, divided into "Luo" and "Kikuyu"; it
is to understand the political and philosophical need to take seriously the politics
of ethnicity, but also, simultaneously, to stand helpless in the face of its too easy,
too expedient, too rapid mobilization. So easy to call forth the name of the Self that
stands in violent contradistinction to the name of the "stranger"/neighbor. It is
to remark upon the Kenyan politician, those who bear the names "Odinga" and

"Kibaki" – it is to confront Kierkegaardian "despair" in the political work these "dark" names can do.

As regards Darfur, to mind come quickly, "Umshishi," "Zurqa," and "Masalit." Names of historic coexistence, names of the neighbor, names that can take on, now, disturbingly, a "strangeness." Or, the most heinous and violent of these enunciations: "Janjawid," the "ruffian" Musa, or his "hordes." *Janjawid* is itself made into a political name: The pejorative *ruffian* is the acknowledgment of disruption, of threat. "Zurqa," the name that became racial by becoming the name of the "black," the African, the Darfurian Muslim who is not Arab. "Zurqa," the name that became a racist moniker. The Other. "Umshishi," they all come out of the land, are deeply attached to and ingrained with the mark of the bloodied, ethnicized, racialized land. It is, however, the name *Janjawid* that is most salient to those in the West because it is already overdetermined. After all, who is the ruffian, the unruly, murderous hordes, but that old trope of the colonial and postcolonial imaginary, the barbarian? The barbarian made famous, and to be feared, first by Cavafy, the Egyptian of Greek descent, and then by J. M. Coetzee? Do we not all live in fear of the barbarian?

In a region where African and Arab have long lived, and now died, together, where bloodlines are difficult to disentangle, the name – the "black" – retains a political meaning. My neighbor's name today might, of course, if it is intolerable to the Janjawiid or to the rebels, mean death. And, yet, what was the name of my neighbor yesterday? Again, we might remind ourselves of the names, if we need any reminding, "Kikuyu" or "Luo," and how little meaning they had just before the outcome of the contested Kenyan parliamentary elections? Likewise, the various people now inhabiting Darfur might be moved to inquire: What was the name of my neighbor in 1910? Or in 1956, the year of independence? More likely than not, that political name was "friend," in a sense that Schmitt might fully recognize: the Fur as friend to the Masalit, the friend as neighbor, the friend as economic collaborator and competitor, the friend with whom political conflict could be confronted in a form that allowed for the retention of difference without violence.

In Darfur, we cannot but conclude, the politics of the name – friend, enemy – is dependent not only upon temporality, that precise time that the name might mean or not mean death – is inveterately linked to the question of land. It is, not to put too metaphoric a point on it, the question of "dar": the land, the kingdom, the place. The power of sovereignty, the capacity, the history, and the dream of tomorrow living again, civilly, turns on the land, on how life is lived on the land. The political and the civil in Darfur is, conclusively, autochthonous. Equal, shared right to the land is fundamental to the end of violence: Only when the land is inhabited equitably, when patterns of life, nomads, farmers, itinerants is enshrined, enjoys the force of law, then civil life can return, fully, to Darfur.

It is also to recognize the vulnerability of the land to nonpolitical forces. More exactly, the disruptive force that can emanate from the drought so that the land itself becomes the most precious resource. The drought brought the famine, the famine produced an ecological disaster that is, invariably, followed by political disaster. Which is to say, death. In a critical way, Darfur is a violence borne of ecological disaster. The drought brought the guns to the Malamit, and with it came, inexorably, the violence. The lack of land, drought, famine, and ecological disaster is what made another political possible. Because of the "natural disaster," a virulent, if always residual, strain of Arab nationalism – emerging out of Qaddafi's Arabist dreams, the Arab Gathering, practiced by Musa Hilal and his Janjawid cronies – articulated itself, the likes of the "Zurqa," the Umshishi can be put in their political place, which is to say, their political nonplace. The place of the uncivil, the place of the nonpolitical, those who live under the name of the politically abject: Fur, Masalit, Zarghawa, and so on.

Claims about the land are inherently uncivil. They are deeply political in that they address issues such as displacement, rights, justice, the right to rights, race and racism. These are claims that cannot be sustained without violence. The dream of the civil, of living together, without – or, more precisely now – after the pejorative, to live with the memory of being labeled "Zurqa" or "Umshishi" – can only be realized through the political. There can be no easy living together after death, in the midst of death. There must be a political living in, living together with, death. The truth of the civil is that it constitutes, in its very powerlessness, in its unsovereignty, the utopian core of the political. If there can be no sovereignty without sovereignty, there can assuredly be no sovereignty that does not desire its own civil incarnation, no sovereign that does not dream of peace. Or, at least, of respite from violence.

That is the work of the civil: not to imagine itself as sovereign, but to demand from the sovereign what is, perversely, idealistically, unknowingly, we might even say, at the embroiled political core of the political. To imagine a sovereign that can sustain itself, not permanently, but at least momentarily, without violence. The end of violence can only emanate from the sovereign. That does not mean, however, that the sovereign will become, of its own accord, civil. Instead, it means that in order to radicalize the sovereignty into "civility," into a life that can sustain life, the civil must argue against itself. The civil can only be achieved through its engagement with the sovereign. The end of violence will only be secured if the Janjawid understand that they are themselves subject to sovereign violence. Moreover, as Jacques Derrida argues in his essay "Force of Law," the Sudanese state must be made "afraid of *founding* violence – that is, violence able to justify, to legitimate (*begründen*), or transform the relations of law (*Rechtsverhältnisse*), and so to present itself as having a right to right and to law [*comme ayant un droit au droit*]."[8] That is, out of the historic political that is Darfur, out of the broad "rebel" movement, there must emerge the threat of a "founding violence": a movement that will assert its axiomatic "right to right and to law." That is, a Darfurian political that is not subject to the sovereign violence of Khartoum; or a Darfurian political that will respond to the North's violence with a violence of its own; a Darfur that will write, enact, and protect its own "law" because it is founded upon resisting the law of Khartoum. The North's law, be that liberal-democratic or even shari'a, only has the force of law when it comes with the protection and power of the sovereign. The law cannot be enforced without power; the state has no power or authority where it has no sovereignty.

The Janjawid will only know that Khartoum is capable of acting against its own if there is the threat, as there was for more than twenty years (1983–2005) in the South, of a "founding" Darfurian violence. The Janjawid must be named what it is: *e'tat voyous*, the "rogue state" that Khartoum has, in ways inadvertently, in others directly, established in order to rule Darfur by violent proxy. The *e'tat voyous* must recognize that it is not a state, that it is itself vulnerable to sovereign violence; or that the *etat voyous* is, because of its violence, responsible for a "founding," which is to say, sovereign, violence. Only the return of violence to the absolute monopoly of the state, under the rule of Al Bashir or someone else or some other force, or the consolidation brought about by a "founding violence" can return Darfur to civility. The latter is, the uncivil history of Sudan's civil wars have taught us, the lesson of the SPLM/A. The threat of a "founding violence," of a sovereign law that is sovereign unto itself (the South) and not Khartoum, is what (more than, we might say, the horrendous loss of life) compelled Al Bashir and his government to restructure the Sudanese political – it is this threat that propelled John Garang to his, albeit tragically brief, position as vice president of Sudan. It is the threat of "founding violence" more than anything that resonates from the triumph of John Garang in 2005. The late SPLM/A leader understood, in Derrida's terms, the political power of the "force of founding violence." As importantly, the sovereign in Khartoum grasped, fully, the kind of threat that the SPLM/A represented because it could, for the Sudanese public North and South, "legitimate" its "founding violence." The South's resistance to Islamicization (though that is not always how it was cast) and the hegemony of the North, made Garang's movement not only nationally viable – and sustainable – but earned it international (which is to say, regional) legitimacy when Libya and Egypt backed its militarized opposition to Khartoum.

Only sovereignty can institute the civil, only sovereignty can restore life to Darfur. That is what must be demanded from Khartoum: the enactment of its sovereignty. Which is to say, Khartoum must be made to act violently against its own Frankensteinian creation. Only sovereignty can address and solve the "problem" of genocide. Sovereignty, in short, must be threatened with the loss of sovereignty. Which poses the question: Can the New Sudan emerge from anywhere but the sovereignty of the Old Sudan? Can life emerge from death? That is the work of the political: to make the sovereign accountable to nothing but its own founding principle: corporate violence. Without sovereign violence there can be, paradoxically, no peace. The task at hand is to compel sovereignty to act violently, to act violently, moreover, against itself in order to retain its sovereignty. The last thing, apparently, that Al Bashir wants – his fear of history, we might properly say – is to be remembered as the sovereign who ceded sovereignty. That, observers argue, is why he struck a deal with the SPLM/A.

In order to achieve a civil, even a provisional, peace the Sudan way is, it could be argued, the politically abject subject must aspire, publically, not to peace but to sovereignty. It must enunciate within its resistance the possibility of a "founding violence." It is only when sovereignty confronts the prescient articulation – the ambition, so to speak – of another sovereignty, that the "offending, repressive" sovereignty accedes to peace. The civil can only be achieved through violence. The work of the civil is not only to make itself the incarnation of violence. It is, rather, to present itself as a viable sovereign – as the sovereign *l'avenir*. The sovereign understands only the language of violence so that the abject (the Darfurian political) must threaten the sovereign in order to live in peace, to make the sovereign, in the first if not the last instance, coextensive with the civil. Violence is the only way to achieve peace that is not Kantian but politically feasible, to make the civil a viable and sustainable modality of life. In order to achieve itself, the civil must militate against itself; it must become other than itself. If there is at the core of every sovereignty the desire for the civil, the obverse must be made to be true: At the core of every civil there is the unspeakable propensity for sovereign-threatening violence.

Notes

[1] Carl Schmitt, *The Concept of the Political*, George Schwab, trans. (Chicago: University of Chicago Press, 1996), p. 29.

[2] The National Congress is the governing official political party of Sudan. Founded in 1998, it contains within it elements of the former National Islamic Front (NIF) organization.

[3] It is widely believed that, with the outbreak of violence in Darfur in 2003, Ali Osman Taha and Chief of the Air Force Abdullah Safi Al-Nur secured Hilal's release for the express purpose of having him conduct the war against the rebels in Darfur.

[4] William Rasch, *Sovereignty and Its Discontents: On the Primacy of Conflict and the Structure of the Political* (Great Britain: Birkbeck Law Press, 2004), p. 21.

[5] See Mansour Khalid's *Nimeiri and the Revolution of Dismay* (London: KPI, 1985) for a critique of the Numieri era.

[6] The idea of New Sudan could be traced back to the program and discourse of the Sudanese left in general and more specifically the Communist party as articulated in the idea of *al quwa al haditha* ("the modern forces"), which always meant the creation of a new Sudan. This was envisioned as a nation where people of the marginalized areas enter into an alliance with the modern forces as represented by organized labor and trade unions, women organization, youth organization, "tribal associations," and left political parties, to restructure the power of the center as controlled by Arabized elites historically supported by traditional and sectarian political parties. This meant the creation of a New Sudan that entails a radical restructuring of power, equal distribution of wealth and national resources between different regions, guaranteeing of gender equality and basic civil and democratic liberties and so forth.

[7] See Richard Kearney's "Dialogue with Emmanuel Levinas," *Face to Face with Levinas*, Richard A. Cohen, ed. (Albany: State University of New York Press, 1986) for a discussion of the encounter with "the Other."

[8] Jacques Derrida, "Force of Law," *Acts of Religion* (New York: Routledge, 2002), p. 268.

17 Power-Sharing or Ethnic Polarization:
The Role of Schoolteachers in Conflict Management in North Darfur[1]

Musa Adam Abdul-Jalil

This essay concentrates on discussing the involvement of schoolteachers (as a sub-elite) in the political structures of North Darfur State and how that leads to ethnic polarization. It aims at discovering the mechanisms by which local conflicts are raised to higher levels and made more complicated through the mediation of elite groups acting on behalf of their ethnic "folk." Thus it produces empirical evidence for discussing the interconnections between local communal politics on one hand and the regional and national on the other. The essay concludes that if power-sharing is introduced against such a background, it may be a recipe for promoting ethnic polarization rather than conflict transformation.

After the end of World War II, there was an expectation that Africa's modern educated elite, who played an important role in the struggle to gain independence for their respective countries from European colonial rule, would deliver the goods of "development" and "democracy" as critical components of modernization. The ascendance to power of figures such as Kwame Nkrumah of Ghana, Kenneth Kaunda of Zambia, and Julius Nyerere of Tanzania was met with considerable optimism both in Africa and worldwide. Several decades after independence, however, most African countries are still suffering from poverty, political instability, and civil wars. It is therefore legitimate to ask a basic question: Why has Africa's educated elite failed so far in their mission, and to what extent can their failure account for the hideous civil wars that are spread all over the continent? In order to answer these questions, a reasonable understanding of the micropolitical processes at the grassroots level must first be achieved. Such an effort aims at understanding the nature of interaction between elite and ordinary people; and, most important, it will reveal the methods of mobilization that the former uses to gain the acceptance of the latter to become representatives for their communities.

Modernization is a model that educated African elites were eager to introduce to their societies. Accordingly, traditional political leaders (i.e., the traditional elite) were considered the greatest obstacle to modernization programs. As a result, members of the educated elite were antagonistic toward traditional chiefs and native administrators and considered them to be part of the colonial legacy that their societies should rid themselves of. Consequently, politics of exclusion were practiced against the traditional elite in the majority of the newly independent African states. The modernization discourse has a lot to do with conflict processes in many African societies that need to be discerned and analyzed. It is a model that traveled to Africa from Europe and has since been widely adopted by African intellectuals and politicians as a necessary tool for transforming the social conditions of underdevelopment in their own societies.

With the advent of independence, the idea of a modern "nation-state" (itself a traveling model) became the only acceptable model according to which educated Africans could imagine the future of their "liberated" societies. Because such a model contradicts the promotion of tribal identities, most educated elites of the 1960s condemned tribal or ethnic identification, especially in urban centers. In Sudan, this attitude was clearly expressed in the writings of intellectuals and in speeches of politicians before and after independence. Amazingly, several decades after the independence of their respective countries, the educated elite in many African countries have come to accept the idea of identification with their ethnic groups more than before. What is even more serious is the adoption of the ruling elite in some countries (e.g., Sudan) of the divide-and-rule tactics that they had condemned in earlier phases of their political careers. Knowing more about the reasons behind such shifts in elite behavior and explaining the contradiction between what they preach and what they practice is both a stimulating and challenging mission for social scientists who are eager to understand processes of conflict management in African societies today.

The failure of democracy to take root in African countries thus far is probably linked to the same set of factors that account for the shift in elite behavior. The educated elite in most African countries has become prey to identity politics. After assuming power, many changed their ideal political vision or abandoned the ideologies that brought them to power and effectively turned into political opportunists who want to survive at any cost. This likely accounts for why many of the conflicts in African countries today are ethnic-based. This is not to say that ethnicity is the root cause of conflict. On the contrary, it is the outcome of it, and the use and abuse of it. This is because ethnicity provides an effective tool for managing conflicts, from the actor's point of view. It gives political actors a golden chance to unite followers and rally them behind a supposedly collective cause. In this sense, educated elites can become political entrepreneurs. Recent political developments in Sudan certainly attest to that. Indeed, the elite and supporters of the National Islamic Front (NIF) in Sudan represent a case in point that illustrates the aforementioned trend.

Both Numeiri and Al Bashir are military officers whose totalitarian regimes tried to apply a philosophy of decentralization for reasons of expediency. They employed divide-and-rule tactics in order to secure political survival amid growing opposition (both local and international). Because of the lack of democracy, members of the educated elite who have political ambitions could not find a way to compete for office except along ethnic/tribal lines. Earlier, people had hoped that their educated sons would bring prosperity to the Darfur region once they came to power. The formation of the "Darfur Renaissance Front" (DRF) on a nonethnic basis by university graduates in 1964 was hailed by many as a chance for the region to stand on par with other parts of Sudan through the efforts of their own educated sons who also shunned tribalism and established a united regional front. Unfortunately, that expectation did not materialize; instead, some of the educated elite became supporters of their own ethnic groups while others openly collaborated with the central government in applying its divide-and-rule tactics designed to keep marginalized regions under control.

This essay is part of a larger project that deals with investigating the role of modern educated elites in the political arena in Darfur, and how in particular they conduct themselves toward existing conflicts whether at the intraregional level or between the region and the center. Darfur is an interesting case study for trying to answer questions related to conflict management processes in which the educated elite are involved and identifying the models that inform political discourse and behavior in such contexts. But this essay mainly concentrates on the political behavior/ activities of schoolteachers, who may be considered a subelite, in the sense that most of them did not receive university education; hence, they cannot easily compete for higher political office at the national level. Despite this clear disadvantage, the effect of schoolteachers on grassroots politics in the rural areas is indisputable. As Lloyd has stated about their counterparts in West Africa, "their achievements in this sphere may well provide a more practical model for their less educated kin than do those of the elite, which may be admired but cannot be copied."[2] Emphasis will be made on the political conduct of schoolteachers at the intraregional and local levels, including their role in conflict management (escalation, prevention, or resolution). Most significantly, this group of subelites, which Darfurians call "half-sleeves" in reference to their humble educational achievement, has been mostly associated with ethnic polarization in Darfur politics.

The last decade of the twentieth century witnessed a steady rise in violence in Darfur with ethnic dimensions in many cases. More recently, in 2003, the whole situation in the region escalated into a full-scale civil war when young people formed two rebel movements and attacked Sudan government forces. The government retaliated by supporting the formation of allied tribal militias of Arab pastoral nomads popularly known as *Janjawid* as a part of its counterinsurgency effort. The confrontation quickly developed into a civil war with accompanying humanitarian crises and international dimensions. Diasporic Darfurian intellectuals succeeded in bringing international attention to the crises. With the help of the African Union (AU) and the United Nations (UN), supported by the United States and leading countries in the European Union (EU), the rebel groups and the government negotiated a peace deal that was signed in Abuja, Nigeria, in May 2006 by only one rebel faction while the rest of the groups resented it and consequently refused to sign. Most recently, in late October 2007 negotiations were reopened in Sirte, Libya, in the hopes that others would join the agreement under a new deal. The Sirte negotiations, however, failed after being boycotted by major participants, including the Sudan Liberation Army (SLA–Abdul Wahid faction) and the Justice and Equality Movement (JEM). The involvement of the educated elite in the peacemaking process reflects the other face of their role in conflict escalation.

This essay attempts to provide answers to some initial questions pertaining to the role of schoolteachers in local politics in Darfur. The main question being asked is: What is the extent of the participation of this group of elites in the political and administrative structures at the state and local levels? Another important question is: Whether and how do they play any roles pertaining to conflict management (escalation, prevention, or resolution)? Connected to that, it is also tempting to ask about the reasons behind the recently observed phenomenon of alliance-building between some educated elites and native administrators. This is important because in the past (especially after independence) the relationship between the two groups was mostly characterized by distrust and antagonism. Finally, one would like to know the reasons behind the resort to an ethnic-based power-sharing model in order to solve problems of conflict within regional and local governance structures.

Methodology and Data Collection

Because the timescale of this topic extends for half a century (from independence to the present), I have used a historical approach to identify various stages and phases in the development of elite involvement in conflict management (prevention, escalation, and resolution) in North Darfur. Research data include historical accounts, documents, and narratives. Extended interviews with schoolteachers were conducted, while limited consultations with members of the general public were made. In addition, a limited number of focus group discussions with teachers (four in total) were conducted in both El Fasher and Khartoum. The Northern Darfur State capital, El Fasher, was the main center for fieldwork operations, as security conditions did not allow me to travel any farther. Moreover, interviews with some Darfur communal elites were carried out in Khartoum, where much of the regional politics is managed. For this reason I shall begin first by reviewing the political trends at the center that ultimately affected and informed political processes in the peripheries.

Numeiri and Populist Democracy

General Ja'far Muhammad al Numeiri took power in Sudan after a coup d'état that was supported by radical socialist parties (namely, the Sudanese Communist, Nasserites, and Arab Bath parties). The new regime wanted to debase the traditional sectarian parties of *Umma* (Arabic, "nation") and Democratic Unionist Party (DUP) by altering politics at the grassroots. Since the stronghold of both parties is in rural areas, a twofold plan for changing the power structure in rural Sudan was devised. The first part of it dealt with eroding the power base of the traditional rural elite. The abolition of native administration and its collateral, the native courts, was the first blow in 1970. This was followed by the enactment of the Unregistered Land Act in 1971. The relevance of the act is that it challenged the power invested in native administrators as customary arbiters in disputes related to land use, tenure, and natural resources management in general.[3]

The second element of the plan for eroding the bases of traditional parties in the rural area was encompassed under the socialist slogan of "giving power to the people." The socialist type of organizing social order is another traveling model that was badly translated into the Sudanese context and had devastating effects. Village councils, people's local councils, and people's local courts were established to replace the abolished structures. Moreover, most of the personnel involved in the old structures were denied places in the newly established institutions. As a result, many young people found themselves in positions of influence. Access to the resources of the state (political and economic) is now mediated through the new elite group. New terminology expressing the ideology of the new polity (socialism, "the people") became the arena for building competence and acquiring tools of political manipulation by the new elite. Because alphabetic literacy was a minimum requirement for obtaining leadership positions in the new institutions, primary schoolteachers became favorable candidates. Furthermore, the fact that schoolteachers in many remote locations were the only educated persons in the village meant that they automatically filled these posts. Indeed, primary schoolteachers filled the majority of the positions in the party offices in the village and town chapters in North Darfur when Numeiri established the Sudan Socialist Union (SSU) as the ruling party.

Seeking to modernize the administrative system in Sudan, the Numeiri regime passed the People's Local Government Act in 1971, according to which the Darfur region was divided into regional, district, and area councils. People's local administration system replaced the Native Administration system (which was a part of the legacy of the colonial era in Sudan) and abolished the jurisdiction and administrative authority of the tribal leaders. Some say this reorganization was the first factor that triggered tribal conflicts on a wider scale in Darfur. In the southern Darfur province alone, sixteen different rural council border disputes and conflicts occurred soon after the implementation of this act. The abolition of Native Administration was followed by a reform in the system of native courts whereby native administrators were excluded from membership. The critical weakness in modernizing native administration lay in the change of emphasis from their previous judicial role (maintaining law and order) to an administrative role of tax collection only, to which political mobilization was later added by the National Islamic Front regime led by Al Bashir. In practice, however, Darfurian tribal leaders continued to be acknowledged as heads of their groups, and the tribe became a political base to promote its members to senior positions in local councils, as well as the regional and national assemblies. Ethnic polarization came to permeate every corner of government offices, since members of the group are considered as representatives of their tribes and are supposed to work for the interests of their tribal folk. Vertical ethnic expansion, from the local level to the regional and even national levels has become an observed phenomenon.

Prior to abolishing Native Administration, the Numeiri regime had already dissolved all political parties in the Sudan. The vacuum was filled with an emerging new social and political force – the Sudanese Socialist Union, the only recognized party by then. These organizations were led by the rural elite such as teachers, small traders, and government employees who occupied the scene in Darfur, resulting in the emergence of new leadership. This leadership played a critical role in reshaping the political scene in Darfur in the years following the promulgation of the Regional Government Act of 1980. For the first time since independence, educated Darfurians (a governor and four ministers) were entrusted with the task of running the bureaucratic machinery in the region. They were given responsibilities to provide public services in Darfur but with inadequate resources.

The Ingaz (Salvation): National Islamic Front Regime of Al Bashir and Muslim Populism

The 1989 coup brought a new group to power in Sudan with a new agenda exactly opposite to that of the Numeiri regime, though adopting the same approach of popular mobilization. The ideology of the new regime was to promote orthodox Islamic practice in public life and to establish an Islamic state in Sudan. In Darfur, rural people were more relaxed in their interpretation of some prescribed prohibitions of Islamic law and its traditions. For example, the tight covering of all limbs for females was not strictly adhered to and the consumption of root beer, brewed from millet and considered a lunchtime meal, known as *khada*, was not uncommon.

Just like the socialists, the Islamists also wanted to debase the traditional parties of Umma and DUP in the rural areas. They thought that because of the favorable feelings of the rural populace toward Islam they could easily win them over to their side. They formed their own ruling party under the name of National Congress Party. Chapters for the new party, called Popular Salvation Committees, were created at the village, locality, and state levels. Again, schoolteachers were best suited to run the machinery of these committees. Many former SSU party activists joined the ruling National Congress Party (NCP) ranks; some even made it to the executive offices of these committees. The Al Bashir regime, however, did not aim at alienating the traditional elite; it tried to co-opt them instead. In Darfur they reinvigorated the native administration system and lured its personnel to join NCP by providing material incentives, including money and residential land blocks in urban centers.

The other popular program introduced by Al Bashir's regime was the formation of Popular Defense Forces (PDF). It was intended as an effective alternative organization to confront the Sudan People's Liberation Army (SPLA) forces and regain control over South Sudan. Moreover, it was associated with high hopes of Islamizing southern Sudanese people, which would have consequently paved the way for expanding Islam in neighboring African countries. The latter became one of the most popularized ideological slogans of the regime enshrined in a grand program known as *al Mashru' al Hadhari*, or "the civilizational project." The PDF program needed continuous mobilization in the rural areas to provide fighters. Darfur proved to be one of the most favorable places to mobilize fighters. Schools were considered instrumental institutions for anchoring this program in the rural area. Thus, schools hosted jihad rallies and exhibitions, and teachers played central roles in such activities. It is interesting to note here that PDF mobilization tried to utilize ethnic identification in order to promote their cause. By arousing ethnic pride, they were able to mobilize more fighters, just as was the case with the early phase of Islamic expansion in Arabia.

In a later stage, Al Bashir simply repeated Numeiri's mistake regarding the formal devolution of authority to the region without real power or adequate resources. This lead to the partial disappointment of ordinary Darfurians in their educated folk, who were unable to deliver what they promised regarding improvement of services. But most significantly it reinforced the existing mistrust between Darfurians and the central government. In 1995, three separate states were created out of Darfur (North, South, and West) in an attempt to establish a system of federal governance in Sudan. The boundaries of the new states were carved according to ethnic considerations. South Darfur became a state where groups claiming Arab identity form the majority of its population. Non-Arab groups dominate North and West Darfur states. The Fur, who gave their name to the region because of their political dominance in the past, became a minority group for the first time in each of the new states. It is noticeable that these developments came after the unsuccessful attempt by the late Yahya Dawood Bolad (a Fur engineering graduate from the University of Khartoum who defected from the National Islamic Front) to gain a foothold for the SPLM/A in the Jebel Marra region of Darfur.

This new development was followed by an increased political manipulation of the native administration by government agencies, and consequently an increased polarization between tribal groups in Darfur. Tribal leaders were entrusted with the task of supplying youth for the PDF as part of the jihad counterinsurgency campaign. Young activists allied to the Ingaz regime were in charge of coordination. As a result, the educated elite of each group became allied with its traditional elite (i.e., Native Administration) in this new phase of political development. It is in this connection that the role of schoolteachers is important to describe and analyze if we are to explain the ethnic polarization that characterizes Darfur politics today, to the extent that power-sharing as a model of conflict resolution has been based on ethnicity (both locally and at the regional level).

The Participation of Teachers in Local Governance and NCP Structures

In order to determine the range and extent of the involvement of schoolteachers in the political arena at the local and state or regional levels, data pertaining to membership in the legislative bodies have been collected from El Fasher. Data for the membership of Darfur Region (Numeiri's regime) and North Darfur State (Al Bashir's regime) assemblies was easily found. Unfortunately, the data for other localities was difficult to find. Security conditions did not allow me to travel outside the state capital. In addition, when war erupted, the documents of most localities were badly treated. Another important warning regarding the quality of the data is that while the formation of regional and state assemblies came as a result of elections, the formation of local councils depended on appointments of the state governor (*wali*). Elections comparatively give a better expression of the popularity of the selected representatives; hence, analysis based on them is more credible. Nonetheless, I have been told that most elections have been "guided" by party preferences. Unfortunately, one has to operate under such unfavorable conditions.

Schoolteachers as Community Representatives

In this section of the essay some data summarized in tables will be presented. As indicated earlier, schoolteachers, especially those working in primary schools, are very involved in the activities of local governance structures.

Starting from the regional level, we can see from Table 1 that the three selected assemblies all included schoolteachers as the largest professional category, with percentages ranging between 46 and 69 percent. The largest category after the teachers is that of administrators (which refers here to a variety of jobs extending from clerks and accountants to retired local government officers). Native administrators who, despite having their traditional jobs abolished by the Numeiri regime, proved to be indispensable to all governments in Sudan because of their experience in local politics, closely follow schoolteachers in their degree of representation. After all, totalitarian regimes need popularity, and these old-timers know how to appeal to the masses; or to put it more directly, they are more experienced in handling the game of politics than the educated elite thought or expected.

Looking at Table 1, it is significant that educated elites with engineering, medical, and agricultural backgrounds do not figure well in the membership of the assemblies. Equally significant is the almost total exclusion of farmers and laborers, even during the supposedly socialist regime of Numeiri. It should be emphasized here that the first regional assembly of 1981 was elected by all Darfurians to represent

Table 1. **Distribution of Darfur Regional and State Assembly Members by Profession**

Profession	People's Regional Assembly/1981	North Darfur State Assembly/1995	North Darfur State Assembly/1999
Teacher	23,46%	32,65%	40,69%
Paramedical	3,6%	3,6%	1,2%
Military	1,2%	1,2%	0,0%
Administrator	8,16%	3,6%	4,7%
Veterinarian	1,2%	0,0%	0,,0%
Engineer	0,0%	0,0%	3,5%
Agriculturalist	2,4%	0,0%	2,3%
Legal	0,0%	1,2%	1,2%
Native administrator	7,14%	4,9%	3,5%
Merchant	3,6%	3,6%	3,5%
Farmer / Pastoralist	0,0%	1,2%	1,2%
Laborer	2,4%	0,0%	0,0%
Unclassified	0,0%	1,2%	0,0%
Total	50,100%	49,100%	58,100%

Source: Composed from field data.

the whole region, which was then unified under one administrative structure. Although Al Bashir's regime constituted an all-Darfur "Committee for National Salvation," I did not include its data here because I have already decided to limit the comparison only to elected assemblies.

The assemblies of 1995 and 1999 represented in this table are only for North Darfur State. It is significant that the proportional representation of schoolteachers during Al Bashir's rule is higher than during Numeiri's period. This is quite understandable, as it is a well-known fact for students of Sudan studies that the Muslim Brothers *al Ihkwan al Muslimin* (who support Al Bashir's regime) used to operate in schools for many years before they were able to climb to positions of power in Sudan. Ideological parties in general find the most conducive environments in schools because the young generation is most suited to accept their revolutionary pledges.

Table 2 shows the distribution of members of local legislative councils according to their professions. The pattern is similar to that of Table 1 in that teachers represent the majority in all six cases with the extremes of 70 percent in Melleit and 35 percent in Um Kaddada. Native administrators figure more prominently here, reaching 35 percent in Al-Waha and 30 percent in Kekabiya. Merchants did better than administrators, except in Melleit and Al-Waha, where they are not represented. On the other hand, paramedicals reached 15 percent in Um Kaddada while unnoticeable in other localities. It is noticeable that members of the Melleit local council represent two professions only: teachers (70 percent) and native administrators

Table 2. **Distribution of North Darfur Localities' Assembly Members by Profession**

Profession	El Fasher	Kutum	Melliet	Um Kaddada	Kebkabiya	Al-Waha
Teacher	56%	60%	65%	35%	55%	45%
Paramedical	3%	0%	0%	15%	0%	0%
Military	10%	5%	0%	0%	0%	5%
Administrator	6%	10%	0%	5%	5%	10%
Veterinarian	0%	0%	0%	0%	0%	0%
Engineer	6%	0%	0%	0%	0%	0%
Agriculturalist	0%	0%	0%	0%	0%	0%
Legal	0%	0%	0%	0%	0%	0%
Native administrator	6%	10%	15%	15%	30%	35%
Merchant	10%	15%	0%	15%	10%	0%
Farmer / Pastoralist	3%	0%	0%	5%	0%	0%
Laborer	0%	0%	0%	0%	0%	0%
Unclassified	0%	0%	20%	10%	0%	5%
Total	100%	100%	100%	100%	100%	100%

Source: Composed from field data

(15 percent). Another noteworthy point to be made here is that there are some cases of teachers who have become native administrators. Because positions in the latter case are prescribed, it means that some teachers belonging to chiefly families have been chosen to succeed their fathers, brothers, or uncles. In the past, such positions would not have been attractive for an educated person.

The latter case warrants two comments. First, teachers are readily absorbed in local political structures because they live and work in the village. This gives them a chance to mix with ordinary people and learn more about their perceptions and ways of behavior. On the other hand, local people consider teachers to be an inch above them because they know more about the outside world and can communicate with government officials in powerful positions far away in the provincial towns or even the national capital. Second, this shows that traditional positions may be manned by more educated personnel in the future. There are already cases of army and police retired generals becoming tribal leaders. I have also come to know of a native administrator who has appointed his son as his deputy. The son holds a master's degree in African studies from the University of Khartoum. This is a similar pattern to what Lloyd reported for northern Nigeria's educated elite.[4]

Leading positions in the organizational structures of political parties tell a lot about the active elements in the political arena. Although desirable, it was not possible to get such data for major political parties in North Darfur. Instead, I was able to find useful data for the NCP. As a ruling party, it provides enough incentives for many who are eager either to occupy positions of power or to safeguard the

Table 3. **Distribution of North Darfur State NCP Assembly Members and Executive Officers by Profession**

Profession	N. Darfur State NCP Assembly	N. Darfur State NCP Executives
Teacher	54,55%	11,69%
Paramedical	2,2%	0,0%
Military	2,2%	1,6%
Administrator	23,24%	2,13%
Veterinarian	1,1%	0,0%
Engineer	1,1%	1,6%
Agriculturalist	2,2%	0,0%
Legal	1,1%	0,0%
Native administrator	6,6%	0,0%
Merchant	5,5%	1,6%
Farmer / Pastoralist	1,1%	0,0%
Laborer	0,0%	0,0%
Unclassified	0,0%	0,0%
Total	98,100%	16,100%

Source: Composed from field data.

interests of their own groups. The latter is always a practical justification for many ambitious individuals who live in the marginalized regions of the Sudan. Their argument is made more credible by the fact that totalitarian regimes make it conditional that people may get their citizenship rights only if they show loyalty to the regime. For this reason, many communities try to have some of their members join the ruling party so that they are not left out.

Table 3 expresses the composition of leading NCP structures according to the professions of its members. As expected, schoolteachers figured high (55 percent in the assembly and 69 percent in the leadership office), followed by administrators, and then native administrators. The latter are not represented in the leadership office because such positions require a reasonable educational background for which most native administrators are not qualified.

The data presented in the tables reflects a high degree of involvement by schoolteachers in the political process. Actually, the proportions indicated in the tables are less than the 80 percent estimate that many informants (both teachers and others) told me in interviews. It seems that a considerable discrepancy exists between perception and reality. One sound explanation would be that teachers are more vocal and comparatively have better skills that make them qualify for leading positions. Consequently, their presence is felt more by others. It is interesting to note in this regard that the current governor (concurrently also NCP chapter president) of North Darfur state is a schoolteacher by profession. His deputy in the NCP leadership office is also a teacher. The deputy speaker of the State assembly is also a teacher. The cabinet of the state government also includes a considerable number of teachers amounting to no less than 30 percent. Such a presence will no doubt make teachers quite instrumental in local and regional politics. It is no wonder therefore that teachers are behind many of the conflict management processes. But more importantly, they are to be found behind most of the interethnic conflicts that have become endemic in Darfur.

Schoolteachers and Ethnic-Based Power-Sharing

Darfur is a territory that is characterized by the multiplicity of its ethnic groups, locally known as "tribes." No simple classification is feasible for these groups; at least this is not the place to attempt it. For the sake of the general argument in this essay one is obliged to mention that Darfur is inhabited by a variety of tribes representing African as well as Arab descent that have undergone a substantial mixing through intermarriage and territorial coexistence. Culturally, the spread of Islam and Arabic language, which acts as a lingua franca, has cemented relations between the indigenous and migrating groups. In addition, the formation of a Sultanate since the seventeenth century brought all groups under a single state apparatus that managed to standardize some administrative and political processes through the structures it created. One of the significant things to be noted about the Darfur Sultanate is the involvement of almost all ethnic groups in its administrative structures. A sort of ethnic federal administration was in place whereby each tribal group or subgroup is associated with a homeland territory (*dar*) under the authority of a hereditary leader. Some camel-herding groups in north Darfur (mainly Mahamid, Ereigat, Etifat, and Mahriya) represent an exception to the rule.[5] Migrant minority groups arriving from outside Darfur are also exceptions. The council of the Sultan in the capital was also composed of tribal representatives.[6] Apart from the position of the grand ruler (Sultan), which was limited to the Keira clan of the Fur tribe, all other positions were open to competition and were mostly circulated over time between men loyal to the throne from various tribal backgrounds. Needless to say, a division of political power between ethnic components of the Darfur region has a long tradition, to which its history attests.

When new administrative and political structures were introduced to the region as part of the modern state apparatus, Darfurians did not lose sight of their political heritage. This is reflected by the fact that representatives of major ethnic groups always had access to some positions of power in the political center stage of the region since the formation of the Sultanate in the mid-seventeenth century. The Sultans were then aware of the dangers brought by the exclusion of some groups from political participation. Following the introduction of decentralized administration by Numeiri in 1981 it was considered legitimate for the first regional government to take into consideration ethnic balances in appointing members of the cabinet. The governor and the speaker of the assembly were Fur, his deputy and one minister were Zaghawa, and two ministers belonged to Arab tribes. The second line positions were equally diversified. In terms of professional background, only one minister was a schoolteacher. When elections were held a year later, competition between the members of the first regional government broke openly along ethnic lines. It was clear that the top political position, which was traditionally a Fur monopoly, is now seriously contested. The educated elite accepted the idea of preserving the tradition of securing chances for political participation for representatives of major ethnic groups, but objected to the Fur's monopolization of the top positions, as indicated by the fact that many educated elites clearly mentioned that the governor and the speaker of the legislative assembly came from one group (Fur).

Under these conditions, schoolteachers became actively engaged in managing election campaigns for the contenders. The seeds of that competition were later reflected in the formation of the Arab Gathering, which in turn initiated the worst ethnic polarization the region has ever witnessed. Harir vividly summarized those developments in his statement: "A division along ethnic lines developed in which ethnic groups rallied around whomever they perceived to be their representatives in the regional cabinet. But as the cabinet itself had developed a factional cleavage, those ethnic groups that shared the position of opposition to the ruler's line aggregated into a broad coalition."[7] It is clear that the new model of power-sharing (regional government) has been translated locally into a competition between groups in a different manner from what the central government originally planned. School-teachers can be considered here as managers of this translation process. It is interesting to note that schoolteachers filled almost all secretarial positions for the regional ministers in Darfur's first regional government.

The same pattern of ethnic competition was expressed at the level of local government and party political structures (especially during the totalitarian regimes of Numeiri and Al Bashir). A typical case is the competition between the Zaghawa, the Tunjur, and Northern Rezeigat Arab camel nomads in 1982 for control of the North Darfur Area Council with its headquarters in Kutum town. Significantly, the majority of council members were primary schoolteachers representing their respective local communities. More than half of the seats and the top executive positions went to representatives who were classified as Zaghawa. The situation soon developed into an open conflict that ended up in strong ethnic polarization. The following description captures the idea very well: "The people of Kutum (mostly Tunjur and Fur) rightly felt excluded by the Zaghawa hegemony over the district level structures of power; and this is why their reaction was so emotionally charged. It took two forms: a bitterness which generated personal hatred to the extent that interethnic friendships, especially where they involved Zaghawa and non-Zaghawa notables, nearly stopped being friendships at all, and strong political mobilization on an ethnic basis."[8] Kutum is one of the oldest towns established by colonial administration as the headquarters for the North Darfur rural council. Its inhabitants feel they are the bearers of the heritage of the Darfur Sultanate. The Tunjur established the first Sultanate, which later fell into the hands of the Fur in 1640. When the Zaghawa dominate the local party and government structures, it means that the people of Kutum become the subjects of a people whose ancestors were the subjects of their ancestors in the past. It does not seem logical to them, especially when they are misrepresented in these structures. In short, it is a typical case of the politics of exclusion at work.

It is worth noting that the Kutum conflict was escalated by SSU committee members, most of whom were schoolteachers on both sides of the ethnic divide. The battle for the seats of the council was finally settled, not according to the rules of law that govern the election process, but according to "behind the scenes dealings" reached through a successful mediation based on retaining the ethnic balance. In other words, there was recognition that some sort of power-sharing is necessary if people are to maintain peaceful coexistence with each other. One may safely deduce from this case that ethnic-based power-sharing arrangements as a temporary solution for conflicts over political office are widely acknowledged in Darfur. Other localities, like Melleit and Kebkabiya, stand as clear evidence for the generality of the Kutum case.

But one burning question remains to be answered: Why could the informal power-sharing arrangements that the people developed locally to settle conflicts not be sustained for longer periods of time? To put it differently: Why is political stability so difficult to achieve in Darfur? The answer to this question lies outside the boundaries of the region. Mohamed and Weddai and Munzoul A. M. Assal have argued convincingly that the constant intervention by the central government to manipulate local politics to its advantage has rendered traditional conflict management mechanisms inefficient and created a situation of periodic revisiting of old conflicts.[9] This is nothing but the reinvention of the old "divide-and-rule" tactics that colonial administrators used to practice in many colonial territories in Africa. That such a model is still in use in postcolonial Africa is a matter that warrants further discussion. But it is certain that Sudan is not alone in this respect. Let me stress once again that schoolteachers figure as the more effective agents through which the center manages its "interventions."

Power-Sharing or Ethnic Polarization?

Broadly defined, power-sharing can be regarded as a system of governance, consisting of practices and institutions that result in broad-based governing coalitions that are generally inclusive of all major ethnic groups. However, most of the current literature on the subject tends to restrict it to situations where open violent conflicts are handled by international mediators who devise special institutional arrangements to guarantee the rights of disadvantaged groups to share power with the rest of the citizens of a country/territory.

Power-sharing solutions are designed to marry principles of democracy with the need for conflict management in deeply divided societies. It involves a wide array of political arrangements in which the major antagonists are assured some permanent political representation, decision-making power, and often autonomous territory in the postconflict stage. In many situations, the international community works proactively to encourage parties to accept brokered power-sharing arrangements instead of violent confrontations that continue to produce human calamities that the same international actors are obliged to handle. As such, power-sharing has become a model that is adopted to solve serious conflicts in so many places around the globe. This does not mean that everywhere the same peace agreement model is adopted, but the same logic is used to lure warring parties to the negotiation table. More often, local adaptations to the model are created.

However, power-sharing is no permanent panacea for conflict. Indeed, some types of power-sharing systems may contain the seeds of their own self-destruction as the search for consensus turns into deadlock by political leaders aware that they hold the power of veto over government action. In many situations power-sharing may be desirable, and necessary, as an immediate exit to serious and protracted conflicts, especially those fought in the name of ethnic or other forms of group identity. In the long run, however, rigid power-sharing is not a durable solution to intractable conflicts. Ideally, power-sharing should give way to democracy, as trust builds between previous enemies. The evolution from formal sharing of power – often by exclusive ethnic groups – to a more socially inclusive and integrated form of representation should be encouraged. In other words, power-sharing – as a model of conflict management – is justified in theory only as a transitional arrangement. Nevertheless, the ability of power-sharing institutions to solve trust and commitment problems has been constantly questioned due to cases of failure. It has been noticed that fundamental tensions exist between the short-term success of power-sharing and its longer-term costs. Critics contend that power-sharing can lead to an inflexible division of spoils; that it can provide political leaders with the means to reinforce societal divisions, and that it stands in the way of real and meaningful democratization. Some even argue that the stability of power-sharing frameworks is contingent on the continued involvement of outside actors.

The Darfur case lends itself to this argument, raising fears about the chances for a sustainable peace agreement under the current conditions of the Sudanese state. What Darfurians will get by way of an internationally mediated peace agreement may not bring peace if it stops only at devising power-sharing arrangements between the Sudan government and Darfur armed movements. If the problem of sharing power at the local level is not addressed, it is likely that a signed peace agreement will only serve as the whistle for the start of a new round of local ethnic-based conflicts. What is expected to be the beginning of the end may ultimately turn out to be the end of the beginning. There is no shortage of spoilers and power brokers at the grassroots level. Schoolteachers are ready everywhere to act as translators of whatever message comes from outside. However, they always make sure that they get their share in the political spoils that are due or else they have their own strategies of resistance. Unfortunately, there are always external actors who are ready to fund.

Notes

1. This essay is based on fieldwork that was supported by a Volkswagen Foundation–funded project called "Traveling Models in Conflict Management" as a part of its African initiative "Knowledge for Tomorrow." I am grateful to the Volkswagen Foundation for its generous support. An earlier draft of this essay was presented at the African Studies Association Annual Meeting in New York in October 2007. I am also grateful to Richard Rottenburg and Carina Ray for reading the first draft of this essay and making important comments and suggestions that enabled me to improve it.
2. P. Lloyd, *Africa in Social Change* (London: Penguin Books, 1972), p. 153.
3. See Musa Adam Abdul-Jalil, "The Dynamics of Customary Land Tenure and Natural Resource Management in Darfur," *Land Reform, Settlement, and Cooperatives* 2 (2006): 8–23.
4. Lloyd, 1972.
5. See Abdul-Jalil, 2006.
6. R. S. O'Fahey, *State and Society in Darfur* (London: Hurst, 1980).
7. Sharif Abdalla Harir, The Politics of "Numbers": Mediatory Leadership and the Political Process among the Beri "Zaghawa" of the Sudan, a Ph.D. thesis, Department of Social Anthropology, University of Bergen (1986), p. 196.
8. Ibid., p. 199.
9. Adam al-Zein Mohamed and Al-Tayeb Ibrahim Weddai, eds., *Perspectives on Tribal Conflicts in Sudan* (Khartoum: University of Khartoum, Institute of Afro-Asian Studies, 1998) (in Arabic). See also Munzoul A. M. Assal. 2006, "It Is All about History Repeating Itself: the State and the Involution of Conflict in Darfur." *Journal of Darfurian Studies*, 1: 6–22 (sample issue); and Salih, M. A. Mohamed. 2005. *Understanding the Conflict in Darfur*. Occasional Paper, Centre of African Studies, University of Copenhagen.

18 A Civil Society Approach to the Darfur Crisis

Al-Tayib Zain Al-Abdin

Introduction

Since ancient times, the Darfur region has been known for its cohesiveness, racial mix, and religiosity; however, since the mid-1970s it has witnessed several inter-ethnic disputes, which were caused by competition over declining natural resources occasioned by the onset of severe drought. The rate of disputes has escalated sharply over the last two decades. By February 2003, Darfur-based rebel groups had turned their guns against the central government, accusing it of marginalizing the region, ignoring its severe conditions, and taking sides in the region's ethnic conflicts. The new conflict developed into a humanitarian crisis with national and international dimensions because of its huge human and material losses that attracted global attention. Media coverage and debates were held all over the world to discuss the problem of Darfur.

Two nongovernmental organizations (NGOs) and two academic institutions in the Sudan decided to organize a serious debate on the problem in an objective and scientific manner. The Sudan Inter-Religious Council (SIRC), Khartoum Centre for Human Rights (KCHR), the Peace Research Institute of the University of Khartoum, and the Centre for Peace and Human Rights Studies of El Fasher University came together to organize a workshop on the crisis in Darfur. The workshop was initially supposed to take place in El Fasher, the capital of Northern Darfur, in order to give the participants a real feeling of the crises in the midst of the troubled region and to show the people of Darfur that other people in Sudan do care for them. However, the governor of Northern Darfur, suspecting that the workshop might give publicity to some of the ideas advocated by the rebels, refused to allow the workshop to take place in El Fasher. Consequently, the organizers shifted the workshop to Khartoum. Even in Khartoum, the government was not happy with the idea. The first vice president, Ali Osman Taha, wrote a letter to the secretary-general of SIRC asking him not to go along with the workshop because it might give the wrong impression that the problem of Darfur is of a religious nature. The secretary-general conveyed to the first vice president that they were well aware of the fact that no religious factor was involved in the problem, that none of the eighteen papers to be discussed dealt with the religious factor, and that this will be further explained at the beginning of the workshop. Nonetheless, most of the government officials boycotted the workshop.

The organizers were convinced to go ahead with the workshop for the following reasons: The two NGOs (Sudan Inter-Religious Council and Khartoum Centre for Human Rights) were working for peaceful religious coexistence and protection of human rights in Sudan, and both objectives were threatened by the conflict in Darfur, which led to a huge loss of innocent lives and to missionary activities undertaken by some relief religious organizations; the two academic institutes were concerned with peace studies, and one of them is literally situated in the middle of the conflict zone. All of this is in addition to the fact that the conflict has become a national crisis and a shame for the country. Finally, since the Darfur conflict has been debated all over the world, it is odd that national organizations should not lead the debate inside the country.

The organizers were careful in their preparations for the workshop to select the topics that covered all aspects of the problem, to assign them to experts who are objective and well informed about their topics, and to invite participants in a balanced way from all groups concerned with the problem inside the country. That approach was fruitful in the balanced and comprehensive recommendations that were approved at the end of the workshop. The workshop was held at the Friendship Hall on November 28–30, 2004, under the slogan "For Peace, Development, and Patching the Social Fabric." The opening session was addressed by Dr. Ali Hassan Taj El Din, the advisor to the President for African Affairs and Chairman of Darfur Forum, Prof. Mohamed Ahmed El Sheikh, the Vice-Chancellor of the University of Khartoum, Dr. Abdullah Abdul Hai, Vice-Chancellor University of El-Fasher, and Prof. al-Tayib Zain al-Abdin (author), the secretary-general of SIRC and head of the Steering Committee. The workshop was attended by a considerable number of leading figures from Darfur, including intellectuals, members of parliament, leaders of the native administration who were specially invited from their respective regions to take part, and student activists. In addition to some government officials, also present were NGOs working in the region and representatives of the media and press who gave good coverage of the proceedings and discussions. Eighteen academic papers were presented in the three-day workshop, written by scholars and experts about the major factors that led to the conflict and its escalation. The researchers focused on finding practical solutions to the complex aspects of the conflict. Each presenter was followed by one or two discussants familiar with the subject and possessing different views. Rich and sometimes heated discussions took place about the various ideas presented on the causes of the conflict, its escalation, and how it can be resolved. The function was a model of civil society cooperation and a contribution to helping solve a national crisis of grave humanitarian dimensions. It was a comprehensive, scientific, and balanced approach that won the appreciation of the different concerned parties. At the end of the workshop, the recommendations were published in leading newspapers and distributed to leaders of political parties, members of parliament, representatives of NGOs working in the region, concerned government agencies, and a translated copy was sent to foreign embassies and UN missions in Khartoum.

Background of the Crisis

The participants in the workshop agreed that the roots of the interethnic conflicts in Darfur, which go back to the preindependence period, were aggravated since the 1970s due to the severe competition between the farmers and the herdsmen over natural resources (water, pasture, and farmland), which started to diminish rapidly at a time when the numbers of people and animals were increasing. This was followed by competition for possession of land, and political and administrative leadership that could decide the outcome of the conflict in favor of one side against the other.

The intensity of the conflict has increased with the movement of some ethnic groups from the areas affected by drought to fertile lands with abundant water.

Because of interethnic relations across international borders, some ethnic groups also came from outside the country to settle in Darfur. The deterioration of natural resources coupled with poor development projects and social services, in addition to the high rate of unemployment and the proliferation of weapons from neighboring countries, all led at first to the phenomenon of armed robbery as a means of living. As a reaction to this phenomenon, some tribal/ethnic militias were created to protect the lives and properties of their fellow tribesmen.

The people of Darfur have their own inherited traditions of resolving interethnic conflicts. When it is a big conflict, they form a broad reconciliatory conference under the supervision of senior native administrators and government officials. Since the late 1980s, these conferences lost their ability to achieve the desired reconciliation due to the increased pattern of conflicts, the changes of social conditions, the complexity of the problems, the high cost of the necessary compensations, and the failure of the government to implement the agreed-upon resolutions. Since February 2003, interethnic conflicts have turned into a political confrontation against the central government and its institutions in the region. It was led by armed groups that accused the government of marginalizing the Darfur region and blamed it for taking sides in the interethnic conflicts. They complained about the lack of development in Darfur, the poor social services, and widespread unemployment.

As a result of the armed conflict in its latest shape, thousands of people were killed, hundreds of villages were burned down, and around 200,000 people took refuge in neighboring Chad. More than one million people left their homes to more secure places inside the region. The Darfur situation constitutes a horrible humanitarian catastrophe that became a topical issue of mass media, parliaments, governments, and NGOs all over the world. It has seriously damaged the reputation of the country in international forums. The problem of Darfur entered the corridors of the UN Security Council, which issued several resolutions that focused on the necessity of protecting the civilians, the delivery of humanitarian relief, and the importance of reaching a political settlement between the disputing parties. Some of the interventions in the crisis were not free of political agendas against the Sudan by some governments and NGOs. Nonetheless, those parties found a weak point in the internal national position that they exploited for their own advantage.

During the course of 2004, more organized negotiations were initiated between the government of Sudan and the armed groups under the supervision of the African Union with the support of the UN and the international community. The Darfur workshop, which was organized by the aforementioned institutions, aimed at discussing the root problems that led to the interethnic disputes and the emergence of the protest movements against the center since the eruption of the October revolution of 1964. The discussions followed a scientific and objective approach, aspiring to find possible solutions to those problems. After three consecutive days of extensive deliberations among the delegates, the workshop reached concrete recommendations to be promoted among the political and civil forces in society, hoping that they will contribute to peacemaking and the achievement of development in that dear part of the country. In drafting these recommendations, we made use of some good suggestions made in earlier workshops, symposia, and meetings held on the Darfur crisis.

The Recommendations
The Political and Administrative Dimension

Since the population of Darfur constitutes 23 percent of the total population of Sudan, since the region has a historically, culturally, and administratively unique character, and since the peace agreement signed between the government of Sudan and the SPLM presents a new political reality in the country that necessarily affects the situation in other regions, we suggest the following recommendations to be implemented to help resolve the crisis in the Darfur:

1. The region should be governed with a full federal system, in which the leaders of the executive body and the legislative assembly are elected by all the people of Darfur. These institutions should be given a mandate and authority similar to what has been stipulated in the Comprehensive Peace Agreement (CPA). They should also be given fixed financial resources that will enable them to develop the region and provide the medical and educational services for their people, so as to bridge the gap between Darfur and the developed regions in the country.

2. The people of Darfur should be given the opportunity to unify their region through a free democratic process under united executive and legislative bodies. At the same time, the local and state levels of government should be preserved, bearing in mind the geographical and social peculiarity of each region and the administrative feasibility.

3. The formation of the states' governments and the legislative assemblies during the transitional period should reflect the general popular agreement. That should be realized through a wide consultation with the political forces in the region, the leaders of the native administration who enjoy popular support, the armed groups, and the intellectuals of Darfur. An agreement should be reached on a joint popular mechanism to be constituted by the government officials, the representatives of armed militias, and the tribal chiefs of Darfur, in order to assure the success of the negotiations and the resolution of problematic issues.

4. The region should be represented during the transitional period in the high constitutional posts, in the federal cabinet, and in the newly established commissions. Its representation in the parliament should reflect the size of its population, and the representatives should be selected on the basis of their professional qualifications and good character.

5. All those who committed criminal atrocities against civilians should be subjected to judicial accountability, and the recommendations given by the National Fact-finding Committee and the report of the International Mission should be implemented under the supervision of a neutral civil board. This process does not prevent the victimized parties from showing pardon and forgiveness in order to preserve the good-neighborly relations between tribes and the repair of the social fabric seeking their reward from Allah (S.W.T.).[1]

6. A committee should be formed to assess the damage caused by the conflict in Darfur, and the victims (individuals and communities) should be compensated for their losses.

7. All those who were detained for political reasons associated with the conflict should be released, and cases of abducted women should be investigated and the victims be returned to their families and provided with psychological and

A Civil Society Approach to the Darfur Crisis

medical care. In addition to that, those who were sacked from the civil and military services should be reinstated in their previous posts.

8. Because the traditional native administration is a deeply rooted system that still has a significant role in organizing the society, the selection of its chiefs should be based upon the consent and approval of the people in the area; it should not be exploited for partisan political gains. It should be given both legal and judicial authority and should be supported morally and enabled financially to perform its effective role. A balance should be struck between its conventional role and the requirements of the new situation in which people are governed by a democratically elected authority with its executive and judicial institutions. The native administration should be activated in the spheres of peaceful coexistence, social reconciliation, and in observing the inherited traditions of herding, farming, and conflict resolution, for the benefit of all sectors in society.

9. A permanent committee should be formed in the different areas with the task of specifying the seasonal passages of cattle (*maraheel*) and their timings, based on a clear map that considers the interests of both farmers and herdsmen. It has to be drawn according to the recognized traditions, the agreements reached during the previous reconciliatory conferences, the spread of drought, and the migration of people. The state and the native administrations should ensure the implementation of the decisions taken by this committee.

The Economic Dimension

Since the deterioration of natural resources and the poor development and services constituted the major reasons behind the conflict in Darfur, the economic factor becomes a principal approach for solving the problem. In this regard, we advance the following suggestions:

1. The deterioration of natural resources in the region should be studied in order to change the lifestyle of herding and farming to suit the available water and plant resources. Consideration should be given to the settlement of nomads and modernizing their cattle breeding to focus on the quality of product rather than the quantity of animals. The farming methods should be improved, the ground-water explored, and the environment should be protected by all means in order to preserve its natural resources.

2. A special commission should be set up to look into land possession in the region in light of the inherited rights that are locally accepted and according to the utilization claims that are rightly acquired. The principle of equal rights to all citizens should be observed irrespective of religion or race in addition to the economic feasibility of exploiting the land. The commission should plan for land uses, specifying the basis for land ownership and taking care of the registration process. The commission has the right to recommend compensation for groups or individuals who lost their inherited or acquired rights as a result of implementing the new regulations.

3. The establishment of a special commission for development and reconstruction of Darfur using local and international funds, so as to build the infrastructure and complete the development projects that have been halted, such as: the Inqaz western highway, the Ghazalah Jawazat and Jebel Marrah projects, the western savanna project, and others.

4. Encouragement of investment and diversification of resources and means of livelihood for ordinary citizens, in accordance with a comprehensive development plan for all states. Introduce small industries that depend on local raw materials and facilitate the marketing of products outside the region.

5. Conduct a study on the possibility of extending a major electricity power line from the new Merowe Dam to Darfur. This would contribute to the provision of the necessary power that would attract investment. The use of alternative power sources, such as solar energy, should also be encouraged, especially in rural areas, so as to further develop living methods and modernize society.

The Security Dimension

Since the lack of security in Darfur has already reached its limits because of the influx of weapons from neighboring countries, the formation of militias, the spread of the phenomenon of armed robbery, and the appearance of the armed opposition, both official and popular efforts should work together to maintain the security all over the region. The situation requires that tranquillity be instilled in the hearts of the displaced and refugees, especially women, children, and elderly people, through the implementation of the following steps:

1. The strict abidance by the cease-fire agreement signed by the government and armed groups in the Ndjamena and Abuja agreements and the Security Protocol, and the withdrawal of all parties from the positions seized after that date. The conflicting parties should extend full cooperation with the international monitors and the African Union forces in protecting the civilians in villages and displaced camps. Women should be recruited within the AU forces to guard the camps and take care of women and children.[2]

2. Necessary measures should be taken to disarm all individuals and groups carrying weapons, outside the regular forces, and the sources of weapons and ammunitions should be dried out. Groups should be encouraged to voluntarily hand over their weapons in exchange for development projects in their areas and payment of compensations, but light weapons may be licensed in a legal way.

3. The authority of the state should be enforced to ensure the rule of law and achieve justice. The immediate settlement of criminal cases before the courts and the quick resolution of administrative and economic problems that confront the executive administration.

4. Scrutinizing individuals to be recruited in the regular forces, giving them good training so that they are suited to perform their duty in a disciplined professional way, without regional or tribal biases.

5. Hastening the implementation of the civil registry for all citizens in the region, controlling migration from neighboring countries, and monitoring the borders through mobile and effective forces. The Sudanese citizenship granted in the region should be revised according to the operative laws and cross-border trade should be allowed to the benefit of citizens in Darfur and those of neighboring countries.

6. The problems of blood money and pending compensations should be resolved according to the established traditions and the resolutions of previous reconciliation conferences. The government should contribute generously to the deserved compensations.

7. The cooperation of all parties (official, popular, and armed groups) to fight against the phenomenon of armed robbery, and to abstain from providing refuge or concealing information about those who committed a crime that could jeopardize the stability and development of the region.

The Humanitarian Dimension

The humanitarian dimension in the crisis of Darfur is a major issue that attracted the attention of the whole world because thousands of people were killed, hundreds of villages were burned down, tens of thousands took refuge in Chad, and hundreds of thousands were displaced inside the country. All this has created a real humanitarian catastrophe. Thus the humanitarian aspect should be given a priority in the solutions for the problem, as most of the victims were the weak members in society, such as women, children, and the elderly. In this regard, we recommend the following:

1. The full abidance by the Humanitarian Protocol, which requires the parties to facilitate the delivery of humanitarian aid for the victims of military operations, to open the roads for humanitarian organizations and not to obstruct their workers, and to protect the camps of the displaced.
2. Secure the delivery of humanitarian needs to all who are affected by the war in their camps, towns, and villages. The distribution of aid to affected persons in different areas should be balanced, and special attention should be given to Sudanese refugees in Chad. The government agencies should monitor and coordinate the works of relief organizations, especially the foreign ones.
3. The voluntary resettlement of the displaced and refugees in their home areas after providing them with security, water, food, shelter, medical care, and education. The scars of war should be removed and the damaged amenities and institutions repaired. In addition to that, sufficient strategic reserves of medicine and food should be stored to avoid any shortage, and early preparations be made for the upcoming agricultural season.
4. The formation of a committee to asses postwar needs, on par with the one constituted by the government and the SPLM in the South. The international community should support this committee, and it may be attached to the Rehabilitation Fund for the Southern region.
5. Provision of intensive and comprehensive programs to heal the physical and psychological wounds of the victims of human violations, and to train them to do jobs that suit them. Victims should be made aware of their human rights and local organizations should be encouraged to help them. The capacity of civil society organizations, including those headed by and for women, should be increased, and their political, economical, cultural, and social roles should be enhanced. They should take part in the decision-making concerning the society at all levels.
6. The establishment of a maternity and childhood fund to alleviate the damages afflicted during the conflict.

The Social Dimension

The society of Darfur is known for its stability, social solidarity, and interracial mix; this is due to their commitment to the values of a shared adherence to Islam as a religion and their established traditions in tolerance and coexistence. However, the fallout from the current conflict has dealt a serious blow to the region's social fabric. That is why a long-term plan is required to patch up the social cohesion taking it back to its former state. In this regard we suggest the following:

1. The promotion of the historical, social, and cultural character of Darfur that unified its people. The institutions of higher education and the organizations of civil society should contribute to this role, and the government should encourage the establishment of corporations and organizations that involve many tribes and that work for the service of all regions.
2. Making use of the educational, religious, and information institutions in order to patch up the social fabric, to overcome the narrow understanding of tribalism, to denounce the call for racial arrogance, exclusiveness, and the rush toward political positions only on the basis of tribal affiliation. The call for violence and sedition among tribes should be criminalized.
3. Care should be taken for general education, improving its services and widening its bases because of its vital influence in shaping and educating the character of the individual. The boarding school system should be returned to big towns, because of its role in cultural and social integration.
4. Involving the local communities and the grassroots entities in the process of social reconciliation and the settlement of pending disputes, and revival of the traditions of tolerance, coexistence, and integration. The culture of peace should be spread among all ranks of society, and the traditions of dispute solving should be given a legal status.
5. Activating the role of the native administration in the settlement of tribal disputes and in the process of social reconciliation, and involving civil society organizations and women in the call for discarding violence and fighting. Contact between Darfurians should be supported across ethnic groups and social entities in the capital city, and their relatives in the regions should be encouraged.
6. The government, the political parties, and the civil society organizations should pledge to support the reconciliation process and peaceful coexistence in Darfur. They should refrain from exploiting tribal fanaticism in the political game. A voluntary and popular entity for all people of Darfur should be created to protect their unity, to support their social fabric, and to contribute to solving the emerging problems and to serve the interests of the region.

Conclusion

The crisis of Darfur has reached its limits in the past few years, but it seems an accidental event compared to the long, peaceful coexistence that was obtained in the region for centuries. Hence, it should be a solvable problem, especially if the people of Darfur themselves realize that there is no better option for them but to live together in that part of the country. If the determination of the wise men and influential leaders in the region is put to work, and the efforts gathered together, they can definitely solve the roots of the problems according to their observed traditions, the new concepts in society, the operative laws, and the social conditions. The government should lead an active role to rectify the social disintegration and build trust, in addition to its role in maintaining security and realizing stability and development of the region.

Notes

[1] S.W.T. is an abbreviation of the words *subhanahu wa ta'ala*. It is an Islamic phrase that means "glorious and exalted is He (Allah)." The phrase, which is in some cases abbreviated to swt, appears in parentheses after the name of Allah in Islamic texts such as the *Qur'an* and the *Hadith*. The uttering of this phrase (such as in the case of the author of this essay) is normally perceived as an act of reverence and devoutness toward Allah.

[2] It should be acknowledged that the situation on the ground has changed since then and the AU force has been gradually replaced by the AU/UN Hybrid force.

19 On the Failure of Darfur Peace Talks in Abuja:
An SLM/A Insider's Perspective

Abaker Mohamed Abuelbashar

Introduction

The origin of the current conflict in Darfur can be traced to two major developments. First, since Sudan became independent, Darfur has suffered from negligence of power sharing and lack of development by successive governments that failed to address the genuine constitutional procedures for the country and the economic disparity between the region and the rest of the Sudan. Second, the policy of deliberate marginalization forced Darfurian people to establish political organizations and movements as early as the late 1950s, demanding economic development for the region and just political representation in the center. But instead of addressing its negligence and associated injustices, successive central governments plunged the region into interethnic conflicts, and thus the ruling elites in Sudan (the Riverian Arabs) have been successful in implementing policies of divide and rule in Darfur. To that end the ruling elites since independence, to varying degrees, have adopted policies of by-proxy war in Darfur, including genocide, ethnic cleansing, and scorched-earth campaigns, which have increasingly become common practice in Darfur by the regime of Omar Hassan Al Bashir.

The Sudan Liberation Movement/Army (SLM/A) took up arms against the Al Bashir regime to protest the lack of government protection against attacks on sedentary groups, and thus SLM/A has been created in response to those challenges and the general policy of marginalization and deprivation by Khartoum governments.

The SLM/A is aware that the current conflict in Darfur is political in nature and cannot be resolved through military means. It recognizes further that a genuine agreement can be reached only through negotiated political settlement to ensure a lasting peace; in that, the SLM/A realizes that the peace agreement put on the table at Abuja on May 5, 2006, was not the right settlement for the people of Darfur to sign.

The Recent History of Political Movements in Darfur

The post-2003 armed and political resistance movements in Darfur reflect the political evolution of the social history of Darfur. Among others, the predecessors of contemporary political movements include the following:

1　The Red Flame (*Al-Laheeb Al-Ahmar*) was established in 1957. This was a movement formed by intellectuals living in Darfur's main cities just one year after the independence of the Sudan, working underground with the main objective of enlightening the people of Darfur about the negligence and lack of development in the region.

2.　The Darfur Development Front (DDF) was established in 1964. Its founders were Ahmed Ibrahim Diraige (chairman), Ali Elhaj Mohamed (vice-chairman), Suleiman Ahmed (secretary), Ali Hassan Taj-Eldeen (deputy secretary), and Mohamed Salih Alfaki (treasurer). Their main objective was to address the issues of deprivation and marginalization, in that the new movement demanded the establishment of socioeconomic development projects in the region and the independence of political decisions without the interference of the center. The DDF may be considered the mother of the recent political movements in Darfur and still has some active members who continue to keep Darfur's issues in the regional and national media alive.

3. The Sooney Movement of June 1966 was led by Darfurian veterans who fought in the civil war in Southern Sudan, but they also recruited policemen, prison guards, and civilians. The founders of the movement were convinced that the civil war in south Sudan was illegal and immoral, and on their return to Darfur they found that DDF was already established as a political movement, but achievement of its objectives was below expectations. They realized that such a movement could not fulfill its aims without strong support of a military wing; therefore, they established the Sooney movement in Darfur to address the same issues raised by DDF, but through other means, including armed resistance. Though the declaration of the movement originated in El Fasher, the historical capital of the Darfur Sultanate, the founders chose the name Sooney, one of Jebel Marra's summits, to indicate the inclusion of all tribes of Darfur in this movement. The main founders were Ahmed Yousif Takana, Bush Alzareef Abu-Kalam, Ishaq Sulieman Ali, Fudol Abaker Teiman, Mohamed Mohamed Naji, Aeid Massaud Ali, Ahmed Abu-Aqiela, Abdelrahman Ali Adam, Albasheir Yousif Ibrahim, Adam Abdelrahman Kharief, and Musa Baraka. This movement was brutally crushed in the early stages of its formation, and almost all its founders were imprisoned for very long periods.

4. Western Sudan People's Organization (WSPO), 1977–1979, was an opposition movement established by the Sudanese diaspora in Libya to challenge other opposition groups led by Northern Sudanese, but their followers were from Western Sudan. Later on, the WSPO became a member of the Sudanese United National Front (UNF), which opposed Numeiri's regime (1969–1985) in the 1970s. The founders were Osman Bushra Mohamed, Mohamed Mansour Abdelgadir, Abubakar Mustafa Zakareia, Ibn-Omar Mohamed Ahmed, and the late Mohamadein Suliman Jar-el-Nabi.

5. The Darfur Popular Uprising (DPU), 1979, was a grassroots uprising in El Fasher, which protested the appointment of General Al-Tayib Al-Mardi as governor of the Region of Darfur. Al-Mardi, who was not from Darfur, was appointed at a time when all other regions in Sudan were governed by men who hailed from the regions they governed.

6. The Darfur People's Demonstration (Khartoum), 1988, was another popular demonstration in the heart of Khartoum that protested government policies that allowed troops of foreign countries, especially Chad, to fight on the soil of Darfur.

7. The Darfur branch of the Sudan People's Liberation Movement/Army (SPLM/A), led by Commander Abdul-Aziz Adam Alhilu, who is currently Deputy Secretary-General, Sudan People Liberation Movement, SPLM. The origins of this movement are found in a deliberate plan to expand the activities of the SPLM/A in Darfur in 1990–1991, which was militarily crushed after the assassination of SPLA Commander Daoud Bolad.

8. Sudan Federal Democratic Alliance (SFDA) was established in January 1994 by Sudanese from the western regions of the country living in diaspora in London.

Their main objective was to replace the opposition group, the National Democratic Alliance (NDA), and to advocate for a different, more stable and inclusive political system so as to address the very problems which brought about the current conflict in Sudan. Founders of SFDA were Ahmed Ibrahim Diraige, chairman and former opposition leader in Sudan; Suleiman Musa Rahall, medical consultant and member from south Kordofan; Abaker Mohamed Abuelbashar (the author), an expert at the Food and Agriculture Organization of the United Nations and member from south Darfur; Sharif Abdalla Harir, lecturer at Bergen University and member from north Darfur; and Ahmed Al-Zubeir Rahall, teacher and member from south Kordofan.

9. The Darfur Liberation Movement first emerged on June 28, 2002, in the Golo town of Jebel Marra, and in February 2003 changed its name to Sudan Liberation Movement/Army (SLM/A), which was led by Abdulwahid Mohamed Ahmed Nour.

10. The Justice and Equality Movement (JEM) also appeared in 2003, led by Dr. Khalil Ibrahim Mohamed. Both movements call for the objectives of the New Sudan, and aim to address the root causes of the conflict and constitutional issues involving the system of governance, human rights, separation of religious and political affairs, and just and fair economic development for marginalized areas. While the SLM/A is a liberal secular movement, JEM has had strong historical links with the National Islamic Front (NIF), a movement that emerged out of the Muslim Brotherhood (al Ikhwan al Muslimiin) movement of Sudan. Nevertheless, it is obvious that the present movements are an evolution of continuous resistance to the deliberate marginalization and negligence of the region.

Objectives of the Peace Talks

The SLM/A is fully convinced that the current conflict in Darfur is of a political nature; therefore, it can only be resolved through a peaceful negotiation process. Accordingly, it accepted and attended all rounds of the Darfur Peace Talks in Abéché, N'Djamena (Chad), and Abuja (Nigeria) to negotiate in good faith with the aim that the talks would address the root causes of the conflict in Darfur in order to reach a fair and just agreement that would smoothly be implemented by its signatories.

The Peace Talks Process

The process of the Inter-Sudanese Peace Talks on the conflict in Darfur started as early as May 2001 in Darfur, even before the SLM/A declared itself by this name. Since then until December 2002, a total of five peace talks were held between the ruling Islamist regime in Khartoum and the SLM/A in different places in Darfur, mainly in El Fasher and the Jebel Marra area. In all of these meetings the movement put three main issues for discussion on the negotiating table:

1. Just political representation for the people of Darfur in the region and the center.
2. Fair economic and social development in Darfur.
3. Cessation of divide-and-rule policies by inciting some tribes against others.

After the SLM/A declared itself as an armed struggle movement, another three meetings were held, and the demands were upgraded. It is worth mentioning that in all of these rounds the Khartoum Islamist regime rejected all demands put forward by the Movement, refusing to admit that the conflict in Darfur is of a political nature. Instead, the Khartoum Islamist regime's propaganda continues to describe the conflict as a tribal war and SLM/A members as armed robbers or bandits.

The following year the Chadian government decided to host and mediate peace talks between Darfurian rebels and the Khartoum government. On September 14, 2003, the venue of the peace talks was moved to Abéché, thus the search for a solution to the conflict was internationalized. The first round under the auspices of African Union (AU) mediation was held in N'Djamena, where a cease-fire agreement was signed on April 8, 2004. After that, an agreement on the modalities for the establishment of the cease-fire commission and deployment of observers in Darfur was signed in Addis Ababa on May 28, 2004. Then the following six successive rounds were held in Abuja where the "The Implementation of the Humanitarian Situation in Darfur" and "Enhancement of the Security Situation in Darfur" protocols were both signed on November 9, 2004. The following year the Declaration of Principles (DOP) for the Resolution of the Sudanese Conflict in Darfur was signed on July 5, 2005. The issues under discussion in the DOP can be classified into three categories.

First, recognition and accommodation of the fact that Sudan is a composition of multiethnic, multireligious, and multicultural groups; affirmation of rights such as tribal land ownership and other historical rights of Darfur; and human rights and citizenship as the basis of civil and political rights and duties.

Second, negotiations on other issues such as power-sharing, wealth-sharing, sustainable development, rehabilitation and reconstruction of Darfur, humanitarian assistance, and security arrangements, etc.

Third, the agreement reached by the parties shall be incorporated into the National Constitution.

To expedite the peace talks process, the chief mediator of the African Union (AU), Salim Ahmed Salim, decided to follow a new policy of negotiation and formed the following three commissions to run concurrently: Power Sharing, Wealth Sharing, and Security Arrangement. Commencing in November 2005, the seventh round of the Peace Talks lasted five and a half months and concluded with the signatures of two parties out of four – the current Sudanese government and SLM/A-Minni Minawi faction, while the SLM/A Abdulwahid Mohamed Nour and JEM withheld their signatures.

Reasons for Rejecting the Abuja Accord

The procedure of negotiation that was adopted by the AU mediation contributed greatly to the failure of the Peace Talks in Abuja, in the sense that the mediation cornered the movements into addressing Darfur-only issues. Also, the international community made it clear that they did not want to see any obstruction to the Comprehensive Peace Agreement (CPA), January 2005, signed by the Islamist regime of the NIF and SPLM/A. Therefore, the AU mediation was unable to accept any proposals from movements related to the resolution of the root causes of the conflict. Later, the AU mediators admitted that this agreement could not take the people of Darfur to a genuine peace settlement, but that it was one step forward toward peace. This was even acknowledged in the preamble of the Darfur Peace Agreement (DPA) signed on May 5, 2006, which states "that the signing of this Agreement shall be a significant step toward a just, peaceful, and lasting political solution to the conflict in Darfur." This is a clear indication of acknowledging the shortcomings of the agreement and its failure to accomplish a final and just settlement. The SLM/A has genuine reasons for rejecting the unfinished and unfair deal presented by the AU mediation. The reasons for rejection may be summarized into the three categories of (A) procedural, (B) legal, and (C) technical.

A. Procedural

As indicated earlier, the AU mediators decided to organize the negotiating agenda into three commissions (Power Sharing, Wealth Sharing, and Security Arrangement) and further decided to proceed in the negotiations of these commissions concurrently. The main concern of the movements that refused to sign was that this kind of procedure would create great confusion and would not lead to fair results, as there are overlapping issues among these commissions. For instance, it was regarded as inadvisable to hold concurrent discussions of the land issue in the three commissions; rather, the movements wanted it to be negotiated first in one commission, preferably Power Sharing, in order to establish a static reference for the other two commissions.

The AU mediation concluded in February 2006 that there was no need for more plenary sessions. Accordingly, it decided to produce one compiled document out of the three commissions for the concerned parties to sign. Since then there have been no more formal negotiations, particularly within the Wealth-Sharing and Power-Sharing commissions. As a result, there were issues left aside without discussion, which gave the SLM/A a legitimate reason for refusing to sign the document.

The compiled document was prepared by the middle of March 2006, and when it was handed to the Darfur Movements on April 25, 2006, they were given an ultimatum to respond and sign it within just five days. Bear in mind that this document includes issues that had not been discussed previously at any level.

The AU mediation proposed calling for the formation of a core team from all parties to resolve the issues of difference, or at least to set up those issues in a compromising form for the top leaders of the parties to make decisions about them. Although the Darfur Movements accepted the proposal, sadly it was not given any chance for survival. One wonders if this had not happened, perhaps the DPA would have been improved in a much better fashion.

The importance of the DPA to the whole nation and to the people of Darfur in particular lies in the fact that it was meant to bring everlasting peace to the region. Because of that and as a matter of normal procedure, the SLM/A officially requested that the AU mediation grant it a three-week grace period in order to study the compiled document in detail before presenting its comments. The AU mediation team rejected the request, which further confirmed to the SLM/A leadership that the AU was adamant about not reaching a genuine peace agreement on Darfur, hence lengthening the suffering of the people.

B. Legal

In the view of the SLM/A, the procedures followed by the AU mediation were illegal. The compiled document presented to the Darfur movements on April 25, 2006, was incomplete in the sense that, on that date, it lacked implementation modalities in all commissions. In addition, three crucial issues were not discussed at all, including implementation mechanisms, general provisions, and guarantees. Above all, the movements had been given an ultimatum of five days to sign the document or leave it. In fact, this procedure is clearly against the globally prevailing negotiation norms, which allow involved parties to negotiate every issue thoroughly in order to reach a compromise that ensures all parties consider themselves winners.

In peace agreements, definitions of key words and phrases are of paramount importance, due to the fact that they constitute legal references during the implementation process of the agreement. However, the SLM/A realized that some words were not given correct definitions, which indicates that the interpretation of such words or phrases can adversely affect the implementation process, e.g., Janjawid, Hawakir (communal land ownership rights), and Masarat (livestock routes).

The fact remains that the NIF regime in Khartoum is accused by the international community of committing genocide and ethnic cleansing in Darfur, and many of its senior members, including officials from Darfur, are suspected by the International Criminal Court of committing war crimes, as well as crimes against humanity. Despite this, the DPA gives the Khartoum Islamist regime (National Congress Party, NCP) absolute power to rule the Darfur region because it holds literally 81 percent of the constitutional and executive posts (state governors, ministers, commissioners, etc.) and 71 percent of legislative seats in Darfur. How can such a government implement an agreement aimed at bringing peace and stability to the region?

There is clear legal offence by the AU mediation in terms of the deletion of some paragraphs of issues already agreed upon by the parties in separate commissions. For example in Article 21 of the Wealth Sharing Commission, which deals with Urgent Programs for Internally Displaced Persons (IDPS), Refugees, and Other War-Affected Persons and Compensation for War-Affected Persons, some paragraphs and subparagraphs that were agreed upon at the discussion stage were completely deleted. These include:

1. A total of five paragraphs under subtitle "Definitions."
2. Paragraph "205. Taking note of the suffering of the individual people of Darfur, and the customary practices of tribal restitution in Darfur, the Commission shall work out principles for appropriate restitution or other compensation for individuals, communities and economic entities. In doing so, the Commission shall take into account, among other considerations [compensation for individuals, communities, and economic entities]." The bracketed portion of the paragraph was deleted.
3. Subparagraph "207 (i) Satisfaction, including public apology."
4. The most critical point was that many paragraphs of the April 25, 2006, document were deleted in the final document of May 5, 2006. A good example is under "Definitions." Almost all words and phrases related to Wealth-Sharing and Power-Sharing commissions were deleted, including definitions of some critical words like Hawakir, Janjawid, and Massaratt, even though their initial definitions brought forward by AU mediation on April 25, 2006, were not accepted in the first place by the movements.

It was agreed that all documents should originate in the English language and that copies must be translated into Arabic and French. Notwithstanding, the Arabic version was presented long after April 25, 2006, and many words and paragraphs were incorrectly translated. A critical example of such a defect is in the Wealth Sharing Commission, where it indicates that IDPs and refugees have no right to compensation. In another instance, the word commission has been mistranslated as committee in Arabic, and in that sense a Compensation Committee shall be established rather than a Compensation Commission.

C. Technical

The security and humanitarian situation has dominated the technical side of the negotiations. This has given the movements the impression that the AU mediation has adopted the agenda of the international community, aiming to (a) safeguard the CPA; (b) help to get Sudanese government approval to bring UN troops to Darfur; and (c) help to bring sufficient aid to the needy people. In this sense, the international community has not committed itself to helping resolve the chronic problems of the Sudan, which underlie the Darfur crisis. Accordingly, less attention has been given to the Power-Sharing commission, which was meant to resolve the root causes of the conflict in Darfur.

Three issues out of nine in the agenda of the Power-Sharing Commission were not discussed at any level of the negotiation process: General Provisions, Implementation Mechanisms, and Guarantees.

There was no inclusion of solutions to the root causes of the political conflict in Darfur. A key goal of the armed uprising of the people of Darfur against the Arabized ruling elites in the center is to stop the damaging policies that threaten to destroy the culture and identity of Darfur. To contribute to the resolution of this issue, the participating Darfur movements pointed out that the following agenda must be accepted as they were originated in the DOP:

1. Tribal land ownership, Hawakir, and other historical rights shall be affirmed within their historical borders.
2. Fair representation in both legislative and executive bodies at a national level and majority representation of the Darfur Movements at a regional level in both legislative and executive organs during the interim period.
3. Participation of the Darfur Movements in the process of disarming the Janjawid with a specific timetable and effective guarantees.

Nevertheless, all these issues have been ignored in the signed DPA. In addition, some essential rights of Darfurians were also not sufficiently addressed. These include:

1. Individual compensation whereby the government of Sudan should put a significant amount of money into the Darfur Compensation Fund following the immediate signing of the DPA.
2. Determining the duration of the interim period.
3. Ensuring that movements shall control their forces over the interim period before the UN's Disarmament, Demobilization, and Reintegration (DDR) program takes place.

All parties at the negotiation process stand on equal footing, in that the signing of the peace agreement gives them legitimate responsibility to carry out the implementation process. According to the final draft of the DPA presented to the negotiating parties for signature, the Darfur movements are represented by only 19 percent in Darfur's executive organs, and by 29 percent in its legislative bodies. This is a clear indication of representation imbalance of the signing parties in this document, and accordingly, the armed movements have had no chance to correct the unjust practices of NCP in the region in order to eliminate the suffering of their people. Finally, there is no provision in the DPA to allow a UN Peacekeeping Force in Darfur after the signing of the agreement.

D. Disintegration of Darfurian Movements

From the very beginning, there was a lack of unity and common vision within the Darfurian movements. The Sudan Liberation Movement/Army first came out under the name of Darfur Liberation Movement in June 2002, then a year later changed its name to SLM/A. Instead of joining the SLM/A to make one strong movement, the Justice and Equality Movement (JEM), which came out in mid-2003, chose to stand as an independent movement, thus creating a state of competition among the armed groups in Darfur over the forthcoming political leader of the region.

In October 2005, a one-sided conference in Hasskanita (Darfur) resulted in the split of the SLM/A into two factions. It was only in November 2005 in N'djamena that a regional mediation from Chad, Libya, and Eritrea played a major role in bringing the leaders of the three movements together to sign a memorandum of understanding that called for negotiation with one team and one list of agreed upon demands.

Though the negotiation began in a good atmosphere in November 2005 in Abuja, it became clear that the memorandum of understanding was a fragile agreement that the movements had little faith in, and the differences of their leaders and their personal ambitions came to surface.

In March 2006, a group of nineteen (G19) members of the negotiating team split from SLM/A faction led by Abdulwahid Mohamnd Nur, adding another hard blow to the crisis of leadership.

Following these developments, the NIF regime in Khartoum realized that the leaders of the Darfur movements were struggling over power sharing, seeking posts for themselves, and not responding to the legitimate demands of the people of Darfur; thus, the NIF regime became adamant about not responding positively to any political demands on the table. Here it is worth mentioning that the international community had done its best to bring together leaders of the movements under one umbrella in order to fulfil the political demands of one greater constituency. But despite their efforts, their plan did not succeed in unifying the fragmented movements. On the contrary, to some extent these efforts contributed to furthering the disintegration among the movements. Thus, the fragmentation based upon personal interests of the leaders contributed to the failure of peace talks in Abuja.

E. The Way Out

There was a way out when the SLM/A offered a proposal immediately after the signature of the agreement aiming to add a supplementary deal to the document that could address unresolved issues, but the AU mediators failed to convince the representative of the Islamist regime in Khartoum, as well as the international community, of the benefits of such a deal.

In a later development, Mr. Jan Pronk, the UN Secretary General Special Envoy to Sudan, supported this proposal by admitting that "... the deal was severely paralysed and needed major additions to bring dissident rebels on board and stop it collapsing ..."[1] Now it is apparent that the DPA is dead, in that not only was the implementation process stuck in the first place (Minni Minawi, the First Assistant to the President of Sudan, admitted that "... I have no regret of signing the DPA but I am regretful of its implementation..."), but also the agreement was rejected by all cross-sections of Darfurian communities. Several demonstrations in protest of the DPA were carried out in the IDP camps in Sudan, refugee camps in eastern Chad, as well as student protests in Khartoum, where eight persons were killed under the brutal treatment of the Islamist government's security agencies in the month of May 2006 alone.

The way out from this dilemma is to transcend the DPA of May 5, 2006, and hold peace talks in a free atmosphere to address the root causes of the conflict, in not only Darfur but the Sudan at large. Among other issues, the following must be given due consideration if the forthcoming negotiations are to bring durable peace and stability to the country:

First, since May 2006, both SLM/A and JEM have been fragmented into several factions, and other movements have been created. In such a situation, what is needed first is the unification of these factions and movements, or at least their collaboration under one umbrella with one negotiating team. In fact, there were several initiatives from the international community aiming to achieve this objective, including initiatives from Eritrea, Chad, Libya, AU-UN, and the Centre for Humanitarian Dialogue (Geneva, Switzerland), Comunita di Sant Egidio (Roma, Italy), and Sudan People's Liberation Movement (Juba, Sudan).

The only successful initiative was the SPLM's invitation to all Darfur resistance movements in Juba, where it hosted from the month of October 2007 over 160 delegates representing about 14 factions and movements for a period exceeding 4 months. Due to the vision and commitment of the SPLM, on November 29, 2007, a unification of 10 factions and movements was born in the name of Sudan Liberation Movement/Army under one military command and political leadership. Names of these factions or movements together with the names of their leaders are as follows:

1. SLM/A led by Commander, Ahmed Abdelshafi Toba
2. SLM/A led by Commander, Mohamed Ali Kelai
3. SLM/A led by Commander, Elhaj Younis Abaker
4. SLM/A led by Commander, Sidiq Abdelkareem Nassir
5. SLM/A led by Ibrahim Ahmed Ibrahim
6. SLM/A led by Commander, Ahmed Adam Abdalla
7. JEM led by Commander, Mohamed Salih Hamid Harba
8. The Armed Popular Resistance for Western Sudan-Kordofan (based in Kordofan region) led by Commander, Mahmoud Khatir Juma
9. The Revolutionary Voice of Truth Movement led by Commander, Ahmed Khalil Ali

10. Sudanese Revolutionary Front led by Musa Hassan Musa. However, after two weeks following the declaration of unification this movement (Musa Hassan Musa) withdrew from the unity process.
11. SLM/A led by Commander, Dr. Saleh Adam Ishaq

The most urgent task needed to forge ahead with any serious peace process is a real coordination and cooperation of the international community with the SPLM to convince and bring the rest of the factions and movements which are out of the unification process under one united movement, or at least two movements – SLM/A and JEM – where coordination is likely to be viable.

Second, to this task is the need to implement the Darfur–Darfur Dialogue and Consultation (DDDC) of the DOP, which is meant to brief the people of Darfur and get their support during the implementation of the peace agreement, but not to give them the right to reopen the negotiation. This dialogue is considered to be the first step toward intertribal reconciliation, which it is hoped will ultimately lead to peaceful coexistence in the region. Armed movements have a legitimate legacy through armed struggle to negotiate on behalf of the people of Darfur, but on the other hand, when taking into consideration the experience of Abuja, it will be more practical if prenegotiation consultation is exercised where armed movements, native administration, civil society, women's organizations, IDPs, and refugees discuss their demands and the future of the region. In doing so, movements will be in a position of getting pre-consent from the people of Darfur, and that will facilitate the implementation process should a peace agreement be signed.

Third is the assertion that issues of land and region are inseparable, and both jointly constitute the core element of the conflict in Darfur. Accordingly, priority must be given to address these issues if a genuine resolution to the conflict is considered a real target to be achieved.

Fourth, the fact remains that, since independence in 1956, successive governments of the Sudan have failed to properly address the root causes of the problem in the country, resulting in creation of conflicts in different parts of the country. It is high time to put an end to the political violence in the country; therefore, the mediation team and the international community as observers or facilitators should give full attention to this issue with clear vision of achieving a just and durable peace settlement.

Fifth, the experience of peace talks in Abuja shows that the AU mediation has proven incompetent in conducting the Darfur peace negotiations; therefore, an experienced organization like the UN or Inter-Governmental Authority for Development (IGAD) is needed to carry out future mediation processes in order to reach a successful peace settlement in Darfur.

Sixth, though African soldiers are well trained, the African Mission in Sudan (AMIS) in Darfur proved that these soldiers are not respected by the NIF regime and its associated Janjawid militias. Ironically, they are considered as an army coming from countries of the same club. Therefore, the UN Peacekeeping Force should be deployed as soon as possible – once a just and durable peace agreement is signed – with a full mandate to use all necessary means to protect civilians and react rapidly to cease-fire violations or provocations by any party. It is highly recommended that this force include a sizable number of European and North American soldiers, as they are better equipped and professionally disciplined.

Notes

This document was first presented in London on Friday, June 30, 2006, and modified in Addis Ababa, Ethiopia, on Friday, February 22, 2008.

[1] See: http://news.bbc.co.uk/2/hi/africa/5142608.stm

SPLM's Demonstration in Solidarity
with People of Darfur Damazin Stadium
Damazin, Sudan, 2007

SPLM-BLUE N

التضامن مع شعب
ارفور

يد

لو

007

ين

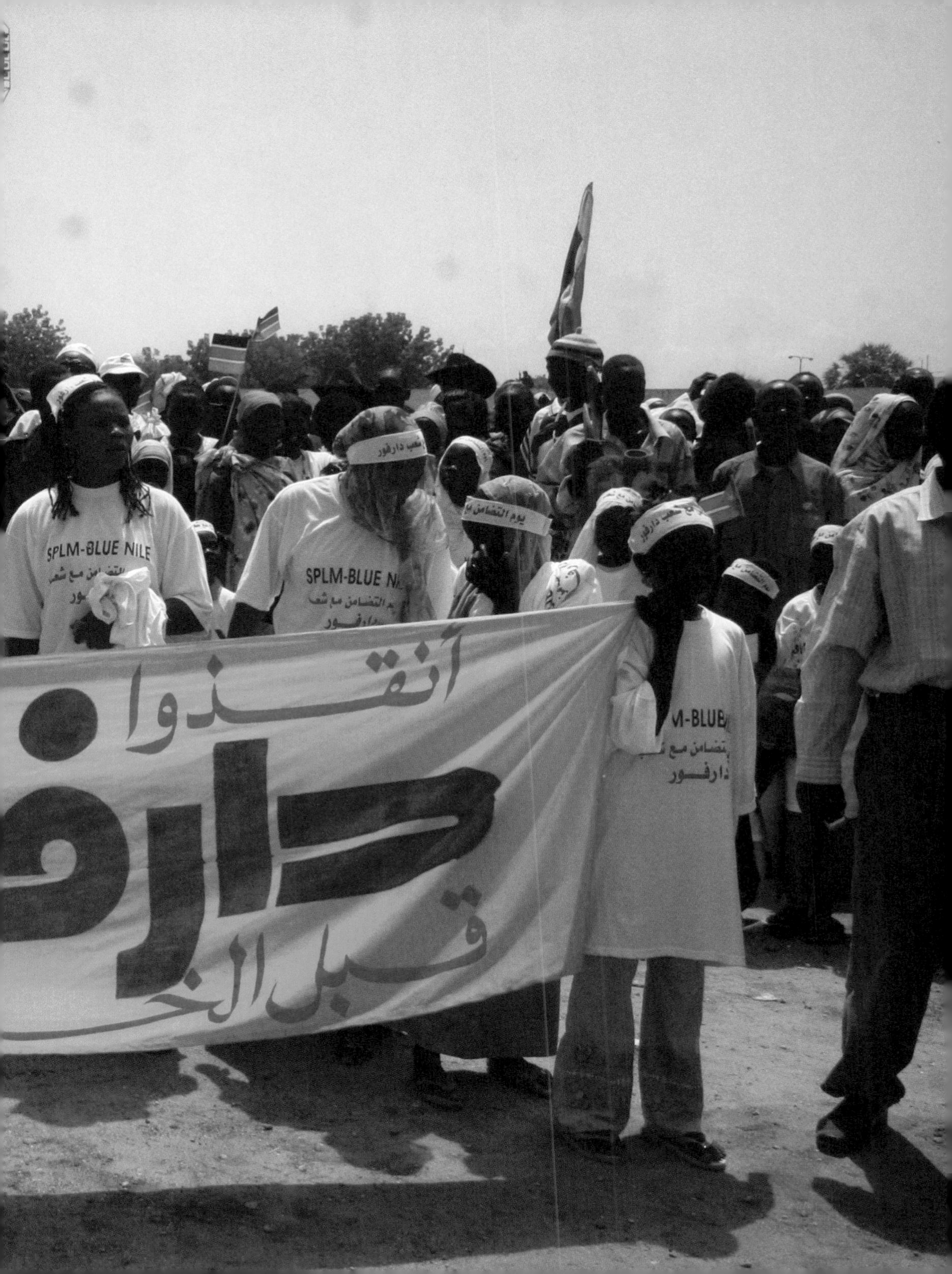
SPLM-BLUE NILE
يوم التضامن
أنقذوا
دارفور

السيدامن مع شعب دارفور

SPLM's Demonstration in Solidarity
with People of Darfur Damazin Stadium
Damazin, Sudan, 2007

Scene from Kalmah Camp
Nyala, 2006

Children Kalmah Camp
Nyala, 2006

Part 2
Appendices

Appendix A

Sudan: Timeline
A Chronology of Key Events

The material presented in this appendix has been adapted from a timeline published by the British Broadcasting Company (BBC) on July 15, 2008.
http://news.bbc.co.uk/go/pr/fr/-1/hi/world/middle_east/country_profiles/827425.stm

1881 Revolt against the Turko-Egyptian administration.

1899–1955   Sudan is under joint British–Egyptian rule.

1956 Sudan becomes independent.

1958 General Abbud leads military coup against the civilian government elected earlier in the year.

1962 Civil war begins in the south, led by the Anya Nya movement.

1964 The October Revolution overthrows Abbud and a national government is established.

1969 Ja'far Numeiri leads the May Revolution military coup.

1971 Sudanese Communist Party leaders executed after short-lived coup against Numeiri.

1972 Under the Addis Ababa peace agreement between the government and the Anya Nya the south becomes a self-governing region.

1978 Oil discovered in Bentiu in southern Sudan.

1983 Civil war breaks out again in the South involving government forces and the Sudan People's Liberation Movement (SPLM/A), led by John Garang.

Islamic Law Imposed

1983 President Numeiri declares the introduction of *Shari'a* (Islamic law).

1985 After widespread popular unrest Numeiri is deposed by a group of officers and a Transitional Military Council is set up to rule the country.

1986 Coalition government formed after general elections, with Sadiq Al Mahdi as prime minister.

1988 Coalition partner the Democratic Unionist Party drafts cease-fire agreement with the SPLM/A, but it is not implemented.

1989 National Salvation Revolution takes over in military coup.

1993 Revolution Command Council dissolved after Omar Al Bashir is appointed president.

US Strike

1995 Egyptian President Mubarak accuses Sudan of being involved in attempt to assassinate him in Addis Ababa.

1998 US launches missile attack on a pharmaceutical plant in Khartoum, alleging that it was making materials for chemical weapons.

· New constitution endorsed by over 96 percent of voters in referendum.

1999   President Bashir dissolves the National Assembly and declares a state
       of emergency following a power struggle with parliamentary speaker,
       Hassan Al-Turabi.

Advent of Oil

1999   Sudan begins to export oil.
2000   President Al Bashir meets leaders of opposition National Democratic Alliance
       for first time in Eritrea.
   ·   Main opposition parties boycott presidential elections. Incumbent Al Bashir
       is reelected for further five years.
2001   Islamist leader Hassan Al-Turabi's party, the Popular National Congress
       (PNC), signs memorandum of understanding with the southern rebel SPLM's
       armed wing, the Sudan People's Liberation Army (SPLA). Al-Turabi is arrested
       the next day, with more arrests of PNC members in the following months.
   ·   Government accepts Libyan/Egyptian initiative to end the civil war after failure
       of peace talks between President Al Bashir and SPLM leader John Garang
       in Nairobi.
   ·   United States extends unilateral sanctions against Sudan for another year,
       citing its record on terrorism and rights violations.
2002   Government and SPLA sign landmark cease-fire agreement providing for six-
       month renewable cease-fire in central Nuba Mountains, a key rebel stronghold.
   ·   Talks in Kenya lead to a breakthrough agreement between the government
       and southern rebels on ending the nineteen-year civil war. The Machakos
       Protocol provides for the South to seek self-determination after six years.
2003   In February, Rebels in western region of Darfur rise up against government,
       claiming the region is being neglected by Khartoum.
   ·   In October, PNC leader Turabi released after nearly three years in detention,
       and ban on his party is lifted.

Uprising in West

2004   In January, army moves to quell rebel uprising in western region of Darfur;
       hundreds of thousands of refugees flee to neighboring Chad.
   ·   In March, UN official says pro-government Arab Janjawid militias are carrying
       out systematic killings of African villagers in Darfur.
   ·   Army officers and opposition politicians, including Islamist leader Hassan
       Al-Turabi, are detained over an alleged coup plot.
   ·   In May, government and southern rebels agree on power-sharing protocols as
       part of a peace deal to end their long-running conflict. The deal follows earlier
       breakthroughs on the division of oil and non-oil wealth.
   ·   In September, the United Nations says Sudan has not met targets for disarming
       pro-government Darfur militias and must accept outside help to protect civilians.
       US Secretary of State Colin Powell describes Darfur killings as genocide.

Peace Agreement

2005   In January, the government and southern rebels sign a peace deal. The agree-
       ment includes a permanent cease-fire and accords on wealth and power sharing.

- UN report accuses the government and militias of systematic abuses in Darfur, but stops short of calling the violence genocide.
- In March, UN Security Council authorizes sanctions against those who violate cease-fire in Darfur. Council also votes to refer those accused of war crimes in Darfur to International Criminal Court.
- In June, government and exiled opposition grouping National Democratic Alliance (NDA) sign reconciliation deal allowing NDA into power-sharing administration.
- President Al Bashir frees Islamist leader Hassan Al-Turabi, detained since March 2004 over alleged coup plot.

Southern Autonomy

2005 Former southern rebel leader John Garang is sworn in as first vice president on July 9. A constitution that gives a large degree of autonomy to the South is signed.
- Vice president and former rebel leader John Garang is killed in a plane crash on August 1. He is succeeded by Salva Kiir. Garang's death sparks deadly clashes in the capital between southern Sudanese and northern Arabs.
- In September, a power-sharing government is formed in Khartoum.
- In October, an autonomous government is formed in the South, in line with the January 2005 peace deal. The administration is dominated by former rebels.

Darfur Conflict

2006 Khartoum government and the main rebel faction in Darfur, the Sudan Liberation Movement, sign a peace accord in May. Two smaller rebel groups reject the deal. Fighting continues.
- In August, Sudan rejects a UN resolution calling for a UN peacekeeping force in Darfur, saying it would compromise sovereignty.
- In October, Jan Pronk, the United Nations' top official in Sudan, is expelled.
- In November, African Union extends mandate of its peacekeeping force in Darfur for six months.
- Hundreds are thought to have died in the heaviest fighting between northern Sudanese forces and their former southern rebel foes since they signed a peace deal last year. Fighting is centered on the southern town of Malakal.
2007 In April, Sudan says it will accept a partial UN troop deployment to reinforce African Union peacekeepers in Darfur, but not a full 20,000-strong force.

War Crimes Charges

2007 In May, International Criminal Court (ICC) issues arrest warrants for a minister and a Janjawid militia leader suspected of Darfur war crimes.
- U.S. President George W. Bush announces fresh sanctions against Sudan.
- In July, UN Security Council approves a resolution authorizing a 26,000-strong force for Darfur. Sudan says it will co-operate with the United Nations–African Union Mission in Darfur (UNAMID).
2007 In October, SPLM temporarily suspends participation in national unity government, accusing Khartoum of failing to honor the 2005 peace deal.
- In December, SPLM resumes participation in national unity government.

2008   United Nations takes over the Darfur peace force in January.
- Within days, Sudan apologizes after its troops fire on a UNAMID.
- Government planes bomb rebel positions in West Darfur, turning some areas into no-go zones for aid workers.
- In February, commander of the UN–AU peacekeepers in Darfur, Balla Keita, says more troops needed urgently in west Darfur.

Abyei Clashes

2008   In March, Russia says it is prepared to provide some of the helicopters urgently needed by UN–AU peacekeepers.
- Tensions rise over clashes between an Arab militia and SPLM in Abyei area on north–south divide, a key sticking point in 2005 peace accord.
- Presidents of Sudan and Chad sign accord aimed at halting five years of hostilities between their countries.

2008   In April, counting begins in national census, which is seen as a vital step toward holding democratic elections after the landmark 2005 north–south peace deal.
- UN humanitarian chief John Holmes says 300,000 people may have died in the five-year Darfur conflict.
- In May, Southern defense minister Dominic Dim Deng is killed in a plane crash in the south.
- Tension increases between Sudan and Chad after Darfur rebel group mounts raid on Omdurman, Khartoum's twin city across the Nile. Sudan accuses Chad of involvement and breaks off diplomatic relations.
- Intense fighting breaks out between northern and southern forces in disputed oil-rich town of Abyei.
- In June, President Al Bashir and southern leader Salva Kiir agree to seek international arbitration to resolve dispute over Abyei.
- In July, ICC's top prosecutor calls for the arrest of President Al Bashir for genocide, crimes against humanity, and war crimes in Darfur; the appeal is the first ever request to the ICC for the arrest of a sitting head of state. Sudan rejects the indictment.

Source

http://news.bbc.co.uk/go/pr/fr/-/1/hi/world/middle_east/
country_profiles/827425.stm

Published: 2008/07/15 09:40:52 GMT
© BBC MMVIII

Appendix B

Press Release/Commentary by SLM/SLA posted on
March 14, 2003, at 13:42:53: EST (-5 GMT)

The Sudan Liberation Movement and Sudan Liberation Army (SLM/SLA):
Political Declaration

Darfur had been an independent state from the sixteenth century to the second decade of the twentieth, when it was coercively annexed to modern-day Sudan. As an independent state, Darfur enjoyed worldwide recognition and had embassies in the capitals of the major empires of that time. If Sudan is seen as the microcosm of Africa, Darfur is the microcosm of Sudan. The peaceful coexistence between its African and Arab tribes, between the sedentary populations and the nomadic ones, and between emigrants from its eastern and western neighbors and indigenous groups was the source of its stability, prosperity, and strength.

However, successive postindependence regimes in Khartoum, both civilian and military, have introduced and systematically adhered to the policies of marginalization, racial discrimination, exclusion, exploitation, and divisiveness. Darfur was made and continues to be a reservoir of cheap labor for central Sudan's agricultural and industrial projects, the major source of lower-ranking soldiers thrown into the fray of the supremacist war waged by Khartoum against south Sudan, Nuba, Fung, Beja, Rashaida, and other marginalized areas, and a fair game for central Sudan's political parties and elite seeking to field nonindigenous parliamentary candidates in safe seats.

The monopolization of power and wealth led to the institutionalization of the hegemonic policies of riverian Sudan's dominating establishment. These were further entrenched through the fueling of ethnic and tribal wars, with the governments in Khartoum providing military assistance to some Arab tribes and organizations to fight against their non-Arab brethren, with whom they have peacefully coexisted for centuries. Rapid desertification, famines, and cross-border population movements from neighboring countries into Darfur have provided Khartoum's regimes with additional ammunition to further its divisive policies between Arab and non-Arabs and sedentary and nomadic groups. These evil policies reached their zenith on the hands of the NIF junta that usurped power in June 1989. The present Khartoum junta has even created a Bantustan-type department of tribal affairs whose mission is to oversee the implementation of Khartoum's divide and rule schemes and channel government assistance to its local allies. These policies have resulted in massive human rights violations amounting to ethnic cleansing and genocide in certain areas of all the three states of Darfur.

The brutal oppression, ethnic cleansing, and genocide sponsored by the Khartoum government left the people of Darfur with no other option but to resort to popular political and military resistance for purposes of survival. This popular resistance has now coalesced into a political movement known as the Sudan Liberation

Movement and its military wing, the Sudan Liberation Army (SLM/SLA), which we are happy to announce today to the Sudanese people and to the world at large.

The Objective of SLM/A
Although the SLM/A has originated from Darfur as a matter of necessity in response to the brutal genocidal policies of the NIF government in that region, we want to affirm and underline that the SLM/A is a national movement that aims along with other like-minded political groups to address and solve the fundamental problems of all of Sudan. The objective of SLM/A is to create a united democratic Sudan on a new basis of equality, complete restructuring and devolution of power, even development, cultural, and political pluralism and moral and material prosperity for all Sudanese.

SLM/A Position on the Unity of Sudan
The SLM/A is of the view that Sudan's unity is of paramount importance, but it should not be maintained and cannot be viable unless it is based on justice and equality for all the Sudanese peoples. Sudan's unity must be anchored on a new basis that is predicated on full acknowledgment of Sudan's ethnic, cultural, social, and political diversity. Viable unity must therefore ultimately be based on the right of self-determination and the free will of the various peoples of Sudan. The fundamental imperatives of a viable unity are an economy and political system that address the uneven development and marginalization that have plagued the country since independence, so that the interests of the marginalized majority are adequately catered for and they are brought to the same level of development of the ruling minority. The SLM/A shall work with all political forces that ascribe to this view.

SLM/A Position on Human Rights and Democracy
The SLM/A shall struggle for the full realization and respect for human rights and democratic pluralism in accordance with international standards leading to equal development and the eradication of political and economic marginalization.

SLM/A Position on System of Governance
The SLM/A shall struggle to achieve a decentralized form of governance based on the right of Sudan's different regions to govern themselves autonomously through a federal or confederal system. At the same time the central government must be completely restructured and recast so that it adequately reflects Sudan's rich diversity as represented by the component regions, which are its stakeholders.

SLM/A Position on the Questions of Identity, Culture, Power, and Wealth
The SLM/A shall struggle to realize a new system of rule that fully respects the cultural diversity in the Sudan and creates new democratic conditions for cultural dialogue and cross-fertilization generating a new view of the Sudanese identity based on Sudanism. Sudanism will provide the Sudanese with the necessary space, regardless of whether they are Arabs or Africans, Christians or Muslims, Westerners or Easterners, Southerners or Northerners to achieve greater cohesiveness on the basis of the simple fact of being Sudanese. This would require restructuring of power and an equal and equitable distribution of both power and wealth in all their dimensions.

SLM/A Position on Religion

Religion is a source of spiritual and moral inspiration for our peoples that serves the needs of our peoples and the entire humankind in their pursuit of peaceful interaction and greater moral and spiritual ascendancy. The state machinery belongs to all Sudanese regardless of their religious or spiritual values and its neutrality must be preserved. Religion and politics belong to two different domains and must be kept in their respective domain, with religion belonging to the personal domain and the state in the public domain, that is, religion belongs to the individual and the state belongs to all of us. In this way, religion cannot become a cause of conflict among citizens of the same country.

SLM/A Position on Armed Struggle and Sudanese Opposition Armed Groups

Armed struggle is one of our means to achieve our legitimate objectives. The SLM/A shall strive to achieve a common vision and programme of action and unity among Sudan's different opposition armed groups as well as with nonarmed political groups with which it shares the same political objectives.

SLM/A Position Regarding Arab Tribes and Groups in Darfur

The Arab tribes and groups are an integral and indivisible component of Darfur social fabric who have been equally marginalized and deprived of their rights to development and genuine political participation. SLM/A firmly opposes and struggles against the Khartoum government's policies of using some Arab tribes and organization such as the Arab Alliance and Quresh to achieve its hegemonic devices that are detrimental both to Arabs and non-Arabs. We call upon all fellow citizens of Darfur from Arab background to join the struggle against Khartoum and its divisive policies, the restoration of our traditional and time-honored peaceful coexistence and the eradication of marginalization. The real interests of the Arab tribes of Darfur are with the SLM/A and Darfur not with the various oppressive and transient governments of Khartoum.

SLM/A Position on Peaceful Solution to the Sudanese Problem

Negotiation for the peaceful resolution of Sudan's conflict is one of our means of struggle to achieve our objective provided that it should be aimed at attaining a comprehensive and just peace. Negotiations must be conducted in good faith and the government must desist from its practices that seek to divide, co-opt, and destroy opposition forces.

SLM/A Position Regarding the NDA and Other Political Forces

SLM/A shall struggle to achieve understanding and common ground with the NDA and other political forces in order to remove the NIF's dictatorial regime and establish a democratic system based on a new political dispensation of freedom, justice, respect for human rights, and equality for all Sudanese. The SLM/A will therefore reach out to establish contact and dialogue with the NDA and other political forces.

SLM/A Appeal for Support

We appeal to the sons and daughters of Darfur, both inside the Sudan and in the diaspora, and to the Sudanese people in general, to give political and moral support to the SLM/A, and despite their poverty and suffering to make financial and material contributions to the SLM/A to enable it to achieve the objective of a free and democratic New Sudan. We appeal to our people in the rural areas, both agriculturalists and pastoral nomads, to rally behind the SLM/A and give the movement their full political and material support. We appeal to our brothers in the regime's armed forces to abandon the regime and join us, or if it is not possible to join us, not to fight us. We appeal to those in various government departments to find ways of supporting the SLM/A. We appeal to our intellectuals to use their pens and pockets to support the SLM/A. We appeal to businessmen to make financial donations. We appeal to our women to organize and find ways to support the SLM/A. We appeal to our youth to join the SLA and contribute their generation's share to rid our people of this dictatorship and establish a new Sudan that belongs equally to all its citizens.

SLM/A Position Regarding Neighboring Countries and International Community

The SLM/A shall strive to build relations of friendship and partnership with the neighboring countries, especially the Republic of Chad, the Great Libyan Jamahiriya, Egypt, and the Central African Republic, as well as all of Sudan's other neighbors. The SLM/A shall seek to create friendly relationships with the international community that will enhance international peace and stability in the world away from Khartoum's policies that have contributed to regional and international instability through its direct involvement in promotion of local, regional, and international terrorism.

SLM/A Appeal for Humanitarian Assistance for Darfur

Finally, on behalf of the people of Darfur, we appeal to the international community to assist the people of Darfur with humanitarian relief to address and ameliorate the serious and deteriorating humanitarian situation in the region. Ethnic cleansing and other gross acts of genocide sponsored by the Khartoum regime have caused massive displacement and suffering in all the three states of Darfur. This has been further compounded by draught and desertification. The population is in dire need of food, human medicine, animal drugs, and other nonfood services.

Signed): _____

Minni Arkou Minnawi
Secretary General, SLM/SLA
Satellite Phone 8821631110628
Darfur, Sudan: March 13, 2003

Appendix C

Justice and Equality Movement (JEM):
Proposal for Peace in Sudan in General and Darfur in Particular

First
Human Rights & Basic Freedoms
1. Commitment to human rights according to the traditions, values, and principles included in the international human rights conventions and treaties.
2. Confirmation of the acknowledgment that Sudan is a multiethnic, multicultural, and multireligious country.
3. Citizenship in Sudan as the basis for rights and duties, including the right to vote and be elected for all leading positions and posts.
4. The system of governance shall be federal and democratic, based on political pluralism, the rule of law, independence of the judiciary, and the principle of separation of powers.
5. Guaranteeing the freedoms of expression, association, formation of political parties, and nongovernmental associations for all the Sudanese, without any discrimination.
6. Guaranteeing the codification of full basic rights for women and children.

Secondly
Participation in Power and Civil Services
1. The adoption of peaceful transition of power as a strategic option, meant to secure the stability and unity of the nation, and transparency and accountability in governance.
2. Assuring the establishment of national and regional criteria and modalities for the distribution of power and wealth, which should positively reflect on the unity and diversity of the nation.
3. The implementation of a federal system of governance for all six regions of the Sudan, which shall allow for democratic self-governing by every region, within a united Sudan. Such regions are: the Central Region, the Northern Region, the Southern Region, the Eastern Region, Darfur Region, and Kordofan Region. The status of the national capital (Khartoum) shall be considered as the 7th special region.
4. Participation by the regions in the central power, which shall be according to a national criterion based on the population of every region, as well as any other criteria to be agreed upon, provided that all the regions shall participate in governing the national capital and occupying the federal public positions in accordance with the population proportion for every region.
5. The restructuring of the armed forces in order to guarantee its national composition and orientation, and limit its role to the defense of the nation, provided that college and other enrollment for recruitment in the armed forces shall be in accordance with the population proportion for every region.

Thirdly

Participation in Public Wealth

1. Commitment to an equitable distribution of the national wealth, according to national modalities and criterion based on the population proportion of every region, as well as any other criteria to be agreed upon.
2. A special proportion of the national wealth shall be allocated to support the development and infrastructures of war-affected regions and areas.
3. Guaranteeing the positive concern and attention by the state toward the Sudanese citizen, who shall be the essence and target of development efforts, particularly in relation to the following:

   (a) Free education.
   (b) Free primary health care and fully free health care for the poor.
   (c) Guaranteeing the right to jobs and equal access to employment at profitable wages.
   (d) Enjoyment of security.

Fourthly

Transitional Measures

1. Release of all detainees, arrested, accused, and convicted persons in relation to political and security cases.
2. The transitional period shall be three years during which the two movements shall retain their forces to assure the implementation of the agreement, provided that the two movements shall have the right to rule Darfur during such transitional period.
3. The formation, at the beginning of the transitional period, of a government of national unity, out of a Supreme Council (to be constituted of the president of the republic and a vice-president representing each region) and a Council of Ministers, provided that the two movements shall have the right to participate in the governance of the Sudan, including the state of Khartoum.
4. General elections shall be held within two years for the election of the president of the republic, the regional governors, members of the national legislature, and members of regional legislatures under regional and international supervision
5. Drafting a national constitution during the transitional period, through a national conference in which all the six regions of Sudan shall participate.
6. The prosecution of war criminals and perpetrators of genocide at international court.

Fifthly

Darfur Region

1. Guaranteeing the unconditional repatriation of all internally displaced persons (IDPs) and Sudanese refugees to their original places of abode, which shall be reconstructed, rehabilitated, and prepared for sustainable living, as well as the provision of full compensation for losses of lives, property, and belongings according to international criteria.
2. Allocation of a substantial proportion of national oil and other financial revenues for the development and reconstruction of Darfur.

3. Recognition of the tribal land ownership and tenure (*hawakir; Hawakir*) at their geographical boundaries and administrative jurisdictions, provided that all Sudanese citizens shall be guaranteed the right to benefit from all lands for cultivation, pasture, or living.
4. Taking necessary steps for the organization of the Sudanese nomad tribal pastoral routes (*massarat*), and the provision of safe passage for their persons and animals.
5. Reinstatement of Darfur geographical and administrative boundaries to those of 1956.
6. An acknowledgment and apology, public and written, by the Khartoum government to the people of Darfur for the war crimes, genocide, and human rights violations committed in Darfur.

Sixthly
International Guarantees

Assuring the provision of international and regional guarantees for the implementation of the peace agreement to be reached by the two movements and the Sudan government.

Seventhly
1. The agreements to be concluded between the Sudan government and the two movements (JEM and SLM) shall be part and parcel of the national constitution.

Appendix D

Sudan People's Liberation Movement (SPLM):
Position on Developments in Darfur, March 20, 2003

The current events in Darfur are a benchmark historical development, which comes at a critical moment in the history of our country. As a major political force in the Sudan, it is incumbent on the Sudan Peoples' Liberation Movement and Sudan Peoples' Liberation Army (SPLM/A) to make its position on the events in Darfur known to the Sudanese people in general and to the people of Darfur in particular, as well as to the international community and hence this statement.

Since its founding in 1983 and in its first political document, the Manifesto, the SPLM/A has based its vision on the fact that the essence of what became known as the "Southern Problem," or "Southern Question," is really a general "Sudanese Problem" represented by the political, economic, and cultural marginalization of the majority of Sudanese people who are denied participation in the exercise of power, access to wealth, and moreover subjected to cultural hegemony. The Sudanese national building project has been an exclusivist project that is based solely on the two parameters of Arabism and Islam. It has never recognized the historical and contemporary diversity of the Sudan. It works to institutionalize the hegemony of a small minority in the center through its system of rule and governance and economic exploitation of the excluded regions. From its inception the SPLM/A called for the restructuring of power, the equitable distribution of wealth, religious tolerance, a democratic dialogue between the cultures of the different ethnic and cultural groups in Sudan, and the creation of a new sociopolitical, economic, and cultural dispensation, which we call the New Sudan.

From the beginning, the SPLM gave priority to political interaction with the people of Darfur as individuals, groups, and tribes. Throughout this period, the SPLM has had some members from among the sons and daughters of Darfur. There was a qualitative development in terms of our concern with Darfur when the movement sent its martyr Engineer Daud Yahya Bolad to Darfur in August 1991, as a result of dialogue between the SPLM/A and the people of Jebel Marra.

The SPLM has always preached that the people of Darfur have a just and genuine cause regardless of whether they are of African or Arab background. Indeed, all of them suffer from political and economic marginalization and consequently do have a vested interest in the restructuring of power, even development and the equal and equitable distribution of wealth. Achieving all these does serve the interest of the masses in Darfur. This is still the position of the SPLM/A; we stand in full solidarity with the people of Darfur in their just struggle to achieve justice and equality for themselves and for all Sudanese.

The current events in Darfur are unfolding at a time when the SPLM/A is negotiating peace with the Sudan government against the backdrop of a window of opportunity for the achievement of a just, genuine, and lasting peace. Despite clear signs of lack of seriousness from the side of the government to continue the process of Machakos, the SPLM/A is determined to take the government to the brink of peace and it is the National Islamic Front (NIF) that will be the reluctant party as they are now, not the SPLM/A. Moreover, the events in Darfur occur as we engage the government in discussing the issue of the three conflict areas of the Nuba Mountains, the Fung Region of Southern Blue Nile, and the Abyei District of the Ngok Dinka. This again vindicates the correctness of our vision, which demands a comprehensive solution and the need to find a correct and genuine political formula for governing the Sudan. In resolving the issue of the three conflict areas a correct formula to address the issues of the other marginalized areas such as Darfur and Eastern Sudan in an effective and positive manner could be found, which in turn would give a new chance for a correct unity of the country and enhance a national consensus that does not exclude other political forces and marginalized regions of the Sudan.

The regime has a real chance to work with the SPLM/A for the success of the Machakos process and the recognition and solution of the other problems such as Darfur within the context of a comprehensive solution and a new Sudanese political dispensation. The SPLM/A believes in and remains committed to a peaceful solution and appeals to the government of Sudan to refrain from seeking a military settlement in Darfur, an approach that has already proven a total failure and a recipe for disaster in Southern Sudan, Nuba Mountains, Southern Blue Nile, and Eastern Sudan. As our own history of the SPLM/A attests, any attempt to misdiagnose the Darfur issue as a security rather than a political problem will result in the erroneous and fatal prescription of a military solution. Violence begets violence, and a military solution will certainly trigger military countermeasures that will only make the situation worse. The NIF government must appreciate the glaring fact that it cannot achieve military victory in Southern Sudan, Nuba Mountains, Southern Blue Nile, Eastern Sudan, and now Darfur. Genuine dialogue to seek a peaceful political settlement that is predicated on addressing the root causes of the political insurrection in Darfur, as it should be the case in other marginalized areas, is the only way forward.

Certain circles in Khartoum have tried to link the SPLM/A with the recent developments in Darfur. The SPLM/A would like to categorically state that it has nothing to do with the inception of the war in Darfur for which the NIF government is solely responsible and accountable. The government is on record as to how the situation in Darfur developed, as they have been depicting it as "armed robbery" over the last ten years. The NIF has also been instigating tribal and racial conflict in the region to fight the so-called armed robbery. Well, the chickens have come home to roost. What the government has been calling armed robbery, which was actually resistance against government policies in the region, has transformed itself into a political movement, and the SPLM/A cannot be blamed for this indigenous Darfur process. Having said that, the SPLM/A remains in full political solidarity with the people of Darfur and their just cause, which the government should neither ignore nor belittle. Ignoring such problems as has happened in the past, in the South, Nuba Mountains, Fung, Beja, and Rashaida, only serves to aggravate them. The responsibilities of the government necessitates that it draws lessons from the mistakes of the past, when dealing with the Darfur issue. Among such mistakes is the NIF government's exploitation of minor contradictions among different tribes in Darfur with the aim of pitting them against each other to divide and rule them. This policy in conjunction with attempts to crush the insurgency using sheer brute force rather than dialogue is responsible for the present developments in Darfur, as it has similarly been the case elsewhere.

The SPLM is convinced that the people of Darfur, who have now taken up arms, have a just cause, which needs to be seriously addressed. It is incumbent upon the SPLM, the NIF government, plus the rest of the political forces to engage in genuine dialogue as the best and correct way to address the situation in Darfur, which by necessity includes talking, and talking in good faith, with those carrying arms in that region. Our concerns and anxieties about the situation in Darfur have been naturally heightened, in view of prospects for success of the Machakos process that would lead to a new political setup of which the SPLM would form a significant part. The situation in Darfur would definitely have an impact, positively or negatively, on the new arrangement and therefore ought to be taken seriously. Should the Machakos process, for example, produce a political agreement and a new (interim) government is formed the SPLM/A would obviously not be a party to any project to fight the people of Darfur.

Finally, the SPLM/A calls on the Sudanese people to extend solidarity with the people of Darfur and demand that the government seek a political solution to the problem in Darfur and further demand the immediate lifting of the siege and denial of services to the people of Northern and Western Darfur. Indeed, the government should look for a comprehensive political settlement that is based on a new Sudanese political dispensation that is inclusive of all of Sudanese regardless of their region of origin, ethnic composition, and cultural grouping.

Dr. Samson L. Kwaje SPLM Commissioner for Information and Official Spokesman of the SPLM/A

Appendix E

National Redemption Front:
Founding Declaration

To our fellow citizens across Darfur and the entire Sudanese nation;
To our comrades in arms in the struggle for just peace;
To all individuals, organizations, and members of the international community who share our indignation at the brutalities of the Khartoum regime.

Driven by our deep commitment to end the suffering of the people of Darfur and the tragic conditions in the refugee and displaced camps in particular;

Committed to end political, economic, cultural and social injustices, and all forms of repression in Darfur as well as other marginalized areas of Sudan;

Aware of the unity of purpose and fundamental objectives of the Darfur armed movements and other political forces in opposition to the government of Khartoum;

Determined to end the genocidal war and ethnic cleansing in Darfur by the Khartoum regime and its militias;

Conscious of the values of solidarity, cooperation, and coordination between our revolutionary movements and other Sudanese opposition forces in the struggle against the hegemony of repressive minority regimes, the tyranny of internal colonialism; and, to free marginalized peoples from the horrors of war, poverty, exclusion, and exploitation.

Cognizant of the after effects of the failed Abuja's process of May 5, 2006.

We, leaders of political and military organizations abstaining from signing the Abuja document, who earlier issued a joint statement in Asmara on June 7, 2006, reaffirm our rejection of that faulty process.

Realizing the virtues of combining efforts and resources to end the suffering of our people, we hereby join hands in establishing the *National Redemption Front (NRF)*, as an instrument for coordinating political, military, diplomatic, and media initiatives.

Fellow Citizens:
We, the revolutionary movements listed below and signatory to this statement:
1. Sudan Liberation Movement/Army (SLM/A);
2. Justice and Equality Movement – Sudan (JEM);
3. Sudan Federal Democratic Alliance (SFDA);

call upon organizations of marginalized communities and other opposition political forces to join NRF in realizing the following principles:
1. Uphold Sudan as multicultural, multireligious, and multiethnic country where diversity constitutes the basis of citizenship for individuals, and unity of our nation.
2. Citizenship is the sole basis for all rights and obligations without discrimination on religious, ethnic, cultural, or regional background.
3. Guarantee all human rights, basic freedoms, rule of law, along with the recognition that accountability and transparency are necessary conditions for good governance.

4. Safeguarding democracy, political pluralism, freedom of expression as fundamental for sharing, and transferring state power.
5. Ensuring priority of human development programs and capacity building as prerequisites for social and sustainable development. Introducing affirmative action in support of free basic social services, health, and education as well as introducing job creation policies.
6. Realizing harmony and interaction between people in various regions, and thereby consolidate national unity by facilitating travel and communication facilities throughout Sudan.

NRF objectives include:
a) Bringing together all Darfurians in their various movements, organizations, groups, and associations within and outside Sudan.
b) Organizing and unifying political, military, diplomatic, legal, media, and various popular initiatives for the realization and protection of the legitimate rights of Darfurians and all Sudanese.
c) Ending the unceasing genocide and prosecuting its perpetrators.
d) Coordination and consolidation of regional and international efforts to end the suffering of our refugees and displaced; and ensure a fair compensation as well as their repatriation to the original regions and villages.
e) Endorse all legitimate demands of the marginalized areas.
f) Advocate a just system for sharing wealth and power between the various regions of Sudan.
g) Realize the full and unimpeded implementation of a federal system; and, ensure regional self-rule.
h) Guarantee a fair participation in administering national political, economic, military, and civil service institutions on the basis of population percentages of various regions.

NRF structure is composed of a leadership council from the leaders of the founding organization with a rotating presidency, and a general-secretariat responsible for the daily executive affairs.

We appeal to all people of Darfur and the marginalized communities of Sudan to join NRF in order to realize justice and lasting peace for all. In conjunction with this declaration, a separate statement on our position regarding the Abuja document will be issued.

Victory to our people and glory to our martyrs.

Signed:
Mr. Ahmed Ibrahim Diraig   Dr. Sharif Harir
Dr Khalil Ibrahim Mohamed   Asmara: June 30, 2006.
Mr. Khamis Abdalla Abakr

Appendix F

The Sudanese Communist Party:
Darfur, the Crisis, and the Tragedy, Position Paper

In the ancient history of Darfur, the existing region was characterized by waves of migrations due to the movements of Arab and African tribes. These waves of migration have significantly influenced both the shape of Darfur's history as well as its norms, traditions, and customs. Clearly, migrants brought with them cultural, social, economic, and religious currents, some of which brought about radical changes in Darfur. Drawn to Darfur's natural and climatic diversity, a number of tribes settled in different parts of the area. Each tribe had its own chief, who managed its affairs independent of any other authority. The tribal customs were the terms of reference that governed relations among different tribes in Darfur. Indeed, Darfur has been known to the world since ancient times. Pharaohs once visited the area, and the Romans attempted to subjugate Darfur in order to exploit its resources. The "40 Days Road" linked Darfur to the Egyptian Governorate of Asute. Moreover, merchants and explorers from across the world visited Darfur as it was one of the important commercial centers on the African continent.

As an independent entity, Darfur has been ruled by various kingdoms and Sultanates, usually named after the dominant tribe, such as Al Dajo Sultanate (between the twelfth and thirteenth centuries A.D.), and Al Tunjur Sultanate (between the end of the thirteenth century and the first half of the fifteenth century A.D.). In 1445, Sultan Suliman Solong established an Islamic state in Darfur, which remained an independent Sultanate until 1874, when it was colonized by the Turko-Egyptian regime following the invasion of Sudan in 1821. Under the new rule, Darfur remained part of Sudan until the Mahdia era. However, following the collapse of the Mahdiyya state after its armies were defeated while resisting the British invasion in the battle of Karari in 1899, Darfur once again became an independent entity with external representation, as well as a member of the League of Nations until 1922. Yet, due to the support given by Sultan Ali Dinar to Turkey in its struggle against the Allies during the First World War, Britain invaded Darfur and forced it to become, yet again, part of Sudan in 1916.

The area of Darfur is approximately half a million square kilometers – the size of Iraq or California in the United States. Also, its size is equivalent to that of France, Holland, and Portugal combined. At the time of Sudan's independence in 1956, Darfur was governed as a single administrative unit known as Darfur Province. However, following its seizure of power on June 30, 1989, the National Islamic Front (NIF) divided Darfur into three states: North Darfur, South Darfur, and West Darfur. The state capitals – El Fasher (North Darfur), Nyala (South Darfur), and Al Ginena (West Darfur) – are the largest towns in Darfur aside from Zalingi, Al Dieen, and Buram.

Darfur has a vast border open to Libya, Chad, and the Central African Republic. Tribal interactions across such vast borders exposed Darfur to existing and renewed conflicts in the region. The victors in these conflicts often advance from Darfur, while the defeated retreat to Darfur to regroup for new attacks. Moreover, Darfur shoulders the burden of the fluctuations in the central government's foreign policy toward its neighbors.

The population of Darfur is six million, represented by nearly one hundred tribes, some of which are of Arab origin, while others are of African origin. African tribes include the Al Fur, Al Zaghawa, Al Masalit, Al Berti, Al Tama, and Al Falata. Arab tribes include the Al Rizegat, Al Ta'yshaa, Al Habania, Beni Helba, Al Misayriyyah, Al Ma'aliyah, and al Salamat. The origin of the name *Darfur* can be traced back to the African tribe of Al Fur, which is the largest and most famous in the region. The word *Darfur* in Arabic means "Home of Al Fur."

All Darfurians are Muslims, and they speak various local languages in addition to Arabic. Due to the nature of its problems and its racial and cultural diversity, Darfur is considered a "mini-Africa."

Darfur is renowned for being the biggest producer and exporter of gum arabic in the world. Also, it is renowned for its substantial animal wealth. Some studies indicate that a huge wealth of oil and other minerals, such as uranium, also exist in Darfur.

View of the Communist Party of Sudan on the Causes of the Conflict in Darfur
The conflict in Darfur is decades older than the date of its recognition by the media and the international community. It is considered to be one of the manifestations of the Sudanese crisis that started with independence and continues until now. We consider the main causes of this conflict to fall into the following two categories:
1. The historical roots of the conflict.
2. The role played by the various consecutive political regimes that governed the Sudan, which eventually resulted in the escalation of the crisis until it was transformed into an international humanitarian tragedy, largely due to the atrocities committed by the NIF, which took over power in the Sudan on June 30, 1989.

Historical Roots of the Conflict
The historical roots of the conflict are of a traditional tribal nature, resulting from the dependency of these tribes on deteriorating natural resources and the use of these resources by both nomads and farmers. In these terms, the conflict is as old as the existence of these tribes and their coexistence together. It was clear that the Darfur tribes did not lack awareness and wisdom to face and resolve these conflicts. From 1957 to present, more than twenty tribal conferences had been convened in Darfur. These conferences summarized the main points of the problem in the following way: (a) respect of the historical rights of these tribes regarding their *Hawakir*; (b) agreement on determining the routes of movements of these tribes (some routes are west of the Jebel Marra mountains, and others are east of the mountains) with a very accurate and precise citation of the fixed natural landmarks for each movement; (c) determination of the time of movement; (d) respect for and adherence to the tribal norms for resolving the intertribal conflicts and to the traditions of hosting or providing a safe haven for other tribes.

The participants in these conferences always come up with sound and practical recommendations, but these recommendations are seldom implemented by either the central or the local authorities. And, as usual, under the present regime, the conferences were transformed into political and public relations shows targeted toward the media. However, had the authorities implemented even some of the recommendations, the security, political, and social situations in Darfur wouldn't have deteriorated to the current level.

Despite the total blackout and tight control over information and media imposed by the NIF government since taking power, there were always eminent warnings in the media related to tribal conflicts in Darfur. For years, the Sudanese newspapers have been reporting news about killing, burning of villages, and stealing of cattle and property in Darfur; but what the newspapers could not report at that time were the most violent crimes committed by the pro-government militias, which resulted in large numbers of victims, the use of highly advanced artillery by the government army, mass rape, and other atrocities. And so, since early times, it became clear that the conflict in Darfur was not between the Arab and the African tribes (Arab vs. "Zurqa"), but it was very clear that Arabs fought Arabs and "Zurqa" fought "Zurqa," and that no tribe or ethnic group is safe from this dangerous situation.

However, it is very important to note that the tribal conflicts in Sudan have outgrown their traditional nature and form, changing from conflicts over diminishing natural resources to conflicts over the natural aspirations toward real participation in power and administration, as well as political decision-making and wealth sharing (these tribes live in the wealth-producing areas).

The Role of the Successive Governing Regimes in the Escalation of the Crisis
Despite its special characteristics and geographical space, the Darfur crisis is regarded as an extension of the general national crisis that has existed in Sudan since its independence. This general national crisis is a direct result of the wrongheaded policies and maltreatments pursued by the successive governments that ruled Sudan during the previous decades. Those authorities focused on their control over power while neglecting the constitutional issues related to building the newly independent Sudan. Among these most distinctive constitutional issues are the following:
1. The suitable form of governance that realizes equitable power sharing in the Sudan among the various national and tribal components, which could lead to healthy political practices.
2. Reviewing the sharing of wealth and development plans so as to alleviate negligence and unfairness toward the underdeveloped areas in the South, West, and East, giving priority to areas of ethnic and social conflicts. This is to be carried out within the context of a scientifically planned economic project that aims to stop the deterioration in the economic surplus–producing areas without exhausting the center.
3. Introduction of political democratic practices that take into consideration the political reality of the Sudan.
4. The issue of the relationship between state and religion.
5. The issue of the Sudanese identity.

The National Islamic Party regime has played a major role in escalating the conflict in Darfur, transforming it into a real tragedy and a great disaster. This role is connected to the strategic plans of the NIF, which aim to build an Arab-Islamic entity in Darfur that extends to Western Africa and constitutes the first line of defense for the Arab-Islamic state in Sudan, the long-held dream of the National Islamic Party. This intention can be seen both in the National Islamic Party's political practices as well as in its developmental plans.

The political practices include the following:
1. Establishment of new administrative bodies without consideration for the conflicts they would cause over land ownership.
2. Division and strife among some local administrations, which were against the central authority, and imposition of new administrations that were in favor of the authority.
3. Distribution of weapons brought by what the government calls "*mujahidin*" from South Sudan to be used in the tribal conflicts.
4. Unequal treatment of the tribes in disarmament procedures and weapons distribution.
5. The situation further deteriorated because of the atrocities committed by the *walis*, or local governors, who wanted to use the tribal historical conflicts to realize political gains for the ruling party. They would award favored tribes a province or an administrative area at the expense of other tribes.
6. Conflicts with the neighboring countries and the tribes' integration in the area resulting in the flow of weapons and warriors.
7. The government policy of soliciting the support of the tribes in neighboring countries and, in return, granting their members Sudanese nationality.
8. Adoption of a clear-cut racial policy through direct involvement of the regime leaders in recruiting, financing, and arming the pro-government *Janjawid* gangsters. These gangs have committed severe atrocities against "Zurqa," including mass murders and massacres, mass rapes, the burning of houses and villages, ethnic cleansing, and so on. The aim of these crimes is the expulsion of millions of "Zurqa" from their fertile homelands and the transfer of ownership of these lands to the class of big businessmen who are either part of the regime or loyal to it. All these crimes have led to intervention by the international community in an attempt to restrain the culprits as well as to enhance solidarity with the Darfur people from all over the world. In this regard, the UN Security Council has adopted many resolutions, including the submission of the case to the International Criminal Court (ICC) to prosecute the Janjawid leaders and the government officials responsible for those crimes.

The development aspects of the causes of Darfur conflict include the following:
1. It is true that reversing the economic backwardness of the region is the basic solution for Darfur's problems, but at the same time, it is very difficult to deceive the people of Darfur by repeating the slogans of the development programs while not implementing them. The people of Darfur have suffered from the failure and collapse of, as well as corruption in, scores of programs such as the Jabal Marra mountain project; the Savanna project; Khor Ramla and Sag Anni'am projects; the closure of Nyala tannery; the negligence of the seasonal maintenance of the clean water streams project, which was technically and financially supported

by the Saxony state of Germany; the abolishing of mobile medical and veterinary clinics project; the suspension of schools and hospitals due to the delay in salary payments; and more. In other words, there were no development projects, and there was a total collapse and failure in the services sector.

2. Darfur tribes who have historical rights to land ownership always very generously provided their lands for the development and revenue-generating projects that benefitted the whole regional population, both nomads and farmers. And, despite the scarcity of natural resources, Darfur can still maintain all its people and animals. The development issue has remained a pressing priority since the October Revolution of 1964, and countless feasibility studies and project files have been accumulated, but the missing link remains the political will to make decisions and to mobilize the human and financial resources for the implementation of the plans and projects.

The NIF regime believed that it could reformulate the Darfurians and their social fabric, norms, and traditions according to the engineered designs of the so-called Islamic Project, but this project has imploded. The first indicator of the project's failure was highlighted when two parliamentarians, both from Darfur, resigned from the NIF block during the 1986–1989 democratic period. The second indicator came after the Islamic Front coup on the June 30, 1989, when a prominent leader in the Islamic Front – a native of Darfur – organized an armed uprising in Darfur but was caught and executed by his fellow brothers in the Islamic Front. The third indicator was the increase of tribal polarization within the Islamic Front with the rise of two groups. The first adopted the name of Quraysh, which is the tribe of the Prophet Muhammad in Mecca, as a symbol of being a descendent of an Arab tribe. The second is the group that produced *The Black Book*, which symbolically affirms their allegiance to an African origin. Then, as a fourth indicator, the volcano erupted in the large rift in the leadership of the Islamic front, which divided it into a ruling National Congress Party led by Omar Hassan Al Bashir and the opposing Peoples Congress Party led by Hassan Al-Turabi.

However, the best summary and assessment of the crisis of the "Islamic Project" in Darfur was offered by one of the founders of the NIF when he wrote:

The security situation in Darfur is deteriorating gradually from bad to worse. The acts of armed robbery have started because of poverty, unemployment, and drought. But then this developed into a tribal conflict between some tribes because of the bankrupt policies of some governors who wanted to use the historical tribal conflicts to achieve political profits for the benefit of the ruling party. The current situation marks the beginning of a civil war in the region under the slogans of political injustice represented in the absence of developmental projects in the region and the lack of education and health services, besides the isolation of the natives of Darfur and preventing them from holding positions of authority in their homeland.

The continuous marginalization of Darfur since independence, the let-down by the traditional political forces who failed to fulfill the demands of the people of Darfur, the policies of the Islamic Front government that are marked by violence and suppression – all these factors encouraged the youth of the tribes in the region to organize themselves and rebel against the status quo through armed resistance to wrench the rights of Darfurian people on equitable sharing of power and wealth, all within the frame of a united Sudan.

On the other hand, the policy of the partial approach to the problems of the Sudan, which was imposed on the country by the international community through concentrating on the civil war in Southern Sudan and recognized the armed group SPLA and the Khartoum government as the only negotiators, encouraged other regions to wage rebellion since it was seen as the only way to attract attention to their demands. Thus, the region of Darfur witnesses a true civil war that raises the slogans of genuine political, social, and economic equality and justice.

The Position of the Communist Party on the Darfur Peace Agreement (DPA)
On May 5, 2006, in the Nigerian capital Abuja, the government of the Sudan and the Sudan Liberation Movement (Mr. Mini Arko Minawi Faction) signed the Darfur Peace agreement (DPA), also known as the Abuja agreement. The agreement was signed after the international community – primarily the United States and the African Union – exerted great pressure on the negotiating parties.

However, many observers are still wondering about the enthusiastic interest of the United States and the West regarding the Darfur issue. In our view, this can be explained through the following points:

1. The Darfur region holds a strategic position that provides a corridor to all the nations of West Africa to the Atlantic Ocean. This region has become a battlefield for the transnational monopolies trying to gain possession of Africa's petroleum and other raw materials with the aid of organizations such as the New Partnership for Africa's Development (NEPAD) and others. The United States plays a major role in this conflict. Also the boundaries of the region extending from Libya passing by Chad to Central Africa have a strategic role in the conflicts of the superpowers in that area. In addition, the civil war in Darfur casts a shadow of danger of spreading the conflict to other regions of the continent.
2. The developments following the occupation of Iraq and Afghanistan forced the United States to present a new face of peace and reconciliation and to attempt to look more humanitarian than it did in the way it dealt with Iraq.
3. The international community is still in a state of shock and guilt due to its silence and inaction about the horrible crimes committed in the conflicts in Rwanda and Burundi. Therefore the Darfur crisis acquired priority in the agendas of regional and worldwide administrators in the form of the United Nations and the Security Council.
4. The international community that supported the peace process of the southern Sudan fears that the continuation of fighting in Darfur could lead to failure of the peace process in the south of the country.
5. There are studies indicating the presence of rich mineral resources of petroleum, uranium, and other minerals in Darfur.

In spite of its reservations and remarks on the DPA, the Communist Party of Sudan considered it as a starting point for the peace process in Darfur. However, the party reaffirmed that the agreement can succeed only if annexes and additions are made to satisfy the demands of the factions that did not sign it, saying that it does not fulfill the basic demand of the people of Darfur. Now, it is well known that in spite of that agreement, the situation in Darfur has deteriorated and the military conflicts increased in number of victims, severity, and destruction. Also, the Communist Party verified its refusal and condemnation of the attempts to threaten the nonsignatory parties, and instead the party insisted on the importance of listening to their demands again and searching for means and ways to reach an agreement with them.

In that context, the Communist Party's reservations on the agreement are as follows:

1. The negotiations in Abuja, and therefore what the agreement entailed, was governed by the Comprehensive Peace Agreement (CPA), between the Sudan People's Liberation Movement (SPLM) and the government of Sudan (GoS), which created an inescapable frame and ceiling that could not be crossed. It is known that the protocols of Machakos and Naivasha extended beyond the issue of the civil war in the south to deal with all aspects of the Sudanese crisis represented in issues such as peace, identity, unity, democracy, system of government, development, and division of resources, the army, security, foreign affairs, and so on. Also, the CPA strived to create basic changes in the structure of the current political system, including self-determination (a single united state or two states) during the transitional period. These changes were determined by two parties only – the Islamic Front government and the SPLM – while all the other political and social forces, including the armed factions in Darfur, were not involved. Therefore, it is not logical to commit the factions of Darfur and confine them within a framework or ceiling to which they did not contribute.

   The Communist Party believes that to solve the national problems and to stop armed confrontation in the country, it is necessary to achieve a comprehensive national consensus that deals with all aspects of the national crises. This can succeed only if all political forces will be actively engaged in this process, both at the level of decision-making and implementation.

2. In the Abuja negotiations, the international community used the same methodology that it adopted at the Naivasha talks. The methodology of a partial approach to the conflict while ignoring the fragility of the resultant solutions, which in all cases will remain as temporary solutions and under real threat, can collapse at any time. It was the same approach used in the Ivory Coast, Cameroon, Sierra Leone, and Chad. This approach does not look at the Sudanese crisis as a whole or as one crisis that manifests itself in many conflicts but breaks up into partial solutions imposed under increased pressure. We believe that this approach is not successful in the case of the Sudan.

3. The international community and the African Union have exerted great pressure with the aim of obtaining signatures of the movements of Darfur. In this regard, the agreement does not differ much from what happened at Naivasha, but here the result was the signing of only one faction of one movement of the warring movements. We wonder, concerning this approach, if the mediators did not notice or had noticed but did not care and did not take into consideration the composition and the structural nature of the armed movements of Darfur and their connection

to the tribal divisions in the region. For everybody, it is clear that the way the agreement was signed will only encourage the continuation of bloody tribal conflicts in the area.

The Position of the Communist Party on the Deployment of United Nations Troops in Darfur

The position of the Communist Party of the Sudan on the deployment of the United Nations troops in Darfur is based on the following factors:

1. A key point is that the deployment of UN troops has become a general and essential demand of the people of Darfur, especially the inhabitants of the displaced person camps, to protect them against the constant attacks of the Janjawid. The African Union troops have failed to provide much protection, and the government troops are considered as a party to the conflict with a very hostile attitude toward the people of Darfur. What is at stake here is the safety of the people of Darfur and their protection from killing and physical liquidation. On such issues there is no room for a compromise. Hence, the party does support the deployment of the UN troops.
2. The deployment of the UN troops in Darfur should take place through wider consultation between the United Nations on one side and the government of Sudan and all the Sudanese political forces on the other side. These consultations should deal with all details related to the tasks, including the composition of these troops.
3. The role of the UN does not end by providing protection to the people of Darfur, but should be extended to achieve the political settlement for the crisis.

Searching for All Means to Resolve the Crisis

In September 2006, the Communist Party sent an envoy to meet the leadership of Darfur armed factions that did not sign the Abuja agreement. Our idea was to discuss the possible means of overcoming the severe tensions and the acute polarizations in the country and to explore the possibilities of laying down the foundations for a sustainable and equitable peace that can prevent the fragmentation of the country.

In the meetings with the leaderships of the movements, we put forward the following points as a basis for discussions and consultations:

1. Darfur is sustaining a real tragedy. This tragedy and disaster have brought about broad international support and interaction. Does this international support not require that the Darfur armed movements try to unify their efforts and forces around a united program, or at least a unified negotiating position that serves the aspiration and demands of the people of Darfur?
2. The Abuja agreement did not stop the war. Not only that, but some figures of the international community have started to warn of its collapse. Also, the deployment of international forces in Darfur has increased the polarization between Sudan government and the international community, which reflects badly on the country. On the other hand, the public statements of some officers of the international community, and especially the UN representatives in the Sudan, paved the way for adding annexes to Abuja agreement that may satisfy those who had initially rejected the agreement. However, these statements received little response from some leaders of the Sudanese regime. As to the Communist Party, despite its

public reservations about the Abuja agreement, the party is not rejecting it; it can see the possibility of improving the agreement by adding new annexes. The party strongly rejects any attempt to threaten or stigmatize the factions that refused to sign with charges of treason. On the contrary, the party can see the importance of listening to the demands of those factions and looking for common grounds with them. However, a question remains: To what extent are those factions ready to react to the positive signals from the UN regarding the possibilities of adding annexes to the agreement? What are their proposals and suggestions in this aspect?

3. At the end of the day, the Sudan is not a government property, nor a property of any of the opposition forces. It is for all. And for that reason the main task will be to exhaust all means and measures to continue the peace process and to reach a national consensus that is capable of stopping the bloodshed and laying the foundations for an equitable peace and democratic transformation in response to the demands of the people of Darfur as well as of all other marginalized territories in the country.

The points raised by the Darfurian factions that met the Party envoy were as follows:

1. Because the Darfur problem is a part of the overall crisis of the Sudan, all Darfur factions showed their readiness to join any project for national unity that could be agreed upon by all Sudanese parties aiming at paving the way for peace, unity, democracy, and equitable development in the country.
2. Their readiness to negotiate annexes with the government to be added to the Abuja agreement.
3. Their negotiating position includes:
   a) To agree upon a mechanism that disarms the Janjawid and secures protection for the civilians.
   b) To agree upon compensations for the affected population, including compensation for loss of life, psychological impact, loss of property, and provision of shelter.
   c) That Darfur shall continue to be one region (not divided into three regions as it is now) under a real federalism of four levels: federal, regional, state, and local.
   d) That Darfur people shall participate in all the central state institutions, both the civil and the military, and that the representation should be according to population density and the parameters of positive discrimination. Some of the factions suggested the formation of a presidential council with a rotating chairmanship or a vice-president from every region.
   e) That 36 percent of the state general budget should be allocated to Darfur, over and above establishing a fund of 6 percent from the national income for 10 years, which is to be allocated for the development of Darfur.
   f) Darfur factions should keep their troops during the transitional period, and those troops should be financed from the central budget.

The Communist Party held several meetings with representatives of the international community and the United Nations to discuss the Darfur problem and the peace process in the country. In these meetings the party confirmed that consultations between the international community and all the Sudanese political parties are necessary and important for the purpose of reaching effective solutions for the country's problems. For such consultations to be useful and of value they should take place at the time of developments and not thereafter. For example, through the early consultations, the issue of referendum on having one Darfur state or three states could have been avoided on the basis that Darfur originally was one united region. Equally true, it was possible to find an acceptable solution for the Abyei problem if, before the resolution of the committee of experts, serious consultations were carried out with all the political parties and with the people of the region, especially the local leaders.

The search for means to resolve the Darfur crisis is not limited to the Communist Party. There are other efforts, including many popular forums in Sudan such as the Darfur Forum, Darfur Lawyers, national and international NGOs, and more. All these bodies are working steadily for the sake of the Darfur issue in terms of launching initiatives that reject the military option, organizing seminars and workshops, helping in the attempts to convene the Darfur–Darfur dialogue or conference, looking at the crisis in its national perspective, trying to unify the Darfurian movements, launching campaigns that address the grave human rights violations and atrocities in Darfur, and providing legal protection for the activists working in Darfur.

The Vision of the Communist Party Toward the Comprehensive Settlement of the Crisis

First, top priority should be given to addressing the disastrous and the tragic situation in the region through immediate measures under the auspices of the United Nations and African Union as agreed to in Addis Ababa. These measures include the following:

1. Deployment of international troops in the region to assist the already deployed African troops in prohibiting all the military operations; protection of refugee camp dwellers and the displaced and ensuring the delivery of aid, food, and medication through safe corridors; imposing a no-fly zone as well as international and regional supervision to the cease fire; introducing an effective mechanism to disarm the region and supervising all means of land transport and entrance points to prevent the smuggling of arms into the region.
2. To introduce effective mechanisms to disarm the Janjawid and bring them to justice.
3. To activate the international mechanism that was assigned to investigate atrocities of ethnic cleansing, genocide, and so on, and to identify the criminals and bring them to justice.
4. To work toward the return of the refugees and the displaced to their homelands and to ensure their protection and compensation for their losses.

Second, the factions that did not sign the Abuja agreement must come to the negotiating table with the government. This should be done under the supervision of the United Nations and the African Union with the purpose of adding annexes to the Abuja agreement.

Third, a Darfurian–Darfurian conference must be organized with the purpose of giving the people of Darfur the chance to address the Abuja agreement and the possible annexes that may be added to it. The resolutions of the conference should be annexed to the peace agreement. The conference should be held in a free and democratic environment, away from the government and with the help of the United Nations.

Fourth, the Communist Party believes that the right approach to the Darfur problem is to recognize it not as just a tribal conflict but as a result of the general crisis of the Sudan, which is characterized by the continuous marginalization of the peripheries, and Darfur is one of these peripheries. Consequently, the problem is political and requires a national political solution. Hence, the idea of convening a national political conference on Darfur becomes a necessity. Such conference is to be attended by all the political forces in the country, including the Darfurian armed movements as well as all sectors of the Darfur people. The conference must embrace all the initiatives attempting to resolve the conflict.

Fifth, Darfur bears the effects of the demographic changes and the geopolitics of the Sudanese state in the western border of the country. This border is a vast, open, and unprotected boundary with the African countries of Chad, Central Africa, and Libya. During the Libyan–Chadian conflict, the factions started their attack from Darfur in Sudan, and the losers took refuge in Darfur to reorganize their troops before attacking again. Central Africa launches frequent attacks through Darfur in revenge for the intervention of the Khartoum government in its internal affairs and conflicts. These vast, open, and unprotected boundaries can only be protected through the policy of good neighborly relations, and that the Sudan should see to it not to be used as a conduit to others' interest in Africa under the name of Islam and Arab Nationalism.

Finally, the Communist Party of the Sudan believes that the solution to the problems of the country can be achieved only through addressing these various problems comprehensivly. The best mechanism for such an approach is convening a national conference attended by all the Sudanese political forces. In this conference, all the agreements – Naivasha, Abuja, The East, Cairo, and so on – should be tabled not to open them for re-discussion but to accommodate the other opinions aimed at further refinement of these agreements, and to participate in monitoring and implementing of these agreements. This will pave the way for the political forces in the conference to adopt a national consensus project, which is the only tool that can save the country. The project should be based on acknowledging ethnic diversity and the facts of unequal development of certain regions of the Sudan, and confront, through democratic means, the problems of inequality in access to power and to national wealth so that the Sudan can be preserved, united, and secured for all of its peoples.

Appendix G

The Darfur Consortium, the UN Security Council, and the International Criminal Court (ICC):
Taking First Steps Toward Justice in Darfur[1]

Abdel Monim Elgak

Since the conflict in Darfur in Western Sudan escalated in April 2003 more than 400,000 people are estimated to have died and more than two million have been forced from their homes. The deliberate targeting of civilians and the wholesale destruction of settlements has been a hallmark of the violence that many have called genocide. In February 2005 a UN Commission of Enquiry found that "[g]overnment forces and militias conducted indiscriminate attacks, including killing of civilians, torture, enforced disappearances, destruction of villages, rape, and other forms of sexual violence, pillaging and forced displacement, throughout Darfur. These acts were conducted on a widespread and systematic basis, and therefore may amount to crimes against humanity."

Over the last fifteen months a group of Africa-focused and Africa-based NGOs, academics, independent legal experts, and parliamentarians has been working, dedicated to finding a solution to this human rights and humanitarian crisis. This group, known as the Darfur Consortium (see www.darfurconsortium.org), was born out of a deep conviction that crimes against humanity were unfolding in Darfur and that the international response to the crisis had been utterly inadequate. At the end of 2004 when the consortium first began to emerge, reflection on the tenth anniversary of the 1994 Rwanda genocide only heightened the concern about international inaction.

Since its emergence in September 2004, the consortium has positioned itself to speak with credibility on the international stage, galvanized a unique advocacy effort across three continents, and impacted action by the international community around questions of accountability and protection in Darfur. One of the most significant achievements of the consortium during 2005 was the part it played in helping to secure the historic first referral by the UN Security Council of the situation in Darfur to the International Criminal Court (ICC) in the last week of March 2005 (Resolution 1593).

This case study will reflect on the experience of the Darfur Consortium – with particular reference to the consortium's work around achieving a referral of the situation in Darfur to the ICC – in order to identify what lessons might be drawn for enhancing civil society engagement within the multilateral sphere.

Birth of the Consortium
The way in which the consortium took shape was deeply influenced by an exploration of the context within which the "question of Darfur" was being discussed in late

2004 in international forums. The establishment of the consortium itself was in many ways a strategic reaction to the recognition that a highly polarized global advocacy climate jeopardized an effective response to Darfur.

With the conflict in Darfur widely and reductively characterized as one pitting "Africans" against "Arabs," perceptions were hostage to ideology and mistrust and exacerbated by post-9/11 geo-politics. Statements and calls for action were viewed as lacking an objective basis, depending on the political allegiance of the messenger. That the United States, for example, had accused the government of Sudan of genocide was often conveniently juxtaposed against the explicit rejection of the charge by regional actors. The result was not only stasis in the international response but also one of escalating violence on the ground.

There was clearly a "gap" in the spectrum of voices that needed to be heard and heeded in the debate on Darfur. First, it was suggested that as the African Union (AU) was playing a leading role in the crisis, brokering the political negotiations and deploying cease-fire monitoring troops on the ground, African civil society could make a vital contribution. Second, it was recognized that the AU provided a unique forum for Arab/North African and sub-Saharan African voices to come together, united by adherence to common goals, including a collective responsibility for the protection of human rights on the continent (Article 3 (h) of the AU Constitutive Act). Independent assessment of, and advocacy around, Darfur by a pan-African group could, *inter alia*, help mitigate the skilful exploitation of fissures in international society around the approach to Darfur and make a unique contribution to helping to understand the crisis and positing solutions.

Creating a Common Framework
Power in Information: Positioning the Consortium Authoritatively
The consortium recognized that it needed to root itself in a firsthand assessment of the situation in Darfur early on. Intensive briefing sessions from Darfurian and Sudanese activists at each of the consortium meetings created an atmosphere within which NGOs from across the continent began to locate themselves as part of a coalition for Darfur. Further, an assessment mission by African human rights activists to Chad and Sudan was conceived as the foundation stone of the development of the consortium's advocacy platform.

Engagement on the ground and directly with Darfurian colleagues was essential not only for establishing a credible basis upon which the consortium could speak. It also provided a process for building consensus within the consortium around contested issues – and particularly so with respect to the ICC referral. There were concerns by some, for example, that triggering the involvement of the ICC in the midst of an ongoing conflict might in fact inflame the violence. Others worried about the stance of North African and Arab states. Further to the mission and to consultation with Darfur activists the consortium was able to argue the opposite: A referral would not be inimical to the peace process; an internationally supported effort to combat impunity was essential to the return of refugees; and it might even have a protective effect. Support for and solidarity with Sudanese and Darfurian activists, civil society groups, and NGOs (including those in the diaspora) was at the heart of the approach.

Mapping the "Outsiders"

The consortium initially focused on the AU as the cohering frame for its work, introducing itself as an NGO effort in support of the major multilateral actor leading the international response to Darfur. It built upon this to reach out to other major multilateral actors with overlapping membership such as the UN Security Council. Targets of the consortium's advocacy over the last year have been a whole range of multilateral institutions, from the African Union (in particular the African Commission on Human and Peoples Rights (ACHPR) to the Arab League, with respect to a series of goals from increasing the representation of women in the political negotiations to improving the local courts system in Darfur. From the outset it was recognized that finding a solution to the crisis in Darfur would require both engagement with a broad range of actors in the multilateral sphere and an understanding of the diversity of political and economic interests and historical entanglements in Darfur.

Negotiating the ICC referral epitomized how multifaceted and nimble the consortium had to be in presenting and arguing its message. At one point in the run up to the final UN Security Council votes on the series of Sudan resolutions, for example, there were signs that African states were retreating from their earlier support for the ICC referral and were circulating a proposal for an "African Alternative" and an "African Panel for Criminal Justice and Reconciliation." The AU, for its part, was uneasy about the ambiguity that might be created around the status of its mission in the event of a UN deployment. At the same time, at the level of the UN Security Council itself, the member states had to square their relationships with the government of Sudan from investment in oil and military equipment to cultural and Pan-Arabism ties.

Creating an "Insider" Consensus: Acknowledging Complexity/Ambiguity and Using Human Rights

The very first publication of the consortium (a background note on the origin of the crisis) acknowledged and emphasized the complexity of the Darfur conflict. It situated the crisis in a comprehensive historical context, and in its multiple cultural, political, and ecological factors: It was misleading, for example, to describe the conflict as pitting "Arabs" against "Black Africans" or as simply arising from tension between pastoralists and farmers. Members of the consortium were one in acknowledging the egregious nature of the violence and suffering unfolding in Darfur. The challenge, however, was how to develop an analysis and pragmatic set of proposals that could help contribute to finding solutions in the midst of such complexity, while avoiding antagonistic, overly politicized, and simplistic positions.

It was agreed that protection of the people of Darfur in accordance with international humanitarian and human rights law would be the key foundation stone of a common advocacy framework. This would cut through ideologies and political allegiances and provide a way to think about the development of a just and peaceful solution to the conflict. The African Union, in which all the key state players had a common membership, had been recently reconstituted as an organization where the protection of human rights was an organizational objective and a right of intervention for the union in cases of "grave circumstances, namely war crimes, genocide and crimes against humanity" (Article 4 (h) AU Constitutive Act). This guiding international human rights and humanitarian law framework was the context in which the decision to embark on advocacy for a referral of the situation in Darfur to the ICC could emerge as a key focus.

Although the consortium decided to prioritize advocacy around an urgent ICC referral, it was viewed as only part of a continuum of necessary steps for the achievement of justice in Darfur. It was agreed that the consortium would pursue a tiered, yet parallel, approach to justice and accountability, including the exploration of possible compensation programs, the regeneration of local tribal mechanisms, and advocating for the establishment of a truth and reconciliation process. Advocacy for the referral as a necessary part of a broader package also turned out to be politically more palatable to some audiences. This comprehensive approach was ultimately adopted by the UN Security Council.

Strategies for Dancing in the Multilateral Sphere
Suppleness of Identity and Roles
The initial gathering of NGOs at the founding meeting in Pretoria in September 2004 included sub-Sahara African NGOs, Africa-focused international NGOs, and Sudanese NGOs and civil society organizations, in addition to one human rights NGO from the North Africa/Arab region. Against the background of a complex advocacy context, much strength lay in this diversity, both in terms of expertise and the capacity to present the Consortium's message through a variety of lenses. A couple of aspects can be highlighted.

1. *The primary "African" identity of the coalition opened doors.* During the ICC referral campaign when alternative "African solutions" were being touted, it was the consortium's identity as encompassing Arab, African, Christian, and Muslim voices coupled with its authoritative connection to Darfur and Sudan, which could argue credibly that the ICC was at once an international *and* an African court, reflecting African policy and practice – and that the people of Darfur deserved to see justice on the basis of their common humanity.
2. *Access to a variety of audiences.* The consortium was made up of both Africa-based and Africa-focused organizations, including international organizations. This not only enriched the variety of strategic perspectives for discussion but also opened doors to a range of audiences. While sub-Sahara African NGOs in the consortium were, for example, generally more knowledgeable about AU structures and politics, the Africa-focused international NGOs were familiar with the UN human-rights mechanisms. In the final weeks of March 2005, the consortium was able to simultaneously conduct a sustained outreach to Security Council member states and other Permanent Missions in New York, monitor the shifting African Union position from Abuja and Addis Ababa, press the position of the consortium with the Arab League summit opening in Algiers, and advocacy before influential governments and missions Abuja, Geneva, London, Khartoum, and Cairo.
3. *Strategic use of lead organizations.* The series of meetings and advocacy activities undertaken by the consortium under the leadership of one of the Egyptian members around the ICC referral in late February in Cairo had an extremely powerful effect on the discussion of the referral in the North Africa requirement.

D. *No requirement for rigid consensus.* On some occasions positions were adopted by groups of consortium members that could not be shared or publicly embraced by all, whether because of political, legal, or security reasons.

E. *A protective umbrella.* Sudanese and Darfurian organizations have been able to closely participate and make central contributions to the work of the consortium, while remaining sheltered when necessary.

The identity of the consortium is an ongoing process of exploration. As more and more organizations have joined and introduced new perspectives and fora to the discussion, there has been an effort to remain flexible and recognize the multiplier effects of different activities. At the same time, there is a recognition that the flexible identity construction and organization of the consortium may have to be rethought.

Adaptive Strategies and Methodologies

Flexibility has also been the hallmark of the consortium in its planning and activities. For example, just a day before two major parallel missions to Sudan and Chad had planned to depart, the government of Sudan decided to revoke the consortium's delegation permission to enter Sudan. When the news came that the UN Commission of Inquiry Report on Darfur had also been published that same day, a new plan was drawn up to build on the convergence of events. It was agreed that a task force would remain in Kampala to generate a detailed analysis of the implications of the report while the Chad mission team and agenda were reconfigured. With sufficient international law expertise delegated to the task force, the mission team determined to focus on eliciting views from the ground on the possible impact of an ICC referral. Furthermore, as the consortium could not travel to Sudan to meet with colleagues in Darfur, arrangements were made for a team of Darfurian activists and lawyers to come to Kampala to confer with the task force and join in the postmission meeting where leading policy makers and thematic experts would help develop an advocacy platform.

Building Capacity and Will for Committed Collaborative Engagement

The consortium has grown in strength and effectiveness over the last year through anchoring the development of its advocacy platform to direct engagement with Darfurian activists, using a multilateral institution (the ACHPR) as a cohering framework for the consortium's program of activities and seeding strong bonds of solidarity and commitment through the organization of an intensive mission and meetings in February, fuelled by meetings of subgroups of the consortium, regular communication and information sharing. Finally, and critically, the consortium was lucky enough to be able to secure the active support of funders, and particularly operational funders, early on in the process. This allowed us to build immediately on the momentum created by the first deliberations of the consortium.

The Continuing Story

The consortium has struggled successfully to understand and negotiate the shifting pressures felt by the multilateral groupings essential to influencing the final decision of the UN Security Council on the ICC referral.

One challenge facing the consortium, and particularly since the referral, has been how to fully engage Arab and North African human rights and civil society NGOs with the situation in Darfur. For some North African NGOs, the AU is not a natural forum and the high-profile engagement of the AU in Darfur has tended to marginalize the role and responsibilities of North African and Arab states in the crisis. Change in the political atmosphere post the ICC referral has also forced the government of Sudan to turn to Arab/North African allies to seek support for a challenge to ICC jurisdiction. One of the most distancing aspects also continues to be the insistence by some on labeling the Darfur conflict as one of "Arabs" versus "Black Africans," which has been coupled with the silence of North African/Arab actors in the face of the escalating violence. These reactions require further exploration and analysis with like-minded NGOs from the North Africa/Arab region. This outreach will be an important focus of the consortium's work in its next phase.

Note

[1] Case study paper prepared for the workshop "Building Bridges – Engaging Civil Society from OIC countries and other Muslim communities with the Multilateral Sphere," organized by the Montreal International Forum (FIM) in partnership with the Institute of Strategic and International Studies (ISIS-Malaysia), January 16–18, 2006, in Hotel Nikko, Kuala Lumpur, Malaysia. The paper was also published in *Respect: Journal for Human Rights' Culture and Issues of Cultural Diversity*, 8th Issue, July 2008 [www.sudan-forall.org].

Appendix H

Darfur Resistance Movements:
A Fact Sheet

At the outbreak of the armed resistance in Darfur in 2003 there were two major organizations, the Sudan Liberation Movement/Army (SLM/A) and the Justice and Equality Movement (JEM). Since then, these two major groups have splintered into several competing factions. The multiplicity of these groups has made it difficult for Darfurians to negotiate with the government based on a united position, and has given the NIF regime an excuse to continue its atrocities and plunge the whole country into an endless abyss of violence. While Darfurian groups are splintered along fault lines shaped by ethnic or clan divisions among their leadership, the NIF regime and its security organs have also played a role in furthering these splits. Pressure from international power brokers and mediators in the aftermath of the Abuja peace talks and the resulting 2006 Darfur Peace Agreement (DPA), which many of the Darfurian rebels refused to sign, has furthered intensified the fragmentation of the Darfur rebel groups. This fragmentation is often a major source of confusion for those interested in familiarizing themselves with the Darfur crisis. Accordingly, as editors, we thought it would be helpful to create this brief fact sheet on the various resistance movements in Darfur.

1. Justice and Equality Movement (JEM)

The Justice and Equality Movement (JEM) is one of the strongest and most efficient among the Darfur rebel groups. Its current leadership includes several Darfurian intellectuals who were former members of the National Islamic Front led by the Islamist leader Hassan Al-Turabi, the intellectual force behind the Islamist military coup that ushered the regime of Omar Hassan Al Bashir into power in 1989. Several JEM leaders sided with Al-Turabi when he broke away from the NIF and created the National Popular Congress (NPC). JEM leadership denies any current linkages with Al-Turabi and has since moved to consolidate a more secular political position that differs radically from that of the NCP. JEM's most prominent leader is Dr. Khalil Ibrahim Muhammad, who recently led an unprecedented major military incursion into Omdurman, the sister-city of the Sudanese capital, Khartoum, that shocked the NIF regime despite its success in squashing the effort. JEM has suffered several splits within it membership, which in turn led to the creation of numerous factions along ethnic or clan lines, such as those led by Idris Azraq and Jibril Abdel Karim Bari.

JEM Break-Away Groups
A. The National Movement for Reform and Development (NMRD)

NMRD is one of JEM's splinter groups that broke away in 2004. It is currently led by Jibril Abdel Karim Bari (a.k.a. Tek), the former JEM Chief of Staff who has since joined the Chadian army as a colonel in the Republican guards of Idris Debi's government. All the leaders of the NMRD are reported to be of Zaghawa origin and more specifically from the Kabka clan. Bari is reported to be on both the ICC and the UN sanctions list for alleged war crimes. Another JEM splinter group led by former JEM commander Mohamed Saleh was reported to have joined NMRD.

B. Other JEM Break-Away Groups
These include less effective groups, such as JEM-Peace Wing, JEM-Field Revolutionary Command, and JEM-Popular Forces Troops.

2. The Sudan Liberation Movement/Army (SLM/A)
SLM/A was originally named the Darfur Liberation Front, which was established in the late 1980s in the aftermath of the major drought of the mid-1980s. Its original ethnic core was Fur, but later on expanded to include other groups such as Zaghawa and Masalit peoples. After the insurrection of 2003, the movement was renamed SLM/A, which indicates a clear affinity with the SPLM/A's vision considering its long history of recruitment among Darfurians as in the case of the earlier SPLA battalion led by Daud Bolad that was crushed in the early 1990s. Clearly influenced by the SPLM/A's ideas and programs, SLM/A leadership advocated a much more secular program that calls for the restructuring of power at the national level to address the demands and aspirations of the marginalized regions of the Sudan.

In the aftermath of the DPA in 2006, the SLM/A split into two major factions mostly along ethnic lines. The first faction is now led by Minni Arkou Minnawi, a Zaghawa who was in charge of its military wing and the only leader who signed the DPA in 2006. The other faction is headed by Abdel Wahid Mohamed Nur, a Fur who was in control of the political wing and refused to sign the DPA. Eventually, several factions also emerged as a result of further fractures within these two majors groups.

A. SLM/A-Minni Arko Minnawi Faction
As mentioned above, this faction is led by Minnawi who signed the Darfur Peace Agreement (DPA) in 2006 and was consequently appointed as a special adviser to the president of Sudan. Many of Minnawi's followers and fighters have since defected and joined other factions who refused to the sign the DPA.

B. SLM/A-Abdel Wahid Faction
As mentioned above, this faction is led by Abdel Wahid Mohamed Nur, who is now based in Paris. Still considered to be among the strongest groups, the SLM/A-Abdel Wahid Faction started to lose some of its followers and fighters, who have since joined break-away groups, including SLM/A-Classic or SLM-Abdel Shafi Faction. Abdel Wahid Mohamed Nur refused to attend the Libyan sponsored peace talks in Sirte, and has since made the deployment of the UN-AU hybrid peacekeeping force in Darfur a pre-condition to any future participation in similar talks.

C. SLM/A-Unity Faction
Led by Abdallah Yehya, the SLM/A-Unity Faction is predominantly Zaghawa from North Darfur. Its fighters are composed of different groups such as Group of 19 (G19). One of its prominent and most popular leaders is Suleiman Jamous, who emerged

as a father figure for the Darfur resistance movements and is now the SLM/A-Unity Faction's coordinator for humanitarian affairs. The group continues to collaborate with the Nur-Faction in consolidating military efforts and political positions vis-à-vis peace negotiations since the DPA in 2006. According to news reports the SLM-Unity Faction has been blamed for the 29 September 2007 attack on an AU base near Haskanita, in which 10 AU soldiers were killed.

D. Other SLM/A Break-Away Groups

Reports from the ground point to the emergence of several groups, such as the Free Will, the Greater Sudan Liberation Movement/Army, and the National Movement for the Elimination of Marginalization, among many others.

3. The National Redemption Front (NRF)

This is the name of the now defunct umbrella group that sought to unite the different Darfurian rebel factions who are opposed to the 2006 DPA, which includes JEM and other splinter groups. Its leadership includes veteran politician and intellectual Ahmad Ibrahim Diraig, the former leader of the Darfur Renaissance Front (DRF) and the Federal Democratic Alliance (FDA), which are all now defunct.

Sources

Sources for this fact sheet include news reports from major media outlets, such as the BBC and Al-Jazeera, and memorandums of the various Darfurian resistance movements and support groups.

Appendix I

The Black Book:
Imbalance of Power and Wealth in Sudan, Part 1

Seekers of Truth and Justice
Translated by Abdullahi Osman El-Tom

March 2004
[Editors' Note]

In reproducing *The Black Book* as an appendix to this volume we decided to include only Part One of the publication and not Part Two due to space limitations. Part Two first appeared in August 2002 and was later reproduced in a communiqué of the Justice and Equality Movement (JEM) in 2004. Using statistical evidence, it methodically documents the inequities in national wealth sharing, services, development, and access to power in the Sudan, particularly during the current reign of "the Government of National Salvation," which formed the subject of Part One's narrative. Part Two provides statistical information drawn from various sources, including official government reports, presidential decrees, and documents from the Sudan Civil Service. For readers who are interested in Part Two, we refer them to JEM's official website: http://www.sudanjem.com/sudan-alt/english/books/ blackbook_part2/bbtwo.htm.

Translator's Introduction

In 2000, a mysterious book appeared in the streets of Khartoum under the title *The Black Book: Imbalance of Power and Wealth in the Sudan*. The mystery of the book was strengthened by its impeccable method of distribution necessitated by the Al Bashir regime's firm grip over information in the country. The launch of the work consisted of a one-off distribution at gates of major mosques following Friday prayers. Soon after, the circulation of the *Book* gained momentum. Photocopying made it available all over the country and abroad. The book soon became the most talked about document in the country even though most readers had never seen an original copy of it. Illiterate people, too, became familiar with the *Book*, as it was debated at every gathering.

The thesis of the *Black Book* is simple but disturbing. Using statistics, the authors claim that Sudan is controlled by only one region (northern region) with just over 5 percent of Sudan's population. Within this hegemonic region, power is monopolized by only three ethnic groups. The *Book* then gives detailed statistics about the hegemony of the Northern Region over the whole country. All Sudan's presidents and prime ministers, for example, came from this Region. Members of this Region also control all key positions in the country, ranging from ministerial posts to heads of banks, developmental schemes, army, police, and so forth.

Part Two of the Black Book did not appear until August 2002. Unlike Part One, this one joined the global world and appeared in a website (Sudanjem.com). Part Two has less talk but more statistics. Altogether, there are more than 200 tables in it.

As of March 2003, some of the activists involved in the preparation of the *Book* took up arms against the government. The armed uprising, referred to as the Darfur Conflict, constitutes Africa's youngest civil war. To date, this war has resulted in 800,000 displaced persons, 120,000 refugees, and no less than 100,000 fatalities.

In translating the *Book* from Arabic, I did my best to remain faithful to the text. Passages that are of no value for the English reader have been eliminated. These passages are either steeped in Arabic metaphors, or elsewhere presuppose some knowledge that is particular to Sudan's history, folklore, and traditions. Retaining them in the text requires substantial explanation that lies beyond my role as a translator.

March 22, 2004

Dedication
To those who filled themselves with haughtiness, arrogance, and feelings of superiority, wishing to silence our *Black Book* or elsewhere replace it with their White Book.
To the Sudanese people who have endured oppression, injustice, and tyranny.
To the majority of the Sudanese people who still suffer marginalization from power and wealth.
To those who work for justice and equality with extreme honesty and self-denial.

Introduction to Part 1
We present our work, "The Black Book: Imbalance of Power and Wealth in the Sudan," as a document that exposes the performance of successive governments that ruled the Sudan in its recent history. This book is not driven by narrow motives that seek to incriminate or blame certain circles in the country. Rather, it is a critical work that documents objective facts that are hard to overlook.

This book is an exposé of the injustice that was visited on the Sudan by the successive governments that have ruled it since independence in 1956. The pattern of injustice remained almost the same throughout, irrespective of the political orientation of the incumbent government: secular, theocratic, dictatorial, or – presumably – democratic. They all displayed blatant favoritism toward one particular circle in the Sudan to the detriment of all others. The favored part of the Sudan attracted disproportionate attention, care, services, and developmental resources from those successive governments. That favored part of the Sudan is the Northern Region, where most of the ruling elite come from.

For the purpose of this Book, we have divided the Sudan into five regions:
1. Northern Region: Current River Nile and Northern States
2. Eastern Region: Gadharif, Kasala, and Red Sea States
3. Central Region: Gezira, Sinnar, Blue Nile, and Khartoum States
4. Southern Region: Upper Nile, Bahr Alghazal, and Equatorial States
5. Western Region: Kordofan and Darfur States

In its blatant favoritism toward the Northern Region, successive governments in the Sudan have systematically breached the rights of its other citizens. They deviated from the principle of treating all citizens as equal. They have accused others of racism, a crime that they have themselves practiced every single day of their reign.

Successive governments of the Sudan have thus lost their credibility and have, therefore, disqualified themselves insofar as support of the Sudanese citizens is concerned.

In presenting this book, we intend to shed light on this unfortunate reality and make it crystal clear for all.

The new millennium is now approaching, full of hope and optimism. Due to its recent history, Sudan meets the new millennium steeped in poverty, illiteracy, disease, and lack of development. Despite this, Sudanese citizens are invited to rise to the challenge by appropriating the same powers that have so far crippled them. Let them do that in collaboration with other global citizens whose rulers have delivered and have prepared them for the new area.

Introducing Sudan

Sudan lies between lines 14 and 38 latitudes East, and 4 and 22 longitudes North of the Equator. It occupies 968,000 square miles. The White Nile, the Blue Nile, and River Nile zigzag their way through it and provide rich sources of water and food. Sudan is surrounded by nine countries: Chad, Central African Republic, the Democratic Republic of Congo, Uganda, Kenya, Ethiopia, Eritrea, Egypt, and Libya. The position of Sudan among these countries is source of wealth but equally of trouble. Sudan also touches the Red Sea with a shore that extends to 309km. Sudan has three distinctive geographical zones. North of Latitude 16 is barren desert. Below Latitude 16 is a region rich in equatorial climate. In between is a savanna belt that gets drier the further you move to the north. These distinctive climatic variations have their impact on Sudan's populations and their cultures.

The last National Census, taken in 1993, put Sudan's population at 24,940,703 with annual growth of 2.6 percent. For the purpose of this document, we divide Sudan into five regions. Each of these regions has its historical, cultural, and administrative particularities. Furthermore, each region consists of a number of provinces (see Table 1).

Table 1. **Populations of Sudan Regions**

Region	States	Population	Percentage of Population
Eastern	Kasala, Gadharif, Red Sea	3,051,958	12.7%
Northern Region	Northern, River Nile	1,291,620	5.4%
Central Region	Gezira, Sinnar, White Nile Blue Nile, Khartoum	8,829,367	36.9%
Western Region	Kordofan, Darfur	7,912,285	33.1%
Southern Region	Upper Nile, Bahr Alghazal Equatorial	2,845,480	11.9%
Total	–	23,930,710	100%

Khartoum, the capital, which we include within the Central Region, has a population of 3,413,034. More than half of this population come from deprived regions of the west and the south, primarily fleeing war and lack of development.

Natural Resources

Sudan is rich in natural resources, particularly agriculture and forestry. It has no less than 120,000,000 acres suitable for agriculture. Only 16,000,000 of that are currently under use. Agriculture is still dependent on rainfalls despite ample underground water. The economy of Sudan now rests on rain-fed agriculture. Major products include peanuts, hibiscus, sesame seeds, watermelon seeds, and gum arabic. Animal resources, like camels, sheep, and cattle, also feature in Sudan's export economy. Recently, petrol and gold have been added to the export wealth while the country still awaits exploitation of other minerals like copper and natural gas.

Administrative Division of the Country

A recent constitutional decree, 1996, divided the Sudan into twenty-six states. These are then grouped into five regions: three in the east, two in the north, five in the center, including the capital Khartoum, six in the west, and ten in the south. Each state has its government and its legislative council. If we exclude the south, which is still a war zone, whatever development we can find in the country has been confined to the north, Khartoum, part of the Central Region, and an even smaller part of the Eastern Region. The entire Western Region now lacks a single developmental scheme that could support one province for a single week. The oil refinery in Alobeid, in the Western Region, is now classified as a national project. As such, its proceeds are controlled by the central government in Khartoum. The oil wells at Abu Jabra and Maglad, also in the Western Region, have also come under similar strategy. Employment of local people is confined to digging these wells. All jobs from drivers and above are filled by labor imported from outside the area. Officers of the security personnel and most of their foot soldiers are carefully selected from one known ethnic category, so that not a single dinar goes to those who do not deserve.

Defining the State and Its Authority

Scholars rarely agree on how to define the state. Nonetheless, a consensus occurs regarding its essence and constituents. Calsen refers to the state as "a constellation of the nation." Others like Degi stress the constituent elements of the state, such as territory, population, and authority. Gamal Albanna, another scholar in this field, identifies five requirements for an Islamic state:
a. Primary aim is to develop the land (*Allah said I am making a Khalifa on the land. Qur'an, Albaqra Sura, Chapter X, verse mm*)
b. An environment that guarantees freedom (no compulsion on faith)
c. Justice as the main axis of state operation (*be just for justice is the essence Almaida Sura* of piety; Prophet Mohamed said: I have declared injustice *haram* ("strongly disallowed") for myself. I also made it haram for all of you so never be unjust)
d. Decision making rests on consultation (seek views of stakeholders first and when you act trust on Allah)

e. Rule based on Allah's *diktat* (Let the rule be based on Allah's words and let Allah be the sole God to be worshiped in the land)

In our modern understanding, a state must display the following:
a. Territory: A defined territory that is endorsed by relevant international authorities.
b. Population: People who live in the specified territory.
c. Ruling authority: The power that is legitimated to administer the territory and its people according to specified laws and institutions. The ruling authority must demonstrate its commitment to work for peace and for meeting basic needs of all within its domain.

Conditions for Accepting the Authority of the Ruler/Governing Power
The authority must demonstrate its commitment to maintain sovereignty of land against foreign intruders; treat its citizens equally; afford them peace and protection; guarantee dignified life; spread freedom and dignity; and must enable its citizens to fully participate in conducting their public affairs. All that is to take place within an environment that is conducive for participation of all without religious, ethnic, skin color, and gender discrimination. The state authority cannot only implement that without commitment to its national laws that regulates and divides powers among different state organs. Most important here is the separation between state powers, and in particular the political, the judicial, and the legislative.

Reflection on State Authorities
Executive Powers
These are vested in specified offices that are delegated to implement state policies regarding economy, politics, social needs, security, and general state-citizen relationship. Executive state organs must be subordinate to and committed to state legislative authorities.

Legislative Authorities
The duty of these bodies is to enact laws regarding state policies in the political, social, economic, and ethical areas. Legislative authorities draw their laws from religious, traditional, natural, and legal conventions. Legislative authorities should be committed to observe these laws that they make and ensure that the state and the public will do likewise.

Judicial Authorities
Their main function is to implement the law, protect the state constitution, and restore justice when disputes occur. These authorities can only function adequately if they maintain and respect their neutrality and independence. Independence of the judiciary should be maintained throughout its entire hierarchy, ranging from its lowest level, like the village court, to its highest level, the Constitutional Court.

Media
Media has only recently surfaced as an important player in modern state apparatus. It has since carved itself a space that has become indivisible from any democratic

state. The media now plays an important role in guarding state laws and constitution, similar to the role traditionally played by legislative powers. Moreover, it has become the avenue for channelling complaints regarding abuse of power, infringement of law by the powerful, corruption, and injustice at large. It has also become a voice for the powerless and a guardian for the dispossessed.

Examples of Imbalance of Division of Powers

State authority is a source of power and a tool for achieving prosperity for all within the nation. Sudan state is no exception in this regard. At its independence, 1956, it declared itself a sovereign state and raised its flag together with other slogans promising full commitment to work for the good of all within the new nation. Discrepancies between slogans and actions, however, appeared as early as the birth of the new state. Politics in Sudan was sectarian and dominated by the two religious houses, the house of the Mahdis and the house of the Mirghani. These two Houses corresponded (and still do) to the two leading political parties: the Umma Party of the Mahdis and the Democratic Unionist Party of the Mirghanis. In some ways, these two Houses inherited colonial powers on golden plates. In order to monopolize power in the country, both of these parties pegged leadership of their parties to that of their respective religious sects. Hence party leader were also sect leaders. The trick was that sect leaders had to come from families of the founding fathers of these religious sects. Moreover, a second strategy was also devised for the same purpose that was of exporting electoral candidates. Important party members from the center were encouraged to stand for elections in areas other than their own. The practice effectively made the emergence of locally born political representatives impossible. These practices ensured domination of the Northern Region over all other regions in the country and established a pattern for dealing with so-called marginalized areas. The pattern also meant that legislative powers remained under personnel who were primarily drawn from the Northern Region.

The pattern described here had, and still has, wide ramifications for political representation in the country. High representation of the Northern Region in the central government remained the same irrespective of knowledge gains in other Regions and changes in the political environment. Throughout its recent history, the Northern Region was represented by well over 50 percent at the central government. Its representation occasionally climbed over 70 percent. From independence to this day, not a single prime minister/president came from any Region other than the Northern Region. Like many third-world countries, Sudan was ruled by several governments that came to power through coups. However, several attempts to overthrow governments failed simply because their leaders came from Regions other than the Northern Region.

Next, we will examine the influence of state on distributions of power in the country. Figures and statistics will be used to explain these distributions.

Ministerial Representation

For the period 1954 to 1964, seventy-three ministerial positions were served in central government in Khartoum. Shares of the different regions are presented in Table 2.

Table 2. **Ministerial Positions, 1954–1964**

No.	Region	Positions	Overall Percentage
1	Eastern Region	1	1.4%
2	Northern Region	58	79%
3	Central Region	2	2.8%
4	Southern Region	12	16%
5	Western Region	0	0%

To place Table 2 within perspective, we have to refer to Sudan's population some decades ago. The 1986 census was the most reliable for our purpose.

Table 3. **Sudan Population Distribution, 1986**

No.	Region	Population	Percentage
1	Eastern Region	2,212,779	11.8%
2	Northern Region	1,016,406	5.4%
3	Central Region	4,958,038	26.5%
4	Southern Region	4,407,450	23.7%
5	Western	6,072,872	32.6%

Note that 5.4 percent of Sudan's population were represented at 79.5 percent, executive/ministerial posts in the Khartoum, the seat of the central government. During that period, five different governments took office, but the pattern remained the same.

Table 4. **National Governments, 1954–1964**

No.	Government	Years	Leader
1	First National Government	Jan. 1954	Alazhari
2	Second National Government	1955	Alazhari
3	Third National Government	1956	Alazhari
4	Kkaleel Government	1958	Khaleel
5	First Military Government	1958–1964	General Aboud

All of the governments listed in Table 4 based their powers on the aforementioned religious sects. General Aboud was no exception.

Following the national uprising in October 1964, Aboud was removed from office, thus making way for a democratic government in 1964–1969. Let us now see what happened to executive representation under democratic Sudan.

Table 5. **Ministerial Positions, 1964–1969**

Region	Positions	Percentage
Eastern	2	2.05%
Northern	55	67.9%
Central	5	6.2%
Southern	14	17.3%
Western	5	6.2%

Total of constitutional posts for this period was eighty-one positions. Strangely enough, the Western and Southern Regions contributed a lot to bringing the interim government under the Presidency of Sir Alkatim, who prepared the country for 1964's elections. Those who were selected as ministers from the Central Regions were of Northern Region origin.

The Reign of Numeiri, 1969–1985
Numeiri's military rule was characterized by internal instability leading to numerous cabinet reshuffles. In total, 115 ministers served in his different cabinets. The regional distribution is given in Table 6.

Table 6. **Ministerial Positions, 1969–1985**

Region	Positions	Percentage
Eastern	4	2.5%
Northern	79	68.7%
Central	19	16.5%
Southern	9	7.8%
Western	4	3.5%

Despite tremendous differences between the politics of Numeiri's and what went before him, domination of the Northern Region seemed to have persevered. Continuous flow of new ministerial blood and the reputation of Numeiri as a man for all Sudan did not dent the supremacy of the Northern Region. This situation increased the hegemony of the Northern Region and sabotaged all attempts to attract development projects for non-Northern Regions. A good example was the defunct Kafra Road, which was meant to connect Libya with El Fashir, the capital of Darfur in the Western Region. The desert highway road was to be financed wholly or partially by Libyan aid. Obstruction against construction of this road is well known to all and had caused tremendous loss of faith in the central government in the Western Region.

Appendix I

Following the demise of Numeiri, a transitional military government took over for a year to prepare the country for election. The new government operated under what came to be known as Transitional Military Council, headed by Swar Aldahab. Table 7 shows the constitution of the Transitional Military Council.

Table 7. **Transitional Military Council, 1985–1986**

Region	Positions	Percentage
Eastern Region	0	0%
Northern Region	21	70%
Central Region	3	10%
Southern Region	5	16.7%
Western Region	1	3.3%

Please note that the Sudanese Army has always been a national institution. That aspect of the army fared rather poorly given the regional representation of the Transititional Military Council.

The council was aided by senior members of the transitional government, but imbalance remained as before.

Second Democracy 1986–1989
The Transitional Military Council kept its word. It organized democratic elections and handed down power to the newly elected Prime Minister, Sadiq Al Mahdi, whose cabinet are presented in Table 8.

Table 8. **Ministerial Positions of Al Madhi's Government, 1986–1989**

Region	Positions	Percentage
Eastern Region	3	2.6%
Northern Region	55	47.4%
Central Region	17	14.7%
Southern Region	15	12.9%
Western Region	26	22.4%

Almahdi was the only leader who came close to perfection in the sense of forming a government in which all regions were reasonably represented, notwithstanding the evident overrepresentation of the North. Although the North was also overrepresented and the cabinet did not reflect the regional distribution of Sudan's population, we would like to acknowledge that Al Madhi deserves praise for having gone further than any other Sudanese leader. Al Mahdi was also the first head of state who allowed the important Ministry of Finance and Economy to be headed by some from the Western and the Central Region. These were Ibrahim Mansour and Omar Al Bashir from the Western Region and Omer Nur Aldayim from the Central Region.

Al Bashir's Government of National Salvation, 1989 to Date
Al Mahdi was overthrown in a bloodless coup in 1989 and a new government took office under the name "Revolution/Government of National Salvation." As the West has been instrumental in the formation of the ideology that inspired Albashir to take over, the Westerners were rewarded without challenging the domination of the North. This was reflected in the constitution of the Military Command Council, which controlled Sudan for Al Bashir's early years (see Table 9).

Table 9. **Revolutionary Command Council, June 1989**

Region	Positions	Percentage
Eastern	0	0%
Northern	10	66.7%
Central	0	0%
Southern	2	13.3%
Western	3	20%

When the power was settled in favor of the new government, the domination of the Northern Region was restored in line with previous political traditions. The new government operated under the slogans: Civilizational project, Islamization of life, equality and justice, and the principle of citizenship. Unfortunately, these slogans soon gave way to unchallenged hegemony of the Northern Region. The evidence for that can be seen in the cumulative high office positions, which continued until the last cabinet reshuffle in 1999. A total of 202 personnel are computed in Table 10.

Table 10. **Constitutional/Ministerial Positions, July 1989–December 1999**

Region	Positions	Percentage
Eastern	6	3%
Northern	120	59.4%
Central	18	8.9%
Southern	30	14.9%
Western	28	13.8%

As Table 10 shows, representation of the Northern Region reached 59.4 percent for a population that constituted only 12.2 percent. As such, the destiny of the remaining 87.8 percent of the population was subordinate to the will of the 12.2 percent who came from the Northern region. The Northern Region itself was not (still is not) a homogeneous entity. In fact, the North contained many groups that were subject to the same level of injustice and marginalization, like the Manaseer and Mahas. The first claimed Arab descent, while the latter were of Nubian origin. In fact, the entire Northern Region was dominated by only three ethnic groups, which also dominated the whole country. These were the Shaygia, the Jaalyeen, and the Danagla.

Table 10 also indicates that the National Salvation government had come to wreck what it had formed before, during its first Military Command Council. In so doing, the government demonstrated its inability to deviate from established patterns of injustice, despite the slogans it raised during its inception. Even in situations when the government appointed some personnel from other regions, it opted for those migrants from the Northern Region. Appointing those of Northern origin resident in other regions was a blatant attempt to deceive people and give the illusion of some air of regional representation.

In December 1999, and following a power struggle between Al Bashir and his ideologue Turabi, the government rushed in a number of presidential decrees. Changes contained in these decrees showed little attempt to avoid tribalism and regionalism as promised in earlier slogans. This was (and still is) evident from the choice of new recruits to high offices, ranging from the Republican Palace to ministers and state governors. To dispel any accusation of bias in our analysis, we present below a list of their new appointees, indicating their portfolios and regions. We will start with the Republican Palace (see Table 11).

Table 11. **Staff of the Republican Palace (December 1999)**

No.	Name	Position	Region
1	F. Marshall Omar A. Al Bashir	President	Northern
1	Ali Osman M. Taha	First Deputy President	Northern
3	George Kangoor Arop	Deputy President	Southern
4	Dr. Riak Mashar	Assistant President	Southern
5	Dr. Ibrahim Ahmed Omer	Assistant President	Northern
6	Lt. General Bakri Hasan Salih	Minister for Presidency of the Republic	Northern
7	Dr. Ahmed Ali Imam	Presidential Advisor	Northern
8	Dr. Nafayi Ali Nafayi	Peace Affairs	Northern
9	Dr. Altayib Mohamed Kheir	Security Affairs	Northern
10	Dr. Suaad Alfatih	Women and Children	Northern
11	Abdel Basit Sabdarat	Legal Politics	Northern
12	Salah Mohamed Salih	Water Resources	Northern

Following defection of Riak Mashar to SPLM, the Palace remained with 11 members, one of them from South Renk (Southern Region) while the rest originated north of Aljaile (town north of Khartoum). Those eleven were left to rule a country that extended from Geneina to Port Sudan and from Nimuli to Halfa. One wonders how those people could have imagined the rest of the country and how many of them had seen a third of it, let alone its entirety.

Where was the justice promised by the government in the field of division of power and where was the transparency often reiterated by official media? What was the role of this immense army of advisors? Had these appointments any purpose other than appeasing relatives and fellow members of ethnic groups? What are the jobs that they could do and that could not be accomplished by ministers of the federal government (as distinct from state governments)?

Below are names of the ministers of the federal government for the post-Turabi Period (December 1999 onward; see Table 12).

Table 12. **Federal Ministers**

Name	Region	
F. Marshall Omar Ahmed Al Bashir	Northern	
Ali Osman Taha	Northern	
George Kangoor Arobe	Southern	
Dr. Riak Mashar	Southern	
Ibrahim Ahmed Omer	Northern	
Dr. Mustafa Osman Ismael	Northern	
Lt. General Abdel Rahman Siralkhatim	Northern	
Dr. Mohamed Kheir Alzibair	Northern	
Dr. Awad Ahmed Aljaz	Northern	
Dr. Zibair Bashir Taha	Northern	
Dr. Abdalla Hasan Ahmed	Northern	
Dr. Qutbi Almahdi	Northern	
Abdel Basit Sabdarat	Northern	
Dr. Abdalla Mohamed Seed Ahmed	Northern	
Ali Ganmar Osman Yasin	Northern	
Kamal Ali Ahmed	Northern	
Badria Sulaiman	Northern	
Abdel Haleem Almuaafi	Central	
Abul Gasim Mohamed Ibrahim	Central	
Dr. Ghazi Salah Aldin Atabani	Central	
Ahmed Ibrahim Altahir	Western	
Lt. General Tigani Adam Tahir	Western	
F. .Marshall Ibrahim Sulaiman	Western	(continued)

Mekki Ali Bilal	Western
Dr. Alhaj Adam Yousif	Western
Mohamed Tahir Bilal	Eastern
Dr. Lam Akol	Southern
Alison Manafi Magaya	Southern
Joseph Malwal	Southern

Based on the information given in Table 12, the regional representation of the federal government is summarized in Table 13.

Table 13. **Regional Representation of the Federal Government, 1999**

Region	No of Positions	Percentage
Eastern Region	1	3.3%
Northern Region	18	60.1%
Central Region	2	6.6%
Southern	4	13.3%
Western Region	5	16.7%

Examples of Imbalance of Division of Wealth

Division of wealth in any society is an important barometer of the legitimacy of its political system. A political system that thwarts its laws to preside over an unfair distribution of wealth is bound to witness rapid erosion of its legitimacy. Modern Sudan is a case in point here. We have carefully monitored the division of wealth in this country over a long time and have come to conclusions that are neither assuring nor comfortable to confront. We have handed our leadership to those with whom we have fought together for our common national objectives. We have paid our allegiance and put our trust behind the appealing slogans they raised and continued to do so until the present time. We have finally come to the conclusion that as we demand restoration of our rights, we are demanding the impossible. We are like a person who tries to straighten a shadow without thinking about the crookedness of the object that casts it in the first place.

During his reign (1958–1964), General Aboud extended the railway line to Nyala, opened two technical schools in Geneina and Nyala and two secondary schools in Alobeid and Port Sudan. Having done that, he then proceeded to redirect the rest of Sudan's wealth for the development of Central and Northern Sudan. Agricultural schemes of Khasm Algirba and New Halfa were given special attention, having been reserved for those who were displaced by the construction of Oswan Dam. The residents of New Halfa were compensated for losing their original homeland and for the mistakes that were committed by previous rulers. However, had they not been indigenous to the Northern Region, they would not have been compensated.

Since independence, Sudan has known several development plans. Among them, we mention the Ten Years Strategic Development Plan, Five Years Development Plan, and Three Years Development Plan. Billions of dollars have been spent on these plans, forming our present foreign debts and a burden on current and future generations. Most of these plans have been located in the central and northern Sudan and we have yet to see a return that benefits all those who are responsible for its costs. Many of the schemes that emerged within these developmental plans have remained a drain on the national economy at the expense of all but the Central and the Northern Regions. A critical look at government budget allocations in recent years shows the perils of such development investment and the special place northern Sudan occupies in the hearts of Sudan's ruling elite. Not a single state in non-northern Sudan exceeded 36 percent of its already budgeted allocations. The Northern states were different. Actual disbursement shows that they never dropped below 60 percent of their planned budget allocations. Apparently, there is a story behind that. The Ministry of Economy and Finance has always been dominated by the Northern Region. Top positions like minister, the deputy minister, secretary generals, and chief administrators usually come from the Northern Region. Even the positions of drivers are also reserved for school dropouts from the north. The rest of the country has to contend with jobs in the Ministry as cleaners, tea makers, guards, etc. In such an environment, it is not surprising that non-northern states find it impossible to receive their allocated budgets while the Northern states have their facilitators at every venue inside the ministry. This is very clear when you look at how universities and higher institutes have been performing. In particular, that is evident from the growth of Universities of Kasala and Kadugli (Eastern and Western Region, respectively) with their peer Universities of Shandi and Atbara (Northern Region). The first category experienced difficulties while the last prospered even when the economy was facing major difficulties. Universities of the north benefited from substantial donations from public companies that were headed by officials from the Northern Region. Their donations were in fact borne by the same taxpayers who come from the whole of the Sudan.

For our purpose here, we will focus on the major characteristics of the Three Years Programme that was ratified by the Government of National Salvation for the years 1999 to 2002.

The Agricultural Sector

The irrigated sector, as distinct from rain-fed sector, of agriculture is an important component of the Sudanese economy. It has been developed with dual aims in mind. First, to boost the export sector through increase in cash products like cotton, peanuts, sesame seeds, and so on. Second, to augment food production as a strategic sector, thus increasing production of millet, maize, rice, lentils, and so on. This sector has been fortunate in attracting substantial funds from national resources as well as borrowed capital from abroad. Substantial expenditure in this sector also goes for infrastructure like dams, roads, bridges, etc. Despite substantial investment in this sector, its revenue to the nation is minuscule compared to that generated by rain-fed agriculture. The latter has remained a backbone of the export sector, contributing peanuts, sesame, gum arabic, hibiscus, and animals. The high cost and low return aspect of the irrigated sector led to its continuous subsidization by the rain-fed sector. We note here that the irrigated sector dominates in Central and Northern Sudan, while rain-fed agriculture features mainly in other parts of the nation.

Lack of investment in areas of rain-fed agriculture has been a major cause of migration to cities, including the capital, Khartoum. The North has, however, been protected against population depletion. Production of wheat has been moved from central Sudan to the north. Movement of wheat to the north has led to the emergence of new dams like Kajabar, Hamadab, and Marawi, and God knows what other dams to follow. Palm trees that were displaced by these dams have been compensated for, and many of them have been transported for transplantation in Khartoum. Compare this level of care with the impact of similar dams and irrigated schemes in the East, like Algash, Tokar, and Sitait. Displacement in these areas still remains unaided to this day. This is despite the fact that the east is among the least underdeveloped parts of the country. Its population suffers disease, hunger, illiteracy, and drought.

Rain-fed Agricultural Sector
Two broad subsectors can be identified here; these are the traditional rain-fed sector and the mechanized rain-fed sector. This sector plays an important role in food production. Its program of work is intended to include investment in agricultural services, pest control, provision of seeds, and agricultural extension in general. A number of schemes were established within this sector with the aim of developing deprived areas and rehabilitating the drought-stricken savanna belt. Rather than augment this sector, the government ordered liquidation of a number of them.

These schemes are:
1. Nuba Mountain Agricultural Corporation
2. Blue Nile Agricultural Corporation
3. White Nile Agricultural Corporation
4. Agricultural Machinery Corporation
5. South Kordofan Agricultural Corporation
6. Mechanised Agriculture Corporation
7. Jebel Mara Rural Development Scheme
8. Western Savannah Corporation

Note that none of these schemes were in the north and that these schemes were liquidated and not sold or privatized. We add that these schemes were developmental and their contribution was not confined to economic gains. As such we are bound to conclude that scrapping of these schemes indicates that development work is a preserve of north Sudan. Others have to contend without it. None of those in power who are calling for equality and development in the country have noticed the plain fact that since Independence, Darfur has not secured a single developmental scheme that could finance a single Local Administrative Area for three months. Moreover, most agricultural schemes in central Sudan are headed by personnel from the north or otherwise those whose origin is in the north. Examples here include the Gezira Scheme, Rahad Scheme, and the Blue Nile Scheme.

In addition to liquidation of public amenities, the government also resorted to aggressive privatization that benefited certain circles. A list of privatized public properties follows:

1. Abu Naama Jute Factory
2. Sata Company
3. Blue Nile Cardboard Factory
4. Port Sudan Cotton Spinning Factory
5. Rabak Ginnery
6. Sudan Mining Corporation
7. Red Sea Hotel
8. Kosti Guest House
9. Sudan Cotton Company
10. White Nile Tannery
11. Ria Sweets Factory
12. Kirrikab Factory for Sweets
13. Khartoum Tannery
14. Kuku Company for Milk
15. Sudan Hotel
16. Atbara Guest House
17. Sudan Trade Bank

Some of these companies were sold to certain institutions and for logical reasons. For example, there was nothing wrong in selling Sudan Hotel to the National Fund for Social Insurance. Other sales were however of dubious nature. Abu Naama Jute Factory was sold for Ls 800m, a sum that was well below its commercial value at the time, considering land, assets, and machineries included in the sale. We were less surprised when we realized that the buyer was none other than Hashim Haju. Other sales also followed the same pattern. In sharp contrast to Hashim Haju, the Sudanese businessman Mohamed Jar Alnabi, who is from the Western Region, had to struggle exceptionally hard to survive with the regime. His effort to establish an oil refinery, a strategic acquisition at the time, did not endear him to the system. Had it not been for his resilience, he would have been driven into exile like the ex-governor of Darfur, Ibrahim Draig.

Sadly, these examples show how the country is run and how the public coffer is manipulated to serve certain individuals and certain areas. Barriers are also erected to prevent leaders from other parts of the Sudan from succeeding. A good example is the endemic problem of drinking water in Alobeid city. It was the governor Ibrahim Alsanusi who decided to confront this problem and had tirelessly worked for a final solution. As an indigenous resident of the area, he was not allowed to reap the result of his work. At the last moment, he was replaced by one of those who deserve to succeed, a governor from the Northern Region.

We all remember the case of Alshafay Ahmed Mohamed, who worked together with his predecessor, Hasan Mohamedain, to establish the National Council. Both of them are from the west and hence had to give way to a northerner to preside over the established council.

Ali Alhaj is another example of the manner in which leaders are penalized for not originating in the north. He was the dynamic figure in the peace negotiations as well as establishment of the federal government system. In each of these successes, he was removed to allow others to crown his success. Despite continuous character assassination, Alhaj remained national in his work and did not give way to racist, regional, or nepotistic temptations.

Agricultural Services

Sudan has great agricultural potentials that are yet to be adequately explored and properly exploited. So far, expenditure on agricultural and horticultural extension has been confined to the irrigated sector. For the farmers in the western, eastern, and southern parts of Sudan, agricultural extension is a riddle for which they do not qualify. Other agricultural services directed at small farmers have also been available only to farmers in northern Sudan. Using the emergency law that has been enacted recently, even the meager resources available to the Western Region have been further eroded. Its only pest control plane has been removed on the grounds that pests did not pose a real threat to agriculture in Sudan. Definition of what constitute pests and grasshoppers as provided by the Agricultural Pest Control Office in Darfur was not convincing enough for the bureaucrats in Khartoum. The result is that the Office lost the plane and its running cost and kept the grasshoppers and other pests.

Natural Resources

Environmental protection and reversal of desertification have been among the salient stated strategies of natural resource policies in the Sudan. Policies have been drafted with the aim of arresting desertification, protecting and promoting forests, locating new sources of cooking fuel, and other similar measures. However, actions on the ground followed a different trend. Jebel Mara forests, rich savannah grass in western Darfur, Blue Nile natural endowment, and the gum arabic belt are all directed to serve the overseers of the federal government and their affiliates in the north.

Animal Resources

As a desert plain, the Northern Region has no significance in the field of animal export. Nonetheless, amid international concern about animal disease, the north was declared – internationally – by the government as an area free of animal diseases. Soon after that, centers of animal exports in the west were moved to the north together with appropriate infrastructural rehabilitation to facilitate that. Officials who contested that were either subjected to threats or enticement to buy into the new policy of the day. Customs tax centers were also moved to the north. Despite difficulties, truck drivers involved in animal export had no choice but to clear their departing products in Dongula in the north. Financial services also had to follow suit. The branch of Sudan Bank in Alashir in the west had to give way to a Bank branch in Dongula despite the fact that Alafshir is a capital of the animal producing region, while Dongula is a capital with no land to support animal wealth and a population that is half of that of El Fashir.

Industrial Sector

Rural industry and industrial villages have been among the fundamentals of development in India and China. The pattern of development is different in the Sudan. Rural areas are emptied of their labour force in favor of bloated cities where the meager industrial development is concentrated. In these industrial centers, power is firmly placed under the grip of the northern elite, who in turn continue depleting other regions of their wealth. This is despite the fact that substantial natural wealth like iron, petrol, gas, gold, and so on is found in these non-northern regions. As long as we continue along this road, it will be a long time before we can see a single industrial scheme outside Central and Northern Sudan. It is in these regions that we find military industry, currency coinage, banknote printing houses, electricity, sugar industries, and so on.

Water and Energy

It is hard to write about expansion in oil drilling and development in the Sudan without a deep feeling of embarrassment. The Ministry of Energy is now, more or less, a homestead of extended families belonging to one ethnic group from the north. This group and its commercial companies have monopolized all the high-paying posts in the venture down to that of drivers. The local people who supposedly own the oil land are to be content with digging trenches and laying the oil pipelines.

Water development is currently reserved for the ever-expanding capital, Khartoum. The rest of the country is left out, dying of thirst as well as of diseases like malaria, kalazar, bilharsiasis, and other waterborne diseases.

Transport and Communication

Current state strategies in the field of transport and communication have the following objectives:
a) Integration and improvement of transport and communication services through continuous maintenance of existing national roads and constructions of new national networks geared toward economic development.
b) Orientation of new investment toward schemes and projects that have clear objectives, leading to increased production.
c) Encouragement of the private sector to invest in transport and communication through sales of public amenities or joint ownership with the state.
d) Making full use of available opportunities, resources, and potentials to that effect.

Despite the obvious importance of transport and communication and their centrality to any developmental plans, they have been relegated to marginal ministries that have no power in the allocation of national budgets. As such, the Department of Transport and Communication has remained subordinate to other ministries, like Economic and Finance, which operate under a different and often contradictory agenda.

While the principle of an integrated transport network is agreeable, the term itself has remained either ill-defined or simply meaningless. It is not at all clear whether the policy of integration is meant to feature at the level of the nation, the state, or a combination of both.

The strategy refers "correctly" to projects and schemes that have clear objectives without being specific as to the delineation of these objectives. Lack of clarity in these issues leaves options open for individual ministers to tune national budgets to their regional and ethnic interests. For example, the Saudi Islamic Bank earmarked funds for the Western Road (Alobeid–El Fashir). That fund was later redirected by the ex-Minister of Finance, Dr. Abdel Wahab Osman, to the Wheat Project in the north. This project came as a policy of indigenizing production of wheat in northern Sudan, a project that competes poorly with the national economic gains of the Western Road. This is despite the fact that previous economic feasibility studies had been in favour of the Alobeid–El Fashir Road and equally the Southern Kordofan Nuba Circular Road.

Education and Other Developmental Services

Tremendous disparities obtain with regard to educational services. While certain areas have seen a progressive increase in the number of children who have progressed to secondary schools, pupils in the marginalized areas have been grounded at the primary level. In the State of Western Darfur, primary schools remained closed for two years for lack of books and staff pay. In fact, books rotted in their stores due to lack of funds. There were more than one and a half million people in the State of Western Darfur. Only 4,211 children were able to sit for the final Primary School Examination. This number is less than the number of primary school leavers in a single Local Administrative Area in the Northern Region. The comparison becomes somewhat bizarre when we realize one Local Administrative Area in Darfur has a population that is equal to that of the entire Northern Region.

At a different level, marginalized regions also suffer at the hand of the State Support Fund. This is a national fund expected to fund state developmental projects. As decreed, no state is to access the fund without sound feasibility studies. While this principle makes sense, it is here that northern control reigns supreme. Poorer states are deprived of costs of feasibility studies and hence credible competition for funding. The result is obvious. The National State Support Fund channels its entire budget to funding projects other than those in the Western, Southern, and Eastern Regions.

National Financial Institutions

The state financial sector is one of those sectors that have remained off-limits for Regions other than the Northern Region. For example, since the establishment of the Bank of Sudan in 1956, and to this day, not a single manager of this bank came from the Eastern, Western, or Southern Region. Those managers who came from the Central Region were in fact members of ethnic groups that originate in the Northern Region. The case of the management of the Bank of Sudan can equally be said for other major Sudanese banks like Khartoum Bank, Sudan Agricultural Bank, and the Industrial Development Bank. Appointment of managers for newly created banks and other recent public financial institutions in the country also followed the same patterns.

Chamber of Zakat (Islamic Tax)

Although this institution is essentially religious, it too could not escape the process of northern ethnification, that is, bringing it under the control of the Shaygia, the Jaalyeen, and the Danagla. A recent power struggle between the Secretary-General and the Manger General of the Chamber of Zakat can be seen within the same process.

Sudan Development Corporation
No Manager General of this institution ever came out of the three ethnic groups (Shaygia, Jaaliyeen, and Danagla) that dominate the region.

Islamic Trust
Throughout the life of Al Bashir's government, this institution has never been led by any manager from outside the Northern Region.

Integration Fund
This fund was originally established for noble reasons. However, when it was placed under directorship of someone from a region other than the favored one, all hell broke loose. All obstacles were placed in front of the non-northern director in order to ensure his failure. This went on despite the impressive profile of the director, who succeeded in attracting Libyan firms for Red Sea fishing, provided badly needed school uniforms, and created employment for a substantial number of people. Despite the appeals of many prominent people, the fund was liquidated and replaced by Sineen Corporation under the same directorship. When Sineen proved its success like its predecessor under the same manager, opposition was revived. A new manager from the "right" region was put in charge. His school-dropout relative now works there and is paid in dollars, not in Sudanese dinars, in a UN-sponsored project.

Control of the Northern Region over public finance also features in other institutions, including the following:
- Application of Shari'a (Islamic Law) Fund
- Philanthropic Corporation for Support of Armed Forces
- Martyr's Organisation
- Call for Jihad
- Bir (Charity) International
- Martyr Zibair Charity Organisation
- Marine Lines
- Philanthropic Insurance Fund

National Insurance Fund
This fund was originally headed by Major General Mahir Sulaiman, who is not from the Northern Region. His success attracted the attention of his relevant federal state minister, who was not pleased by what he saw. Confrontation followed and the fund was subsequently restored to the control of the Northern Region.

When we raise issues of injustice, corruption, and mismanagement, we get accused of racism. Others are free to abuse their position and enrich themselves at the expense of the taxpayers in the open. Let us give one example known to many in the country. A general director of a well-known public company was moved to head another public company. He requested payment of $17,000 as travel expenses for himself and his family against his new company. He also demanded payment of the same expenses from the previous company, insisting payment be made outside the state. He also applied for two years house rent in cash and 7 million Sudanese pounds for furniture, in addition to his salary of 10 million pounds a month. All was paid to him to the last penny. Now, this explains why higher jobs have to be reserved only for those from the Northern Region and that there is little or nothing left for other regions.

Committee for Division of Resources

The discovery of petrol and resumption of its export introduced a new type of wealth into the nation. This new wealth was territory bound and could not be simply relocated to the Northern Region. Something had to be done to ensure flow of wealth to the North and there was no dearth of genius thinking in our leadership. It was easy. A presidential decree was to take care of it. Here is the decree in full:

> Decree No 334, Year 1999: Creation of a National Committee, for drafting proposal for division of national wealth between Federal Government and State governments.
> Following examination of the recommendations of the Minister for Federal Relations and the decision of the Council of Ministers No. 839, Year 1998 regarding constitution of a National Committee for division of national resources between the Federal Government and state governments, and in accordance with Constitutional Articles 113, 114, and 115, the President decrees the following: Establishment of a National Committee for the purpose of drafting proposals for division of national wealth between the Federal and State Governments. The committee consists of the following:

Table 14. **National Committee for Division of National Wealth**

No	Name	Position	Region [added by authors]
1	Abdel RahimMohamed Hamdi	Chair	Northern
2	Dr. Taj Alsir Mahjoub	Secretary and Member	Northern
3	Dr.Taj Alsir Mustafa	Member	Northern
4	M. General Abul Qasim M. Ibrahim	Member	Northern
5	Dr. Khalid Sir Alkhitim	Member	Northern
6	Farah Hasan	Member	Northern
7	Dr. Ahmed Majzoub Ahmed	Member	Northern
8	Abdel Wahab Ahmed Hamza	Member	Northern
9	Dr. Jumaa Kindi Komi	Member	Western
10	Dr. Swar Aldahab Ahmed Iesa	Member	Northern
11	Jamie Leemy	Member	Southern
12	Dr. Ali Abdalla Ali	Member	Northern
13	Dr. Awad Alseed Alkarsabi	Member	Northern
14	Moses Mashar	Member	Southern

15	Ahmed Ibrahim Turuk	Member	Eastern
16	Dr. Izzaldin Ibrahim Altigani	Member	Northern
17	Dr. Mohamed Kheir Alzibair	Member	Northern
18	Gindeel Ibrahim	Member	Northern
19	Fareed Omer Medani	Member	Northern
20	Badr Aldin Taha	Member	Central
21	Sheikh Beesh Kore	Member	Southern
22	Omer Taha Abu Samra	Member	Northern
23	Dr. Bidoor Abu Affan	Member	Northern
24	Tariq Mubarak	Member	Northern
25	Hasan Jiha Ali	Member	Northern

Table 15. **Summary of Table 14, Division of National Wealth**

Region	Seats	Percentage
Eastern	1	4%
Northern	19	76%
Central	1	4%
Southern	3	12%
Western	1	4%

The hegemony of the Northern Region over all other regions is obvious (Table 15). Such a powerful position enables the committee to become yet another tool for furthering the interests of the Northern Region.

Future Visions

The injustice and mal-division of power and wealth in the Sudan have eroded the sense of belonging to a unified society where all could aspire to share benefits as well as duties and responsibilities. The situation in which citizens compromise their personal interests in return for peaceful coexistence with others in their society is what early philosophers called "social contract." Inability of our leaders to respect this simple fact has undermined the very fabric of Sudanese society. Ensuing problems include the following.

I. Internal Immigration

Emigration is not natural and is rarely built into the culture of most Sudanese societies. Most rural Sudanese prefer to remain in their homes surrounded by their familial human and nonhuman surroundings. However, rural people are also thinking individuals who have to evaluate their options and ensure reasonable future prospects for themselves and their future generations. The current pattern of development in country consists of continuous transfer of surplus from rural areas to cities and from marginalized regions to the Northern Region. Not surprisingly, rural villages, particularly in marginalized regions, are emptied of their human resources. Young people in particular vacate these rural centers in their desperate attempt to flee poverty, illiteracy, and ill health. At the same time, shantytowns continue growing, forming belts of poverty around every city in the country. This has serious implications at both ends.

Rural areas have been depleted of their human resources, particularly the young, energetic, and creative. Cities in turn cannot cope as their resources, employment opportunities, and services collapse under the pressure of ever-growing populations.

II. Education Loss

Educational services have so far been concentrated in Khartoum, the Northern Region, and certain parts of the Central Region. Within these locales, the cost of education has been beyond the reach of the average citizen. In fact, education has become more and more confined to the rich, including families of high government employees. Much more recently, education has been devolved and placed under state authorities. Many states rose to the challenge and used the then rationed sugar to finance their own state education. That policy did not last for long. The government moved to remove sugar from the list of rationed items and left it to the open market. Obviously, that deprived states of the revenue raised by tax on sugar, thus resulting in the collapse of the educational system in all marginalized states. To this day, not a single leader called for examination of this costly problem with a view to overcoming it. We are bewildered about previous slogans of compulsory education and free education that preceded it and equally free medicine. It is our contention that the Northern Region is deliberate in inflicting illiteracy and ignorance on others as part of its project of hegemony over the Sudan.

III. Spread of Diseases

The Eastern Region gives a good example of the collapse of the health system in the Sudan and the impotence of those who are in charge in Khartoum. Kasala and Gadharif cities offer health services to patients that are four times their capacity – by national standards. They both depend on internally generated and charity funds in offering their services. National health system and national disease prevention have receded to feature only on national TV programs. Instead, the government introduced the so-called national health insurance for those who can pay for it. The policy led to the mushrooming of health hotels, some rated at five stars and above for the haves and forget about the have-nots.

The entire state of Western Darfur has two medical specialists in the field of obstetrics and gynecology, one in Geneina and the other in Zalengay. They are to serve a population of 1,650,000 aided by few medical students who visit the area for training and for escaping mandatory military service.

Let us give one example to highlight the dearth of health services in Darfur. The city of Geneina got its first X-ray machine in 1978. It lasted for seven or so years. Since the 1980s, patients requiring X-rays had to leave for Nyala or Khartoum for X-rays, a trip of two to six days for those who could not afford air tickets.

Erosion of Peace and Harmony

The continuous feeling of injustice, favoritism in job allocations, removal of employees from their jobs to leave room for designated individuals, and so on, have all created a sense of exclusion and lack of belonging. This has led marginalized people either to opt out of the society or to turn to violence to redress their perceived maltreatment. Loss of faith in authority and leadership is eating fast at the very fabric of the Sudanese society.

Regional Associations

Continuous marginalization of certain groups and loss of faith in all those in power have resulted in new ways of campaigning for basic rights. Among others, this has led to mushrooming of ethnic and regional groups acting in desperate attempts to remind leaders of their role regarding distribution of power and wealth in the country, albeit in a peaceful manner. Thus we have the Bija Association, the Nuba Mountain Associations, and Darfur Associations, in addition to lobby groups from within the National Parliament.

Armed Movements

Over the years, various regional armed movements appeared in the Sudan in response to injustices perpetrated by successive Khartoum governments. These movements include Anyana I and II, Sudan Liberation Movement, Sudan's People Liberation Force, Ingessana Coalition, and Nuba Mountain Freedom Movement. For all of these groups, the "independence" of the country was no more than a replacement of one master by another.

Loss of Credibility

Loss of credibility is certainly the worst outcome of imbalance of power and of wealth in the Sudan. Lack of faith in the Khartoum government has been a phenomenon felt in all regions, with the North being the only exception. Since independence, Sadiq Al Madhi's second tenure as prime minister (1986–1989) was perhaps the only exception whereby some efforts had been shown in its mild attempt to be somewhat inclusive. Other governments have simply pursued policies of entrenching domination of the north and few areas in the center over all other regions. The last government (Al Bashir's National Salvation) is certainly the worst of them all. It combined politics with ethnicity and Islam to concentrate power and wealth in the North. In this project, regionalism goes hand in hand with racism, and is often disguised under an Islamic flag to realize government goals. It is not only that Sudan is further dissected into clearly demarcated power-regions; cities are also falling under the same onslaught. They are to be ruled by their inhabitants who originate in the North.

Islamic Rule

Since its accession to power, this government has been selling itself as a champion of Islam. Its major slogan has been to construct a state built on "Knowledge/Science and Submission to Islam." Such a state is expected to be a model of justice, equality, and faith. We hereby offer our understanding of the five major criteria for an Islamic state:

I. Land Development (I'mar Alarad)

As stated in the Qur'an, man is the successor of God on earth and is entrusted with its development (*I'mar*). The state or the government is the body that is in charge of this, and is thus obliged to devise and implement and monitor all relevant policies. In so doing, the state is to guarantee equality of all in front of the laws in the designated land. In accordance with God's decrees, the state should ensure prevalence of justice, protection of the weak, and eradicate oppression and the excesses of the powerful. The state is obliged to fight nepotism, favoritism, and unfair enrichment of the few at the expense of the many. Only through this can the state claim to be an adequate representative and a true successor to God.

II. Freedom

The second criterion of an Islamic state is freedom as enshrined in the Qur'an ("Let there be no compulsion in religion: Truth stands out Clear from Error." The Cow, verse 256). The divine order presupposes freedom, treating the individual as a thinking citizen capable of making his/her own choice. Only through enabling people to make their choice can we guarantee true debate and exchange of different views that can lead to effective use of resources and continuous development. Islam teaches us to exchange views in a free environment that is cleared of the autocracy and arrogance of rulers, an environment in which the ruler is subordinate to the consensus based on views of ordinary citizens. This was the method used by the Prophet and his immediate successors. Abu Bakr, the first successor of the Prophet, once said: "Support me if I do well and correct me when I make mistakes." His successor, Omer, also followed the same philosophy. As narrated, a woman opposed one of his decisions and quoted the Qur'an to support her argument. Omer listened and obliged, saying, "Omer erred while a woman delivered the right view. All of you are more knowledgeable than Omer." This is why early Islamic states prospered and extended their borders from the Indian to the Atlantic oceans.

Arrogant leaders who refuse to listen to their subjects are ultimately bound to depend on oppressive institutions if they are to preserve their power. In their pursuit of remaining in power, these leaders, hypocritically, preach the word of God and His Prophet amid corruption, injustice, and tyranny. They however never recall the words of the Prophet: "If Fatima, the daughter of [Mohammed] is to steal, I will certainly amputate her hands as we do to other thieves." Such a level of justice requires an environment of freedom in which citizens guide their leaders in the fight against corruption, nepotism, and injustice.

III. Justice

The third criterion of an Islamic state is working for justice. Justice is the essence of good leadership. With its presence, a non-Muslim king can guarantee his success in a Muslim community. In its absence, even the most Muslim king is bound to fail. The high place accorded to justice is indicated by its use as one of the most beautiful names of Allah.

Justice that we require in the Sudan is that which includes division of resources in accordance with equality of all citizens as members of the same country. Resources are to be divided according to clearly laid-down priorities that are transparent and evident to all. Such an approach ensures consensus and evades feelings of deceit. Control over public wealth should be open to all according to their experience, qualifications, and commitment to national interests. It should not be a preserve of a select minority whose members collaborate to protect the corrupt and shield the incompetent. While stories of corruption in many public financial institutions are rampant in the state, the response of the government seems to have focused on a limited number of banks. So far all of these banks and financial institutions seem to have links to regions other than the Northern Region.

Justice presupposes opening high offices to all qualified citizens. This is not the case in the Sudan. The presidency of the state, for example, has always been monopolized by certain ethnic groups. This has been the case throughout the independent history of the Sudan. The position of the head of the judicial system has also fallen under the same menace of ethnic domination.

VI. Shura (Consultation)
We introduce *shura*, or "consultation," as the fourth criterion of Islamic rule. Islam stipulates the use of consultation for all public decisions, big and small alike. The shura is a right of all citizens in an Islamic state, and the ruler is clearly instructed to avoid monopoly over decision-making. The following are clearly stated in Islamic jurisprudence:
a) The ruler is obliged to consult widely prior to taking any major decision. Consultation allows the ruler to examine various views that are not available to a single individual, no matter how wise he or she is. Consultation also allows the ruler to avoid pitfalls of emotional and personal inclinations.
b) Absence of consultation leads to abuse of power and breeds arrogance. Major decisions are public matters and should not be left to a single individual. The duty of all citizens to contribute to such consultation is so crucial in Islam that it is elevated to the level of Jihad: "The best of Jihad is a word of truth to an unjust ruler." In a modern state, civic societies, organizations, media, and so on are all obligated to speak out and contribute to the decision-making process.

IV. Adoption of Divine Governance
Our fifth criterion of an Islamic rule is its conformity with divine laws as enshrined in the Qur'an, the prophetic traditions and other good sources of Islamic jurisprudence. In this system, submission must be made to God alone and this applies to the ruler and ruled alike. The rule here is nothing but a means of entrenching the rule of God. Islam grants the ruler rights, but that comes with corresponding responsibilities. So heavy are these responsibilities and that is what led Omer, the second successor of Prophet Mohammed, to lament: "I wish the mother of Omer had never given birth to me," or elsewhere: "You are all shepherds and every one of you is responsible for his flock (i.e., subjects) in front of Allah."

The ruler must constantly remember that he has to defend himself on the Day of Judgment. Those who are related to the ruler should not abuse that relationship. Early Islamic rulers had always seen such a relationship as a liability and never an asset. A relative of a ruler is the first to be called to action and first to be scrutinized for mistakes. Such was the case with Abdullah, the son of Successor Omer who was the first to be investigated and the last to receive his legitimate share in his community.

Harvest of Destruction

We would like to step back and contemplate on our rulers and assess the reasons behind their incessant control over power and their use of every possible means to retain it. Here are our conclusions:

I. Those who are in charge seem to have succumbed to their inner instinct for power and domination over others. Their thirst for power has gone out of control as they have lost the most important bridle and that is fear of God and the after-death punishment.

   Success in monopolizing power for so long gave members of this group an illusion that their rise to power is natural and is a direct result of their superior capabilities, tribes, and regional origin. Nothing better illustrates this more than their popular saying that they will never hand in the Sudan to anybody except to Jesus and the Messiah at the end the current world (referring to the Biblical story about the end of the world). Despite their deceptive talk about Islam, those people have never learned the simple Islamic teaching that it is God that gives power to some and takes it from others; that it is God's kingdom that lasts, not that of His creatures.

II. In the last ten years or so, corruption has become so widespread that it has acquired semi-legal status. Corrupt government officials are often described as being involved in establishing themselves or forming personal wealth. Public office has become a means of acquiring villas, expensive cars, or extra wives. Corruption has become so indivisible from the state that the judicial powers have to be tuned to protect the inner circle of the favored ruling elite. Thus *shari'a* (Islamic) laws are interpreted to strike those who encroach on private property and spare those who steal from the public coffer. The result is obvious. Amputation, flogging, and extended prison sentences became the punishment of the destitute and dispossessed, who are likely to steal a transistor radio, a watch, or a camel. The same laws and hence punishment do not apply to those who steal public money no matter how huge are their unlawful gains. The latter group of thieves consists of government officials, mostly among the favoured few. Not surprisingly, poverty of the many grew in tandem with the growth of wealth as illustrated by substantial increase in new villas, expensive cars, and luxurious lifestyle. This trend is very much facilitated by the unwritten code that enabled a small minority to control almost all key financial positions in the country and at the same time preside over the judicial system.

III. While enriching themselves, our ruling elite also devised a system in which nobody else succeeds in the economic sphere. The rule is simple: "Starve your dog and he will follow you," forgetting that it is God who provides sustenance and that He can change fortunes overnight. Moreover, the ruling elite also made sure that success in any public office can only be achieved if the occupant is a Northerner. Otherwise, all obstacles are erected to guarantee failure of the government offical. This pattern has been clear in the following cases:

A) The old colonial dictum "divide and rule" has been refashioned by our leaders and used in various ways to achieve their objectives. It is combined with other tactics, including rewards and punishment, character assassination, and embellishment of poppets. Turning ethnic groups against each other has been a dominant feature of this current regime. Examples here are the Hadandwa against the Beni Amir, the Ara'ar against the Bashshareen, and the Halanga against the Rashida in the Eastern Region. The Southern Region has also been placed under the same destructive policy. Thus you witness the Dinka against the Nuer, the Nuer against the Shiluk, the Manari against the Zande, and so forth. The Western Region also has its share of this divisive policy, culminating in conflicts between the Nuba and the Misairiya, the Slamat and the Silaihat, the Zaghawa and the Rizaigat, and so forth. Much more recently, a broader gulf has been created in Darfur between the so-called Arab Alliance (Arab Gathering) on one hand, and the "Zurqa" (black) on the other. The national security offices and media have also been employed to stimulate such conflicts. This has often appeared in the form of false statements attributed to certain groups threatening their neighbors.

B) Character assassination of leaders who raise their voices against injustice has also been a favored tactic for this government. The case of Colonel Malwal, the southern leader, is known to all in the Sudan. He was removed from the Command Council of the government following false accusations stage-managed by certain circles within the regime.

When this government came to power, General Bakri Almak rose to become the governor of the Eastern Region. False accusations similar to those levelled against Colonel Malwal were devised to remove him from office. The only reason we can come up with is that he comes from the wrong region (i.e., the Central Region).

Khartoum State also saw similar dirty plays. Khartoum has always been seen as an extension of the Northern Region. That became clear when Badr Aldin Yhia, who is Khartoumese, became state governor of Khartoum. He was subjected to vicious attack using the might of the government-controlled media. Attacks continued until he was finally driven out of office. He was replaced by Dr. Majzoub Alkhalifa, who is a Northerner, and even better, famous for his chauvinistic inclination toward the Jaalyeen ethnic group.

Conclusion

This document, which is factual in its data and clear in its representation, is compiled under the slogan of justice. Our choice is inspired by the fact that "justice" is derivative of one of the ninety-nine names of Allah. Justice and equality are our demand. Remaining within Islamic slogans, which this government claim to raise, we indicate that justice and equality are essential to the full realization of Islamic rule. That can only be realized if we are prepared to speak out for justice. Prophet Mohammed once said: "Support your brother whether he is just or otherwise." In so saying, he does not mean standing with injustice. Rather, what he meant is that you take your unjust brother by the hand, and direct him to where justice lies. This is our approach to our brothers in the Northern Region.

Sudan was not ideal at its independence in 1956. Resources were poorly divided among different provinces at the time. By the 1970s some progress had been made, and gaps between provinces started narrowing. The last two decades have been different. Resources were moved to concentrate in the Northern and Central Regions, leading to impoverishment of other regions. As a result, marginalized regions became zones of out-migration. People had to move in search of food, work, and services, all of which concentrated in the Central and Northern Regions.

Destruction of marginalized regions has become a feature of Sudan, particularly during the reign of the current regime. Much worse are the marginalized regions that are ruled by governors who do not come from the Northern Region. The State of Western Darfur and the State of Southern Kordofan provide a good example in this regard. They were both brought to their knees simply because their governors happen to be from within these states. When they were replaced by governors from the "right" northern ethnic groups, funds were released, and the states became somewhat functional. So acute was this problem that a pillar of the government in Khartoum declared federal funding for western states can only be released following his personal approval, verbal or written. Such policies are bound to lead to alienation and subsequent loss of faith in Sudan as a united country. We hereby appeal to those who are in charge to think hard. We understand that justification has always been made to behave in a specific way, but the road to move forward is clear. Our northern brothers must be ready to compromise and be fair in dealing with national issues. They must open up government positions to all according to their qualifications, competence, and experience. They must stop abusing their positions and halt directing illegitimate resources to their own home areas. Finally, they must follow the – just – slogans they raise in their public speeches.

The current regime took over in 1989 to augment the project of Sudan as a model of an Islamic state. Muslim countries everywhere are looking at our experience. Its failure is a failure of Islam as much as it is a failure of Sudan as a nation. It is time to set things right. We appeal to those who are in charge to unite and commit themselves to justice, protection of individual rights, and promotion of the national interest.

Lastly, we would like to promise our readers more detailed information in Part II of this work.

Notes

1 Directory of Federal Rule, Sudan.
2 People Councils publications.
3 Presidential/Republican decrees.
4 Public Administration regulations.
5 Sudan National Census, 1993.
6 Mekki Othman, 1997. Finance Ministers Whom I Knew. (No Publishing House).
7 IMF publications.

8 Institute for Arab Planning. Kuwait. March 1997.
9 National Fund for Social Insurance, Sudan.
10 Sudan Sea Lines publications.
11 Newspaper articles.
12 Diplomatic publications, Jordan.
13 Bank of Sudan publications.
14 World Bank publication.

Appendix J

Black Book of Sudan:
Imbalance of Power and Wealth in Sudan (in Arabic): A Review

Abdullahi Osman El-Tom

Most of the recent literature on the civil war, political turmoil, and social upheavals in the Sudan is written in Arabic. At least three reasons explain this tendency. First, Arabic is the official language of the Sudan, the main spoken language among its diverse nationalities and ethnic groups. Second, the Arabicization (*tarib*, in Arabic, refers to the use of Arabic as a language of instruction) of higher education means that English is gradually losing ground to Arabic. Third, the Sudan government's orientation courts the Arab World and perceives Arabism as the edifice of Sudanese nationalism regardless of the fact that the majority of the Sudanese peoples are of an African or Afro-Arab origin. For all three reasons, Arabic language became dominant even in regions such as Southern Sudan, the Nuba Mountains, and Darfur, where Arabism, apparently an ideology of dominance, is resisted and its political designs rejected by peoples of non-Arab origin.

Evidently, the discourse of power and the struggle for providing the symbols of a dominant identity cannot be separated from issues such as language and religion. Nor can these issues be separated from the twin domains of wealth-sharing and equitable resource distribution and their discontent. However, this review article does not focus on the common theme of identity politics. Its objective is more mundane; that is, it is an attempt to avail the non-Arabic reader of a glimpse of a mysterious new Arabic publication titled *The Black Book: Imbalance of Power and Wealth in Sudan*, which appeared in 2000. The authors of the book have opted to remain anonymous, calling themselves "The Seekers of Truth and Justice." The place of publication has also been withheld. *The Black Book*, as we will refer to it the rest of this review, has no copyright either.

The mystery of *The Black Book* is compounded by its impeccable method of distribution that was executed with military precision. A one-off distribution of the book took place at Friday prayers in the Capital and in most major cities in the country, thus beating the government's tight grip on information circulation.

According to one source, top officials, including personnel of the Presidential Palace, received copies on their desks on the same day. Within weeks of its release, the book now popularly known as *The Black Book* (al-kitab al-aswad) became a topic of discussion at every venue in the country. Its success in tapping the grassroots imagination in a way that is unparalleled by any other literary work in the recent history of the country has made it the envy of every author in the land. The distribution of the book took on a life of its own through spontaneous photocopying. The book has no copyright. Indeed, its free duplication constituted the greatest bulk of its distribution, as most readers have never seen the original copy of the book. Translation of the book into English for southern Sudanese readers and others has greatly expanded its readership both inside and outside Sudan.

The Main Thesis

The authors spelled out the aim of their publication in the following passage:

> This publication unveils the level of injustice practiced by successive governments, secular and theocratic, democratic or autocratic, since the independence of the country in 1956 to this date (p.1; all translations are ours unless otherwise stated).

The authors then proceed to the distribution of various types of powers among population blocs in the country. Using the 1986 Official Census, Sudan's Regional populations are shown in the first two columns of Table 1.

Table 1. **Population and Representation, 1986**

Regions	Population	Percentage	Representation	Percentage
Northern	1,026,406	5.4%	58	79.5%
Eastern	2,222,779	11.8%	1	1.4%
Central	4,908,038	26.5%	2	2.8%
Southern	4,407,450	23.7%	12	16.4%
Western	6,072,872	32.6%	0	0%

The table reveals that the Northern Region, with a population of 5.4 percent of the total population of the Sudan, provided 79.5 percent of national representation. The figures illustrate the inequitable distribution of regional representatives and the political dominance of the minority Northern Sudanese who historically dominated the country's economy as well.

The authors then move on to examine the regional status of the occupants of the constitutional posts for the first five national governments from 1956 to 1964. Given that these are the early governments, we may be tempted to throw the blame on flawed structures inherited from colonial regimes. The Northern Region has maintained a representation of more than 50 percent and occasionally exceeded 70 percent. Since independence, not a single president has come from outside the Northern Region, while many military coups have failed simply because their leaders came from outside the fortunate region (p. 11)[1] – for instance, the 1977, 1980, and 1991 military coups.

An impressive array of statistics has been compiled regarding regional representations in successive governments from 1964 to date. These are as follows: First multiparty democracy (MD1,1964–1969), Numeiri regime (1969–1985), Military Provisional Council (MPC, 1985–1986), second multiparty democracy (MD2, 1986–1989), NIF/National Salvation 1 (NS1, 1989–1999), and National Salvation 2 (NS2, 1999–present). The ministerial representation in these governments is given in Table 2.

Table 2. **Ministerial Representation in Governments, 1964–2000**

Gov/Region	Northern		Central		Western		Southern		Western	
	Number	Percent-age	Number	Percent-age	Number	Percent-age	Number	Percent-age	Number	Percent age
MD1	55	67.9%	2	2.5%	5	6.2%	14	17.3%	5	6.2%
Numeiri	79	68.7%	4	2.5%	19	16.5%	9	7.8%	4	3.5%
MPC	21	70.0%	0	0%	3	10%	5	16.7%	1	3.3%
MD2	55	47.4%	3	2.6%	17	14.7%	15	12.9%	26	22.4%
NS1	120	59.%	6	3%	18	8.9%	30	14.9%	28	13.8%
NS2	18	60.%	1	3.3%	2	6.6%	4	13.3%	5	16.7%

Note: The list here refers to federal (national) ministers as opposed to state/*wilaie* ministers.

The Black Book here gives some credit to the then-Prime Minister Sadiq Al Mahdi and his democratic government in 1986–1989 (Table 2, MD2) for increasing the representation of marginalized groups in the country. This is taken as a testimony that liberal democracy goes some way toward tackling the dilemma of representation (p. 14).

Although *The Black Book* stresses the domination of the entire Sudan by the Northern Region, it does not take these regions as undifferentiated entities. The most startling element in the thesis is the claim that just three ethnic groups within the Northern Region in effect dominate the country. The authors state that "This tiny population of the North contains several marginalized ethnic groups like the Manseer and the Mahas. The former represents the marginalized Sudanese Arabs, while the latter represent the marginalized Nubian tranche. These and others are dominated by just three ethnic groups within the Northern Region, the Shaygia, the Jaalieen, and the Danagla" (pp. 15–16).

The Black Book allots substantial space to the performance of the current government, perhaps due to its repeated claim to nonsectarianism, justice, and equality. Statistics presented, however, reveal a spectacular conformity with the previous pattern of distribution of power prevalent in the Sudan. Regional composition of the Military Command Council at the time of the takeover of power by the present Government of National Salvation (GNS, 1989) is given in Table 3.

Table 3. **Revolutionary Command Council, 1989**

Region	Number of Representatives	Percentage
Northern	10	66.7%
Eastern	0	0%
Central	0	0%
Southern	2	13.3%
Western	3	20.0%

Once the power was consolidated, a return to normal politics became evident in the distribution of ministerial positions (p.15). This distribution is given in Table 4.

Table 4. **Ministerial Positions of the GNS, 1989**

Region	Number of Representatives	Percentage
North	120	59.9%
Eastern	6	3.0%
Central	18	8.9%
Southern	30	14.9%
Western	28	13.8%

The recent political demise of Hassan Al-Turabi (December 1999), the spiritual leader of the National Islamic Front (now Popular National Congress), was a cause of euphoria for the majority of the Sudanese people. The authors of *The Black Book*, however, see little cause for celebration. The power distribution is evident at the level of the presidential palace positions, the federal ministerial posts, and state governors. To save space, I will present a summary of the regional distribution of powers at the presidential palace, combined with computation of federal ministers (Table 5).

One would have assumed that the imbalance shown would not feature at the level of state governors, provincial commissioners, and regional ministers. The *Black Book*, however, states otherwise, as shown in Table 6.

Table 5. **Presidential and Federal Ministerial Posts**

Region	Presidential		Federal Ministerial	
	Number	Percentage	Number	Percentage
North	10	83.3%	18	60.1%
Eastern	0	0%	1	3.3%
Central	0	0%	2	6.6%
Southern	2	16.6%	4	13.3%
Western	0	0%	5	16.7%

Using similarly powerful statistical support, the authors arrive at the same conclusion regarding the legislative power in the Sudan. Although the domination of the North has remained a prime feature, the authors concede that liberal democracy and its elected parliaments give marginalized areas a better representation (p. 25). In the case of appointed legislative bodies, the authors conclude many of those appointed in non-northern regions are in fact of northern origin but have been living in other regions.

Table 6. **Governors, Commissioners, and State Ministers**

Region	Governors		Commissioners		Ministers	
	Number	Percentage	Number	Percentage	Number	Percentage
North	9	69.2%	160	51%	240	47.5%
Eastern	2	12.5%	13	13%	9	1.8%
Central	2	12.5%	27	27%	25	4.9%
Southern	Excluded	–	69	69%	160	31.7%
Western	3	18.8%	47	47%	71	14.1%

Legal System

The Black Book acknowledges the important role attached to the legal profession in the making of any modern state. It equally praises the history of the Sudanese legal profession and its pursuit of justice and equality. However, the legal profession has also been subject to the insidious hands of the northern power brokers, as the publication states. In the words of the authors: "the leadership of the legal system at the level of the Minister for Justice and the Attorney General has been controlled by the executive powers which are characterized by nepotism and discrimination among the members of the nation" (p. 28). Table 7 shows the regional affiliation of heads of the legal system in postindependence Sudan.

Table 7. **Sudanese Attorney Generals**

Region	Number	Percentage
North	8	67%
Eastern	0	0%
Central	3	33%
Southern	0	0%
Western	0	0%

The Media

The media, too, has not escaped the assault of *The Black Book*. It is described as dominated by the north and playing its tunes. This, as *The Black Book* claims, is evident at the level of news, art, and appreciation of music and lyrics and evolution of culture. In short, the media has projected the culture of the north and elevated it to a national culture at the expense of other parts of the Sudan (pp. 28–33). With extreme sarcasm, *The Black Book* narrates how the *jihad* itself did not escape the wrath of the northernization process: "Examine with us the documentary films on Mujahideen which are produced by the Popular Defence Forces and (National) charity corporations. Look at the pictures and scrutinize the names. Wouldn't you be certain that all the Mujahideen in the Sudan are from the Northern Region? That the defending army and its martyrs who fall every day are equally from the same region? And the weddings of these martyrs are classified in tandem with their corresponding levels of citizenship; first, second, and third" (pp. 32–33). The involvement in "jihad" and the sacrifice it entails are, however, different according to *The Black Book* as shown in Table 8.

Table 8. **Number of "Martyrs" for a Certain Period for Present Government**

Area	Number of Martyrs
South Darfur	1923
North Darfur	1212
West Darfur	713
Northern	111
River Nile	196
Western Kordofan	1796

Strict control over the media meant that the agendas are determined by the north. Those who wished otherwise are subjected to character assassination, often involving the usual racist card. A number of leaders were quoted as an example of this exclusionary mechanism, including Daoud Bolad, Faroug Adam, Ali Al Haj, and Jar Al Nabi (pp. 33–37).

Wealth (Mal-) Distribution

The Black Book contends that distribution of resources in Sudan has always been skewed in favor of the Northern Region. This pattern has been copper-fastened by the northern control over public finance in the country: "[…] The Ministry of Finance has become an estate belonging to the Northern Region. Excluding some Board directors inside the Ministry, you would not find even 5 percent of its staff from outside the northern Region. Appointment of staff in the Ministry is primarily reserved for the citizens of the north. Those from other Regions have to contend with tea-making and cleaning services. Even the drivers are also recruited from northern school dropouts whose family members are working in the Ministry" (p. 39).

The Black Book concludes that this pattern of employment has its bearings on the approval of government allocations for developmental schemes across the nation, which again favors the Northern Region: "No (non-northern) state has ever exceeded 36 percent of its allocated budget while actual expenditure of the two northern states has never dropped below 60 percent of their annual approved allocations. This has left the northern states in continuous position for attracting extra funds originally destined for other states" (p. 39).

In line with this pattern, *The Black Book* bemoans the liquidation of eight developmental schemes, none of which was in the north: "These schemes were not sold or privatized but simply cancelled despite the fact that they were developmental in nature and had an impact on the life of ordinary citizens of these states … To date and since independence, not a single scheme has been established in the Western state which is capable of supporting one province for a period of one month" (p. 43).

Seventeen public enterprises (schemes, corporations, etc.) were privatized in recent years. It is implied in *The Black Book* that the privatization of these public amenities was characterized by nepotism, corruption, and open defiance of national interests (pp. 43–44).

Other issues raised in *The Black Book* that we are not able to summarize include topics such as agricultural services, natural resources, animal resources, industrial sector, energy and water, transport and communication, development and public services, and banking and economic corporations.

Committee for Distribution of Wealth

The start of petrol production and export has introduced a new dimension to Sudan's economy. This necessitated formation of what has come to be known as the National Council for Distribution of Resources. Regional membership of the council is given in Table 9.

Table 9. **The National Council for Distribution of Resources**

Region	Number of Representatives	Percentage
Northern	19	76%
Eastern	1	4%
Central	1	4%
Southern	3	12%
Western	1	4%

Needless to say, *The Black Book* sees the composition of this council firmly in line with the pattern of northern domination of the country.

In its last chapter, *The Black Book* explores the consequences of the alleged "imbalance in the scale of justice," a term used as a subtitle for the publication. It says:

Loss of government credibility has been one of the prime consequences of this injustice. All governments since Independence and up until Al Mahdi's rule of [1986–1989] (which is the only government that made some effort towards a better distribution of wealth) have adopted a single path, that of entrenching the power and resources in the north and small part of the centre. The government of National Salvation, however, has come to affirm the ethnic and regional domination of the north over the rest of the country… (pp. 58–59).

Comments and Analysis

The Black Book is certainly very controversial. In the words of Francis Deng (1989), "What is not said is what divides."[2] The success of *The Black Book* in making a persuasive discussion of what is not talked about made it an instant grassroots topic. Indeed, its method of reaching the public is a unique case worthy of being studied by every student of mass media. In many ways, its speed of dissemination has probably surpassed alternative media in comparable settings with strict official control over information. An informant working in a public photocopying office claimed that he had duplicated eleven copies for his friends in five different cities. An owner of a photocopying shop in Khartoum said, "This book came to us from heaven. I made no less that one hundred copies for our customers. We sometimes charged them more due to the risk involved in duplicating illegal documents."

The mystique of *The Black Book* is further boosted by the high level of illiteracy in the Sudan, as most people knew about it and its contents through word of mouth, apparently the most powerful tool of mass media even in the modern world. A company manager in Khartoum declared:

> As I was coming out from the mosque, somebody handed me a copy of a book. I threw it in my car and forgot about it. Suddenly everybody started talking about *The Black Book*. It was three days later when I realized I was one of those who received a copy. I read it and found nothing new. Well, I had already mastered the contents of *The Black Book* from my neighbors even before reading it.

Naturally, *The Black Book* is met with different feelings ranging from admiration, embarrassment, and disbelief to fear, contempt, and anger. Wherever one stands, it is hard to think as though *The Black Book* has never been published. This is clear from the response of most major political players in the country. Both government and opposition parties, including Turabi's faction, contend that *The Black Book* raises an important issue of injustice. The mess highlighted in *The Black Book* is, however, common throughout policies and actions of all governments and political parties. Hence the criticism is general and so is the responsibility. Indeed, every party in the country is now claiming to be the better candidate for setting things right.

Following the demise of Al-Turabi in December 1999, an intense power struggle ensued in the country. The government as well as Al-Turabi's factions toured the country for support. Delegates that toured the western regions found that three issues dominated the public agenda: the western highway project; pay of public servants, in particular, teachers; and *The Black Book*.

Needless to say, the distribution of *The Black Book* sparked frantic investigation by the security apparatus. It was rumored that several junior officials were fired from their posts in the Presidential Palace due to the appearance of *The Black Book* on the desks of top officials, including the president. Writers, journalists, academics, and publishing houses were subjected to security investigations during which fonts of computer software, typewriters, etc., were checked. The investigation was fruitless and the authors remained unknown.

Al-Turabi declared that he senses an Islamic touch in *The Black Book*. Others say it is the work of frustrated scholars from the Western Region. The *Sudan Democratic Gazette* seems to favor this view. Yet others say people who have been close to power must have authored this publication and had access to classified information.

Certain observations can, however, be made about *The Black Book* that may shed some light on its authors. First, its language reflects some sort of an Islamic vision common among the Islamic parties in the country. This is further affirmed by the attempt of *The Black Book* to read the situation within a clearly defined Islamic Sudan.

Second, the grievances of the western Sudan and its leaders seem to be paramount and disproportional to other marginalized Regions the *Book* tries to defend, including the south.

Third, there is a distinct lack of sympathy for the north. This is despite the fact that following the logic of the book, its numerous ethnic groups are dominated by the "Powerful Three" northern ethnic groups: the Shaigia, the Jaaliyeen, and the Danagla.

Fourth, confining *The Black Book* to an Arabic version implies that the South had little or no input in its publication. The subsequent translation of the book into English has, however, now made it available to non-Arabic readers.

Fifth, the distribution of *The Black Book* reflects a style of organization, discipline, and execution that is far beyond the competence of organizations other than the NIF. Nonetheless, *The Black Book* is unlikely to be the product of the mainstream NIF.

Public Reaction

The fact that *The Black Book* is written in Arabic gave it an immediate public response, for the material it contains cannot be ignored by Sudan's tense and severely divided identities. A similar response was echoed earlier in relation to the role of discursive narratives in the making of competing identities in the Sudan. In examining writings of fifteen Sudanese authors of various ethnic origins, Mohamed Salih laments, "caught between ethnic and national identity crises, Sudanese authors who publicly expressed ethnic sentiments were denounced for fear that they might frustrate the nation-building project that embarked violently on creating one nation-state (Arabist in its orientation), one religion (Islam as an ideological inspiration), and one language (Arabic as a dominant discourse) despite the ethnic and cultural diversity of the country. The result was the development of an increasingly agonized intellectual milieu, with split identities which are often privately ethnic and publicly nationalist."[3]

In the process of writing this review, we interviewed a very small number of Sudanese across the ethnic divide in order to sample their response to *The Black Book*. Although the majority of the Sudanese population may not share their views, they give an impression, no matter how partial, of the significance of the book and its ability to engage people in a noteworthy political debate on the nature and structure of the Sudanese polity. The reactions of members of the general public are as follows.

A bank official from Darfur commented on *The Black Book* as follows:

A man went to the court and was asked to present his case in writing. Being illiterate, he commissioned a scribe to write his case. When the case is documented, the scribe said: Let me read it to you to see if you are happy with it. Upon reading the document, the man started weeping. The scribe said:

Why do you cry? I am only reading what you have just told me. The customer said: I knew I was subjected to injustice but I never knew it was that bad.

The banker continued:

This is how I felt in reading *The Black Book*. We all knew that we were taken for a ride and that we have been discriminated against. I was so angry that I wanted to go out and beat up the first northerner I met. Well, I might be exaggerating but for the first time, I have the information to prove that we are done.

Another reader from Kordofan commented:

Now we have the information in front of our eyes, and if we say the system is unjust, then we cannot simply be accused of being racists. What we want is plain and simple: a Sudan which is for everybody and in which we are all equal including the specified three ethnic groups.

A teacher from Darfur residing in the Central Region commented:

I like those guys because they wrote from the heart and in a language which we can all follow. They knew what they are talking about and they don't put it in the way you intellectuals do. Not a single politician was able to dispute what is said so far.

A taxi driver from the North:

There has never been any justice for you westerners. But you are not alone in that. We in Halfa suffer even more than you. Even the southerners have a better deal than us despite the Jihad against them. At least you are able to speak out. We are relegated to nothing but cooking for those guys. A cook is a cook even if he works in the kitchen of the [Presidential] Palace.

A politician from Kordofan said:

I thoroughly enjoyed the book. We have always raised the issue of injustice, but *The Black Book* was able to prove it with clear and straight statistics. It occasionally went too far giving munitions to racists and tribalists. What is the point when the case is already made? The highway, the petrol revenue, Al Obeid Water Project, the injustice is unmistakable.

A security man from Darfur, living and working in Khartoum, narrated:

I read the book three times. Things shouldn't have been said in this way. We know that the system has never been fair, but we should avoid stirring troubles. Strangely enough, I have never been able to dispute what is said.

I thought the government would, but they kept quiet. Even the northern journalists just said the book is racist but stopped there.

A lawyer of mixed parentage (Darfur/River Nile) said:

I was so embarrassed reading *The Black Book*. Where are all these politicians we admired? Can't they see all this? Having said that, I would like to think that *The Black Book* got it wrong. How did they manage to find the ethnic origins of all those who are listed? We can establish the ethnic affiliation of the members of this government, but can we be sure about those who were in power even before I was born? I think part of *The Black Book* is cooked, but I cannot prove it. I hope someone else does.

A pensioner from Darfur narrated:

It has finally been said loud and clear. We knew this for years and years. Here it is for those who do not know. I cannot imagine any present or future leader being able to ignore the contents of this book. I am glad it came out and would love to know who are the authors. They are great.

A civil servant (from Kordofan working in Khartoum) commented:

The Black Book is definitely the work of [Al-Turabi] and his boys. What did he do when he was in power? He only made it worse. Now he is trying to embarrass the government. We know that type of printing is only available for [Al-Turabi's] people. *The Black Book* is certainly well written and has important information, but the timing is not right. Sudan is now facing war staged by the whole world and we should unite. No, this book doesn't help at all.

Judged by its popularity, *The Black Book* could certainly be rated as one of the most important political publications in contemporary Sudan. It is unthinkable that any present politician will act as though it has not been published. Indeed, it is a publication that would be foolish to ignore. The compilation of the statistics is worthy of note and has given *The Black Book* a power that is hard to challenge. The main thesis of *The Black Book* remains intact no matter how many mishaps are detected in the publication.

The latter part of *The Black Book* is, however, less organized and often carelessly presented. Some claims are not substantiated, and it is not good enough to state points whose evidence lies outside the text, for example, in newspaper articles, government decisions, etc. Occasionally, *The Black Book* relies on anecdotal knowledge. For example, the claim that equipment owned by the Western Highway Project was diverted to the Northern Highway Project is not corroborated by evidence in *The Black Book*. One may say everybody knows this, but still evidence is missing in the publication. Other examples here include treatment of Jar Al Nabi, Farouq, and the governor's house in Al Obeid (the HQ of Kordofan State). Supportive evidence for these claims might be available in newspaper articles and official documents. Nonetheless, lack of presentation of these documents weakens the argument considerably.

In several passages, the book launches into personal vendetta. This should have been avoided. *The Black Book* also fails to distinguish between government policies and idiosyncratic behavior and corruption enacted by certain individuals. Surely not every action that went against the alleged marginalized regions or performed by officials from the north is rooted in government policies. This point is not fully observed in *The Black Book*.

Despite this, one has to concur with the main view of *The Black Book* that a minority within the Northern Region has dominated the Sudan and that a move toward a more inclusive Sudan is wanting. The implications of *The Black Book* on the current debate on the future of the Sudan are significant and this is what we intend to allude to in the closing pages of this review article.

Concluding Remarks

The Black Book touches a raw nerve in the Sudanese identity construction debate by deconstructing the political use of identity politics in cementing the dominant discourse of power. The potency of the discourse espoused by *The Black Book* is embedded in a politics of difference expressed in an economic reality characterized by inequality and social injustice. It signals a shift in Sudanese conceptualizations of their political reality from an abstract notion of difference based on cultural and ethnic cleavages to tangible material differences projected in the unsettling task of choosing between competing definitions of what informs the genesis of a collective Sudanese identity, if that common identity has ever existed. Behind the glow of the nation-building project and its discontent there exists a tragic tale of social, political, and economic exclusion. It is a tale of a nation divided not only in terms of the constitutive elements of identity politics, but also the resonance of the political economy that usurps the cultural meaning of distributive justice.

The fact that *The Black Book* of the Sudan has come from unknown sources and is authored by unknown "people" who advocate the grievances of forgotten people says much about the nature of the political space available to those brave enough to interrogate injustice. It says little about the dominant social forces behind this episode, although these social forces could be regionally and ethnically diverse, but working collectively within the boundaries of a dominant discourse that rejects those who fail to keep silent. This is not surprising in situations where the search for identity in conflict-ridden states is an important ingredient in the making of political boundaries that serve to reproduce subjugation or dominance.

In the Sudan, and probably elsewhere, identity construction is not a simple assertion of cultural or ethnic difference. It bestows meaning on the ideology of dominance on which economic difference thrives, while its nature is denied, hence pushed to obscurity. Engaging obscurity and redeeming it from the possibility of deconstructing the myth of community or nation is in itself a very powerful counterdiscourse and a politically informed ideological strand built around the narrators' capacity to unravel the bedrock of injustice. *The Black Book of the Sudan* has done exactly that, and in a discourse proved capable of alienating its opponents. Its consequences will certainly outlive the eternity of its ghost publishers since ghosts are immortal.

Notes

1 This page number, along with all others that appear in this essay, refer to the page numbers in the original version of *The Black Book*, not the page numbers of the portion of *The Black Book* reproduced in Appendix I. We decided to leave the page numbers in this essay in the event that people want to cross-reference the original version of *The Black Book*.

2 An article with the same title is published in Gunnar Sørbø and A. G. M. Ahmed, *Management of the Conflict in the Sudan* (Bergen: University of Bergen Press, 1989), pp. 10–18.

3 Mohamed, M. A. Salih, "Other Identities: The Politics of Sudanese Discursive Narratives," *Identities: The Journal of Global Power and Culture* 2, no. 2 (1999): 29.

Appendix K

Arab Congregation [Gathering] and the Ideology of Genocide in Darfur, Sudan

Abdullahi Osman El-Tom

This essay presents six documents related to *Al Tajamu' Al Arabi*, loosely translated here as the "Arab Congregation." Other translations are: the Arab Coalition, Arab Gathering, Arab Alliance, and Arab Congress.

The Arab Congregation was probably formed in the early 1980s, but gained momentum later in the decade. Darfur has been a major site of operation of the Arab Congregation. This basic fact disguises the broader aim and geographic spread of the organization. Within Sudan, the Arab Congregation aims at displacing and controlling indigenous populations of the entire country though modestly starting with the six states of the western regions and provinces of Kordofan and Darfur.

At the broader regional level of Sub-Saharan Africa, tentacles of the Arab Congregation have spread as far as Chad, Cameroon, Central African Republic, Niger, and possibly beyond. The geographical spread of the organization indicates that the Arab Congregation of Western Sudan is merely a small cog within a wider network of national and regional dimensions. At the national level, the Arab Congregation of Western Sudan is sponsored and operates as a conduit for *Kayan Al Shamal* (KASH) or the Northern Entity in English.[1] KASH was formed in 1976 when the government of dictator Numeiri was nearly toppled by a Kordofan army officer, who in today's language in the Sudan would be classed as "black" and non-Arab. KASH was then formed to ensure that, irrespective of the ideology behind the government of Khartoum, democratic, fascist, military, socialist, religious fanatic, or otherwise, the leadership remains in the hands of the Northern Region. But KASH is an exclusive club, open only for the three elite ethnic groups of the Northern Region. This is what various circles, including the Arab Congregation, referred to as *Al Thalooth* – i.e., the Tripartite Coalition. The Tripartite Coalition, which has been ruling the Sudan since independence, encompasses barely three ethnic groups: the *Shaiqiyya* (ex-President Sir Alkhatim, current Vice President Taha), the *Ja'aliyyin* (President Albashir), and the *Danaqla* (ex-President Ja'far Numeiri, ex-Prime Minister Sadiq Al Mahdi, and former Vice President Alzubair). For the last forty years or so, KASH has spearheaded the project of Arab-Islamization of the Sudan, and in their pursuit of their project, they needed foot soldiers supplied by various bodies, including the Arab Congregation. The hegemony of the Northern Region over Sudan is so clear-cut and requires no rerun in this article.[2]

The might of the geopolitical dimension of the Arab Congregation was chillingly demonstrated in Darfur in the early 1980s. Following the collapse of Numeiri's regime, the Khartoum government connived with Muammar al-Qaddafi of Libya in his disastrous gamble in Chad to turn Darfur into one of their daring crusades to push the so-called Islamic Belt into Black Africa. Having been kicked out of Chad,

Qaddafi proceeded to locate his Islamic Legion under the command of Acheikh Ibn Omar in Massalit land, western Darfur. The Islamic Legion, whose recruits were from Chad, Mali, Niger, and as far away as Mauritania, devastated the area and its indigenous inhabitants. Settlers of the Islamic Legion in Darfur were later to play a prominent role as *Janjawid*, effectively executing Musa Hilal's call to "change the demography of Darfur and empty it of African tribes."[3] Attempts to change the demography of Darfur are still going on to this day. As recently as July 2007, Bloomfield accused the government of Sudan of "cynically trying to change the demography of the whole region." Monitoring the Chadian-Sudanese borders, Bloomfield wrote:

> An internal UN report, obtained by *The Independent*, show that up to 30,000 Arabs have crossed the border in the past three months. Most arrived with all their belongings and large flocks. They were greeted by Sudanese Arabs who took them to empty villages cleared by the government and Janjawid forces [...] further 45,000 Arabs from Niger have also crossed over.[4]

At least three conclusions can be drawn so far, each of which connects with a general misconception about the current conflict in Darfur. First, the Darfur conflict cannot be reduced to a strife that is internal to Darfur and as an outcome of environmentally generated scarcity of resources. Rather, the conflict is part and parcel of national and regional dynamics and aspirations.

Second, the Janjawid are not a by-product of the present Darfur conflict. Their current involvement in the Darfur war is a mere culmination of decades of atrocities in the region as well as in other parts of the Sudan, such as Abeye in southern Sudan.

Third, the reading that the Khartoum government unleashed the Janjawid following the rebellion in Darfur is factually incorrect. On the contrary, the Darfur rebellion took place due to several reasons, including the atrocities of the Janjawid against indigenous Darfurians.

The Documents

In the following pages, I will present several documents, all of them translated by myself. Notes made by the author on the text are placed between brackets while official translation of Qur'anic verses is used throughout. Some of these documents have been commented upon in English in other sources, but they have never been made available in their entirety to the English reader. Therefore, the value of this article lies in the inclusion of the documents and not in my own analysis as such.

As the documents presented here are of clandestine nature, their sources have remained unconventional to this day. Documents 1 and 2 are the exception. Document 1 was published in the Sudanese daily newspaper *Al-Ayam*, October 5, 1987, while Document 2 is currently posted at www.amiralnour.googlepages.com. Documents 3–6 have not been published and are circulated through personal exchange of their photocopies. Occasionally, these documents are copied by hand for further circulation. The author has obtained all of these documents through normal post or fax and is, therefore, not in a position to point to their exact sources.

Document 1
"Arab Coalition
Foundation Statement/Bian Assasi
[October 1987]

"In the Name of God, Most Gracious, Most Merciful" – Holy Qur'an
Sayed [title meaning "Mr."] Prime Minister [Sadiq Al Mahdi]

The Arab race known today as Arab tribes in Darfur entered the Sudan together
with the Arab waves that arrived in the fifteenth century. Despite their division into
numerous groups, these tribes belong to one origin.

These tribes settled in two areas in Darfur Region. One faction settled in an
area constituting 88 percent of the province of South Darfur. The other faction settled
in the province of North Darfur; namely, the greatest part of its northern, middle,
eastern, and western territories. In the province of North Darfur, Arab settlement
constitutes 55 percent of the province. The Arab tribes now form more than 70 percent
of the population of Darfur Region.

Over the centuries that followed their entry into Sudan and their settlement
in Darfur, these Arab tribes have played a pivotal role in the formation of the identity
of the Region. In this part of the nation, Darfur Arabs have been the makers of
civilization that formed the real and actual existence of this region. That they have
done through their involvement in politics religion and language and in a manner
that led to the moulding of present Sudan.

Darfur Arabs have also been instrumental in the Mahdist Revolution, having
fought, excelled, and died in defence of Sudan. Throughout other periods, Darfur
Arabs have contributed to political, economic, social, civilizational, and cultural
advancement of Darfur in particular and Sudan in general.

We reaffirm that we have defended and we will continue to defend the unity
of Sudan, and with utmost belief and strength. We will remain united and avoid any
fragmentation and guard the wholeness of Sudan at all times.

Sayed Prime Minister
Scholars of political systems define regional governance in different ways. However,
they all concur that regional governance calls for handing over power to the people
of the concerned region to undertake political, administrative, and economic reforms.
Regional governance stipulates that the tribes of the region take over the running
of the region and manage their affairs using their available capable cadres. In this
regard we state with regret that we have been deprived of our right of leadership,
representation, and participation in decision-making in this region. We have become
a majority but with no weight and subjects but not citizens. This has been the case
despite the following:
1. We represent 70 percent of the population of the region.
2. Our educated members constitute 40 percent of the total educated members
    of the region. We have hundreds of university graduates and tens of others who
    have obtained Masters and Ph.D. degrees in numerous specializations.
3. Our contribution to the national budget amounts to no less than 15 percent.

4. Our contribution to Darfur Region exceeds 90 percent.
5. We contribute a lion's share to the army and in sacrifice to the nation.
6. We have contributed fourteen representatives to the Constitutional Assembly (*Jam'iya Ta'sisiya*) who have effectively represented us, the Arabs. We have equally contributed eighteen members to the Constitutional Assembly (*Jam'iya Ta'sisiya*) [note irregularity in the last two sentences].

Mr Prime Minister:
All that we have said confirms the political, social, and economic weight of Darfur Arab tribes. We therefore demand to be represented at a minimum of 50 percent in the regional constitutional posts and in the regional representation to the central government.

We are worried that should the neglect of representation of the Arab race prevail, things may go out of control and matters may pass from the hands of the wise to the ignorant. Consequences of that will be unpalatable. Injustice visited by a kin is more painful than a stab of a sword.

Finally, we assure every Sudanese citizen that we are not calling for fragmentation and disunity. We are calling for justice and equality. Long live Sudan, united and under freedom and democracy.

Interim Committee, Mandated by the Arab Congregation:
Signed: 1. Abdalla Masar; 2. Sharif Ali Jagar; 3. Ibrahim Yagoub; 4. Hesain Hasan Basha; 5. Nazir Hanid Beito; 6. Tajeldin Ahmed Alhilo; 7. Ayoub El Baloula; 8. Mohamed Khawif Alshitali; 9. Zakaria Ibrahim Abu Lehao; 10. Mohamed Zakaria Daldoum; 11. Nazir Alhadi Eisa Dabaka; 12. Altayib Abu Shama; 13. Sindika Dawood; 14. Haroun Ali Sanusi; 15. Dr. Omer Abdel Jabbar; 16. Abdalla Yahia; 17. Sulaiman Jabir Abbaker; 18. Nazir Mohamed Yagoub Alumda; 19. Hamid Mohamed Kheiralla; 20. Mohamed Aldouma Omer; 21. Abdelrahman Ali Abdelnabi; 22. Ahmed Shahata Ahmed; 23. Abubaker Abbo Amin; 24. Jabir Ahmed Alreyyah; [End of text].

Document 2 [5]
Qoreish [Quraysh] 2 [6]
Extremely Confidential

"In the Name of God, Most Gracious, Most Merciful.
Say: O God!
Lord of Power
To whom Thou pleasest
And Thou strippest off Power
From whom Thou pleasest:
Thou enduest with honour
Whom Thou pleasest,
And Thou bringest low
Whom Thou pleasest:
In Thy hand is all Good.
Verily, over all things
Thou hast power" [7]

God, the Almighty Is Most Truthful.

In Qoreish 1, we have covered the birth of the new Qoreish and some of its programs. However, new political realities, with internal and external dimensions, necessitate taking a moment of reflection to recall objectives, review plans, and consolidate achievements for realization of your noble aims. As you know, the *Ja'aliyyin*, the *Danagla*, and the *Shaiqiyya* have prevented us ruling Sudan for almost a century. Despite their adopted Arab cloak, these three ethnic groups are nothing but a hybrid, both racially and culturally, and are part and parcel of the Nubian Egyptian fabric. These groups intend to cling to power forever. As we have just learned, these groups have vowed to retain power and rotate it among themselves.

Qoreish is currently passing through a difficult period. All of us, and especially the two partners in Kordofan and Darfur, are requested to rise above opinionated and sectarian divisions so that we can achieve our noble objectives and retain gains that have been realized to date. To achieve our objectives, it is necessary to hold fast to the following:

a. Aiming at the year 2020 as the latest date.
b. Objectives are those stated in Qoreish 2020 (i.e., to control Sudan).
c. Provisional objective: to control the six western States of Sudan.
d. Plans, programs, and methods:

1. Internal to Sudan Recommendations

− Giving special attention to education, both vertically and horizontally; and preparation of highly qualified cadre in all specializations, including politics, economics, media, security, and military profession.
− Establishment of an economic institution/foundation.
− Enlightened recruitment into the army and security apparatus.
− Continuation of the plan of pretentious cooperation with the current regime.
− Retention of established working relations with some of the central figures who belong to the ruling tripartite coalition [*Ja'aliyyin, Danagla*, and *Shaiqiyya*].
− Coordination with our cousins in central and eastern Sudan.
− Affirmation of the tribes of the north-south intersection zone, their support, armament, and training; making use of Popular Defence Force [at the time, pro-government militias], Mujahidiin, and Peace Forces.
− Encouragement of all those who are able to fight to join Sudan Peace Force.
− Retention of channels of communication with the Dinka.
− Complete commitment to principles enshrined in Shaheen Operation of south Kordofan.
− Containment of friction between Nuhood and Alfula townships (Kordofan) and urging of relatives across the nation to avoid internal strife, which depletes energy.
− Avoidance of raising the oil issue before its actual extraction.
− Containment of consequences of Nyala inter-Arab conflict as far as possible and working for release of detained – Arab – cavalries.
− Securing of stuffiest pastures for nomads in Sudan, Chad, and Central Africa.
− Fighting traditions of land rights like *hawakir* (indigenous traditional titles to land) and *Dar* (tribal land), by all means.

- Projection of our strife against non-Arab tribes in the west as a national defence against extension of southern rebellion into the west.
- Widening the gap and demolition of trust between the center and the non-Arab tribes. That can be done by pushing leaders of the non-Arab groups to the extreme in expressing their grievances regarding injustice of the central government in the west (Darfur and Kordofan) and by enlightened collaboration with them in their racist and regionalist tendencies.
- Working for an increase of our constitutional posts in the center and in the States.
- Securing of achievements of Jamous (Buffalo) Programme in western Darfur with all its calculated consequences.
- Continuation of Teraifi 1 and Reraifi 2 in their aim of entrenching members of Qoreish in Darfur.
- Adequate preparation for elections in the six Western States.
- Remaining vigilant regarding discipline and avoiding callous behaviour like talking about the Nation of the Baggara.
- Payment of attention to positive media by our leaders.
- Necessity of upgrading financial performance of Qoreish.
- Prominent leaders of Qoreish shall remain within the National Congress, three from Qoreish [?] and making decisions as necessitated by daily events.[8]

2. External Recommendations:
- Strengthening of coordination and consultation with members of Qoreish in neighboring countries.
- Promotion of strategic thinking as founded by Albaqalani Aseel and Sheikh Ibn Omer.
- Promotion of Camel Race Programme and using it to strengthen relations with Arab brothers in the Countries of the Arab-Gulf, and with the help of God we will succeed.

"*And We wished to be*
Gracious to those who were
Being depressed in the land
To make them leaders (in faith)
And make them heirs
To establish a firm place
For them in the land,
And to show Pharaoh, Haman,
And their hosts, at their hands,
The very things against which
They were taking precautions"
(Qur'an; Ali 1983: 1002–1003)
God, the Almighty is Most Truthful.
[End of text]

Document 3

The Arab Congregation
Administration of Military Operations

"In the Name of God, Most Gracious, Most Merciful.
And hold fast,
All together, by the Rope
Which God (stretches out
For you), and be not divided
Among yourselves" (Qur'an; Ali 1983: 149).

All corporate members who have taken oath under leadership of the Arab
Congregation are instructed to convene intensive meetings in order to embark on
execution of all commitments/resolutions that have been made and implemented by
leadership of the Executive Committee. First meetings shall include all Arab tribes
that reside near the areas designated for extermination/*ibada* and burning. *'Umdas*
[mayors] and Sheikhs are to commit their subjects under oath of secrecy so that the
matter remains completely confidential. Following initial contacts, general meetings
shall be convened to include Arab and non-Arab tribes and volunteers from other
groups. Assistance of non-Arab tribes like the Zaghawa shall be commissioned, thus,
making use of them in war procedures, military training, and geographical knowledge
[original word: "studies"] of the area. In this way, the matter will not be evident
for those targeted for extermination/ibada.

The following recommendations have been endorsed:

1. Dispossession of the Fur of all their cattle and other animals through the use
   of all available means.
2. Assassination of Fur leaders, representatives, and intellectuals and restriction
   of the remaining Fur in cities, jails and murdering all those who can be killed.
3. Destruction of all means of transport, including fast ambulance services in order
   to prevent reporting of incidences to the police and to disrupt communication –
   of the victims – with the government.
4. Establishment of camps of the Arab fighters on top of mountains so that they
   remain beyond reach or entry of the attackers.
5. Starting military operations in larger and more fortified areas, using
   disproportionately large number of fighters.
6. Posting of those who have arrived from western nations/Chad, in particular
   members of Idris Jamous and Hesain Habri, in the following areas: (a) Wadi Salih,
   (b) Mukjar, and (c) Wadi Kaja.
7. Posting of fighters of Popular Defence Force who came from Kordofan (i.e., the
   Miseiriya) in the following locations: (a) Jebel Marrah, (b) South and southwest Kas,
   and (c) Wadi Bari.

All under-oath members are hereby instructed to firmly commit themselves to all
agreed resolutions until we achieve victory. You are to know that our enemies are
drawing on the support of the unbelievers and that is why we assigned our forces
to different locations and in a way that fits the military situation.

Committee of Arab Congregation in the Region
Administration of Military Operations, 1992.
[End of text].

Document 4[9]
The Arab Congregation
Strictly Confidential

Mr_____

The Executive Committee of the Arab Congregation held a meeting for the purpose of evaluation of activities of all members and for reviewing the situation following appointment of Ministers of Regional Government from among the "*Zurqa*" population. The meeting agreed that we never obtain a position in Darfur without recourse to (armed) struggle and unity among ourselves. This is a difficult and critical time and can only be endured by determined men. To achieve objectives of the Congregation, the Supreme Committee of the Arab Congregation made the following decisions.

Committed members of the Congregation and who are under oath are to:

1. Incite troubles for the regional government and use all possible means to subvert implementation of its policies and reform programs.
2. Work to paralyze delivery of public services in the areas of the "*Zurqa*" population and agitate them and make them feel that the government is impotent and incapable of delivering even the minimum life requirements.
3. Double the number of our volunteers in the areas of the "*Zurqa*." Our duty necessitates creation of insecurity in these areas, halting of production, and liquidation of "*Zurqa* leaders.*"
4. Work to create tribal conflicts among the "*Zurqa*" so that they will never unite.
5. Those members of the Congregation who occupy leading positions are instructed to:
   a) Ensure concentration of public services in areas of influence of the Arab Congregation.
   b) Not to appoint children of the "*Zurqa*" in important posts and at the same time to create obstacles in the face of those members of the "*Zurqa*" community who occupy executive and administrative positions whenever it is possible.
   c) Work by all ways and means to disrupt stability of schools in areas of the "*Zurqa*." [End of Text]

Document 5
The Arab Congregation
Coordination Council of The Arab Congregation
Political Committee

Date: November 15, 2003
Subject: Report on visits of Political Committee to the localities of Buram, Tulus, Reheid Albirdi, and Iddalfursan.

The committee left for Buram Monday November 10, 2003, and reached its destination at 10:30 pm. The committee started its work immediately by holding meetings with relevant community and local administration/tribal leaders, politicians, executive officials, and notables.

Members of the committee started the meeting clarifying mission and objectives of the visit. Exploration of views of hosts followed. Host speakers relayed their satisfaction with the visit and affirmed their agreement with the mission even though the initiative was somewhat late.

Discussion focused on ambiguous issues that needed some clarification by the committee members. The committee was able to make all necessary clarifications.

The following recommendations and points were agreed upon:
1. That the project of the Arab Congregation must proceed with resolute and effective power so that the end result will be wholly achieved.
2. Making maximum use of learned people/scientists who command wisdom, prudence, and knowledge of economics.
3. Ensuring just allocation of resources and access to power at both local and national levels, especially under the expected peace agreement [which became the Comprehensive Peace Agreement (CPA)].
4. Working to speedily overcome intertribal conflicts among Arab groups.
5. Considering the issue at hand within the framework of religion, *shari'a*, and reconciliatory Islamic goodness.
6. Propagating the plan across the Sudan.
7. Changing the name of the state [meaning Darfur Region or State of South Darfur] to a suitable name.
8. Being attentive to importance of media, documentation, and research.
9. After issuing of recommendations, Brother Omer Ali Alghali, Deputy Nazir of Buram Locality, was chosen to coordinate between the people of his locality and the Coordination Council of the Arab Congregation.
10. That was followed by appointment of the Secretary of the National Congress (the ruling party) to collect signatures of members of the Local *Shura* (Consultation) Council and send them to Nyala at the earliest opportunity.
11. At the end of the meeting, all present attested under oath to work together for the success of the unification concept.

On the following day, the committee paid a visit to Nazir Salah Ali Alghali to explain the concept in detail and to which he was fully in agreement.

The committee also paid a visit to the house, which was also headquarters, of the Commissioner of the Local Council who gave the project his absolute support. The Commissioner was asked to assist the Secretary of the National Congress in the collection of signatures and in provision of transport for members of the Consultative Commission, whenever requested.

On November 11, 2003, the committee visited Tullus Fallata Nazirite and held a meeting with tribal administration, politicians, and government executive officials. The commissioner addressed the meeting, thanking the Coordination Council represented by the visiting committee. He further elaborated on the dangerous state of affairs and the necessity for unification before presenting the committee members to the meeting. After elaborate deliberations, the following recommendations were agreed upon:
1. All agreed on the idea of unification and the necessity of its implementation.
2. Setting up of an information committee.

3. Necessity of working for extended presence in the Republic of Chad.
4. Publicizing the idea among university students.
5. Opening up of migratory corridors and resting areas/seasonal camping zones for nomads.
6. Integration and organization of executive and political work.
7. Establishment of strong and good relations with the federal government.
8. Formulation of a system of exchange of security plans and intelligence – with the government.
9. Institution of appropriate economic planning to secure unity.
10. Activation and development of native administration.
11. Preparation of clear memorandum of association/congregation.
12. Abiding by strict secrecy.

'Umda [Mayor] Yousif Omer Khatir was appointed Coordinator for Tullus Local Council. The Secretary of the National Congress was nominated to collect signatures of the members of Consultative Commission [Shura] and send them to Nyala as soon as possible. The Commissioner of Tullus was urged to provide transport for the Consultative Commission members whenever demanded. The committee then met with Nazir Ahmed Alsammani Albasher who affirmed the unity project but added further recommendations:
1. There is a need to bring together all Arab leaders, expose them to the idea of unity, and commit them to its implementation.
2. Urge Nazir Madibbo of the Rizeigat to take this matter seriously with all other leaders in the area.

On November 12, 2003, the committee visited Reheid Albirdi Locality where they met with tribal leaders, politicians, and notables. The hosts pledged their unanimous support to the unity project and affirmed their willingness to work for its full realization. The following recommendations were made in the meeting:
1. Advertise the unity to the public since it is a noble project.
2. Commit to secrecy of information, particularly with regard to internal local plans.
3. Give a clear name for the unity.
4. Give a clear goal/target and work for its implementation.
5. Switch from defensive to offensive stance and take initiative to refute gossip, lies, and rumors that harm the Congregation.
6. Careful study of events in order to secure success of actions.
7. Cleanliness (self-denial, steadfastness) in dealing with others.
8. Remove Popular [Defence?] Police Force from States of Darfur as they are involved in numerous violations.
9. Work out a well-studied economic plan to support the project.
10. Complete taking over authority in South Darfur using mechanical majority.
11. Change the name Darfur to a suitable one.
12. Review the issue of the National Service with Khartoum in all aspects.
13. Encourage the sons of the Arab tribes to get recruited into the armed forces, the police, and the security bodies.

After taking oath, Brother Yousif Mohamed Yousif was elected to act as a coordinator for the Locality, while the Secretary of the National Congress in the area was nominated to collect signatures of the Consultative Commission and send them to Nyala. It is worth noting that the meeting was attended by all (Arab) families and clans, especially the Salamat who reside in Reheid Albirdi.

On Thursday November 13, 2003, the committee held a meeting with tribal leaders, notables, and politicians in Iddalfursan. After explaining the purpose of the visit, the committee listened attentively to views of their hosts. The following recommendations were then made in the meeting:

1. Employment of (Arab) university graduates in government institutions.
2. Setting up of information and research committees.
3. Guarding and development of the principles embodied in the project.
4. Protection of politicians of all concerned/Arab tribes by all means.
5. Changing the names of Darfur states into more logical ones.
6. Strengthening the social fabric of the Arabs and arrangement of exchange visits among them.
7. Laying clear economic foundations and principles.
8. Publicizing Arab actions/achievements without reservations.
9. Organizing the Janjawid for benevolent actions and for protection of the tribes.
10. Unreserved obedience to the Arab leaders, especially the Coordination Commission.
11. Arbitration to solve interstate problems between all races to attain harmony and gain respect of others.
12. Paying attention to external and particularly border trade.
13. Committing to secrecy of information.
14. Utilization of university graduates and research results.
15. Employment of graduates in government institutions [repeated, 1]
16. Improvement of administrative and executive system in the capital of South Darfur and strengthening of native administration at all levels.
17. Reviewing of planned settlement [not clear of whom] to Goz Dongo and also reviewing the water project approved in the name of Iddalfursan.
18. Reviewing of immigration to Nyala.

This was followed by taking oath and by nomination of Dabaka Isa Dabaka to act as Coordinator for the Locality. The Secretary of the National Congress to the Locality was asked to collect signatures of members of the Consultative Council and send them to Nyala. [End of text]

Document 6[10]

In the name of God, Most Gracious, Most Merciful

Subject: Intelligence Report No. 310

Sayed (Mr.) Head of Intelligence and Security Department.
Greetings of peace and Allah's blessings.

Reference to your message marked "top secret" dated August 6, 2004, and concerning removal of nine mass graves (*maqabir jama'iya*) in Darfur states; killing of any who poses a threat to content of this instruction; and possibility of giving evidence to UN, EU, and AU delegates coming to investigate mass graves, we hereby inform your Excellency of the following:

- Eight mass graves have been unearthed, removed, and completely burnt under supervision of a committee of the National Security System, Arab Congregation committee, and the Secretary-General of the State of North Darfur. The operation was conducted under protection of our forces and for whom nothing under the sun is impossible.
- We have not been able to reach the ninth designated mass grave in Wadi Salih, State of West Darfur. We appeal to your Excellency to address Administration of Military Operations to approve an airplane so that we can remove Wadi Salih mass grave, possibly containing 1200 – one thousand two hundred – remains [extra word illegible].
- We salute your Excellency, the National Salvation Revolution and the Arab Congregation.

[Repeat of Military Stamp as above left – no date inscribed; signed on left corner as follows]
Lieutenant: Hajaj Ahmed Rabih [Signature left of name]
Head of Field Division of the Light, the Fast, and the Fearful Forces, and member of Implementation Mechanism of The Arab Congregation.
[On the bottom right hand margin, comments written in a different hand read:]
For information of Military and Security Intelligence Instructions:
Graves in Wadi Salih have been unearthed within twenty-four hours using a plane, Nyala Airport to Wadi Salih. Relocation and burning shall proceed under utmost secrecy and shall not include [two words not legible].
Intelligence Division, 29th August" [Signature follows, exact name not legible; End of Document].

Discussion

The question of authenticity must arise in handling clandestine documents such as those presented in this article. Document 1, which appeared in the form of a letter addressed to Prime Minister Al Mahdi, went public and was published in national newspapers. All other documents are meant to be secret and were marked so. More often than not, participants in the meetings were sworn on the Qur'an to ensure just that.

It is hard to doubt the authenticity of the presented documents. Excellent, though brief, comments on some of them appeared in Julie Flint and Alex de Waal's 2005 publication, *Darfur: A Short History of a Long War*.[11] Harir and Sulaiman have also referred to some of them, although the latter writer relegated his comments to the footnotes of his publication.[12]

It is difficult to discern consensus of the Arab Coalition on these documents, particularly the inflammatory and racist Documents 2, 3, 4, and 5. While it is obvious that these documents reflect the work of a supremacist sector of the Arab Coalition, it is not easy to comprehend the conspicuous absence of their public condemnation among Arab groups. Moreover, racist principles contained in most of these documents seemed to have enjoyed wide support in the current Darfur conflict and are well in tune with the perception of black people in the Arab culture of northern Sudan.[13] I will return to this issue after some comments on the documents.

The appointment of Ahmed Diraig as a Governor for Darfur during Numeiri's rule in 1983 caused a stir among the Arabs of Darfur. As Diraig belonged to the Fur, the ethnic group that gave the region its name, the Arabs of Darfur saw that as a setback of their dream of dominating the region. Clandestine inflammatory cassettes circulated among members of Darfur's Arabs, some of whom were blatantly militant and racists. But the Arab groups were yet to organize into a coherent political force. That came later during Sadiq Al Mahdi's presidency later in the decade.

In October 1987, a coalition of twenty-seven Arab Groups sent an open letter to Prime Minister Al Mahdi, addressing him as one of their own and who had in some way betrayed them. The letter, signed by twenty-seven people with three names later withdrawn, referred clearly to the background where the Arabs have assisted Khartoum government in its war against the South, only to be let down by passing over the Darfur governorship to their opponents under the leadership of Tigani Sisi. The letter stated that the Arabs constituted a 70 percent majority in Darfur and demanded control over the region, together with adequate representation in the central government. The Arab Groups ended their letter with a clear warning that should their demands be ignored, matters might pass from the wise to the ignorant and with dire consequences.

In some ways, Document 1 can be said to have marked the official inauguration of the Arab Congregation. Exaggeration of the size of the Arab population is very clear. If the Arabs constituted 70 percent of Darfur's population, they would have simply controlled the region through the same election that had given power to Al Mahdi. Ibrahim, a formidable scholar who has monitored Darfur people over several decades, reverses the figures, giving the Arabs 30 percent and African ethnic groups 70 percent of the population.[14] But what is more ominous is that the letter indicated a worrying sense of superiority, a divine right to monopolize power, and readiness to use all methods to achieve its stated objective. Moreover, the letter implied that support of riverian Sudan had been secured but was not delivered (see also Qoreish 2 in Document 2).

Since its letter to Al Mahdi, the Arab Congregation went from strength to strength but has since passed its leadership to the "ignorant," if we are to use the Congregation's own expression. Subsequent communications of the Arab Congregation became steeped in a discourse of racial purity, a term that has long been relegated to the dustbin of history. Remarkably, and despite its intellectual inaccuracy, race has become central to understanding the Darfur conflict. In his thoughtful article on Darfur, Lumamba challenges analysts not to avoid the issue of race like a plague and face the ultimate truth that although race is a social construction and has no biological basis, it has been the backbone of the ideology that underpinned the conflict in Darfur and Sudan. Both the Arab Congregation and their surrogate parents, the riverian Arabs, share this ideology.[15]

At a different level, the results of the election that took place during the third democracy (1986–1989) shattered the Congregation's dream in a different way. Their claim to constitute a clear majority in Darfur was falsified and did not translate into parliamentary seats. To add insult to injury, Al Mahdi proceeded to appoint a non-Arab Darfurian (Tigani Sisi) to the governorship of Darfur. Although organized attacks by members of the Arab Congregation were reported as early as 1982, they became more incessant during the late 1980s.[16] At the same time, the Arab Congregation intensified the release of its edicts that provided ideological backing to their violence. This period also witnessed renewed emphases on Arab racial purity coupled by lumping together all indigenous Darfurians under the rubric of "Zurqa." So intense was the campaign of the Arab Congregation in this regard that non-Arab Darfurians began to see themselves as an undifferentiated mass of "Zurqa." The hybridity of race that was once alluded to by many indigenous people was finally laid to rest.

The Arab Congregation's ideological campaign of violence became less clandestine by using available technologies: cassettes, photocopying, and faxes. As the documents show, the edicts regularly called for the destruction of public services aimed at the "Zurqa," killing of "Zurqa" elites, mobilization of Arab militias, occupation of land, and inciting conflict.

At the organizational level, the Arab Congregation elected its offices in the guise of high councils, executive, political, and military committees. Moreover, links began to be forged among all Arabs of western Sudan (Kordofan and Darfur), within Sudan at large, and at the geopolitical stage spanning neighboring countries, North Africa, and the Middle East. This is chillingly demonstrated in what has come to be called Qoreish 2, released probably in the early 1990s, to follow Qoreish 1, which the author has not been able to acquire as of this publication.

Qoreish 2 subscribes to an assumed Arab racial purity that is now exclusively a preserve of components of the Arab Congregation. Riverian allies and those who championed the project of Arab-Islamization of the Sudan are dismissed in the edict as no more than hybrid Nubians and Egyptians. Much worse, they are guilty of depriving the Qoreishi and true descendents of prophet Muhammad of legitimately ruling the Sudan. In fact, the relationship between the Arab Congregation and the Tripartite Coalition, in particular, has constituted a marriage of convenience characterized by love and hate. The Tripartite Coalition sees its members as the civilized heirs of the colonial project of modernization and for which the Arab Congregation is badly suited. In its most recent form, government propaganda code named this project "the Civilizational Orientation." In the eyes of the Tripartite Coalition, the Arab Congregation is no more than a bunch of nomads, steeped in savagery and fit only for use as foot soldiers. Nonetheless, they are indispensible in carrying out full implementation of the Arab-Islamic project. If Western powers/the international community torpedoed phase one of this project in the Christian south of the Sudan, phase two of it must succeed in Darfur. It will be accomplished, even if it takes considerable delaying maneuvers, or to use Condoleezza Rice's term, "Khartoum's cat and mouse tactics" with the international community.

In a recent development, Abdel Rahim Hamdi, guru economist and El Bashir's former Minister for Economy and Finance, advised that future investment and development in the Sudan should bypass Darfur and focus on the northern Dongola-Sennar-Kordofan axis. Hamdi concluded that this triangle represents the hard core of historic and future Arab-Islamic Sudan. Following segregation of the south, taken as a given by Hamdi, this triangle guarantees power for the National Congress Party of Al Bashir in future democratic Sudan. The Arabs of Darfur have a lot to contemplate in their alliance with the Riverian people of Sudan.[17]

In examining these documents, one must avoid the temptation of treating them as work of a lunatic fringe that has little impact on what has happened and is still happening in Darfur. For any nation to be able to massacre anywhere between 200,000 to 550,000 people, mostly noncombatants, and in just over four to five years, it requires a sustained ideology and discourse capable of turning a substantial sector of its population into conniving killers. It is within this context that we should read these documents. And as long as the carnage in Darfur has called in the interference of the International Criminal Court, it is futile to waste time debating whether we have genocide at hand or not. What is pertinent is that these documents have been part and parcel of a culture that is favorable to the committal of genocide.

Comparing the Darfur situation with other countries that witnessed genocide, crimes against humanity, and other heinous atrocities, one finds similar edicts that were central to formation of an ideology that sustained the killing. Rwanda, Bosnia, Holocaust Germany, and the Anfal of Iraq were all accompanied by similar campaigns. For the purpose of this article I will restrict myself to Rwanda, whose Hutu ideology mimics, though with some differences, the contents of Arab Congregation documents. The Hutu ideology that led to the Rwandan genocide was enshrined in what was publicized as the "Ten Commandments of the Hutu." Below are the points of convergence between the Congregation documents and the Ten Commandments:

1. **Hutu Ten Commandments:**
   Point 5 of the Commandments reads:
   – All strategic positions, political, administrative, economic, and military, and security should be entrusted to Hutu.

   The Arab Congregation documents read:
   – Enlightened recruitment into the army and security apparatus (Document 1, point 1.3).
   – Encouragement of those who are able to fight to join Popular Defence Force, Mujahideen Force, and Peace Force (Document 1, point 1.8).
   – Not to appoint children of the "Zurqa" in important posts and at the same time... (Document 4, point "b").
   – Encourage the sons of the Arab tribes to get recruited into the armed forces, police, and security bodies (Document 5, point 13).

2. **Hutu Ten Commandments:**
   Point 6 reads:
   – The education sector (school pupils, students, teachers) must be majority Hutu.

   The Arab Congregation documents read:
   – Giving special attention to education, both vertically and horizontally... (Document 1, point 1.1).

- Work to paralyze delivery of public services in the areas of the "Zurqa" population (Document 4, point 3).
- Ensure concentration of public services in the areas of influence of the Arab Congregation (Document 4, point a).
- Work by all ways and means to disrupt stability of schools in areas of the "Zurqa" (Document 4, point c).

3. Hutu Ten Commandments:
Passages in point 9 read:
- The Hutu, wherever they are, must have unity and solidarity, and be concerned with the fate of their Hutu brothers.
- The Hutu inside and outside Rwanda must constantly look for friends and allies for the Hutu cause, starting with their Bantu brothers.

The Arab Congregations documents read:
- Coordination with our cousins in central and eastern Sudan.
- Strengthening of coordination and consultation with members of Qoreish in neighboring countries (Document 2, point 2.1).
- Promotion of Camel Race Program and using it to strengthen relations with Arab brothers in the Gulf countries (Document 2, point 2.3).
- Working to speedily overcome intertribal conflicts among the Arabs (Document 5, 4).
- ... under oath to work together for the success of the unification project (Document 5, point 11).
- All agreed on the idea of the unification project and necessity of its implementation.
- Advertise the unity to the [Arab] public since it is a noble project ... Give a clear name for the unity (Document 5, points 1 and 4).

4. Hutu Ten Commandments:
Point 10 reads:
- ... the Hutu ideology must be taught to every Hutu at every level. Every Hutu must spread this ideology widely.

Documents of the Arab Congregation read:
- Propagating the thought across Sudan (Document 5, point 6).
- Spreading the idea among university students (Document 5, point 4).
- There is a need to bring together all Arab leaders, expose them to the idea of unity, and commit them to its implementation (Document 5, point 1).

5. Finally, the Hutu Commandment restricts its call for having no mercy on the Tutsi. The Arab documents are much more explicit, referring to killings, assassinations, and extermination.

Darfur Crisis: From Culturecide to Genocide
The Arab Congregation documents contained in this essay were not formed in a vacuum. Rather, they are part of a discourse that has characterized the formation of Sudan's nationhood. The very constitution of Sudan as an Arab-Islamic entity

presupposes that all other cultures, indigenous or otherwise, have to give way to Arab Islamic cultures and in the way defined by the hegemonic power in the country. Genocides are not new to Sudan. Ignoring distant history, they featured in the Mahdiyya rule (Berber), in the south of Sudan, the Nuba Mountains, the conflictual zone of Abyie, and now in Darfur. While genocides in the Sudan have been intermittent, the destruction of African cultures (culturecide) has accompanied the formation of Sudan since the colonial period. British rule protected the south of the Sudan against Arab-Muslim encroachment of north but did not extend the same guardianship to other indigenous African cultures.[18]

As far as other parts of the Sudan, including Darfur, were concerned, they were simply handed over to riverian Sudan to oversee the destruction of their cultures. If the European and the Islamic Arab worlds agree on one thing in Africa, it is their conviction that black African cultures have nothing to offer, do not merit survival, and the sooner they vanish, the better. Leaving the European world aside, Sudan's Arab-Islamic project has its regional dimension that transcends national borders. Black Africa south of the Sahara is all too familiar with the incessant expansion of Arab-Islamic cultures at the expense of its indigenous counterparts. What is more perplexing is that this process has gone unchallenged for so long. Much worse, it has been taken as inevitable and desirable and has commanded the support of national and Arab leaders. Writing in this respect, Prunier notes:

> [...] in the 1980s, Colonel [Qaddafi] and Prime Minster [Sadiq Al Mahdi] gave an answer: Darfur was poor and backward because it was insufficiently [A]rabized. It had missed out in the great adhesion to the Muslim Umma because its Islam was primitive and insufficiently Arabic.[19]

As Darfur is entirely Muslim, it is the Arabization of its populations that occupied the minds of Khartoum rulers. Let us leave the alleged inferiority of Darfur Islam aside and focus on Arabization. The machinery of the state was used for that purpose: the school, the judicial system, the media, the mosque, and of course the market. All these institutions played their roles in disseminating Arab-Islamic culture while at the same time denigrating its rival, the indigenous cultures. Even the landscape itself did not escape this cultural onslaught. Towns had to be renamed to please Riverian Arab-Islamic taste. Thus Id al-Ghanam became Id al Fursan, the town Broosh became 'Uroosh, Kattal became Dar Alsalam, Khoor Mareesa became Zamzam, and so forth.[20] The fact that these towns acquired their names for historical and cultural reasons is immaterial. Part of the process is of course to rewrite history and obliterate local heritage. If the indigenous people needed any history, they can look beyond the Red Sea and retrieve it from the early Islamic period in the Middle East or the like. Not surprisingly, schools and classrooms came to be known as Al-Zahra, Omer, Osman, Abubakar, Safa, Marwa, Al-Humayra', and so forth – names that make these establishments indistinguishable from any school nomenclature in Saudi Arabia.[21] While there is nothing wrong in drawing on Islamic symbols, it is their exclusivity that makes a mockery of local history.

In looking at symbolic nomenclature, Arabism often transcends Islam. This is belied by the very fact that the plight of the Muslims in Darfur attracted little sympathy in the Arab-Islamic world. Running the risk of blaming the victim, the locals, too, have participated in pillaging their culture, a common feature of oppressed groups. Arab politics provided a rich source of names for boys in Darfur but also for Sudan at large, sometimes commensurate with eras in which Arab rulers and dictators lived. Thus Faisal (Saudi), Najeeb, Jamal, Anwar (Egypt), Sabah (Kuwait), and Qaddafi are now common names in Darfur. As for girls in Darfur, they are not fortunate. Male chauvinist gender relations offer them scant opportunity. Arab soap operas, mostly Egyptian, stand ready to fill this void. Hence you have new popular names for girls like Rania, Hanan, Sameera, Shahr Zad, and Nabeela, all lifted from Egyptian movie stars. These new names rarely feature among older generations in Darfur, instead more likely to be Khadija, Fatna, Ashsha, Mariam, Zeinab, Kaltuma, and their derivatives. The former category is Arabic while the latter is distinctively Islamic. Those whose names bear a Darfur accent also have to oblige. Thus, Abbaker became Abu Bakr, Isakha turned into Ishag, and Adoama retuned to read Adam.

The Genocide Connection

The connection between the Arab documents and the Janjawid genocide actions in Darfur is unmistakably evident. In sociological terms, genocide can be defined as "a form of violent social conflict, or war, between armed power and organizations that aim to destroy, in part or in whole, social groups and those groups and other actors who resist this destruction."[22]

In Lemkin's format, genocide involves the destruction of social groups, a fact that challenges popular perceptions of mass killing as an essential component of genocide. As Shaw explains, destruction is aimed at uprooting essential foundations of the life of such social groups.[23] Without exhausting social fields expounded by Lemkin, the assault includes destroying political, economic, and social/cultural/moral aspects of targeted social groups.

At the political level, the Arab documents were very clear about the intention of the group to destroy the political system of their enemies. To begin with, the target groups were stripped of their legitimacy to rule themselves. The right to rule the region(s) is a divine outcome of the "biological" descent of the Arab groups; the descent that connects them directly with the prophet. The right of the Arab groups for political domination is further asserted by alleged majority status and by having migrated into the area when it was empty of indigenous populations. Both of these claims are factually incorrect. As practical steps toward effecting political control, members of the Arab Congregation are called in the documents to enroll en masse in all relevant strategic institutions like the army, police, Popular Defence, and Peace Force, Security, etc.

At a different level, the documents call for the assassination of leaders of the target groups, not to appoint their members in high offices, and to set them against each other as well as against the government. All these measures are likely to destroy the political viability of the indigenous population.

In the economic field, the target groups are to be attacked at various levels. As the documents show, there is a clear mobilization for seizing properties of the "Zurqa," appropriating their land, disrupting public services, and creating instability that makes economic advancement impossible.

In the social and cultural fields, the Arab Congregation documents are again instructive regarding destruction of the non-Arab populations. Many of the points raised here already point to that direction, that is, social and cultural disruption of the target population. Denial of political and economic autonomy poses a formidable threat to the social and cultural survival of these groups. Furthermore, the documents call for setting "Zurqa" communities in conflict against each other, killing their leaders, wrecking their educational system, and reducing their populations to a state of utter dependency in the guise of landless refugees and internally displaced people (IDPs). In short, the aim of the document is to ensure that the "Zurqa" no longer constitute functioning communities.

Those who see mass killings as an essential defining feature of genocide can turn to Documents 3 and 6. The term *Ibada*, accurately translated as "annihilation," "extermination," or "eradication," occurs twice in Document 3. It is noteworthy that the first time the term *Ibada* appeared in the Arab Congregation communication was in 1992, in Document 3. Document 6 refers to a desperate attempt to hide evidence of mass killings prior to a visit of international investigators. Interestingly, international institutions and Western governments have often been accused of doing so little to protect the people of Darfur. Document 6 shows their actions, no matter how feeble, have thrown Darfur genocidaires into panic. As such, it is possible to conclude that international intervention must have reduced genocide actions and saved human lives.

In reading through the documents, one is struck by the paramountcy given to secrecy. In fact, these documents were nothing but secret. Coordination of the work with government security, army, and political machinery made it difficult for these documents and their contents to remain confidential. Evil as it may be, destruction of villages and depopulation of entire areas were openly discussed by both government officials and members of the Arab Congregation. The case of Attal Mannan, former governor of South Darfur, is revealing in this regard. Attal Mannan is also reputed to be the head of KASH (Northern Entity), referred to earlier in the article. At the height of the Darfur war in 2005, the then-governor roared in a public rally in Sheiryia town, "the Zaghawa have to look for another planet to live on." His speech openly supported the attempts of Arab Janjawid to drive the Zaghawa out of the area.

The Arab Congregation's actions and movements cannot be kept secret for another reason. The intensity of security surveillance in Darfur makes it impossible for the Arab Congregation to operate out of government sight. As allies in the Darfur war at least, the need for coordination makes secrecy unnecessary if not totally counterproductive.

Concluding Remarks

This essay examines a number of documents issued by the Arab Congregation and its branches over the last two decades. While these documents are available in Arabic, this article presents them to the English reader in their entirety. This is where the value of this essay resides. Hence, the essay does not attempt an exhaustive analysis of the documents. That job is left to the reader as well as to different work in a different space.

Documents contained in this article should be read as complementary to the discourse of genocide in Darfur. They provide an ideology that made Darfur's genocide possible. At the same, the ideology underlining these documents is not a recent phenomenon. Rather, it has been set in motion ever since Sudan was declared an Arab-Islamic state. Moreover, Sudan's project is part of a continental project that seeks to expand Arab influence, expressed as the Arab Belt farther south into Sub-Saharan Africa.

Notes

1. Abdullahi Osman El-Tom, "Darfur People: Too Black for the Arab-Islamic Project of Sudan," Part II, *Irish Journal of Anthropology* 9, no. 1 (2006): 12–18.
2. See Justice and Equality Movement (JEM), *The Black Book: Imbalance of Power and Wealth in Sudan*, Parts I and II, English Translation, UK: JEM, 2004; Abdullahi Osman El-Tom, "The Black Book of Sudan: Imbalance of Power and Wealth in Sudan," *Journal of African National Affairs* 1, no. 2 (2003): 25–35; also in *Review of African Political Economy* 30, no. 97: 501–511 (joint authorship with M. A. Salih); and Fouad Ibrahim, *Background to the Present Conflict in Darfur*, Discussion Paper, Germany: University of Bayruth, 2004.
3. Julie Flint and Alexander de Waal, "Darfur: Ideology in Arms – The Imergence of Darfur's *Janjawid*," *The Daily Star*, August 29, 2005; Julie Flint, and Alexander de Waal, *Darfur: A Short History of a Long War* (London: Zed Books, 2006).
4. Steve Bloomfield, "Arabs from Chad, Niger Pile into Sudan's Darfur-UN," July 18, 2007, www.sudantribune.com.
5. Document undated, possibly 1987; Flint and de Waal, 2005, refer it to on pages 98 and 99.
6. Qoreish [transliteration: *Quraysh*], Prophet Muhammed's tribe, was the original and most dominant tribe in Mecca at the time of the appearance of Islam. The Qoreish aristocracy were known for their initial fierce opposition to Prophet Muhammad and to his message in the early days of Islam.
7. Qur'an; also Yusuf, A. Ali, *The Holy Qur'an: Text, Translation and Commentary* (Brentwood, MD: Amana Corp, 1983), p. 129.
8. The question mark indicates a lack of clarity in the original Arabic document.
9. This document appeared in a circular letter format intended to be sent to several officials. No date was affixed to the document, but it was possibly sent in 1993.
10. The top left corner of this document has a stamp bearing the name "The Light (*El-Khafifa*), the Fast (*El-Sariya*), and the Fearful (*El-Muriya*) Forces, 28/8/2004." The top right bears a stamp with the government official emblem, possibly of the head of a bird, with an ilegible inscription and no date.
11. Flint Julie and Alexander de Waal, *Darfur: A Short History of a Long War* (London: Zed Books, 2006).
12. See Sharif Harir, "The Arab Belt Versus African Belt in Darfur," paper presented at the conference on *"Short Cut to Decay": The Case of the Sudan*. (Centre for Development Studies, University of Bergen, 1992). Mohamed Sulaiman, *Sudan: Wars of Resources and Identity* (Cambridge: Cambridge University Press 2000); in Arabic).
13. See Al-Baqir Afif Mukhtar, "The Crisis of Identity in Northern Sudan: A Dilemma of a Black People with a White Culture," in *Race and Identity in the Nile Valley: Ancient and Modern Perspectives*, C. Fluehr-Lobban and K. Rhodes, ed. (Trenton, NJ: The Red Sea Press, 2004); and Fouad Ibrahim, "Strategies for a De-Escalation of Violence in Darfur, Sudan," Special Issue of *Global Development Options* 4 (2005): 29–52.
14. See Ibrahim, 2005, p. 1.
15. Harakati Shaja Lumamba, "Darfur: A Wake up Call for Africa," *Tinabanu* 3, no. 1 (2007, Forthcoming).
16. See Flint and de Waal, 2006, p. 52.
17. Abdel Rahim Hamdi, "Future of Foreign Investment in Sudan: A Working Paper for the National Congress Party," *Sudan Studies Association Newletter* 24, no. 1 (2005): 11–14, http://www.sudanstudies.org/ssanewsletter.html.
18. In the early 1920s, the British colonial administration, as part of its divide-and-rule policy, enacted what came to be known as the Closed District Ordinance Act of 1920, which barred the freedom of movement between the Northern and Southern provinces of Sudan. The South was administered as a "Closed District," meaning that it was an isolated area and entry to it by any Northerner was highly restricted and prohibited by law.
19. Gérard Prunier, *Darfur: The Ambiguous Genocide* (Ithaca, NY: Cornell Univeristy Press, 2005), p. 162; quoted in Lumamba, 2007.
20. *Khoor Mareesa* in English translates to "stream or small river of beer." *Mareesa* is a local beer normally homemade from millet or sorgham and known to have rich nutritional value. *Zamzam* is originally the name of the famous well in Mecca, which is located near the *Ka'aba* (Bayt Allah Al Haram), and its water is believed by some Muslims to be divinely blessed.
21. These are mostly names of either the Prophet Muhammad's closest companions or famous Muslim personalities from the early days of Islam in the Arabian Peninsula.
22. Adapted from Martin Shaw, *What Is Genocide?* (Cambridge: Polity Press, 2007), p.154.
23. Shaw, 2007: 19; and R. Lemkin, *Axis Rule in Occupied Europe: Laws of Occupation, Analysis of Government, Proposal for Redress*, New York: Carneige Endowment for International Peace, 1944.

Appendix L

Resolution 1593 (2005):
Security Council Refers Situation in Darfur, Sudan, to Prosecutor of International Criminal Court, Adopted by Vote of Eleven in [Favor] to None Against, with Four Abstentions (Algeria, Brazil, China, and United States)

31/03/2005 / Press Release / SC/8351
Security Council / 5158th Meeting (Night)

Acting under Chapter VII of the United Nations Charter, the Security Council decided this evening to refer the situation prevailing in Darfur since July 1, 2002, to the prosecutor of the International Criminal Court (ICC).

Adopting resolution 1593 (2005) by a vote of 11 in favour, none against with 4 abstentions (Algeria, Brazil, China, United States), the Council decided also that the government of the Sudan and all other parties to the conflict in Darfur would cooperate fully with the court and prosecutor, providing them with any necessary assistance.

The council decided further that nationals, current or former officials or personnel from a contributing state outside the Sudan which was not a party to the Rome Statute would be subject to the exclusive jurisdiction of that contributing state for all alleged acts or omissions arising out of or related to operations in the Sudan authorized by the council or the African Union, unless such exclusive jurisdiction had been expressly waived by that contributing state.

Inviting the court and the African Union to discuss practical arrangements that would facilitate the court's work, including the possibility of conducting proceedings in the region, the council encouraged the court, in accordance with the Rome Statute, to support international cooperation with domestic efforts to promote the rule of law, protect human rights, and combat impunity in Darfur. It also emphasized the need to promote healing and reconciliation, as well as the creation of institutions, involving all sectors of Sudanese society, such as truth and/or reconciliation commissions, in order to complement judicial processes and thereby reinforce the efforts to restore long-lasting peace.

Speaking in explanation of position after the vote were the representatives of the United States, Algeria, China, Denmark, Philippines, Japan, United Kingdom, Argentina, France, Greece, United Republic of Tanzania, Romania, Russian Federation, Benin, and Brazil.

The representative of the Sudan also addressed the council.
The meeting began at 10:40 P.M. and ended at 11:55 P.M.

Council Resolution

Security Council resolution 1593 (2005) reads, as follows:

"*The Security Council,*

"*Taking note* of the report of the International Commission of Inquiry on violations of international humanitarian law and human rights law in Darfur (S/2005/60),

"*Recalling* article 16 of the Rome Statute under which no investigation or prosecution may be commenced or proceeded with by the International Criminal Court for a period of 12 months after a Security Council request to that effect,

"*Also recalling* articles 75 and 79 of the Rome Statute and encouraging States to contribute to the ICC Trust Fund for Victims,

"*Taking note* of the existence of agreements referred to in Article 98–2 of the Rome Statute,

"*Determining* that the situation in Sudan continues to constitute a threat to international peace and security,

"*Acting* under Chapter VII of the Charter of the United Nations,

"1. *Decides* to refer the situation in Darfur since [July 1, 2002] to the Prosecutor of the International Criminal Court;

"2. *Decides* that the Government of Sudan and all other parties to the conflict in Darfur shall cooperate fully with and provide any necessary assistance to the Court and the Prosecutor pursuant to this resolution and, while recognizing that States not party to the Rome Statute have no obligation under the Statute, urges all States and concerned regional and other international organizations to cooperate fully;

"3. *Invites* the Court and the African Union to discuss practical arrangements that will facilitate the work of the Prosecutor and of the Court, including the possibility of conducting proceedings in the region, which would contribute to regional efforts in the fight against impunity;

"4. *Also encourages* the Court, as appropriate and in accordance with the Rome Statute, to support international cooperation with domestic efforts to promote the rule of law, protect human rights and combat impunity in Darfur;

"5. *Also emphasizes* the need to promote healing and reconciliation and encourages in this respect the creation of institutions, involving all sectors of Sudanese society, such as truth and/or reconciliation commissions, in order to complement judicial processes and thereby reinforce the efforts to restore long-lasting peace, with African Union and international support as necessary;

"6. *Decides* that nationals, current or former officials or personnel from a contributing State outside Sudan which is not a party to the Rome Statute of the International Criminal Court shall be subject to the exclusive jurisdiction of that contributing State for all alleged acts or omissions arising out of or related to operations in Sudan established or authorized by the Council or the African Union, unless such exclusive jurisdiction has been expressly waived by that contributing State;

"7. *Recognizes* that none of the expenses incurred in connection with the referral, including expenses related to investigations or prosecutions in connection with that referral, shall be borne by the United Nations and that such costs shall be borne by the parties to the Rome Statute and those [s]tates that wish to contribute voluntarily;

"8.*Invites* the Prosecutor to address the Council within three months of the date of adoption of this resolution and every six months thereafter on actions taken pursuant to this resolution;

"9.*Decides* to remain seized of the matter."

Action on Text

The draft resolution was adopted by a vote of eleven in favor with four abstentions (Algeria, Brazil, China, and United States).

Following the vote, Anne Woods Patterson (United States) said her country strongly supported bringing to justice those responsible for the crimes and atrocities that had occurred in Darfur and ending the climate of impunity there. Violators of international humanitarian law and human rights law must be held accountable. Justice must be served in Darfur. By adopting today's resolution, the international community had established an accountability mechanism for the perpetrators of crimes and atrocities in Darfur. The resolution would refer the situation in Darfur to the International Criminal Court for investigation and prosecution.

While the United States believed that a better mechanism would have been a hybrid tribunal in Africa, it was important that the international community spoke with one voice in order to help promote effective accountability. The United States continued to fundamentally object to the view that the court should be able to exercise jurisdiction over the nationals, including government officials, of states not party to the Rome Statute. Because it did not agree to a council referral of the situation in Darfur to the court, her country had abstained on the vote. She decided not to oppose the resolution because of the need for the international community to work together in order to end the climate of impunity in the Sudan, and because the resolution provided protection from investigation or prosecution for United States nationals and members of the armed forces of non-state parties.

The United States was and would be an important contributor to the peace-keeping and related humanitarian efforts in the Sudan, she said. The language providing protection for the United States and other contributing States was precedent-setting, as it clearly acknowledged the concerns of states not party to the Rome Statute and recognized that persons from those states should not be vulnerable to investigation or prosecution by the court, absent consent by those states or a referral by the council. In the future, she believed that, absent consent of the state involved, any investigations or prosecutions of nationals of non-party states should come only pursuant to a decision by the council.

Although her delegation had abstained on the council referral to the court, it had not dropped, and indeed continued to maintain, its long-standing and firm objections and concerns regarding the court, she continued. The Rome Statute was flawed and did not have sufficient protection from the possibility of politicized prosecutions. Non-parties had no obligations in connection with that treaty, unless otherwise decided by the council, upon which members of the organization had conferred primary responsibility for the maintenance of international peace and security.

She was pleased that the resolution recognized that none of the expenses incurred in connection with the referral would be borne by the United Nations, and that instead such costs would be borne by the parties to the Rome Statute and those that contributed voluntarily. That principle was extremely important. Any effort to retrench on that principle by the United Nations or other organizations to which the United States contributed could result in its withholding funding or taking other action in response.

The council included, at her country's request, a provision that exempted persons of non-party states in the Sudan from the ICC prosecution. Persons from countries not party who were supporting the United Nations' or African Union's efforts should not be placed in jeopardy. The resolution provided clear protection for United States persons. No United States person supporting operations in the Sudan would be subject to investigation or prosecution because of this resolution. That did not mean that there would be immunity for American citizens that acted in violation of the law. The United States would continue to discipline its own people when appropriate.

Abdallah Baali (*Algeria*) said his country believed strongly in the crucial importance of combating impunity if peace and stability were to take root – a need that was even more vital in the case of Darfur, where relations between various communities had been destroyed over the years. It was, therefore, important that the fight against impunity had the equal goal of re-establishing harmony among the peoples of Darfur while serving the cause of peace.

He said that any international *démarche* toward those ends must be reinforced in a way that guaranteed a fair and transparent trial process; brought justice for the victims by restoring their rights and providing reparations for their moral and material suffering; contributed toward national reconciliation, a political settlement of the crisis and the consolidation of peace and stability throughout the Sudan; and promoted the support of all Sudanese in that process, including, in particular, securing the cooperation of the government.

Because of those factors, the African Union was best placed to carry out so delicate an undertaking because it could provide peace, while also satisfying the need for justice, he said. President Olusegun Obasanjo had made a proposal, on behalf of the African Union, based on the need to secure peace without sacrificing the need for justice. Regrettably, for the sake of reconciliation, the council had neither considered that proposal nor assessed its potential to enable its members to combat impunity. One could not claim to support the African Union while brushing aside its proposals without deigning even to consider them. At the eruption of the Darfur conflict, it had been none other than the African Union that had deployed its soldiers and begun negotiating the various complex issues involved. What was true of the Sudan was true all over Africa, and Algeria regretted that for the sake of compromise at any cost those who defended the principle of universal justice had, in fact, confirmed that even in the council there could be a double standard.

Wang Guangya (China), explaining his delegation's abstention, said that China had followed the situation in Darfur closely and supported a political solution. Like the rest of the international community, China deplored deeply the violations of international humanitarian law and human rights law and believed that the perpetrators must be brought to justice. The question before the council was what was the most appropriate way to do so. While ensuring justice, it was important to sustain the hard-won gains of the North–South peace process.

He said his country would have preferred that the perpetrators stand trial in Sudanese courts, which had recently taken action against people involved in human rights violations in Darfur. China did not favor the referral to the International Criminal Court without the consent of the Sudanese government. In addition, China, which was not a party to the Rome Statute, had major reservations regarding some of its provisions and had found it difficult to endorse the council authorization of that referral.

Ellen Margrethe Løj (Denmark) said that it had been two months since the council had received the report of the Commission of Inquiry, which had strongly recommended referring the situation in Darfur to the ICC. The court had the mandate, capacity and funding necessary to ensure swift and effective prosecution. She was encouraged that the council had voted to adopt a resolution to bring an internationally recognized follow-up to the crimes in Darfur. She recognized the difficulty of some delegations to accept the text and appreciated the flexibility shown.

Denmark had only been able to support the text after some alterations were made, she said. Regarding the formulation on existing agreements referred to in article 98–2 of the Rome Statute, she noted that that reference was purely factual and referred to the existence of such agreements. Thus, the reference was in no way impinging on the Rome Statute. The result was a valid compromise leading to the first referral of a situation to the ICC. She looked forward to the court taking the first steps to ending the culture of impunity in Darfur.

Lauro Baja (Philippines) noted that today's was the third resolution borne out of the council's consideration of Darfur. He had voted for the resolution in response to the urgency and gravity of the crimes, which the council and the international community were obliged to address. Any failure of action two months after the presentation of the report would have reduced the council to irrelevance in ending impunity and protecting human rights and international humanitarian law.

He shared the concerns of some regarding the manner in which the resolution was arrived at. Once again, veto threats prevented the expression of a clear and robust signal from the council. That was why calls for council reform were growing louder with each passing day. He also believed that the ICC was a fatality in the resolution. Did the council have the prerogative to mandate the jurisdiction of the court?

Kenzo Oshima (Japan) said he had voted in favor of the resolution because impunity for serious violations of human rights and crimes against humanity must not be allowed. Japan supported in principle the referral to the ICC within the appropriate time-frame, although it was not a party to the Rome Statute and would have much preferred more agreement among council members.

Emyr Jones Parry (United Kingdom) said that by tonight's vote the council had acted to ensure accountability for the crimes committed in Darfur. The United Kingdom hoped to send a salutary warning to other parties who may be tempted to commit similar human rights violations. The United Kingdom welcomed the adoption of the two other resolutions on the Sudan this week and called for a redoubling of efforts on behalf of peace and justice for the people of Darfur, and the Sudan as a whole, who had suffered enough. The three resolutions were a substantial contribution toward that end.

César Mayoral (Argentina) said he had voted in support of the resolution on the basis of the report to the council by the High Commissioner for Human Rights, who stated clearly what had been crimes against humanity in Darfur. The legal context for dealing with such violations was the ICC. He understood that the ICC would be the proper place to combat impunity. The resolution gave strong support to the court and demonstrated significant progress within the United Nations to ensure the functioning of an international system for human rights, for which the court was an essential tool.

He noted that it was the first time the council had referred to the court a situation involving crimes over which the court had jurisdiction. It was a crucial precedent. The letter and spirit of the Rome Statute must be respected, taking into account the legitimate concerns of States. Accordingly, he regretted that the council had to adopt a text that provided an exemption to the court, and hoped that that would not become normal practice. The exemption referred to in Operative Paragraph 6 applied only to those states not party to the Rome Statute.

Jean-Marc de la Sabliere (France) said the events in Darfur were deeply troubling, and the greatest concern was the plight of the people there. The Secretary-General's reports had provided a detailed picture of those atrocities. The council had a duty to take action. Its policy must include three elements. The first was the need to assist the African Union to strengthen its mandate for protection and monitoring. The council had done that by adopting resolution 1590 last week. Then, there was the need to exert pressure on the warring parties to fulfil their obligations and achieve a political settlement. The council did that by adopting resolution 1591 a few days ago. Finally, it was necessary to put an end to impunity. That was what the council had done today.

The commission's report recommended the referral of the situation in Darfur to the ICC, he said. The Secretary-General and the High Commissioner for Human Rights had asked the council to urgently provide a positive outcome following that recommendation. Referring the issue to the ICC was the only solution. It was necessary to do right by the victims, and doing so would prevent those violations from continuing. That was why France had been the initiator of the resolution and voted in its favor. He was gratified by the adoption of this historic resolution, by which the council, for the first time, referred a situation to the ICC.

Thus, the council had sent a strong message to all those in Darfur who had committed or were tempted to commit atrocious crimes, and to the victims. The international community would not allow those crimes to remain unpunished. It also marked a turning point and sent a message farther than Darfur. His delegation had been ready to acknowledge immunity from the ICC for nationals from states not party to the Rome Statute. He reaffirmed his confidence in the ICC and hoped that those clauses concerning immunity from the court would be dropped very soon.

Adamantios Th. Vassilakis (Greece) stressed that impunity must not be allowed to go unpunished and that was why his country had turned to the ICC. It would have preferred a text that did not make exceptions, but it was better than one that allowed violations to go unpunished. The text strengthened the council's authority, as well as that of the ICC, which would have the possibility of showing its competence. The three recently adopted resolutions on Darfur would assist in restoring peace in the Sudan.

Augustine Mahiga (United Republic of Tanzania) said that every new delay in the adoption of the resolution represented a failure to serve the interests of justice, and his delegation regretted that the text took on matters that did not concern the council. It did not permit any avoidance of the ICC's authority, and the United Republic of Tanzania hoped that the international community would not abandon the people of the Sudan, particularly those of Darfur.

Mihnea Ioan Motoc (Romania) said that text spoke for itself in showing the way the council could come together to address serious issues. The adoption of resolution 1593 was a stand against impunity and an expression of confidence in the ICC to handle complex cases, like the one the council was referring to it today. At the end of the day, the council had sent a message that there was no way that anyone anywhere could get away without retribution for grave crimes. By deciding to refer Darfur to the ICC, the council had enhanced its conflict prevention and resolution capabilities. Upholding the ICC by adopting the resolution would be to no avail unless states remained supportive of the court as it exercised its prerogatives.

Andrey Denisov (Russian Federation) said that council members had reaffirmed that the struggle against impunity was one of the elements of long-term stability in Darfur. All those responsible for grave crimes must be punished, as pointed out in the report of the Commission of Inquiry. The resolution adopted today would promote an effective solution to the fight against impunity.

Joel Adechi (Benin) said the vote was a major event in the context of the international community's attempts to ensure there was no impunity for violations of international humanitarian law in the past decade. Benin had voted in favor of the resolution because it was party to the Rome Statute and also because the worsening of the situation in Darfur meant that the council must take action to end the suffering of the civilians, ending impunity by providing impartial justice. Benin had also voted in favor out of respect for human dignity and the right to life. The African Union recognized that the international community had a responsibility to protect civilians when they were not protected by their own governments. The resolution must help them to achieve their legitimate dream of an end to their suffering and enable them to look ahead to the future with serenity.

Council President Ronaldo Mota Sardenberg (Brazil), speaking in his national capacity, said his country was in favor of the resolution, but had been unable to join those who had voted in favor. However, Brazil was ready to cooperate fully with the ICC whenever necessary. The court provided all the necessary checks and balances to prevent politically motivated prosecutions, and any fears to the contrary were both unwarranted and unhelpful.

However, there were limits to the responsibilities of the council vis-à-vis international instruments, and Brazil had consistently maintained that position since the negotiations on the Rome Statute. But the court remained the only suitable institution to deal with the violations in the Sudan. Brazil had been unable to support Operative Paragraph 6, which recognized exclusive jurisdiction. It would not strengthen the role of the ICC.

Elfatih Mohamed Ahmed Erwa (Sudan) said that, once more, the council had persisted in adopting unwise decisions against his country, which only served to further complicate the situation on the ground. The positions over the ICC were well known. The Darfur question had been exploited in light of those positions. It was a paradox that the language in which the resolution was negotiated was the same language that had buffeted the council before on another African question. The resolution adopted was full of exemptions. He reminded the council that the Sudan was also not party to the ICC, making implementation of the resolution fraught with procedural impediments. As long as the council believed that the scales of justice were based on exceptions and exploitation of crises in developing countries and bargaining among major powers, it did not settle the question of accountability in Darfur, but exposed the fact that the ICC was intended for developing and weak countries and was a tool to exercise cultural superiority.

The council, by adopting the resolution, had once again ridden roughshod over the African position, he said. The initiative by Nigeria, as chair of the African Union, had not even been the subject of consideration. Also, the council had adopted the resolution at a time when the Sudanese judiciary had gone a long way in holding trials, and was capable of ensuring accountability. Some here wanted to activate the ICC and exploit the situation in Darfur. Accountability was a long process that could not be achieved overnight. The council was continuing to use a policy of double standards, and sending the message that exemptions were only for major powers. The resolution would only serve to weaken prospects for settlement and further complicate the already complex situation.

Appendix M

Resolution 1706 (2006):
United Nations – Security Council
S/RES/1706 (2006),
Adopted by the Security Council at Its
5519th Meeting, on August 31, 2006

The Security Council,

Recalling its previous resolutions concerning the situation in the Sudan, in particular resolutions 1679 (2006) of May 16, 2006, 1665 (2006) of March 29, 2006, 1663 (2006) of March 24, 2006, 1593 (2005) of March 31, 2005, 1591 (2005) of March 29, 2005, 1590 (2005) of March 24, 2005, 1574 (2004) of November 19, 2004, 1564 (2004) of September 18, 2004 and 1556 (2004) of July 30, 2004, and the statements of its president concerning the Sudan.

Recalling also its previous resolutions 1325 (2000) on women, peace and security, 1502 (2003) on the protection of humanitarian and United Nations personnel, 1612 (2005) on children and armed conflict, and 1674 (2006) on the protection of civilians in armed conflict, which reaffirms inter alia the provisions of paragraphs 138 and 139 of the 2005 United Nations World Summit outcome document, as well as the report of its Mission to the Sudan and Chad from June 4–10, 2006.

Reaffirming its strong commitment to the sovereignty, unity, independence, and territorial integrity of the Sudan, which would be unaffected by transition to a United Nations operation in Darfur, and to the cause of peace, *expressing its determination* to work with the Government of National Unity, in full respect of its sovereignty, to assist in tackling the various problems confronting the Sudan and that a United Nations operation in Darfur shall have, to the extent possible, a strong African participation and character,

Welcoming the efforts of the African Union to find a solution to the crisis in Darfur, including through the success of the African Union–led Inter-Sudanese Peace Talks on the Conflict in Darfur in Abuja, Nigeria, in particular the framework agreed between the parties for a resolution of the conflict in Darfur (the Darfur Peace Agreement), *commending* the efforts of the signatories to the Darfur Peace Agreement, *expressing* its belief that the Agreement provides a basis for sustained security in Darfur, *reiterating* its welcome of the statement of May 9, 2006, by the representative of the Sudan at the United Nations Security Council Special Session on Darfur of the Government of National Unity's full commitment to implementing the Agreement, *stressing* the importance of launching, with the African Union, the Darfur–Darfur dialogue and consultation as soon as possible, and *recognizing* that international support for implementation of the agreement is critically important to its success.

Commending the efforts of the African Union for the successful deployment of the African Union Mission in the Sudan (AMIS), as well as the efforts of member states and regional and international organizations that have assisted it in its deployment, and AMIS's role in reducing large-scale organized violence in Darfur, *recalling* the decision of the African Union Peace and Security Council of March 10, 2006, and its decision of June 27, 2006, as outlined in paragraph 10 of its Communiqué that the African Union is ready to review the mandate of AMIS in the event that the ongoing consultations between the Government of National Unity and the United Nations conclude on an agreement for a transition to a United Nations peacekeeping operation, *stressing* the need for AMIS to assist implementation of the Darfur Peace Agreement until transition to the United Nations force in Darfur is completed, *welcoming* the decision of the African Union Peace and Security Council of June 27, 2006, on strengthening AMIS's mandate and tasks, including on the protection of civilians, and *considering* that AMIS needs urgent reinforcing.

Reaffirming its concern that the ongoing violence in Darfur might further negatively affect the rest of the Sudan as well as the region, in particular Chad and the Central African Republic, and *stressing* that regional security aspects must be addressed to achieve long lasting peace in Darfur,

Remaining deeply concerned over the recent deterioration of relations between the Sudan and Chad, calling on the governments of the two countries to abide by their obligations under the Tripoli Agreement of February 8, 2006, and the agreement between the Sudan and Chad signed in N'djamena on July 26, 2006, and to begin implementing the confidence-building measures which they have voluntarily agreed upon, welcoming the recent re-establishment of diplomatic relations between the Sudan and Chad, and calling upon all states in the region to cooperate in ensuring regional stability.

Reiterating its strong condemnation of all violations of human rights and international humanitarian law in Darfur, and *calling upon* the Government of National Unity to take urgent action to tackle gender-based violence in Darfur including action toward implementing its Action Plan to Combat Violence Against Women in Darfur with particular focus on the rescission of Form 8 and access to legal redress.

Expressing its deep concern for the security of humanitarian aid workers and their access to populations in need, including refugees, internally displaced persons and other war-affected populations, and *calling upon* all parties, in particular the Government of National Unity, to ensure, in accordance with relevant provisions of international law, the full, safe and unhindered access of relief personnel to all those in need in Darfur as well as the delivery of humanitarian assistance, in particular to internally displaced persons and refugees.

Taking note of the communiqués of January 12, March 10, May 15, and June 27, 2006, of the Peace and Security Council of the African Union regarding transition of AMIS to a United Nations operation.

Taking note of the report of the Secretary-General on Darfur dated July 28, 2006 (S/2006/591).

Determining that the situation in the Sudan continues to constitute a threat to international peace and security.

1. *Decides*, without prejudice to its existing mandate and operations as provided for in resolution 1590 (2005) and in order to support the early and effective implementation of the Darfur Peace Agreement, that UNMIS's mandate shall be

expanded as specified in paragraphs 8, 9, and 12 following, that it shall deploy to Darfur, and therefore invites the consent of the Government of National Unity for this deployment, and *urges* member states to provide the capability for an expeditious deployment.

2. *Requests* the Secretary-General to arrange the rapid deployment of additional capabilities for UNMIS, in order that it may deploy in Darfur, in accordance with the recommendation contained in his report dated July 28, 2006.

3. *Decides* that UNMIS shall be strengthened by up to 17,300 military personnel and by an appropriate civilian component including up to 3,300 civilian police personnel and up to 16 Formed Police Units, and *expresses its determination* to keep UNMIS's strength and structure under regular review, taking into account the evolution of the situation on the ground and without prejudice to its current operations and mandate as provided for in resolution 1590 (2005).

4. *Expresses* its intention to consider authorizing possible additional temporary reinforcements of the military component of UNMIS, at the request of the Secretary-General, within the limits of the troop levels recommended in paragraph 87 of his report dated July 28, 2006.

5. *Requests* the Secretary-General to consult jointly with the African Union, in close and continuing consultation with the parties to the Darfur Peace Agreement, including the Government of National Unity, on a plan and timetable for transition from AMIS to a United Nations operation in Darfur; *decides* that those elements outlined in paragraphs 40 to 58 of the Secretary-General's report of 28 July 2006 shall begin to be deployed no later than 1 October 2006, that thereafter as part of the process of transition to a United Nations operation additional capabilities shall be deployed as soon as feasible and that UNMIS shall take over from AMIS responsibility for supporting the implementation of the Darfur Peace Agreement upon the expiration of AMIS's mandate but in any event no later than December 31, 2006;

6. *Notes* that the Status of Forces Agreement for UNMIS with the Sudan, as outlined in resolution 1590 (2005), shall apply to UNMIS' operations throughout the Sudan, including in Darfur.

7. *Requests* the Secretary-General to take the necessary steps to strengthen AMIS through the use of existing and additional United Nations resources with a view to transition to a United Nations operation in Darfur; and *authorizes* the Secretary-General during this transition to implement the longer-term support to AMIS outlined in the report of the Secretary-General of July 28, 2006, including provision of air assets, ground mobility package, training, engineering and logistics, mobile communications capacity and broad public information assistance.

8. *Decides* that the mandate of UNMIS in Darfur shall be to support implementation of the Darfur Peace Agreement of May 5, 2006, and the N'djamena Agreement on Humanitarian Cease-fire on the Conflict in Darfur ("the Agreements"), including by performing the following tasks:

   a. To monitor and verify the implementation by the parties of Chapter 3 ("Comprehensive Cease-fire and Final Security Arrangements") of the Darfur Peace Agreement and the N'djamena Agreement on Humanitarian Cease-fire on the Conflict in Darfur.

   b. To observe and monitor movement of armed groups and redeployment of forces in areas of UNMIS deployment by ground and aerial means in accordance with the Agreements.

c. To investigate violations of the Agreements and to report violations to the Cease-Fire Commission; as well as to cooperate and coordinate, together with other international actors, with the Cease-Fire Commission, the Joint Commission, and the Joint Humanitarian Facilitation and Monitoring Unit established pursuant to the Agreements including through provision of technical assistance and logistical support.

d. To maintain, in particular, a presence in key areas, such as buffer zones established pursuant to the Darfur Peace Agreement, areas inside internally displaced persons camps and demilitarized zones around and inside internally displaced persons camps, in order to promote the re-establishment of confidence, to discourage violence, in particular by deterring use of force.

e. To monitor transborder activities of armed groups along the Sudanese borders with Chad and the Central African Republic in particular through regular ground and aerial reconnaissance activities.

f. To assist with development and implementation of a comprehensive and sustainable programme for disarmament, demobilization and reintegration of former combatants and women and children associated with combatants, as called for in the Darfur Peace Agreement and in accordance with resolutions 1556 (2004) and 1564 (2004).

g. To assist the parties, in cooperation with other international actors, in the preparations for and conduct of referendums provided for in the Darfur Peace Agreement.

h. To assist the parties to the Agreements in promoting understanding of the peace accord and of the role of UNMIS, including by means of an effective public information campaign, targeted at all sectors of society, in coordination with the African Union.

i. To cooperate closely with the Chairperson of the Darfur–Darfur Dialogue and Consultation (DDDC), provide support and technical assistance to him, and coordinate other United Nations agencies' activities to this effect, as well as to assist the parties to the DDDC in addressing the need for an all-inclusive approach, including the role of women, toward reconciliation and peace building.

j. To assist the parties to the Darfur Peace Agreement, in coordination with bilateral and multilateral assistance programs, in restructuring the police service in the Sudan, consistent with democratic policing, to develop a police training and evaluation program, and to otherwise assist in the training of civilian police.

k. To assist the parties to the Darfur Peace Agreement in promoting the rule of law, including an independent judiciary, and the protection of human rights of all people of the Sudan through a comprehensive and coordinated strategy with the aim of combating impunity and contributing to long-term peace and stability and to assist the parties to the Darfur Peace Agreement to develop and consolidate the national legal framework.

l. To ensure an adequate human rights and gender presence, capacity and expertise within UNMIS to carry out human rights promotion, civilian protection and monitoring activities that include particular attention to the needs of women and children.

9. *Decides* further that the mandate of UNMIS in Darfur shall also include the following:
   a. To facilitate and coordinate in close cooperation with relevant United Nations agencies, within its capabilities and in its areas of deployment, the voluntary return of refugees and internally displaced persons, and humanitarian assistance *inter alia* by helping to establish the necessary security conditions in Darfur.
   b. To contribute toward international efforts to protect, promote and monitor human rights in Darfur, as well as to coordinate international efforts toward the protection of civilians with particular attention to vulnerable groups including internally displaced persons, returning refugees, and women and children.
   c. To assist the parties to the Agreements, in cooperation with other international partners in the mine action sector, by providing humanitarian demining assistance, technical advice, and coordination, as well as mine awareness programs targeted at all sectors of society.
   d. To assist in addressing regional security issues in close liaison with inter-national efforts to improve the security situation in the neighboring regions along the borders between the Sudan and Chad and between the Sudan and the Central African Republic, including through the establishment of a multi-dimensional presence consisting of political, humanitarian, military, and civilian police liaison officers in key locations in Chad, including in internally displaced persons and refugee camps, and if necessary, in the Central African Republic, and to contribute to the implementation of the Agreement between the Sudan and Chad signed on July 26, 2006.
10. *Calls upon* all member states to ensure the free, unhindered and expeditious movement to the Sudan of all personnel, as well as equipment, provisions, supplies and other goods, including vehicles and spare parts, which are for the exclusive and official use of UNMIS in Darfur.
11. *Requests* the Secretary-General to keep the council regularly informed of the progress in implementing the Darfur Peace Agreement, respect for the cease-fire, and the implementation of the mandate of UNMIS in Darfur, and to report to the council, as appropriate, on the steps taken to implement this resolution and any failure to comply with its demands.
12. Acting under Chapter VII of the Charter of the United Nations:
   a. *Decides* that UNMIS is authorized to use all necessary means, in the areas of deployment of its forces and as it deems within its capabilities:
      i. To protect United Nations personnel, facilities, installations and equipment, to ensure the security and freedom of movement of United Nations personnel, humanitarian workers, assessment and evaluation commission personnel, to prevent disruption of the implementation of the Darfur Peace Agreement by armed groups, without prejudice to the responsibility of the government of the Sudan, to protect civilians under threat of physical violence.
      ii. In order to support early and effective implementation of the Darfur Peace Agreement, to prevent attacks and threats against civilians.
      iii. To seize or collect, as appropriate, arms or related material whose presence in Darfur is in violation of the Agreements and the measures imposed

by paragraphs 7 and 8 of resolution 1556, and to dispose of such arms and related material as appropriate;

b. *Requests* that the Secretary-General and the governments of Chad and the Central African Republic conclude status-of-forces agreements as soon as possible, taking into consideration General Assembly resolution 58/82 on the scope of legal protection under the Convention on the Safety of United Nations and Associated Personnel, and *decides* that pending the conclusion of such an agreement with either country, the model status-of-forces agreement dated October 9, 1990 (A/45/594), shall apply provisionally with respect to UNMIS forces operating in that country.

13. *Requests* the Secretary-General to report to the council on the protection of civilians in refugee and internally displaced persons camps in Chad and on how to improve the security situation on the Chadian side of the border with Sudan.

14. *Calls upon* the parties to the Darfur Peace Agreement to respect their commitments and implement the Agreement without delay, *urges* those parties that have not signed the Agreement to do so without delay and not to act in any way that would impede implementation of the Agreement, and *reiterates* its intention to take, including in response to a request by the African Union, strong and effective measures, such as an asset freeze or travel ban, against any individual or group that violates or attempts to block the implementation of the Agreement or commits human rights violations.

15. *Decides* to remain seized of the matter.

Appendix N

International Criminal Court, The Office of the Prosecutor Situation in Darfur, the Sudan
Prosecutor's Application for Warrant of Arrest under Article 58, Against Omar Hassan Ahmad Al Bashir

Summary of the Case:

I. The Application

Upon investigation of crimes allegedly committed in the territory of Darfur, the Sudan, on or after July 1, 2002, the Prosecution has concluded that there are reasonable grounds to believe that Omar Hassan Ahmad Al Bashir (hereafter referred to as "Al Bashir") bears criminal responsibility for the crime of genocide under Article 6 (a) of the Rome Statute, killing members of the Fur, Masalit, and Zaghawa ethnic groups (also referred to as "target groups"), (b) causing serious bodily or mental harm to members of those groups, and (c) deliberately inflicting on those groups conditions of life calculated to bring about their physical destruction in part; for crimes against humanity under Article 7 (1) of the statute, committed as part of a widespread and systematic attack directed against the civilian population of Darfur with knowledge of the attack, the acts of (a) murder, (b) extermination, (d) forcible transfer of the population, (f) torture, and (g) rapes; and for war crimes under Article 8 (2)(e)(i) of the statute, for intentionally directing attacks against the civilian population as such, and (v) pillaging a town or place.

The prosecution does not allege that Al Bashir physically or directly carried out any of the crimes. He committed crimes through members of the state apparatus, the army and the Militia/Janjawid in accordance with article 25 (3)(a) of the statute (indirect perpetration or perpetration by means).

At all times relevant to this application, Al Bashir has been President of the Republic of the Sudan, exercising both *de jure* and *de facto* sovereign authority, Head of the National Congress Party, and Commander in Chief of the Armed Forces. He sits at the apex of, and personally directs, the state's hierarchical structure of authority and the integration of the Militia/Janjaweed within such structure. He is the mastermind behind the alleged crimes. He has absolute control.

The evidence establishes reasonable grounds to believe that Al Bashir intends to destroy in substantial part the Fur, Masalit, and Zaghawa ethnic groups as such. Forces and agents controlled by Al Bashir attacked civilians in towns and villages inhabited by the target groups, committing killings, rapes, torture, and destroying means of livelihood. Al Bashir has thus forced the displacement of a substantial part of the target groups and attacked them in the camps for internally displaced persons (IDPs), causing serious and bodily harm – through rapes, tortures, and forced displacement in traumatizing conditions – and deliberately inflicting on a substantial part of those groups conditions of life calculated to bring about their physical destruction.

Al Bashir's conduct simultaneously constitutes genocide against the Fur, Masalit, and Zaghawa ethnic groups, crimes against humanity and war crimes against any civilian population in the area, including members of the target groups.

The case proposed in this application is the second case in the situation and covers crimes committed in Darfur from March 2003 to the date of filing this application. This case is not being investigated or prosecuted by the government of the Sudan (GoS).

II. Background and Scope of the Investigation
Jurisdiction

Security Council Resolution 1593 (2005), which affirmed that justice and accountability are critical to achieve lasting peace and security in Darfur.

Investigation

Since the start of the investigation, the prosecution has collected statements and evidence during 105 missions conducted in 18 countries. Throughout the investigation, the prosecutor has examined incriminating and exonerating facts in an independent and impartial manner.

For the purpose of the application, the prosecution has relied primarily on: (1) witness statements taken from eyewitnesses and victims of attacks in Darfur; (2) recorded interviews of GoS officials; (3) statements taken from individuals who possess knowledge of the activities of officials and representatives of the GoS and of the Militia/Janjawid in the conflict in Darfur; (4) documents and other information provided by the GoS upon request of the prosecution; (5) the Report of the UN Commission of Inquiry (UNCOI) and other materials provided by the UNCOI; (6) the Report of Sudanese National Commission of Inquiry (NCOI) and other materials provided by the NCOI; and (7) documents and other materials obtained from open sources.

Throughout the investigation the prosecution monitored the security of victims and witnesses and implemented protective measures. The prosecution and the Victims and Witness Unit of the Registry continue to monitor and assess the risks to victims and witnesses.

Admissibility

The case proposed in this application is the second case in the situation and covers crimes committed in Darfur from March 2003 to the date of filing. In accordance with the principle of "complementarity," at all times the prosecution has assessed the existence of national proceedings in the Sudan in relation to those crimes. However, this case is not being investigated or prosecuted by the GoS. There are not national proceedings in the Sudan against the perpetrators of crimes relevant to this application. The prosecution is aware of the incarceration of officers who refused to comply with Al Bashir's orders to commit genocide.

III. Summary of the Evidence and Information provided in the Prosecution's Application

Consistent with the requirements of Article 58 (2)(d) of the Statute, the Prosecution furnished in the Application "a summary of the evidence" sufficient to establish "reasonable grounds to believe" that Omar Hassan Ahmad Al Bashir committed crimes within the jurisdiction of the Court.

a. The Context in Which Crimes Were Committed

Since he assumed power in June 1989, Al Bashir has engaged in political and military struggles with groups both in Khartoum and in the peripheries of the Sudan seen as threats to his power. In Darfur, he assessed that the Fur, Masalit, and Zaghawa ethnic groups, as socially and politically dominant groups in the province, constituted such threats: they challenged the economic and political marginalization of their region, and members of the three groups engaged in armed rebellions.

Al Bashir set out to quell those movements through armed force and, over the years, also employed a policy of exploiting real or perceived grievances between the different tribes struggling to prosper in the difficult Darfur environment. He promoted the idea of a polarization between tribes aligned with the government, whom he labeled "Arabs," and the three groups he perceived as the main threats, whom he labeled "Zurgas" or "Africans." The image is only one of many devices used by Al Bashir to disguise his crimes. Both victims and perpetrators are "Africans" and speak "Arabic."

In March 2003, after negotiations and armed action both failed to end in Darfur a rebellion whose members belonged mostly to the three target groups, Al Bashir decided and set out to destroy in part the Fur, Masalit, and Zaghawa groups, on account of their ethnicity. His motives were largely political. His pretext was a "counter-insurgency." His intent was genocide.

The Fur, Masalit, and Zaghawa speak Arabic and share with the majority of the Darfur population the same religion (Islam). Coexistence and intermarriage have blurred differences. However, historically they occupied specific territories (Dar Fur, Dar Masalit, and Dar Zaghawa), and also spoke their own languages, different from one another and from Arabic. Members of the groups see themselves, and are seen by their attackers, as different ethnic groups.

b. The Crimes

Genocide by Killing Members of the Target Groups

From March 2003 up to the date of filing, Al Bashir's orders giving carte blanche to his subordinates to quell the rebellion and take no prisoners triggered a series of brutal attacks against the Fur, Masalit, and Zaghawa groups. The Armed Forces, often acting together with Militia/Janjawid, singled out for attack those villages and small towns inhabited mainly by members of the target groups. The attackers went out of their way to spare from attack villages inhabited predominantly by other tribes considered aligned with the government, even where they were located very near villages inhabited predominantly by members of the targeted groups.

The prosecution has charted all the known attacks that have taken place from 2003–2008 on an interactive map of Darfur, showing towns, villages and the tribal composition of the inhabitants (available on the ICC OTP website). The results show that the overwhelming majority of villages attacked were inhabited mainly by the target groups. They were clearly selected for attack.

The Armed Forces and Militia/Janjawid carried out such attacks jointly and in a similar pattern throughout the entire period, up to the date of filing. Typically, the Armed Forces would arrive in trucks and land cruisers mounted with Dshkas, and the Militia/Janjawid would arrive on camels and horseback. These joint forces would then surround the village and on occasion, the Air Force would be called upon to drop bombs on the village as a precursor to the attacks. The ground forces would then enter the village or town and attack civilian inhabitants. They kill men, children, elderly, and women; they subject women and girls to massive rapes. They burn and loot the villages.

The targets are not rebel forces, but the Fur, Masalit, and Zaghawa communities. Attacks are typically launched against civilian targets, and do not cease until the town or village, in its entirety, has been victimized and its population forcibly displaced, regardless of the lack of rebel presence or the lack of any valid military objective. Witnesses have also described instances in which rebels were known to be located outside of towns or villages, but attackers from the Armed Forces and Militia/Janjawid bypassed those locations to attack the towns or villages instead.

An armed conflict has existed in Darfur since 2003. The government has the right to use force to defend itself against insurgents. However, the crimes covered in the application are not the collateral damage of a military campaign. At all times relevant to the application Al Bashir specifically and purposefully targeted civilians who were not participants to any conflict with the intent to destroy them, as a group.

In Darfur 35,000 people have been killed outright in such attacks; an overwhelming majority of them are from the three target groups.

The Fate of the Displaced Persons
Almost the entire population of the target groups has been forcibly displaced following the attacks. Data from refugee camps in Chad and camps for internally displaced persons ("IDP camps") within Darfur confirm that most of those displaced belong to the target groups.

As of December 2007, the total number of Sudanese people from Darfur in refugee camps in Chad was approximately 235,000. Of those, there were approximately 110,000 Zaghawa and approximately 103,000 Masalit. Only approximately 7,750 members of the Fur had reached Chad, due to their geographical location in the south of Darfur.

According to information, the Fur represent 50 percent up to the totality of some IDP camps in Darfur. In South Darfur, Kalma camp, near Nyala, which hosts around 92,000 IDPs, there are an estimated 46 to 50,000 Fur, 9,000 Zaghawa, and 5,000 Masalit. In West Darfur, Nertiti (Jebel Marra) hosts mostly Fur (about 32,000); Hassa Hissa near Zalingei hosts about 85 percent Fur (42,500), 10 percent Zaghawa (5,000), 5 percent Masalit (2,500) and smaller tribes. The Fur represent 99 percent (about 30,000) of the population of Hamadiya camp near Zalingei and 90 percent (about 16,000) in Deleig camp near Wali Sadih.

In the view of the UNCOI in January 2005, there would be no policy of genocide if "the populations surviving attacks on villages ... live together in areas selected by the government ... where they are assisted." Notwithstanding the evidence that genocide was committed by killing and the infliction of serious bodily and mental harm, the current evidence also shows that the target groups, far from being assisted, are also attacked in the camps. Such attacks, as described next, against such an overwhelming majority of members of the target groups, are a clear indication of Al Bashir's genocidal intent.

Genocide by Causing Serious Mental Harm to Members of the Target Group
As a result of the attacks to the villages, at least 2,700,000 people, most of them members of the target groups, have been forcibly expelled from their homes. As survivors fled the attacks, they were pursued into deserts, killed or left to die. Those who managed to reach the outskirts of bigger cities and what would become IDP camps are submitted to physical and mental harm, and generally conditions calculated to slowly bring about their destruction.

(i) Thousands of women and girls belonging to the target groups were and continue to be raped in all three states of Darfur by members of the Militia/Janjawid and Armed Forces since 2003. Girls as young as five years old have been raped. A third of the rapes are rapes of children. Underreporting of rape is widespread. Nonetheless, periodic reports and testimonies conclude that rape has been committed systematically and continuously for 5 years. Women and girls going to collect firewood, grass or water are repeatedly raped by Militia/Janjawid, Armed Forces, and other GoS security agents: "[W]hen we see them, we run. Some of us succeed in getting away, and some are caught and taken to be raped – gang-raped. Maybe around 20 men rape one woman ... [...] These things are normal for us here in Darfur. These things happen all the time. I have seen rapes, too. It does not matter who sees them raping the women – they don't care. They rape women in front of their mothers and fathers." Rape is an integral part of the pattern of destruction that the government of the Sudan is inflicting upon the target groups in Darfur. As described by the ICTR in the Akayesu case, they use rape to kill the will, the spirit, and life itself.

Particularly in view of the social stigma associated with rape and other forms of sexual violence among the Fur, Masalit, and Zaghawa, these acts cause significant and irreversible harm, to individual women, but also to their communities.

(ii) Massive forced displacement was, and continues to be, conducted in such a manner as to traumatize the victims and prevent the reconstitution of the group. Al Bashir's criminal plan has violently uprooted at least 2.7 million civilians – principally members of the target groups – from lands on which they and their ancestors had been living for centuries. Victims suffer the trauma of being forced to witness their own homes and possessions destroyed and/or looted and family members raped and/or killed. The victims thereafter endure the anguish of learning that, in many cases, prior homelands have been occupied and resettled by members of other communities – and thus, there is no prospect of ever returning. Organized insecurity in and around the camps by Al Bashir's forces and agents, including through spying and harassment by members of the Humanitarian Aid Commission (HAC), exacerbates the fear of IDPs. The cumulative effect of these

Appendices

crimes is that many of the surviving members of the target groups, particularly those in IDP camps, suffer serious mental and/or psychological harm.

Genocide by Deliberate Infliction on Members of the Target Groups Conditions of Life Calculated to Bring about the Physical Destruction of the Group in Whole or in Part

i. The attacks on villages across Darfur from March 2003 to the present were designed not only to kill members of the target groups and force them from their lands, but also to destroy the very means of survival of the groups as such. They destroy food, wells and water pumping machines, shelter, crops and livestock, as well as any physical structures capable of sustaining life or commerce. They destroy farms and loot grain stores or set them on fire. The goal is to ensure that those inhabitants not killed outright would not be able to survive without assistance.

ii. The survivors are not only forced out of their homes, they are also pursued into inhospitable terrain. A victim in the desert overheard one attacker say to another: "Don't waste the bullet, they've got nothing to eat and they will die from hunger."

iii. In addition to persecuting the victims, the attackers spoil their land, now occupied by new settlers: "This land is liberated and you have no land and no right to cultivate on liberated areas." Usurpation of the land is often the final blow to the capacity of the target groups to survive in Darfur. Land has always been identified as a key issue by Al Bashir himself. In his April 2003 address to the Armed Forces and PDF troops at El Fasher airport, Al Bashir declared, "I only want land." Having removed the target groups from their land and destroyed their means of survival, Al Bashir encourages and facilitates resettlement of the land by other tribes more supportive of the government, often affiliated with Militia/Janjawid. The scale of displacements was done in the knowledge of the devastating impact it would have on the fabric of the groups, whose identity is linked with the land. When they were removed from the land, the tribal structure was weakened.

iv. They also attack the target groups in the camps. Al Bashir and his subordinates systematically refuse to provide any meaningful aid, and hinder other efforts to bring humanitarian aid to the 2,450,000 civilians displaced. Thus after forcibly expelling members of the target groups from their homes, they subject them to, at best, a subsistence diet and the reduction of essential medical services below minimum requirements.

In the IDP camps, where most of the target groups' members fled, Al Bashir has organized the destitution, insecurity and harassment of the survivors. The Ministry for Humanitarian Affairs provides no meaningful government aid to those displaced, and consistently obstructs or blocks humanitarian assistance from the international community. The Ministry for Humanitarian Affairs blocks the publication of nutrition surveys, delays the delivery of aid, expels relief staff denouncing such acts, denies visas and travel permits, and imposes unnecessary bureaucratic requirements on aid workers. This has the effect of reducing nutrition and access to medical services for protracted periods of time.

Appendix N

Militia/Janjawid, which Al Bashir has recruited, armed and purposefully refused to disarm, are stationed in the vicinity of the camps and, with other GoS agents, they subject IDPs to abuses, including killings, rapes, and other sexual violence. While the authorities argue that there are armed rebels in the camps, the evidence shows that those attacked are unarmed civilians.

The overall effect of physical attack, forced displacement, destruction of means of livelihood, and denial of humanitarian assistance was that mortality rates among civilians, including principally members of the target groups, remained at critical levels. Between April and June 2004, as deaths directly caused by violence decreased, mortality rates among displaced populations in Darfur remained elevated because of deficient humanitarian assistance. Overall, at least 100,000 civilians – mostly members of the targeted groups – have already endured "slow death" since March 2003.

Crimes Against Humanity

Charges of crimes against humanity are also required to represent the full extent of criminal activity in Darfur since 2003, namely the acts of murder, rape, forcible displacement, and extermination committed against members of the target groups and other, smaller ethnic groups, such as the Tunjur, Erenga, Birgid, Misseriya Jebel, Meidob, Dajo, and Birgo. While the attacks against these groups were carried out on discriminatory grounds, there is insufficient evidence at this time to substantiate a charge of genocide in respect of these groups.

War Crimes

At all times relevant to the charges, the government of the Sudan has been engaged in a military campaign conducted in Darfur against rebel armed forces including the SLM/A and the JEM. Both rebel groups mainly recruit from the Fur, Masalit, and Zaghawa tribes. As is well known, the GoS has relied on Militia/Janjawid.

Al Bashir also committed, through other persons, the war crime of pillaging towns and villages in Darfur, including but not limited to Kodoom, Bindisi, Mukjar, Arawala, Shataya, Kailek, Buram, Muhajeriya, Siraf Jidad, Silea, Sirba, Abu Suruj, and villages in the area of Jebel Mun.

c. The Personal Responsibility of Omar Hassan Ahmad Al Bashir

Al Bashir controls and directs the perpetrators. The commission of those crimes on such a scale, and for such a long period of time, the targeting of civilians and in particular the Fur, Masalit and Zaghawa, the impunity enjoyed by the perpetrators, and the systematic cover-up of the crimes through public official statements, are evidence of a plan based on the mobilization of the state apparatus, including the armed forces, the intelligence services, the diplomatic and public information bureaucracies, and the justice system.

Al Bashir designed a plan that includes: the dismissal of staff opposed to crimes and the appointment of key personnel to implement the crimes, most significantly Ahmed Harun; the integration of the Militia/Janjawid, their leaders formally appointed into the Sudanese structure of authority; the unified implementation of attacks against the target groups in villages through the Security Committees at the locality level, reporting to State Security Committees, reporting, during 2003–2005 to Ahmed Harun as head of the Darfur Security Desk and member of the National Security Council; the sophisticated system of obstacles to the delivery of humanitarian aid; the misinformation campaign; and the deliberate failure to punish perpetrators.

Al Bashir controls the implementation of such a plan through his formal role at the apex of all state structures and as commander in chief and by ensuring that the heads of relevant institutions involved report directly to him through formal or informal lines. His control is absolute.

Because the magnitude of the crimes attracted national and international scrutiny, Al Bashir consistently denies, conceals and distances himself and his subordinates from the crimes committed. Throughout the time period relevant to this application, Al Bashir personally and through his subordinates denies that crimes are taking place. Al Bashir uses the Sudanese Intelligence and Security Service (known as NISS) to further manipulate local and international public opinion concerning Darfur through the NISS-controlled Sudan Media Centre (SMC), which was established in December 2002 and disseminates directives to all officials to contribute to the campaign by highlighting stories about voluntary returns of IDPs, and by conveying that Darfur is a safe place where people can lead a normal life.

Given the international attention to Darfur, genocide by imposing conditions calculated to bring about physical destruction, in combination with a studied misinformation strategy, is an efficient strategy to achieve complete destruction. By preventing the truth about the crimes from being revealed; by concealing his crimes under the guise of a "counter-insurgency strategy," or "inter-tribal clashes," or the "actions of lawless autonomous militia"; by threatening Sudanese citizens – and trying to blackmail the international community – into silence, Al Bashir makes possible the commission of further crimes.

Al Bashir denies victims access to the criminal justice system, while using the system against those who did not comply with his genocidal orders. Al Bashir protects, promotes and provides impunity to his subordinates, in order to secure their willingness to continue committing crimes. He could authorize investigations of members of the armed and security forces, but the only officers investigated are those who refused to participate in crimes. Al Bashir promoted notorious perpetrators (Musa Hilal, Shukurtallah, Abdallah Masar, and General Ismat), but his most telling acts concern ICC indictee Ahmed Harun.

Ahmad Harun as Minister of State for the Interior, responsible for the Darfur Security Desk, recruited and mobilized the Militia/Janjawid, relying on experience he had gained in mobilizing tribal militias in South Sudan in the 1990s. On various occasions, Ahmad Harun publicly acknowledged his mission to destroy the target groups, stating that Al Bashir had given him the power to kill whomever he wanted and that, "for the sake of Darfur, they were ready to kill three quarters of the people in Darfur, so that one quarter could live." After the court's decision of April 27, 2007, Al Bashir traveled to Darfur with Harun and announced publicly that he would never hand over Harun to the ICC; on the contrary, Harun would continue working in Darfur to implement his orders. The decision to maintain Harun in such positions as Minister of State for Humanitarian Affairs, where he was able to affect the victims in the camps; as Chair of a committee on human rights violations in the south and north, in which he could provide perpetrators with a guarantee of impunity; as a member of the UNAMID national monitoring group, where he was able to affect the deployment of peacekeepers; these are all clear indications of Al Bashir's complete protection of those who committed genocidal acts under his direct orders.

d. Al Bashir's Mens Rea

Al Bashir has genocidal intent. His forces and agents submitted a substantial part of each target group – living in IDP camps – to conditions calculated to destroy each group in part.

In attacks, Al Bashir forces consistently made statements such as "the Fur are slaves, we will kill them"; "You are Zaghawa tribes, you are slaves"; "You are Masalit. Why do you come here, why do you take our grass? You will not take anything today." The language used by perpetrators of rape made also clear the genocidal intent underlying their actions: "After they abused us, they told us now we would have Arab babies, and if they could find any Fur woman, they would rape them again to change the color of their children." Perpetrators of other crimes have used language which is not just ethnically derogatory, but evidencing an intention to destroy: "You are blacks, no blacks can stay here, and no black can stay in Sudan …The power of Al Bashir belongs to the Arabs and we will kill you until the end"; "we will kill all the black"; "we will drive you out of this land"; "we are here to eradicate blacks (nuba)"; "This is your end. The government armed me."

The systematic targeting of victims based on their membership in a particular group; the actual destructions; the deliberate failure to differentiate between civilians and persons of military status; the perpetration of acts which violate the very foundation of the groups such as massive rapes or massive expulsion from the land with no possibility to return or reconstitute as a group; the utterances of perpetrators on the ethnicity of the victims during the attacks; the sophisticated strategy of concealing crimes; and the evidence of a plan are many indicators from which *mens rea* of genocide is the only possible inference.

Assessed against all those factors, the only reasonable inference available based on the evidence is that Al Bashir intends to destroy substantial parts of the Fur, Masalit, and Zaghawa groups, as such.

III. Ensuring the Appearance of Al Bashir

Under article 58 of the statute, if the pre-trial chamber is satisfied that there are reasonable grounds to believe that a person has committed crimes within the juris-diction of the court, the chamber may issue upon the application of the prosecution either a warrant of arrest or a summons to appear. The prosecution, by this application, submits that the evidence and information summarized before give reasonable grounds to believe that the person, Al Bashir, committed the crimes alleged. The prosecution respectfully requests the issuance of an arrest warrant.

There are circumstances that could lead it to modify its assessment. The Prosecution submits that a summons to appear could be an alternative pursued by the court should the government of the Sudan, which would serve and follow up on the summons, and the individual concerned, express their willingness to pursue this route.

Appendix O

Sudanese Law Related to Rape from Section 15 of the Criminal Act of 1991

The following is an English-language version of the statutes related to rape from the Sudanese Criminal Act of 1991, Section 15 ("Offences of [Honor], Reputation and Public Morality, Adultery [Zina]"). Although there is no officially sanctioned English translation of Sudanese law, the version is used by the various UN agencies and commissions. The definition of rape as "nonconsensual adultery" is problematic because zina encompasses any sexual penetration between individuals not married to one another.

In the Name of Allah, the Gracious, the Merciful
The Criminal Act 1991
Be it here bypassed by the National Salvation Revolution Command Council in accordance with the provisions of the third Constitutional Decree 1989, as follows:

Part XV
Offences of [Honor], Reputation and Public Morality
Adultery (Zina)
145.
(1) There shall be deemed to commit adultery:
    (a) Every man, who has sexual intercourse with a woman,
        without there being a lawful bond between them;
    (b) Every woman, who permits a man to have sexual intercourse with her,
        without there being a lawful bond, between them.
(2) Sexual intercourse takes place by the penetration of the whole glans,
    or its equivalent into the vulva.
(3) There shall not be deemed, to be lawful bond, marriage which, by consensus,
    is ruled void.

Penalty for Adultery
146.
(1) Whoever commits the offence of adultery shall be punished with:
    (a) Execution, by lapidation [stoning], where the offender is married (*muhsan*);
    (b) One hundred lashes, where the offender is not married (non-muhsan).
(2) The male, unmarried offender may be punished, in addition to whipping, with
    expatriation for one year.
(3) Being "muhsan" means having a valid persisting marriage at the time of the
    commission of adultery; provided that such marriage has been consumated [*sic*].
(4) Whoever commits adultery, in the Southern states, shall be punished, with
    imprisonment, for a term, not exceeding one year, or with fine, or with both, and
    where the offender is (muhsan), with imprisonment, for a term, not exceeding
    three years; a fine; or both.

Whoever commits the offence of adultery shall be punished by execution by lapidation where the offender is married.
Laws without Justice: An Assessment of Sudanese Laws Affecting Survivors of Rape.

Remittance of the Penalty of Adultery

147.

Penalty of adultery shall be remitted for any of the following two reasons:

(a) If the offender retracts his confession before execution of the penalty, where the offence is proved by confession only.

(b) If the witnesses retract their testimony thereby lessening the *nisab* of such testimony.

Offence of Sodomy

148.

(1) There shall be deemed to commit sodomy, every man who penetrates his glans, or the equivalent thereof, in the anus of a woman, or another man's, or permits another man to penetrate his glans, or its equivalent, in his anus.

(2) (a) Whoever commits the offence of sodomy shall be punished with a whipping of 100 lashes, and he may also be punished by imprisonment for a term not exceeding 5 years;

(b) Where the offender is convicted for the second time, he shall be punished, with a whipping of 100 lashes and with imprisonment for a term not exceeding 5 years;

(c) Where the offender is convicted for the third time, he shall be punished with death or with life imprisonment.

Rape

149.

(1) There shall be deemed to commit the offence of rape whoever makes sexual intercourse, by way of adultery or sodomy, with any person without his consent.

(2) Consent shall not be recognized, where the offender has custody or authority over the victim.

(3) Whoever commits the offence of rape shall be punished with a whipping of 100 lashes and with imprisonment for a term not exceeding 10 years, unless rape constitutes the offence of adultery or sodomy, which is punishable with death.

Gross Indecency

151.

(1) There shall be deemed to commit the offence of gross indecency, whoever commits any act contrary to another person's modesty or does any sexual act with another person not amounting to adultery or sodomy, and he shall be punished with whipping, not exceeding forty lashes, and he may also be punished by imprisonment for a term not exceeding one year or by a fine.

(2) Where the offence of gross indecency is committed in a public place or without the consent of the victim, the offender shall be punished with whipping not

exceeding eighty lashes, and he may also be punished by imprisonment for a term not exceeding two years or by a fine.

Indecent and Immoral Acts

152.

(1) Whoever commits in a public place an act or conducts himself in an indecent manner or in a manner contrary to public morality or wears an indecent or immoral dress that causes annoyance to public feelings, shall be punished by whipping, not exceeding forty lashes, by a fine, or by both.

(2) The act shall be deemed contrary to public morality if it is so considered in the religion of the doer or the custom of the country where the act occurs.

Scene from Bindisi Market.
Bindisi, 2006

Acronyms/Abbreviations

AU	The African Union
BC	The Beja Council (Eastern Sudan Political Opposition Organization)
BDF	Botswana Defense Force
CPA	Comprehensive Peace Agreement
DDDC	Darfur–Darfur Dialogue and Consultation
DoP	Declaration of Principles
DDF	Darfur Development Front (*Jabhat Nahdat Darfur*)
DDR	Disarmament, Demobilization, and Reintegration
DPA	Darfur Peace Agreement
DRC	Democratic Republic of Congo
DRDF	Darfur Reconstruction and Development Fund
DRF	Darfur Renaissance Front
DUP	Democratic Unionist Party
EF	Eastern Front
FGM	Female Genital Mutilation
GBV	Gender-Based Violence
GONGOs	Governmental Non-Governmental Organizations
GoS	Government of Sudan
HAC	Humanitarian Aid Commission
ICC	International Criminal Court
IDPs	Internally Displaced People
IGAD	Intergovernmental Authority on Development
IGAAD	Intergovernmental Authority on Drought and Development
ILO	International Labor Organization
IMF	International Monetary Fund
INGOs	International Nongovernmental Organizations
JEM	Justice and Equality Movement (Darfur)
JEM-CL	Justice and Equality Movement–Collective Leadership
KASH	*Kayan Al-Shimal* (Northern Entity)
KCHR	Khartoum Centre for Human Rights
MSF	*Medicins sans Frontiers* (Doctors without Borders)
MNRD	National Movement for Development and Reforms
NCP	National Congress Party
NDA	National Democratic Alliance
NGOs	Nongovernmental Organizations
NIF	National Islamic Front
NRF	National Redemption Front (*jabhat alkhals alwatani*)
PCP	People's Congress Party or Popular Defense Council
PDF	Popular Defense Force
PSC	Popular Salvation Council
RAMP	Riverian Arab-Muslim Power
RI	Refugees International
RPF	Rwanda Patriotic Front
SADC	Southern African Development Community
SCCED	Special Criminal Court for the Events in Darfur
SCP	Sudanese Communist Party
SIHA	Strategic Initiative for the Women in the Horn of Africa
SFDA	Sudan Federal Democratic Alliance

SIRC	Sudan Inter-Religious Council
SLA/M	Sudan Liberation Army/Movement (Darfur)
SOAT	Sudan Organization against Torture
SPLM/A	Sudan People's Liberation Movement/Army
SSU	Sudan Socialist Union
SUDCO	Sudan Social Development Organization
TRC	Truth and Reconciliation Commission
TUA	Trade Unions Alliance
UNAMID	United Nations–African Union Mission in Darfur
UNHCR	United Nations High Commission for Refugees
UNMIS	United Nations Mission in Sudan
UNSC	United Nations Security Council
UP	Unionist Party
URFF	United Revolutionary Forces Front
VAW	Violence against Women
WSPO	Western Sudan People's Organization
WNAC	White Nile Agricultural Corporation

Glossary

This is a selected glossary of relevant terms, mostly Arabic words or words from other Sudanese languages, that appear throughout this book. With the exception of a few key terms we decided not to include those that are widely known and have been fully explained in the essays included in this volume, as well as the major texts on Darfur cited in the Introduction, the Selected Bibliography, and Comprehensive Bibliography.

Ansar: An Arabic word, which literally means "followers" or "protectors." The Ansar are known in the history of Sudan as the members of the early Mahdist movement in the late nineteenth century. Now *Ansar* refers to the Sudanese Muslim Sect currently headed by Al-Sadiq Al Mahdi, the great grandson of the Imam Muhammad Ahmad Al Mahdi, the leader of the Mahdist Revolution and the founder of its state (1881–1898). The Ansar sect is also the patron of the Umma Party, which has become its contemporary political wing. The Mahdist revolution was considered one of the progenitors of modern Sudanese nationalism. Many Darfurians supported the Mahdist movement and fought as part of its forces against Turko-Egyptian colonialism and remain committed to its contemporary political party.

Baggara (Baqqarah): An Arabic name that literally means "Those of the Cow" or the "People of the Cow." It refers to Sudanese Arabized pastoralists who are cattle herders. Non-Arabized groups can become Baggara through acquisition of cattle and inter-marriage. Currently the term *Baggara* refers to two major groups: the Misayriyya of South Kordofan and the Rizeigat of South Darfur.

Berti: Among the so-called African groups, the Berti are a Muslim non-Arabized people of the North Darfur province.

International Commission of Inquiry on Darfur: The committee appointed by the then-UN Secretary-General Kofi Anan (1997–2006) to investigate war crimes in Darfur in 2004. Its report fell short of labeling the situation in Darfur "genocide," although it put the responsibility squarely on the government of Sudan for its crimes against humanity in the region and for violating international law.

Dar: Arabic word for "homeland" or "country." Traditionally it refers to land designated by a Sultan as homeland for a specific ethnic group such as Dar Masaalit, Dar Fur, and Dar Zaghawa (see also *Hakura* below).

El Fasher (Elfashir): Capital of North Darfur state.

Fur: One of the major "non-Arabized" ethnic groups of the Darfur region, commonly referred to in the Western media as the major "African" ethnic group of Darfur. *Darfur* is a composite word (*Dar Fur*), which means "land of the Fur." A Muslim people, the Fur, under the leadership of Suleiman Solong, established the historical Sultanate of Darfur, which governed Darfur between 1596 and 1916.

El Geneina: Capital of West Darfur state.

Hakura (Hawakeer; Hawakir plural): The *hakura* is an important aspect of Darfur's ethnically based land tenure and ownership system. Historically, land-grants were awarded by the Sultan to an individual, while a *dar* was the homeland granted to a specific ethnic group during the British colonial period on the basis of certain historical claims. As explained by Alex de Waal, "historically, hakura and dar are overlapping concepts, but the reinvented hakura is much closer to the colonial concept of dar than to the historic hakura of the Sultanate." ("Making Sense of Darfur": http://www.ssrc.org/blogs/darfur/2008/03/07/land-in-the-dpa-a-false-agreement/)

IGAD (IGAAD): IGAD is the Intergovernmental Authority on Development (IGAD) in Eastern Africa, which was created by seven countries (Djibouti, Eritrea, Ethiopia, Kenya, Somalia, Sudan, and Uganda) in 1996 to supersede the Intergovernmental Authority on Drought and Development (IGADD), which was founded in 1986. It is known for its role in brokering the Comprehensive Peace Agreement of 2005, which brought a formal end to the North–South civil war in Sudan.

Janjawid (Janjaweed): The paramilitary militia recruited from the Arabized pastoralists groups in Darfur by the NIF regime to use in its counterinsurgency war against non-Arabized groups in Darfur, such as the Fur, Masaalit, and Zaghawa. They are known for committing heinous crimes against Darfur's non-Arabized groups. The origin of the term *Janjawid* is controversial. While in the context of the current conflict in Darfur it is often interpreted as a composite of the Arabic words *Jin* ("spirit" or "devil") and *jawad* ("horse"); prior to this it was used in Darfur to depict individuals or groups who were thought to be rude, impolite, bad-mannered, and so on. Others have suggested that it was also used to refer to bands of young men involved in banditry.

Jebel Marra (Jabal Marrah): Famous mountain range in Darfur known for its temperate climate and predictably high levels of rainfall. As drought-induced competition for land has created instability in Darfur, its desirable climate has made Jebel Marra one of the region's most fiercely contested areas. Located in the center of the Darfur region, Jebel Marra is most closely associated with the Fur people.

Jihad: While the Western mainstream media refers to it solely as the violent doctrine of declaring war against non-Muslims or "infidels," this Arabic word literally means "struggle." Historically the term *jihad* has two connotations: It refers to the nonviolent spiritual struggle for Islam or against worldly desires, and it also carries the meaning of a violent struggle against injustices and oppression, illegitimate power, and/or against perceived nonbelievers.

Khatmiyya: A Sudanese Muslim sect, which has become the major patron for the Democratic Unionist Party (DUP), a major force in contemporary Sudanese politics. Its current spiritual leader is Mualana Muhammad

'Utman Al-Mirghani. The Khatmiyya are traditional rivals of the Ansar.

Masaalit (Masalit): Comprised predominately of sedentary farmers, like the rest of Darfur's inhabitants, the Masaalit are Muslims who are often categorized as an "African" ethnic group.

Murahhalin (Murahalin): The first paramilitary militia to be recruited from the Arabized pastoralists (Misayriyya-Baggra) in provinces to the north of Bahr-el-Ghazal, by the Sudanese government during the military dictatorship of Numeiri, to fight Dinka and destabilize their communities to deprive the SPLM/A of its social base. The term literally means "people on the move" or "nomads" in Arabic.

Naivasha Agreement: A series of protocols that resulted in the Comprehensive Peace Agreement of 2005 that ended the second phase of the North–South civil war in Sudan, which lasted for more than twenty years (1983–2005). It was negotiated in Naivasha, Kenya, and mediated for more than ten years by IGAD. It is now referred to as the Comprehensive Peace Agreement (CPA), which has opened up the possibility for democracy and civil liberties in Sudan.

National Islamic Front (NIF): The current Islamist party, now known as the National Congress Party (NCP), which has its origin in the Islamic Brotherhood movement (*Harakt al-Ikhwan al-Muslimin*). It is known to be the major political power behind the 1989 coup that brought the government of Omar Hassan Al Bashir to power. The party was further fragmented into multiple factions in early 2000. However, the current regime still refers to itself as the "NIF system" or "INGAZ regime" (Salvation government).

Nyala: Capital of South Darfur state.

Qabila: An Arabic word that is most often translated as "tribe"; however, as understood in Arabic, *qabila* does not connote the negative stereotypes often associated with the term *tribe*.

Shari'a (Islamic Law): Considered by Muslims to be the divine and ultimate law that regulates and governs public and private lives. In Sudan it refers to the strictly enforced legal code introduced in 1983 during the Numeiri regime and orchestrated by Hassan Al Turabi, then a prominent attorney and leader of the NIF, which brought the current regime to power in 1989.

Hamdis Triangle (Also Known in Arabic as Muthalath Hamdi/thaluth Hamdi): This triangle normally refers to the three Arabized ethnic groups – Ja'aliyyin, Danagla, and Shayqiyya – who have dominated state power in Sudan since independence. The term is linked to Abdelrahim Hamdi, a former finance minister in the NIF regime, and a leading member of the NCP who popularized the phrase in a memo that asserted the importance of focusing development projects in the central and northern parts of Sudan occupied by these three Arabized ethnic groups. As a result, critics of the NIF's policies also sometimes refer to this as "Hamdi's Privileged Triangle."

Tunjur: Prior to the rise of the Sultanate of Darfur, the Tunjur were a ruling dynasty in Darfur (ca. 1200–1600). Often categorized as an "African" ethnic group, like the rest of Darfur's inhabitants, the Tunjur are Muslims.

Zaghawa: This seminomadic group is found in both Darfur and eastern Chad. They call themselves "Beri" and are often categorized as an "African" ethnic group. Like the rest of Darfur's inhabitants, they are Muslims.

Zurqa (singular "Azraq"): A pejorative term used widely by Arabized Darfurians to refer to non-Arabized, or "black," Darfurians. In Arabic it literally means "blue," which is used in Sudan to reference "black" as a skin color.

Comprehensive Bibliography

Books and Articles

Abdul-Jalil, Musa Adam. "Some Political Aspects of Zaghawa Migration and Resettlement." In *Rural–Urban Migration and Identity Change Case Studies from the Sudan;* Fouad N. Ibrahim and Helmut Ruppert, eds. Bayreuth: Druckhaus Bayreuth, Verlagsgesellchaft, 1988.

—. "The Dynamics of Customary Land Tenure and Natural Resource Management in Darfur." *Land Reform, Settlement, and Cooperatives* 2 (2006).

Ablorh-Odjidja, E. "It Is Darfur Again and the Misery Goes On." *Accra Mail* (October 8, 2007).

—. "The All African Darfur Force." *Accra Mail* (August 22, 2007).

Abubakar, Abdul-Rahman. "Darfur–Senate Summons Yayale, Agwai." *Daily Trust* (October 3, 2007).

Abubakar, Jibrin. "Darfur Peace Talks Postponed." *Daily Trust* (August 25, 2005). "Sudanese Officials, Darfur Rebels in Talks." *Business Day (*October 4, 2005).

Adelaja, Abiodun, and Lere Ojedokun. "AU'll Resolve Darfur Crisis–President." *Daily Champion* (August 18, 2004).

Adoba, Iyefu. "Darfur: Peace Talks Kick Off with Consultations in Abuja." *This Day* (October 23, 2004).

African Rights. *Facing Genocide: The Nuba of Sudan*. London: African Rights, 1995.

Agger, I. *The Blue Room: Trauma and Testimony Among Refugee Women*. London: Zed Books, 1992.

Ahmed, Abdel Ghaffar M. *Anthropology in the Sudan: Reflections by a Sudanese Anthropologist*. Utrecht: International Books, 2002.

Ahmed, Abdel Ghaffar M., and Leif Manger, eds. *Understanding the Crisis in Darfur: Listening to Sudanese Voices*: University of Bergen, Centre for Development Studies, 2006.

Ahmed, Abdel Ghaffar M., and Gunnar M. Sorbo, eds. *The Management of the Crisis in the Sudan*. Bergen: University of Bergen, 1989.

Ajibade, Tunji. "Darfur and Martin Agwai's Many Challenges." *Daily Trust* (September 24, 2007).

Akinsanmi, Gboyega. "7 Local Soldiers Killed in Darfur." *This Day* (October 1, 2007).

Akosile, Ambibola. "Darfur–Amnesty Urges UN on Civilians' Safety." *This Day* (November 1, 2006).

—. "Darfur–Falana Tasks FG, AU on Sanctions." *This Day* (May 2, 2007).

Albino, Oliver. *The Sudan: A Southern Viewpoint*. London: Oxford University Press, 1970.

Ali, Taisir Mohamed. "The Road to Jouda." *Review of African Political Economy* 26: 1–14.

Ali, Yusuf, A., *The Holy Qur'an: Text, Translation and Commentary*. Brentwood, MD: Amana Corp, 1983.

Alier, Abel. *Southern Sudan: Too Many Agreements Dishonoured*. New York: Ethica Press, 1990, 1992.

Al-Karsani, Awad Al-Sid. "Beyond Sufism: The Case of Millennial Islam in the Sudan." In *Muslim Identity and Social Change in Sub-Saharan Africa*, Louis Brenner, ed. Bloomington: Indiana University Press, 1993.

Al-Mubarak, M. *Tarikh Darfur al-syasi (The Political History of Darfur)*, second edition. Khartoum: Khartoum University Press, 1995.

al-Rahim, Muddathir Abd. "Arabism, Africanism and Self-Identification in the Sudan." In Y. F. Hasan, *Sudan in Africa*. Khartoum: Khartoum University Press, 1971.

Alsop, Rachel, Annette Fitzsimons, and Kathleen Lennon, eds. *Theorizing Gender*. Cambridge: Polity, 2003.

al-Zein Mohamed, Adam, and Al-Tayeb Ibrahim Weddai, eds. *Perspectives on Tribal Conflicts in Sudan*. Khartoum: University of Khartoum, Institute of Afro-Asian Studies, 1998. (in Arabic).

Amnesty International. *Sudan, Darfur. Rape as a Weapon of War: Sexual Violence and Its Consequences*. New York: Amnesty International, 2004.

Arou, Mom Kou, and B. Yongo-Bure, eds. *North-South Relations in the Sudan since the Addis Ababa Agreement*. Khartoum: Institute of African and Asian Studies & Khartoum University Printing Press, 1988.

Assal, Manzoul. *Darfur: An Annotated Bibliography of Social Research*. Bergen: Bric/The University of Bergen, 2005.

—. "It Is All about History Repeating Itself: The State and the Involution of Conflict in Darfur." *Journal of Darfurian Studies*, 1: 6–22 (2006).

—. "National and International Responses to the Crisis of Darfur." *The Ahfad Journal: Women and Change*, 24 (1).

Awad, Hashim. *Why the Bread Basket Is Empty?* Seminar Paper, Development Studies and Research Center, University of Khartoum, 1984.

Ayoub, Mona Mohammed Taha. *Resolution Conference Between Fur and Arabs as an Example of Tribal Conflict Resolution in Sudan*, M.Sc. Thesis, Afro-Asian Institute, University of Khartoum, 1992.

Badal, Raphael K. *Oil and Regional Sentiment in Southern Sudan*. Department of Geography, Syracusde University Discussion Paper No. 80 (June 1983).

Badri, Balghis, and El Zein Mohammed, Adam. *The Rezeigat–Zaghawa Conflict in Darfur Region*. A Fund for Peace Report, Washington, 2000.

Baguma, Steven. "Kabarebe Speak Out on UN Darfur Mission." *The New Times* (April 27, 2006).

—. "Police Hailed over Darfur Mission." *The New Times* (February 23, 2006).

Bales, K. *Disposable People: New Slavery in the Global Economy*. Berkeley, CA: University of California Press, 1999.

Bank of Sudan. *Annual Report*. 1960–1988.

Barth, Frederik. "Economic Spheres in Darfur." In *Themes in Economic Anthropology*, Raymond Firth, ed. London: Tavistock, 1967.

Baya, Philister. "Seeking a Refuge or Being a Displaced: Analysis of a Southern Woman's Personal Experience." In *The Tragedy of Reality: Southern Sudanese Women Appeal for Peace*, M. Elsanousi, ed. Khartoum: Open Learning Organization, 1999.

Bayingana, John. "2,000 More RDF Set for Darfur." *The New Times* (June 29, 2005).

Akanga, Eleneus. "More RDF Soldiers for Troubled Darfur." *The New Times* (February 13, 2006). "RDF to Send More Troops to Darfur." *The New Times* (June 18, 2006).

Beck, K. "Nomads of Northern Kordufan and the State: From Violence to Pacification." *Nomadic Peoples* 38 (1996).

Beshir, M. *The Southern Sudan: Background to Conflict*. New York: Praeger, 1965.

Bigabo, Patrick. "AU Awards Pioneer Darfur-RDF Troops." *The New Times* (August 10, 2005).

—. "Gen. Kabarebe Lauds RDF on Darfur." *The New Times* (October 6, 2005).

—. "Genocide in Darfur, Says Rice." *The New Times* (July 22, 2005).

Biryabarema, Elias. "NGO Accuses Sudan of Darfur Rapes." *The Monitor* (July 20, 2004).

Bob, Ali. "Islam, the State and Politics in the Sudan," *Northeast African Studies* 12, no. 2–3 (1990).

Britt, Joseph. "Arab Genocide, Arab Silence." *The Washington Post* (July 13, 2005): A21.

Burr, J. Millard, and Collins, R. O. *Darfur: The Long Road to Disaster*. Princeton: Markus Wiener Publishers, 2008.

Butler, Judith. *Gender Trouble: Feminism on the Subversion of Identity*. New York and London: Routledge, 1990.

Chawai, Elkanah. "Darfur: How Far Can Abuja Talks Go?" *Daily Trust* (October 10, 2005).

Chawai, Elkanah, and Idris Ahmed. "Abuja Joins in Global Rally for Darfur." *Daily Trust* (September 18, 2006).

Cobham, Alex. "Causes of Conflict in Sudan: Testing the Black Book," QEH Working Paper Series No. 121: 9.

Cordell, Dennis D. "The Savanna Belt of North-Central Africa." In *History of Central Africa*, David Birmingham and Phyllis M. Martin, eds. London and New York: Longman, 1983.

Cunnison, Ian. *Baggara Arabs: Power and the Lineage in a Sudanese Nomad Tribe*. Oxford: Clarendon Press, 1966.

Dahab, Mohammed Eisa Ismail. "Darfur–Solution Must Come from Africans." *New Vision* (October 1, 2006).

Dak, Ayul Abwol. *Who Benefits from the Agricultural Schemes of Northern Upper Nile?* Development Studies and Research Center, University of Khartoum, Post-Graduate Diploma Thesis, 1989.

Daly, M. W. *Darfur's Sorrow: A History of Destruction and Genocide*. Cambridge: Cambridge University Press, 2007.

de Vries, Hent, and Samuel Weber, eds. *Violence, Identity and Self-Determination* Stanford CA: Stanford University Press, 1997.

de Waal, Alex. "Racism and Nature: Roots of Darfur Crisis." *New Vision* (August 2, 2004).

—. "Some Comments on Militias in Contemporary Sudan." In *Civil War in the Sudan*, M. Daly and A. A. Sikainga, eds. London: Taurus, 1994.

—. "Tragedy in Darfur: On Understanding and Ending the Horror." *Boston Review*. Volume 29, Number 5 (Oct./Nov.), 2004.

—. *War in Darfur and the Search for Peace.* Cambridge, MA: Harvard University Press, 2007.

—. *Famine That Kills: Darfur, Sudan.* Revised edition, Oxford Studies in African Affairs. Oxford: Oxford University Press, 2005.

de Waal, Alexander, and Julie Flint. *Darfur: A Short History of a Long War.* London: Zed Books, 2005.

—. *The Forsaken People.* Washington: The Brookings Institution, 1995.

Deng, Francis M. *The Cry of the Owl.* New York: Lilian Barber Press, 1989.

—. *The Dinka of the Sudan.* Illinois: Waveland, 1972.

Deng, F., and R. Cohen. *Masses in Flight: The Global Crisis of the Internally Displaced.* Washington: The Brookings Institution, 1998.

Deng, Francis M., and Prosser Gifford, eds. *The Search for Peace and Unity in the Sudan.* Washington: The Wilson Center Press, 1987.

Department of Statistics. *A Report on the Census of Pump Schemes*, Vol. 1. Khartoum, 1967.

Development Alternatives and Area Studies Vol. 243 No. 3 & 4 (September-December, 2005): 74–93.

Doornbos, Paul. "On Becoming Sudanese." In *Sudan: State, Capital, and Transformation*, T. Barnett and A. Abdelkarim, eds. London: Croom Helm, 1988.

Dudu, C. "Southern Sudanese Displaced Women: Losses and Gains." In *The Tragedy of Reality: Southern Sudanese Women Appeal for Peace*, M. Elsanosi, ed. Khartoum: Sudan Open Learning Organization, 1999.

Duffield, Mark. *Maiurno: Capitalism and Rural Life in Sudan.* London: Ithaca Press, 1981.

Duru, Nnamdi. "Nigerian Troops Leave for Sudan." *This Day* (August 31, 2004).

Eastmond, M. "Reconstructing Life: Chilean Women and the Dilemmas of Exile." In *Migrant Women: Crossing Boundaries and Changing Identities*, G. Bujis, ed. Oxford: Berg, 1993.

Ehigiator, Kenneth. "200 Soldiers Leave for Darfur." *Vanguard* (October 8, 2007).

—. "Darfur–Nwachukwu Tasks FG." *Vanguard* (October 3, 2007).

Eisenbruch, M. "From Post-Traumatic Stress Disorder to Cultural Bereavement: Diagnosis of Southeast Asian Refugees." *Social Sciences & Medicine* 3 (1991).

Ekpunobi, Cosmas, Daniel Idonor, and Yabolisa Ofoka. "Tension in Senate over Darfur Killings." *Daily Champion* (October 3, 2007).

El-Battahani, Atta. *Tribal Peace Conferences in Sudan: The Role of Joudiyya Institution in Darfur.* Zurich: ECOMAN, 1999.

El-Mahdi, Saeed Mohamed. *Introduction to Land Law of the Sudan.* Khartoum: Khartoum University Press, 1979.

Elmi, Asha Hagi, et al., "Give Women of Darfur and Chad a Hearing." *East African* (September 11, 2007).

El-Sammani, Mohamed O., et al., *A Strategy for Development Project in Darfur.* Khartoum: UNDP, 2004.

El-Tom, Abdullahi Osman. "The Black Book of Sudan: Imbalance of Power and Wealth in Sudan." *Journal of African International Affairs* vol. 1 no. 2 (2003): 25–35.

—. "Darfur People: Too Black for the Arab-Islamic Project of Sudan." Part II, *Irish Journal of Anthropology* 9, no. 1 (2006).

—. "The Black Book of Sudan: Imbalance of Power and Wealth in Sudan." *Journal of African National Affairs* 1, no. 2 (2003).

Ewald, Janet J. *Soldiers, Traders and Slaves: State Formation and Economic Transformation in the Greater Nile Valley, 1700–1885.* Madison: University of Wisconsin Press, 1990.

Eze, Chinedu. "Nigeria Sends More Soldiers to Darfur." *This Day* (October 8, 2007).

Flint, Julie. "Darfur's Armed Movements." In *War in Darfur and the Search for Peace*, Alex de Waal, ed. Cambridge, MA: Harvard University Press, 2007.

Fouad, Ibrahim. "Strategies for a De-Escalation of Violence in Darfur, Sudan," *Global Development Options* 4 (2005).

Garang, John de Mabior. *The Call for Democracy in Sudan*. New York/London: Kegan Paul International Ltd., 1992.

Gberie, Lansana. "A Test Case for Humanitarian Intervention." *Concord Times* (October 1, 2004).

Goldstone, Richard. "A Dangerous Silence as Darfur Screams." *Business Day* (December 11, 2006).

Grawert, Elke. *Making a Living in Rural Sudan: Production of Women Labour Migration of Men*, and *Politics for Peasants' Needs*. New York, St. Martin Press, 1998.

Gure, Joel. "Understanding the Darfur Conflict." *Vanguard* (August 19, 2004).

Haaland, Gunnar, "Nomadization as an Economic Career among the Sedentaries in the Sudan Savannah Belt." In *Essays in Sudan Ethnography*, I. Cunnison and W. Jones, eds. London: Hurst, 1972.

—. "Economic Determinants in Ethnic Processes." In *Ethnic Groups and Boundaries*, Frederik Barth, ed. London: Allen and Unwin, 1969.

Habib, A. "Effects of Displacement on Southern Women's Health and Food Habits." *Ahfad Journal* vol. 12, no. 2 (1995).

Hackett, B. *Pray God and Keep Walking: Stories of Women Refugees*. London: McFarland & Company Publishers, 1996.

Hamid, Sulayman. *Darfur: Wadh' Al-Niqat 'Ala Al-Huruf*. Khartoum: Midan Books, 2004.

Harir, S. "Arab Belt versus African Belt: Ethno-Political Conflict in Darfur and the Regional Cultural Factors." In *Short Cut to Decay: The Case of the Sudan*, T. Tvedt and Sharif Harir, eds. Uppsala: The Nordic Africa Institute, 1994.

—. "Militarization of the Conflict, Displacement and the Legitimacy of the State: A Case from Darfur, Western Sudan." Paper presented to Center for Development Studies, University of Bergen, Norway 1992.

—. "Racism in Islamic Discourse! Retreating Nationalism and Upsurging Ethnicity in Dar Fur, Sudan." Paper presented to Center for Development Studies, University of Bergen, Norway (1993).

Hasan, Yusuf Fadl. *Sudan in Africa*. Khartoum: University Press, 1971.

Hooper, C. *Manly States: Masculinities, International Relations, and Gender Politics*. New York: Columbia University Press, 2000.

Howell, John. *Local Government and Politics in the Sudan*. Khartoum: Khartoum University Press, 1974.

Human Rights Watch Report. "Sexual Violence and Its Consequences among Displaced Persons in Darfurand Chad." April 2005.

Ibe, Paul. "Darfur: Confab Raises Panel to Harmonise Govt., Rebel's Position." *This Day* (August 27, 2004).

Ibrahim, Fouad. *Desertification in North Darfur*. Hamburg: Hamburger Geographisher Studien 35, 1980.

Idris, Amir H. *Sudan's Civil War: Slavery, Race and Formational Identities*. Lewiston, NY: Edwin Mellen Press, 2001.

Indra, D. ed. *Engendering Forced Migration*. New York: Berghahn, 1998.

International Crisis Group. "Darfur Rising: Sudan's New Crisis." *Africa Report* No. 76, March 25, 2004.

International Labor Office (ILO). *Appropriate Farm Equipment Technology for Small-Scale Traditional Sector: Synthesis Report*. Addis Ababa, 1983.

International Monetary Fund (IMF). *Sudan: Final Review under the Medium-Term Staff-Monitored Program and the 2002 Program*. Washington, June 2002.

Jalal Hashim, Mohammad. *To Be or Not to Be: Sudan at Crossroads*. http://www.sudanjem.com/sudan-alt/english/books/TOBEORNOTTOBE/20040418_books_TOBEORNOTTOBE.htm (2004).

Johnson, Douglas H. *The Root Causes of Sudan's Civil Wars*. Oxford: James Currey, 2003.

—. "Nationalism, Independence, and the First Civil War 1942–1972." In *The Root Causes of Sudan's Civil Wars*. Oxford: James Curry, 2003.

Jok, Jok Madut. *War and Slavery in Sudan*. Philadelphia: University of Pennsylvania Press, 2001.

Justice and Equality Movement (JEM). *The Black Book: Imbalance of Power and Wealth in Sudan*, Parts I and II, English Translation, UK: JEM, 2004.

Kagame, George. "Sudan Envoy Commends RDF in Darfur." *The New Times* (January 25, 2007).

Kani, Ahmed Mohammed. *The Intellectual Origin of Islamic Jihad in Nigeria*. London: Al Hoda, 1988.

Kapila, Mukesh. UN Report on the Situaton in Darfru, Khartoum: UNDP, 2005.

Kapteijns, Lidwien, and Jay Spaulding. *After the Millennium: Diplomatic Correspondence from Wadai and Dar Fur on the Eve of Colonial Conquest, 1885–1916*. Lansing: Michigan State University Press, 1988.

—. *Mahdist Faith and Sudanic Tradition: The History of the Masalit Sultanate 1870–1930*. London: Kegan Paul International Series, 1985.

Kapteijns, Lidwien. *Mahdist Faith and Sudanic Tradition: The History of the Masalit Sultanate 1870–1930*. London: Kegan Paul International Series, 1985.

Kawu, Is'haq Modibbo. "Darfur–On the Margins of the AU Summit." *Daily Trust* (August 13, 2007).

Kearney, Richard. "Dialogue with Emmanuel Levinas." *Face to Face with Levinas*, Richard A. Cohen, ed. Albany: State University of New York Press, 1986. Jacques Derrida, J. "Force of Law." In *Acts of Religion*. New York: Routledge, 2002.

Khalid. Mansour. *War and Peace in Sudan: The Tale of Two Countries*. London: Kegan Paul, 2003.

Khalid, Monsour, ed. *John Garang Speaks*. New York/London: Kegan Paul International Ltd, 1987.

Kimanuka, Oscar. "Darfur's Plight Is Like Rwanda's." *East African* (October 9, 2007). Nyago, Kintu. "Bigotry Still Assaults Black African." *The Monitor* (August 5, 2004).

Kimenyi, Felly. "Brown Extols Rwanda on Growth, Darfur." *The New Times* (October 8, 2007).

—. "Gov't, U.S. Discuss Darfur." *The New Times* (March 17, 2007).

—. "New RDF Battalion for Darfur This Month." *The New Times* (October 10, 2007).

Ki-Moon, Ban. "Darfur Crisis Defies Easy Solutions." *The Nation* (September 20, 2007).

—. Ban. "The Conflict in Darfur Beyond What We Think." *New Times* (September 19, 2007).

—. "The Real Work Begins in Darfur." *The Reporter* (June 25, 2007).

Komolafe, Babajide, and Clifford Amuzuo. "Darfur–Time for AU to Act, Say Serap, IAP." *Vanguard* (September 18, 2007).

Kukathas, Chandran. "Are There Any Cultural Rights?" *Political Theory* vol. 20, no. 1 (1992).

—. "Cultural Rights Again: A Rejoinder to Kymlicka." *Political Theory* vol. 20, no. 4 (1992).

Kursany, Ibrahim, "Peasants of the Nuba Mountains Region," *Review of African Political Economy* No. 26: 15–34.

Kushner, T., and K. Knox. *Refugees in an Age of Genocide*. London: Frank Cass, 1999.

Kuwa, Yusuf. "Things Would No Longer Be the Same." In *The Right to Be Nuba: The Story of a Sudanese People's Struggle for Survival*, S. Rahhal, ed. Trenton, NJ: Red Sea Press, 2002.

Kymlicka, Will. *The Rights of Minority Cultures*. Oxford: Oxford University Press, 1995.

La Rue, G. Michael. "Land and Social Stratification in Darfur, 1785–1875: The Hakura System." In *The State and the Market: Studies in the Economic and Social History of the Third World*, Clive Dewey. ed. (New Delhi: Manohar, 1987).

Leaning, Jennifer. "Diagnosing Genocide– The Case of Darfur." *New England Journal of Medicine* 351, no. 8.

Leckie, Scott. "Another Step Towards Indivisibility: Identifying the Key Features of Violations of Economic, Social, and Cultural Rights." *Human Rights Quarterly* 20 no. 1 (1998).

Levey, Geoffrey Brahm. "Equality, Autonomy, and Cultural Rights." *Political Theory* 25 no. 2. (1997).

Lloyd, P. *Africa in Social Change*. London: Penguin Books, 1972.

Logoron, Stephen Lomeling, et. al. *The Agricultural Bank of Sudan: Twenty-Five Years of Agricultural Credit, 1959–1984*. Development Studies and Research Center, University of Khartoum, Group Research, 1985.

Lohor, Josephine. "Darfur: Obasanjo Meets Parties to Peace Talks." *This Day* (August 21, 2004).

—. "Final Meeting on Darfur for Abuja Soon." *This Day* (May 18, 2005).

—. "Obasanjo, El Bashir Meet to End Darfur Crises." *This Day* (July 21, 2006).

Long, Lynellyn. *Ban Vinai: The Refugee Camp*. New York: Columbia University Press, 1993.

Loveless, Jeremy. Displaced Populations in Khartoum. Report for Save the Children Denmark. Channel Research, 1999.

MacKinnon, Catharine. "Rape, Genocide, and Women's Human Rights." In *Violence Against Women: Philosophical Perspectives*. Stanley French et al., eds. Ithaca, NY: Cornell University Press, 1998.

MacMichael, H. A. *A History of the Arabs in the Sudan*. Cambridge: Cambridge University Press, 1922.

Madut, Abalgak Them. *Regional Distribution of Agricultural Credit in Sudan*. Development Studies and Research Center, University of Khartoum, M.A. Thesis, 1986.

Mafeje, Archie. "The Ideology of 'Tribalism," *The Journal of Modern African Studies* Vol. 9, No. 2 (Aug. 1971).

Malwal, B. "Sources of Conflict in the Sudan." Paper presented at the United States Institute of Peace, Washington, DC, 1993.

Mamdani, Mahmood. "The Politics of Naming: Genocide, Civil War, Insurgency," *London Review of Books*, 8 March 2007.

—. *Famine that Kills: Darfur, Sudan*. New York: Oxford University Press, 2004.

Mazimpaka, Magnus K. "Over 600 RDF Return From Darfur." *The New Times* (February 22, 2007).

Mazimpaka, Magnus K. "Another RDF Soldier Dies in Darfur." *The New Times*. (April 12, 2007).

Mbitiru, Chege. "Darfur Attack Confirms Old Fears." *The Nation* (October 8, 2007).

—. "Darfur the Loser as Row Rages." *The Nation* (September 11, 2006).

McFerran, Ann. "Curse of the Janjaweed," *The Sunday Times* (September 23, 2007).

McGregor, et al., "Why Don't More Women Report Sexual Assault to the Police?" *Canadian Medical Association* 162, no. 5 (2000).

Miller, et al. "Victim Costs of Violent Crime and Resulting Injuries," *Health Affairs* 12, no. 4 (1993).

Mills, Sara. *Discourse*. London and New York: Routledge, 1997.

Ministry of Finance and Economic Planning. *The Six-Year Plan of Economic and Social Development 1977/78–1982/83*. Juba, 1977.

—. *The Ten-Year Plan of Economic and Social Development 1961/62–1970/71*. Khartoum: Government Printing Press, 1962.

Ministry of National Planning. *The Six-Year Plan of Economic and Social Development 1977/78–1982/83*. Khartoum: Government Printing Press, 1977.

—. *The Five-Year Plan of Economic and Social Development of the Democratic Republic of the Sudan for the Period 1970/71–1974/75*. Khartoum: Government Printing Press, 1970.

Mohamed, A., and Belgis Bedri. *Inter-Communal Conflicts in Sudan Cases, Resolution Mechanisms and Transformation: A Case Study of Darfur Region*. Omdurman: Ahfad University, 2005.

Mohamed, M.A., and Sharif Harir. "The Genesis of National Disintegration." In *Short-Cut to Decay: The Case of the Sudan*, Sharif Harir and Terje Tvedt, eds. Uppsala: Nordiska Afrikainstitutet, 1994.

Mohamed, A. et al. *Development Is the Key for Peace in Darfur*. Khartoum: Centre for Development and Peace Studies (Juba)/ Fredrich Ebert Stiftung, 2003.

Morawska, E. "Intended and Unintended Consequences of Forced Migrations: A Neglected Aspect of East Europe's Twentieth Century History." *International Migration Review* vol. 34, no. 4 (2000).

Morris-Jones, Sophia. "Amnesty Demonstrates for Citizens in Darfur." *Ghanaian Chronicle* (September 19, 2007).

Morton, James. *The Poverty of Nations*. London: British Academic Press, 1994.

Mukhtar, Al-Baqir Afif. "The Crisis of Identity in Northern Sudan: A Dilemma of a Black People with a White Culture." In *Race and Identity in the Nile Valley: Ancient and Modern Perspectives*, C. Fluehr-Lobban and K. Rhodes, eds. Trenton, NJ: The Red Sea Press, 2004.

Mukombozi, Robert. "Government, AU in Talks over Darfur." *The New Times* (May 4, 2007).

Mukombozi, Robert, and Edwin Musoni. "Darfur—Worry over 'Pullout.'" *The New Times* (March 23, 2007).

Mukose, Abubaker. "Sudan Bishops Decry Deaths." *New Vision* (August 30, 2004).

Mulama, Joyce. "Rights—Sudan: Women Boost Darfur Talks." *Inter Press Service* (December 22, 2005).

Mulera, Muniini K. "It's Genocide in Darfur." *The Monitor* (August 9, 2004).

Munyaneza, James. "Bin Laden Calls for Jihad Against Darfur Peacekeepers." *The New Times* (October 26, 2007).

—. "General Karake Takes Up Darfur Hybrid Force Post." *The New Times* (September 17, 2007).

—. "Rwanda Almost Pulled Out of Darfur." *The New Times* (December 13, 2006).

—. "Rwanda May Withdraw from Darfur—Kagame." *The New Times* (March 14, 2007).

Muramila, Gasheegu. "Govt Affirms Darfur Loyalty." *The New Times* (August 22, 2007).

Murunga, Ambrose. "Darfur Is Burning as We Fiddle." *The Nation* (September 16, 2006).

Musoni, Edwin. "Fallen Darfur Peacekeepers' Bodies Flown In." *The New Times* (November 1, 2007).

Muthuma, Gitau. "The Darfur Crisis: Are Accords Enough?" *The New Times* (March 14, 2005).

Mutua, Makau. "Racism at the Root of Darfur Crisis." *The East African Standard* (July 26, 2004).

Mwaura, Peter. "Darfur Attracting 'Undue' Attention." *The Nation* (November 19, 2004).

Myrdal, Gunnar. *Economic Theory of Underdeveloped Regions*. London: Methuen & Co. Ltd., 1969.

Niblock, Tim. *Class & Power in Sudan: The Dynamics of Sudanese Politics, 1898–1985*. Albany: State University of New York Press, 1987.

Njenga, Gitau Wa. "Kenyans in UK Protest over Killings." *The East African Standard* (June 1, 2004).

Nordstrom, Carloyn. *Another Kind of War Story*. Philadelphia: University of Pennsylvania Press, 1997.

Nour, Babikir Osman Abdel. *Financing Rural Development in Sudan*. A paper presented in a conference on Alternative Policies for Sudan, Cairo, Egypt, 2000.

Nurkse, R. *Problems of Capital Formation in Underdeveloped Countries*. New York: Oxford University Press, 1953.

O'Fahey, R. S. "A Complex Ethnic Reality with a Long History." *International Herald Tribune* (May 15, 2004).

—. *State and Society in Dar Fur*. London: C. Hurst & Company, 1980.

O'Fahey, R.S., and J. L. Spaulding. *Kingdoms of the Sudan*. London: Methuen & Co. Ltd., 1974.

Ochayi, Chris. "Fresh 680 Troops Leave for Darfur." *Vanguard* (October 9, 2007).

Ochieng, Zachary. "Darfur Crisis Blanks Out Many Unresolved Conflicts." *East African* (August 7, 2007).

Odaudu, Samuel. "AU, Darfur and the Price of Peace-Keeping." *Leadership* (October 15, 2007).

Odipo, Dominic. "State Silence over Darfur Says a Lot About Itself." *The East African Standard* (April 2, 2007).

Oduho, Joseph, and Deng, William. *The Problem of the Southern Sudan*. London: Oxford University Press, 1963.

Ojeifo, Sufuyan, and Juliana Taiwo. "Darfur—FG Sends Azazi to Assess Situation." *This Day* (October 3, 2007).

Oji, George. "Darfur—Reject Deployment, Be Sanctioned, Soldiers Warned." *This Day* (October 11, 2007).

Okerafor, Tony. "Will the UN Enter Darfur." *Daily Champion* (September 8, 2006).

Okoiti, Okiya. "AU Decision on Darfur Misguided." *The Nation* (August 27, 2007).

Olaleye, Olawale. "Darfur—'Nigerian Soldiers are Outstanding.'" *This Day* (November 5, 2007).

Ologbondiyan, Kola. "Darfur: Senate Okays Obasanjo's Troops Deployment." *This Day* (August 20, 2004).

Oluoch, Fred. "Gadaffi Blows Hot and Cold On Darfur Issue." *The East African*. November 12, 2007.

—. "How the Conflict Is Affecting Prospects of Peace in S. Sudan." *The East African* (September 15, 2004).

Omonobi, Kingsely. "155 Soldiers for Darfur Peace Mission." *Vanguard* (August 31, 2004).

—. "7 Soldiers Killed, 10 Missing in Darfur." *Vanguard* (October 2, 2007).

Omonobi, Kingsley, and Umoru Henry. "Darfur–Corpses of Slain Soldiers Arrive for Burial Today." *Vanguard* (October 5, 2007).

Onunaiju, Charles. "Darfur Talks: Commission on Power Sharing Holds First Session." *Daily Trust* (December 2, 2005).

Oshidari, Kenro, and Felix Bamezon. "Darfur Crisis Snowballing Across Central Africa." *The East African* (April 3, 2007).

Ozoemena, Charles, and Habib Yacoob. "Sudan's Peace Talks Adopt 4-Point Agenda on Darfur." *Vanguard* (August 25, 2004).

Pact of the League of Arab States, Article 8. U.N. doc. A/C. 6/L.111 [also in U.N. Treaty Series (vol. LXX): 237–263.

Piet, Bame. "BDF to Send Troops to Darfur." *Mmegi* (February 6, 2006).

—. "Botswana to Airlift Troops to Darfur." *Mmegi* (March 15, 2006).

Powell, Eve Troutt. *A Different Shade of Colonialism: Egypt, Great Britain and the Mastery of the Sudan*. Berkeley: University of California Press, 2003.

Power, Samantha. "A Reporter at Large: Dying in Darfur." *The New Yorker* (August 30, 2004).

Prendergast, John, and Colin Thomas-Jensen. "Echoes of Genocide in Darfur, Eastern Chad." *East African* (September 25, 2007).

Prunier, Gérard. *Darfur: The Ambigious Genocide*. Ithaca, NY: Cornell Univeristy Press, 2005.

Rabbah, Nazik E. "The Role of National Government and Native Administration in Conflict Resolution in Darfur Region" M.Sc. Thesis, Faculty of Economics and Social Studies, University of Khartoum, 1998.

Rasch, William. *Sovereignty and Its Discontents: On the Primacy of Conflict and the Structure of the Political*. Great Britain: Birkbeck Law Press, 2004.

Regional Ministry of Finance and Economic Affairs, ed. *Proceedings of the Conference on Development in the Southern Region of the Sudan*. Juba, 1984.

Reyna, S. P. *Wars without End: The Political Economy of a Precolonial African State*. Hanover, NH: University Press of New England, 1990.

Rogaia Mustafa, Abusharaf. "Sudanese." In *Encyclopedia of Medical Anthropology: Health and Sickness in the World's Cultures*, C. Ember and M. Ember, eds. New York: Plenum, 2004.

Ruiz, H. "The Sudan: Cradle of Displacement." In *The Forsaken People*, F. Deng and R. Cohen, eds. Washington: The Brookings Institution, 1997.

Rünger, Mechtild. *Land Law and Land Use Control in Western Sudan: The Case of Southern Darfur*. London: Ithaca Press, 1987.

Rutazigwa, Alphonse. "Senate Hails Darfur Peacekeepers" *The New Times* (July 2, 2007).

Sahgal, G., and Nira Yuval-Davis, eds. *Refusing Holy Orders Women and Fundamentalism in Britain*. London: Virago, 1992.

Salih, M. A. Mohamed. 2005. *Understanding the Conflict in Darfur*. Occasional Paper, Centre of African Studies, University of Copenhagen.

Santandrea, Stefano. *A Tribal History of the Western Bahr el Ghazal*. Bologna: Nigrizia, 1964.

Scheper-Hughes, Nancy, and Bourgios, Philippe. *Violence in Peace and War: An Anthology*. Oxford: Blackwell Publishing, 2004.

Schmitt, Carl. *The Concept of the Political*, George Schwab, trans. Chicago: University of Chicago Press, 1996.

Sen, Amartya. *Development as Freedom*. New York: Knopf, 1999.

Shaw, Martin. *What Is Genocide?* Cambridge MA: Polity Press, 2007.

Shewareged, Bruck. "Will the Darfur Peace Hold?" *The Reporter* (September 2, 2006).

Sikainga, Ahmad Alawad. *Slaves into Workers: Emancipation and Labor in Colonial Sudan*. Austin: University of Texas, 1996.

Soeken, et al. "Randomized Response Technique: Applications to Research on Rape." *Psychology of Women Quarterly* 10, no. 2 (1986).

Southern Development Investigation Team. *Natural Resources and Development*. London/Khartoum: 1954.

Sudan Demographics and Health Survey. Baltimore: Institute for Resource Development/Macro International, Inc., 1995.

Sudan Peoples Liberation Army/Movement. *Manifesto*. Bilpam, 1983.

Suleiman, Toba. "UNHCR Raises Alarm on Refugee Influx." *This Day* (December 14, 2004).

Suliman, Mohammed. *al-Sudan: Hiroub al-Mawarid Wa al-Hawiya* Sudan: Resources, Identity, and War. London: Cambridge Academic Press, 2000.

—. *Darfur Harb Al-Mawarid Wa-Al-Hawiyah*. First ed. London: Cambridge Publishing House, 2004.

—. "Ethnicity from Perception to Cause of Violent Conflicts: The Case of the Fur and Nuba Conflicts in Western Sudan." Paper presented at the CONTICI International Workshop, Bern, Switzerland, July 8–11, 1997.

—. *War in Darfur*. London: IFAA Publications, 1994.

Swiss, et al. "Violence Against Women During the Liberian Civil Conflict." *Journal of the American Medical Association* 279, no. 8 (1998).

Taiwo, Juliana. "680 Soldiers Head for Darfur." *This Day* (October 9, 2007).

—. "Darfur–Dead Soldiers for Burial Tomorrow." *This Day* (October 4, 2007).

—. "Political Will Panacea to Darfur Crisis–Agwai." *This Day* (September 24, 2007).

—. "Tears As Soldiers Killed in Darfur Get Heroic Burial." *This Day* (October 6, 2007).

Tajudeen, Abdul Raheem. "The Root of Chaos in Darfur." *New Vision* (August 12, 2004).

Teklu, Dagnachew. "Sudan Accepts Hybrid Force for Darfur–AU." *Daily Monitor* (June 13, 2007).

—. "UN, AU Start Serious Consultation on Darfur Issue." *Daily Monito* (June 12, 2007).

Theobald, Alan Buchan. *Ali Dinar, Last Sultan of Darfur, 1898–1916*. London: Longmans, 1965.

Tubiana, Jerome. "Darfur: A War for Land?" In *War in Darfur and the Search for Peace*. Alex de Waal, ed. Cambridge, MA: Harvard University Press, 2007.

Tully, Dennis. "The Decision to Migrate in Sudan." *Cultural Survival Quarterly* 7.4 (1983): 17–18.

Turner, Terrence. *The Kayapo*. The Disappearing World Series: Granada TV, 1997.

UNESCO. *Cultural Rights as Human Rights*. Paris: UNESCO, 1970.

—. Defending Cultural Rights. UNESCO Asia and Pacific Regional Bureau for Education, Bangkok, Thailand.

UNHCR. Sexual Violence against Women: Guidelines for Prevention and Response. Geneva, Switzerland, 1995.

Van Rensberg, Patrick. "African Leaders Play the Fiddle While Sudan Burns." *Mmegi* (July 16, 2004).

Wafawarova, Reason. "Darfur, AU and Global Politics." *The Herald* (October 31, 2007).

Wanyeki, L. Muthoni. "Yes, Let Africans Sort Out Darfur Crisis." *The East African* (August 24, 2004).

Warburg, Gabriel R. *Historical Discord in the Nile Valley*. Evanston, IL: Northwestern University Press, 1993.

Whande, Tanonoka Joseph "Darfur Disgraces the African Union." *Mmegi* (February 26, 2007).

Willemse, Karin "On Globalization, Gender and the Nation-State. Muslim Masculinity and the Urban Middle-Class Family in Islamist Sudan." In *The Gender Question in Globalization. Changing Perspectives and Practices*, Tine Davids and Francien van Driel, eds. Burlington, VT: Ashgate Publishers, 2005.

—. *One Foot in Heaven: Narratives on Gender and Islam in Darfur, West Sudan*. Leiden: Brill Publishers, 2007.

Yamba, C. Bawa. *Permanent Pilgrims: The Role of Pilgrimage in the Lives of West African Muslims in Sudan*. Washington: Smithsonian Press, 1995.

Yongo-Bure, B. *Economic Development of Southern Sudan*. Lanham, MD: University Press of America, 2007.

—. "The Agricultural Bank of Sudan and the Sudanese Peasant" *Journal of*

Newspaper Articles

"Abuja Hosts Rally for Darfur." *This Day* (September 17, 2006).

"Agwai Appointed Darfur Force Commander by AU" *This Day* (May 25, 2007).

Akinsanmi, G. "Darfur–10 Soldiers Missing." *This Day* (October 2, 2007).

Akwiwu, B.A. "Genocide in Sudan." *This Day* (May 14, 2004).

Andrew, Ahiante. "Sudan: AU Meets in Abuja, Aug 23." *This Day* (August 12, 2004).

"Annan Seeks to Evade Sudan Blame." *Addis Tribune* (June 25, 2004).

"Arabian Shame." *The Washington Post* (August 12, 2005): A18.

"Army Arrests Darfur Rebels as New Peace Talks Resume." *The East African Standard* (June 13, 2005).

"AU Summit Opens Today." *New Vision* (July 6, 2004).

"Change of Guard in BDF Darfur Mission." *Mmegi* (August 7, 2006).

"China and Darfur Crisis." *Daily Champion* (April 5, 2007).

"CPP Joins Protests Against the Murder of Africans." *Accra Mail* (July 23, 2004).

"Darfur Peace Talks Resume in Abuja." *Nigeria First* (June 13, 2005).

"Darfur Peace Talks: Obasanjo Urges Coope-ration." *Nigeria First* (September 15, 2004). Ojedokun, Lere. EU Team Visits Obasanjo Over Darfur Crisis." *Daily Champion* (October 16, 2004).

"Darfur Peacekeeping Row Divides Sudan." *The Herald* (July 3, 2006).

"Darfur: Parties Unite on Peace Resolution." *Daily Trust* (December 1, 2005).

"Darfur—AU, FG, Tasked on Human Rights." *This Day* (September 19, 2007).

"Darfur—Galvanise the Hybrid Force." *This Day* June 28, 2007.

El-Hassan, Yahya. "Sudanese Women as War Victims." *PANA* (March 6, 2000).

"Emi Release 'Voices for Darfur' DVD." *The Ethiopian Herald* (September 7, 2005).

"Ending Darfur Crisis." *The Daily Observer* July 10, 2007.

"Fallen RDF Darfur Peacekeepers Buried." *The New Times* (November 4, 2007).

"Female IDP's Raped and Beaten in Darfur." *Media Institute of Southern African* (December 9, 2004).

"Festering War in Darfur." *Daily Champion* (March 10, 2006).

"France Calls for Speedy Deployment of Darfur Force." *Daily Monitor* (July 30, 2007).

"Free Darfur—Or Forget about African Union." *Accra Mail* (August 20, 2007).

"IAP, Serap Task Yar'Adua on Darfur." *Vanguard* (September 15, 2007).

Ifionu, Okey. "Darfur As Another Blood-stain." *This Day* (August 12, 2004).

"Konare Appoints Darfur Force Commander." *Ethiopian Herald* (May 25, 2007).

"Konare Expresses Concern over Deteriorating Situation." *Addis Tribune* (December 30, 2004).

Mamdani, Mahmood. "Darfur Crisis." *New Vision* (March 19, 2007).

"Nigerian Soldier in Darfur." *Daily Champion* (October 8, 2007).

"Obasanjo Confers on Darfur, Leaves for US." *Nigeria First* (December 2, 2004). "Obasanjo Tours War-Ravaged Darfur." *Nigeria First* (January 10, 2005).

"Obasanjo Hopeful on Resolution of Sudan Conflict." *Nigeria First* (November 22, 2004).

"Obasano in Libya for Darfur Talks." *Nigeria First* (October 19, 2004).

Piet, Bame. "BDF to Send Troops to Darfur." *Mmegi* (February 6, 2006).

"Premier, Albright Hold Talks on Somalia, Darfur." *The Daily Monitor* (December 4, 2006).

"President Mediates at Darfur Peace Talks." *Nigeria First* (August 24, 2004).

"Proposals Submitted for a Cease-Fire Commission." *Addis Tribune* (May 7, 2004). Greece Gives 100,000 Euro to AU for Humanitarian Support." *Daily Monitor*. (September 16, 2004).

"PSC Adopts Communique on Darfur Crisis." *Addis Tribune* (August 13, 2004).

"Racism at the Root of Darfur Crisis." *The East African Standard* (July 26, 2004).

"Ray of Light in Darfur?" *The Nation* (June 14, 2007).

"RDF Could Leave Darfur." *The New Times* (September 5, 2006).

Review of Books, 8 March 2007.

"Saving Darfur." *Daily Champion* (August 10, 2004).

"Sudan Accused of 'Ethnic Cleansing.'" *The East African* (May 10, 2004).

"Sudan Govt, Rebls Adopt African Union Agenda for Peace." *Vanguard* (August 25, 2004).

"Sudan Strives to Keep Darfur Pledges." *New Era* (August 12, 2004).

"Sudan to Disarm Arab Militias." *This Day* (July 5, 2004).

"Sudan: AU Meets in Abuja, Aug 23." *This Day* (August 12, 2004).

"Sudanese Govt, Darfur Rebels Sign Peace Accord in Abuja." *Nigeria First* (July 6, 2005).

"Sudanese Parties Sign Security and Humanitarian Protocol." *Nigeria First* (November 10, 2004).

"The Chairperson of AU Expresses Concerns over Violation of Accord." *Addis Tribune* (April 30, 2004).

"The Darfur Crisis—BDF's Major Tiro Dies on Darfur Mission." *The Voice* (October 9, 2007).

"UN Diplomats to Hold Darfur Talks with Sudan and African Union." *The Ethiopian Herald* (November 12, 2006).

"UN Okays Hybrid Force for Darfur." *This Day*. (November 17, 2006).

Online Sources

"Aid agency warns on Darfur rapes." http://news.bbc.co.uk/2/hi/africa/5280286.stm, August 24, 2006; "Women demand end to Darfur rapes," http://news.bbc.co.uk/2/hi/africa/6165017.stm, December 10, 2006.

Amnesty International. *Sudan Report*. 2001, www.amnesty.org.

"An unequal Sudan." http://weekly.ahram.org.eg/2006/797/re64.htm, Issue No. 797 (June 1–7, 2006).

"Clutching at Straws." http://weekly.ahram.org.eg/2006/792/re4.htm, Issue No. 792 (April 27–May 3, 2006).

"Content Providers." http://allafrica.com/publishers.html?language=en, cited on June 26, 2008.

"Darfur on the backburner." http://weekly.ahram.org.eg/2005/729/re4.htm, Issue No. 729 (February 10–16, 2005).

"Darfur Rebels May Unite but Talks Still Tough." Wednesday April 9, 2008, *Sudan Tribune*, Tuesday November 13, 2007, http://www.sudantribune.com/spip.php?page=imprimable&id_article=24712, accessed April 9, 2008.

"Darfur: A Deadly Paradox." *The Nation* July 29, 2004, http://www.thenation.com

"Dateline Darfur." http://weekly.ahram.org.eg/2004/697/fr2.htm, Issue No. 697 (July 1–7, 2004).

"Deadlocked." http://weekly.ahram.org.eg/2004/707/re6.htm, Issue No. 707 (September 9–15, 2004).

"Deadly Lesson for the AU." *The Nation* (October 1, 2007).

"Divisive Darfur." http://weekly.ahram.org.eg/2005/770/re102.htm, Issue No. 770 (November 24–30, 2005).

"Dying for Darfur." http://weekly.ahram.org.eg/2006/805/re113.htm, Issue No. 805 (July 27–August 2, 2006).

"Ending the Darfur silence," *The Boston Globe*, http://www.boston.com/news/globe/editorial_opinion/editorials/articles/2006/04/30/ending_the_darfur_silence/ (April 30, 2006).

Henshaw, Amber. "Sudan rape laws 'need overhaul.'" http://news.bbc.co.uk/2/hi/africa/6252620.stm (June 29, 2007).

"Khartoum's bare knuckle." http://weekly.ahram.org.eg/2006/778/re9.htm, Issue No. 778 (January 19–26, 2006).

"Open to Abuse." http://weekly.ahram.org.eg/2007/867/re93.htm, Issue No. 867 (October 18–24, 2007).

"Pinning hopes on peace." http://weekly.ahram.org.eg/2004/718/re7.htm, Issue No. 718 (November 2–December 1, 2004).

"Principles and Personalities." http://weekly.ahram.org.eg/2003/670/re8.htm, Issue No. 670 (December 25–31, 2003).

"Raging rivalries." http://weekly.ahram.org.eg/2006/804/re3.htm, Issue No. 804 (July 20–26, 2006).

"Rectitude for Darfur." http://weekly.ahram.org.eg/2005/736/re6.htm, Issue No. 736 (March 31–April 6, 2005).

"Sentencing to Death by Stoning of Two Women on Adultery Charges." World Organization Against Torture, Geneva, March 9, 2007, http://www.omct.org/index.php?id=EQL&lang=eng&actualPageNumber=1&articleSet=Appeal&articleId=6911&PHPSESSID=2c740df6f87caeff97ae9d65851825e9.

"Sudan at the crossroads." http://weekly.ahram.org.eg/2004/713/re4.htm, Issue No. 713 (October 21–27, 2004).

"Sudanese spats." http://weekly.ahram.org.
eg/2007/877/reg202.htm, Issue No. 877
(December 27, 2007–January 2, 2008).

"Talking Darfur to Death." *The New York
Times*, http://www.nytimes.com/2007/03/31/
opinion/31sat1.html (March 31, 2007).

"Talking heads, Sudanese style."
http://weekly.ahram.org.eg/2003/637/re11.
htm, Issue No. 637 (May 8–14, 2003).

"Talks about talks." http://weekly.ahram.org.
eg/2004/678/re6.htm, Issue No. 678
(February 19–24, 2004).

"The deafening silence." *The Independent*,
http://www.independent.co.uk/opinion/lea
ding-articles/leading-article-the-deafening-
silence-794426.html (March 12, 2008).

"The horrors of Darfur." http://weekly.ahram.
org.eg/2004/698/re72.htm, Issue No. 698
(July 8–4, 2004).

"The land question." http://weekly.ahram.org.
eg/2006/794/sc21.htm, Issue No. 794
(May 11–17, 2006).

"Turning the tables." http://weekly.ahram.org.
eg/2005/775/re182.htm, Issue No. 775
(December 29, 2005–January 4, 2006).

"UN attacks Darfur 'fear and rape.'"
http://news.bbc.co.uk/2/hi/africa/3690232.
stm, September 25, 2004; "UN accuses
Sudan over Darfur rape."
http://news.bbc.co.uk/2/hi/africa/4728231.
stm (July 29, 2005).

"Yesterday's men and tomorrow's."
http://weekly.ahram.org.eg/2005/747/re3.
htm, Issue No. 747 (June 16–22, 2005).

Darfur Crisis
A Selected Bibliography

Eric Kofi Acree

This bibliography provides basic references to further assist readers in understanding the history, culture, and politics related to the current conflict in Darfur. It is interdisciplinary and varied in content, but by no means exhaustive. It includes books, articles, online resources, videos/DVDs, and major websites related to the issue of Darfur.

Books

Darfur-History, Conflict, and Genocide

Ahmed, Abdel Ghaffar M. *Understanding the Crisis in Darfur: Listening to Sudanese Voices*. Bergen, Norway: BRIC, University of Bergen, 2006.

Apsel, Joyce, ed. *Darfur: Genocide Before Our Eyes*. New York: Institute for the Study of Genocide, 2005.

Burr, J. Millard and Robert O. Collins. *Darfur the Long Road to Disaster*. Princeton, NJ: Markus Wiener, 2006.

Daly, M. W. *Darfur's Sorrow: A History of Destruction and Genocide*. Cambridge; New York: Cambridge University Press, 2007.

De Waal, Alexander. *Famine That Kills: Darfur, Sudan*. Oxford: Oxford University Press, 2005.

De Waal, Alexander. *War in Darfur and the Search for Peace*. Cambridge, MA; London: Global Equity Initiative, Harvard University; Justice Africa, 2007.

Flint, Julie and Alexander De Waal. *Darfur: A New History of a Long War*. London; New York: Zed Books, 2008.

Flint, Julie and Alexander De Waal. *Darfur: A Short History of a Long War*. London; New York: Zed Books, 2005.

International Crisis Group. *Darfur: The Failure to Protect*. ICG Africa Report; no. 89; Policy Report; Variation: Policy Report (International Crisis Group). Nairobi; Brussels: International Crisis Group, 2005.

Jeffries, William. *The Darfur Crisis*. New York: Nova Science Publishers, Inc., 2008.

Lefkow, Leslie. *Darfur in Flames: Atrocities in Western Sudan*. New York: Human Rights Watch, 2004.

O'Fahey, R. S. *The Darfur Sultanate: A History*. New York: Columbia University Press, 2008.

Prunier, Gerard. *Darfur: The Ambiguous Genocide: Revised and Updated Edition*. Ithaca, NY: Cornell University Press, 2005.

Totten, Samuel and Eric Markusen. *Genocide in Darfur: Investigating the Atrocities in the Sudan*. New York: Routledge, 2006.

Van Ardenne, Agnes and others. *Explaining Darfur: Lectures on the Ongoing Genocide*. Amsterdam: Vossiuspers UvA, 2006.

Darfur–Personal Narratives

El-Tom, Abdullahi Osman. *Growing Up in Darfur, Sudan*. Khatoum: Sudanese Studies Center, 2007.

Hari, Daoud. *The Translator: A Tribesman's Memoir of Darfur*. New York: Random House, 2008.

Darfur–Bibliographies

Assal, Munzoul A. M. *An Annotated Bibliography of Social Research on Darfur*. Bergen, Norway: BRIC, University of Bergen, 2005.

Sudan–Conflict and War

Burr, J. Millard and Robert O. Collins. *Africa's Thirty Years War: Libya, Chad and the Sudan (1963–1993)*. Boulder, CO: Westview Press, 1994.

Deng, Francis Mading. *War of Visions: Conflict of Identities in the Sudan*. Washington, D.C.: Brookings Institution, 1995.

Idris, Amir H., *Conflict and Politics of Identity in Sudan*. New York: Palgrave Macmillan, 2005.

Iyob, Ruth, and Gilbert M. Khadiagala. *Sudan: The Elusive Quest for Peace*. Boulder, CO: Lynne Rienner Publishers, Inc., 2006.

Johnson, Douglas Hamilton, *The Root Causes of Sudan's Civil Wars*. Bloomington: Indiana University Press, 2003.

Online Resources

Brickhill, Jeremy. *Protecting Civilians Through the Peace Agreements: Challenges and Lessons of the Darfur Peace Agreement*. Pretoria: Institute for Security Studies, 2007, http://www.iss.co.za/index.php?link_id=14 &slink_id=4506&link_type= 12&slink_type= 12&tmpl_id=3 (accessed July 29, 2008).

Hoile, David. *Darfur in Perspective*. Padstow, Cornwall, UK: T. J. International, 2005, http://www.espac.org/pdf/Darfur-Book-New-Edition.pdf (accessed July 29, 2008).

ICG Africa Briefing Paper; no. 43; Policy Briefing (International Crisis Group). Nairobi; Brussels: International Crisis Group, 2006, http://www.crisisgroup.org/home/index.cfm?id=4442 (accessed July 29, 2008).

International Crisis Group. *Darfur: Revitalising the Peace Process*. Africa Report; no. 125; Policy Report; Variation: ICG Africa Report; no. 125; Policy Report (International Crisis Group). Nairobi; Brussels: International Crisis Group, 2007, http://www.crisisgroup.org/home/index.cfm?id=4769 (accessed July 29, 2008).

—. *A Strategy for Comprehensive Peace in Sudan*. Africa Report; no. 130; Policy Report; Variation: ICG Africa Report; no. 130; Policy Report (International Crisis Group). Nairobi; Brussels: International Crisis Group, 2007, http://www.crisisgroup.org/home/index.cfm?id=4961 (accessed July 29, 2008).

—. *Darfur's Fragile Peace Agreement*. Africa Briefing; no. 39; Policy Briefing; Variation: ICG Africa Briefing Paper; no. 39; Policy Briefing (International Crisis Group). Nairobi; Brussels: International Crisis Group, 2006, http://www.crisisgroup.org/home/index.cfm?id=4179 (accessed July 29, 2008).

—. *Getting the UN into Darfur*. Africa Briefing; no. 43; Policy Briefing; Variation: Lindsay, Tony and Conflict Studies Research Centre (Great Britain). *Darfur: A Cultural Handbook*. Special Series; 07/13. Watchfield, Swindon: Defence Academy of the United Kingdom, Conflict Studies Research Centre, 2007, http://www.isn.ethz.ch/pubs/ph/details.cfm?lng=en&ord61=alphaNavi&ord60=PublicationDate&id=43307 (accessed July 29, 2008).

Online Government Documents, United States

United States. Congress. House. Committee on Foreign Affairs. *Calling on the League of Arab States to Acknowledge the Genocide in the Darfur Region of Sudan and to Step up Their Efforts to Stop the Genocide in Darfur; Calling on the Government of the Socialist Republic of Vietnam to Immediately and Unconditionally Release Father Nguyen Van Ly, Nguyen Van Dai, Le Thi Cong Nhan, and Other Political Prisoners and Prisoners of Conscience, and for Other Purposes; and Commemorating the 200th Anniversary of the Abolition of the Transatlantic Slave Trade: Markup before the Committee on Foreign Affairs, House of Representatives*, 110th Cong., 1st sess., on H. Con. Res. 7, H. Res. 243 and H. Res. 272, April 19, 2007. Washington: U.S. G.P.O., 2007, http://purl.access.gpo.gov/GPO/LPS84375 (accessed July 29, 2008).

—. *Current Situation in Darfur: Hearing before the Committee on Foreign Affairs, House of Representatives*, 110th Cong., 1st sess., April 19, 2007. Washington: U.S. G.P.O., 2007, http://purl.access.gpo.gov/GPO/LPS83947 (accessed July 29, 2008).

—. *The Escalating Crisis in Darfur: Are There Prospects for Peace?: Hearing before the Committee on Foreign Affairs*, House of Representatives, 110th Cong., 1st sess., February 8, 2007. Washington: U.S. G.P.O., 2007, http://purl.access.gpo.gov/GPO/LPS81464 (accessed July 29, 2008).

United States. Congress. House. Committee on International Relations. *The Crisis in Darfur: A New Front in Sudan's Bloody War; and Condemning the Government of the Republic of the Sudan for Its Attacks Against Innocent Civilians in the Impoverished Darfur Region of Western Sudan: Hearing and Markup before the Committee on International Relations*, House of Representatives, 110th Cong., 2nd sess., on H. Con. Res. 403, May 6, 2004. Washington: U.S. G.P.O., http://purl.access. gpo.gov/GPO/LPS53644 (accessed July 29, 2008).

United States. Congress. Senate. Committee on Foreign Relations. *Darfur Revisited: The International Response: Hearing before the Committee on Foreign Relations*, United States Senate, 109th Cong., 1st sess., September 28, 2005. Washington: U.S. G.P.O., 2007, http://purl.access.gpo.gov/GPO/LPS81787 (accessed July 29, 2008).

United States. Congress. Senate. Committee on the Judiciary. Subcommittee on Human Rights and the Law. *Genocide and the Rule of Law: Hearing before the Subcommittee on Human Rights and the Law of the*

Committee on the Judiciary, United States Senate, 110th Cong., 1st sess., February 5, 2007. Washington: U.S. G.P.O., 2007, http://purl.access.gpo.gov/GPO/LPS82841 (accessed July 29, 2008).

United States. Government Accountability Office. *Darfur Crisis: Death Estimates; Death Estimates Demonstrate Severity of Crisis, but Their Accuracy and Credibility Could Be Enhanced: Report to Congressional Requesters.* Washington, D.C.: U.S. Government Accountability Office, 2006, http://purl.access.gpo.gov/GPO/LPS77420 (accessed July 29, 2008).

—. *Darfur Crisis: Progress in Aid and; Progress in Aid and Peace Monitoring Threatened by Ongoing Violence and Operational Challenges: Report to Congressional Requesters.* Washington, D.C.: U.S. Government Accountability Office, 2006, http://purl.access.gpo.gov/GPO/LPS77449 (accessed July 29, 2008).

United Nations Documents
www.unmis.org/English/documents.htm

Special Journal Issue on Darfur Crisis
Alvarez, Alex et al., eds. "Special Issue on Darfur." Special issue, *Genocide Studies and Prevention* 1, no. 1 (2006).

Articles
Ahmad, Khabir. "Crisis in Sudan Set to Worsen as Annual Rains Approach." *The Lancet* 363, no. 9420 (May 8, 2004): 1530.

Bacon, Kenneth H. "Hiding Death in Darfur: Why the Press Was So Late." *Columbia Journalism Review* (September/October 2004): 9–10.

Burton, John W. "Development and Cultural Genocide in Sudan." *Journal of Modern African Studies* 29, no. 3 (September 1991): 511–520.

Cobham, Alex. "Causes of Conflict in Sudan: Testing the Black Book." *The European Journal of Development Research* 17, no. 3 (September 2005): 462–480.

Collins, Greg. "Incorporating Africa's Conflicts into the War on Terror." *Peace Review* 19, no. 3 (July/September 2007): 397–406.

Crook, John R. "President and Secretary of State Characterize Events in Darfur as Genocide." *The American Journal of International Law* 99, no. 1 (January 2005): 266–267.

—. "U.S. Proposes New Regional Court to Hear Charges Involving Darfur, Others Urge ICC." *The American Journal of International Law* 99, no. 2 (April 2005): 501–502.

—. "United States Abstains on Security Council Resolution Authorizing Referral of Darfur Atrocities to International Criminal Court." *The American Journal of International Law* 99, no. 3 (July 2005): 691–693.

de Pas, Remco van. "Darfur–Dependent Population at Risk of Another Catastrophe." *British Medical Journal* 333, no. 7573 (October 21, 2006): 846.

Depoortere, Evelyn and others. "Violence and Mortality in West Darfur, Sudan (2003–04): Epidemiological Evidence from Four Surveys." *The Lancet* 364, no. 9442 (October 9–15, 2004): 1290–1291.

De Waal, Alex. "Briefing: Darfur, Sudan: Prospects for Peace." *African Affairs* 104, no. 414 (January 2005): 127–135.

De Waal, Alex. "Darfur and the failure of the responsibility to protect." International Affairs 83, issue 6 (November 2007) 1039–1054.

De Waal, Alex. "Darfur: The Inside Story." *New African* 461 (April 2007): 28–33.

Dhooge, Lucien J. "Condemning Khartoum: The Illinois Divestment Act and Foreign Relations." *American Business Law Journal* 43, no. 2 (Summer 2006): 245–316.

Elsea, Zachary. "Facing Genocide." *Harvard International Review* 26, no. 3 (Fall 2004): 11–12.

Flint, Julie. "In the Name of Islam." *Africa Report* 40, no. 3 (May/June 1995): 34–37.

Fluehr-Lobban, Carolyn and Richard Lobban. "The Sudan Since 1989: National Islamic Front Rule." *Arab Studies Quarterly* 23, no. 2 (Spring 2001): 1–9.

Gompert, David C. "For a Capability to Protect: Mass Killing, the African Union and NATO." *Survival* 48, no. 1 (2006): 7–18.

Grono, Nick. "Briefing—Darfur: The International Community's Failure to Protect." *African Affairs* 105, no. 421 (October 2006): 621–631.

Guthmann, Jean-Paul and others. "A Large Outbreak of Hepatitis E among a Displaced Population in Darfur, Sudan, 2004: The

Role of Water Treatment Methods." *Clinical Infectious Diseases* 42, no. 12 (June 15, 2006): 1685–1691.

Hagan, John and Alberto Palloni. "Death in Darfur." *Science* 313, no. 5793 (September 15, 2006): 1578–1579.

Hagan, John, Wenona Rymond-Richmond, and Patricia Parker. "The Criminology of Genocide: The Death and Rape of Darfur." *Criminology* 43, no. 3 (August 2005): 525–562.

Hampton, Tracey. "Agencies Speak Out on Rape in Darfur." *The Journal of the American Medical Association (JAMA)* 294, no. 5 (August 3, 2005): 542–544.

Heinze, Eric A. "The Rhetoric of Genocide in U.S. Foreign Policy: Rwanda and Darfur Compared." *Political Science Quarterly* 122, no. 3 (Fall 2007): 359–383.

Holland, Emily. "Murder the Men, Rape the Women." *Jane* volume 11, issue 6 (August 2007): 26–28.

Islam, M. Rafiqul. "The Sudanese Darfur Crisis and Internally Displaced Persons in International Law: The Least Protection for the most Vulnerable." *International Journal of Refugee Law* 18, no. 2 (July 2006): 354–385.

Jentleson, Bruce W. "A Responsibility to Protect." *Harvard International Review* 28, no. 4 (Winter 2007): 18–23.

Kasfir, Nelson. "Sudan's Darfur: Is It Genocide?" *Current History* 104, no. 682 (May, 2005): 195–202.

Kinnock, Glenys. "The Victims of Mass Rape, Need Our Help." *New Statesman* 135, issue 4777 (January 30, 2006): 14.

Leaning, Jennifer. "Diagnosing Genocide – The Case of Darfur." *The New England Journal of Medicine* 351, no. 8 (August 19, 2004): 735–738.

Luban, David. "Calling Genocide by Its Rightful Name: Lemkin's Word, Darfur, and the UN Report." *Chicago Journal of International Law* 7, no. 1 (Summer 2006): 303–320.

Mans, Ulrich. "Briefing: Sudan: The New War in Darfur." *African Affairs* 103, no. 411 (April 2004): 291–294.

Marchal, Roland. "Chad/Darfur: How Two Crises Merge." *Review of African Political Economy* 33, no. 109 (Sep, 2006): 467-482.

Mohammed, Adam Azain. "Sudan: Women & Confict in Darfur." *Review of African Political Economy* 30, no. 97 (September 2003): 479–510.

Nasong'o, Shadrack Wanjala, and Rapando Godwin. "Lack of Consensus on Constitutive Fundamentals: Roots of the Sudanese Civil War and Prospects for Settlement." *African and Asian Studies* 4, no. 1/2 (2005): 51–82.

Otunnu, Olara A. "The Secret Genocide." *Foreign Policy* 155 (July/August 2006): 44–46.

Patrick, Erin. "Intent to Destroy: The Genocidal Impact of Forced Migration in Darfur, Sudan." *Journal of Refugee Studies* 18, no. 4 (December 2005): 410–429.

Piiparinen, Touko. "The Lessons of Darfur for the Future of Humanitarian Intervention." *Global Governance* 13, no. 3 (July–September 2007): 365–390.

Prunier, Gérard. "The Politics of Death in Darfur." *Current History* 105, no. 691 (May 2006): 195–202.

Slim, Hugo. "Dithering over Darfur? A Preliminary Review of the International Response." *International Affairs* 80, no. 5 (October 2004): 811–828.

Soyinka, Wole and David L. Phillips. "Don't Forget Darfur." *New Perspectives Quarterly* 23, no. 4 (Fall 2006): 57–59.

Steidle, Brian. "Ceasefire, Sudan Style: A Photographic Essay on Darfur." *World Policy Journal* 22, no. 1 (Spring 2005): 1–8.

Stephenson, Joan. "Crisis in Sudan." *JAMA* 292, no. 3 (July 21, 2004): 323.

Stompor, John. "The Darfur Dilemma: U.S. Policy toward the ICC." *Georgetown Journal of International Affairs* 7, no. 1 (Winter 2006): 111–119.

Straus, Scott. "Darfur and the Genocide Debate." *Foreign Affairs* 84, no. 1 (January/February 2005): 123–133.

Udombana, Nsongurua J. "Still Playing Dice with Lives: Darfur and Security Council Resolution 1706." *Third World Quarterly* 28, no. 1 (2007): 97–116.

—. "When Neutrality Is a Sin: The Darfur Crisis and the Crisis of Humanitarian Intervention in Sudan." *Human Rights Quarterly* 27, no. 4 (November 2005): 1149–1199.

Wagner, Justin. "The Systematic Use of Rape as a Tool of War in Darfur: A Blueprint for International War Crimes Prosecutions."

Georgetown Journal of International Law 37, no. 1 (Fall 2005): 193–243.

Welling, J. J. "Non-Governmental Organizations, Prevention, and Intervention in Internal Conflict: Through the Lens of Darfur." *Indiana Journal of Global Legal Studies* 14, no. 1 (Spring 2007): 147–179.

Williams, Paul D. "Military Responses to Mass Killing: The African Union Mission in Sudan." *International Peacekeeping* 13, no. 2 (June 2006): 168–183.

Video/DVD

Bain, Aisha, Jen Marlowe, and Adam Shapiro. *Darfur Diaries Message from Home.* Los Angeles: Cinema Libre Studio, 2006.

Braun, Ted. *Darfur Now*. United States: Warner Home Video, 2008.

Clooney, N. and others. *A Journey to Darfur*. Nostalgia Network, AmericanLife TV Network, et al., 2007.

Docherty, Neil and Lisa Ellenwood. *On Our Watch*. PBS Video, 2007.

Elsanhouri, Taghreed. *All about Darfur*. San Francisco: California Newsreel, 2005.

Freedman, Paul and others. *Sand and Sorrow: A New Documentary about Darfur*. New York: HBO Video, 2008.

Jackson, Judy. *In Search of International Justice*. Judy Films Inc, History Television, & Bullfrog Films. Oley, PA: Bullfrog Films, 2006.

Koppel, T. *Sudan in Crisis*. ABC News Productions, & Films for the Humanities. Princeton, N.J: Films for the Humanities & Sciences, 2006.

Websites

24 Hours for Darfur:
http://www.24hoursfordarfur.org/

Africa Action: Campaign to Stop Genocide in Darfur: http://www.africaaction.org/campaign_new/darfur.php

Amnesty International–Sudan:
http://www.amnesty.org/en/region/africa/east-africa/sudan

Human Rights Watch–Sudan:
http://hrw.org/doc/?t=africa&c=sudan

Human Rights Watch–Darfur:
http://www.hrw.org/doc?t=africa&c=darfur

International Crisis Group–Darfur Crisis:
http://www.crisisgroup.org/home/index.cfm?id=3060&l=1

Justice Africa Sudan:
http://www.justiceafricasudan.org/

Making Sense of Darfur:
http://www.ssrc.org/blogs/darfur/category/darfur/

Save Darfur:
http://www.savedarfur.org/

Sudan Net:
http://www.sudan.net/

Sudan People's Liberation Movement:
http://www.splmtoday.com/

Sudanese Online:
http://www.sudaneseonline.com/

Sudanile:
http://www.sudanile.com/

SudanJem.com:
http://www.sudanjem.com/en/index.php

Sudan Tribune Newspaper:
http://www.sudantribune.com/

Web Bibliographies

Children of Darfur Exhibit, Eastern Washington Exhibit: http://www.ewu.edu/x23579.xml.

Darfur, United States Holocaust Memorial Museum: http://www.ushmm.org/research/library/bibliography/index.php?content=darfur.

Darfur Crisis Bibliography, Caruso Yuusuf, Columbia University Libraries: http://www.columbia.edu/cu/lweb/indiv/africa/cuvl/darfurbib.html.

Library of Congress Subject Headings

Genocide–Sudan–Darfur

Genocide–Sudan–Darfur–International Cooperation

Atrocities–Sudan–Darfur

Humanitarian Assistance–Sudan–Darfur

Genocide–Darfur (Sudan)

Atrocities–Darfur (Sudan)

Crimes Against Humanity–Darfur (Sudan)

Darfur (Sudan)–Politics and government

Sudan–History

Sudan–History–Civil War

Sudan–History–Darfur Conflict, 2003–

Darfur (Sudan)–Ethnic Relations

Darfur (Sudan)–History 20th Century

Darfur (Sudan)–Politics and Government

Civil War–Sudan–Darfur

Ethnic Conflict–Sudan–Darfur

Notes on Contributors

Musa Adam Abdul-Jalil is a Professor in the Department of Sociology and Social Anthropology, Faculty of Economic and Social Studies at the University of Khartoum. He received his B.Sc. Honors in social anthropology and sociology from the University of Khartoum in 1974 and his Ph.D. in social anthropology from the University of Edinburgh (UK) in 1980. Additionally, he completed postdoctoral training in law and society studies at the University of California, Berkeley. His research and published work focus on ethnicity and conflicts over natural resources, most specifically, over land. His most recent publication is the co-edited volume *Development Is Key for Peace and Development in Darfur* (Khartoum/ Friedrich Ebert Stiftung, 2006; in Arabic).

Issam A. Abdel Hafiez is a prominent painter, graphic designer, and photographer who lives and works in Khartoum, Sudan. His artwork has been exhibited in Africa, the Middle East, Europe, and the United States. He is also a photojournalist whose work has appeared in several Sudanese and Arab newspapers and magazines.

Abaker Mohamed Abuelbashar is a leading member of the Sudan Liberation Movement/Army (SLM/A). He was born in Nyala, South Darfur, and graduated from the University of Khartoum in 1976 with a B.Sc. in economics and politics and holds diplomas in agricultural economics from the University of Reading (UK), and in agriculture and rural development from Wye College, University of London (UK) 1988. Abuelbashar worked for Civil Aviation in Khartoum for two years, then for the United Nations' Food and Agriculture Organization in the Yemen Arab Republic for eight years. Upon his return from Yemen, he worked in Darfur for the Western Savannah Development Project. In 1990 he left Sudan, seeking political asylum in the United Kingdom. Since then he has become a political activist dedicated to working jointly with others to resolve the root causes of Sudan's problems. Abuelbashar joined the SLM/A in November 2003, and in 2004–2006 attended all rounds of the Abuja (Nigeria) Peace Talks, where he led the SLM/A team in the negotiations of the Wealth Sharing Commission.

Rogaia Mustafa Abusharaf is a Professor in the Department of Anthropology at Qatar University. Abusharaf is also a Sir Williams Luce Fellow at the Durham University School of Government and International Affairs (UK), leading an initiative on international politics and the "woman question" in the Muslim world. A Sudanese anthropologist, she has worked on policy recommendations for improving the condition of war-displaced women. Her primary fields of interest are security, human rights protection, and the cultural strategies adopted by women to cope with the trauma of violence and dislocation. Abusharaf's work has received support from the Guggenheim and Rockefeller foundations, as well as from the Andrew Mellon Foundation and the MIT Center for International Studies. She is the author of numerous publications, including *Wanderings: Sudanese Migrants and Exiles in North America* (Cornell University Press, 2002), and the editor of *Female Circumcision: Multicultural Perspectives* (University of Pennsylvania Press, 2006). Her latest book is forthcoming from University of Chicago Press in spring 2009 and is titled *Becoming Displaced: Gender, Politics and the Body in a Sudanese Squatter Settlement.*

Eric Kofi Acree is Director of the John Henrik Clarke Africana Library at Cornell University. He has been with Cornell since 2002. In addition to being the Director of the Africana Library, Acree is the Africana subject specialist for Cornell University Library (CUL) and is responsible for providing reference and bibliographic instruction and consultation in the area of Africana Studies. Prior to Cornell, he held a number of significant positions within the Undergraduate Library at the University at Buffalo (US). He received his MLS degree from the School of Information and Library Studies at the University at Buffalo. He has published several annotated and selected bibliographies, including one on "Lynching, Visuality, and Empire" in *Nka: Journal of Contemporary Art* (No. 20, Fall 2006).

Ali B. Ali-Dinar is the Associate Director of the African Studies Program at the University of Pennsylvania. An expert on web technology and online archiving, he is also a founder of the Darfur Information Center and editor of its website (www.dafurinfo.org). He has published extensively on issues related to Sudanese identity, information technology in Africa, and the current situation in Darfur. He received his doctorate from the University of Pennsylvania, master's degree from the Institute of African and Asian Studies in Khartoum, Sudan, and his bachelor's degree from the University of Khartoum. Ali-Dinar is also a prominent advocate for the people of Darfur and a prominent activist for peace, justice, and democracy in Sudan.

Munzoul A. M. Assal is an Associate Professor of Anthropology at the University of Khartoum. His major research has focused on refugees and internally displaced persons (IDPs). Major publications include *Sticky Labels or Rich Ambiguities? Diaspora and Challenges of Homemaking for Somalis and Sudanese in Norway* (Bric/University of Bergen, 2004), *Diaspora within and without Africa: Homogeneity, Heterogeneity, Variation* (co-editor; The Scandinavian Institute of African Studies, 2006), *An Annotated Bibliography of Social Research on Darfur* (Bric/ University of Bergen, 2005), and *Anthropology in the Sudan* (co-editor; International Books, 2003).

Alex de Waal is a researcher, writer, and activist on African issues. He is a fellow of the Global Equity Initiative, Harvard; director of the Social Science Research Council program on AIDS and social transformation; and director of Justice Africa in London. In his twenty-year career, de Waal has studied the social, political, and health dimensions of famine, war, genocide, and the HIV/AIDS epidemic, especially in the Horn of Africa and the Great Lakes. He has been at the forefront of mobilizing African and international responses to these problems. De Waal's books include *Famine that Kills: Darfur, Sudan, 1984–5* (Oxford University Press, 1989), and *Facing Genocide: The Nuba of Sudan* (African Rights, 1995). He is the editor and lead author of *Islam and Its Enemies in the Horn of Africa* (Indiana, 2004), *AIDS and Power: Why There Is No Political Crisis Yet* (Zed, 2006), *War in Darfur and the Search for Peace* (Harvard University Press, 2007), and most recently author, with Julie Flint, of *Darfur: A New History of a Long War* (Second Edition; Zed Books, 2008). De Waal earned his doctorate in social anthropology from Oxford University.

Atta El-Battahani is Associate Professor of political science and political economy at the University of Khartoum. He is also a manager of the International Institute for Democracy and Electoral Assistance, Sudan Project. El-Battahani was educated at Khartoum University and Sussex University (UK). During 2003–2006 he was head of the Department of Political Science and a member of the faculty of economics at the University of Khartoum. He is also a founding member of the Amnesty International Khartoum Group (1987–1989), and a founding and leading member of the Sudanese Civil Society Network for Poverty Alleviation (SCSNPA; 2002–2005). He has more than twenty-five years of experience as a researcher and has published widely on issues of governance and conflict in Sudan. His areas of research include development-related implications of ethnic and religious conflicts in African societies; governance and state institutional reform in Africa and the Middle East; conflict and cooperation in the Nile Valley; gender politics; and peripheral capitalism and political Islam in Sub-Saharan Africa.

Kamal El Gizouli is a Sudanese lawyer, poet, writer, journalist, and human-rights activist. He studied law and international relations at Kiev State University in the former Soviet Union. Kamal El Gizouli's publications include three major collections of poetry, including the critically acclaimed

Omdurman Comes on the Eight O'clock Train. He has published five other books and hundreds of articles on diverse topics, ranging from culture and politics, literature and literary criticism to issues of peace, democracy, civil war, and human rights. His writings have appeared in local and foreign newspapers and magazines such as *El Sahafa*, *El Ray Al'aam*, *Al Sudani*, Sudanile.com, *El Bayan*, *The Democratic*, and *Modern Discussion*. Several of his publications focus on the problems of marginalization and ethnic and cultural diversity in Sudan. El Gizouli is a founding member of the Sudanese Writers' Union and served as its Secretary-General until 2007. He is an honorary member of Pen International. As a human-rights activist, El Gizouli's contributions range from being a founding member of the Sudanese Organization for Human Rights and The Sudanese Monitor for Human Rights to being the coordinator of the Movement for the Freedom of Conscience and member of the Board of Trustees and Directors of the Sudanese Centre for Legal Studies. He also serves as a consultant for the Cairo Institute for Human Rights' Studies.

Abdel Monim Elgak is a Sudanese national who has been working on human rights and democratization issues in Sudan and in the Arab region for the last seven years. Currently, Monim-Elgak is the Regional Program Coordinator of the Strategic Initiative for Women in the Horn of Africa (SIHA Network). An anthropologist by training with degrees from the University of Khartoum and the American University in Cairo, he specializes in identity, gender, urban anthropology, and globalization. He has also worked with youth groups in Sudan and Egypt in promoting human rights issues and engaging in peace building, democratization, and human rights. During the last year Monim-Elgak has worked with NGOs in the Arab region to raise awareness of the current situation in Darfur, particularly contributing to the activities of the Darfur Consortium, a new and growing coalition of African and Africa-based NGOs dedicated to finding a solution to the humanitarian and human rights crisis in Darfur.

Abdullahi Osman El-Tom is a Sudanese Anthropologist living in Ireland. He is currently the head of the Department of Anthropology at the National University of Ireland in Maynooth. Over the years, El-Tom has written widely on issues relating to Darfur, Sudan, and Africa. He is also a leading member of the Justice and Equality Movement (JEM) of Darfur and participated in the African Union-sponsored Peace Talks on Darfur, held at Abuja, Nigeria, 2004–2006. His most recent book is *Growing Up in Darfur* (Sudanese Studies Centre, 2007).

Grant Farred is a Professor in the Africana Studies and Research Center and English Department at Cornell University. He earned his Ph.D. from Princeton University in 1997, an M.A. from Columbia University in 1990, and a B.A. from the University of the Western Cape, in Cape Town, South Africa, in 1988. He also taught at Williams College, Michigan University, and Duke University. He has served as general editor of the prestigious journal of critical cultural studies *South Atlantic Quarterly* (SAQ) since 2002. His books include *Midfielder's Moment: Coloured Literature and Culture in Contemporary South Africa* (Westview Press, 1999), *What's My Name? Black Vernacular Intellectuals* (University of Minnesota Press, 2003), *Phantom Calls: Race and the Globalization of the NBA* (Prickly Paradigm Press, 2006), and his most recent, *Long Distance Love: A Passion for Football* (Temple University Press, 2007).

Adrienne L. Fricke works on human rights and gender issues in the Middle East and Africa. A fluent Arabic and French speaker, she recently completed a clinical fellowship at Harvard Law School's Human Rights Program. Ms. Fricke is a consultant to numerous nongovernmental organizations and in 2007 led a field mission to Sudan to investigate the impact of Sudan's laws on survivors of rape. Ms. Fricke previously served on the Coalition for International Justice's Atrocities Documentation Team, with whom she traveled to eastern Chad to interview refugees from Darfur. In addition to her J.D. from the University of Pennsylvania, she holds an M.A. in Near Eastern Studies from New York University and a B.A. in African Studies from Yale University.

Fahima A. Hashim is a Sudanese women's rights activist and founding director of Salmmah Women's Resource Centre of Khartoum and a board member of the Global Alliance Against Traffic in Women (GAATW). Salmmah is an autonomous women and gender resource center, which provides women and men with knowledge and information based on feminist ideology, violence against women, and sexuality. Hashim's main focus is on mobilizing and empowering women, youth groups, and institutions to influence policies and achieve an effective positive change.

Salah M. Hassan is Goldwin Smith Professor and Director of Africana Studies and Professor of African and Diaspora Art History and Visual Culture at Cornell University in Ithaca, New York. He is editor and founder of *Nka: Journal of Contemporary African Art*, and consulting editor for *African Arts* and *Atlantica*. He has authored and edited several books, including *Diaspora, Memory, Place: David Hammons, Maria Magdalena Campos-Pons, and Pamela Z* (Prestel, 2008); *Power and Nationalism in Modern Africa* (Carolina Academic Press, 2008); *Unpacking Europe* (NAi Publishers, 2001); *Authentic/Ex-Centric* (Forum for African Arts, 2001); *Gendered Visions: The Art of Contemporary Africana Women Artists* (1997) and *Art and Islamic Literacy Among the Hausa of Northern Nigeria* (Edwin Mellen Press, 1992). He has contributed to numerous art journals and anthologies, including *The Art of African Fashion* (Africa World Press, 1998); *Women, Patronage, and Self-Representation in Islamic Societies*, edited by D. Fairchild Ruggles (State University of New York Press, 1999); *Reading the Contemporary: African Art from Theory to Marketplace*, edited by Olu Oguibe and Okwui Enwezor (MIT Press, 1999); and most recently *Looking Both Ways*, edited by Laurie Farrell (Snoeck Publishers, 2003). Hassan has curated several international exhibitions, including Unpacking Europe,

at Museum Boijmans Van Beuningen in Rotterdam, December 2001–March, 2002; Authentic/Ex-Centric at the 49th Venice Biennale (2001); EV+A 2001 Expanded, Limerick, Ireland; Self and Other at Apex Art Gallery, New York, 2000.

Amira M. Khair is an activist and specialist on sexual and gender-based violence in conflict situations. She has a master's degree in social science with a major in political science from Nehru Institute of Social Sciences, India. She currently works and lives in The Netherlands. She has worked with the UN Mission in Sudan as a human rights officer monitoring, evaluating, and documenting violation cases throughout the South Darfur state. She has also worked with Medica Mondiale in Cologne, Germany; Sudan Organization Against Torture; Khartoum Centre for Human Rights & Environmental Development; and the Amel Centre for Treatment and Rehabilitation of Victims of Torture. Khair has worked extensively training international organizations on effective methods for investigating gender-based crimes in armed conflicts.

Mansour Khalid is former Sudan Minister of Foreign Affairs and councilor and advisor to the late John Garang, the founder and leader of the Sudan People's Liberation Movement/Army (SPLM/A), and currently a member of the Political Bureau of Sudan People's Liberation Movement (SPLM). He has also served as Sudan's Minister of Youth and Culture and Minister of Education. As a foreign minister during former Numeiri's regime, Khalid negotiated the first peace agreement that ended the North–South civil war in 1972. He is also the author of several books, including *The Government They Deserve* (Taylor and Francis, 1986), *Numeiri and the Revolution of Dis-May* (1984), and *War and Peace in Sudan: A Tale of Two Countries* (2003).

Mahmood Mamdani is the Herbert Lehman Professor of Government in the departments of Anthropology and Political Science at Columbia University in the United States. He served as the President of the

Council for Development of Social Research in Africa (CODESRIA) Dakar, Senegal. He attended the University of Pittsburgh, receiving a B.A. in 1967, and went on to get an M.A. and A.A.L.D. at the Fletcher School of Law and Diplomacy at Tufts University in Boston in 1969. He studied for his Ph.D. at Harvard, receiving his doctorate in 1974. His book *Citizen and Subject: Contemporary Africa and the Legacy of Late Colonialism* (James Currey Ltd., 1996) won the 1998 Herskovits Award of the African Studies Association of the USA. In 2001, he was one of nine scholars to present at the Nobel Peace Prize Centennial Symposium. His recent books include *Good Muslim, Bad Muslim: America, the Cold War and the Roots of Terror* (Pantheon, 2004); and *When Victims Become Killers: Colonialism, Nativism and Genocide in Rwanda* (Princeton University Press and David Phillip, 2001).

Carina E. Ray is Assistant Professor in the History Department of Fordham University in New York City, where she teaches African and Black Atlantic History. Ray received her B.A. with honors from the University of California at Santa Cruz and her M.A. and Ph.D. in African History from Cornell University. She is currently working on a book titled *Policing Sexual Boundaries: The Politics of Race in Colonial Ghana*, which focuses on the creation and contestation of sexual boundaries between Africans and Europeans in the Gold Coast (colonial Ghana). She is a columnist for *New African* magazine, the oldest Pan-African monthly magazine in print. As part of her efforts to make Africa's history accessible to a broad audience, each month her column, "Lest We Forget," reflects on various aspects of Africa's past in relationship to its present and future.

Karin Willemse holds a Ph.D. in anthropology and is Associate Professor in the Department of History at the Erasmus University Rotterdam, The Netherlands, and former Chair of the Netherlands Feminist Studies Association (LOVA). She conducted research in Darfur in the 1980s and 1990s, which culminated in the publication of *'One Foot in Heaven': Narratives on Gender and Islam in Darfur, West-Sudan* (Brill, 2007). She is the author of numerous articles on Darfur and gender, including '"In my father's house': Gender, Islam and the construction of a gendered public sphere in Darfur, Sudan," which was published in the *Journal for Islamic Studies* (2007). Currently she is engaged in a research project in Khartoum as one of four major cities in Africa in which the construction of modern identities by youth in Islamic societies is being studied.

Benaiah Yongo-Bure is Associate Professor of Social Science at Kettering University in Flint, Michigan, where he teaches Economics and Social Science. He received his B.A. with Honors from Makerere University, Kampala, Uganda, and his M.A. and Ph.D. in economics from Dalhousie University, Halifax, Canada. In February 2007 Yongo-Bure's most recent book, *Economic Development of Southern Sudan*, was published by University Press of America. He previously taught economics and economic development at the University of Khartoum, Sudan, and economics and peace and conflict studies at Wayne State University in Detroit, Michigan.

Al-Tayib Zain Al-Abdin is Professor of Political Science and Advisor to the Vice Chancellor at University of Khartoum and served as General Secretary of the Sudan Inter-Religious Council (SIRC). He taught political science at the Institute of Afro-Asian Studies, University of Khartoum, and served as Chancellor of the University of Africa in Khartoum, Sudam. He earned his Ph.D. from Cambridge University (UK) in 1975. He was a leading member of the Islamist movement in Sudan and one of its most prominent critical intellectuals. He has published extensively on issues of Islam and interreligious dialogue, democracy, and development in Sudan, and as a columnist for daily newspapers in Khartoum.

Index

Index